UNITED NATIONS JURIDICAL YEARBOOK 2019

UNITED NATIONS • NEW YORK, 2026

ST/LEG/SER.C/57

UNITED NATIONS PUBLICATION
Sales No. E.26.V.7
ISBN 978-92-1-107405-5
eISBN 978-92-1-157620-7
ISSN 0082-8297
eISSN 2412-1223

CONTENTS

FOREWORD

By its resolution 1814 (XVII) of 18 December 1962, the General Assembly requested the Secretary-General to publish a *Juridical Yearbook* which would include certain documentary materials of a legal character concerning the United Nations and related intergovernmental organizations, and by its resolution 3006 (XXVII) of 18 December 1972, the General Assembly made certain changes in the outline of the *Yearbook*. The present volume, which is the fifty-seventh of the series, has been prepared by the Codification Division of the Office of Legal Affairs.

Chapters I and II contain selected legislative texts and treaties, or provisions thereof, concerning the legal status of the United Nations and related intergovernmental organizations.

Chapter III contains a general review of the legal activities of the United Nations and related intergovernmental organizations, based on information provided by each organization.

Chapter IV contains selected treaties concerning international law concluded under the auspices of the organizations concerned during the year in question, whether or not they entered into force in that year in view of the sometimes considerable time lag between the conclusion of the treaties and their entry into force.

Chapter V contains selected decisions of administrative tribunals of the United Nations and related intergovernmental organizations.

Chapter VI reproduces selected legal opinions of the United Nations and related intergovernmental organizations.

Chapter VII includes a list of judgments, advisory opinions and selected decisions rendered by international tribunals in 2019.

Chapter VIII contains decisions given in 2019 by national tribunals relating to the legal status of the various organizations.

Finally, the bibliography, which is prepared under the responsibility of the Office of Legal Affairs by the Dag Hammarskjöld Library, lists works and articles of a legal character relating to the work of the United Nations and related intergovernmental organizations.

Several documents published in the *Juridical Yearbook* were supplied by the organizations or Governments concerned at the request of the Secretariat. Treaty provisions, legislative texts and judicial decisions may have been subject to minor editing by the Secretariat.

This volume will appear on the United Nations Juridical Yearbook's website at http://legal.un.org/unjuridicalyearbook/.

ABBREVIATIONS

2030 Agenda	2030 Agenda for Sustainable Development
CPPNM	Convention on the Physical Protection of Nuclear Material, 2005
AMISOM	African Union Mission in Somalia
AMR	antimicrobial resistance
ARN	Aircraft Registration Network (ICAO)
ASEAN	Association of Southeast Asian Nations
ASP	Assembly of States Parties to the Rome Statute of the International Criminal Court
ATT	Arms Trade Treaty
AUC	African Union Commission
BIMCO	Baltic and International Maritime Council
BINUH	United Nations Integrated Office in Haiti
Biological Weapons Convention	Convention on the Prohibition of the Development, Production and Stockpiling of Bacteriological (Biological) and Toxin Weapons and on Their Destruction
BWM Convention	International Convention for the Control and Management of Ships' Ballast Water and Sediments, 2004
CAR	Central African Republic
CARICOM	Caribbean Community
CCLM	Committee on Constitutional and Legal Matters (FAO)
CCM	Convention on Cluster Munitions
CCW	Convention on Prohibitions or Restrictions on the Use of Certain Conventional Weapons Which May Be Deemed to Be Excessively Injurious or to Have Indiscriminate Effects
CEB	United Nations System Chief Executives Board for Coordination
CELAC	Community of Latin American and Caribbean States
CESAIR	Commission of Experts of the Supervisory Authority of the International Registry (ICAO)
Chicago Convention	Convention on International Civil Aviation, 1944
CICIG	International Commission Against Impunity in Guatemala
CITES	Convention on International Trade in Endangered Species of Wild Fauna and Flora
CLCS	Commission on the Limits of the Continental Shelf
CMF	Combined Maritime Forces

CNMC	Cameroon-Nigeria Mixed Commission
CNS	Convention on Nuclear Safety, 1994
COMHAFAT	Convention on Fisheries Cooperation Among African States Bordering the Atlantic Ocean
COPESAALC	Commission for Inland Fisheries and Aquaculture of Latin America and the Caribbean (FAO)
COPPESAALC	Commission for Small-Scale and Artisanal Fisheries and Aquaculture of Latin and Aquaculture of Latin America and the Caribbean (FAO)
CPLP	Community of Portuguese-speaking Countries
CPPNM	Convention on the Physical Protection of Nuclear Material, 1979
CTBT	Comprehensive Nuclear-Test-Ban Treaty
CTBTO	Comprehensive Nuclear-Test-Ban Treaty Organization
CTC	Counter-Terrorism Committee (Security Council)
CTED	Counter-Terrorism Committee Executive Directorate (United Nations)
CWC	Convention on the Prohibition of the Development, Production, Stockpiling and Use of Chemical Weapons and on their Destruction, 1992
DPRK	Democratic People's Republic of Korea
ECA	Emissions control area (IMO)
ECCAS	Economic Community of Central African States
ECOWAS	Economic Community of West African States
EU	European Union
EuFMD	European Commission for the Control of Foot-and-Mouth Disease
EUFOR ALTHEA	European Union Force ALTHEA
EUROFISH	International Organization for the Development of Fisheries in Europe
FAO	Food and Agriculture Organization of the United Nations
FAL Convention	Convention on Facilitation of International Maritime Traffic, 1965
FDLR	Democratic Liberation Forces of Rwanda
FFA	Pacific Islands Forum Fisheries Agency
FIPS Instruments	Faster Implementation of Project Start-up Instruments (IFAD)
GCP	FAO Government Cooperation Programme
GISIS	Global Integrated Shipping Information System (IMO)
GNA	Government of National Accord (Libya)
HNS Convention	2010 Convention on Liability and Compensation for Damage in Connection with the Carriage of Hazardous and Noxious Substances by Sea

IAEA	International Atomic Energy Agency
IBRD	International Bank for Reconstruction and Development
ICAO	International Civil Aviation Organization
ICBA	International Center for Biosaline Agriculture
ICC	International Criminal Court
ICCAT	International Convention for the Conservation of Atlantic Tunas
ICS	International Chamber of Shipping
ICTR	International Criminal Tribunal for Rwanda
ICTY	International Criminal Tribunal for the former Yugoslavia
IFAD	International Fund for Agricultural Development
IGAD	Intergovernmental Authority on Development
IGO	Intergovernmental organization
ILC	International Law Commission
ILO	International Labour Organization
IMF	International Monetary Fund
IMO	International Maritime Organization
IMLI	IMO International Maritime Law Institute
IMRF	International Migration Review Forum (IOM)
IMO	International Maritime Organization
INLEX	International Expert Group on Nuclear Liability (IAEA)
INTERTANKO	International Association of Independent Tanker Owners
IOM	International Organization for Migration
IOTC	Indian Ocean Tuna Commission
ITLOS	International Tribunal for the Law of the Sea
ITPGRFA	International Treaty on Plant Genetic Resources for Food and Agriculture, 2001
ITU	International Telecommunication Union
IUU	Illegal, unreported and unregulated (fishing)
Kinshasa Convention	Central African Convention for the Control of Small Arms and Light Weapons, Their Ammunition and All Parts and Components That Can Be Used for Their Manufacture, Repair and Assembly
LEB	ICAO Legal Affairs and External Relations Bureau
LEG	Legal Committee (IMO)
LEGN	Development Law Branch, FAO Legal Office
London Convention	Convention on the Prevention of Marine Pollution by Dumping of Wastes and Other Matter, 1972

LVFO	Lake Victoria Fisheries Organization
MARPOL	International Convention for the Prevention of Pollution from Ships, 1973
MASS	Maritime Autonomous Surface Ships
MEPC	Marine Environment Protection Committee (IMO)
Mine-Ban Convention	Convention on the Prohibition of the Use, Stockpiling, Production and Transfer of Anti-personnel Mines and on Their Destruction
MINUJUSTH	United Nations Mission for Justice Support in Haiti
MINURSO	United Nations Mission for the Referendum in Western Sahara
MINUSMA	United Nations Multidimensional Integrated Stabilization Mission in Mali
MINUSCA	United Nations Multidimensional Integrated Stabilization Mission in the Central African Republic
MINUSTAH	United Nations Stabilisation Mission in Haiti
MISCA	African-led International Support Mission in the Central African Republic
MONUC	United Nations Organization Mission in the Democratic Republic of the Congo
MONUSCO	United Nations Organization Stabilization Mission in the Democratic Republic of the Congo
MLC	Maritime Labour Convention, 2006
MSC	Maritime Safety Committee (MSC) (IMO)
NATO	North Atlantic Treaty Organisation
NEPPO	Near East Plant Protection Organization
NGO	Non-governmental organization
NPT	Treaty on the Non-Proliferation of Nuclear Weapons, 1970
OCHA	Office for the Coordination of Humanitarian Affairs
OECD	Organisation for Economic Co-operation and Development
OHCHR	Office of the High Commissioner for Human Rights (United Nations)
OLA	Office of Legal Affairs (United Nations)
OPCW	Organisation for the Prohibition of Chemical Weapons
OPCW-JIM	Organization for the Prohibition of Chemical Weapons – United Nations Joint Investigative Mechanism
OSCE	Organization for Security and Cooperation in Europe
OSES	Office of the Special Envoy for the Sahel
OSESGY	Office of the Special Envoy of the Secretary-General for Yemen
OTP	Office of the Prosecutor (ICC)

PSMA	Agreement on Port State Measures to Prevent, Deter and Eliminate Illegal, Unreported and Unregulated Fishing, 2009
PTC	Pre-Trial Chamber (ICC)
RPAS	Remotely piloted aircraft systems
RPASP	RPAS Panel (ICAO)
RSA	Revised Supplementary Agreement Concerning the Provision of Technical Assistance by the IAEA
RSE	Regulatory scoping exercise
RSGLEG	Research Subgroup on Legal Aspects (ICAO)
SADC	Southern African Development Community
SDGs	Sustainable Development Goals
SFF Guidelines	Voluntary Guidelines for Securing Sustainable Small-scale Fisheries in the Context of Food Security and Poverty Eradication (FAO)
SEMG	Somalia and Eritrea Monitoring Group
SOLAS	International Convention for the Safety of Life at Sea, 1974
SSGC	Secretariat Study Group on Cybersecurity (ICAO)
TCP	FAO Technical Cooperation Programme
TPNW	Treaty on the Non-Proliferation of Nuclear Weapons
UNAMA	United Nations Assistance Mission in Afghanistan
UNAMI	United Nations Assistance Mission for Iraq
UNAMID	African Union/United Nations Hybrid Operation in Darfur
UNAT	United Nations Appeals Tribunal
UNCITRAL	United Nations Commission on International Trade Law
UNDOF	United Nations Disengagement Observer Force
UNDP	United Nations Development Programme
UNDT	United Nations Dispute Tribunal
UNECA	United Nations Economic Commission for Africa
UNECE	United Nations Economic Commission for Europe
UNEP	United Nations Environment Programme
UNESCO	United Nations Educational, Scientific and Cultural Organization
UNFCCC	United Nations Framework Convention on Climate Change
UNFICYP	United Nations Peacekeeping Force in Cyprus
UNFPA	United Nations Population Fund
UN Habitat	United Nations Human Settlements Programme
UNHAS	United Nations Humanitarian Air Service
UNHCR	Office of the United Nations High Commissioner for Refugees

UNICEF	United Nations Children's Fund
UNIDO	United Nations Industrial Development Organization
UNIDROIT	International Institute for the Unification of Private Law
UNIFIL	United Nations Interim Force in Lebanon
UNIOGIBIS	United Nations Integrated Peacebuilding Office in Guinea-Bissau
UNISFA	United Nations Interim Security Force for Abyei
UNITAR	United Nations Institute for Training and Research
UNLIREC	United Nations Regional Centre for Peace, Disarmament and Development in Latin America and the Caribbean
UNMHA	United Nations Mission to Support the Hudaydah Agreement
UNMIK	United Nations Interim Administration Mission in Kosovo
UNMIL	United Nations Mission in Liberia
UNMISS	United Nations Mission in the Republic of South Sudan
UNMOGIP	United Nations Military Observer Group in India and Pakistan
UNOAU	United Nations Office to the African Union
UNOCA	United Nations Regional Office for Central Africa
UNODC	United Nations Office on Drugs and Crime
UNOP	United Nations Office for Partnerships
UNOWA	United Nations Office for West Africa
UNOWAS	United Nations Office for West Africa and Sahel
UNRCCA	United Nations Regional Centre for Preventive Diplomacy for Central Asia
UNRCPD	United Nations Regional Centre for Peace and Disarmament in Asia and the Pacific
UNREC	United Nations Regional Centre for Peace and Disarmament in Africa
UNRGID	United Nations Representative to the Geneva International Discussions
UNSCO	United Nations Special Coordinator for the Middle East Peace Process
UNSCOL	United Nations Special Coordinator for Lebanon
UNSMIL	United Nations Support Mission in Libya
UNSOM	United Nations Assistance Mission in Somalia
UN-Space	Inter-Agency Meeting on Outer Space Activities
UNSU	United Nations Staff Union
UNTOC	United Nations Convention against Transnational Organized Crime, 2000
UNTSO	United Nations Truce Supervision Organization
UNU	United Nations University

UN-Women	United Nations Entity for Gender Equality and the Empowerment of Women
UPU	Universal Postal Union
UNVMC	United Nations Verification Mission in Colombia
VGGT	Voluntary Guidelines on the Responsible Governance of Tenure (FAO)
VPRS	Victims Participation and Reparations Section (ICC)
WHO	World Health Organization
WMO	World Meteorological Organization
WFP	World Food Programme
WOAH	World Organization for Animal Health
WTO	World Trade Organization
XBT	Cross-Border Transferability (ICAO)

Part One

LEGAL STATUS OF THE UNITED NATIONS AND RELATED INTERGOVERNMENTAL ORGANIZATIONS

Chapter I

LEGISLATIVE TEXTS CONCERNING THE LEGAL STATUS OF THE UNITED NATIONS AND RELATED INTERGOVERNMENTAL ORGANIZATIONS

Belgium

1. Federal level: Act of 25 November 2018 ratifying the Additional Protocol to the Supplementary Agreement to the Convention on the Privileges and Immunities of the United Nations between the Kingdom of Belgium and the United Nations, signed in Brussels on 22 January 1976, done at Brussels on 11 July 2012, and New York on 11 July 2012, Moniteur Belge, 9 September 2019*

[...]

The Chamber of Representatives has adopted and we approve the following:

Article 1. The present Act regulates a matter referred to in article 74 of the Constitution.

Article 2. The Additional Protocol, to the Supplementary Agreement to the Convention on the Privileges and Immunities of the United Nations between the Kingdom of Belgium and the United Nations, signed in Brussels on 22 January 1976, done at Brussels on 11 July 2012 and at New York on 11 July 2012, shall have full and complete effect.

[...]

2. Federal level: Addendum to the Act of 8 April 1953 ratifying the Convention on the Privileges and Immunities of the Specialized Agencies, adopted in New York on 21 November 1947, by the General Assembly of the United Nations, at its second session, Moniteur Belge, 21 August 2019**

[...]

1. Article V and section 25, paragraphs 1 and 2 (I) of article VII of the Convention shall extend to the representatives of Associate Members participating in the work of the

---

* Translation from the original in French.

** Translation from the original in French.

Organization in accordance with the Statutes of the World Tourism Organization (hereinafter referred to as "the Statutes").

2. Representatives of Affiliate Members, participating in the activities of the Organization in accordance with the Statutes, shall be granted:

(*a*) All facilities in order to safeguard the independent exercise of their official functions;

(*b*) Maximum expeditiousness in the processing of their applications for visas, where required and when accompanied by a certificate that they are travelling on the business of the Organization. In addition, such persons shall be granted facilities for speedy travel.

3. Experts, other than officials coming within the scope of article VI of the Convention, serving on organs and bodies of, or performing missions for, the Organization, shall be accorded such privileges and immunities as are necessary for the independent and effective exercise of their functions, including the time spent on journeys in connection with service on organs and bodies or missions. In particular they shall be accorded:

(*a*) Immunity from personal arrest or seizure of their personal baggage;

(*b*) In respect of words spoken or written or acts done by them in the performance of their official functions, immunity from legal process of every kind, such immunity to continue notwithstanding that the persons concerned are no longer serving on organs and bodies of, or employed on mission for, the Organization;

(*c*) Inviolability for all papers and documents relating to the work on which they are engaged for the Organization;

(*d*) For the purposes of their communications with the Organization, the right to use codes and to receive papers or correspondence by courier or in sealed bags;

(*e*) The same facilities in respect of currency or exchange restrictions and in respect of their personal baggage as are accorded to officials of foreign Governments on temporary official missions.

4. Privileges and immunities are granted to the experts in the interests of the Organization and not for the personal benefit of the individuals themselves. The Secretary-General of the Organization shall have the right and the duty to waive the immunity of any expert in any case where, in his or her opinion, the immunity would impede the course of justice and it can be waived without prejudice to the interests of the Organization.

5. Notwithstanding paragraph 2 above, paragraphs 3 and 4 above shall apply to representatives of Affiliate Members performing missions for the Organization as experts.

6. The privileges and immunities, exemptions and facilities referred to in section 21 of the standard clauses shall also be accorded to the Deputy Secretary-General of the Organization, his or her spouse and minor children.

[…]

Chapter II

TREATIES CONCERNING THE LEGAL STATUS OF THE UNITED NATIONS AND RELATED INTERGOVERNMENTAL ORGANIZATIONS*

A. Treaties concerning the legal status of the United Nations

1. Status of the Convention on the Privileges and Immunities of the United Nations. Approved by the General Assembly of the United Nations on 13 February 1946**

In 2019, no State acceded to the Convention. As at 31 December 2019, there were 162 States parties to the Convention.***

2. Agreements relating to missions, offices and meetings

(*a*) Exchange of letters constituting an agreement between the United Nations Office for Project Services (UNOPS) and the Independent State of Papua New Guinea on the establishment of a UNOPS office in Papua New Guinea. Copenhagen, 19 October 2018 and Waigani, 8 February 2019****

I

Copenhagen, 19 October 2018

Excellency,

I have the honour to refer to the proposed establishment of an Office of the United Nations Office for Project Services (UNOPS) in the Independent State of Papua New Guinea. It is to be recalled that by General Assembly decision 48/501, UNOPS was established as a subsidiary organ of the United Nations to provide, *inter alia*, sustainable project, procurement and infrastructure management services for the benefit of the member countries of the United Nations.

---

* In light of the large number of treaties concluded, only a selection of the relevant treaties is reproduced herein.

** United Nations, *Treaty Series*, vol. 1, p. 15, and vol. 90, p. 327 (corrigendum to vol. 1).

*** For the list of States parties to the Convention, see *Multilateral Treaties Deposited with the Secretary-General*, available on the website http://treaties.un.org.

**** Entered into force on 8 February 2019 by the exchange of the said letters, in accordance with their provisions. United Nations registration no. I-55788.

I also have the honour to refer to the Standard Basic Assistance Agreement between the Government of Papua New Guinea and the United Nations Development Programme (UNDP), concluded on 7 April 1981 (the "Agreement"), and propose that the terms of the Agreement apply, *mutatis mutandis*, to UNOPS and its property, funds, assets, and officials, and to all persons performing services on behalf of UNOPS, while UNOPS is present in Papua New Guinea.

Moreover, I have the honour to propose that in applying the Agreement, *mutatis mutandis*, the Government confirms that the treatment afforded to UNOPS shall be no less favourable than that afforded to any accredited diplomatic mission or international organization in Papua New Guinea.

Furthermore, the Government shall provide to UNOPS and its personnel, throughout Papua New Guinea, such security as is required for the effective performance of its activities. To this end, the appropriate authorities of Papua New Guinea shall ensure the security and protection of the premises and personnel, and exercise due diligence to ensure that the tranquillity of the premises is not disturbed by the unauthorized entry of persons or groups of persons from outside or by disturbances in its immediate vicinity.

I propose that upon receipt of your confirmation in writing of the above, this Exchange of Letters shall constitute an Agreement between the United Nations and the Government of the Independent State of Papua New Guinea, which shall enter into force on the date of your reply, regulating matters relating to, and arising out of, the establishment and proper functioning of the UNOPS Office in Papua New Guinea.

Please accept, Excellency, the assurances of my highest consideration.

[*Signed*]

GRETE FAREMO

United Nations Under-Secretary-General and Executive Director of UNOPS

II

8 February 2019

Dear Executive Director,

I have the honour to refer to your letter dated 19 October 2018 on the proposed establishment of an Office of the United Nations Office for Project Services (UNOPS) in the Independent State of Papua New Guinea. It is noted that by General Assembly decision 48/501, UNOPS was established as a subsidiary organ of the United Nations to provide, *inter alia*, sustainable project, procurement and infrastructure management services for the benefit of the member countries of the United Nations.

I also have the honour to refer to the Standard Basic Assistance Agreement between the Government of Papua New Guinea and the United Nations Development Programme (UNDP), concluded on 7 April 1981 (the "Agreement"), and propose that the terms of the Agreement apply, *mutatis mutandis*, to UNOPS and its property, funds, assets, and officials, and to all persons performing services on behalf of UNOPS while UNOPS is present in Papua New Guinea.

It is agreed that in applying the Agreement, *mutatis mutandis*, the Government confirm that the treatment afforded to UNOPS shall be no less favourable than that afforded to any accredited diplomatic mission or international organization in Papua New Guinea.

Furthermore, the Government shall provide to UNOPS and its personnel throughout Papua New Guinea, such security as required for the effective performance of its activities. To this end, the appropriate authorities of Papua New Guinea shall ensure the security and protection of the premises and personnel, and exercise due diligence to ensure that the tranquillity of the premises is not disturbed by the unauthorized entry of persons or groups of persons from outside or by disturbance in its immediate vicinity.

It is agreed that upon receipt of my confirmation of the above, this Exchange of Letters shall constitute an Agreement between the United Nations and the Government of the Independent State of Papua New Guinea, which shall enter into force on the date of my reply, regulating matters relating to, and arising out of, the establishment and proper functioning of the UNOPS Office in Papua New Guinea.

Please accept, Excellency, the assurances of my highest consideration.

[*Signed*]

HONOURABLE RIMBINK PATO, OBE MP

Minister for Foreign Affairs and Trade

(*b*) Exchange of letters constituting an agreement between the United Nations and the Government of the Kingdom of Morocco concerning arrangements for the Africa Region Midterm Review of the Vienna Programme of Action for the Landlocked Developing Countries for the Decade 2014–2024, held at Marrakesh, Morocco, on 18 and 19 March 2019. New York, 15 March 2019*

I

15 March 2019

Excellency,

I have the honour to refer to the arrangements concerning the organization of the Africa Region Midterm Review of the Vienna Programme of Action for the Landlocked Developing Countries for the Decade 2014–2024, (hereinafter referred to as “the Meeting”). The Meeting organized by the United Nations represented by the Office of the High Representative for the Least Developed Countries, Landlocked Developing Countries and Small Island Developing States (hereinafter referred to as “the United Nations”) in cooperation with the Government of the Kingdom of Morocco (hereinafter referred to as “the Government”), will be held at the Hotel Barcelo Palmeraie Marrakesh, Morocco on 18 and 19 March 2019.

The Meeting falls within the mandate stipulated in the General Assembly resolution 69/137 on the follow up and implementation of the Vienna Programme of Action for Landlocked Developing Countries for the Decade 2014–2024 and General Assembly resolution 72/232 that

* Entered into force on 15 March 2019 by the exchange of the said letters, in accordance with their provisions. United Nations registration no. I-55802.

calls for the organization of a comprehensive high-level midterm review on the implementation of the Vienna Programme of Action to be preceded by regional review meetings.

With the present letter, I wish to obtain your Government's acceptance of the following:

1. The Meeting will be attended by the following participants:

(*a*) up to 17 representatives of the landlocked developing countries including the Chairman of the Group of Landlocked Developing Countries;

(*b*) up to 25 representatives of donor countries and transit developing countries;

(*c*) up to 5 local participants;

(*d*) up to 13 officials from the United Nations; and

(*e*) up to 10 experts from permanent missions in New York including co-facilitators of the Midterm Review of the Vienna Programme of Action, international, regional and sub-regional organizations and corridor management organizations, the private sector, academia and other civil society organizations.

2. The total number of participants will be approximately 70. The final list of participants will be determined by the United Nations in consultation with the Government prior to the holding of the Meeting.

3. The Meeting will be conducted in English, and French.

4. The United Nations will be responsible for:

(*a*) Covering costs and issuing round trip air tickets and payment of daily subsistence allowance and terminal expenses for (i) up to 17 representatives from landlocked developing countries as specified in sub-paragraph l(*a*), (ii) up to 19 representatives from transit countries as specified in sub-paragraph 1 (*b*); up to 10 experts from Permanent Missions in New York, international, regional and sub-regional organizations and corridor management organizations as specified in sub-paragraph l(*e*); and up to 13 officials from the United Nations as specified in sub-paragraph l(*d*);

(*b*) Overall substantive support to the organization and running of the Meeting that will include: (i) the preparation of appropriate documentation; and (ii) the identification of speakers and moderators;

(*c*) The invitation of participants as specified in sub-paragraphs l(*a*), (*b*), (*d*) and (*e*);

(*d*) Provision of coffee and tea breaks one during the morning sessions and one in the afternoon sessions for the duration of the meeting;

(*e*) Provision of interpretation services in the following languages of the Meeting: English, and French; and

(*f*) Preparation and printing of the Report of the Meeting and its distribution to the Meeting's participants and wider dissemination.

5. The cost of air fares, daily subsistence allowance, and terminal expenses for those not covered under sub-paragraph 4(*a*) will be the responsibility of the participants or their respective organizations.

6. As the Meeting will be convened by the United Nations, I wish to propose that the following terms shall apply:

(*a*) The Convention on the Privileges and Immunities of the United Nations adopted by the General Assembly on 13 February 1946 ("the Convention"), to which the Kingdom of Morocco is a party, shall be applicable in respect of the Meeting. In particular, representatives of States shall enjoy the privileges and immunities accorded under Article IV of the Convention. The participants shall enjoy the privileges and immunities accorded to experts on mission for the United Nations by articles VI and VII of the Convention. Officials of the United Nations participating in or performing functions in connection with the Meeting shall enjoy the privileges and immunities provided under articles V and VII of the Convention. Officials of the Specialized Agencies participating in the Meeting shall be accorded the privileges and immunities under articles VI and VIII of the Convention on the Privileges and Immunities of the Specialized Agencies, adopted by the General Assembly on 21 November 1947;

(*b*) Without prejudice to the provisions of the Convention, all participants in the Meeting shall enjoy immunity, as necessary in respect of words spoken or written in connection with their official participation in the Meeting;

(*c*) All participants and all persons performing functions in connection with the Meeting shall have the right of unimpeded entry into and exit from Morocco;

(*d*) Visas and entry permits, where required, shall be granted free of charge and as speedily as possible, on the condition that the general entry formalities of entering the territory of the Kingdom of Morocco have been legally fulfilled. When applications are made four weeks before the opening of the Meeting, visas shall be granted not later than two weeks before the opening of the Meeting. If the application is made less than four weeks before the opening, visas shall be granted as speedily as possible and no later than three days before the opening. Arrangements shall be made to ensure that visas for the duration of the Meeting are delivered at the airport of arrival to those who are unable to obtain them prior to their arrival. Exit permits, where required, shall be granted free of charge, as speedily as possible as and in any case not later than three days before the closing of the Meeting.

7. The Government shall furnish police protection as may be required to ensure the effective functioning of the Meeting in an atmosphere of security and tranquillity free from any interference of any kind. While such police services shall be under the direct supervision and control of a senior officer provided by the Government, this officer shall work in close co-operation with a designated senior official of the United Nations.

8. The Government shall be responsible for dealing with any action, claim or other demand against the United Nations relating to:

(*a*) injury to persons or damage to or loss of property in the Meeting premises provided by or under control of the Government for the Meeting;

(*b*) injury to persons or damage to or loss of property caused by or incurred in using any transport services that are provided for the Meeting by or under the control of the Government;

(*c*) the employment for the Meeting of personnel provided or arranged for by the Government; and

the Government shall indemnify and hold harmless the United Nations and its officials in respect of any such action, claim or other demand unless the Government and the United Nations agree that such damage, injury or loss is the result of gross negligence or willful misconduct on the part of the officials of the United Nations.

9. Any dispute concerning the interpretation or implementation of this Agreement, except for a dispute subject to Section 30 of the Convention or to any other applicable

agreement, shall be resolved by negotiations or any other agreed mode of settlement. Any such dispute that is not settled by negotiation or any other agreed mode of settlement shall be submitted at the request of either Party for a final decision to a tribunal of three arbitrators, one of whom shall be appointed by the Secretary-General of the United Nations, one by the Government and the third, who shall be the Chairperson, by the other two arbitrators. If either Party does not appoint an arbitrator within three months of the other Party having notified the name of its arbitrator, or if the first two arbitrators do not within three months of the appointment or nomination of the second one of them appoint the Chairperson, then such arbitrator shall be nominated by the President of the International Court of Justice at the request of either Party to the dispute. Except as otherwise agreed by the Parties, the tribunal shall adopt its own rules of procedure, provide for the reimbursement of its members and the distribution of expenses between the Parties, and take all decisions by a two-thirds majority. Its decisions on all questions of procedure and substance shall be final and, even if rendered in default of one of the Parties, be binding on both of them.

10. I further propose that upon receipt of your Government's confirmation in writing of the above, this exchange of letters shall constitute an Agreement between the United Nations and the Kingdom of Morocco regarding the hosting of the Meeting, which shall enter into force on the date of your reply and shall remain in force for the duration of the Meeting from 18 to 19 March 2019, and for such additional period as is necessary for its preparation, completion of its work, and for the resolution of any matters arising out of the Agreement.

Please accept Excellency, the assurances of my highest consideration.

[*Signed*]

FEKITAMOELOA KATOA 'UTOIKAMANU

Under-Secretary-General, and High Representative

II

The Permanent Mission of the Kingdom of Morocco presents its compliments to the United Nations Office of the High Representative for the Least Developed Countries, Landlocked Developing Countries and Small Island Developing States (UN-OHRLLS) and has the honor to inform that the lasted draft Host Country Agreement for the Regional African Meeting on the midterm review on the implementation of the Vienna Programme of Action to be held be held on 18 and 19 March 2019, in Marrakech, sent to this mission on the 14th of March 2019 (Letter: OHRLLS-2019–00045) is agreed to by the Government of the Kingdom of Morocco.

The Permanent Mission of the Kingdom of Morocco to the United Nations avails itself of this opportunity to renew to the United Nations Office of the High Representative for the Least Developed Countries, Landlocked Developing Countries and Small Island Developing States the assurance of its highest appreciation.

New York, 15 March 2019

(c) Exchange of letters constituting an agreement between the United Nations and the Government of Kazakhstan concerning the hosting of the seminar on fostering cooperation and enhancing consultation mechanisms among the existing nuclear-weapon-free zones, to be held in Nur-Sultan (Kazakhstan) from 28 to 29 August 2019. New York, 29 May 2019 and 14 June 2019*

I

29 May 2019

Excellency,

1. I have the honor to refer to the arrangements concerning the organization of the "Two-day seminar on fostering cooperation and enhancing consultation mechanisms among the existing nuclear-weapon-free zones" (hereinafter referred to as "the Seminar"). The Seminar falls within the scope of the mandate of the United Nations General Assembly resolution A/RES/73/71 (5 December 2018) and directly contributes to the fulfillment of Action 5 ("Strengthening and consolidating nuclear-weapon-free zones") of Secretary-General António Guterres' Disarmament Agenda.

2. The Seminar is organized by the United Nations, represented by the United Nations Office for Disarmament Affairs (hereinafter referred to as "the United Nations"), in co-operation with the Government of the Republic of Kazakhstan, through the Ministry of Foreign Affairs of Kazakhstan (hereinafter referred to as "the Government"). The Seminar will be held at a suitable location determined and provided by the Ministry of Foreign Affairs in Nur-Sultan (former Astana), Kazakhstan, from 28 to 29 August 2019.

3. The purpose of the Seminar is to identify and discuss measures that the States Parties to the existing nuclear-weapon-free zones (NFWZ's) and Mongolia and relevant organizations might undertake in order to facilitate, enhance and systematize inter-zonal cooperation. The Seminar participants will attempt to elaborate a list of recommendations for implementing the identified measures, which will be conveyed in the format of an outcome document to the Fourth Conference of Nuclear-Weapon-Free Zones and Mongolia (to be held on 24 April 2020 in New York). Eventually, the Seminar findings are expected to contribute to strengthening disarmament initiatives and the non-proliferation regime, and to provide impetus to the development of new zones.

4. The Seminar will be attended by the following participants to be invited by the United Nations:

(*a*) Two (2) representatives from a national ministry/agency or relevant regional organization/institution authorized as the acting Focal Point (coordinator) from each nuclear-weapon-free zone (Latin America and the Caribbean, South Pacific, Africa, Southeast Asia and Central Asia);

(*b*) One (1) representative from Mongolia;

(*c*) Up to five (5) additional Government representatives from Kazakhstan;

(*d*) One (1) representative from the International Atomic Energy Agency;

(*e*) One (1) representative from the Comprehensive Nuclear-Test-Ban Treaty Organization;

* Entered into force on 17 June 2019 by the exchange of the said letters, in accordance with their provisions. United Nations registration no. I-55829.

(*f*) One (1) representative from the United Nations Institute for Disarmament Research;

(*g*) One (1) representative from the Vienna Center for Disarmament and Non-Proliferation;

(*h*) Up to three (3) representatives from the United Nations Office for Disarmament Affairs;

(*i*) One (1) representative from the James Martin Center for Nonproliferation Studies.

The total number of participants will be approximately twenty-four (24). The list of participants will be determined by the United Nations in consultation with the Government prior to the holding of the Seminar.

5. The working language of the Seminar will be English. In this regard no formal interpretation services and/or equipment will be provided by the organizers for the purposes of the Seminar. Participants may provide their own interpreters and/or equipment at their own expense following a formal request to the United Nations Office for Disarmament Affairs at least two months prior to the start-date of the Seminar for the purpose of processing the necessary arrangements related to the Seminar.

6. The United Nations will be responsible for:

(*a*) the arranging and provision of round-trip air travel tickets and accommodation for the participants specified in paragraphs 4 (*a*), (*b*), (*d*), (*e*), (*f*), (*g*) and (*h*) above, in accordance with United Nations rules and regulations;

(*b*) the preparation of the substantive content and the agenda of the Seminar;

(*c*) the preparation of the *aide-mémoire*, the participant package including documents related to the work of the Seminar, the press release and other relevant materials;

(*d*) the registration of and liaison with participants from outside Kazakhstan.

7. The Government will be responsible for:

(*a*) the designation of a senior official from the Ministry of Foreign Affairs of Kazakhstan to deliver opening and closing remarks at the Seminar;

(*b*) the provision, including costs, of conference facilities (incl. audio system, power point, visual equipment *etc.*) and meeting services;

(*c*) the provision, including costs, of lunch, refreshments, and a dinner-reception for all participants during the Seminar;

(*d*) the provision of visas and entry permits, where required, to enter Kazakhstan for all participants where necessary;

(*e*) the provision, including costs, of personnel to assist with logistics during the Seminar, as needed;

(*f*) the arranging and provision of local transportation for participants between the airport, their accommodation and the location where the Seminar shall take place.

8. The costs associated with the participation of those participants who are not covered by paragraphs 6 and 7 of this letter, including airfare, accommodation and meals, will be the responsibility of the participants and/or their sponsoring organizations.

9. I wish to propose that the following terms shall apply to the Seminar:

(a) (i) The Convention on the Privileges and Immunities of the United Nations adopted by the General Assembly on 13 February 1946 ("the Convention"), to which Kazakhstan is a party, shall be applicable in respect of the

Seminar. In particular, representatives of States shall enjoy the privileges and immunities accorded under Article IV of the Convention. The participants invited by the United Nations shall enjoy the privileges and immunities accorded to experts on mission for the United Nations under articles VI and VII of the Convention. Officials of the United Nations participating in or performing functions in connection with the Seminar shall enjoy the privileges and immunities provided under articles V and VII of the Convention;

(ii) Without prejudice to the provisions of the Convention, all participants and persons performing functions in connection with the Seminar shall enjoy such privileges and immunities, facilities and courtesies as are necessary for the independent exercise of their functions in connection with the Seminar;

(iii) Personnel provided by the Government pursuant to this Agreement shall enjoy immunity from legal process in respect of words spoken or written or any act performed by them in their official capacity in connection with the Seminar.

(*b*) All participants and all persons performing functions in connection with the Seminar shall have the right to unimpeded entry and exit from Kazakhstan. Visas and entry permits, where required, shall be granted free of charge and as speedily as possible. If the application is made four weeks before the opening of the Seminar or earlier, visas shall be granted not later than two weeks before the opening of the Seminar. If the application is made less than four weeks before the opening, visas shall be granted as speedily as possible and not later than three days before the opening. Arrangements shall also be made to ensure that visas for the duration of the Seminar are delivered at the airport of arrival to those who are unable to obtain them prior to their arrival. Exit permits, where required, shall be granted free of charge, as speedily as possible and in any case not later than three days before the closing of the Seminar.

10. The Government shall furnish such police protection as may be required to ensure the effective functioning of the Seminar in an atmosphere of security and tranquillity free from interference of any kind. While such police services shall be under the direct supervision and control of a senior officer provided by the Ministry, this Officer shall work in close cooperation with a designated senior official of the United Nations.

11. The Government shall be responsible for dealing with any action, claim or other demand against the United Nations or its officials and arising out of:

(*a*) injury to persons or damage to or loss of property in the Seminar premises that are provided by or are under the control of the Government;

(*b*) injury to persons or damage to or loss of property caused by, or incurred in using, the transport services that are provided by or are under the control of the Government;

(*c*) the employment for the Seminar of personnel provided or arranged for by the Government.

And the Government shall indemnify and hold harmless the United Nations and its officials in respect of any such action, claim or other demand.

12. Any dispute concerning the interpretation or implementation of this agreement, except for a dispute subject to Section 30 of the Convention or to any other applicable agreement, shall, unless the parties otherwise agree, be resolved by negotiations or any

other agreed mode of settlement. Any such dispute that is not settled by negotiations or any other agreed mode of settlement shall be submitted at the request of either party for a final decision to a tribunal of three arbitrators, one of whom shall be appointed by the Secretary-General of the United Nations, one by the Government, and the third, who shall be the Chairperson, by the other two arbitrators. If either party does not appoint an arbitrator within three months of the other party having notified the name of its arbitrator or if the first two arbitrators do not within three months of the appointment or nomination of the second one of them appoint the Chairperson, then such arbitrators shall be nominated by the President of the International Court of Justice at the request of either party to the dispute. Except as otherwise agreed by the parties, the tribunal shall adopt its own rules of procedure, provide for the reimbursement of its members and the distribution of expenses between the parties, and take all decisions by a two-thirds majority. Its decisions on all questions of procedure and substance shall be final and, even if rendered in default of one of the parties, be binding on both of them.

13. I further propose that upon receipt of your Government's confirmation in writing of the above, this exchange of letters will constitute an agreement between the United Nations and Kazakhstan on the hosting of the Seminar, which shall enter into force on the date of your reply and will remain in force for the duration of the Seminar, and for such additional period as is necessary for the completion of its work and for the resolution of any matters arising out of the Agreement.

Please accept, Excellency, the assurances of my highest consideration.

[*Signed*]

IZUMI NAKAMITSU

Under-Secretary-General

High Representative for Disarmament Affairs

II

14 June 2019

Dear Izumi,

With reference to your letter of 29 May, 2019, I have the honor to inform you that the Ministry of Foreign Affairs of the Republic of Kazakhstan confirms its agreement with and acceptance of the proposed terms and conditions for the parties related to the organizing of the "Two-day seminar on fostering cooperation and enhancing consultation mechanisms among the existing nuclear-weapon-free zones", in Nur-Sultan during 28–29 August, 2019.

We therefore understand and agree that your above-mentioned letter and this confirmation will constitute the Agreement between the United Nations and the Government of the Republic of Kazakhstan on the hosting of the seminar.

Please accept the assurances of my highest consideration.

[*Signed*]

KAIRAT UMAROV

Ambassador Extraordinary and Plenipotentiary

Permanent Representative of Kazakhstan to the United Nations

(*d*) Agreement between the Government of the Republic of Kenya and the United Nations Population Fund regarding the arrangements for "The Nairobi Summit on ICPD25: Accelerating the Promise". New York, 31 May 2019 and Nairobi, 21 June 2019*

Whereas the United Nations Population Fund ("UNFPA") was established as a subsidiary organ of the General Assembly of the United Nations by Assembly resolution 3019 (XXVII) of 18 December 1972 to support and supplement the national efforts of developing countries at solving their population problems, to improve their economic development and to promote social progress and better standards of life;

Whereas the year 2019 marks the twenty-fifth anniversary of the adoption of the Programme of Action at the International Conference on Population and Development ("ICPD PoA") in 1994;

Whereas the Republic of Kenya (the "Government") and UNFPA wish to convene a conference entitled "The Nairobi Summit on ICPD25: Accelerating the Promise" (the "Nairobi Summit") in Nairobi, Kenya, to bring together stakeholders and galvanize commitments towards accelerating the achievement of the ICPD PoA and contributing to the achievement of the Sustainable Development Goals;

Now Therefore, UNFPA and the Government (each a "Party" and together the "Parties") hereby agree as follows:

Article I. Date and place of the Nairobi Summit

The Nairobi Summit shall be held at the Kenyatta International Convention Centre in Nairobi, Kenya, from 12 to 14 November, 2019.

Article II. Attendance at the Nairobi Summit

1. Participants of the Nairobi Summit shall comprise the following:

(*a*) Representatives of Member States and Observers of the United Nations;

(*b*) Representatives of organizations that have received standing invitations from the United Nations General Assembly to participate in the capacity of observers;

(*c*) Officials of the Specialized and related agencies of the United Nations;

(*d*) Representatives of other intergovernmental organization;

(*e*) Representatives of intergovernmental and subsidiary organs of the United Nations;

(*f*) Representatives of non-governmental and civil society organizations;

(*g*) Officials of the United Nations, including its Funds and Programmes;

(*h*) Other persons and groups invited by the Parties or contracted by UNFPA; and

(*i*) Representatives of the private and business sectors.

2. The public meetings of the Nairobi Summit shall be open to representatives of national, regional and international media accredited by the Parties.

---

* Entered into force on 21 June 2019 by signature, in accordance with article XIV. United Nations registration no. I-55977.

Article III. Premises, equipment, utilities and supplies

1. UNFPA shall obtain the necessary premises for the Nairobi Summit at its own expense at the Kenyatta International Convention Centre and such other premises it deems necessary to accommodate various activities and events related to the Nairobi Summit ("Nairobi Summit area"). Notwithstanding the foregoing, the Government shall provide appropriate support to UNFPA in obtaining and otherwise dealing with the Kenyatta International Convention Centre by, *inter alia*, coordinating and facilitating discussions between UNFPA and the Kenyatta International Convention Centre as needed.

2. The Government shall ensure the availability of facilities for representatives of the media as referred to in article 11.2 above, in particular, to the extent required by the United Nations. In addition, the Government shall coordinate with the Kenyatta International Convention Centre to ensure the availability of a press working area, a briefing room for correspondents, radio and television studios and areas for interviews and programme preparation.

3. The Government shall ensure the availability of all necessary utility services, including local telephone communications, of the secretariat of the Nairobi Summit and its communications by telex, telefax, telephone and electronic communications system (inclusive of internet and email) between the secretariat of the Nairobi Summit and United Nations offices when such communications are authorized by or on behalf of the secretariat of the Nairobi Summit. The Government shall further ensure the availability of all necessary and adequate internet services, including and not limited to wireless network facilities, throughout the duration of the Nairobi Summit for use by the participants of the Nairobi Summit.

4. The United Nations flag shall be displayed at the entrance to the Kenyatta International Convention Centre from the opening day of the Nairobi Summit until its end, in accordance with United Nations practice, and may be displayed at other designated places as agreed by the Government and the United Nations.

Article IV. Accommodation

The Government shall endeavour to ensure that adequate accommodation in hotels and residences near the venue will be available at competitive commercial rates for persons participating in or attending the Nairobi Summit.

Article V. Medical facilities

1. Medical facilities adequate for first aid in emergencies shall be provided by the Government within the area of the Nairobi Summit.

2. For serious emergencies, the Government shall ensure immediate transportation and admission to a hospital. The cost of any hospitalization shall be solely borne by the patient.

Article VI. Protocol and Transportation

1. The Government shall provide transport between the designated airport and the Nairobi Summit area and principal hotels for UNFPA staff members servicing or participating in the Nairobi Summit upon their arrival and departure. At the time of signature of this Agreement, the Parties estimate the number of such UNFPA staff members to be around three hundred (300).

2. The Government shall endeavour to ensure the availability of transport at competitive commercial rates for all participants attending the Nairobi Summit between the designated airport, the principal hotels and the Nairobi Summit area.

3. The Government shall provide an adequate number of cars with drivers for official use by the principal officers of UNFPA and the secretariat of the Nairobi Summit, as well as such other local transportation as is required by the secretariat in connection with the Nairobi Summit.

4. The Government shall provide protocol services to the leaders of delegations and such other high-level participants as agreed between the Parties attending the Nairobi Summit.

Article VII. Right of Entry and Exit

1. All persons referred to in article II above shall have the right of entry into and exit from the, Republic of Kenya, and no impediment shall be imposed on their transit to and from the Nairobi Summit area.

2. Visas and entry permits, where required, shall be granted free of charge, as speedily as possible and not later than two (2) weeks before the date of the opening of the Nairobi Summit, provided the application for the visa is made at least three weeks before the opening of the Nairobi Summit. The Government shall give due consideration to applications that are made after this period. Arrangements shall also be made to ensure that visas for the duration of the Nairobi Summit are given at specified point of entry to participants who were unable to obtain them prior to their arrival.

Article VIII. Security

1. The Government shall furnish such security and protection as may be required to ensure the effective functioning of the Nairobi Summit in an atmosphere of security and tranquillity free from interference of any kind. While such security services shall be under the direct supervision and control of a senior officer provided by the Government, this officer shall work in close co-operation with a designated senior official of UNFPA and the United Nations.

2. The access to and the security within the Kenyatta International Convention Centre shall be under the direct supervision and control of a designated senior official of the United Nations Department of Safety and Security (UNDSS) who will work in close cooperation with the senior security officer provided by the Government. The modalities of cooperation between the United Nations and the Government on security matters will be spelled out in a Memorandum of Understanding. All other external areas shall remain the responsibility of the Government.

3. UNFPA and the Government shall cooperate in the preparation of a comprehensive security plan based on the Government's security assessment of the Nairobi Summit. This security plan shall be the framework upon which all tasks relating to security will be executed.

Article IX. Local personnel

1. The Government shall appoint a liaison officer who shall be responsible, in consultation with UNFPA, for making and carrying out the administrative and personnel arrangements for the Nairobi Summit as required under this Agreement.

2. The Government shall recruit and provide an adequate number of personnel as agreed between the Parties, including drivers for the cars referred to in article VI, paragraphs 1 and 3. The exact requirements in this respect will be agreed by the Parties in writing. Some of the persons shall be available at least one (1) week before the opening of the Nairobi Summit and until a maximum of six (6) days after its close, and to maintain such night-time services, as required by the United Nations.

Article X. Financial Arrangements

Each Party will be responsible for its own costs incurred in preparing for and holding the Nairobi Summit, including costs associated with each Party's responsibilities as detailed in this Agreement, unless otherwise provided for elsewhere in this Agreement. For avoidance of doubt, the Government shall provide the security, transportation and protocol services as detailed in articles VI(*l*) and (3) and VIII above at its own expense. Any co-financing arrangements as may be agreed between the Parties will be the subject of a separate written agreement.

Article XI. Liability

1. The Government shall be responsible for dealing with any action, claim or other demand against the United Nations, including UNFPA, or its officials, agents and personnel and arising out of:

(*a*) personal injury, or property loss or damage caused by, or incurred in using, the transportation referred to in article VI (1) and (3) that is provided by the Government; and

(*b*) the employment of personnel arranged for or provided by the Government for the Nairobi Summit referred to in articles VIII and IX.

2. The Government shall indemnify and hold harmless the United Nations, including UNFPA, and its officials, agents and personnel in respect of any such action, claim or other demand.

3. To the extent possible and appropriate, UNFPA shall advise the participants listed in article II above to obtain necessary medical and travel insurances for their attendance at the Nairobi Summit.

Article XII. Privileges and Immunities

1. The Convention on the Privileges and Immunities of the United Nations, adopted by the General Assembly on 13 February 1946, to which the Republic of Kenya is a party, shall be applicable in respect of the Nairobi Summit. In particular, the representatives of States referred to in article II, paragraph 1 (*a*), above, shall enjoy the privileges and immunities provided under article IV of the Convention, the officials of the United Nations, including its Funds and Programmes referred to in article II, paragraph 1 (*g*), above, shall enjoy the privileges and immunities provided under articles V and VII of the Convention and any experts on mission for the United Nations in connection with the Nairobi Summit shall enjoy the privileges and immunities provided under articles VI and VII of the Convention.

2. The representatives or observers referred to in article II, paragraph 1 (*b*), (*d*), (*e*), (*f*), (*h*), and (*i*), above, shall enjoy immunity from legal process in respect of words spoken or written and any act performed by them in connection with their participation in the Nairobi Summit.

3. The representatives of the specialized or related agencies, referred to in article II, paragraph 1 (*c*), above, shall enjoy the privileges and immunities provided by the Convention on the Privileges and Immunities of the Specialized Agencies or the Convention on the Privileges and Immunities of the United Nations, *mutatis mutandis*, as appropriate.

4. Without prejudice to the preceding paragraphs of the present article, all persons performing functions in connection with the Nairobi Summit, including those referred to in article VIII and all those invited to the Nairobi Summit, shall enjoy the privileges, immunities and facilities necessary for the independent exercise of their functions in connection with the Nairobi Summit.

5. For the purpose of the Convention on the Privileges and Immunities of the United Nations, Kenyatta International Convention Centre specified in article III, paragraph 1, above, shall be deemed to constitute premises of the United Nations in the sense of article II, section 3 of the Convention and access thereto shall be subject to the authority and control of the United Nations. The premises shall be inviolable for the duration of the Nairobi Summit, including the preparatory stage and the winding-up.

6. The Government of Kenya shall allow tax-free and duty-free temporary importation of all equipment and supplies for use at the Nairobi Summit in accordance with the applicable tax laws in Kenya, to the extent that such Jaws are not inconsistent with the Convention on the Privileges and Immunities of the United Nations.

7. UNFPA shall be exempt from all direct and indirect taxes, including value added tax, in connection with the Nairobi Summit in accordance with applicable tax law in Kenya to the extent that such Jaws are not inconsistent with the Convention on the Privileges and Immunities of the United Nations.

Article XIII. Settlement of disputes

Any dispute concerning the interpretation or the application of this Agreement, except for a dispute subject to section 30 of the Convention on the Privileges and Immunities of the United Nations or of any other applicable agreement, shall, unless the Parties otherwise agree, be resolved by negotiations or any other agreed mode of settlement. Any such dispute that is not settled by negotiations or any other agreed mode of settlement shall be submitted at the request of either Party for a final decision to a tribunal of three arbitrators, one of whom shall be appointed by the Secretary-General of the United Nations, one by the Republic of Kenya and the third, who shall be the Chairperson, by the other two arbitrators. If either Party does not appoint an arbitrator within three months of the other Party having notified the name of its arbitrator or if the first two arbitrators do not within three months of the appointment or nomination of the second one of them appoint a Chairperson, then such arbitrator shall be nominated by the President of the International Court of Justice at the request of either party to the dispute. Except as otherwise agreed by the Parties, the tribunal shall adopt its own rules of procedure, provide for the reimbursement of its members and the distribution of expenses between the Parties, and take all decisions by a two-thirds majority. Its decision on all questions of procedure and substance shall be final and, even if rendered in default of one of the parties, be binding on both of them.

Article XIV. Final provisions

1. This Agreement may be modified by written agreement between the United Nations and the Government.

2. This Agreement will enter into force immediately upon signature by the Parties and will remain in force for the duration of the Nairobi Summit. Individual provisions of this Agreement shall survive the expiration or termination of this Agreement to the extent necessary as agreed by both UNFPA and Government of Kenya.

Signed for UNFPA in New York, United States of America on this [31] day of [May] 2019 and for the Government of Kenya in Nairobi, Kenya on this [21st] day of [June] 2019 in duplicate in English.

For the Government of the Republic of Kenya	For the United Nations Population Fund
[*Signed*]	[*Signed*]
AMB. MONICA JUMA, DPhil, CBS	DR. NATALIA KANEM
Cabinet Secretary for Foreign Affairs	Executive Director

(*e*) Agreement between the United Nations Office for Project Services and the Kingdom of Tonga concerning the establishment of an Office in Nuku'alofa, Kingdom of Tonga. Nuku'alofa, 8 July 2019*

Whereas, the United Nations Office for Project Services ("UNOPS") was established by the United Nations General Assembly decision 48/501 of 19 September 1994 to provide, inter alia, management and other support services for the benefit of the member countries of the United Nations, impartially, efficiently and on a cost reimbursement basis;

Whereas, UNOPS is part of the United Nations;

Whereas, the Kingdom of Tonga ("Host Country") wishes to request assistance from UNOPS for the benefit of its people;

Whereas, the Host Country, insofar as it is not already bound to do so, shall apply to UNOPS, their property, funds and assets, and to their officials, including all UNOPS personnel operating under this Agreement in respect of the United Nations, the Convention on the Privileges and Immunities of the United Nations and the Kingdom of Tonga's Diplomatic Privileges Act, executed on 10 September, 1948.

Now, therefore UNOPS and the Host Country have entered into this Agreement in a spirit of friendly co-operation:

Article I. Definitions

1. For the purposes of this Agreement,

---

* Entered into force on 8 July 2019 by signature, in accordance with article XXIX(5). United Nations registration no. I-55919.

(*a*) "Archives" means all records, correspondence, documents, manuscripts, computer records, still and motion pictures, film and sound recordings, and any other records belonging to or held by the Office in furtherance of its functions;

(*b*) "Executive Director" means the Executive Director of UNOPS, who is responsible and accountable to the Secretary-General of the United Nations for all UNOPS functions, activities, and services;

(*c*) "Experts on Mission" means persons, other than Officials of the Office, performing missions at the request of or on behalf of the Office;

(*d*) "General Convention" means the Convention on the Privileges and Immunities of the United Nations adopted by the General Assembly on 13 February 1946;

(*e*) "Head of the Office" means the official who is in charge of the Office in the Host Country;

(*f*) "Host Country" means Kingdom of Tonga or Tonga;

(*g*) "Office" means the UNOPS Office in the Host Country;

(*h*) "Officials of the Office" means all of the UNOPS staff members assigned to the Office irrespective of their nationality, with the exception of those who are locally recruited and paid hourly rates, as provided for in United Nations General Assembly resolution 76(1) of 7 December 1946;

(*i*) "Party" means UNOPS or the Host Country, individually;

(*j*) "Parties" means UNOPS and the Host Country, collectively;

(*k*) "Persons Performing Services" means service contractors, operational experts, volunteers, consultants, judicial or natural persons, and their employees, who provide services to the Office, other than Officials of the Office and Expert on Mission;

(*l*) "Premises of the Office" means the building or part of building or used permanently or temporarily by the Office in accordance with this Agreement or any Supplementary Agreements entered into between the Office and the Host Country;

(*m*) "Property of the Office" means all property, including funds, income and other assets belonging to or held or administered by the Office in furtherance of its functions;

(*n*) "Secretary-General" means the Secretary-General of the United Nations;

(*o*) "Telecommunications" means any emission, transmission or reception of written or verbal information, images, sound or information of any nature by wire, radio, satellite, optical, fibre or any other electronic or electromagnetic means.

Article II. Establishment of the Office

The seat of the Office shall be established in Nuku'alofa, Tonga, to permit UNOPS to carry out its activities and services.

Article III. Juridical Personality

1. The Office shall possess juridical personality in Tonga. It shall have the capacity:

(*a*) to contract;

(*b*) to acquire and dispose of immovable and movable property;

(*c*) to institute legal proceedings.

2. For the purposes of this agreement, the Office shall be represented by the Head of the Office.

Article IV. Purpose and Scope of the Agreement

1. (*a*) This Agreement regulates the status of the Office in the Host Country, in particular of its Premises, Officials, Experts on Mission and Persons Performing Services to the Office;

(*b*) The Modalities of Assistance rendered by the Office to the Host Country shall be determined in separate project specific agreements between the Office and the Host Country;

(*c*) The Host Country confirms that the treatment afforded to the Office shall not be less favourable than that afforded to any other accredited foreign mission in the Host Country;

(*d*) Any holding in or outside Nuku'alofa, Tonga, which may be used with the concurrence of the Host Country for meetings, seminars, training courses, symposiums, workshops and similar activities organized by the Office shall be temporarily included in the Premises of the Office and shall be deemed to be covered by this Agreement for the duration of such meetings, training courses, symposiums, workshops and similar activities organized by the Office.

Article V. Application of the General Convention

The Host Country and UNOPS agree to apply the General Convention to the Office, its Archives, Property, Telecommunications and to its Officials, Experts on Mission and Persons performing services to the Office in the Host Country.

Article VI. Inviolability of the Office

1. The Office and its Property, Archives and Telecommunications, wherever located and by whomsoever held, shall be inviolable and enjoy immunity from every form of legal process, except when in a particular case such immunity has been expressly waived in accordance with the General Convention. However, no waiver of immunity from legal process shall extend to any measure of execution.

2. No officer or official of the Host Country or person exercising any public authority within the Host Country, shall enter the Premises of the Office to perform any duties therein except with the consent of, and under the conditions approved by the Head of the Office. In case of a fire or other emergency requiring prompt protection action, the consent of the Head of the Office to any necessary entry into the premises shall be presumed if he or she cannot be reached in time.

3. The Premises of the Office can be used for meetings, seminars, exhibitions and other related purposes which are organized by the Office or other United Nations entities.

4. The Premises of the Office shall not be used in any manner incompatible with the purpose and scope of the Office, as set forth in Article IV above.

Article VII. Security and Protection

1. The Host Country shall ensure the security and protection of the Premises of the Office and exercise due diligence to ensure that the tranquillity of the Premises is not disturbed by the unauthorized entry of persons or groups of persons from outside or by

disturbances in its immediate vicinity. If so requested by the Head of Office, the Host Country shall provide adequate police force necessary for the preservation of law and order in the Office premises or in its immediate vicinity, and for the removal of persons therefrom.

2. The Host Country shall take effective and adequate action which may be required to ensure the appropriate security, safety and protection of persons referred to in this Agreement, indispensable for the proper functioning of the Office free from interference of any kind.

Article VIII. Public Services

1. The Host Country shall facilitate, upon request of the Head of the Office and under terms and conditions not less favourable than those accorded by the Host Country to any accredited foreign mission, access to the public services needed by the Office such as, but not limited to utility, power and communications services.

In cases where public services referred to in paragraph 1, above, are made available to the Office by the Host Country or where the prices thereof are under their control, the rate for such services shall not exceed the lowest comparable rates accorded to accredited foreign missions in the Host Country.

In case of *force majeure*, resulting in a complete or partial disruption of the above-mentioned services, the Office shall, for the performance of its functions, be accorded the same priority given to essential governmental agencies and organs.

The provisions of this Article shall not prevent the reasonable application of fire protection or sanitary regulations of the Host Country.

Article IX. Communications Facilities

1. The Office shall enjoy, for its official communications, treatment not less favourable than that accorded by the Host Country to any other accredited diplomatic mission in the Host Country, in the matter of priorities, rates and taxes on mails, cables, telegrams, radiograms, telephotos, telephone and other communication and press rates for information to the press and radio.

2. The Host Country shall secure the inviolability of the official communications of the Office, whatever the means of the communications employed, and shall not apply any censorship to such communications.

3. The Office shall have the right to operate communication equipment, including satellite facilities and to use codes and to dispatch and receive correspondence by couriers and bags. The bags must bear visibly the emblem of UNOPS or any other United Nations entity and may contain only documents or articles intended for official use, and the courier shall be provided with a courier certificate issued by UNOPS or any other United Nations entity.

Article X. Funds, Assets and Other Property

1. The Office, its funds, assets and other property, wherever located and by whomsoever held, shall enjoy immunity from every form of legal process except when in a particular case such immunity has expressly been waived in accordance with General Convention. It is understood, however, that no waiver of immunity shall extend to any measure of execution.

2. The property and assets of the Office shall be exempt from restrictions, regulations, controls and moratoria of any nature.

3. Without being restricted by financial controls, regulations or moratoria of any kind, the Office:

(*a*) may hold and use funds, currency or negotiable instruments of any kind and maintain and operate accounts in any currency and convert any currency held by it into any other currency;

(*b*) shall be free to transfer its funds or currency from the Host Country to another country, or within the Host Country, to the United Nations or any other agency;

(*c*) shall enjoy the most favourable, legally available rate of exchange for its financial transactions.

Article XI. Exemption from Taxes, Duties, Import or Export Restrictions

The Office, its assets, funds and other property shall enjoy:

(*a*) Exemption from all direct and indirect taxes and levies, fees, tolls and duties; it being understood, however, that the Office shall not request exemption from taxes which are in fact no more than charges for public utility services rendered by the Host Country or by a corporation controlled by the Host Country at a fixed rate according to the amount of services rendered, and which can be specifically identified, described and itemized;

(*b*) Exemption from customs duties, charges and all other levies, as well as from limitations and restrictions on the import or export of materials imported or exported by the Office for its official use, it being understood that tax free imports cannot be sold in the Host Country except under conditions agreed to by the Host Country;

(*c*) Exemption from all limitations and restrictions on the import or export of publications, still and moving pictures, films, tapes, diskettes and sound recordings imported, exported or published by the Office within the framework of its official activities.

Article XII. Participants in Meetings Organized by the Office

1. Representatives of Member States of the United Nations invited to meetings, seminars, training courses, symposiums, workshops and similar activities organized by the Office and any other United Nations entity shall, while exercising their functions, enjoy the privileges and immunities as set out in Article IV of the General Convention.

2. The Host Country shall respect the complete freedom of expression of all participants of meetings, seminars, training courses, symposiums, workshops and similar activities organized by the Office and any other United Nations entity.

3. All participants and persons performing functions in connection with the meetings, seminars, training courses, symposiums, workshops and similar activities organized by the Office and any other United Nations entity shall enjoy such privileges, immunities and facilities as are necessary for the independent exercise of their participation and functions, in particular in respect of words spoken and acts done in connection with such meetings, seminars, training courses, symposiums, workshops and similar activities.

Article XIII. Officials of the Office

1. Officials shall enjoy the following privileges, immunities and facilities in the Host Country:

(*a*) Immunity from legal process in respect of words spoken or written and all acts performed by them in their official capacity. Such immunity shall continue in force after termination of employment with the Office;

(*b*) Immunity from personal arrest or detention and from seizure of their personal and official effects and baggage for acts performed in the discharge of their functions except in case of *flagrante delicto*. In such cases the Host Country shall immediately inform the Head of the Office of the arrest, detention or seizure;

(*c*) Exemption from taxation on the salaries and emoluments paid to them by the Office and any other United Nations entity; exemption from taxation on all income and property, for themselves and for their spouses and dependent members of their families, in so far as such income derives from sources, or in so far as such property is located outside the Host Country;

(*d*) Exemption from any military service obligations or any other obligatory service in the Host Country;

(*e*) Exemption, for themselves and for their spouses and dependent members of their families, from immigration restrictions or alien registration procedures;

(*f*) Exemption for themselves for the purpose of official business from any restriction on movement and travel inside the Host Country and a similar exemption for themselves and for their spouses and dependent members of their families for recreation in accordance with arrangements agreed upon between the Head of Office and the Host Country;

(*g*) In regard to foreign exchange, including holding accounts in foreign currencies, enjoyment of the same facilities as are accorded to members of diplomatic missions accredited to the Host Country;

(*h*) The same protection and repatriation facilities with respect to themselves, their spouses, and dependent members of their families as are accorded in time of international crisis to diplomatic envoys;

(*i*) The right to import for their personal use, free of duties, taxes (including value added and sales tax) and other levies, prohibitions and restrictions on imports:

i. their furniture and other personal effects;

ii. a motor vehicle, in accordance with existing regulations of the Host Country applicable to members of foreign missions of comparable ranks. This right is renewable every three years. A vehicle imported pursuant to this Agreement may be sold under conditions agreed with the Host Country.

(*j*) Officials shall be entitled, on the termination of their functions in the Host Country, to export their furniture and personal effects, including motor vehicles, without duties and taxes.

2. Officials of the nationality of the Host Country or with permanent residency status in the Host Country shall enjoy only those privileges and immunities provided for in Section 18 of the General Convention.

3. In accordance with the provisions of Section 17 of the General Convention, the Host Country shall be periodically informed of the names of the officials assigned to the Office.

Article XIV. Head of the Office and Senior Officials

1. The Head of Office shall be the principal channel of communication with the Host Country on all UNOPS matters. The Head of Office shall have full responsibility and ultimate authority, on behalf of the Executive Director, for the UNOPS activities and services in all its aspects in the Host Country. The Head of Office shall maintain liaison on behalf of UNOPS with the appropriate organs of the Host Country, and shall inform it of the policies, criteria and procedures of UNOPS. The Head of Office shall assist the Host Country, as may be required, in the preparation of requests for UNOPS assistance.

2. The Head of Office may also be designated as the UNOPS Representative in the Host Country.

3. Without prejudice to the provisions of the above Article, the Head of the Office shall enjoy during his or her residence in the Host Country the privileges, immunities and facilities granted to heads of accredited foreign missions to the Host Country. Furthermore, without prejudice to the provisions of the above Article, all officials assigned to the Office, having the rank of P/L-5 or above, shall be accorded the privileges, immunities and facilities granted to diplomatic staff at missions accredited to the Host Country. Their names shall be included in the diplomatic list held by the Host Country.

4. The privileges, immunities and facilities referred to above shall also be accorded to a spouse and dependent members of the family of the Officials concerned.

Article XV. Experts on Mission

1. Experts on Mission shall be granted the privileges, immunities and facilities specified in Articles VI and VII of the General Convention.

2. Experts on Mission shall be granted exemption from taxation on the salaries and other emoluments paid to them by the Office, and may be accorded such additional privileges. immunities and facilities as maybe agreed upon between UNOPS and the Host Country.

3. Experts on Mission of the nationality of the Host Country or with permanent residency status in the Host Country shall enjoy only those privileges and immunities that come within the scope of Articles VI and VII of the General Convention.

Article XVI. Persons Performing Services

The Host Country shall grant all persons performing services for or on behalf of the Office the same privileges and immunities as Officials assigned to the Office.

Article XVII. Locally-recruited personnel assigned to hourly rates

1. The terms and conditions of employment for persons recruited locally and assigned to hourly rates shall be in accordance with the relevant United Nations resolutions, decisions, regulations and rules and policies of the United Nations.

2. Personnel recruited in the Host Country and assigned to hourly rates shall be accorded immunity from legal process in respect of words spoken or written and all acts performed by them in their official capacity. Such immunity shall continue to be accorded after termination of employment with the Office.

Article XVIII. Waiver of Immunity

Privileges and immunities referred to in this Agreement are granted in the interest of the United Nations and not for the personal benefit of the persons to which such privileges and immunities are being granted. The right and the duty to waive the immunity of these persons, in any case where it can be waived without prejudice to the interests of the United Nations shall lie with the Secretary-General of the United Nations.

Article XIX. Entry into, exit from, movement and sojourn within the Host Country

All persons referred to in this Agreement including all participants in meetings, seminars, training courses, symposiums, workshops and similar activities organized by the Office shall have the right of unimpeded entry into, exit form, sojourn and free movement within the Host Country. Visas, entry permits or licenses, where required, shall be granted as promptly as possible and free of charge.

Article XX. United Nations Laissez-Passer, Certificates and Visas

1. The Host Country shall recognize and accept the United Nations *laissez-passer* issued to Officials of the Office and any other United Nations entity as a valid travel document.

2. In accordance with the provisions of Section 26 of the General Convention, the Host Country shall recognize and accept the United Nations certificate issued to Experts on Mission and other persons travelling on business for UNOPS or any other United Nations entity.

3. All persons referred to in this Agreement shall be granted facilities for speedy travel. Visas, entry permits or licenses, where required, shall be granted free of charge and as promptly as possible to the persons referred to in this Agreement, their dependents and other persons invited to the Office in connection with the official work and activities of the Office.

Article XXI. Identification Cards

1. At the request of the Head of the Office, the Host Country shall issue identification cards to all persons referred to in this Agreement, certifying their status under this Agreement.

2. Upon the demand of an authorized official of the Host Country, persons referred to in this Agreement shall be required to present, without having to surrender, their identification cards.

Article XXII. Flags, Emblem and Markings

The Office shall be entitled to display the United Nations flag, logo, emblem and markings in the Office premises and on vehicles used for official purposes.

Article XXIII. Social Security

1. The United Nations Joint Pension Fund shall enjoy legal capacity in the Host Country and shall enjoy the same exemptions, privileges and immunities as the United Nations itself. Benefits received from the Pension Fund shall be exempt from taxation.

2. The Host Country agree that, owing to the fact that Officials of the Office are subject to the United Nations Staff Regulations and Rules, including Article VI thereof, which establish a comprehensive social security scheme. Officials of this Office, irrespective of nationality, shall be exempt from the laws of the host country on mandatory coverage and

compulsory contributions to the social security schemes of Host Country during their appointment with the Office.

3. The provisions above shall apply *mutatis mutandis* to the members of families forming part of the household of Officials of the Office, unless they are employed or self-employed in the Host Country or receive social security benefits from the Host Country.

Article XXIV. Access to the labour market for family members and issuance of visas and residence permits to household employees

1. The Host Country shall grant working permits for spouses of Officials assigned to the Office and their children forming part of their household who are under 21 years of age or economically dependent.

2. The Host Country shall issue visas and residence permits and any other documents, where required, to household employees of officials assigned to the Office as speedily as possible.

3. The Host Country undertakes to assist Officials, Experts on Mission and Persons Performing Services to the Office, as much as possible, in obtaining premises for use as residences.

Article XXV. Cooperation with the Host Country

1. Without prejudice to the privileges and immunities accorded by this Agreement, it is the duty of all persons enjoying such privileges and immunities to respect the laws and regulations of the Host Country, and not to interfere in the internal affairs of the Host Country.

2. Without prejudice to the privileges and immunities referred to in this Agreement, the Office shall cooperate at all times with the Host Country to facilitate the proper administration of justice, secure the observance of police regulations and prevent the occurrence of any abuse in connection with the facilities, privileges and immunities accorded to persons referred to in the present Agreement.

Article XXVI. Liability

1. The Host Country shall bear all risks of operations of the Office under this Agreement. It shall be responsible for dealing with claims which may be brought by third parties against UNOPS, its Officials, Experts on Mission, Persons Performing Services or participants of meetings, seminars, training courses, symposiums, workshops and similar activities organized by the Office and any other United Nations entity, and shall hold them harmless in respect of claims or liabilities arising from operations under this Agreement.

2. The foregoing provision shall not apply in case of gross negligence or wilful misconduct of the Office or the above-mentioned persons.

Article XXVII. Supplemental Agreements

1. Arrangements of an administrative and financial nature concerning the Office may be made by supplemental agreements, as appropriate.

2. The Parties may enter into any other supplemental agreements as the Parties may deem appropriate.

Article XXVIII. Settlement of disputes

1. UNOPS shall make provisions for the settlement of:

(*a*) Disputes arising out of contracts and disputes of a private law character to which the Office is a party;

(*b*) Disputes involving any person referred to in this Agreement, who enjoys immunity, if such immunity has not been waived.

2. Any dispute between the Office and the Host Country arising out of, or relating to this Agreement or any Supplemental Agreement, which is not settled by negotiation or another agreed mode of settlement, shall, at the request of either Party, be submitted to an arbitral tribunal of three arbitrators. Each Party shall appoint one arbitrator, and the two arbitrators so appointed shall appoint a third, who shall be the chairperson of the Tribunal. If, within sixty (60) days of the request for arbitration, a Party has not appointed an arbitrator, or if, within thirty (30) days of the appointment of two arbitrators, the third arbitrator has not been appointed, either Party may request the President of the International Court of Justice to appoint the arbitrator referred to. The Tribunal shall determine its own procedures and all decisions shall require the agreement of at least two arbitrators. The fees and expenses of the tribunal shall be borne by the Parties as assessed by the Tribunal. The arbitral award shall contain a statement of the reasons on which it is based and shall be final and binding on the Parties.

Article XXIX. Final Provisions

1. If the Host Country enters into any agreement with another United Nations entity or intergovernmental organization containing terms and conditions more favourable than those extended to the Office under the present Agreement, such terms and conditions shall be extended to the Office at its request, by means of a supplemental agreement.

2. This Agreement may be modified by written agreement between the Parties hereto. Any relevant matter for which no provision is made in this Agreement shall be settled by the Parties under the relevant resolutions and decisions of the appropriate organs of the United Nations. Each Party shall give full and sympathetic consideration to any proposal advanced by the other Party under this paragraph.

3. This Agreement may be terminated by either Party by written notice to the other and shall terminate six months after receipt of such notice. Notwithstanding any such notice of termination, this Agreement shall remain in force to allow the completion of the Office's operations of in the Host Country, the liquidation of its Properties, to settle all pending matters relating to the implementation of this Agreement and the resolution of any dispute between the Parties in relation to this Agreement.

4. The obligations assumed by the Host Country shall survive the termination of this Agreement, to the extent necessary to permit orderly withdrawal of the Property and Archives, of the Office and of its Officials, Expert on Missions and other relevant persons under this Agreement.

5. This Agreement shall be subject to the signature of both Parties. It shall enter into force on the date of the last signature thereof.

In Witness Whereof, the undersigned, duly appointed representatives of the Parties, have signed the present Agreement between UNOPS and Kingdom of Tonga on this 8th day of July, 2019, in the English language, in two originals.

For UNOPS	For the Kingdom of Tonga
[*Signed*]	[*Signed*]
Ms. Grete Faremo United Nations Under-Secretary General and Executive Director of UNOPS	Hon. Samuela Akilisi Pohiva Prime Minister, Kingdom of Tonga

(*f*) Agreement between the United Nations and the Government of the Republic of Haiti on the status of the United Nations Integrated Office in Haiti ("BINUH"). Port-au-Prince, 12 October 2019*

I. Definitions

1. For the purpose of the present Agreement the following definitions shall apply:

(*a*) "BINUH" means the United Nations Integrated Office in Haiti, established in accordance with Security Council resolution 2476 (2019) of 25 June 2019 with the mandate described in the above-mentioned resolution, based on the recommendations contained in the letter of the Secretary-General dated 13 May 2019 addressed to the President of the Security Council (S/2019/387).

BINUH shall consist of:

(i) The "Special Representative" appointed by the Secretary-General of the United Nations with the consent of the Security Council. Any reference to the Special Representative in the present Agreement shall, except in paragraph 25, include any members of BINUH to whom he or she delegates a specified function or authority;

(ii) United Nations staff members assigned by the Secretary-General to BINUH, including locally recruited staff;

(iii) United Nations Volunteers assigned to BINUH;

(iv) Police and corrections advisers and other non-United Nations staff members who carry out missions for BINUH;

(*b*) "Members of BINUH" means the Special Representative of the Secretary-General and all persons listed in paragraph 1 (*a*) (ii), (iii) and (iv);

(*c*) "The Government" means the Government of Haiti;

(*d*) "The territory" means the territory of Haiti;

* Entered into force provisionally on 12 October 2019 by signature, in accordance with paragraph 59. United Nations registration no. I-55978.

(*e*) "The Convention" means the Convention on the Privileges and Immunities of the United Nations adopted by the General Assembly of the United Nations on 13 February 1946, to which the Republic of Haiti is a party;

(*g*) "Contractors" means persons, other than members of BINUH, engaged by the United Nations, including juridical as well as natural persons and their employees and sub-contractors, to perform services and/or supply equipment, provisions, supplies, materials and other goods in support of BINUH activities. Such contractors shall not be considered third-party beneficiaries to the present Agreement;

(*h*) "Vehicles" means vehicles in use by the United Nations and operated by members of BINUH and contractors in support of BINUH activities;

(*i*) "Vessels" means vessels in use by the United Nations and operated by members of BINUH, participating States and contractors in support of BINUH activities;

(*j*) "Aircraft" means aircraft in use by the United Nations and operated by members of BINUH, participating States and contractors in the context of BINUH activities.

II. Application of the present Agreement

2. Unless specifically provided otherwise, the provisions of the present Agreement and any obligation undertaken by the Government or any privilege, immunity, facility or concession granted to BINUH or any member thereof or to contractors shall apply throughout the territory of Haiti.

III. Application of the Convention

3. BINUH, its property, funds and assets and its members, including the Special Representative, shall enjoy the privileges and immunities specified in the present Agreement and in the Convention.

[*IV is missing in the authentic French text*]

V. Status of BINUH

4. BINUH and its members shall refrain from any action or activity incompatible with the impartial and international nature of their duties or inconsistent with the spirit of the present arrangements. BINUH and its members shall respect all local laws and regulations. The Special Representative shall take all appropriate measures to ensure the observance of those obligations.

5. The Government undertakes to respect the exclusively international nature of BINUH.

United Nations flag and distinctive United Nations identification

6. The Government recognizes the right of BINUH to display, within Haiti, the United Nations flag on its headquarters, camps or other premises, vehicles, vessels or otherwise, as decided by the Special Representative.

7. Vehicles, vessels and aircraft of BINUH shall carry a distinctive United Nations identification, which shall be notified to the Government.

Communications

8. BINUH shall enjoy the facilities with respect to communications provided in article III of the Convention and shall, in coordination with the Government, use such facilities as may be required for the performance of its task. Issues with respect to communications which may arise and which are not specifically provided for in the present Agreement shall be dealt with pursuant to the relevant provisions of the Convention.

9. Subject to the provisions of paragraph 8:

(*a*) BINUH shall have the right to install and operate United Nations radio stations in order to broadcast information relating to its mandate. It shall also have the authority to install and to operate radio sending and receiving stations, as well as satellite systems, to connect appropriate points within the territory with each other and with United Nations offices in other countries, and to exchange data by telephone, voice, facsimile and other electronic means with the United Nations global telecommunications network. United Nations radio stations and telecommunication services shall be operated in accordance with the International Telecommunication Convention and Regulations, and the frequencies on which any such station may be operated shall be allocated by the Government without delay;

(*b*) BINUH shall enjoy, within the territory, the right to unrestricted communication by radio (including satellite, mobile and hand-held radio), telephone, electronic mail, facsimile or any other means, and of establishing the necessary facilities for maintaining such communications within and between its premises, including the laying of cables and landlines and the establishment of fixed and mobile radio sending, receiving and repeater stations. The frequencies on which the radio will operate shall be decided upon in cooperation with the Government and shall be allocated without delay. It is understood that connections with the local system of telephones, facsimile machines and other electronic data transmission methods may be made only after consultation and in accordance with arrangements with the Government, it being further understood that the use of the local system of telephones, facsimile machines and other electronic data transmission methods will be charged at the most favourable rate;

(*c*) BINUH may make the necessary arrangements, through its own facilities, for the processing and transport of personal mail addressed to or emanating from its members. The Government shall be informed of the nature of such arrangements and shall not interfere with or apply censorship to the mail of BINUH or its members. In the event that postal arrangements applying to personal mail of members of BINUH are extended to the transfer of currency or the transport of packages and parcels, the conditions under which such operations are conducted shall be agreed with the Government.

Travel and transport

11.[*] BINUH and its members and contractors shall enjoy, together with vehicles, including vehicles of contractors used exclusively for the provision of services to BINUH, vessels, aircraft and equipment, freedom of movement without delay throughout the territory. That freedom shall, with respect to large movements of personnel, stores, vehicles or

[*] The authentic French text contains two paragraphs numbered as 11 and no paragraph 10.

aircraft through airports or on railways or roads used for general traffic within the territory, be coordinated with the Government. The Government undertakes to supply BINUH, where necessary, with maps and other information, including with regard to dangers and impediments, which may be useful in facilitating its movements.

11. BINUH vehicles and vessels shall not be subject to Haitian registration and licensing regulations, but must carry third-party insurance.

12. BINUH and its members and contractors, together with their vehicles, including those used exclusively for the provision of services to BINUH, vehicles and aircraft, may use roads, bridges, canals and other waters, port facilities, airfields and airspace without the payment of charges, tolls, landing fees, parking or overflight fees, or port fees or charges, including wharfage and pilotage charges. However, BINUH will not claim exemption from charges which are in fact charges for services rendered, it being understood that such charges shall be calculated at the most favourable rates.

Privileges and immunities of BINUH

13. BINUH, as a subsidiary organ of the United Nations, enjoys the status, privileges and immunities of the United Nations in accordance with the Convention. The Government recognizes the right of BINUH in particular:

(*a*) To import, free of duty or other restrictions, equipment, provisions, supplies, fuel and other goods which are for its exclusive and official use or for resale in the commissaries provided for hereinafter;

(*b*) To establish, maintain and operate commissaries at its headquarters, camps and posts for the benefit of its members but not of locally recruited personnel. Such commissaries may provide goods of a consumable nature and other articles to be specified in advance. The Special Representative shall take all necessary measures to prevent the abuse of such commissaries and the sale or resale of such goods to persons other than members of BINUH, and shall give sympathetic consideration to observations or requests of the Government concerning the operation of the commissaries;

(*c*) To clear ex customs and excise warehouse, free of duty or other restrictions, equipment, provisions, supplies, fuel and other goods which are for its exclusive and official use or for resale in the commissaries provided for above;

(*d*) To re-export or otherwise dispose of equipment that is still usable, all unconsumed provisions, supplies, fuel and other goods so imported or cleared ex customs and excise warehouse which are not transferred, or otherwise disposed of, on terms and conditions to be agreed upon, to the competent local authorities of the State of Haiti or to an entity nominated by them.

To the end that importation, clearances, transfer or exportation may be effected with the least possible delay, a mutually satisfactory procedure, including documentation, shall be agreed between BINUH and the Government at the earliest possible date.

V. Facilities for BINUH and its contractors

Premises required for conducting the operational and administrative activities of BINUH

14. The Government shall provide, without cost to BINUH and in agreement with the Special Representative, such areas for headquarters and other premises as may be necessary for the conduct of its operational and administrative activities. Without prejudice to the fact that all such premises remain Haitian territory, they shall be inviolable and subject to the exclusive control and authority of the United Nations. The Government shall guarantee unrestricted access to such premises.

15. The Government undertakes to assist BINUH as far as possible in obtaining, or to provide, where applicable, water, electricity and other facilities free of charge, or, where this is not possible, at the most favourable rate and, in the case of interruption or threatened interruption of service, to give, as far as is within its powers, the same priority to the needs of BINUH as to essential government services. Where such utilities or facilities are not provided free of charge, payment shall be made by BINUH on terms to be agreed with the relevant authorities. BINUH shall be responsible for the maintenance and upkeep of facilities so provided.

16. BINUH shall have the right, where necessary, to generate, within its premises, electricity for its use and to transmit and distribute such electricity.

17. The United Nations alone may consent to the entry of any government officials or of any other person not a member of BINUH to the premises of BINUH.

Provisions, supplies and services, and sanitary arrangements

18. The Government agrees to grant expeditiously all authorizations, permits and licences necessary for the importation and exportation of equipment, provisions, supplies, materials and other goods exclusively used in support of BINUH, including in respect of importation or exportation by contractors, free of any restrictions and without the payment of duties, charges or taxes, including value-added tax on purchases.

19. The Government undertakes to assist BINUH as far as possible in obtaining from local sources the equipment, provisions, supplies, fuel, materials and other goods and services required for its subsistence and operations. In respect of equipment, provisions, supplies, materials and other goods purchased locally by BINUH or by contractors for the official and exclusive use of BINUH, the Government shall make appropriate administrative arrangements for the reimbursement of, or exemption from, duties or taxes included in the price. The Government shall exempt BINUH and its contractors from general sales taxes in respect of all official local purchases. In making purchases on the local market, BINUH shall, on the basis of observations made and information provided by the Government in that respect, avoid any adverse effect on the local economy.

20. For the proper performance of the services provided by contractors, other than Haitian nationals resident in Haiti, in support of BINUH, the Government agrees to provide contractors with facilities concerning their entry into and departure from Haiti, as well as their repatriation in time of crisis. For this purpose, the Government shall promptly issue to contractors, free of charge and without any restrictions, all necessary visas, licences or permits. Contractors, other than Haitian nationals resident in Haiti, shall be accorded exemption from taxes on the services provided to BINUH, including corporate, income, social security and other similar taxes arising directly from the provision of such services.

21. BINUH and the Government shall cooperate with respect to sanitary services and shall extend to each other the fullest cooperation in matters concerning health, particularly with respect to the control of communicable diseases, in accordance with international conventions.

Recruitment of local personnel

22. BINUH may recruit locally such personnel as it requires. Upon the request of the Special Representative, the Government undertakes to facilitate the recruitment of qualified local staff by BINUH and to accelerate the process of such recruitment.

Currency

23. The Government undertakes to make available to BINUH, against reimbursement in mutually acceptable currency, local currency required for its use, including the pay of its members, at the exchange rate most favourable to BINUH.

VI. Status of the members of BINUH

Privileges and immunities

24. The Special Representative, the Deputy Special Representative, the head of the United Nations police and such high-ranking members of the Special Representative's staff as may be agreed upon with the Government shall have the status specified in sections 19 and 27 of the Convention, provided that the privileges and immunities therein referred to shall be those accorded to diplomatic envoys by international law.

25. Officials of the United Nations assigned to BINUH, as well as United Nations Volunteers who shall be assimilated thereto, remain officials of the United Nations entitled to the privileges and immunities of articles V and VII of the Convention.

26. Police and corrections advisers, and civilian personnel other than United Nations officials whose names are, for the purpose, notified to the Government by the Special Representative shall be considered as experts on mission within the meaning of article VI of the Convention.

27. Unless otherwise specified in the present Agreement, locally recruited members of BINUH shall enjoy the immunities concerning official acts and exemption from taxation and national service obligations provided for in sections 18 (*a*), (*b*) and (*c*) of the Convention.

28. Members of BINUH shall be exempt from taxation on the pay and emoluments received from the United Nations and any income received from outside Haiti. They shall also be exempt from all other direct taxes, except municipal rates for services enjoyed, and from all registration fees and charges.

29. Members of BINUH shall have the right to import, free of duty, their personal effects, in connection with their arrival in and departure from Haiti. They shall be subject to the laws and regulations governing customs and foreign exchange with respect to personal property not required by them by reason of their presence in Haiti with BINUH. Special facilities will be granted by the Government for the speedy processing of entry and exit formalities for all members of BINUH, upon prior written notification. On departure from Haiti, members of BINUH may, notwithstanding the above-mentioned exchange regulations, take with them such funds as the Special Representative certifies were received

in pay and emoluments from the United Nations and are a reasonable residue thereof. Special arrangements shall be made for the implementation of the present provisions in the interests of the Government and the members of BINUH.

30. The Special Representative shall cooperate with the Government and shall render all assistance within his or her power in ensuring the observance of the customs and fiscal laws and regulations of Haiti by the members of BINUH, in accordance with the present Agreement.

Entry, residence and departure

31. The Special Representative and members of BINUH shall, whenever so requested by the Special Representative, have the right to enter into, reside in and depart from Haiti.

32. The Government undertakes to facilitate the entry into and departure from Haiti of the Special Representative and members of BINUH, and shall be kept informed of such movement. For that purpose, the Special Representative and members of BINUH shall be exempt from passport and visa regulations and immigration inspection and restrictions, as well as from payment of any fees or charges, on entering or departing from the territory. They shall also be exempt from any regulations governing the residence of aliens in Haiti, including registration, but shall not be considered as acquiring any right to permanent residence or domicile in Haiti.

33. Upon such entry or departure, members of BINUH shall only be required to have a personal identity card issued in accordance with paragraph 34 of the present Agreement, except in the case of first entry, when a United Nations laissez-passer, a national passport or a personal identity card issued by the United Nations shall be accepted in lieu of the said identity card.

Identification

34. The Special Representative shall issue to each member of BINUH, before or as soon as possible after such member's first entry into the territory, as well as to all locally recruited personnel and contractors, a numbered identity card, which shall show the bearer's name and photograph. Except as provided for in paragraph 34 of the present Agreement, such identity card shall be the only document required of a member of BINUH.

35. Members of BINUH, as well as locally recruited personnel and contractors, shall be required to present, but not to surrender, their BINUH identity cards upon demand of an appropriate official of the Government.

Uniform and arms

36. Police advisers and corrections advisers shall wear, while performing official duties, the national uniform of their respective States, with standard United Nations accoutrements. United Nations Security Officers and Field Service Officers may wear the United Nations uniform. The wearing of civilian dress by the above-mentioned members of BINUH may be authorized by the Special Representative at other times. Police advisers and United Nations Security Officers designated by the Special Representative may possess and carry arms while on duty, in accordance with their orders. Those carrying weapons while on official duty, other than United Nations Security Officers designated by the Special Representative, must be in uniform while on official duty.

Permits and licences

37. The Government agrees to accept as valid, without tax or fee, a permit or licence issued by the Special Representative for the operation by any member of BINUH, including locally recruited personnel, of BINUH transport capabilities and for the practice of any profession or occupation in connection with the functioning of BINUH, provided that no licence to drive a vehicle shall be issued to any person who is not already in possession of an appropriate and valid licence.

38. The Government agrees to accept as valid, and where necessary to validate, free of charge and without any restrictions, licences and certificates issued by appropriate authorities in other States in respect of aircraft and vessels, including those operated by contractors exclusively for BINUH. Without prejudice to the foregoing, the Government further agrees to grant expeditiously, free of charge and without any restrictions, necessary authorizations, licences and certificates, where required, for the acquisition, use, operation and maintenance of aircraft and vessels.

39. Without prejudice to the provisions of paragraph 36, the Government further agrees to accept as valid, without tax or fee, a permit or licence issued by the Special Representative to a member of BINUH for the carrying or use of firearms or ammunition in connection with the functioning of BINUH.

Arrest and transfer of custody and mutual assistance

40. The Special Representative shall take all appropriate measures to ensure the maintenance of discipline and good order among members of BINUH, as well as locally recruited personnel. To this end, United Nations Security Officers shall police the premises of BINUH and such areas where its members are deployed. Such personnel shall be employed subject to arrangements with the Government and in liaison with it only insofar as such employment is necessary to maintain discipline and order among members of BINUH.

41. The personnel mentioned in paragraph 40 above may take into custody any other person on the premises of BINUH. Such other person shall be delivered immediately to the nearest appropriate official of the Government for the purpose of dealing with any offence or disturbance on such premises.

42. Subject to the provisions of paragraphs 24 and 26, officials of the Government may take into custody any member of BINUH:

(*a*) When so requested by the Special Representative; or

(*b*) When such a member of BINUH is apprehended in the commission or attempted commission of a criminal offence. Such person shall be delivered immediately, together with any weapons or other item seized, to the nearest appropriate representative of BINUH, whereafter the provisions of paragraph 48 shall apply mutatis mutandis.

43. When a person is taken into custody under paragraph 41 or paragraph 42 (*b*), BINUH or the Government, as the case may be, may make a preliminary interrogation but may not delay the transfer of custody. Following such transfer, the person concerned shall be made available upon request to the arresting authority for further interrogation.

44. BINUH and the Government shall assist each other in carrying out all necessary investigations into offences in respect of which either or both have an interest, in the

production of witnesses and in the collection and production of evidence, including the seizure of and, if appropriate, the handing over of items connected with an offence. The handing over of any such items may be made subject to their return within the terms specified by the authority delivering them. Each shall notify the other of the disposition of any case in the outcome of which the other may have an interest or in which there has been a transfer of custody under the provisions of paragraphs 41 to 43.

Safety and security

45. The Government shall ensure that the provisions of the Convention on the Safety of United Nations and Associated Personnel are applied to and in respect of BINUH and its property, assets and members. In particular:

(*a*) The Government shall take all appropriate measures to ensure the security of the members of BINUH. In particular, it shall take all appropriate steps to protect the members of BINUH and their equipment and premises from attack or any action that prevents them from discharging their mandate. This is without prejudice to the fact that such premises are inviolable and are subject to the exclusive control and authority of the United Nations;

(*b*) If members of BINUH are detained in the performance of their duties and their identity has been established, they shall not be subjected to interrogation and shall be promptly released and returned to the United Nations. Pending their release, such personnel shall be treated in accordance with universally recognized human rights standards;

(*c*) The Government shall establish the following acts as crimes under its national law and make them punishable by appropriate penalties taking into account their grave nature:

(i) Murder, kidnapping or any other attack upon the person or liberty of any member of BINUH;

(ii) Violent attack on the official premises, private residence or means of transport of any member of BINUH likely to endanger his or her person or liberty;

(iii) Threat to commit such an attack with the aim of compelling a physical or juridical person to perform or to refrain from performing any act;

(iv) Attempt to commit such an attack;

(v) Any act constituting participation or complicity in any such attack or attempted attack, or in organizing or ordering others to commit such an attack.

(*d*) The Government shall establish its jurisdiction over the crimes set out in paragraph 45 (*c*) above:

(i) When the crime was committed in its territory;

(ii) When the alleged offender is a national of the country;

(iii) When the alleged offender, other than a member of BINUH, is present in its territory, unless he or she has been extradited to the State in whose territory the crime was committed, to the State of his or her nationality, to the State of his or her habitual residence if he or she is a stateless person or to the State of nationality of the victim.

(*e*) The Government shall ensure the prosecution, without exception and without delay, of persons accused of acts described in paragraph 45 (c) above who are present in its territory (if the Government does not extradite them), as well as persons subject to its criminal jurisdiction who are accused of other acts against BINUH or its members which, if committed against the forces of the Government or against the civilian population, would have rendered such acts liable to prosecution.

46. Upon the request of the Special Representative, the Government shall provide such security as is necessary to protect BINUH, its property and its members during the exercise of their functions.

Jurisdiction

47. All members of BINUH, including locally recruited personnel, shall be immune from legal process in respect of words spoken or written and all acts performed by them in their official capacity. Such immunity shall continue even after they cease to be members of or employed by BINUH and after the expiration of the other provisions of the present Agreement.

48. Should the Government consider that any member of BINUH has committed a criminal offence, it shall promptly inform the Special Representative and present to him or her any evidence available to it. Subject to the provisions of paragraph 24, the Special Representative shall conduct any necessary supplementary inquiry and then agree with the Government whether or not criminal proceedings should be instituted. Failing such agreement, the question shall be resolved as provided in paragraph 54 of the present Agreement.

49. If any civil proceeding is instituted against a member of BINUH before any court of Haiti, the Special Representative shall be notified immediately, and he or she shall certify to the court whether or not the proceeding is related to the official duties of such member:

(*a*) If the Special Representative certifies that the proceeding is related to official duties, such proceeding shall be discontinued and the provisions of paragraph 52 of the present Agreement shall apply;

(*b*) If the Special Representative certifies that the proceeding is not related to official duties, the proceeding may continue. If the Special Representative certifies that a member of BINUH is unable, because of official duties or authorized absence, to protect his or her interests in the proceeding, the court shall, at the defendant's request, suspend the proceeding until the elimination of the disability, but for not more than 90 days. Property of a member of BINUH that is certified by the Special Representative to be needed by the defendant for the fulfilment of his or her official duties shall be free from seizure for the satisfaction of a judgment, decision or order. The personal liberty of a member of BINUH shall not be restricted in a civil proceeding, whether to enforce a judgement, decision or order, to compel an oath or for any other reason.

Deceased members

50. The Special Representative or the Secretary-General shall have the right to take charge of and dispose of the body of a member of BINUH who dies in Haiti, as well as that member's personal property located within Haiti, in accordance with United Nations procedures.

VII. Limitation of liability of the United Nations

51. Third-party claims for property losses or damage or for personal injury, illness or death arising from or directly attributed to BINUH, except for those arising from

operational necessity, which cannot be settled through the internal procedures of the United Nations, shall be settled by the United Nations in the manner provided for in article 52 of the present Agreement, provided that the claim is submitted within six months following the occurrence of the loss, damage or injury, or, if the claimant did not know or could not have reasonably known of such loss or injury, within six months from the time he or she discovered the loss or injury, but in any event not later than one year after the termination of the mandate of BINUH. Upon determination of liability as provided in the present Agreement, the United Nations shall pay compensation within such financial limitations as have been approved by the General Assembly in its resolution 52/247 of 26 June 1998.

VIII. Settlement of disputes

52. Except as provided in paragraph 54, any dispute or claim of a private law character not relating to damage attributable to the operational needs of BINUH to which BINUH or any member thereof is a party and over which the courts of Haiti do not have jurisdiction because of any provision of the present Agreement shall be settled by a standing claims commission to be established for that purpose. One member of the commission shall be appointed by the Secretary-General of the United Nations, one member by the Government and the Chairperson jointly by the Secretary-General and the Government. If no agreement as to the Chairperson has been reached by the two parties within 30 days of the appointment of the first member of the commission, the President of the International Court of Justice may, at the request of either party, appoint the Chairperson. Any vacancy on the commission shall be filled by the same method prescribed for the original appointment, provided that the 30-day period there prescribed shall start as soon as there is a vacancy in the chairpersonship. The commission shall determine its own procedures, provided that any two members shall constitute a quorum for all purposes (except for a period of 30 days after the creation of a vacancy) and all decisions shall require the approval of any two members. The awards of the commission shall be final. The awards of the commission shall be notified to the parties and, if against a member of BINUH, the Special Representative or the Secretary-General of the United Nations shall use his or her best endeavours to ensure compliance.

53. All disputes concerning the terms of employment and conditions of service of locally recruited personnel shall be settled in accordance the regulations and rules of the United Nations.

54. All disputes between BINUH and the Government concerning the interpretation or application of the present Agreement shall, unless otherwise agreed by the parties, be submitted to a tribunal of three arbitrators. The provisions relating to the establishment and procedures of the claims commission shall apply, mutatis mutandis, to the establishment and procedures of the tribunal. The decisions of the tribunal shall be final and binding on both parties.

55. All differences between the United Nations and the Government arising out of the interpretation or application of the present arrangements which involve a question of principle concerning the Convention shall be dealt with in accordance with the procedure of section 30 of the Convention.

IX. Supplemental arrangements

56. The Special Representative and the Government may conclude in writing supplemental arrangements to the present Agreement.

X. Liaison

57. The Special representative and the Government shall take appropriate measures to ensure close and reciprocal liaison at every appropriate level.

XI. Miscellaneous provisions

58. Wherever the present Agreement refers to the privileges, immunities and rights of BINUH and to the facilities Haiti undertakes to provide to BINUH, the Government shall have the ultimate responsibility for the implementation and fulfilment of such privileges, immunities, rights and facilities by the appropriate local authorities.

59. The present Agreement shall be applied provisionally upon signature by the United Nations and the Government, and shall enter into force upon notification by the Government of the completion of the internal procedures.

60. The present Agreement shall remain in force until the departure of the final element of BINUH, except that:

(*a*) The provisions of paragraphs 47, 50, 54 and 55 shall remain in force;

(*b*) The provisions of paragraphs 51 and 52 shall remain in force until all claims made in accordance with the provisions of paragraph 51 have been settled.

In Witness Whereof the undersigned, being the duly authorized plenipotentiary of the Government and the duly appointed representative of the United Nations, have, on behalf of the parties, signed the present Agreement.

Port-au-Prince, 12 October 2019

For the United Nations	For the Government of Haiti
[*Signed*]	[*Signed*]
Helen Ruth Meagher La Lime	Bocchit Edmond
Special Representative of the Secretary-General in Haiti	Minister for Foreign Affairs and Worship

3. United Nations Development Programme

Standard Basic Assistance Agreement (*SBAA*) between the United Nations Development Programme (UNDP) and the Government of the Republic of Fiji. Suva, 25 February 2019*

Whereas the General Assembly of the United Nations has established the United Nations Development Programme (hereinafter called the UNDP) to support and supplement the national efforts of developing countries at solving the most important

* Entered into force on 25 February 2019 by signature, in accordance with article XIII. United Nations registration no. I-55641.

problems of their economic development and to promote social progress and better standards of life; and

Whereas the Government of the Republic of Fiji wishes to request assistance from the UNDP for the benefit of its people;

Now Therefore the Government and the UNDP (hereinafter called the Parties) have entered into this Agreement in a spirit of friendly co-operation.

Article I. Scope of this Agreement

1. This Agreement embodies the basic conditions under which the UNDP and its Executing Agencies shall assist the Government in carrying out its development projects, and under which such UNDP-assisted projects shall be executed. It shall apply to all such UNDP assistance and to such project documents or other instruments (hereinafter called Project Documents) as the Parties may conclude to define the particulars of such assistance and the respective responsibilities of the Parties and the Executing Agency hereunder in more detail in regard to such projects.

2. Assistance shall be provided by the UNDP under this Agreement only in response to requests submitted by the Government and approved by the UNDP. Such assistance shall be made available to the Government, or to such entity as the Government may designate, and shall be furnished and received in accordance with the relevant and applicable resolutions and decisions of the competent UNDP organs, and subject to the availability of the necessary funds to the UNDP.

Article II. Forms of Assistance

1. Assistance which may be made available by the UNDP to the Government under this Agreement may consist of:

(*a*) The services of advisory experts and consultants, including consultant firms or organizations, selected by and responsible to, the UNDP or the Executing Agency concerned;

(*b*) The services of operational experts selected by the Executing Agency, to perform functions of an operational, executive or administrative character as civil servants of the Government or as employees of such entities as the Government may designate under Article I, paragraph 2, hereof;

(*c*) The services of members of the United Nations Volunteers (hereinafter called volunteers);

(*d*) Equipment and supplies not readily available in Fiji (hereinafter called the country);

(*e*) Seminars, training programmes, demonstration projects, expert working groups and related activities;

(*f*) Scholarships and fellowships, or similar arrangements under which candidates nominated by the Government and approved by the Executing Agency concerned may study or receive training; and

(*g*) Any other form of assistance which may be agreed upon by the Government and the UNDP.

2. Requests for assistance shall be presented by the Government to the UNDP through the UNDP resident representative in the country (referred to in paragraph 4(*a*) of this Article), and in the form and in accordance with procedures established by the UNDP

for such requests. The Government shall provide the UNDP with all appropriate facilities and relevant information to appraise the request, including an expression of its intent with respect to the follow-up of investment-oriented projects.

3. Assistance may be provided by the UNDP to the Government either directly, with such external assistance as it may deem appropriate, or through an Executing Agency, which shall have primary responsibility for carrying out UNDP assistance to the project and which shall have the status of an independent contractor for this purpose. Where assistance is provided by the UNDP directly to the Government, all references in this Agreement to an Executing Agency shall be construed to refer to the UNDP, unless clearly inappropriate from the context.

4. (*a*) The UNDP may maintain a permanent mission, headed by a resident representative, in the country to represent the UNDP therein and be the principal channel of communication with the Government on all Programme matters. The resident representative shall have full responsibility and ultimate authority, on behalf of the UNDP Administrator, for the UNDP programme in all its aspects in the country, and shall be team leader in regard to such representatives of other United Nations organizations as may be posted in the country, taking into account their professional competence and their relations with appropriate organs of the Government. The resident representative shall maintain liaison on behalf of the Programme with the appropriate organs of the Government, including the Government's co-ordinating agency for external assistance, and shall inform the Government of the policies, criteria and procedures of the UNDP and other relevant programmes of the United Nations. The resident representative shall assist the Government, as may be required, in the preparation of UNDP country programme and project requests, as well as proposals for country programme or project changes, assure proper coordination of all assistance rendered by the UNDP through various Executing Agencies or its own consultants, assist the Government, as may be required, in co-ordinating UNDP activities with national, bilateral and multilateral programmes within the country, and carry out such other functions as may be entrusted to him or her by the Administrator or by an Executing Agency;

(*b*) The UNDP mission in the country shall have such other staff, as the UNDP may deem appropriate to its proper functioning. The UNDP shall notify the Government from time to time of the names of the members, and of the families of the members, of the mission, and of changes in the status of such persons.

Article III. Execution of Projects

1. The Government shall remain responsible for its UNDP-assisted development projects and the realization of their objectives as described in the relevant Project Documents, and shall carry out such parts of such projects as may be stipulated in the provisions of this Agreement and such Project Documents. The UNDP undertakes to complement and supplement the Government's participation in such projects through assistance to the Government in pursuance of this Agreement and the Work Plan forming part of such Project Documents, and through assistance to the Government in fulfilling its intent with respect to investment follow-up. The Government shall inform UNDP of the Government Co-operating Agency directly responsible for the Government's participation in each UNDP-assisted project. Without prejudice to the Government's overall

responsibility for its projects, the Parties may agree that an Executing Agency shall assume primary responsibility for execution of a project in consultation and agreement with the Co-operating Agency, and any arrangements to this effect shall be stipulated in the project Work Plan forming part of the Project Document together with arrangements, if any, for transfer of such responsibility, in the course of project execution, to the Government or to an entity designated by the Government.

2. Compliance by the Government with any prior obligations agreed to be necessary or appropriate for UNDP assistance to a particular project shall be a condition of performance by the UNDP and the Executing Agency of their responsibilities with respect to that project. Should provision of such assistance be commenced before such prior obligations have been met, it may be terminated or suspended without notice and at the discretion of the UNDP.

3. Any agreement between the Government and an Executing Agency concerning the execution of the UNDP-assisted project or between the Government and an operational expert shall be subject to the provisions of this Agreement.

4. The Co-operating Agency shall as appropriate and in consultation with the Executing Agency assign a full-time director for each project who shall perform such functions as are assigned to him or her by the Co-operating Agency. The Executing Agency shall as appropriate and in consultation with the Government appoint a Chief Technical Adviser or Project Co-ordinator responsible to the Executing Agency to oversee the Executing Agency's participation in the project at the project level. The Chief Technical Adviser or Project Co-ordinator shall supervise and co-ordinate activities of experts and other Executing Agency personnel and be responsible for the on-the-job training of national Government counterparts. The Chief Technical Adviser or Project Co-ordinator shall be responsible for the management and efficient utilization of all UNDP-financed inputs, including equipment provided to the project.

5. In the performance of their duties, advisory experts, consultants and volunteers shall act in close consultation with the Government and with persons or bodies designated by the Government, and shall comply with such instructions from the Government as may be appropriate to the nature of their duties and the assistance to be given and as may be mutually agreed upon between the UNDP and the Executing Agency concerned and the Government. Operational experts shall be solely responsible to, and be under the exclusive direction of, the Government or the entity to which they are assigned, but shall not be required to perform any functions incompatible with their international status or with the purposes of the UNDP or of the Executing Agency. The Government undertakes that the commencing date of each operational expert in its service shall coincide with the effective date of his or her contract with the Executing Agency concerned.

6. Recipients of fellowships shall be selected by the Executing Agency. Such fellowships shall be administered in accordance with the fellowship policies and practices of the Executing Agency.

7. Technical and other equipment, materials, supplies and other property financed or provided by the UNDP shall belong to the UNDP unless and until such time as ownership thereof is transferred, on terms and conditions mutually agreed upon between the Government and the UNDP, to the Government or to an entity nominated by it.

8. Patent rights, copyright rights, and other similar rights to any discoveries or work resulting from UNDP assistance under this Agreement shall belong to the UNDP. Unless

otherwise agreed by the Parties in each case, however, the Government shall have the right to use any such discoveries or work within the country free of royalty or any charge of similar nature.

Article IV. Information concerning Projects

1. The Government shall furnish the UNDP with such relevant reports, maps, accounts, records, statements, documents and other information as it may request concerning any UNDP-assisted project, its execution or its continued feasibility and soundness, or concerning the compliance by the Government with its responsibilities under this Agreement or Project Documents.

2. The UNDP undertakes that the Government shall be kept currently informed of the progress of its assistance activities under this Agreement. Either Party shall have the right, at any time, to observe the progress of operations on UNDP-assisted projects.

3. The Government shall, subsequent to the completion of a UNDP-assisted project, make available to the UNDP at its request information as to benefits derived from and activities undertaken to further the purposes of that project, including information necessary or appropriate to its evaluation or to evaluation of UNDP assistance, and shall consult with and permit observation by the UNDP for this purpose.

4. Any information or material which the Government is required to provide to the UNDP under this Article shall be made available by the Government to an Executing Agency at the request of the Executing Agency concerned.

5. The Parties shall consult each other regarding the publication, as appropriate, of any information relating to any UNDP-assisted project or to benefits derived therefrom. However, any information relating to any investment-oriented project may be released by the UNDP to potential investors, unless and until the Government has requested the UNDP in writing to restrict the release of information relating to such project.

Article V. Participation and contribution of Government in execution of Project

1. In fulfillment of the Government's responsibility to participate and co-operate in the execution of the projects assisted by the UNDP under this Agreement, it shall contribute the following in kind to the extent detailed in relevant Project Documents:

(*a*) Local counterpart professional and other services, including national counterparts to operational experts;

(*b*) Land, buildings, and training and other facilities available or produced within the country; and

(*c*) Equipment, materials and supplies available or produced within the country.

2. Whenever the provision of equipment forms part of UNDP assistance to the Government, the latter shall meet charges relating to customs clearance of such equipment, its transportation from the port of entry to the project site together with any incidental handling or storage and related expenses, its insurance after delivery to the project site, and its installation and maintenance.

3. The Government shall also meet the salaries of trainees and recipients of fellowships during the period of their fellowships.

4. If so provided in the Project Document, the Government shall pay, or arrange to have paid, to the UNDP or an Executing Agency the sums required, to the extent specified in the Project Budget of the Project Document, for the provision of any of the items enumerated in paragraph 1 of this Article, whereupon the Executing Agency shall obtain the necessary items and account annually to the UNDP for any expenditures out of payments made under this provision.

5. Monies payable to the UNDP under the preceding paragraph shall be paid to an account designated for this purpose by the Secretary-General of the United Nations and shall be administered in accordance with the applicable financial regulations of the UNDP.

6. The cost of items constituting the Government's contribution to the project and any sums payable by the Government in pursuance of this Article, as detailed in Project Budgets, shall be considered as estimates based on the best information available at the time of preparation of such Project Budgets. Such sums shall be subject to adjustment whenever necessary to reflect the actual cost of any such items purchased thereafter.

7. The Government shall as appropriate display suitable signs at each project identifying it as one assisted by the UNDP and the Executing Agency.

Article VI. Assessed programme costs and other items payable in local currency

1. In addition to the contribution referred to in Article V, above, the Government shall assist the UNDP in providing it with assistance by paying or arranging to pay for the following local costs or facilities, in the amounts specified in the relevant Project Document or otherwise determined by the UNDP in pursuance of relevant decisions of its governing bodies:

(*a*) The local living costs of advisory experts and consultants assigned to projects in the country;

(*b*) Local administrative and clerical services, including necessary local secretarial help, interpreter-translators, and related assistance;

(*c*) Transportation of personnel within the country; and

(*d*) Postage and telecommunications for official purposes.

2. The Government shall also pay each operational expert directly the salary, allowances and other related emoluments which would be payable to one of its nationals if appointed to the post involved. It shall grant an operational expert the same annual and sick leave as the Executing Agency concerned grants its own officials, and shall make any arrangement necessary to permit him or her to take home leave to which he or she is entitled under the terms of his or her service with the Executing Agency concerned. Should his or her service with the Government be terminated by it under circumstances which give rise to an obligation on the part of an Executing Agency to pay him or her an indemnity under its contract with him or her, the Government shall contribute to the cost thereof the amount of separation indemnity which would be payable to a national civil servant or comparable employee of like rank whose service is terminated in the same circumstances.

3. The Government undertakes to furnish in kind the following local services and facilities:

(*a*) The necessary office space and other premises;

(*b*) Such medical facilities and services for international personnel as may be available to national civil servants;

(*c*) Simple but adequately furnished accommodation to volunteers; and

(*d*) Assistance in finding suitable housing accommodation for international personnel, and the provision of such housing to operational experts under the same conditions as to national civil servants of comparable rank.

4. The Government shall also contribute towards the expenses of maintaining the UNDP mission in the country by paying annually to the UNDP a lump sum mutually agreed between the Parties to cover the following expenditures:

(*a*) An appropriate office with equipment and supplies, adequate to serve as local headquarters for the UNDP in the country;

(*b*) Appropriate local secretarial and clerical help, interpreters, translators and related assistance;

(*c*) Transportation of the resident representative and his or her staff for official purposes within the country;

(*d*) Postage and telecommunications for official purposes; and

(*e*) Subsistence for the resident representative and his or her staff while in official travel status within the country.

5. The Government shall have the option of providing in kind the facilities referred to in paragraph 4, above, with the exception of items (*b*) and (*e*).

6. Monies payable under the provisions of this Article, other than under paragraph 2, shall be paid by the Government and administered by the UNDP in accordance with Article V, paragraph 5.

Article VII. Relation to assistance from other sources

In the event that assistance towards the execution of a project is obtained by either Party from other sources, the Parties shall consult each other and the Executing Agency with a view to effective co-ordination and utilization of assistance received by the Government from all sources. The obligations of the Government hereunder shall not be modified by any arrangements it may enter into with other entities co-operating with it in the execution of a project.

Article VIII. Use of Assistance

The Government shall exert its best efforts to make the most effective use of the assistance provided by the UNDP and shall use such assistance for the purpose for which it is intended. Without restricting the generality of the foregoing, the Government shall take such steps to this end as are specified in the Project Document.

Article IX. Privileges and Immunities

1. The Government shall apply to the United Nations and its organs, including the UNDP and United Nations subsidiary organs acting as UNDP Executing Agencies, their property, funds and assets, and to their officials, including the resident representative and other members of the UNDP mission in the country, the provisions of the Convention on the Privileges and Immunities of the United Nations.

2. The Government shall apply to each Specialized Agency acting as an Executing Agency, its property, funds and assets, and to its officials, the provisions of the Convention

on the Privileges and Immunities of the Specialized Agencies, including any Annex to the Convention applicable to such Specialized Agency. In case the International Atomic Energy Agency (the IAEA) acts as an Executing Agency, the Government shall apply to its property, funds and assets, and to its officials and experts, the Agreement on the Privileges and Immunities of the IAEA.

3. Members of the UNDP mission in the country shall be granted such additional privileges and immunities as may be necessary for the effective exercise by the mission of its functions.

4. (*a*) Except as the Parties may otherwise agree in Project Documents relating to specific projects, the Government shall grant all persons, other than Government nationals employed locally, performing services on behalf of the UNDP, a Specialized Agency or the IAEA who are not covered by paragraphs 1 and 2, above, the same privileges and immunities as officials of the United Nations, the Specialized Agency concerned or the IAEA under Sections 18, 19 or 18 respectively of the Conventions on the Privileges and Immunities of the United Nations or of the specialized agencies, or of the Agreement on the Privileges and Immunities of the IAEA;

(*b*) For purposes of the instruments on privileges and immunities referred to in the preceding parts of this Article:

(1) All papers and documents relating to a project in the possession or under the control of the persons referred to in sub-paragraph 4(*a*), above, shall be deemed to be documents belonging to the United Nations, the Specialized Agency concerned, or the IAEA, as the case may be; and

(2) Equipment, materials and supplies brought into or purchased or leased by those persons within the country for purposes of a project shall be deemed to be property of the United Nations, the Specialized Agency concerned, or the IAEA, as the case may be.

5. The expression "persons performing services" as used in Articles IX, X and XIII of this Agreement includes operational experts, volunteers, consultants, and juridical as well as natural persons and their employees. It includes governmental or non-governmental organizations or firms which UNDP may retain, whether as an Executing Agency or otherwise, to execute or to assist in the execution of UNDP assistance to a project, and their employees. Nothing in this Agreement shall be construed to limit the privileges, immunities or facilities conferred upon such organizations or firms or their employees in any other instrument.

Article X. Facilities for execution of UNDP assistance

1. The Government shall take any measures which may be necessary to exempt the UNDP, its Executing Agencies, their experts and other persons performing services on their behalf from regulations or other legal provisions which may interfere with operations under this Agreement, and shall grant them such other facilities as may be necessary for the speedy and efficient execution of UNDP assistance. It shall, in particular, grant them the following rights and facilities:

(*a*) prompt clearance of experts and other persons performing services on behalf of the UNDP or an Executing Agency;

(*b*) prompt issuance without cost of necessary visas, licenses or permits;

(*c*) access to the site of work and all necessary rights of way;

(*d*) free movement within or to or from the country, to the extent necessary for proper execution of UNDP assistance;

(*e*) the most favourable legal rate of exchange;

(*f*) any permits necessary for the importation of equipment, materials and supplies, and for their subsequent exportation;

(*g*) any permits necessary for importation of property belonging to and intended for the personal use or consumption of officials of the UNDP, its Executing Agencies, or other persons performing services on their behalf, and for the subsequent exportation of such property; and

(*h*) prompt release from customs of the items mentioned in sub-paragraphs (*f*) and (*g*), above.

2. Assistance under this Agreement being provided for the benefit of the Government and people of Fiji, the Government shall bear all risks of operations arising under this Agreement. It shall be responsible for dealing with claims which may be brought by third parties against the UNDP or an Executing Agency, their officials or other persons performing services on their behalf, and shall hold them harmless in respect of claims or liabilities arising from operations under this Agreement. The foregoing provision shall not apply where the Parties and the Executing Agency have agreed that a claim or liability arises from the gross negligence or willful misconduct of the above-mentioned individuals.

Article XI. Suspension or termination of assistance

1. The UNDP may by written notice to the Government and to the Executing Agency concerned suspend its assistance to any project if in the judgement of the UNDP any circumstance arises which interferes with or threatens to interfere with the successful completion of the project or the accomplishment of its purposes. The UNDP may, in the same or a subsequent written notice, indicate the conditions under which it is prepared to resume its assistance to the project. Any such suspension shall continue until such time as such conditions are accepted by the Government and as the UNDP shall give written notice to the Government and the Executing Agency that it is prepared to resume its assistance.

2. If any situation referred to in paragraph 1 of this Article shall continue for a period of fourteen days after notice thereof and of suspension shall have been given by the UNDP to the Government and the Executing Agency, then at any time thereafter during the continuance thereof, the UNDP may by written notice to the Government and the Executing Agency terminate its assistance to the project.

3. The provisions of this Article shall be without prejudice to any other rights or remedies the UNDP may have in the circumstances, whether under general principles of law or otherwise.

Article XII. Settlement of disputes

1. Any disputes between the UNDP and the Government arising out of or relating to this Agreement which is not settled by negotiation or other agreed mode of settlement shall be submitted to arbitration at the request of either Party. Each Party shall appoint one arbitrator, and the two arbitrators so appointed should appoint a third, who shall be the chairman. If within thirty days of the request for arbitration either Party has not appointed an arbitrator or if within fifteen days of the appointment of two arbitrators the third arbitrator has not been appointed, either Party may request the President of the International

Court of Justice to appoint an arbitrator. The procedure of the arbitration shall be fixed by the arbitrators, and the expenses of the arbitration shall be borne by the Parties as assessed by the arbitrators. The arbitral award shall contain a statement of the reasons on which it is based and shall be accepted by the Parties as the final adjudication of the dispute.

2. Any dispute between the Government and an operational expert arising out of or relating to the conditions of his or her service with the Government may be referred to the Executing Agency providing the operational expert by either the Government or the operational expert involved, and the Executing Agency concerned shall use its good offices to assist them in arriving at a settlement. If the dispute cannot be settled in accordance with the preceding sentence or by other agreed mode of settlement, the matter shall at the request of either Party be submitted to arbitration following the same provisions as are laid down in paragraph 1 of this Article, except that the arbitrator not appointed by either Party or by the arbitrators of the Parties shall be appointed by the Secretary-General of the Permanent Court of Arbitration.

Article XIII. General Provisions

1. This Agreement shall enter into force upon signature by the Parties. It shall continue in force until terminated under paragraph 3, below. Upon the entry into force of this Agreement, it shall supersede existing Agreements concerning the provision of assistance to the Government out of UNDP resources and concerning the UNDP office in the country, and it shall apply to all assistance provided to the Government and to the UNDP office established in the country under the provisions of the Agreements now superseded.

2. This Agreement may be modified by written agreement between the Parties hereto. Any relevant matter for which no provision is made in this Agreement shall be settled by the Parties in keeping with the relevant resolutions and decisions of the appropriate organs of the United Nations. Each Party shall give full and sympathetic consideration to any proposal advanced by the other Party under this paragraph.

3. This Agreement may be terminated by either Party by written notice to the other and shall terminate sixty days after receipt of such notice.

4. The obligations assumed by the Parties under Articles IV (concerning project information) and VIII (concerning the use of assistance) hereof shall survive the expiration or termination of this Agreement. The obligations assumed by the Government under Articles IX (concerning this Agreement. The obligations assumed by the Government under Articles IX (concerning privileges and immunities), X (concerning facilities for project execution) and XII (concerning settlement of disputes) hereof shall survive the expiration or termination of this Agreement to the extent necessary to permit orderly withdrawal of personnel, funds and property of the UNDP and of any Executing Agency, or of any persons performing services on their behalf under this Agreement.

In Witness Whereof the undersigned, duly appointed representatives of the United Nations Development Programme and of the Government, respectively, have on behalf of the Parties signed the present Agreement in the English language in two copies at *[SUVA]* this *[25th]* day of *[February 2019]*.

For the United Nations Development Programme

[*Signed*]

MR. BAKHODIR BURHANOV

UNDP Resident Representative a.i

For the Government of the Republic of Fiji

[*Signed*]

MAJOR GEN (RET'D) IOANE NAIVALURUA

Permanent Secretary for Foreign Affairs

4. Office of the High Commissioner for Human Rights

Agreement between the Government of the Republic of the Sudan and the United Nations Office of the High Commissioner for Human Rights concerning the establishment of a country office in Sudan. New York, 25 September 2019*

1. *Reaffirming* the purposes and principles of the Charter of the United Nations, in particular those under article 1, paragraph 3 in regard to achieving international cooperation in solving international problems of an economic, social, cultural, or humanitarian character, and in promoting and encouraging respect for human rights and for fundamental freedoms for all without distinction as to race, sex, language, or religion;

2. *Recognizing* the importance of observing the provisions contained in the Universal Declaration of Human Rights, the International Covenant on Civil and Political Rights, the International Covenant on Economic, Social and Cultural Rights, and other international human rights instruments;

3. *Considering* further the Vienna Declaration and Programme of Action adopted by the World Conference on Human Rights on 25 June 1993, the Beijing Declaration and Platform for Action adopted by the Fourth World Conference on Women on 15 September 1995, the Durban Declaration and Programme of Action adopted by the World Conference against Racism, Racial Discrimination, Xenophobia and Related Intolerance on 8 September 2001, and the 2005 World Summit Outcome adopted by the General Assembly on 16 September 2005;

4. *Bearing* in mind the mandate conferred on the United Nations High Commissioner for Human Rights by the General Assembly of the United Nations in its resolution 48/141 of 20 December 1993, in promoting and protecting human rights and the mandate of the Office of the High Commissioner for Human Rights (OHCHR);

5. *Considering* that the Country Office established pursuant to this Agreement has significant potential in promoting and protecting fundamental human rights, as well as facilitating the implementation of human rights commitments undertaken, including those contained in the international human rights treaties signed and ratified by the Government of Sudan;

6. *Considering* that the Government of the Republic of Sudan has expressed its consent to the establishment of an OHCHR Country Office in Sudan within the mandate

* Entered into force on 25 September 2019 by signature, in accordance with article XXVIII. United Nations registration no. I-55976.

conferred on OHCHR by the General Assembly of the United Nations in its resolution 48/141 of 20 December 1993;

7. *Considering* the commitment of the Government of the Republic of Sudan, reflected in the Constitutional Document signed on 17 August 2019, to facilitate the work of OHCHR in Sudan;

8. *Considering* that Sudan has acceded, without any reservation, on 21 March 1977, to the Convention on the Privileges and Immunities of the United Nations of 13 February 1946;

9. Have agreed as follows:

Article I: Definitions

10. For the purpose of this Agreement the following definitions shall apply:

(*a*) "Host Country" means the Republic of Sudan (or "Sudan");

(*b*) "Government" means the Government of the Republic of Sudan;

(*c*) "OHCHR" means the Office of the United Nations High Commissioner for Human Rights;

(*d*) "Parties" refers to the Government and the United Nations;

(*e*) "Country Office" means the OHCHR Office in Khartoum, Sudan, and any other sub-offices which may be additionally established in Sudan, in consultation with the Government;

(*f*) "Convention" means the Convention on Privileges and Immunities of the United Nations adopted by the General Assembly of the United Nations on 13 February 1946;

(*g*) "Agreement" means the current agreement signed between the Government and OHCHR;

(*h*) "Premises of the Country Office" means the building or part of building occupied permanently or temporarily by the Country Office or by meetings convened in Sudan by the Country Office, and as defined in this Agreement or in any Supplementary Agreements entered into with the Government;

(*i*) "Archives of the Country Office" means all records, correspondence, documents, manuscripts, computer records, still and motion pictures, film and sound recordings, belonging to or held by the Country Office in furtherance of its functions;

(*j*) "Property of the Country Office" means all property, including funds, income and other assets belonging to the Country Office or held or administered by the Country Office in furtherance of the functions of the Country Office;

(*k*) "Representative of the High Commissioner" means the United Nations official in charge of directing and supervising the activities of the Country Office of OHCHR, on behalf and under the authority of the High Commissioner for Human Rights;

(*l*) "Competent Authorities" means local, regional and central governmental authorities of Sudan, whether civil, police, security, military or other;

(*m*) "Officials" means the Representative of the High Commissioner and all members of the OHCHR Country Office staff, irrespective of nationality, with the exception of persons who are recruited locally and assigned to hourly rates, as provided for in the United Nations General Assembly resolution 76(I) of 7 December 1946;

(*n*) "Experts on Mission" means individuals, other than officials of the United Nations mentioned under paragraph (*k*) and (*m*), who are performing missions at the request of or on behalf of the OHCHR Country Office;

(*o*) "Persons Providing Services" means service contractors, operational experts, volunteers, consultants and juridical as well as natural persons and their employees;

(*p*) "OHCHR Personnel" means Officials, other OHCHR officials, persons recruited locally and assigned to hourly rates, Experts on Mission and Persons Providing Services on behalf of OHCHR;

(*q*) "Secretary-General" means the Secretary-General of the United Nations;

(*r*) and "Telecommunications" means any emission, transmission or reception of written or verbal information, images, sound or information of any nature by wire, radio, satellite, optical, fibre or any other electronic or electromagnetic means.

Article II: Purpose of this Agreement

11. The Government agrees to the establishment of the OHCHR Country Office in Sudan.

12. The purpose of the present Agreement is to regulate the conditions and modalities relative to the functioning of the OHCHR Country Office, its status and the status of OHCHR Personnel and Premises, and to facilitate its activities in cooperation with the Government.

13. The Government confirms that the treatment afforded to the Country Office shall be equal and the same as that afforded to any other accredited foreign mission in the Host Country.

Article III: Application of the Convention

14. The Convention shall be applicable to the Country Office, its properties, funds and assets and to its Officials, Persons Providing Services and Experts on Mission in the Republic of Sudan.

Article IV: Legal personality

15. OHCHR shall possess legal personality in the Republic of Sudan, and shall have the capacity:

(*a*) to contract;

(*b*) to acquire and dispose of immovable and movable property; and

(*c*) to institute legal proceedings.

16. For the purpose of this Article, the Country Office shall be represented by the Representative of the High Commissioner.

Article V: Mandate and functions of the Country Office

17. In accordance with the Charter of the United Nations and the mandate of the United Nations High Commissioner for Human Rights as set out in the General Assembly resolution 48/141 of 20 December 1993, the Country Office shall advise and assist the Government of Sudan on the formulation and implementation of policies, programmes and measures for the promotion and protection of human rights in Sudan. To this end, the Country Office shall provide advisory services and technical assistance to the Government

and other relevant actors with a view to implementing international human rights norms, in particular, international human rights instruments ratified by Sudan, and outcomes of the processes of international human rights mechanisms.

18. The Country Office shall observe the human rights situation in Sudan, and consult and assist the relevant authorities, as well as various national human rights institutions, civil society organizations and other relevant bodies for the purpose of promoting and protecting human rights.

19. The Country Office shall report to the High Commissioner, who may decide to publish reports, including on the activities of the Country Office, as well as the human rights situation in Sudan, in accordance with the High Commissioner's mandate. Prior to publication, reports shall be shared with the Government in order to allow the Government to provide comments within a specific deadline.

20. The Country Office shall also provide training activities and disseminate human rights information to government officials, as well as national human rights institutions, civil society organisations and other relevant actors.

21. In all its actions, the Country Office shall be guided by the principles of the United Nations, especially the principles of impartiality, independence, objectivity and transparency.

Article VI: Inviolability of the Country Office

22. The Country Office shall be located in Khartoum, Republic of Sudan. To accomplish its mandate, the OHCHR shall be able to establish auxiliary offices in Darfur, South Kordofan, Blue Nile and East Sudan, and other premises on the territory of Sudan, in consultation with the Government. The Premises of the Country Office shall be inviolable. Premises used on a temporary basis for meetings organized by the Country Office shall be considered, during the period of the meetings, Premises of the Country Office and covered by the same status.

23. The property, funds and assets of the Country Office, wherever located and by whomsoever held, shall be immune from search, requisition, confiscation, expropriation and any other form of interference, whether by executive, administrative, judicial or legislative action.

24. The Archives of the Country Office, and in general all documents belonging to or held by it, shall be inviolable, wherever located.

25. The Competent Authorities shall not enter the Country Office Premises, except with the express consent of the Representative of the High Commissioner and under conditions agreed to by him or her. In case of a fire or other emergency requiring prompt protection action, the consent of the Representative of the High Commissioner for any necessary entry into the Premises shall be presumed if he or she cannot be reached in time.

Article VII: Security and Protection

26. The Competent Authorities shall ensure the security and protection of the Premises of the Country Office and exercise due diligence to ensure that the tranquillity of the Country Office Premises is not disturbed by the unauthorized entry of persons or groups of persons from outside or by disturbances in its immediate vicinity. If so requested by the Representative of the High Commissioner, the Competent Authorities shall provide adequate police force necessary for the preservation of law and order in the Country Office Premises or in its immediate vicinity, and for the removal of persons therefrom.

27. The Competent Authorities shall take effective and adequate action which may be required to ensure the appropriate security, safety and protection of persons referred to in this Agreement, indispensable for the proper functioning of the Country Office free from interference of any kind.

Article VIII: Public services

28. The Competent Authorities shall facilitate, upon request of the Representative of the High Commissioner and under terms and conditions not less favourable than those accorded by the Government to any accredited foreign mission, access to the public services needed by the Country Office such as, but not limited to, utility, power and communications services.

29. In cases where public services referred to in paragraph 28, above, are made available to the Country Office by the Competent Authorities or where the prices thereof are under their control, the rate for such services shall not exceed the lowest comparable rates accorded to accredited foreign missions.

30. In case of force majeure, resulting in a complete or partial disruption of the above-mentioned services, the Country Office shall, for the performance of its functions, be accorded the same priority given to essential governmental agencies and organs.

31. The provisions of this Article shall not prevent the reasonable application of fire protection or sanitary regulations of the Host Country.

Article IX: Funds, assets and other property

32. The Country Office, its property, funds and assets wherever located and by whomsoever held, shall enjoy immunity from every form of legal process, except insofar as in any particular case, the Secretary-General of the United Nations has expressly waived its immunity, it being understood that no waiver of immunity shall extend to any measure of execution.

33. The property, funds and assets of the Country Office shall not be subject to any financial controls, regulations or moratoria and the Country Office may freely:

(*a*) Hold and use funds, currency or negotiable instruments of any kind and maintain and operate accounts in any currency and convert any currency held by it into any other currency;

(*b*) Transfer its funds or currency from one country to the other or within Sudan;

(*c*) Enjoy the most favourable, legally available rate of exchange for its financial transactions.

Article X: Exemption from taxation, duties, import or export restrictions

34. The Country Office, its funds, assets, income and other property shall be exempt from:

(*a*) All direct and indirect taxes and levies, fees, tolls and duties, including value added tax; it being understood, however, that the Country Office shall not request exemption from taxes which are in fact no more than charges for public utility services rendered by the Competent Authorities or by a corporation under the laws and regulations of the Host Country at a fixed rate according to the amount of services rendered, and which can be specifically identified, described and itemized;

(*b*) Customs duties and prohibitions and restrictions on articles imported or exported by the Country Office for its official use. It is understood, however, that articles imported under such exemptions will not be sold in Sudan except under conditions agreed upon with the Government;

(*c*) Customs duties and prohibitions and restrictions on imports and exports in respect of its publications, still and motion pictures, tapes, diskettes, as well as film and sound recordings.

Article XI: Communications

35. The Country Office shall enjoy, in respect of its official communications and its means of communications generally, treatment not less favourable than that accorded by the Government to any diplomatic mission or other intergovernmental organization in matters of establishment and operation, priorities, tariffs and taxes, in particular regarding the following forms of communication: mail, telegrams, faxes, satellite connections, telephone, and other communications, as well as rates for communication through the press and radio.

36. The Government shall secure the inviolability of the official communications and correspondence of OHCHR and shall not apply any censorship to communications and correspondence, Such inviolability shall extend, inter alia, to printed materials, photographs and electronic material.

37. The Country Office shall have the right to operate communication equipment, including satellite facilities and to use codes and to dispatch and receive correspondence either by courier or in sealed bag pouches, all of which shall have the same privileges and immunities as diplomatic couriers and bags. The OHCHR Personnel have the right to communicate with OHCHR Headquarters in Geneva, OHCHR offices in other countries and OHCHR Personnel in the field in Sudan *via* radio, telephone, telegram, satellite, mail or any other communication means.

Article XII: Participants in United Nations Meetings

38. Representatives of Members of the United Nations invited to meetings, seminars, training courses, symposiums, workshops and similar activities organized by the Country Office and other related organizations shall, while exercising their functions, enjoy the privileges and immunities as set out in Article IV of the Convention.

39. The Government, in accordance with relevant United Nations principles and practices and the present Agreement, shall respect the complete freedom of expression of all participants of meetings, seminars, training courses, symposiums, workshops and similar activities organized by the Country Office and other related organizations, to which the Convention shall be applicable. All participants and persons performing functions in connection with the meetings, seminars, training courses, symposiums, workshops and similar activities organized by the Country Office and other related organizations shall enjoy such privileges, immunities and facilities as are necessary for the independent exercise of their participation and functions. In particular, all participants and persons performing services in connection with the meetings, seminars, training courses, symposiums, workshops and similar activities organised by the Country Office and other related organizations shall be immune from legal process in respect of words spoken and acts done in connection with such meetings, seminars, training courses, symposiums, workshops and similar activities.

Article XIII: Status of Officials of the Country Office

40. Officials of the Country Office shall enjoy the following privileges, immunities and facilities in the Host Country:

(*a*) Immunity from legal process with respect to words spoken or written and all acts performed by them in their official capacity. Such immunity shall continue to be accorded after termination of employment with the United Nations;

(*b*) Immunity from personal arrest or detention and from seizure of their personal and official effects and baggage except in case of flagrante delicto, and in such cases the Competent Authorities shall immediately inform the Representative of the High Commissioner of the arrest, detention or seizure;

(*c*) Immunity from inspection and seizure of their baggage;

(*d*) Exemption from taxation on the salaries and all other remuneration paid to them by the United Nations; exemption from taxation on all income and property, for themselves and for their spouses and dependent members of their families, in so far as such income derives from sources, or in so far as such property is located outside the Host Country;

(*e*) Exemption from military service duties or any national service obligation;

(*f*) Exemption, with respect to themselves, their spouses and dependent members of their families, from immigration restrictions and alien registration;

(*g*) The same privileges in respect of exchange facilities as accorded to officials of comparable ranks forming part of the diplomatic missions accredited in the Host Country;

(*h*) The same protection and repatriation facilities with respect to themselves, their spouses and dependent members of their families as are accorded to diplomatic envoys in time of international crisis;

(*i*) The right to import free of duty and other levies their furniture, personal effects and all household appliances, at the time of first taking up their post in the Host Country which may be done in one or more shipments, and thereafter from time to time necessary additional to or replacements for such furniture and effects;

(*j*) Import free of custom and excise duties limited quantities of certain articles intended for personal use or consumption and not for gift or sale;

(*k*) Import or acquire in the Host Country a motor vehicle free of customs and excise duties, including value-added tax, according to the regulations applicable in the Host Country to diplomatic representatives accredited in the country and/or resident members of international organisations. A vehicle imported pursuant to this Agreement may be sold under conditions agreed with the Host Country;

(*l*) Officials shall be entitled, on the termination of their functions in Sudan, to export their furniture and personal effects, including motor vehicles, without duties and taxes.

41. Officials of Sudanese nationality or with permanent resident status in the Host Country shall enjoy only those privileges and immunities provided for in Section 18 of the Convention.

42. The Country Office may recruit Officials from within the Host Country as required. The recruitment will be done in accordance with United Nations rules and regulations regarding recruitment and selection of staff.

43. The Representative of the High Commissioner shall be granted the privileges and immunities, exemptions and facilities normally accorded to Heads of diplomatic missions accredited in the Host Country. Furthermore, without prejudice to the other provisions of this Agreement, all Officials assigned to the Country Office, having the rank

of P/L-5 or above, shall be accorded the privileges, immunities and facilities granted to diplomatic staff at missions accredited to the Host Country.

44. The name of the Representative of the High Commissioner shall be included in the diplomatic list by the Ministry of Foreign Affairs of Sudan.

45. The privileges, immunities and facilities referred to in paragraph 40 above shall also be accorded to a spouse and dependent members of the family of the Official concerned.

Article XIV: Experts on Mission

46. Experts on Mission are granted the privileges, immunities and facilities mentioned in articles VI and VII of the Convention.

47. Experts on Mission shall be granted exemption from taxation on the salaries and other emoluments paid to them by OHCHR, and may be accorded such additional privileges, immunities and facilities as may be agreed upon between the Parties.

Article XV: Persons Providing Services

48. The Government shall grant all Persons Providing Services for or on behalf of the Country Office the same privileges and immunities as Officials of the Country Office.

Article XVI: Personnel recruited locally and assigned to hourly rates

49. Personnel recruited in Sudan and assigned to hourly rates to perform services for the Country Office shall be accorded immunity from legal process in respect of words spoken or written and all acts performed by them in their official capacity. Such immunity is granted in the interest of the United Nations and not for the personal benefit of such persons. It shall continue to be accorded after the persons concerned cease to be employed by the Country Office.

50. The terms and conditions of the employment of persons recruited locally and assigned to hourly rates shall be governed by the relevant United Nations resolutions, decisions, regulations and rules and policies of the competent organs of the United Nations.

Article XVII: Waiver of Immunity

51. Privileges and immunities referred to in Articles XIII through XVI above are granted to the relevant personnel or experts on mission in the interest of the United Nations and not for their personal benefit. The right and the duty to waive the immunity of these persons, in any case where it can be waived without prejudice to the interests of the United Nations, shall lie with the Secretary-General of the United Nations.

Article XVIII: Freedom of movement and access to useful information

52. All persons referred to in this Agreement, including all participants in meetings, seminars, training courses, symposiums, workshops and similar activities organized by the Country Office, shall have the right of unimpeded entry into, exit from, sojourn and free movement within the Host Country.

53. OHCHR and OHCHR Personnel enjoy full freedom of movement, throughout Sudan. In order to facilitate the exercise of freedom of movement, the Government will facilitate access when needed, especially in areas where traffic is restricted or difficult.

Freedom of movement includes freedom of observation and monitoring and the following prerogatives, exercised pursuant to the Country Office's mandate:

(*a*) Access, without requirement for prior authorization, to all places of arrest, detention, or interrogation. OHCHR Personnel shall be allowed to converse in private, freely and without impediment, with any person arrested, detained, or interrogated, or otherwise present in such places, in accordance with international human rights instruments. The Competent Authorities shall thereafter be notified of such access;

(*b*) Direct contact with the Competent Authorities;

(*c*) Direct contact with individuals, representatives of associations, nongovernmental organizations and other members of civil society, private institutions, hospitals and medical centres, and media entities;

(*d*) Access to all documents and materials necessary for the proper functioning of the Country Office's activities, including official records for which the Government shall grant the necessary permits, except for official documents to which access is restricted under the legislation of Sudan.

Article XIX: Laissez-Passer, Certificates and Visas

54. The Government shall recognize and accept the United Nations Laissez-Passer issued to OHCHR Personnel as a valid travel document, equivalent to a passport.

(*a*) In accordance with the provisions of Article VII, Section 26 of the Convention, the Government shall recognize and accept the United Nations Certificates issued by the United Nations to Experts on Mission and other persons travelling to Sudan on behalf of OHCHR;

(*b*) All persons referred to in this Agreement shall be granted all facilities that ensure speedy travel. Visas, entry and exit permits, where required, shall be granted free of charge and as promptly as possible to the persons referred to in this Agreement, their dependents and other persons invited to the Country Office in connection with the official work and activities of the Country Office;

(*c*) Similar facilities to those specified in paragraph (b) above shall be accorded to experts on mission and other persons who, though not the holders of United Nations laissez-passer, are confirmed by the Office as travelling on official business of the United Nations.

Article XX: Flags, emblems and distinctive signs

55. The Country Office may fly or display the United Nations and OHCHR flags and/or emblems on its Premises and official vehicles, and make them visible in any other manner agreed upon by the Parties.

Article XXI: Identification

56. At the request of the Representative of the High Commissioner, the Minister of Foreign Affairs shall issue to OHCHR Personnel appropriate identity documents certifying that, as OHCHR Personnel and in conformity with the Convention and the present Agreement, they enjoy privileges and immunities as well as freedom of movement, observation and monitoring and access to relevant information and to any document or

material necessary for the accomplishment of their functions, and the implementation of the Country Office's activities, further to the present Agreement.

57. OHCHR Personnel shall, upon request, show, but not be required to surrender, their identity documents to any authorized Government official.

58. At the final departure of the person(s) referred to in paragraph 56 above or when the relevant person has ceased to perform his or her functions, the identity card(s) referred to in paragraph 56 above shall be promptly returned by the Country Office to the Ministry of Foreign Affairs.

Article XXII: Social Security

59. The United Nations Joint Pension Fund shall enjoy legal capacity in the Host Country and shall enjoy the same exemptions, privileges and immunities as the United Nations itself. Benefits received from the Pension Fund shall be exempt from taxation.

60. The United Nations and the Government agree that, owing to the fact that Officials of the United Nations are subject to the United Nations Staff Regulations and Rules, including Article VI thereof, which establish a comprehensive social security scheme, the United Nations, the Country Office and its Officials, irrespective of nationality, shall be exempt from the laws of the Host Country on mandatory coverage and compulsory contributions to the social security schemes of the Host Country during their appointment with the United Nations.

61. The provisions of the preceding paragraph shall apply *mutatis mutandis* to the members of families forming part of the household of persons referred to in said paragraph, unless they are employed or self-employed in the Host Country or receive social security benefits from the Host Country.

Article XXIII: Access to the labour market for family members and issuance of visas and residence permits to household employees

62. The Competent Authorities shall grant working permits for spouses of Officials assigned to the Country Office whose duty station is in the Host Country, and their children forming part of their household who are under 21 years of age or economically dependent. The Competent Authorities shall issue visas and residence permits and any other documents, where required, to household employees of Officials assigned to the Country Office as speedily as possible.

63. The Government undertakes to assist Officials, Experts on Mission and Persons Providing Services assigned to the Country Office, as far as possible, in obtaining premises for use as residences.

Article XXIV: Cooperation between the Government and the High Commissioner for Human Rights

A. *Obligations of the Government*

64. The Government undertakes to respect the status of OHCHR and OHCHR Personnel, and to ensure that no one associated or cooperating with OHCHR is subjected in any way to abuses, threats, sanctions, reprisals or prosecution for such association or cooperation.

65. In all those cases where this Agreement refers to the privileges, immunities and rights of the Country Office and OHCHR Personnel, as well as to the facilities that the Government undertakes to grant, the Government shall ensure that the Competent Authorities of the Host Country respect such privileges, immunities and rights, and grant the facilities mentioned.

66. The Government shall disseminate this Agreement, in particular to national and regional civilian, police, law enforcement, security and military authorities.

B. Obligations of OHCHR

67. The privileges and immunities accorded under the present Agreement are granted in the interests of the United Nations, and not for the personal benefit of the persons concerned. The Secretary-General of the United Nations has the right and the duty to waive the immunity of any individual referred in to Articles XIII, XIV, XV, and XVI in any case where, in his opinion, such immunity would impede the course of justice and can be waived without prejudice to the interests of the United Nations.

68. OHCHR, without prejudice to their recognized privileges and immunities, shall cooperate at all times with the Competent Authorities of Sudan to facilitate the proper administration of justice, secure the observance of police regulations, and prevent the occurrence of any abuse in connection with the privileges, immunities, exemptions, facilities, rights and advantages accorded under the present Agreement.

69. OHCHR Personnel, without prejudice to their recognized privileges and immunities, shall respect the laws of the Host Country and refrain from any action or activity incompatible with the impartial and international nature of their functions.

Article XXV: Liability

70. The Government shall bear all risks of operations arising under this Agreement. It shall be responsible for dealing with claims which may be brought by third parties against the United Nations, including OHCHR, the Country Office or its OHCHR Personnel or participants of meetings, seminars, training courses, symposiums, workshops and similar activities organized by the Country Office and other related organizations under this Agreement, and shall hold them harmless in respect of claims or liabilities arising from operations under this Agreement. The foregoing provision shall not apply where the Parties are agreed that a claim or liability arises from the gross negligence or wilful misconduct of the above-mentioned individuals.

Article XXVI: Settlement of disputes

71. Any dispute between the Parties relating to the interpretation and application of the present Agreement or any supplementary agreement, with the exception of disputes subject to the dispute settlement provisions of section 30 of the Convention or any other applicable agreement, shall be settled by negotiation or by other mode of settlement agreed by the Parties.

72. In case a dispute cannot be settled by way of negotiation or another mode of settlement agreed by the Parties, each Party shall appoint one arbitrator, and the two arbitrators so appointed shall appoint a third, who shall be the chairman. If within thirty days of the request for arbitration either Party has not appointed an arbitrator or if within fifteen days of the appointment of two arbitrators the third arbitrator has not been appointed,

either Party may request the President of the International Court of Justice to appoint an arbitrator. The procedure for arbitration shall be fixed by the arbitrators, and the expenses of the arbitration shall be borne by the Parties as assessed by the arbitrators. The arbitral award shall contain a statement of the reasons on which it is based and shall be accepted by the Parties as the final adjudication of the dispute.

Article XXVII: Supplemental Agreements

73. Arrangements of an administrative and financial nature concerning the Country Office may be made by supplemental agreements, as appropriate.

74. The Parties may enter into any other supplemental agreements as the Parties may deem appropriate.

Article XXVIII: Entry into force, duration and termination

75. This Agreement shall enter into force upon signature by both Parties.

76. The Agreement shall be amended by mutual consent through the exchange of written communications expressing the Parties' intention to that effect.

77. This Agreement shall remain in force for an indefinite period. It may be terminated upon mutual agreement of the Parties. In this case, the Agreement remains in force for a period of six months to allow the conclusion and cessation of the Country Office activities in the country.

78. The obligations assumed by the Government shall survive the termination of this Agreement, to the extent necessary to permit orderly withdrawal of property, funds and assets of the Country Office and Officials assigned to it by virtue of this Agreement.

79. This Agreement has been concluded and signed in New York, on 25 September 2019, in two original copies in English.

For the Government of the Republic of Sudan

[*Signed*]

ASMAA MOHAMMED ABDULLAH

Minister of Foreign Affairs

For the Office of the United Nations High Commissioner for Human Rights

[*Signed*]

MICHELLE BACHELET

United Nations High Commissioner for Human Rights

5. United Nations Entity for Gender Equality and the Empowerment of Women

(*a*) Exchange of letters constituting an agreement between the Government of the People's Republic of Bangladesh and the United Nations Entity for Gender Equality and the Empowerment of Women ("UN Women") on the application *mutatis mutandis* of the Standard Basic Assistance Agreement ("SBAA"), concluded between the Government of Bangladesh and the United Nations Development Programme, to UN Women, its premises, property and assets as well as to its personnel in the People's Republic of Bangladesh. New York, 17 September 2012, Dhaka, 22 January 2014, New York, 15 July 2014, Dhaka, 21 August 2014, New York, 9 October 2014 and Dhaka, 9 June 2019*

I

17 September 2012

Excellency,

I have the honour to refer to the presence and operations of UN Women, the United Nations Entity for Gender Equality and the Empowerment of Women, established pursuant to General Assembly Resolution 64/289 of 2 July 2010. By this resolution the General Assembly decided, *inter alia*, to transfer the mandates, functions and assets of the United Nations Development Fund for Women (UNIFEM) to UN Women.

Accordingly, with the present letter, I wish to propose that the Standard Basic Assistance Agreement ("SBAA") concluded between your Government and the United Nations Development Programme, which entered into force on 25 November 1986, shall apply *mutatis mutandis* to UN Women, its premises, property, and assets as well as to its personnel in the People's Republic of Bangladesh.

I further propose that upon receipt of your acceptance of the above proposal in writing, this exchange of letters shall constitute an Agreement between your Government and UN Women, as of the date of your reply.

I would greatly appreciate your Excellency's early confirmation of these arrangements. I attach a draft reply that your Government might wish to consider for this confirmation.

Please accept, Excellency, the assurances of my highest consideration.

[*Signed*]

MICHELLE BACHELET

Under Secretary-General and Executive Director

II

22 January 2014

I have the honour to refer to your letter dated 17 September 2012 addressed to my predecessor/the Foreign Minister of Bangladesh.

---

* Entered into force on 9 June 2019 by the exchange of the said letters, in accordance with their provisions. United Nations registration no. I-55832.

Accordingly, with the present letter, I wish to agree to your proposal that the Standard Basic Assistance Agreement (SBAA) concluded between the Government of Bangladesh and United Nations Development Programme, which entered into force on 25 November 1986, shall apply *mutatis mutandis* to UN Women, its premises, property, assets as well as to its personnel in Bangladesh. In addition to the provisions of the SBAA following provisions would also be applicable for UN Women:

i) Any future revision of the SBAA mutually agreed between GoB and UNDP would also apply, *mutatis mutandis*, for UN Women automatically without further requirement of letters of exchange. However, a letter from the Government notifying the revisions would be sent to the UN Women;

ii) The Country Representative of UN Women shall communicate to the Government a list of the UN Women's officials (including spouses and other dependants) on quarterly basis and inform it of any change in between in this list;

iii) The UN Women shall submit information on a quarterly basis on the locally recruited staff members in the prescribed format provided by the Ministry of Foreign Affairs. In case of new recruitment or termination of service of locally recruited staff members, the UN Women shall promptly inform the Ministry of Foreign Affairs and provide necessary particulars;

iv) Local rules and regulations shall apply on UN Women, its staff members and operation, unless otherwise exempted under SBAA.

Upon receipt of your acceptance of the terms of this letter in writing, this exchange of letters shall constitute an Agreement between the Government of Bangladesh and UN Women, as of the date of your reply.

Yours sincerely,

[*Signed*]

Foreign Minister/State Minister for Foreign Affairs

Government of the People's Republic of Bangladesh

III

15 July 2014

Excellency,

I have the honour to refer to the presence and operations of the United Nations Entity for Gender Equality and the Empowerment of Women (UN Women), established pursuant to General Assembly Resolution 64/289 of 2 July 2010. By this resolution the General Assembly decided, *inter alia*, to transfer the mandates, functions and assets of the United Nations Development Fund for Women (UNIFEM) to UN Women.

I further have the honour to refer to letter from Ms. Michelle Bachelet of 17 September 2012 regarding the application, *mutatis mutandis*, of the Standard Basic Assistance Agreement ("SBAA") concluded between the Government of the People's Republic of Bangladesh and the United Nations Development Programme (UNDP), to UN Women, its premises, property, assets and personnel in Bangladesh, and to the concurrence of the Government conveyed to our office by your Ministry on 22 January 2014.

In relation to the specific points raised by the Government, I am pleased to confirm the understanding between the Government and UN Women as follows:

(*a*) any further revision of the SBAA mutually agreed between the Government of Bangladesh and UNDP would also apply, *mutatis mutandis*, for UN Women without further requirement of letters of exchange, subject to the receipt by UN Women of a letter from the Government notifying the revisions;

(*b*) UN Women will follow the practice of notifying the Government from time to time of the names of all its officials assigned to serve in Bangladesh, including locally recruited staff, in a manner consistent with any administrative arrangements as may be agreed between the Government and the United Nations and its subsidiary entities;

(*c*) persons enjoying the privileges and immunities established in the General Convention and in the Agreement between the Government of Bangladesh and UN Women shall be required to respect the laws of Bangladesh, comply with their legal obligations of a private nature and not to interfere in internal affairs; and that the United Nations and UN Women shall cooperate at all times with the appropriate authorities of Bangladesh in order to facilitate the administration of justice, ensure the observance of police regulations and prevent the abuse of the facilities, privileges and immunities granted to the persons mentioned in the Agreement.

In light of the above agreement, I look forward to receiving confirmation that the appropriate steps have been taken to ensure full recognition of the presence and operations of UN Women in the People's Republic of Bangladesh so that the office may be in a position to deliver important assistance to the Government and the people of Bangladesh.

Please accept, Excellency, the assurances of my highest consideration.

Yours sincerely,

[*Signed*]

PHUMZILE MLAMBO-NGCUKA

Under-Secretary-General and Executive Director

IV

21 August 2014

Excellency,

I have the honour to refer to your letter dated 15 July 2014.

Accordingly, with the present letter, I wish to agree to your proposal that the Standard Basic Assistance Agreement (SBAA) concluded between the Government of Bangladesh and United Nations Development Programme, which entered into force on 25 November 1986, shall apply *mutatis mutandis* to UN Women, its premises, property, assets as well as to its personnel in Bangladesh. In addition to the provisions of the SBAA, following provisions would also be applicable for UN Women:

i) Any further revision of the SBAA mutually agreed between the Government of Bangladesh and UNDP would also apply, mutatis mutandis, for UN Women without further requirement of letters of exchange. However, a letter from the Government notifying the revisions would be sent to the UN Women;

ii) UN Women will follow the practice of notifying the Government from time to time of the names of all its officials assigned to serve in Bangladesh, including locally recruited staff, in a manner consistent with any administrative arrangements agreed as or may be agreed in future between the Government and the United Nations and its subsidiary entities;

iii) Persons enjoying the privileges and immunities established in the General Conventions and in the Agreement between the Government of Bangladesh and UN Women shall be required to respect the laws of Bangladesh, comply with their legal obligations of a private nature and not to interfere in internal affairs; and that the United Nations and UN Women shall cooperate at all times with the appropriate authorities of Bangladesh in order to facilitate the administration of justice, ensure the observance of police regulations and prevent the abuse of the facilities, privileges and immunities granted to the persons mentioned in the Agreement.

Upon receipt of your acceptance of the terms of this letter in writing, this exchange of letters shall constitute an Agreement between the Government of Bangladesh and UN Women, as of the date of your reply.

Please accept, Excellency, the assurances of my highest consideration.

[*Signed*]

ABUL HASSAN MAHMOOD ALI, MP

V

9 October 2014

Excellency,

This is in reference to your letter dated 21 August 2014 concerning the applicability of the Standard Basic Assistance Agreement (SBAA) concluded between your Government and the United Nations Development Programme *mutatis mutandis* to the activities of UN Women in the People's Republic of Bangladesh.

I would like to express my gratitude to you and your Government for the continued support to UN Women's efforts in promoting gender equality and women's empowerment globally and in the People's Republic of Bangladesh. The commitment of your Government in raising the profile of this significant issue in Bangladesh is well respected and acknowledged.

UN Women confirms its acceptance of the terms contained in your letter dated 21 August 2014, in addition to the provisions of the SBAA, as follows:

i) Any further revision of the SBAA mutually agreed between the Government of Bangladesh and UNDP would also apply, mutatis mutandis, for UN Women without further requirement of letters of exchange. However, a letter from the Government notifying the revision would be sent to the UN Women;

ii) UN Women will follow the practice of notifying the Government from time to time of the names of all its officials assigned to service in Bangladesh, including locally recruited staff, in a manner consistent with any administrative arrangements agreed as or may be agreed in future between the Government and the United Nations and its subsidiary entities;

iii) Persons enjoying the privileges and immunities established in the General Conventions and in the Agreement between the Government of Bangladesh and UN Women shall be required to respect the laws of Bangladesh, comply with their legal obligations of a private nature and not to interfere in internal affairs; and that the United Nations and UN Women shall cooperate at all times with the appropriate authorities of Bangladesh in order to facilitate the administration of justice, ensure the observance of police regulations and prevent the abuse of the facilities, privileges and immunities granted to the persons mentioned in the Agreement.

Accordingly, upon your receipt of this acceptance, confirmation of which we should be grateful to receive, this exchange of letters shall constitute an Agreement between the People's Republic of Bangladesh and UN Women as of the date of this letter.

Please accept, Excellency, the assurances of my highest consideration.

[*Signed*]

PHUMZILE MLAMBO-NGCUKA

Under-Secretary-General and Executive Director

VI

09 June 2019

Excellency,

I would like to refer to your letter dated 09 October 2014 conveying your acceptance of the terms, as put forth by my predecessor through letter of 21 August 2014. Through the letter, three additional provisions were stipulated to be applicable to UN Women along with the Standard Basic Assistance Agreement (SBAA) concluded between the Government of Bangladesh and the United Nations Development Programme (UNDP) *mutatis mutandis* to the activities of the UN Women in the People's Republic of Bangladesh.

Since we both are in terms with the Agreement, I hereby confirm that your letter dated 09 October 2014 and my acknowledgement conveyed herein, should therefore, be regarded as constituting an agreement between the UN Women and the Government of Bangladesh regarding UN Women's activities in the People's Republic of Bangladesh as a separate UN entity.

Please accept, Excellency, the assurances of my highest consideration.

[*Signed*]

DR. A. K. ABDUL MOMEN, MP

(*b*) Exchange of letters constituting an agreement between the Government of the Kingdom of Bahrain and the United Nations Entity for Gender Equality and the Empowerment of Women ("UN Women") on the application *mutatis mutandis* of the Standard Basic Assistance Agreement ("SBAA"), concluded between the Government of the Kingdom of Bahrain and the United Nations Development Programme, to UN Women, its premises, property and assets as well as to its personnel in the Kingdom of Bahrain. New York, 17 December 2018 and Manama, 18 June 2019*

I

17 December 2018

Excellency,

I have the honour to refer to the presence and operations of the United Nations Entity for Gender Equality and the Empowerment of Women (UN Women), established pursuant to the General Assembly Resolution 64/289 of 2 July 2010. By this resolution the General Assembly decided, *inter alia*, to transfer the mandates, functions and assets of the United Nations Development Fund for Women (UNIFEM) to UN Women.

Accordingly, with the present letter, I wish to propose that the Standard Basic Assistance Agreement ("SBAA") concluded between your Government and the United Nations Development Programme, which entered into force on 3 August 1978, shall apply *mutatis mutandis* to UN Women, its premises, property, and assets as well as to its personnel in the Kingdom of Bahrain.

I further propose that upon receipt of your acceptance of the above proposal in writing, this exchange of letters shall constitute an Agreement between your Government and UN Women, as of the date of your reply.

I would greatly appreciate your Excellency's early confirmation of these arrangements. For ease of reference, I attach a draft reply that your Government might wish to consider for this confirmation.

Please accept, Excellency, the assurances of my highest consideration.

[*Signed*]

PHUMZILE MLAMBO-NGCUKA

Under-Secretary-General and Executive Director

II

18 June 2019

Your Excellency,

I have the pleasure to refer to your letter of December 11, 2018, which reads as follows:

---

* Entered into force on 18 June 2019 by the exchange of the said letters, in accordance with their provisions. United Nations registration no. I-55831.

"I have the honour to refer to the presence and operations of the United Nations Entity for Gender Equality and the Empowerment of Women (UN Women), established pursuant to the General Assembly Resolution 64/289 of 2 July 2010. By this resolution the General Assembly decided, *inter alia*, to transfer the mandates, functions and assets of the United Nations Development Fund for Women (UNIFEM) to UN Women.

Accordingly, with the present letter, I wish to propose that the Standard Basic Assistance Agreement ("SBAA") concluded between your Government and the United Nations Development Programme, which entered into force on 3 August 1978, shall apply *mutatis mutandis* to UN Women, its premises, property, and assets as well as to its personnel in the Kingdom of Bahrain.

I further propose that upon receipt of your acceptance of the above proposal in writing, this exchange of letters shall constitute an Agreement between your Government and UN Women, as of the date of your reply."

I can confirm that the Kingdom of Bahrain is in agreement with your proposal, and accordingly Your Excellency's letter dated December 11, 2018, together with this reply, shall be regarded as constituting an Agreement on the matter, as of the date hereof.

Please accept, Excellency, the assurances of my highest consideration.

[*Signed*]

KHALID BIN AHMED BIN MOHAMED AL KHALIFA

Minister of Foreign Affairs, Kingdom of Bahrain

B. Treaties concerning the legal status of intergovernmental organizations related to the United Nations

1. Convention on the Privileges and Immunities of the Specialized Agencies[*]

As at 31 December 2019, there were 129 States parties to the Convention.[**]

2. International Labour Organisation

An agreement concerning the organization of the 14th African Regional Meeting in Abidjan, Côte d'Ivoire, 3–6 December 2019, was concluded between the International Labour Organization and the Government of the Republic of Côte d'Ivoire.

3. International Atomic Energy Agency

Status of the Agreement on the Privileges and Immunities of the International Atomic Energy Agency, 1959[***]

In 2019, Côte d'Ivoire, Georgia, Lesotho, and Paraguay became Parties to the Agreement. By the end of the year, there were 90 Parties.

4. Food and Agriculture Organization

(*a*) Agreements regarding FAO Representations and Offices

The legal status, privileges and immunities enjoyed by the Food and Agriculture Organization (FAO)'s offices, its personnel and assets are confirmed in agreements concluded with the host countries. Agreements were concluded for the establishment of FAO Partnership and Liaison Offices[1] with the Government of the State of Kuwait on 3 December 2019, and with the Government of the Republic of Korea on 18 March 2019.

---

[*] United Nations, *Treaty Series*, vol. 33, p. 261.

[**] For the list of the States parties to the Convention, see *Multilateral Treaties Deposited with the Secretary-General*, available on the website of the Treaty Section of the United Nations Office of Legal Affairs: http://treaties.un.org.

[***] United Nations, *Treaty Series*, vol. 374, p. 147. For the list of the States parties to the Convention, see *Multilateral Treaties Deposited with the Secretary-General*, available on the website of the Treaty Section of the United Nations Office of Legal Affairs: http://treaties.un.org.

[1] The establishment of a Partnership and Liaison Office is primarily proposed for middle-to high-income countries interested in strengthening FAO's presence in their country on a cost-sharing basis, and is geared towards an in-country partnership for implementing the applicable Country Programming Framework (CPF) and establishing a trust fund portfolio to provide technical assistance to other countries, including through South-South and Triangular Cooperation.

(*b*) Agreements for hosting meetings of FAO Bodies

For the purpose of holding international conferences and meetings of FAO bodies outside FAO Headquarters and premises, the FAO normally concludes agreements specifying the privileges and immunities and other facilities that the Organization and participants (delegations and observers) will enjoy for the purpose of the meeting, and to address any potential liabilities of the Organization. These agreements are based on a standard Memorandum of Responsibilities, which reflects the usual requirements of UN System Organizations for such meetings, including the provision of visas to all participants. During 2019, Memoranda of Responsibilities were concluded with Canada, Chile, China, Costa Rica, Egypt, Ethiopia, France, Greece, India, Kazakhstan, Lebanon, Morocco, Nigeria, Norway, Spain, Uganda, and Vanuatu, for hosting sessions of FAO Governing and Statutory Bodies, and their subsidiary organs, to be held in 2019 and 2020.

5. United Nations Educational, Scientific and Cultural Organization

(*a*) Agreements relating to conferences, seminars and other meetings

For the purpose of holding international conferences on the territory of member States, UNESCO concluded various agreements that contained the following provisions concerning the legal status of the Organization:

> *"Privileges and Immunities*
>
> The Government of [name of the State] shall apply, in all matters relating to this meeting, the provisions of the Convention on the Privileges and Immunities of the Specialized Agencies of the United Nations as well as Annex IV thereto to which it has been a party from [date].
>
> In particular, the Government shall not place any restriction on the entry into, sojourn in, and departure from the territory of [name of the State] of all persons, of whatever nationality, entitled to attend the meeting by virtue of a decision of the appropriate authorities of UNESCO and in accordance with the Organization's relevant rules and regulations.
>
> *Damage and accidents*
>
> As long as the premises reserved for the meeting are at the disposal of UNESCO, the Government of [name of State] shall bear the risk of damage to the premises, facilities and furniture and shall assume and bear all responsibility and liability for accidents that may occur to persons present therein. The [name of State] authorities shall be entitled to adopt appropriate measures to ensure the protection of the participants, particularly against fire and other risks, of the above-mentioned premises, facilities and furniture. The Government of [name of State] may also claim from UNESCO compensation for any damage to persons and property caused by the fault of staff members or agents of the Organization."

UNESCO also concluded a number of agreements that contained provisions slightly deviating from the aforementioned clauses, including an agreement with Thailand for the 26th Ordinary Session of the UNESCO International Bioethics Committee (IBC), the 11th Ordinary Session of the UNESCO World Commission on the Ethics of Scientific Knowledge and Technology (COMEST), and the Conference on the Ethics of Science & Technology and Sustainable Development, which contained the following provisions:

"Privileges and Immunities

The Government of Thailand will apply, mutatis mutandis, the provisions of the Convention on the Privileges and Immunities of the Specialized Agencies of the United Nations, as well as Annex IV thereto relating to UNESCO. The Government of Thailand shall take all necessary measures to facilitate the entry into and sojourn in its territory and shall place no impediment in the way of the departure from its territory of the persons who are entitled, regardless of nationality, to the Meeting by virtue of a decision of the appropriate authorities of UNESCO and in accordance with the Organization's relevant rules and regulations. The Government of Thailand shall ensure that no impediment is placed in the way of their transit to or from the place of their official duty or business and shall afford them any necessary protection in transit.

Damage and accidents

The Government of Thailand shall be responsible for dealing with any action, claim or other demand against UNESCO or its officials and arising out of injury to persons or damage to or loss of property in the premises of the Meeting that are provided by or are under the control of the Government for the Meeting. However, the Government of Thailand shall not bear responsibility and liability for damages caused by gross negligence or willful misconduct of such persons. The Government of Thailand shall adopt appropriate measures to ensure the protection, particularly against fire and other risks, of the above-mentioned premises, facilities, furniture and persons. It may also claim from UNESCO compensation for any damage to persons and property caused by the fault of staff members or agents of the Organization."

(*b*) Constitutional amendments

At its 40th session (12–27 November 2019), the General conference adopted a resolution on the UNESCO Constitution, amending section A, paragraph 1 and adding the new section C, paragraph 14 to article V (insertions are shown in bold italic, deletions in strikethrough). It also decided that these amendments shall come into effect as of its 41st session.

"Article V. Executive Board

A. *Composition*

1. (*a*) The Executive Board shall be elected by the General Conference and it shall consist of fifty-eight Member States. The President of the General Conference shall sit *ex officio* in an advisory capacity on the Executive Board.

(*b*) *A Member State shall not be eligible as a Member of the Executive Board if the total amount of contributions due from it exceeds the total amount of contributions payable by it for the current year and the immediately preceding calendar year. The General Conference may nevertheless permit such a Member State to be eligible as a Member of the Executive Board if it is satisfied that failure to pay is due to conditions beyond the control of the Member State.*

(*c*) Elected States Members of the Executive Board are hereinafter referred to as "Members" of the Executive Board.

[...]

C. Voting rights

14. (*a*) *Each Member of the Executive Board shall have one vote.*

(*b*) *A Member State shall have no vote if the total amount of contributions due from it exceeds the total amount of contributions payable by it for the current year and the immediately preceding calendar year. The General Conference may nevertheless permit such a Member State to vote if it is satisfied that failure to pay is due to conditions beyond the control of the Member State.*"

6. Universal Postal Union

(*a*) Memorandum of understanding between the Universal Postal Union ("UPU") and the Burgendy School of Business signed on 25 June and 29 July 2019*

"VII. Final provisions

Nothing contained in this MoU shall be deemed a waiver of any of the privileges or immunities enjoyed by the UPU.

(...)"

(*b*) Memorandum of understanding between the Universal Postal Union ("UPU") and the Global Alliance of Data-Driven Marketing Associations signed on 30 June and 29 July 2019**

"VII. Final provisions

1. Nothing contained in this MoU shall be deemed a waiver of any of the privileges or immunities enjoyed by the UPU.

(...)"

7. United Nations Industrial Development Organization

(*a*) Application of the Convention on the Privileges and Immunities of the Specialized Agencies in respect of UNIDO***

In 2019, the Islamic Republic of Iran and Trinidad and Tobago deposited notifications with the Secretary-General of the United Nations in his capacity as depositary undertaking to apply the provisions of the Convention to United Nations Industrial Development Organization (UNIDO).

* Entered into force on 29 July 2019.

** Entered into force on 29 July 2019.

*** For more information on the General Convention, see above subchapter 1.

(*b*) Provisions of treaties or other international agreements relating to the legal status, privileges and immunities of UNIDO which came into force in 2019

(i) *Trust fund arrangement between UNIDO and the Ministry of Foreign Affairs of the Republic of Korea regarding the implementation of a project entitled "Developing sustainable settlements for Afghan refugees in the Islamic Republic of Iran"**

"PROJECT DOCUMENT

(...)

H. LEGAL CONTEXT

The Government of the Islamic Republic of Iran as a member state of UNIDO has agreed to apply to all the UNIDO projects the Standard Technical Assistance Agreement concluded between the United Nations and the Specialized Agencies and the Government on 2 February 1956."

(ii) *Agreement between UNIDO and the Government of the United Arab Emirates relating to the arrangements for the eighteenth session of the General Conference of UNIDO signed on 15 and 29 August 2019***

"*Article X. Privileges and immunities*

1. In accordance with article 21 of the Constitution of UNIDO, the Convention on the Privileges and Immunities of the Specialized Agencies, adopted by the General Assembly on 21 November 1947, which the United Arab Emirates has undertaken to apply to UNIDO, shall be applicable in respect of the Conference.

2. In particular, the representatives, alternates, advisers and experts of States or of the intergovernmental organs referred to in article II, paragraph 1 (*a*), (*b*) and (*c*), and article II, paragraph 5 (*a*) and (*b*) above, shall enjoy the privileges and immunities provided under article V of the Convention.

3. The officials of UNIDO performing functions in connection with the Conference referred to in article II, paragraph 4, of this Agreement shall enjoy the privileges and immunities provided under articles VI and VIII of the Convention on the Privileges and Immunities of the Specialized Agencies and any experts on mission for UNIDO in connection with the Conference shall enjoy the privileges and immunities provided under Annex XVII to that Convention.

4. The officials of the United Nations performing functions in connection with the Conference referred to in article II, paragraph 4, of this Agreement shall enjoy the privileges and immunities provided under articles V and VII of the Convention on the Privileges and Immunities of the United Nations and any experts on mission for the United Nations in connection with the Conference shall enjoy the privileges and immunities provided under articles VI and VII of that Convention.

* Entered into force on 14 August 2019.

** Entered into force on 29 August 2019.

5. The representatives or observers referred to in article II, paragraph 1 (*e*), (*f*), (*g*) and (*h*), and in article II, paragraph 5 (*c*) and (*d*) above, shall enjoy immunity from legal process in respect of words spoken or written and any act performed by them in connection with their participation in the Conference.

6. The personnel provided by the Government under article IX of this Agreement shall not be rendered liable for performing their duly authorized responsibilities in connection with the Conference.

7. The representatives of the specialized or related agencies, referred to in article II, paragraph 1 (*d*), above, shall enjoy the privileges and immunities provided under the Convention on the Privileges and Immunities of the Specialized Agencies.

8. Without prejudice to the preceding paragraphs of the present article, all persons performing functions in connection with the Conference and all those participating in the Conference, shall enjoy the privileges, immunities and facilities necessary for the independent exercise of their functions in connection with the Conference.

9. All persons referred to in article II shall have the right of entry into and exit from the territory of the United Arab Emirates, and no impediment shall be imposed on their transit to and from the Conference area. They shall enjoy facilities for obtaining visas and entry permits, free of charge, as speedily as possible. Exit permits, where required, shall be granted free of charge, as speedily as possible, and in any case not later than three days before the closing of the Conference.

10. For the purpose of the Convention on the Privileges and Immunities of the Specialized Agencies, the Conference premises specified in article IV, paragraph 1, above, shall be deemed to constitute premises of UNIDO within the meaning of section 5 of article Ill of the Convention and access thereto shall be subject to the authority and control of UNIDO. The premises shall be inviolable for the duration of the Conference, including the preparatory stage and the winding-up.

11. All persons referred to in article II above shall have the right to take out of the United Arab Emirates at the time of their departure, without any restrictions, any unexpended portions of the funds they brought into the United Arab Emirates in connection with the Conference and to reconvert any such funds at the same rate at their departure.

12. The Government shall allow the temporary importation, tax and duty free, of all equipment, including technical equipment accompanying representatives of information media, and shall waive import duties and taxes on supplies necessary for the Conference. It shall issue without delay any necessary import and export permits for this purpose.

[...]

Article XII. Settlement of disputes

[...]

3. Any such dispute that involves a question regulated by the Convention on the Privileges and Immunities of the Specialized Agencies shall be dealt with in accordance with section 32 of article IX of that Convention.

4. Any such dispute that involves a question regulated by the Convention on the Privileges and Immunities of the United Nations shall be dealt with in accordance with section 30 of that Convention."

(iii) *Agreement between UNIDO and the Government of Ethiopia regarding the implementation of a project in Ethiopia entitled "Capacity development for sustainable agro-industrialization" signed on 11 October 2019*[*]

"6. This Agreement shall be interpreted in a manner that ensures it is consistent with the provisions of the Basic Agreement and the provisions of the 1947 Convention on the Privileges and Immunities of the Specialized Agencies (the "Convention"), provided, however, that if Ethiopia has not acceded to said Convention in respect of UNIDO, the Government agrees to apply to UNIDO the provisions of the 1946 Convention on the Privileges and Immunities of the United Nations (the "General Convention").

7. Nothing contained in or relating to this Agreement shall be deemed a waiver, express or implied, of any of the privileges and immunities of the United Nations, including the UN Partner, under the Convention, the General Convention, the Basic Agreement, or otherwise."

(iv) *Letter of agreement between UNIDO and the Swiss Federal Council regarding the implementation of a project entitled "Market access facilitation for typical agrifood products, phase II—Tunisia" signed on 8 and 18 November 2019*[**]

"23. Nothing in or relating to this letter of agreement shall be deemed to be a waiver of any of the privileges and immunities of UNIDO and no provision of this letter of agreement shall be interpreted or applied in a manner, or to an extent, inconsistent with such privileges and immunities."

8. International Organization for Migration

In 2019 the International Organization for Migration (IOM) entered into cooperation and privileges and immunities agreements with each of the following States: Kingdom of Bahrain (25 April 2019, and an amendment on 30 April 2019), State of Eritrea (16 July 2019), Kingdom of Tonga (16 July 2019), Federal Republic of Somalia (14 December 2019) and State of Qatar (2 December 2019).

9. Organisation for the Prohibition of Chemical Weapons

In 2019, the Organisation for the Prohibition of Chemical Weapons (OPCW) continued to negotiate privileges and immunities agreements with Member States in accordance with paragraph 50 of article VIII of the Convention in order to ensure their effective entry into force. The total number of such agreements concluded by the Organisation stood at 55 at the end of the reporting period.

During 2019, the OPCW concluded a number of international agreements, including technical agreements, voluntary contribution agreements, agreements concerning the provision of Junior Professional Officers for appointment with the OPCW, and exchanges of letters and memoranda of understanding, which entail substantial undertakings at the

[*] Entered into force on 11 October 2019.

[**] Entered into force on 18 November 2019.

policy level or are intended to facilitate the day-to-day work of the Technical Secretariat in support of the objectives of the Convention.

10. International Criminal Court

(*a*) Rome Statute of the International Criminal Court*

On 4 March 2019, Malaysia deposited with the Secretary-General of the United Nations its instrument of accession to the Rome Statute of the International Criminal Court (the "Rome Statute"). The Rome Statute would enter into force for Malaysia on 1 June 2019 in accordance with article 126(2) of the Rome Statute. However, on 5 April 2019, the Government of Malaysia decided to withdraw its instrument of accession to the Rome Statute. According to the Secretary-General of the United Nations, Malaysia's decision to withdraw its instrument of accession to the Rome Statute was effected on 29 April 2019.**

(*b*) Amendment(s) to the Rome Statute

On 6 December 2019, the Assembly of States Parties ("ASP") adopted at the 9th plenary meeting, by consensus, resolution ICC-ASP/18/Res.5 on amendments to article 8 of the Rome Statute of the International Criminal Court.*** In this resolution, the ASP decided to adopt the amendment to article 8, paragraph 2(*e*), of the Rome Statute contained in annex I to the resolution, which is to be inserted as article 8(2)(*e*)(xix) of the Rome Statute, and the relevant elements to be added to the Elements of Crimes, as provided in annex II to the resolution. The two annexes referred to in the resolution provide as follows:

Annex I: Amendment to be inserted as article 8-2-e)-xix) of the Rome Statute

"Intentionally using starvation of civilians as a method of warfare by depriving them of objects indispensable to their survival, including wilfully impeding relief supplies."

Annex 2: Elements of crime of new article 8-2-e)-xix) of the Rome Statute

"1. The perpetrator deprived civilians of objects indispensable to their survival.

2. The perpetrator intended to starve civilians as a method of warfare.

3. The conduct took place in the context of and was associated with an armed conflict not of an international character.

4. The perpetrator was aware of factual circumstances that established the existence of an armed conflict."

---

* United Nations, *Treaty Series*, vol. 2187, p. 3.

** See https://treaties.un.org/doc/Publication/CN/2019/CN.185.2019-Eng.pdf.

*** See https://asp.icc-cpi.int/iccdocs/asp_docs/ASP18/ICC-ASP-18-Res5-ENG-article-8-resolution-10Dec19-1300.cln.pdf.

(*c*) Ratification/Acceptance of amendments to the Rome Statute

(i) *Amendment to article 8(2)(e) of the Rome Statute concerning the insertion of paragraphs (xiii), (xiv) and (xv)*[*]

Paraguay accepted the amendment to article 8(2)(*e*) of the Rome Statute on 5 April 2019.

(ii) *Amendments on the crime of aggression (article 8 bis of the Rome Statute)*[**]

On 5 April 2019, Paraguay accepted the amendments to the Rome Statute on the crime of aggression. On 25 September 2019, Ecuador ratified the amendments to the Rome Statute on the crime of aggression.

(iii) *Amendment to the article 124 of the Rome Statute*[***]

Slovenia and Belgium ratified the amendment to article 124 of the Rome Statute on 2 April 2019 and 16 May 2019, respectively.

(iv) *Amendment to article 8 of the Rome Statute concerning the insertion of articles 8(2)(b)(xxvii) and 8(2)(e)(xvi) relating to weapons which use microbial or other biological agents, or toxins*[****]

Luxembourg and Slovakia ratified the amendment to article 8 of the Rome Statute on 2 April 2019 and 19 June 2019, respectively.

(v) *Amendment to article 8 of the Rome Statute concerning the insertion of articles 8(2)(b)(xxviii) and 8(2)(e)(xvii) relating to weapons the primary effect of which is to injure by fragments which in the human body escape detection by X-rays*[*****]

Luxembourg and Slovakia ratified the amendment to article 8 of the Rome Statute on 2 April 2019 and 19 June 2019, respectively.

(vi) *Amendment to article 8 of the Rome Statute concerning the insertion of articles 8(2)(b)(xxix) and 8(2)(e)(xviii) relating to blinding laser weapons*[******]

Luxembourg and Slovakia ratified the amendment to article 8 of the Rome Statute on 2 April 2019 and 19 June 2019, respectively.

---

[*] See https://treaties.un.org/doc/Publication/CN/2010/CN.533.2010-Eng.pdf.

[**] See https://asp.icc-cpi.int/iccdocs/asp_docs/RC2010/AMENDMENTS/CN.651.2010-ENG-CoA.pdf.

[***] See https://asp.icc-cpi.int/iccdocs/asp_docs/Publications/Compendium/UN.orgdoc.RS-a124.CN.7.2016-ENG.pdf.

[****] See https://asp.icc-cpi.int/iccdocs/asp_docs/ASP16/CN.116.2018-Eng.pdf.

[*****] See https://asp.icc-cpi.int/iccdocs/asp_docs/ASP16/CN.125.2018-Eng.pdf.

[******] See https://asp.icc-cpi.int/iccdocs/asp_docs/ASP16/CN.126.2018-Eng.pdf.

(*d*) Agreement on the Privileges and Immunities of the International Criminal Court

During the reporting period for 2019, the status of the Agreement on the Privileges and Immunities of the International Criminal Court has not changed.

Part Two

LEGAL ACTIVITIES OF THE UNITED NATIONS AND RELATED INTERGOVERNMENTAL ORGANIZATIONS

Chapter III

GENERAL REVIEW OF THE LEGAL ACTIVITIES OF THE UNITED NATIONS AND RELATED INTERGOVERNMENTAL ORGANIZATIONS

A. General review of the legal activities of the United Nations

1. Membership of the United Nations

As of 31 December 2019, the number of Member States of the United Nations was 193.

2. Peace and Security

(*a*) Peacekeeping operations and missions[1]

(i) *Peacekeeping operations and missions established in 2019*

There were no peacekeeping missions or operations established in 2019.

(ii) *Changes in the mandate and/or extensions of time limits of ongoing peacekeeping operations or missions in 2019*

a. Cyprus

The United Nations Peacekeeping Force in Cyprus (UNFICYP) was established by Security Council resolution 186 (1964) of 4 March 1964.[2] By resolutions 2453 (2019) of 30 January 2019 and 2483 (2019) of 25 July 2019, the Security Council decided to extend the mandate of UNFICYP until 31 July 2019 and 31 January 2020, respectively.

b. Syrian Arab Republic and Israel

The United Nations Disengagement Observer Force (UNDOF) was established by Security Council resolution 350 (1974) of 31 March 1974.[3] By resolutions 2477 (2019) of

[1] The operations and missions are listed in chronological order as per their date of establishment.

[2] For more information on UNFICYP, see https://unficyp.unmissions.org/en and https://peacekeeping.un.org/en/mission/unficyp. See also the reports of the Secretary-General on the United Nations operation in Cyprus (S/2019/562, S/2020/23 and S/2020/682).

[3] For more information on UNDOF, see https://undof.unmissions.org and https://peacekeeping.un.org/en/mission/undof. See also the reports of the Secretary-General on UNDOF (S/2019/248, S/2019/467, S/2019/774, S/2019/923 and S/2020/219).

26 June 2019 and 2503 (2019) of 19 December 2019, the Security Council decided to renew the mandate of UNDOF until 31 December 2019 and 30 June 2020, respectively.

c. Lebanon

The United Nations Interim Force in Lebanon (UNIFIL) was established by Security Council resolutions 425 (1978) and 426 (1978) of 19 March 1978.[4] By resolution 2485 (2019) of 2 August 2019, the Security Council decided to extend the mandate of UNIFIL until 31 August 2020.

d. Western Sahara

The United Nations Mission for the Referendum in Western Sahara (MINURSO) was established by Security Council resolution 690 (1991) of 29 April 1991.[5] By resolutions 2468 (2019) of 30 April 2019 and 2494 (2019) of 30 October 2019, the Security Council decided to extend the mandate of MINURSO until 31 October 2019 and 31 October 2020, respectively.

e. Democratic Republic of the Congo

The United Nations Organization Mission in the Democratic Republic of the Congo (MONUC) was established by Security Council resolution 1279 (1999) of 30 November 1999. As of 1 July 2010, MONUC was renamed United Nations Organization Stabilization Mission in the Democratic Republic of the Congo (MONUSCO).[6]

By resolution 2463 (2019) of 29 March 2019, the Security Council, acting under Chapter VII of the Charter of the United Nations, decided to extend until 20 December 2019 the mandate of MONUSCO, including, on an exceptional basis and without creating a precedent or any prejudice to the agreed principles of peacekeeping, its Intervention Brigade. It decided that MONUSCO's authorized troop ceiling would be comprised of 16,215 military personnel, 660 military observers and staff officers, 391 police personnel, and 1,050 personnel of formed police units. It also decided that the strategic priorities of

---

[4] For more information on UNIFIL, see https://unifil.unmissions.org/ and https://peacekeeping.un.org/en/mission/unifil. See also the twenty-ninth, thirtieth, and thirty-first semi-annual report of the Secretary-General to the Security Council on the implementation of Security Council resolution 1559 (2004) (S/2019/343, S/2019/819 and S/2020/329); the reports of the Secretary-General on the implementation of Security Council resolution 1701 (2006) (S/2019/237, S/2019/574, S/2019/889 and S/2020/195); and the letter dated 1 August 2019 from the Secretary-General addressed to the President of the Security Council (S/2019/619).

[5] For more information on MINURSO, see https://minurso.unmissions.org and https://peacekeeping.un.org/en/mission/minurso. See also the reports of the Secretary-General on the situation concerning Western Sahara (S/2019/282, S/2019/787 and S/2020/938).

[6] For more information on MONUSCO, see https://monusco.unmissions.org/en and https://peacekeeping.un.org/en/mission/monusco. See also the reports of the Secretary-General on MONUSCO (S/2019/218, S/2019/575, S/2019/776, S/2019/905 and S/2020/214); the reports of the Secretary-General on the implementation of the Peace, Security and Cooperation Framework for the Democratic Republic of the Congo and the Region (S/2019/229, S/2019/783 and S/2020/272); the statement by the President of the Security Council of 2 August 2019 (S/PRST/2019/6); the letter dated 15 February 2019 from the Secretary-General addressed to the President of the Security Council (S/2019/159); and the exchanges of letter between the Secretary-General and the President of the Security Council dated 29 November 2019 (S/2019/917) and 3 December 2019 (S/2019/918).

MONUSCO were to contribute to the (*a*) protection of civilians, as described in paragraph 29(i) of resolution 2463 (2019) and (*b*) support to the stabilisation and strengthening of State institutions in the DRC and key governance and security reforms, as described in paragraph 29(ii) of the same resolution.

By resolution 2502 (2019) of 19 December 2019, the Security Council, acting under Chapter VII of the Charter of the United Nations, decided to extend until 20 December 2020 the mandate of MONUSCO, including, on an exceptional basis and without creating a precedent or any prejudice to the agreed principles of peacekeeping, its Intervention Brigade. It decided that MONUSCO's authorised troop ceiling will comprise 14,000 military personnel, 660 military observers and staff officers, 591 police personnel, and 1,050 personnel of formed police units, and further agreed to a temporary deployment of an additional 360 personnel of formed police units provided they were deployed in replacement of military personnel, as proposed by the Secretary-General in his report S/2019/905.

f. Republic of the Sudan (Darfur)

The African Union-United Nations Hybrid Operation in Darfur (UNAMID) was established and authorized by Security Council resolution 1769 (2007) of 31 July 2007.[7] Acting under Chapter VII of the Charter of the United Nations, by resolution 2479 (2019) of 27 June 2019, the Security Council decided to extend the mandate of UNAMID until 31 October 2019. It decided that UNAMID should continue to implement its mandate as set out in resolution 2429 (2018), and further decided to extend, temporarily and exceptionally, the period of drawdown for UNAMID's military personnel outlined in paragraph 5 of resolution 2429 (2018), in order to maintain the Mission's self-protection capacities.

By resolution 2495 (2019) of 31 October 2019, acting under Chapter VII of the Charter of the United Nations, the Security Council decided to extend until 31 October 2020 the mandate of UNAMID. It decided that until 31 March 2020 UNAMID should maintain its current troop and police ceilings, and further decided that during this period UNAMID should maintain all team sites for mandate implementation, with the exception of its sector headquarters in South Darfur, which should be closed in line with paragraph 5 of resolution 2495 (2019), whilst being prepared for the timely and responsible closure of additional team sites following a decision of the Security Council.

By the same resolution, the Security Council expressed its intention, taking into account the findings of the Special Report requested in paragraph 6 of resolution 2495 (2019), to decide by 31 March 2020, courses of action regarding the responsible drawdown and exit of UNAMID, and further expressed its intention to adopt a new resolution at the same time, establishing a follow-on presence to UNAMID.

---

[7] For more information on UNAMID, see https://unamid.unmissions.org/en and https://peacekeeping.un.org/en/mission/unamid. See also the reports of the Secretary-General on UNAMID (S/2019/44 and S/2019/305); the special report of the Chairperson of the African Union Commission and the Secretary-General on UNAMID (S/2019/445 and S/2019/816); and the exchange of letters between the Secretary-General and the President of the Security Council (S/2019/366, S/2019/367, S/2019/731, S/2019/732 and S/2020/72).

g. Republic of the Sudan and Republic of South Sudan (Abyei)

The United Nations Interim Security Force for Abyei (UNISFA) was established by Security Council resolution 1990 (2011) of 27 June 2011.[8] By resolution 2465 (2019) of 12 April 2019, the Security Council decided to extend UNISFA's mandate modification set forth in resolution 2024 (2011) and paragraph 1 of resolution 2075 (2012) until 15 October 2019. It decided that this should be the final such extension unless the Governments of Sudan and South Sudan took the specific measures described in paragraph 3 of resolution 2465 (2019). The Council also decided that as of 15 October 2019, the authorized troop ceiling for UNISFA should decrease by 557 troops, unless it decided to extend the mandate modification set forth in resolution 2024 (2011) and paragraph 1 of resolution 2075 (2012).

By resolution 2469 (2019) of 14 May 2019, the Security Council decided to extend until 15 November 2019 the mandate of UNISFA as set out in paragraph 2 of resolution 1990 (2011) and acting under Chapter VII of the Charter of the United Nations, further decided to extend until 15 November 2019 the tasks of UNISFA as set out in paragraph 3 of resolution 1990 (2011). It decided to reduce the authorized troop ceiling to 3,550 and also decided that as of 15 October 2019, the authorized troop ceiling should decrease by a further 585 troops, unless it decided to extend the mandate modification set forth in resolution 2024 (2011) and paragraph 1 of resolution 2075 (2012), in accordance with paragraphs 1 and 3 of resolution 2465 (2019). It also decided to increase the authorized police ceiling established in resolution 1990 (2011) to 640 police personnel, including 148 individual police officers and three formed police units.

By resolution 2492 (2019) of 15 October 2019, the Security Council decided to extend until 15 November 2019 UNISFA's mandate modification set forth in resolution 2024 (2011) and paragraph 1 of resolution 2075 (2012).

By resolution 2497 (2019) of 14 November 2019, the Security Council decided to extend the mandate of UNISFA as set out in paragraph 2 of resolution 1990 (2011) until 15 May 2020 and acting under Chapter VII of the Charter of the United Nations, further decided to extend until 15 May 2020 the tasks of UNISFA as set out in paragraph 3 of resolution 1990 (2011). It decided to extend until 15 May 2020 UNISFA's mandate modification set forth in resolution 2024 (2011) and paragraph 1 of resolution 2075 (2012), which provided for UNISFA's support to the Joint Border Verification and Monitoring Mechanism (JBVMM), and further decided that this should be the final such extension unless the parties take the specific measures described in paragraph 3 of resolution 2497 (2019).

By the same resolution, the Security Council maintained the authorized troop ceiling at 3,550 and decided to allow postponement in the withdrawal of 295 troops above the authorized troop ceiling until 15 May 2020. It also maintained the authorized police ceiling at 640 police personnel, including 148 individual police officers and three formed police units, requested the United Nations to take necessary steps to deploy additional police sequentially in order to meet the authorized police ceiling of 640, and expressed its intention to reduce the authorized police ceiling as the Abyei Police Service was gradually

---

[8] For more information on UNISFA, see https://unisfa.unmissions.org and https://peacekeeping.un.org/en/mission/unisfa. See also reports of the Secretary-General on the situation in Abyei (S/2019/319, S/2019/817 and S/2020/308); and letter dated 20 September 2019 from the Secretary-General addressed to the President of the Security Council (S/2019/768).

established and providing effective law enforcement throughout the Abyei area. It further requested the Secretary-General to appoint a civilian Deputy Head of Mission for UNISFA and add additional civilian staff within existing resources to further facilitate liaison between and engagement with the parties in a manner consistent with the Agreement on Temporary Arrangements for the Administration and Security of the Abyei Area of June 2011, including agreement to establish the Abyei Police Service.

h. Republic of South Sudan

The United Nations Mission in the Republic of South Sudan (UNMISS) was established by the Security Council in resolution 1996 (2011) of 8 July 2011.[9] By resolution 2459 (2019) of 15 March 2019, the Security Council, acting under Chapter VII of the Charter of the United Nations, decided to extend the mandate of UNMISS until 15 March 2020 and authorized UNMISS to use all necessary means to perform the following tasks: (*a*) protection of civilians; (*b*) creating the conditions conducive to the delivery of humanitarian assistance; (*c*) monitoring, and investigating human rights; and (*d*) supporting the Implementation of the Agreement and the Peace Process.

By the same resolution, the Security Council decided to maintain the overall force levels of UNMISS with a troop ceiling of 17,000 troops, including a Regional Protection Force (RPF) at levels to be set by the Secretary-General but not to exceed 4,000, and maintaining the police ceiling of 2,101 police personnel, including individual police officers, formed police units and 78 correction officers. It authorized the RPF to use all necessary means, including undertaking robust action where necessary and actively patrolling, to accomplish the RPF mandate. It also expressed its intention to consider all appropriate measures against those who take actions that undermine the peace, stability, and security of South Sudan.

i. Mali

The United Nations Multidimensional Integrated Stabilization Mission in Mali (MINUSMA) was established by Security Council resolution 2100 (2013) of 25 April 2013.[10] By resolution 2480 (2019) of 28 June 2019, the Security Council, acting under Chapter VII of the Charter of the United Nations, decided to extend the mandate of MINUSMA until 30 June 2020. It decided that MINUSMA should continue to comprise up to 13,289 military personnel and 1,920 police personnel. It also decided that MINUSMA's mandate should include the following priority tasks: (*a*) support to the implementation of the Agreement on Peace and Reconciliation in Mali; (*b*) support to stabilization and restoration of State

---

[9] For more information on UNMISS, see https://unmiss.unmissions.org and https://peacekeeping.un.org/en/mission/unmiss. See also the reports of the Secretary-General on South Sudan (S/2019/191, S/2019/491, S/2019/722,S/2019/936) and S/2020/145); the statement by the President of the Security Council dated 8 October 2019 (S/PRST/2019/11).

[10] For more information on MINUSMA, see https://minusma.unmissions.org/en and https://peacekeeping.un.org/en/mission/minusma. See also the reports of the Secretary-General on the situation in Mali (S/2019/207, S/2019/262, S/2019/454, S/2019/782 and S/2019/983), the statement by the President of the Security Council of 3 April 2019 (S/PRST/2019/2) and the letter dated 27 December 2019 from the Secretary-General addressed to the President of the Security Council (S/2019/1004).

authority in the Centre; (*c*) protection of civilians; (*d*) good offices and reconciliation; (*e*) promotion and protection of human rights; and (*f*) humanitarian assistance.[11]

j. Central African Republic

The United Nations Multidimensional Integrated Stabilization Mission in the Central African Republic (MINUSCA) was established by Security Council resolution 2149 (2014) of 10 April 2014.[12] By resolution 2499 (2019) of 15 November 2019, the Security Council decided to extend the mandate of MINUSCA until 15 November 2020. It decided that MINUSCA should continue to comprise up to 11,650 military personnel, including 480 Military Observers and Military Staff Officers, and 2,080 police personnel, including 400 Individual Police Officers and 1,680 formed police unit personnel, as well as 108 corrections officers and recalled its intention to keep this number under continuous review. It further decided that MINUSCA's strategic objective was to support the creation of the political, security and institutional conditions conducive to the sustainable reduction of the presence of, and threat posed by, armed groups through a comprehensive approach and proactive and robust posture without prejudice to the basic principles of peacekeeping.

The Council also decided that the mandate of MINUSCA should include the following priority tasks: (*a*) protection of civilians; (*b*) good offices and support to the peace process, including the implementation of the Peace Agreement, elections, national reconciliation, social cohesion and transitional justice at national and local levels; (*c*) 2020/2021 elections, (*d*) facilitate the creation of a secure environment for the immediate, full, safe and unhindered delivery of humanitarian assistance; and (*e*) protection of the United Nations.

(iii) *Other ongoing peacekeeping operations or missions*

a. India and Pakistan

The United Nations Military Observer Group in India and Pakistan (UNMOGIP) was established by resolutions 39 (1948) of 20 January 1948 and 47 (1948) of 21 April 1948, to supervise, in the State of Jammu and Kashmir, the ceasefire between India and Pakistan, as well as to observe, to the extent possible, developments pertaining to the strict observance of the ceasefire of 17 December 1971 and to report thereon to the Secretary-General.[13] UNMOGIP continued to operate in 2019.

---

[11] Letter dated 27 December 2019 from the Secretary-General addressed to the President of the Security Council (S/2019/1004).

[12] For more information on MINUSCA, see https://minusca.unmissions.org/en and https://peacekeeping.un.org/en/mission/minusca. See also the reports of the Secretary-General on the situation in the Central African Republic (S/2019/147, S/2019/498, S/2019/822 and S/2020/124).

[13] For more information on UNMOGIP, see https://unmogip.unmissions.org and https://peacekeeping.un.org/en/mission/unmogip.

b. Middle East

The United Nations Truce Supervision Organization (UNTSO) was established by Security Council resolution 50 (1948) of 29 May 1948 to supervise the observation of the truce in Palestine.[14] UNTSO continued to operate in 2019.

c. Kosovo

The United Nations Interim Administration Mission in Kosovo (UNMIK) was established by resolution 1244 (1999) of 10 June 1999 to help ensure conditions for a peaceful and normal life for all inhabitants of Kosovo and advance regional stability in the western Balkans.[15] UNMIK continued to operate in 2019.

(iv) *Peacekeeping missions or operations concluded in 2019*

a. Haiti

The United Nations Mission for Justice Support in Haiti (MINUJUSTH) was established by Security Council resolution 2350 (2017) of 13 April 2017, upon completion of the mandate of the United Nations Stabilization Mission in Haiti (MINUSTAH).[16] By resolution 2466 (2019) of 12 April 2019, the Security Council, acting under Chapter VII of the Charter of the United Nations, decided to extend the mandate of MINUJUSTH for a final period of six months until 15 October 2019. It requested the Secretary-General to initiate the necessary planning for an appropriate integrated United Nations system presence in Haiti, including a Special Political Mission, and beginning on 16 October 2019, with the capacity and expertise to coordinate the activities of United Nations agencies, funds and programmes, to cooperate with the donor community, and to continue to support the efforts of the Government of Haiti in peace consolidation and long-term development after MINUJUSTH has withdrawn; and further requested the Secretary-General to prepare for and begin the gradual, phased withdrawal of MINUJUSTH personnel in advance of 15 October 2019 as appropriate, ensuring a seamless transition.[17]

---

[14] For more information on UNTSO, see http://untso.unmissions.org and https://peacekeeping.un.org/en/mission/untso.

[15] For more information on UNMIK, see https://unmik.unmissions.org and https://peacekeeping.un.org/en/mission/unmik. See also the reports of the Secretary-General on UNMIK (S/2019/102, S/2019/461, S/2019/797 and S/2020/255).

[16] For more information on MINUJUSTH see https://minujusth.unmissions.org/en and https://peacekeeping.un.org/en/mission/minujusth. See also reports of the Secretary-General on the United Nations Mission for Justice Support in Haiti (S/2019/198, S/2019/563 and S/2019/805) and letter dated 13 May 2019 from the Secretary-General addressed to the President of the Security Council (S/2019/387).

[17] For the integrated United Nations system presence in Haiti after the conclusion of MINUJUSTH, see subsection (*b*)(i)b below on the United Nations Integrated Office in Haiti (BINUH).

(*b*) Political and peacebuilding missions[18]

(i) *Political and peacebuilding missions established in 2019*

a. Yemen (City of Hodeidah)

By resolution 2452 (2019) of 16 January 2019, the Security Council decided to establish a Special Political Mission, the United Nations Mission to support the Hodeidah Agreement (UNMHA), to support the implementation of the Agreement on the City of Hodeidah and Ports of Hodeidah, Salif and Ras Issa as set out in the Stockholm Agreement, circulated as S/2018/1134, for an initial period of six months from the date of adoption of the resolution.[19] It further decided that, to support the parties in implementing their commitments in accordance with the Hodeidah Agreement, UNMHA should undertake the following mandate: (*a*) to lead, and support the functioning of, the Redeployment Coordination Committee, assisted by a secretariat staff by United Nations personnel, to oversee the governorate-wide ceasefire, redeployment of forces, and mine action operations, (*b*) to monitor the compliance of the parties to the ceasefire in Hodeidah governorate and the mutual redeployment of forces from the city of Hodeidah and the ports of Hodeidah, Salif and Ras Issa, (*c*) to work with the parties so that the security of the city of Hodeidah and the ports of Hodeidah, Salif, and Ras Issa is assured by local security forces in accordance with Yemeni law, and (*d*) to facilitate and coordinate United Nations support to assist the parties to fully implement the Hodeidah Agreement.

By resolution 2481 (2019) of 15 July 2019, the Security Council decided to extend the mandate of UNMHA until 15 January 2020.

b. Haiti

By resolution 2476 (2019) of 25 June 2019, the Security Council requested the Secretary-General to establish the United Nations Integrated Office in Haiti (BINUH) beginning on 16 October 2019 and for an initial period of 12 months headed by a Special Representative of the Secretary-General of the United Nations to be appointed as swiftly as possible who would also play a good offices, advisory, and advocacy role at the political level including the following key tasks: (*a*) advising the Government of Haiti in promoting and strengthening political stability and good governance; (*b*) assisting the Government of Haiti with its efforts to: (i) plan and execute free, fair, and transparent elections; (ii) reinforce the capacity of the Haitian National Police, develop an inclusive approach with all sectors of society to reduce community violence, and in particular gang violence; (iii) develop an inclusive approach with all sectors of society to reduce community violence, and in particular gang violence; (iv) address human rights abuses and violations and comply with international human rights obligations; (v) improve penitentiary administration and management and oversight of prison facilities; and (vi) strengthen the justice sector. It

---

[18] The political and peacebuilding missions are listed in chronological order as per their date of establishment.

[19] For more information on UNMHA, see https://unmha.unmissions.org/ and https://dppa.un.org/en/mission/unmha-hudaydah-agreement (Note that some sources, such as the website of the Department of Political and Peacebuilding Affairs use the alternative spelling of "Hudaydah Agreement"). See also the letters the Secretary-General addressed to the President of the Security Council reviewing the UNMHA (S/2019/485, S/2019/823 and S/2020/524).

underscored the need for the activities of BINUH and the United Nations Country Team in Haiti, which would assume MINUJUSTH's programmatic and technical assistance role after 15 October 2019, to be fully integrated, and stressed the need for a seamless, successful, and responsible transition to BINUH to ensure continuity.

c. Bolivia

The Secretary-General sent a Personal Envoy to Bolivia on 14 November 2019 during the crisis and violent incidents that followed the general elections of October 2019 to engage with all national actors and offer United Nations support to find a peaceful resolution to the crisis, including through credible and inclusive elections.[20] The Personal Envoy joined facilitation efforts by the Episcopal Conference of Bolivia, the European Union and Spain in a dialogue among the main political actors that resulted in the de-escalation of the crisis. Under the facilitators' auspices, on 22 November 2019, the main parties reached an agreement in which they requested the United Nations system to undertake peace consolidation activities "to help protect life; contain and prevent violence; ensure respect for human rights; promote dialogue; and guarantee the holding as soon as possible of a transparent, credible and inclusive electoral process".

(ii) *Changes in the mandate and/or extensions of the time limits of ongoing political and peacebuilding missions in 2019*

a. Afghanistan

The United Nations Assistance Mission in Afghanistan (UNAMA) was established by Security Council resolution 1401 (2002) of 28 March 2002.[21] By resolutions 2460 (2019) of 15 March 2019 and 2489 (2019) of 17 September 2019, the Security Council decided to extend the mandate of UNAMA until 17 September 2019 and 17 September 2020, respectively.

The Security Council further decided in resolution 2460 (2019) that UNAMA and the Special Representative of the Secretary-General would continue to lead and coordinate the international civilian efforts with a particular focus on the following priorities: (*a*) providing outreach as well as good offices to support the peace process, (*b*) supporting the organization of elections, (*c*) promoting coherent support by the international community to the development and governance priorities of the Government of Afghanistan, (*d*) supporting regional cooperation, (*e*) continuing to cooperate with and strengthen the capacity of the Government of Afghanistan and civil society in the protection and promotion of human rights, (*f*) supporting the importance of gender equality and women's and girls' empowerment, (*g*) continuing to report on violations and abuses against children and to support efforts to strengthen the protection of children affected by armed conflict, and (*h*) closely coordinating and cooperating, where relevant, with the non-combat Resolute Support Mission.

---

[20] See press release https://www.un.org/sg/en/content/sg/personnel-appointments/2019-11-14/mr-jean-arnault-of-france-personal-envoy-of-the-secretary-general-for-bolivia. For more information on the Personal Envoy, see https://dppa.un.org/en/mission/personal-envoy-bolivia.

[21] For more information on UNAMA, see http://unama.unmissions.org and https://dppa.un.org/en/mission/unama.

b. Iraq

The United Nations Assistance Mission for Iraq (UNAMI) was established by Security Council resolution 1500 (2003) of 14 August 2003.[22] By resolution 2470 (2019) of 21 May 2019, the Security Council decided to extend the mandate of UNAMI until 31 May 2020. It decided further that the Special Representative of the Secretary-General and UNAMI, at the request of the Government of Iraq, and taking into account the letter from the Minister of Foreign Affairs of Iraq to the Secretary-General,[23] should, *inter alia*, prioritize the provision of advice, support, and assistance to the Government and people of Iraq on advancing inclusive, political dialogue and national and community-level reconciliation.

c. Guinea Bissau

The United Nations Integrated Peacebuilding Office in Guinea-Bissau (UNIOGBIS) was established by Security Council resolution 1876 (2009) of 26 June 2009.[24] By resolution 2458 (2019) of 28 February 2019, the Security Council decided to extend the mandate of UNIOGBIS for a period of 12 months beginning on 1 March 2019 until 28 February 2020. It also decided that as of the June 2019, UNIOGBIS should operate as a streamlined good offices special political mission, led by a Special Representative at the Assistant Secretary-General level. It also requested UNIOGBIS, including through the use of the good offices and political support of the Special Representative, to focus, in particular, on the following priorities: (*a*) supporting the full implementation of the Conakry Agreement and the Economic Community of West African Stats Roadmap; (*b*) supporting, through good offices the electoral process to ensure inclusive, free and credible legislative elections and presidential election in 2019; and (*c*) providing support, including technical assistance, to national authorities in expediting and completing the review of Guinea-Bissau's Constitution.

d. Libya

The United Nations Support Mission in Libya (UNSMIL) was established by Security Council resolution 2009 (2011) of 16 September 2011.[25] By resolution 2486 (2019) of 12 September 2019, the Security Council decided to extend until 15 September 2020 the mandate of UNSMIL, under the leadership of the Special Representative of the Secretary-General, as an integrated special political mission, in full accordance with the principles of national ownership to exercise mediation and good offices to support: (i) an inclusive political process and security and economic dialogue; (ii) continued implementation of the Libyan Political Agreement; (iii) consolidation of the governance, security and economic

---

[22] For more information about UNAMI, see https://iraq.un.org/en/132447-united-nations-assistance-mission-iraq-unami. See also the reports of the Secretary-General pursuant to resolution 2421 (2018) (S/2019/101 and S/2019/365) and the reports of the Secretary-General pursuant to resolution 2470 (2019) (S/2019/660, S/2019/903 and S/2020/140)).

[23] S/2019/414.

[24] For more information on UNIOGBIS, see http://uniogbis.unmissions.org. See also the reports of the Secretary-General on developments in Guinea-Bissau and the activities of UNIOGBIS (S/2019/115, S/2019/664 and S/2020/105).

[25] For more information on UNSMIL, see https://unsmil.unmissions.org. See also the reports of the Secretary-General on UNSMIL (S/2019/19, S/2019/682 and S/2020/41).

arrangements of the Government of National Accord, including support for economic reform in collaboration with international financial institutions; (iv) a possible ceasefire; and (v) subsequent phases of the Libyan transition process, including the constitutional process and the organisation of elections. It further decided that UNSMIL, within operational and security constraints, should undertake the following tasks: (i) support to key Libyan institutions; (ii) support, on request, for the provision of essential services and delivery of humanitarian assistance, in accordance with humanitarian principles; (iii) human rights monitoring and reporting; (iv) support for securing uncontrolled arms and related materiel and countering their proliferation; and (v) co-ordination of international assistance, and provision of advice and assistance to GNA-led efforts to stabilise post-conflict zones, including those liberated from Da'esh.

e. Somalia

The United Nations Assistance Mission in Somalia (UNSOM) was established by Security Council resolution 2102 (2013) of 2 May 2013 under the leadership of a Special Representative of the Secretary-General.[26] By resolution 2461 (2019) of 27 March 2019, the Security Council decided to extend UNSOM's mandate as set out in paragraph 1 of resolution 2158 (2014) until 31 March 2020.

f. Colombia

The United Nations Verification Mission in Colombia (UNVMC) was established by Security Council resolution 2366 (2017) of 10 July 2017 headed by a Special Representative of the Secretary-General of the United Nations.[27] Following a request by the President of Colombia, presented in a letter dated 12 July 2019 requesting an extension of the mandate of the Verification Mission as agreed by the Government of Colombia and the People's Alternative Revolutionary Force (FARC), the Security Council decided, by resolution 2487 (2019) of 12 September 2019 to extend, to 25 September 2020, the mandate of the Verification Mission and reporting requirements in accordance with its resolutions 2366 (2017), 2377 (2017), and 2435 (2018), headed by a Special Representative of the Secretary-General of the United Nations.

---

[26] For more information on UNSOM, see https://unsom.unmissions.org and https://dppa.un.org/en/mission/unsom. See also the reports of the Secretary-General on Somalia (S/2019/393, S/2019/661, S/2019/884 and S/2020/121); the exchange of letters between the Secretary-General and the President of the Security Council (S/2019/140 and S/2019/141); and the letter dated 6 May 2019 from the Secretary-General addressed to the President of the Security Council (S/2019/372).

[27] For more information on UNVMC, see https://colombia.unmissions.org/en and https://dppa.un.org/en/mission/un-verification-mission-colombia. See also the reports of the Secretary-General on the United Nations Verification Mission in Colombia (S/2019/265, S/2019/530, S/2019/780, S/2019/988 an S/2020/239).

(iii) *Other ongoing political and peacebuilding missions in 2019*

a. Cyprus

The Office of the Special Adviser to the Secretary-General on Cyprus was established in March 1964.[28] The Office continued to operate throughout 2019.[29]

b. Middle East

The Office of the United Nations Special Coordinator for the Middle East Peace Process (UNSCO) was established by the Secretary-General in June 1994.[30] UNSCO continued to function in 2019.

c. Western Sahara

The Personal Envoy of the Secretary-General for Western Sahara was established on 19 March 1997.[31] The Personal Envoy continued to function in 2019.

d. Lebanon (UNSCOL)

The Office of the United Nations Special Coordinator for Lebanon (UNSCOL) was originally established in 2000 as the Personal Representative of the Secretary-General for Southern Lebanon.[32] The mandate was expanded to include coordination of United Nations political activities for the whole of Lebanon and the title changed to Personal Representative for Lebanon in 2005, and to Special Coordinator for Lebanon in 2007, respectively.[33] UNSCOL continued to function in 2019.[34]

e. Central Asia

The United Nations Regional Centre for Preventive Diplomacy for Central Asia (UNRCCA) was established on 10 December 2007 by a letter dated 7 May 2007 from the

---

[28] For more information on the Office of the Special Adviser, see https://uncyprustalks.unmissions.org/en and https://dppa.un.org/en/mission/special-adviser-cyprus.

[29] For an overview of the activities of the Office of the Special Adviser in 2019, see the reports of the Secretary-General on his mission of good offices in Cyprus (S/2019/322, S/2019/883 and S/2020/685).

[30] For more information on UNSCO, see https://unsco.unmissions.org and https://dppa.un.org/en/mission/unsco.

[31] Letter dated 17 March 1997 from the Secretary-General addressed to the President of the Security Council (S/1997/236). For more information on the Personal Envoy, see https://dppa.un.org/en/mission/personal-envoy-western-sahara.

[32] For more information on UNSCOL, see https://unscol.unmissions.org/ and https://dppa.un.org/en/mission/unscol.

[33] Letters dated 14 November 2005 and 8 February 2007, respectively, from the Secretary-General to the President of the Security Council (S/2005/725 and S/2007/85).

[34] See thirty-ninth, fortieth and forty-first report of the Secretary-General on Security Council resolution 1701 (2006) (S/2019/237, S/2019/574 and S/2019/889).

Secretary-General to the President of the Security Council (S/2007/279).[35] UNRCCA continued to function in 2019.[36]

f. Geneva International Discussions

The Geneva International Discussions commenced on 15 October 2008 in accordance with the six-point agreement of 12 August 2008 and implementing measures of 8 September 2008, following the hostilities of August 2008.[37] The Discussions were co-chaired by the European Union, the Organization for Security and Cooperation in Europe, and the United Nations. The United Nations Representative to the Geneva International Discussions (UNRGID) served as the United Nations Co-Chair of the Discussions. The Discussions continued in 2019, with the 47th, 48th, 49th and 50th rounds taking place in Geneva in 2019.

g. African Union

The United Nations Office to the African Union (UNOAU) was established by the General Assembly in resolution 64/288 of 24 June 2010 on 1 July 2010 to enhance the partnership between the United Nations and the African Union in the area of peace and security.[38] UNOAU continued to operate in 2019.[39]

h. Central Africa

The United Nations Regional Office for Central Africa (UNOCA),[40] located in Libreville, Gabon, was established in March 2011 through an exchange of letters in August 2010 between the Secretary-General and the Security Council and began its operations on 2 March 2011.[41] UNOCA continued to operate in 2019.[42]

---

[35] For more information on UNRCCA, see http://unrcca.unmissions.org and https://dppa.un.org/en/mission/unrcca.

[36] Letter dated 27 November 2019 from the Representative of the Dominican Republic to the United Nations addressed to the President of the Security Council (S/2019/910).

[37] For more information on UNRGID, see https://dppa.un.org/en/mission/unrgid.

[38] For more information on UNOAU, see https://unoau.unmissions.org and https://dppa.un.org/en/mission/unoau.

[39] Reports of the Secretary-General on Strengthening the partnership between the United Nations and the African Union on issues of peace and security in Africa, including on the work of the United Nations Office to the African Union (S/2019/759 and S/2020/860).

[40] For more information on UNOCA, see https://unoca.unmissions.org/ and https://dppa.un.org/en/mission/unoca.

[41] Exchange of letters between the Secretary-General and the President of the Security Council dated 11 December 2009 (S/2009/697) and 30 August 2010 (S/2010/457).

[42] Reports of the Secretary-General on the situation in Central Africa and the activities of UNOCA (S/2019/430, S/2019/913 and S/2020/463). See also the letter dated 1 August 2019 from the Secretary-General addressed to the President of the Security Council (S/2019/625) and the statement by the President of the Security Council of 12 September 2019 (S/PRST/2019/10).

i. Syria

On 16 February 2012, the General Assembly in its resolution 66/253 requested the Secretary-General to provide support to the efforts of the League of Arab States aimed at promoting a peaceful solution to the Syrian crisis, including through the appointment of a special envoy. On 23 February and 17 August 2012, the Secretary-General of the United Nations and the Secretary-General of the League of Arab States appointed a Joint Special Envoy and a Joint Special Representative, respectively. On 10 July 2014, the Secretary-General of the United Nations appointed a Special Envoy for Syria.[43] The Office of the Special Envoy continued its operations throughout 2019.[44]

j. Yemen

In April 2011, the Secretary-General appointed a Special Adviser to support him in exercising his good offices in Yemen.[45] On 18 June 2012, the Secretary-General established the Office of the Special Envoy of the Secretary-General for Yemen (OSESGY).[46] Following that the Security Council requested in resolution 2216 (2015) of 14 April 2015 the Secretary-General to intensify his good offices role, the Secretary-General on 23 April 2015, appointed a new Special Envoy for Yemen at the level of Under-Secretary-General.[47] The Office of the Special Envoy to the Secretary-General on Yemen continued its operations throughout 2019.[48]

k. Great Lakes Region

On 24 February 2013, the Peace, Security and Cooperation Framework for the Democratic Republic of the Congo (DRC) and the region was signed by 11 countries, namely Angola, Burundi, the Central African Republic, the Republic of Congo, the DRC, Rwanda, South Africa, South Sudan, Tanzania, Uganda and Zambia. In 2014, Kenya and Sudan became the 12th and 13th signatories of the Framework, respectively. The United Nations acted as one of the Guarantors of the Framework, and its implementation was supported by the Office of the Special Envoy of the Secretary-General for the Great Lakes region.[49] The Office of the Special Envoy continued its operations throughout 2019.[50]

---

[43] For more information on the Office of the Special Envoy, see https://specialenvoysyria.unmissions.org/ and https://dppa.un.org/en/mission/special-envoy-syria.

[44] For an overview of the activities of the Office of the Special Envoy in 2019, see Statement by the President of the Security Council of 8 October 2019 (S/PRST/2019/12). See also the letter dated 26 September 2019 from the Secretary-General addressed to the President of the Security Council (S/2019/775).

[45] For more information on the Office, see https://osesgy.unmissions.org/ and https://dppa.un.org/en/mission/special-envoy-yemen.

[46] Exchange of letters between the Secretary-General and the President of the Security Council (S/2012/469 and S/2012/470).

[47] Exchange of letters between the Secretary-General and the President of the Security Council (S/2015/283 and S/2015/284).

[48] Statement of the President of the Security Council on the developments in Yemen (S/PRST/2019/9).

[49] For more information on the Office of the Special Envoy, see https://ungreatlakes.unmissions.org/en and https://dppa.un.org/en/mission/special-envoy-great-lakes-region.

[50] Reports of the Secretary-General on Implementation of the Peace, Security and Cooperation Framework for the Democratic Republic of the Congo and the Region (S/2019/229, S/2019/783 and S/2020/272).

l. Burundi

In 2015, the Security Council in resolution 2248 (2015) of 12 November 2015 welcomed the decision of the Secretary-General to appoint a Special Adviser on Conflict Prevention, including in Burundi, to work with the government of Burundi and other concerned stakeholders, as well as sub-regional, regional and other international partners, in support of an inclusive inter-Burundian dialogue and peaceful resolution of conflict and in support of national efforts to build and sustain peace. The mandate was amended by the Security Council in its resolutions 2279 (2016) of 1 April and 2303 (2016) of 29 July 2016. The Special Adviser was succeeded by the appointment of the Special Envoy for Burundi on 5 May 2017 at the Under-Secretary-General level, to lead and coordinate the political efforts of the United Nations in Burundi.[51] The Special Envoy for Burundi continued to exercise his functions throughout 2019.[52]

m. West Africa and the Sahel

The United Nations Office for West Africa and the Sahel (UNOWAS) was established in January 2016 on the basis of an exchange of letters between the Secretary-General and the Security Council, merging the former Office of the Special Envoy for the Sahel (OSES) and the United Nations Office for West Africa (UNOWA).[53] UNOWAS began its operations on 12 February 2016 and continued its operations throughout 2019.[54]

n. Myanmar

On 26 April 2018, the Secretary-General appointed a Special Envoy on Myanmar, following the request of the General Assembly in resolution 72/248 of 24 December 2017, to continue to provide good offices and to pursue discussions relating to Myanmar, and to offer assistance to the Government of Myanmar.[55] The General Assembly, in its resolution 73/264 of 22 December 2018, requested the Secretary-General to extend the appointment of the Special Envoy and submit the report of the Special Envoy covering all relevant issues addressed in the resolution to the General Assembly at its seventy-fourth session, and to provide all assistance necessary to enable the Special Envoy to effectively discharge

---

[51] Letter dated 3 May 2017 from the Secretary-General addressed to the President of the Security Council (S/2017/396).

[52] For more information on the Office of the Special Envoy, see https://oseb.unmissions.org/en. For an overview of the activities of the Special Envoy in 2019, see the Report of the Secretary-General on the situation in Burundi (S/2019/837).

[53] Letter dated 14 January 2016 from the Secretary-General addressed to the President of the Security Council (S/2016/88) and letter dated 28 January 2016 from the President of the Security Council addressed to the Secretary-General (S/2016/89). For more information on UNOWAS, see https://unowas.unmissions.org/ and https://dppa.un.org/en/mission/unowas. See also the reports of the Secretary-General on the activities of UNOWAS (S/2019/549 and S/2019/1005); the statement by the President of the Security Council on UNOWAS of 08 August 2019 (S/PRST/2019/7).

[54] Statement by the President of the Security Council of 7 August 2019 (S/PRST/2019/7). See also letter dated 19 November 2019 from the Secretary-General addressed to the President of the Security Council (S/2019/896) and the exchange of letters between the Secretary-General and the President of the Security Council dated 19 December 2019 (S/2019/1009) and 27 December 2019 (S/2019/1010).

[55] For more information on the appointment of the Special Envoy on Myanmar, see: https://press.un.org/en/2018/sga1802.doc.htm.

her mandate and to brief Members States every six months, or as otherwise requested or as warranted by the situation on the ground.[56] The Office of the Special Envoy of the Secretary-General on Myanmar continued to function in 2019.[57]

o. Horn of Africa

In October 2018, the Secretary-General expanded the remit of the Special Envoy for the Sudan and South Sudan to cover the Horn of Africa region, defined for this purpose to comprise the members of the Intergovernmental Authority on Development (IGAD).[58] The Special Envoy for the Horn of Africa continued to function in 2019.

(iv) *Political and peacebuilding missions concluded in 2019*

a. Greece and the former Yugoslav Republic of Macedonia

From 1993 to 2019, the negotiations aimed at resolving the name dispute between Greece and, at the time, the former Yugoslav Republic of Macedonia had been convened under the auspices of the Personal Envoy of the Secretary-General for Greece and the former Yugoslav Republic of Macedonia.[59] In 2019, the Secretary-General reported the outcome of the efforts of the parties concerned to resolve their difference and remaining issues under the auspices of the Secretary-General. The efforts of the parties resulted in the conclusion of the Final Agreement for the Settlement of the Differences as Described in the United Nations Security Council Resolutions 817 (1993) and 845 (1993), the Termination of the Interim Accord of 1995, and the Establishment of a Strategic Partnership between the Parties on 17 June 2018 (also known as the Prespa Agreement). The parties had agreed to, among other things, the name "Republic of North Macedonia". The Secretary-General was informed of the entry into force of the Final Agreement on 12 February 2019.[60]

b. International Commission Against Impunity in Guatemala

On 12 December 2006, the United Nations and the government of Guatemala signed the Agreement on the Creation of an International Commission against Impunity in Guatemala (CICIG).[61] According to the Agreement, CICIG's mandate is comprised of three

---

[56] For more information about the Special Envoy, see https://dppa.un.org/en/mission/special-envoy-myanmar.

[57] See, *e.g.* Letter dated 30 December 2019 from the Chargé d'affaires a.i. of the Permanent Mission of Equatorial Guinea to the United Nations addressed to the President of the Security Council (S/2019/1015) and Letter dated 2 March 2020 from the Permanent Representative of Peru to the United Nations addressed to the President of the Security Council (S/2020/171).

[58] Exchange of letters between the Secretary-General and the President of the Security Council (S/2018/955 and S/2018/979). For more information on the Special Envoy, see https://dppa.un.org/en/mission/special-envoy-horn-of-africa.

[59] For more information on the Personal Envoy, see https://dppa.un.org/en/mission/personal-envoy-greece-former-yugoslav-republic-of-macedonia.

[60] Identical letters dated 13 February 2019 from the Secretary-General addressed to the President of the General Assembly and the President of the Security Council (A/73/745–S/2019/139).

[61] United Nations, *Treaty Series*, vol. 2472, p. 47. For more information on CICIG, see https://www.cicig.org/ and https://dppa.un.org/en/mission/cicig.

main objectives: (1) the investigation of the existence of illicit security forces and clandestine security organizations that commit crimes that affect the fundamental rights of the citizens of Guatemala, and identify the structures of these illegal groups as well as their activities, operating modalities and sources of financing; (2) helping Guatemala to disband clandestine security structures and illegal security groups, and promoting the investigation, criminal prosecution and punishment of crimes committed by the members of such groups; and (3) making recommendations to Guatemala regarding public policies to be adopted to eradicate and prevent the re-emergence of clandestine security structures and illegal security forces. The Agreement established an initial two-year mandate of the CICIG which was renewed four times, for the last time from 4 September 2017 to 3 September 2019.[62]

(*c*) Other bodies

(i) *Cameroon-Nigeria Mixed Commission*

The Cameroon-Nigeria Mixed Commission (CNMC) was established by the Secretary-General, pursuant to a Joint Communiqué of the Presidents of Nigeria and Cameroon adopted in Geneva on 15 November 2002, to facilitate the implementation of the 10 October 2002 ruling of the International Court of Justice on the Cameroon-Nigeria boundary dispute.[63] The mandate of CNMC included supporting the demarcation of the land boundary and delineation of the maritime boundary, facilitating the withdrawal and transfer of authority along the boundary, addressing the situation of affected populations and making recommendations on confidence-building measures. CNMC continued its work in 2019.[64]

(ii) *Monitoring mechanism for Syria*

The United Nations monitoring mechanism for Syria was established by Security Council resolution 2165 (2014) to monitor, under the authority of the United Nations Secretary-General and with the consent of the relevant neighbouring countries of Syria, the loading of all humanitarian relief consignments of the United Nations humanitarian agencies and their implementing partners at the relevant United Nations facilities. By resolution 2449 (2018) of 13 December 2018, the Security Council decided to renew its decisions in paragraphs 2 and 3 of Security Council resolution 2165 (2014) concerning humanitarian assistance for a further period of twelve months, until 10 January 2020. The monitoring mechanism continued its work in 2019.[65]

---

[62] United Nations, *Treaty Series*, vol. 3276, p. 1.

[63] Joint Communiqué Establishing the Cameroon-Nigeria Mixed Commission (CNMC) (SG/SM/8495). *Land and Maritime Boundary between Cameroon and Nigeria (Cameroon* v. *Nigeria: Equatorial Guinea intervening), Judgment, I. C. J. Reports 2002*, p. 303.

[64] For more information on CNMC, see https://unowas.unmissions.org/cameroon-nigeria-mixed-commission. See also the Reports of the Secretary-General on Activities of the United Nations Office for West Africa and the Sahel (S/2019/549 and S/2019/1005).

[65] For more information on the Monitoring Mechanism, see the reports of the Secretary-General on the Implementation of Security Council resolutions 2139 (2014), 2165 (2014), 2191 (2014), 2258 (2015), 2332 (2016), 2393 (2017), 2401 (2018) and 2449 (2018) (S/2019/157, S/2019/321, S/2019/508, S/2019/674, S/2019/820, S/2019/949 and S/2020/141).

(iii) *International Commission of Inquiry for Mali*

In a letter dated 19 January 2018 from the Secretary-General to the President of the Security Council (S/2018/57), the Secretary-General, in response to a request made by the Government of Mali on 5 April 2016, and taking into consideration article 46 of the Agreement on Peace and Reconciliation in Mali, decided to establish an International Commission of Inquiry to investigate allegations of abuses and serious violations of international human rights law and international humanitarian law, including allegations of conflict-related sexual violence, committed in the territory of Mali from 1 January 2012 to the date of the establishment of the Commission for a period of one year. The Commission was also mandated to, *inter alia*, establish the facts and circumstances concerning the commission of such abuses and violations, including those that may constitute international crimes, and identify those allegedly responsible for such abuses and violations.[66] The Commission effectively commenced its work on 22 October 2018 but, owing to various challenges, was granted an extension by the Secretary-General, who authorized it to complete its work on 19 June 2020.[67] The Commission continued its work in 2019.[68]

(*d*) Missions of the Security Council

(i) *West Africa*

In a letter dated 8 February 2019, the President of the Security Council informed the Secretary-General that the Council had decided to send a mission to West Africa (Côte d'Ivoire and Guinea-Bissau) from 13 to 17 February 2019, outlining in an annex to the letter the mission's terms of reference.[69]

The mission to Côte d'Ivoire would, *inter alia*, take stock of the ongoing transition in Côte d'Ivoire, as well as in Liberia and Sierra Leone, and to support the work of the United Nations Office for West Africa and the Sahel (UNOWAS) for conflict prevention and peacebuilding in the Mano River subregion and the respective United Nations country teams in those three countries. The mission to Guinea-Bissau would, *inter alia*, engage with key stakeholders involved in the political crisis in Guinea-Bissau, evaluate the compliance of UNIOGBIS with its mandate and evaluate the efforts made by the Guinea-Bissau authorities to implement and review national laws and mechanisms to more effectively combat transnational organized crime, in particular drug trafficking and money-laundering.

The mission submitted to the Security Council a report on its work.[70]

---

[66] For more information on the Commission, see https://www.un.org/en/our-work/commission-of-inquiry-for-mali.

[67] Report of the International Commission of Inquiry for Mali. Annex to the letter dated 17 December 2020 from the Secretary-General addressed to the President of the Security Council (S/2020/1132).

[68] Report of the Secretary-General on the situation in Mali (S/2018/1174).

[69] Letter dated 8 February 2019 from the President of the Security Council addressed to the Secretary-General (S/2019/123).

[70] Report of the Security Council mission to Côte d'Ivoire and Guinea-Bissau (S/2019/303).

(ii) *Sahel*

In a letter dated 20 March 2019, the President of the Security Council informed the Secretary-General that the Council had decided to send a mission to the Sahel (Mali and Burkina Faso) from 21 to 25 March 2019, outlining in an annex to the letter the mission's terms of reference.[71]

The mission to Mali would, *inter alia*, prepare for the meeting of the Security Council aimed at discussing the way forward regarding the implementation of the Agreement and the future of MINUSMA, assess the implementation of the priority measures referenced in paragraph 4 of resolution 2423 (2018), as well as of the commitments contained in the Pact for Peace signed between the Government of Mali and the United Nations. The mission to Burkina Faso would, *inter alia*, assess the current security situation in Burkina Faso, including regarding the evolving threat posed by terrorism and transnational organized crime and hear from the Burkinabe rotating presidency of the Group of Five for the Sahel on its priorities.

The mission briefed the Security Council on its work during the 8492nd meeting of the Security Council.[72]

(iii) *Iraq and Kuwait*

In a letter dated 27 June 2019, the President of the Security Council informed the Secretary-General that the Council had decided to send a mission to the Sahel (Mali and Burkina Faso) from 27 to 30 June 2019, outlining in an annex to the letter the mission's terms of reference.[73]

The mission would, *inter alia*, observe and support the efforts of the United Nations Assistance Mission for Iraq to implement its mandate in line with resolutions 2470 (2019) and 2107 (2013) and other related Security Council resolutions.

The mission briefed the Security Council on its work during the 8571st meeting of the Security Council.[74]

(iv) *Colombia*

In a letter dated 10 July 2019, the President of the Security Council informed the Secretary-General that the Council had decided to send a mission to Colombia from 11 to 14 July, outlining in an annex to the letter the mission's terms of reference.[75]

The mission would, *inter alia*, observe and support the efforts of the United Nations Verification Mission in Colombia to implement its mandate, in line with Council resolutions 2366 (2017), 2377 (2017) and 2435 (2018).

---

[71] Letter dated 20 March 2019 from the President of the Security Council addressed to the Secretary-General (S/2019/252).

[72] See S/PV.8492.

[73] Letter dated 27 June 2019 from the President of the Security Council addressed to the Secretary-General (S/2019/533).

[74] See S/PV.8571.

[75] Letter dated 10 July 2019 from the President of the Security Council addressed to the Secretary-General (S/2019/557).

The mission submitted to the Security Council a report on its work.[76]

(v) *Africa*

In a letter dated 16 October 2019, the President of the Security Council informed the Secretary-General that the Council had decided to send a mission to Africa (Ethiopia and South Sudan) from 19 to 23 October 2019, outlining in an annex to the letter the mission's terms of reference.[77]

The mission would, *inter alia*, observe and support the efforts of UNMISS to implement its mandate in line with resolution 2459 (2019) and other related Council resolutions.

(*e*) Action of Member States authorized by the Security Council

(i) *Bosnia and Herzegovina*

The European Union Force Althea (EUFOR ALTHEA) was initially authorized by Security Council resolution 1575 (2004) of 22 November 2004.[78] By resolution 2496 (2019) of 5 November 2019, the Security Council, acting under Chapter VII of the Charter of the United Nations, authorized the Member States acting through or in cooperation with the EU to establish for a further period of twelve months, starting from the date of the adoption of this resolution, a multinational stabilization force (EUFOR ALTHEA). It also authorized the Member States acting under paragraphs 3 and 4 above to take all necessary measures to effect the implementation of and to ensure compliance with annexes 1-A and 2 of the Peace Agreement,[79] and to take all necessary measures to ensure compliance with the rules and procedures governing command and control of airspace over Bosnia and Herzegovina with respect to all civilian and military air traffic. Moreover, it authorized Member States to take all necessary means, at the request of either EUFOR ALTHEA or the NATO Headquarters, in defence of the EUFOR ALTHEA or NATO presence respectively, and to assist both organizations in carrying out their missions. It also recognized the right of both EUFOR ALTHEA and the NATO presence to take all necessary measures to defend themselves from attack or threat of attack. It also decided to renew the authorization provided by paragraph 11 of its resolution 2183 (2014) for a further period of twelve months starting from the date of adoption of this resolution.

---

[76] Report of the Security Council mission to the Republic of Colombia, 11–14 July 2019 (S/2019/827).

[77] Letter dated 16 October 2019 from the President of the Security Council addressed to the Secretary-General (S/2019/825).

[78] For more information on the European Union military mission in Bosnia and Herzegovina (EUFOR), see https://www.euforbih.org/index.php/en. See also the letter dated 1 May 2019 from the Secretary-General addressed to the President of the Security Council (S/2019/364) and the reports of the High Representative for Implementation of the Peace Agreement on Bosnia and Herzegovina, reproduced as annexes to letters of the Secretary-General addressed to the President of the Security Council (S/2019/364, S/2019/843 and S/2020/345, annexes).

[79] General Framework Agreement for Peace in Bosnia and Herzegovina and the Annexes thereto, attachment to letter dated 29 November 1995 from the Permanent Representative of the United States of America to the United Nations addressed to the Secretary-General (S/1995/999).

(ii) *Somalia*[80]

The African Union Mission in Somalia (AMISOM) was initially authorized by the Security Council, acting under Chapter VII of the Charter of the United Nations, in resolution 1744 (2007) of 20 February 2007.[81] By resolution 2472 (2019) of 31 May 2019, the Security Council, acting under Chapter VII of the Charter of the United Nations, decided to authorise the Member States of the African Union (AU) to maintain the deployment of AMISOM until 31 May 2020, including a minimum of 1,040 AMISOM police personnel including five Formed Police Units, and to reduce the level of uniformed AMISOM personnel by 1000 to a maximum level of 19,626, by 28 February 2020, in line with the Transition Plan, and the handover to Somali security forces, unless the Security Council decides to adjust the pace of the reduction taking into account conditions set out in the Transition Plan. It further decided that AMISOM should be authorised to take all necessary measures, in full compliance with participating States' obligations under international law, including international humanitarian law and international human rights law, and in full respect for the sovereignty, territorial integrity, political independence and unity of Somalia, to carry out its mandate.

It also decided to authorise AMISOM to pursue the strategic objectives of (*a*) conducting a gradual handing over of security responsibilities from AMISOM to the Somali security forces with the aim of Somali security institutions taking the lead by 2021; (*b*) reducing the threat posed by Al Shabaab and other armed opposition groups with a view to enabling a stable, federal, sovereign and united Somalia; (*c*) assisting the Somali security forces to provide security for the political process at all levels, stabilisation efforts, reconciliation, and peacebuilding and providing relevant support to Somali police and authorities to create a secure environment in the build up to elections with the aim of fully handing over security responsibility to Somali security institutions. It decided to authorise AMISOM to carry out a set of priority tasks to achieve the above-mentioned objectives, *inter alia*, maintaining a presence in the sectors set out in AMISOM's Concept of Operations; mentoring and assisting Somali security forces and securing key supply routes including to areas recovered from Al Shabaab.

(iii) *Central African Republic*

French forces had initially been authorized by the Security Council, acting under Chapter VII of the Charter of the United Nations, in resolution 2127 (2013) of 5 December 2013 to take all necessary measures to support the African-led International Support Mission in the CAR (MISCA) and, by resolution 2149 (2014) of 10 April 2014, acting under Chapter VII of the Charter of the United Nations, to use all necessary means to provide operational support to elements of MINUSCA, from the commencement of the activities of MINUSCA until the end of its mandate.[82]

---

[80] See subsection (j) below on acts of piracy off the coast of Somalia.

[81] For more information on AMISOM, see https://amisom-au.org/. See also the letters dated 20 March 2019, 10 May 2019, 24 May 2019, 19 August 2019, and 4 October 2019 from the Secretary-General to the President of the Security Council (S/2019/255, S/2019/388, S/2019/440 and S/2019/671).

[82] For reports on the activities carried out by the French armed forces in the Central African Republic in support of MINUSCA, see the note verbales from the Permanent Mission of France to the

By resolution 2499 (2019) of 15 November 2019, the Security Council, acting under Chapter VII of the Charter of the United Nations, authorised French armed forces, within the provisions of their existing bilateral agreement with the CAR and the limits of their capacities and areas of deployment, at the request of the Secretary-General, to use all the means to provide operational support to elements of MINUSCA when under serious threat, from the date of adoption of this resolution, and requested France to ensure reporting to the Council on the implementation of this mandate and to coordinate its reporting with that of the Secretary-General referred to in paragraph 54 of that resolution.

(iv) *Mali*

French forces had initially been authorized by Security Council, acting under Chapter VII of the Charter of the United Nations, in resolution 2164 (2014) of 25 June 2014 to use all necessary means to intervene in support of elements of MINUSMA when under imminent and serious threat upon request of the Secretary-General.[83] By resolution 2480 (2019) of 28 June 2019, the Security Council, acting under Chapter VII of the Charter of the United Nations, decided to extend this authorization until the end of MINUSMA's mandate as authorized in the resolution.

(*f*) Sanctions imposed under Chapter VII of the Charter of the United Nations[84]

(i) *Somalia*

The Security Council Committee established pursuant to resolution 751 (1992) of 24 April 1992 concerning Somalia was mandated to oversee the general and complete arms embargo imposed by Security Council resolution 733 (1992) and to undertake the tasks set out by the Security Council resolutions 751 (1992), 1356 (2001) and 1844 (2008).[85] Following the adoption of resolution 1907 (2009), which imposed a sanctions regime on Eritrea and expanded its mandate, the Committee decided on 26 February 2010 to change its name to "Security Council Committee pursuant to resolution 751 (1992) and 1907 (2009) concerning Somalia and Eritrea".[86] With the adoption of resolution 2444 (2018) of

United Nations, annexed to the letters from the Secretary-General addressed to the President of the Security Council dated 4 April 2019, 31 October 2019 and 2 March 2020 (S/2019/294, S/2019/855 and S/2020/173, respectively). On MINUSCA, see subchapter (*a*)(ii)(j) above.

[83] For more information, see the letters dated 19 October 2018, 19 November 2018, and 4 April 2019 from the Secretary-General addressed to the President of the Security Council transmitting a note verbale from the Permanent Mission of France to the United Nations with a report on the activities carried out by French armed forces in support of MINUSMA (S/2019/252, S/2019/1004, and S/2020/285, respectively).

[84] The sanctions imposed under Chapter VII of the Charter of the United Nations are listed in chronological order according to the date of adoption of the respective Security Council resolutions. For more information on the sanction regimes established by the Security Council, see the Security Council's website relating to subsidiary organs at https://main.un.org/securitycouncil/en/sanctions/information.

[85] For more information on the Committee, see https://www.un.org/securitycouncil/sanctions/751.

[86] Report of the Security Council Committee pursuant to resolutions 751 (1992) and 1907 (2009) concerning Somalia and Eritrea, in annex of Letter dated 31 December 2010 from the Chairman of the

14 November 2018, which terminated the Eritrea sanctions regime, the Committee's name was changed to "Security Council Committee pursuant to resolution 751 (1992) concerning Somalia". The Security Council Committee submitted, on 20 December 2019, a report on its work in 2019 to the Security Council.[87]

By resolution 2498 (2019) of 15 November 2019, the Security Council, acting under Chapter VII of the Charter of the United Nations, reaffirmed the existing arms embargo on Somalia with certain exceptions and decided to impose an improvised explosive devices components ban. It also decided to renew the provisions set out in paragraph 15 of resolution 2182 (2014) until 15 November 2020 and the Panel on Somalia until 15 December 2020 , respectively.

(ii) *ISIL (Da'esh) and Al-Qaida*

The 1267 Committee was first established by Security Council resolution 1267 (1999) of 15 October 1999 and sets forth a sanctions regime concerning the Taliban. The regime was modified and strengthened by subsequent resolutions, including resolutions 1333 (2000), 1390 (2002), 1455 (2003), 1526 (2004), 1617 (2005), 1735 (2006), 1822 (2008), 1904 (2009),1989 (2011) and 2253 (2015) so that the sanctions measures would be applicable to designated individuals and entities associated with Al-Qaida and Islamic State in Iraq and the Levant (ISIL, also known as Da'esh), wherever located. The Committee continued its operations in 2019 and submitted, on 20 December 2019, a report on its work in 2019 to the Security Council.[88]

By resolution 2462 (2019) of 28 March 2019, the Security Council, acting under Chapter VII of the Charter of the United Nations, urged all States to participate actively in implementing and updating the ISIL (Da'esh) and Al-Qaida Sanctions List and to consider including, when submitting new listing requests, individuals and entities involved in the financing of terrorism. It requested the Counter-Terrorism Committee and the Committee established pursuant to resolutions 1267 (1999), 1989 (2011) and 2253 (2015) to hold, within 12 months, a joint special meeting on terrorist financing threats and trends as well as on the implementation of the provisions of this resolution.

(iii) *1518 Sanctions Committee (Iraq)*

The Security Council Committee established pursuant to resolution 1518 (2003) of 24 November 2003 to continue to identify senior officials of the former Iraqi regime and their immediate family members who are subject to the measures imposed by paragraph 23 of resolution 1483 (2003). The Committee updates the lists of individuals and entities that have already been identified by the Committee established pursuant to resolution 661

Security Council Committee pursuant to resolutions 751 (1992) and 1907 (2009) concerning Somalia and Eritrea addressed to the President of the Security Council (S/2010/688).

[87] Report of the Security Council Committee pursuant to resolution 751 (1992) concerning Somalia (S/2019/978).

[88] Report of the Security Council Committee pursuant to resolutions 1267 (1999) and 1989 (2011) and 2253 (2015) concerning Al-Qaida and associated individuals and entities (S/2019/980). For more information on the 1267 Committee, see: https://un.org/securitycouncil/en/sanctions/1267.

(1990).[89] The Committee continued its operations throughout 2019 and submitted, on 19 December 2019, a report on its work in 2019 to the Security Council.[90]

(iv) *Democratic Republic of the Congo*

The Security Council Committee established pursuant to resolution 1533 (2004) of 12 March 2004 to oversee the sanctions measures imposed by relevant Security Council resolutions continued its operations in 2019 and submitted, on 19 December 2019, a report on its work in 2019 to the Security Council.[91]

By resolution 2478 of 26 June 2019, the Security Council, acting under Chapter VII of the Charter of the United Nations, decided to renew until 1 July 2020 the measures as set out in paragraphs 1 to 6 of resolution 2293 (2016). It also decided to extend until 1 August 2020 the mandate of the Group of Experts, as set forth in paragraph 6 of resolution 2360.

(v) *Republic of the Sudan (Darfur)*

The Security Council Committee established pursuant to resolution 1591 (2005) of 29 March 2005 to oversee the relevant sanctions measures concerning the Sudan and to undertake the tasks set out by the Security Council in sub-paragraph 3 (*a*) of the same resolution continued its operations in 2019 and submitted, on 20 December 2019, a report on its work in 2019 to the Security Council.[92]

By resolution 2455 (2019) of 7 February 2019, the Security Council, acting under Chapter VII of the Charter of the United Nations, decided to extend until 12 March 2020 the mandate of the Panel of Experts, originally appointed pursuant to resolution 1591 (2005). It also expressed its intention to review the mandate and take appropriate action regarding the further extension of the mandate no later than 12 February 2020.[93]

(vi) *1636 Sanctions Committee (Lebanon)*

The Security Council Committee established pursuant to resolution 1636 (2005) of 31 October 2005 to register individuals designated by the International Independent Investigation Commission or the Government of Lebanon as suspected of involvement in

---

[89] The Security Council Committee established pursuant to resolution 661 (1990) was terminated by resolution 1483 (2003) of 22 May 2003.

[90] Report of the Security Council Committee established pursuant to resolution 1518 (2003) (S/2019/963). For more information on the Committee, see https://main.un.org/securitycouncil/en/sanctions/1518.

[91] Report of the Security Council Committee established pursuant to resolution 1533 (2004) concerning the Democratic Republic of the Congo (S/2019/965). For more information on the Committee, see https://www.un.org/securitycouncil/sanctions/1533.

[92] Report of the Security Council Committee established pursuant to resolution 1591 (2005) concerning the Sudan (S/2019/975). For more information on the Committee, see https://main.un.org/securitycouncil/en/sanctions/1591.

[93] Final report of the Panel of Experts submitted in accordance with paragraph 2 of resolution 2400 (2018) (S/2019/34).

the 14 February 2005 terrorist bombing in Beirut, Lebanon, that killed former Lebanese Prime Minister Rafiq Hariri and 22 others. The Committee continued its work in 2019.[94]

(vii) *Democratic People's Republic of Korea*

The Security Council Committee established pursuant to resolution 1718 (2006) on 14 October 2006 to oversee the relevant sanctions measures concerning the Democratic People's Republic of Korea (DPRK) and to undertake the tasks set out in paragraph 12 of that same resolution and in resolutions 1874 (2009), 2087 (2013) and 2094 (2013), continued its operations in 2019 and submitted, on 20 December 2019, a report on its work to the Security Council.[95]

By resolution 2464 (2019) of 10 April 2019, the Security Council, acting under Article 41 of Chapter VII of the Charter of the United Nations, decided to extend until 24 April 2020 the mandate of the Panel of Experts, as specified in paragraph 26 of resolution 1874 (2009) and modified in paragraph 29 of resolution 2094 (2013), decided that this mandate should apply also with respect to the measures imposed in resolution 2270 (2016), 2321 (2016), 2356 (2017), 2371 (2017), 2375 (2017), and 2397 (2017). The Security Council also expressed its intent to review the mandate and take appropriate action regarding further extension no later than 24 March 2020.[96]

(viii) *Libya*

The Security Council Committee established pursuant to resolution 1970 (2011) concerning Libya on 26 February 2011 to oversee the relevant sanctions measures continued its operations in 2019 and submitted, on 20 December 2019, a report on its work in 2019 to the Security Council.[97]

By resolution 2473 (2019) of 10 June 2019, the Security Council, acting under Chapter VII of the Charter of the United Nations, decided to extend the authorizations as set out in resolution 2420 for a further 12 months from the date of resolution 2473.

(ix) *Afghanistan (Taliban)*

The Security Council Committee established pursuant to resolution 1988 (2011) on 17 June 2011 to oversee the relevant sanctions measures and to undertake the tasks set out by

---

[94] For more information on the Committee, see https://main.un.org/securitycouncil/en/sanctions/1636.

[95] Report of the Security Council Committee established pursuant to resolution 1718 (2006) (S/2019/971). For more information on the Committee, see https://main.un.org/securitycouncil/en/sanctions/1718.

[96] Report of the Panel of Experts established pursuant to resolution 1874 (2009) (S/2019/691).

[97] Report of the Security Council Committee established pursuant to resolution 1970 (2011) concerning Libya (S/2019/972). For more information on the Committee, see https://main.un.org/securitycouncil/en/sanctions/1970.

the Security Council in paragraph 30 of the same resolution continued its operations in 2019 and submitted, on 19 December 2019, a report on its work in 2019 to the Security Council.[98]

In resolution 2501 (2019) of 16 December 2019, acting under Chapter VII of the Charter of the United Nations, the Security Council decided that all States should continue to take the measures required by paragraph 1 of resolution 2255 with respect to individuals and entities designated prior to the date of adoption of resolution 1988 (2011) as the Taliban, as well as other individuals, groups, undertakings and entities associated with the Taliban in constituting a threat to the peace, stability and security of Afghanistan as designated by the Committee established in paragraph 35 of resolution 1988 in the 1988 Sanction List. It also decided that the 1267/1988 Analytical Support and Sanctions Monitoring Team, established pursuant to paragraph 7 of resolution 1526 (2004), should continue to support the Committee for a period of twelve months from the date of expiration of the current mandate in December 2019.

(x) *Guinea-Bissau*

The Security Council Committee established pursuant to resolution 2048 (2012) on 18 May 2012, to monitor the implementation of the measures imposed by resolution 2048 (2012), to designate the individuals subject to the measures and to consider requests for exemptions, continued its operations in 2019 and submitted, on 6 February 2019, a report on its work in 2019 to the Security Council.[99]

By resolution 2458 (2019) of 28 February 2019, the Security Council decided to review the sanctions measures established pursuant to resolution 2048 (2012) seven months from the adoption of resolution 2458 (2019), and also requested the Secretary-General to submit to the Security Council regular reports every six months on the implementation of resolution 2458 (2019) and to submit a report within six months, with a briefing to the Committee established pursuant to resolution 2048 (2012), on the progress made regards to the stabilization of the country and restoration of constitutional order and recommendations on the continuations of the sanctions regime in the post-elections environment, in line with paragraph 12 of resolution 2048 (2012).

(xi) *Central African Republic*

The Security Council Committee concerning the Central African Republic (CAR) established pursuant to resolution 2127 (2013) of 5 December 2013 continued its operations in 2019 and submitted, on 19 December 2019, a report on its work in 2019 to the Security Council.[100]

---

[98] Report of the Security Council Committee established pursuant to resolution 1988 (2011) (S/2019/970). For more information on the Committee, see https://main.un.org/securitycouncil/en/sanctions/1988.

[99] Report of the Security Council Committee established pursuant to resolution 2048 (2012) concerning Guinea-Bissau (S/2019/966). For more information on the Committee, see https://www.un.org/securitycouncil/sanctions/2048.

[100] Report of the Security Council Committee established pursuant to resolution 2127 (2013) concerning the Central African Republic (S/2019/973). For more information, see https://main.un.org/securitycouncil/en/sanctions/2745.

By resolution 2454 (2019) of 31 January 2019, the Security Council, acting under Chapter VII of the Charter of the United Nations, decided to renew the measures and provisions as set out in paragraphs 1 to 19 of resolution 2399 (2018) until 31 January 2020. It also decided to extend the mandate of the Panel of Experts as set out in paragraphs 30 to 39 of the same resolution until 29 February 2020 and expressed its intention to review the mandate and take appropriate action regarding its further extension no later than 31 January 2020.[101]

By resolution 2488 (2019) of 12 September 2019, the Security Council, acting under Chapter VII of the Charter of the United Nations, decided, pursuant to its intention as expressed in paragraph 10 of resolution 2454 (2019) to review the arms embargo measures on the CAR authorities, to adjust the measures imposed by paragraph 1 of resolution 2399 (2018) and extended by paragraph 1 of resolution 2454 (2019), such that, until 31 January 2020, they should not apply to certain supplies as listed in paragraph 2 of this resolution.

(xii) *Yemen*

The Security Council Committee established pursuant to resolution 2140 (2014) of 26 February 2014, to monitor the implementation of the measures imposed by the resolution, continued its operations in 2019 and submitted, on 19 December 2019, a report on its work in 2019 to the Security Council.[102]

By resolution 2456 (2019) of 26 February 2019, the Security Council, acting under Chapter VII of the Charter of the United Nations, decided to renew until 26 February 2020 the measures imposed by paragraphs 11 and 15 of resolution 2140 (2014), reaffirmed the provisions of paragraphs 12, 13, 14 and 16 of resolution 2140 (2015), and further reaffirmed the provisions of paragraphs 14 to 17 of resolution 2216 (2015); applicable to individuals or entities designated by the Committee or in the annex to resolution 2216 (2015). It also decided to extend until 28 March 2020 the mandate of the Panel of Experts as set out in paragraph 21 of resolution 2140 (2014) and paragraph 21 of resolution 2216 (2015).[103]

(xiii) *South Sudan*

The Security Council Committee established pursuant to resolution 2206 (2015) of 3 March 2015 to monitor the implementation of the measures imposed by the resolution continued its operations in 2019 and submitted, on 19 December 2019, a report on its work in 2019 to the Security Council.[104]

---

[101] See the midterm and final report of the Panel of Experts on the Central African Republic extended pursuant to Security Council resolution 2399 (2018) (S/2019/608 and S/2019/930, respectively) and the letter dated 26 July 2019 from the Secretary-General addressed to the President of the Security Council (S/2019/609).

[102] Report of the Security Council Committee established pursuant to resolution 2140 (2014) (S/2019/969). For more information, see https://www.un.org/securitycouncil/en/sanctions/2140. See also the letter dated 18 March 2019 from the Secretary-General addressed to the President of the Security Council (S/2019/247).

[103] See the final report of the Panel of Experts prepared in accordance with paragraph 6 of resolution 2456 (2019) (S/2020/326).

[104] See the report of the Security Council Committee established pursuant to resolution 2206 (2015) concerning South Sudan (S/2019/967). For more information, see https://www.un.org/securitycouncil/

By resolution 2471 (2019) of 30 May 2019, the Security Council, acting under Chapter VII of the Charter of the United Nations, decided to renew until 31 May 2020 the measures imposed by paragraphs 9 and 12 of resolution 2206 (2015) and to renew until 31 May 2020 the measures imposed by paragraph 4 of resolution 2428 (2018). It also decided to extend until 30 June 2020 the mandate of the Panel of Experts as established by paragraph 18 of resolution 2206 (2015).[105]

(xiv) *Mali*

The Security Council Committee established pursuant to resolution 2374 (2017) of 5 September 2017 to monitor the implementation of the measures imposed by the resolution continued its operations in 2019 and submitted, on 20 December 2019, a report on its work in 2019 to the Security Council.[106]

By resolution 2484 (2019) of 29 August 2019, the Security Council, acting under Chapter VII of the Charter of the United Nations, decided to renew until 31 August 2020 the measures as set out in paragraphs 1 to 7 of resolution 2374 (2017). It also decided to extend until 30 September 2020 the mandate of the Panel of Experts, as set out in paragraphs 11 to 15 of resolution 2374 (2017).

(*g*) Terrorism

(i) *General Assembly*

On 12 December 2019, the General Assembly, upon recommendation of the First Committee, adopted resolution 74/43 entitled "Measures to prevent terrorists from acquiring weapons of mass destruction" without a vote.[107] In that resolution, the General Assembly appealed to all Member States to consider early accession and ratification of the International Convention for the Suppression of Acts of Nuclear Terrorism, and encouraged State parties to the Convention to review its implementation.

On 18 December 2019, upon the recommendation of the Third Committee, the General Assembly adopted resolution 74/147 entitled "Terrorism and human rights", without a vote. In this resolution, the General Assembly strongly condemned all terrorist acts as criminal and unjustifiable, and expressed grave concern at their detrimental effects on the enjoyment of all human rights. It urged States to fully comply with their obligations under international law while countering terrorism, in particular international human rights law, international refugee law and international humanitarian law, with regard to the absolute prohibition of torture and other cruel, inhuman or degrading treatment or

sanctions/2206.

[105] See the interim report of the Panel of Experts on South Sudan submitted pursuant to resolution 2471 (2019) (S/2019/897) and the letter dated 2 July 2019 from the Secretary-General addressed to the President of the Security Council (S/2019/544).

[106] Report of the Security Council Committee established pursuant to resolution 2374 (2017) concerning Mali (S/2019/968).

[107] See also the Report of the Secretary-General on Measures to prevent terrorists from acquiring weapons of mass destruction (A/74/140).

punishment. It also urged States to take measures to ensure that counter-terrorism laws and implementing measures were consistent with and were applied in a manner that fully respected the rights enshrined in the Universal Declaration of Human Rights and the obligations of States under international human rights law, in particular the International Covenant on Civil and Political Rights, with a view to ensuring respect for the principles of legal certainty and legality.

On 18 December 2019, upon the recommendation of the Third Committee, the General Assembly adopted resolution 74/175 entitled "Technical assistance provided by the United Nations Office on Drugs and Crime related to counter-terrorism", without a vote. In this resolution, the General Assembly urged Member States that had not yet done so to consider becoming parties to the existing international conventions and protocols related to counter-terrorism, and requested the United Nations Office on Drugs and Crime, within its mandate and in close coordination with the relevant entities of the United Nations Global Counter-Terrorism Coordination Compact, to continue to provide technical assistance to Member States, upon request, for the ratification and legislative incorporation of those international legal instruments. It requested the United Nations Office on Drugs and Crime, in cooperation with the International Criminal Police Organization (INTERPOL) and other relevant entities of the United Nations Global Counter-Terrorism Coordination Compact, to continue to provide technical assistance to Member States, upon request, to collect, record and share biometric data in order to responsibly and properly identify terrorists, including foreign terrorist fighters, in compliance with domestic law and international law, welcomed the publication of the United Nations Compendium of Recommended Practices for the Responsible Use and Sharing of Biometrics in Counter-Terrorism, developed within the Working Group on Border Management and Law Enforcement relating to Counter-Terrorism, and stressed the importance of populating and making full use of the databases of INTERPOL in this regard.

On 18 December 2019, upon the recommendation of the Sixth Committee, the General Assembly adopted resolution 74/194 entitled "Measures to eliminate international terrorism", without a vote.[108] It reiterated its call upon all States to adopt further measures in accordance with the Charter of the United Nations and the relevant provisions of international law to prevent terrorism and strengthen international cooperation. It further called upon all States to bring to justice or, where appropriate, extradite, on the basis of the principle of extradite or prosecute, the perpetrators of terrorist acts. The General Assembly further urged all States to accede to several international conventions on the suppression of terrorism and related activities.

(ii) *Security Council counter-terrorism and non-proliferation committees*

a. Counter-Terrorism Committee

The Counter-Terrorism Committee (CTC) was established pursuant to Security Council resolution 1373 (2001) of 28 September 2001, in the wake of the 11 September terrorist attacks in the United States of America, to bolster the ability of United Nations

---

[108] See also the Report of the Secretary-General on Measures to Eliminate International Terrorism (A/74/151).

Member States to prevent terrorist acts both within their borders and across regions.[109] By resolution 1535 (2004) of 26 March 2004, the Security Council established the CTED to assist the work of the CTC and coordinate the process of monitoring the implementation of resolution 1373 (2001). The Committee continued its operations in 2019.

b. 1540 Committee (non-proliferation of weapons of mass destruction to non-State actors)

On 28 April 2004, the Security Council adopted resolution 1540 (2004) by which it decided that all States would refrain from providing any form of support to non-State actors that attempt to develop, acquire, manufacture, possess, transport, transfer or use nuclear, chemical or biological weapons and their means of delivery, and established a Committee to report on the implementation of the same resolution. The mandate of the Committee was subsequently extended by resolutions 1673 (2006), 1810 (2008) and 1977 (2011) until 25 April 2021. The Committee continued its operations in 2019.[110]

(*h*) Humanitarian law and human rights in the context of peace and security

(i) *Children and armed conflict*

The Security Council Working Group on Children and Armed Conflict was established by Security Council resolution 1612 (2005) of 26 July 2005 to review reports of the monitoring and reporting mechanism on children and armed conflict.[111] The Working Group continued its operations in 2019 and submitted, on 20 December 2019, a report of its activities in 2019 to the Security Council.[112]

Regarding the situation in Somalia, the Security Council, in resolution 2461 (2019) of 27 March 2019, strongly condemned the continued violations and abuses against children including the continued recruitment and use of children, rape and sexual violence and abduction, especially by Al-Shabaab in Somalia. It urged all parties to the conflict to take appropriate measures to end and prevent further such violations and abuses, and to identify those responsible for such violations and abuses, to consider as victims those children who had been released or otherwise separated from armed forces and armed groups. In resolution 2472 (2019) of 31 May 2019, the Security Council called on the Somali authorities to take action on preventing the killing and maiming, abduction, the recruitment, re-recruitment and use of, sexual violence against children in armed conflict, and to hold perpetrators to account.[113]

---

[109] See also Security Council resolution 1624 (2005) of 14 September 2005. For more information, see https://www.un.org/securitycouncil/ctc/.

[110] Review of the implementation of resolution 1540 (2004) for 2019 (S/2019/986, annex). For more information on the 1540 Committee, see https://www.un.org/en/sc/154.

[111] See the report of the Secretary-General on children and armed conflict (A/74/845–S/2020/525).

[112] Report of the Security Council Working Group on Children and Armed Conflict (S/2019/981, annex).

[113] Conclusions on children and armed conflict in Somalia of the Working Group on Children and Armed Conflict (S/AC.51/2017/2).

Regarding the situation in the Democratic Republic of the Congo, the Security Council, in resolution 2463 (2019) of 29 March 2019, strongly condemned recruitment and use of children and abductions of children and humanitarian personnel by armed groups and militias. It demanded that all armed groups cease immediately violations and abuses against children, and further demanded that their members immediately and permanently disband, lay down their arms, reject violence and release children from their ranks. In resolution 2502 (2019) of 19 December 2019, the Security Council requested MONUSCO to take fully into account child protection as a cross-cutting issue throughout its mandate and to assist the Government of the DRC in ensuring that the protection of children's rights is taken into account.

In resolution 2467 (2019) of 23 April 2019, the Security Council expressed deep concern over the slow progress in addressing and eliminating sexual violence in situations of armed conflict in particular against women and children.

In resolution 2474 (2019) of 11 June 2019, the Security Council expressed concern about the dramatic increase in persons reported missing as a result of armed conflict, especially women and children. It called upon parties to armed conflict to pay the utmost attention to cases of children reported missing as a result of armed conflict, and to take appropriate measures to search for and identify those children.

In resolution 2480 (2019) of 28 June 2019, on the situation in Mali, the Security Council decided that MINUSMA's mandate should include providing specific protection for women and children affected by armed conflict. It urged all parties to implement the conclusions on Children And Armed Conflict in Mali adopted by the Security Council working group on 19 June 2018, and further urged all armed groups to establish and implement action plans to end and prevent all six grave violations against children, as identified by the Secretary-General, including the recruitment and use of children and sexual violence against children.

In resolution 2489 (2019) of 17 September 2019, on the situation in Afghanistan, the Security Council decided that UNAMA and the Special Representative of the Secretary-General should focus on continuing to report on violations and abuses against children and to support efforts to strengthen the protection of children affected by armed conflict.

In resolution 2499 (2019) of 15 November 2019, on the situation in the CAR, the Security Council urged all parties to armed conflict in the CAR, including armed groups, to end all violations and abuses committed against children, in violation of applicable international law. It further called upon the CAR authorities to respect their obligations under the Optional Protocol to the Convention on the Rights of the Child on the Involvement of Children in Armed Conflict that they ratified on 21 September 2017.

The General Assembly adopted resolution 73/155 of 10 January 2019, entitled "Rights of the child", without a vote. The General Assembly called upon States to protect children affected by armed conflict, in particular from violations of international humanitarian law and human rights law, and to ensure that they receive timely, effective humanitarian assistance, noting the efforts taken to end impunity by ensuring accountability and punishing perpetrators, and further called upon the international community to hold those responsible for violations accountable, *inter alia*, through the International Criminal Court.

(ii) *Women and peace and security*[114]

In resolution 2453 (2019) of 30 January 2019, on the situation in Cyprus, the Security Council stressed the importance of the full and effective participation of civil society and women in particular at all stages of the peace process.

In resolution 2461 (2019) of 27 March 2019, on the situation in Somalia, the Security Council urged the Federal Government of Somalia and Federal Member States to increase representation and participation of women and youth at all decision-making levels.

In resolution 2463 (2019) of 29 March 2019, on the situation in the DRC, the Security Council requested MONUSCO to take fully into account gender considerations as a crosscutting issue throughout its mandate and to assist the Government of the DRC and other relevant stakeholders in ensuring the equal and meaningful participation and full involvement and representation of women at all levels for the maintenance and promotion of peace and security.

In resolution 2466 (2019) of 12 April 2019, on the situation in Haiti, the Security Council reaffirmed the importance for MINUJUSTH taking fully into account gender mainstreaming as a cross-cutting issue throughout its mandate and to assist the Government of Haiti in ensuring the full and effective participation, involvement, and representation of women at all levels.

In resolution 2467 (2019) of 23 April 2019, the Security Council urged Member States to strengthen access to justice for victims of sexual violence in conflict and post-conflict situations, including women and girls, who were particularly targeted. It also called upon parties to conflict to ensure that ceasefire and peace agreements contain provisions that stipulate sexual violence in conflict and post-conflict situations as a prohibited act, particularly in provisions relating to disengagement, and ensure further that women are present and meaningfully participate in political pre-negotiation and negotiation processes.

In resolution 2469 (2019) of 14 May 2019, on the situation in Sudan and South Sudan, the Security Council urged the two Governments immediately to take steps to implement confidence-building measures among the respective communities in the Abyei Area, ensuring women are involved at all stages.

In resolution 2472 (2019) of 31 May 2019, on the situation in Somalia, the Security Council reaffirmed the important role of the full, equal, meaningful and effective participation of all Somalis, including women, youth, persons with disabilities, Internally Displaced Persons (IDPs) and refugees in the prevention and resolution of conflicts, reconciliation processes, peacebuilding and elections and other political processes.

In resolution 2476 (2019) of 25 June 2019, on the situation in Haiti, the Security Council requested that BINUH mainstream gender considerations as a cross-cutting issue throughout its mandate and assist the Government of Haiti in ensuring the full, meaningful, and effective participation, involvement and representation of women at all levels. It further reaffirmed the importance of gender expertise and capacity strengthening in executing the mission mandate in a gender-responsive manner.

In resolution 2480 (2019) of 28 June 2019, on the situation in Mali, the Security Council called upon all parties in Mali to ensure full, effective and meaningful participation of women in the mechanisms established by the Agreement to support and monitor its implementation.

---

[114] See the report of the Secretary-General on women and peace and security (S/2019/800).

In resolution 2483 (2019) of 25 July 2019, on the situation in Cyprus, the Security Council recalled its resolution 2453 (2019) and called upon the two leaders to increase their support to, and ensure a meaningful role for, civil society engagement in peace efforts, in particular strengthening the participation of women's organisations and youth in the process.

In resolution 2485 (2019) of 29 August 2019, on the situation in Lebanon, the Security Council requested UNIFIL to take fully into account gender considerations as a cross-cutting issue throughout its mandate and to assist the Lebanese authorities in ensuring the full and effective participation, involvement and representation of women at all levels of decision-making in all efforts for the maintenance and promotion of peace and security.

In resolution 2486 (2019) of 12 September 2019, on the situation in Libya, the Security Council requested UNSMIL to take fully into account a gender perspective throughout its mandate and to assist the Government of National Accord (GNA) in ensuring the full, effective and meaningful participation of women in the democratic transition, reconciliation efforts, the security sector and in national institutions, as well as the protection of women and girls from sexual and gender-based violence, in line with resolution 1325 (2000).

In resolution 2489 (2019) of 17 September 2019, on the situation in Afghanistan, the Security Council decided that UNAMA and the Special Representative of the Secretary-General should focus on supporting the full, safe, equal, effective and meaningful participation, engagement and leadership of women in all levels of decision-making, including in peace talks and overall peacebuilding strategies at the national and subnational levels.

In resolution 2493 (2019) of 29 October 2019, the Security Council urged Member States to commit to implementing the Women, Peace and Security agenda and its priorities by ensuring and promoting the full, equal and meaningful participation of women in all stages of peace processes, including through mainstreaming a gender perspective, and remain committed to increasing the number of civilian and uniformed women in peacekeeping at all levels and in key positions. It called on Member States to promote all the rights of women, including civil, political and economic rights, and urged them to increase their funding on women, peace and security including through more aid in conflict and post-conflict situations for programmes that further gender equality and women's economic empowerment and security, as well as through support to civil society, and to support countries in armed conflict and post-conflict situations. It also requested the Secretary-General to ensure the full implementation of the Women, Peace and Security agenda.

In resolution 2499 (2019) of 15 November 2019, on the situation in the CAR, the Security Council decided that the mandate of MINUSCA should include providing specific protection for women and children affected by armed conflict, including through the deployment of Child Protection Advisers, Women Protection Advisers and Gender Advisers and by adopting a gender-sensitive, survivor-centred approach in this regard, especially to provide the best assistance to survivors of sexual violence.

In resolution 2502 (2019) of 19 December 2019, on the situation in the DRC, the Security Council requested MONUSCO to assist the Government of the DRC and other relevant stakeholders in creating a legal, political and socio-economic environment conducive to ensuring the full, effective and meaningful participation and full involvement and representation of women at all levels, and survivors of sexual and gender-based violence, for the maintenance and promotion of peace and security, protection of civilians, including by engaging women's networks as partners in protection, support to DDR and SSR efforts, and support to stabilisation efforts through, inter alia, the provision of civilian and uniformed gender and women protection advisers and focal points at headquarters and field levels, participation of women civil society leaders and organization members with regards to conflict prevention and resolution, public institutions and decision-making.

(iii) *Protection of civilians in armed conflict*[115]

In resolution 2474 (2019) of 11 June 2019, the Security Council reaffirmed its strong condemnation of the deliberate targeting of civilians or other protected persons in situations of armed conflict, and called upon all parties to armed conflict to put an end to such practices, in accordance with their obligations under international humanitarian law.

In resolution 2475 (2019) of 20 June 2019, the Security Council urged all parties to armed conflict to take measures, in accordance with applicable international law obligations to protect civilians, including those with disabilities, and to prevent violence and abuses against civilians in situations of armed conflict, including those involving killing and maiming, abduction and torture; as well as rape and other forms of sexual violence in conflict and post-conflict situations. It emphasized the need for States to end impunity for criminal acts against civilians, including those with disabilities, and to ensure that such persons have access to justice and effective remedies and, as appropriate, reparation.

In resolution 2463 (2019) of 29 march 2019, on the situation in the DRC, the Security Council reiterated its condemnation of the violence witnessed in the DRC, especially those involving attacks on the civilian population, United Nations and associated personnel and humanitarian actors, as well as medical personnel and facilities, summary executions and maiming, sexual and gender-based violence and recruitment and use of children, abductions of children and humanitarian personnel, attacks on schools and hospitals in violation of applicable international law by armed groups and militias, the use of civilians as human shields, the forced displacement of significant numbers of civilians, extrajudicial executions and arbitrary arrests, and further reiterated that those responsible must be held accountable.

In resolution 2499 (2019) of 15 November 2019, on the situation in the CAR, the Security Council demanded that all armed groups reject violence, cut off all ties with terrorist organizations and transnational organized crime and take concrete steps to prevent human rights abuses against civilians.

(iv) *Youth*

In resolution 2453 (2019) of 30 January 2019, regarding the situation in Cyprus, the Security Council recalled its resolution 2430 (2018) and called upon the two leaders to increase their support to, and ensure a meaningful role for, civil society engagement in peace efforts, in particular strengthening the participation of women's organisations and youth in the process.

In resolution 2457 (2019) of 27 February 2019, regarding the conflicts in Africa, the Security Council reaffirmed the important and positive contribution of youth to the efforts for the maintenance and promotion of peace and security and the role they play in the prevention and resolution of conflicts. It encouraged all those involved in the planning for

[115] See also the report of the Secretary-General on the protection of civilians in armed conflict (S/2020/366).

disarmament, demobilization and reintegration to consider the needs of youth affected by armed conflict, including youth unemployment.

In resolution 2461 (2019) of 27 March 2019, regarding the situation in Somalia, the Security Council reaffirmed the importance of the full, equal and effective participation of all Somalis, including women, youth, persons with disabilities, Internally Displaced Persons (IDPs) and refugees in the prevention and resolution of conflicts, peacebuilding and elections.

Regarding the situation in the DRC, the Security Council, in resolutions 2502 (2019) of 19 December 2019 and 2463 (2019) of 29 March 2019, reaffirmed the important role of women and youth in the prevention and resolution of conflicts, and in peacebuilding, and stressed the importance of their full, effective and meaningful participation in all efforts for the maintenance of and promotion of peace and security in the DRC.

In resolution 2472 (2019) of 31 May 2019, on the situation in Somalia, the Security Council reaffirmed the important role of the full, equal, meaningful and effective participation of all Somalis, including women, youth, persons with disabilities, Internally Displaced Persons (IDPs) and refugees in the prevention and resolution of conflicts, reconciliation processes, peacebuilding and elections and other political processes.

In a statement by the President of the Security Council of 12 December 2019,[116] the Security Council reaffirmed that States must respect, promote and protect the human rights of all individuals, including youth.

(*i*) Comprehensive assessment of United Nations peace operations

In a statement by the President of the Security Council of 7 May 2019,[117] the Security Council, *inter alia*, underscored the importance of peacekeeping as one of the most effective tools available to the United Nations in the promotion and maintenance of international peace and security. It reaffirmed the basic principles of peacekeeping, such as consent of the parties, impartiality, and non-use of force, except in self-defence and defence of the mandate.

In a statement by the President of the Security Council of 20 August 2019,[118] the Security Council, *inter alia*, reaffirmed its strong condemnation of violations of international humanitarian law committed by all parties to armed conflict, as well as violations and abuses of international human rights law, as applicable, and called upon all parties to comply with their legal obligations. It also urged States which had not yet done so to consider becoming parties, at the earliest possible date, to the Additional Protocols to the Geneva Conventions, and to take appropriate steps to implement their obligations under these instruments.

(*j*) Piracy

(i) *General Assembly*

The General Assembly adopted resolution 74/19 of 10 December 2019, entitled "Oceans and the law of the sea", without reference to a Main Committee and by a recorded vote with 135 in favour, 1 against and 3 abstentions. The Assembly urged all States,

---

[116] S/PRST/2019/15.

[117] S/PRST/2019/4.

[118] S/PRST/2019/8.

in cooperation with the International Maritime Organization, to actively combat piracy and armed robbery at sea by adopting measures in accordance with international law and by adopting national legislation. The Assembly encouraged States to ensure effective implementation of international law applicable to combating piracy, as reflected in the United Nations Convention on the Law of the Sea and called upon States to take appropriate steps under their national law to facilitate, in accordance with international law, the apprehension and prosecution of those who were alleged to have committed acts of piracy. The Assembly recognized national, bilateral and trilateral initiatives, as well as regional cooperative mechanisms, in accordance with international law to address piracy, and called upon States to give immediate attention to adopting, concluding, and implementing cooperation agreements at the regional level on combating piracy and armed robbery against ships. The Assembly further called upon States to become parties to several conventions related to the safety of maritime navigation, and urged States parties to ensure the effective implementation of these instruments.

(ii) *Security Council*

In resolution 2500 (2019) of 4 December 2019, the Security Council, welcoming the report of the Secretary-General submitted pursuant to Security Council resolution 2442 (2018) on the implementation of that resolution and on the situation with respect to piracy and armed robbery at sea off the coast of Somalia[119] and acting under Chapter VII of the Charter of the United Nations, decided that, for a further period of twelve months from the date of resolution 2500 (2019) to renew the authorizations as set out in paragraph 14 of resolution 2442 (2018) granted to States and regional organizations cooperating with Somali authorities in the fight against piracy and armed robbery at sea off the coast of Somalia, for which advance notification had been provided by Somali authorities to the Secretary-General.

By the same resolution, the Security Council decided that the arms embargo on Somalia imposed by paragraph 5 of resolution 733 (1992) and further elaborated upon by paragraphs 1 and 2 of resolution 1425 (2002) and modified by paragraphs 33 to 38 of resolution 2093 (2013) did not apply to supplies of weapons and military equipment or the provision of assistance destined for the sole use of Member States, international, regional, and sub-regional organizations undertaking measures in accordance with paragraph 14 above, as most recently reaffirmed by OP 19(*b*) of resolution 2498 (2019). It also called upon all States to take appropriate actions under their existing domestic law, or develop legislative processes, to prevent the illicit financing of acts of piracy and the laundering of its proceeds, and decided to keep these matters under review, including, as appropriate, the establishment of specialized anti-piracy courts in Somalia with substantial international participation and/or support as set forth in resolution 2015 (2011).

(*k*) Migrant smuggling and human trafficking

(i) *General Assembly*

The General Assembly adopted resolution 74/19 of 10 December 2019, entitled "Oceans and the law of the sea", without reference to a Main Committee and by a recorded

[119] S/2019/867.

vote with 135 in favour, 1 against and 3 abstentions. The Assembly encouraged States, acting nationally or through relevant global or regional organizations, as appropriate, to provide technical assistance and capacity-building to flag, port and coastal States, upon request, to enhance their capabilities to prevent smuggling of migrants and human trafficking by sea. It also called upon States, in that context, to take measures in accordance with relevant international obligations to prevent and combat all forms of trafficking in persons, to identify victims of human trafficking, including among migrant flows, and to provide trafficking victims with appropriate protection and assistance, according to their national law and policy. It further called upon States to become parties to several conventions related to the smuggling of migrants and human trafficking, and urged States parties to take appropriate measures to ensure the effective implementation of these instruments.

The General Assembly adopted resolution 74/148 of 18 December 2019 entitled "Protection of migrants", on the recommendation of the Third Committee and without a vote. The Assembly encouraged Member States that had not already done so to enact national legislation and to take further effective measures to combat human trafficking and smuggling of migrants, recognizing that these crimes may endanger the lives of migrants or subject them to harm, servitude, exploitation, debt bondage, slavery, sexual exploitation or forced labour, and also encouraged Member States to strengthen international cooperation to prevent, investigate and combat such trafficking in persons and smuggling of migrants and to identify and disrupt financial flows related to these activities.

(ii) *Security Council*

By resolution 2491 (2019) of 3 October 2019, the Security Council, regarding the situation in Libya and off the coast of Libya, acting under Chapter VII of the Charter of the United Nations, decided to renew the authorisations as set out in paragraphs 7, 8, 9 and 10 of resolution 2240 (2015), for a further period of twelve months from the date of adoption of this resolution, reaffirmed paragraph 11 thereof and otherwise reiterates its resolutions 2240 (2015), 2312 (2106), 2380 (2017) and 2437 (2018) and its Presidential Statement S/PRST/2015/25.

3. Disarmament and related matters[120]

(*a*) Disarmament machinery

(i) *Disarmament Commission*

The United Nations Disarmament Commission, a subsidiary organ of the General Assembly with a general mandate on disarmament questions, comprises all Member States of the United Nations.

The Commission held its organizational session for 2019 in New York on 12 February and 2 April 2019 but was unable to adopt the draft provisional agenda for the organizational

[120] For more information about disarmament and related matters see *The United Nations Disarmament Yearbook*, vol. 44, 2019 (United Nations Publication, Sales No.: E.20.IX.3, for part I, and Sales No.: E.20.IX.7, for part II), which is also available at https://disarmament.unoda.org/en.

session due to unresolved procedural issues.[121] As a result, the Commission could not convene its substantive session in 2019, and Member States were only able to hold informal meetings.[122]

(ii) *Conference on Disarmament*

The Conference on Disarmament, established in 1979 as the single multilateral disarmament negotiating forum of the international community, was a result of the first special session on disarmament of the General Assembly in 1978.

The Conference was in session from 21 January to 29 March, 13 May to 28 June and 29 July to 13 September 2019.[123] At its 1475th plenary meeting on 21 January 2019, the Conference adopted its agenda for the 2019 session,[124] which included, *inter alia*, the items "Cessation of the nuclear arms race and nuclear disarmament", "Prevention of nuclear war, including all related matters", "Prevention of an arms race in outer space", "Effective international arrangements to assure non-nuclear-weapon States against the use or threat of use of nuclear weapons", "New types of weapons of mass destruction and new systems of such weapons; radiological weapons", "Comprehensive programme of disarmament" and "Transparency in armaments".

Throughout the 2019 session, despite efforts from successive Presidents of the Conference and delegations, the Conference did not succeed in reaching consensus on a programme of work in 2019.[125] On 3 September 2019, the Conference adopted its annual report and transmitted it to the General Assembly for its consideration.[126]

(iii) *General Assembly*

On 12 December 2019, upon the recommendation of the First Committee, the General Assembly adopted the following resolutions concerning institutional activities relating to disarmament machinery:

- resolution 74/56 entitled "Convening of the fourth special session of the General Assembly devoted to disarmament", by a recorded vote of 179 in favour to none against, with 4 abstentions;
- resolution 74/69 entitled "United Nations Regional Centre for Peace and Disarmament in Asia and the Pacific", without a vote;
- resolution 74/70 entitled "United Nations regional centres for peace and disarmament", without a vote;

---

[121] See verbatim record of the 375th meeting of the Disarmament Commission (A/CN.10/PV.375) and press release, Disarmament Commission Postpones Holding of Organizational Meeting (available at https://press.un.org/en/2019/dc3800.doc.htm). See also GA decision 74/511 (recorded in A/74/49 (Vol. II)).

[122] See Draft Schedule of Informal Meetings of the United Nations Disarmament Commission (2019) at https://front.un-arm.org/wp-content/uploads/2019/04/schedule-of-informal-meetings-041519.pdf.

[123] *Official Records of the General Assembly, Seventy-fourth Session, Supplement No. 27* (A/74/27), paras. 2–3.

[124] *Ibid.*, para. 14.

[125] *Ibid.*, para. 16.

[126] *Ibid.*, para. 47.

- resolution 74/71 entitled "United Nations Regional Centre for Peace and Disarmament in Africa", without a vote;
- resolution 74/72 entitled "United Nations Regional Centre for Peace, Disarmament and Development in Latin America and the Caribbean", without a vote;
- resolution 74/73 entitled "Regional confidence-building measures: activities of the United Nations Standing Advisory Committee on Security Questions in Central Africa", without a vote;
- resolution 74/74 entitled "Report of the Conference on Disarmament", without a vote.

On 12 December 2019, the General Assembly also adopted decision 74/511 entitled "2020 session of the Disarmament Commission (decision)", without a vote.

(*b*) Nuclear disarmament and non-proliferation issues

(i) *Limitation of nuclear weapons*

a. Treaty on the Non-Proliferation of Nuclear Weapons

The Preparatory Committee for the 2020 Review Conference of the Parties to the Treaty on the Non-Proliferation of Nuclear Weapons (NPT) held its third session from 29 April to 10 May 2019 in New York.[127] During this session, States parties reiterated their commitment to the Treaty and its goals, as well as to pursuing a successful outcome at the 2020 Review Conference.[128] The Committee organized its meetings into three clusters: (*a*) non-proliferation of nuclear weapons, disarmament and international peace and security; (*b*) non-proliferation of nuclear weapons, safeguards and nuclear-weapon-free zones; and (*c*) the inalienable right of all States parties to the Treaty to the development, research, production and use of nuclear energy for peaceful purposes, without discrimination and in conformity with articles I and II of the Treaty. The clusters addressed three specific issue areas, respectively: (*a*) nuclear disarmament and security assurances; (*b*) regional issues, such as the Middle East and the implementation of the 1995 resolution on the Middle East; and (*c*) peaceful uses of nuclear energy and other provisions of the Treaty.

In 2019, no States signed, ratified or acceded to the NPT, therefore the number of signatory States remained unchanged at 93 and the number of ratifying or acceding States at 191.[129]

b. Comprehensive Nuclear-Test-Ban Treaty

On 13 February 2019, Zimbabwe ratified the Comprehensive Nuclear-Test-Ban Treaty (CTBT), bringing the number of ratifications to 168. The number of signatories of the Treaty remained unchanged at 184.[130]

---

[127] See the final report of the Preparatory Committee for the 2020 Review Conference of the Parties to the Treaty on the Non-Proliferation of Nuclear Weapons (NPT/CONF.2020/1).

[128] NPT/CONF.2020/PC.III/WP.49.

[129] The treaty text and adherence status are available at https://treaties.unoda.org/t/npt/participants. On 10 January 2003, the Democratic People's Republic of Korea (DPRK) announced its withdrawal from the Treaty in a public statement. States parties to the Treaty continue to express divergent views regarding the status of the DPRK under the NPT.

[130] The treaty text and adherence status are available at http://disarmament.un.org/treaties/t/ctbt.

The fifty-second and fifty-third sessions of the Preparatory Commission for the Comprehensive Nuclear-Test-Ban Treaty Organization (CTBTO) were held from 17 to 18 June and from 25 to 27 November 2019, respectively.[131]

In 2019, there was no Ministerial Meeting of the Friends of the Comprehensive Nuclear Test-Ban Treaty.[132]

On 25 September 2019, the eleventh biennial Conference on Facilitating the Entry into Force of the Comprehensive Nuclear-Test-Ban Treaty (also known as an "Article XIV conference") was held in New York. In the Final Declaration, the ratifying States and other States signatories affirmed that a universal and effectively verifiable Treaty constituted a fundamental instrument in the field of nuclear disarmament and non-proliferation and also affirmed the vital importance and urgency of the entry into force of the Treaty.[133]

c. Treaty on the Prohibition of Nuclear Weapons

In 2019, 11 States signed the Treaty on the Prohibition of Nuclear Weapons and 15 States ratified it, bringing the number of signatory States to 80, and the number of States parties to 34.[134]

d. Nuclear arms control instruments

On 2 February 2019, the United States of America provided its six-month notice of withdrawal from the Treaty between the United States of America and the Union of Soviet Socialist Republics on the Elimination of Their Intermediate-Range and Shorter-Range Missiles of 1987 (Intermediate-Range Nuclear Forces Treaty or INF Treaty).[135] On 4 March 2019, the Russian Federation formally suspended its implementation of the Treaty.[136] The withdrawal of the United States of America took effect on 2 August 2019.[137]

e. International Atomic Energy Agency

The International Atomic Energy Agency (IAEA) held its sixty-third General Conference of member States from 16 to 20 September 2019 in Vienna.[138] The Conference adopted 15 resolutions and 13 decisions[139] relating to the work of IAEA in key areas, including on measures to strengthen international cooperation in nuclear, radiation and nuclear security; strengthening the Agency's activities related to nuclear science, technology and

---

[131] See the annual report of the CTBTO, https://www.ctbto.org/sites/default/files/2022-08/00-ctbto_ar_2019_en.pdf.

[132] https://www.ctbto.org/our-mission/ministerial-meetings.

[133] CTBT-Art.XIV/2019/6.

[134] The treaty text and adherence status are available at https://treaties.unoda.org/t/tpnw. See also the Report of the Secretary-General on the Treaty on the Prohibition of Nuclear Weapons (A/75/139) and General Assembly resolution 74/41.

[135] See https://2017-2021.state.gov/remarks-to-the-press-12/.

[136] See http://en.kremlin.ru/events/president/news/59939.

[137] See https://2017-2021.state.gov/u-s-withdrawal-from-the-inf-treaty-on-august-2-2019/. See also *The United Nations Disarmament Yearbook*, vol. 44, 2019, part II, p. 22.

[138] For more information, see https://www.iaea.org/about/policy/gc/gc63/gc-at-glance. See also section B.1 of this chapter.

[139] GC(63)/RES/DEC(2019).

applications; implementation of the Agreement between the Agency and the Democratic People's Republic of Korea; and application of IAEA safeguards in the Middle East.

(ii) *General Assembly*

On 12 December 2019, upon the recommendation of the First Committee, the General Assembly adopted the following resolutions concerning nuclear weapons and non-proliferation:

- resolution 74/26 entitled "African Nuclear-Weapon-Free Zone Treaty", without a vote;
- resolution 74/27 entitled "Treaty for the Prohibition of Nuclear Weapons in Latin America and the Caribbean (Treaty of Tlatelolco)", without a vote;
- resolution 74/30 entitled "Establishment of a nuclear-weapon-free zone in the region of the Middle East", by a recorded vote of 175 in favour to 2 against, with 3 abstentions;
- resolution 74/31 entitled "Conclusion of effective international arrangements to assure non-nuclear-weapon States against the use or threat of use of nuclear weapons", by a recorded vote of 122 in favour to none against, with 64 abstentions;
- resolution 74/36 entitled "Follow-up to nuclear disarmament obligations agreed to at the 1995, 2000 and 2010 Review Conferences of the Parties to the Treaty on the Non-Proliferation of Nuclear Weapons", by a recorded vote of 118 in favour to 43 against, with 19 abstentions;
- resolution 74/41 entitled "Treaty on the Prohibition of Nuclear Weapons", by a recorded vote of 123 in favour to 41 against, with 16 abstentions;
- resolution 74/42 entitled "Humanitarian consequences of nuclear weapons", by a recorded vote of 144 in favour to 13 against, with 28 abstentions;
- resolution 74/44 entitled "Reducing nuclear danger", by a recorded vote of 123 in favour to 49 against, with 15 abstentions;
- resolution 74/45 entitled "Nuclear disarmament", by a recorded vote of 120 in favour to 41 against with 22 abstentions;
- resolution 74/46 entitled "Towards a nuclear-weapon-free world: accelerating the implementation of nuclear disarmament commitments", by a recorded vote of 137 in favour to 33 against, with 16 abstentions;
- resolution 74/47 entitled "Ethical imperatives for a nuclear-weapon-free world", by a recorded vote of 135 in favour to 37 against, with 13 abstentions;
- resolution 74/48 entitled "Nuclear-weapon-free southern hemisphere and adjacent areas", by a recorded vote of 148 in favour to 5 against, with 30 abstentions;
- resolution 74/50 entitled "Nuclear disarmament verification", by a recorded vote of 178 in favour to 1 against, with 5 abstentions;
- resolution 74/54 entitled "Follow-up to the 2013 high-level meeting of the General Assembly on nuclear disarmament", by a recorded vote of 142 in favour to 34 against, with 10 abstentions;
- resolution 74/58 entitled "Prohibition of the dumping of radioactive wastes", without a vote;

- resolution 74/59 entitled "Follow-up to the advisory opinion of the International Court of Justice on the legality of the threat or use of nuclear weapons ", by a recorded vote of 138 in favour to 33 against, with 15 abstentions;
- resolution 74/63 entitled "Joint courses of action and future-oriented dialogue towards a world without nuclear weapons ", by a recorded vote of 160 in favour to 4 against, with 21 abstentions;
- resolution 74/68 entitled "Convention on the Prohibition of the Use of Nuclear Weapons", by a recorded vote of 118 in favour to 50 against, with 15 abstentions;
- resolution 74/75 entitled "The risk of nuclear proliferation in the Middle East", by a recorded vote of 152 in favour to 6 against, with 24 abstentions; and
- resolution 74/78 entitled "Comprehensive Nuclear-Test-Ban Treaty", by a recorded vote of 182 in favour to 1 against, with 4 abstentions.

On 12 December 2019, the General Assembly also adopted decision 74/509 entitled "Treaty banning the production of fissile material for nuclear weapons or other nuclear explosive devices", by a recorded vote of 181 in favour to 1 against, with 4 abstentions; and decision 74/510 entitled "Treaty on the South-East Asia Nuclear-Weapon-Free Zone (Bangkok Treaty)", without a vote.

(iii) *Security Council*

On 10 April 2019, the Security Council adopted resolution 2464 (2019) (on the topic of the Democratic People's Republic of Korea) in which it decided, acting under Article 41 of Chapter VII of the Charter of the United Nations, to extend until 24 April 2020 the mandate of the Panel of Experts, as established pursuant to resolution 1874 (2009) and modified in paragraph 29 of resolution 2094 (2013). It also decided that this mandate should apply also with respect to the measures imposed in resolution 2321 (2016), 2321 (2016), 2356 (2017), 2371 (2017), 2375 (2017), and 2397 (2017) and expressed its intent to review the mandate and take appropriate action regarding further extension no later than 27 March 2020.[140]

(*c*) **Biological and chemical weapons issues**

(i) *Biological Weapons Convention*

From 29 July to 8 August 2019, the Meeting of Experts to the Convention on the Prohibition of the Development, Production and Stockpiling of Bacteriological (Biological) and Toxin Weapons and on Their Destruction (Biological Weapons Convention) took place in Geneva. The Meeting of Experts addressed the following topics: cooperation and assistance, with a particular focus on strengthening cooperation and assistance under article X;[141] review of developments in the field of science and technology related to

---

[140] For more information on the sanctions imposed on the Democratic People's Republic of Korea under Chapter VII of the Charter of the United Nations, see section A.2(*e*)(vi) of this chapter.

[141] BWC/MSP/2019/MX.1/2.

the Convention;[142] strengthening national implementation;[143] assistance, response and preparedness;[144] and institutional strengthening of the Convention.[145]

The annual Meeting of States Parties to the Biological Weapons Convention took place in Geneva from 3 to 6 December 2019.[146] During the Meeting, participants reached agreement on measures to address structural and financial issues. The Meeting also considered the annual report of the Implementation Support Unit[147] and considered progress towards universalization of the Biological Weapons Convention.[148]

In 2019, the United Republic of Tanzania ratified the Biological Weapons Convention, bringing the number of States parties to 183. The number of signatory States remained at 109.[149]

(ii) *Chemical Weapons Convention*

The twenty-fourth session of the Conference of the States Parties to the Convention on the Prohibition of the Development, Production, Stockpiling and Use of Chemical Weapons and their Destruction, 1992 (Chemical Weapons Convention)[150] was held from 25 to 29 November 2019 in The Hague. The Conference considered, *inter alia*, the status of implementation of the Chemical Weapons Convention, fostering of international cooperation for peaceful purposes in the field of chemical activities, the OPCW Programme for Africa and the engagement with chemical industry and the scientific community. On 29 November 2019, the Conference considered and adopted the report of its twenty-fourth session.[151]

The ninetieth,[152] ninety-first,[153] and ninety-second[154] sessions of the Executive Council of the OPCW were held from 12 to 15 March, 9 to 12 July and 8 to 11 October 2019, respectively. The sixty-second,[155] sixty-third[156] and sixty-fourth[157] meetings of the Executive Council of the OPCW were held on 14 January, 25 February and 10 May, respectively.

In 2019, the number of States parties to the Chemical Weapons Convention remained at 193.[158]

---

[142] BWC/MSP/2019/MX.2/2.

[143] BWC/MSP/2019/MX.3/2.

[144] BWC/MSP/2019/MX.4/2.

[145] BWC/MSP/2019/MX.5/2.

[146] See also the Report of the 2019 Meeting of States Parties (BWC/MSP/2019/7).

[147] BWC/MSP/2019/4.

[148] BWC/MSP/2019/3.

[149] The treaty text and adherence status are available at https://treaties.unoda.org/t/bwc.

[150] United Nations, *Treaty Series*, vol. 1974, p. 45.

[151] OPCW, "Report of the Twenty-Fourth Session of the Conference of the States Parties 25–29 November 2019", document C-24/5.

[152] See https://www.opcw.org/ec-90.

[153] See https://www.opcw.org/resources/documents/executive-council/ec-91.

[154] OPCW, "Report of the ninety-second session of the Executive Council", document EC-92/5.

[155] See https://www.opcw.org/resources/documents/executive-council/EC-M-62.

[156] See https://www.opcw.org/sixty-third-meeting-executive-council.

[157] See https://www.opcw.org/sixty-fourth-meeting-executive-council.

[158] For more information, see https://www.opcw.org/about-us/member-states.

(iii) *General Assembly*

On 5 December 2019, the General Assembly adopted three resolutions relating to biological and chemical weapons in 2019, on the recommendation of the First Committee, namely resolution 74/40, entitled "Implementation of the Convention on the Prohibition of the Development, Production, Stockpiling and Use of Chemical Weapons and on Their Destruction", by a recorded vote of 151 in favour to 8 against, with 21 abstentions; resolution 74/43, entitled "Measures to prevent terrorists from acquiring weapons of mass destruction", without a vote; and resolution 74/79 entitled "Convention on the Prohibition of the Development, Production and Stockpiling of Bacteriological (Biological) and Toxin Weapons and on Their Destruction", without a vote.[159]

(iv) *Security Council*

On 10 April 2019, the Security Council adopted resolution 2464 (2019) concerning non-proliferation and the Democratic People's Republic of Korea. The Security Council determined that the proliferation of nuclear, chemical and biological weapons, as well as their means of delivery, continue to constitute a threat to international peace and security.

(*d*) Conventional weapons issues

(i) *International trade in conventional arms*

The fifth Conference of States Parties to the Arms Trade Treaty (ATT)[160] was held in Geneva from 26 to 30 August 2019. A number of decisions were adopted by the Conference, concerning, *inter alia*, the Voluntary Trust Fund, the Working Group on Effective Treaty Implementation and the topic of the significance of transparency and reporting under the Treaty.[161]

In 2019, five States deposited their instruments of ratification or accession. Accordingly, the total number of States parties increased to 105.[162]

In a communication received on 18 July 2019, the United States of America, a signatory to the treaty, informed the Secretary-General of the United Nations that the United States did not intend to become a party to the treaty and that it considered that it had no legal obligations arising from its signature on 25 September 2013.[163]

On 12 December 2019, on the recommendation of the First Committee, the General Assembly adopted the following resolutions:

- resolution 74/49 entitled "The Arms Trade Treaty", by a recorded vote of 153 in favour to 1 against, with 28 abstentions;

---

[159] See also the note by the Secretary-General on Cooperation between the United States and the Organization for the Prohibition of Chemical Weapons (A/73/97).

[160] United Nations, *Treaty Series*, registration no. 523373.

[161] ATT, "Final Report of the Fifth Conference of States Parties to the Arms Trade Treaty", document ATT/CSP5/2019/SEC/536/Conf.FinRep.Rev1.

[162] The treaty text and adherence status are available at https://treaties.unoda.org/t/att. See also *The United Nations Disarmament Yearbook*, vol. 44, 2019, part II, p. 75.

[163] https://treaties.unoda.org/t/att/declarations/USA_un_SIG.

- resolution 74/51 entitled "Assistance to States for curbing the illicit traffic in small arms and light weapons and collecting them", without a vote;
- resolution 74/53 entitled "Transparency in armaments", by a recorded vote of 157 in favour to none against, with 23 abstentions;
- resolution 74/60 entitled "The illicit trade in small arms and light weapons in all its aspects", without a vote.

(ii) *Convention on Certain Conventional Weapons*

The 2019 Meeting of the High Contracting Parties to the Convention on Prohibitions or Restrictions on the Use of Certain Conventional Weapons which may be deemed to be Excessively Injurious or to have Indiscriminate Effects (Convention on Certain Conventional Weapons) was held in Geneva from 13 to 15 November 2019.[164] The Meeting took note of the conclusions and recommendations of the Group of Governmental Experts on Emerging Technologies in the Area of Lethal Autonomous Weapons Systems.[165] At the Meeting, several States raised concerns over the discussion of the use of explosive weapons in populated areas in this forum. The Convention had 125 contracting parties at the end of 2019.[166]

With regard to the Protocol on Non-Detectable Fragments (Protocol I), the number of contracting parties remained at 118 in 2019.[167]

With regard to the Protocol on Prohibitions or Restrictions on the Use of Mines, Booby-Traps and Other Devices, as amended on 3 May 1996 (Amended Protocol II)[168] annexed to the Convention on Conventional Weapons, the twenty-first Annual Conference of the High Contracting Parties to Amended Protocol II was held on 12 November 2019 in Geneva following the meeting of the Group of Experts of the High Contracting Parties to Amended Protocol II on 22 August 2019. The Conference, *inter alia*, decided that, in 2019, the Amended Protocol II Group of Experts should review the operation and status of the Protocol and consider matters arising from the national annual reports, and consider measures to increase the rate of national reporting and the consistency of the current reporting methodology in the framework of Amended Protocol II.[169] In 2019, with Benin expressing consent to be bound by Amended Protocol II, the number of contracting parties to the Protocol reached 106.[170]

With regard to the Protocol on Prohibitions or Restrictions on the Use of Incendiary Weapons (Protocol III), the number of contracting parties remained at 115 in 2019.[171]

---

[164] Final Report (CCW/MSP/2019/9).

[165] CCW/GGE.1/2019/3.

[166] The Convention's text and adherence status are available at https://treaties.unoda.org/t/ccw/participants.

[167] The protocol text and adherence status are available at https://treaties.unoda.org/t/ccw_p1/.

[168] United Nations, *Treaty Series*, vol. 2048, p. 93.

[169] See the Final document (CCW/AP.II/CONF.21/5).

[170] The protocol text and adherence status are available at https://treaties.unoda.org/t/ccw_p2a.

[171] The protocol text and adherence status are available at https://treaties.unoda.org/t/ccw_p3/.

With regard to the Protocol on Blinding Laser Weapons (Protocol IV), in 2019, with Benin expressing consent to be bound by Protocol IV, the number of contracting parties to the Protocol reached 109.[172]

The thirteenth Conference of the High Contracting Parties to Protocol V on Explosive Remnants of War[173] was held on 11 November 2019 in Geneva[174] following the Meeting of Experts of the High Contracting Parties to Protocol V on Explosive Remnants of War on 23 August 2019. The Conference considered, *inter alia*, article 4 of the Protocol, entitled "Recording, retaining and transmission of information"; national reporting; and victim assistance. In 2019, with Benin expressing consent to be bound by Protocol V, the number of contracting parties to the Protocol reached 96.[175]

(iii) *Convention on Cluster Munitions*

The Ninth Meeting of States Parties to the Convention on Cluster Munitions[176] was held from 2 to 4 September 2019 in Geneva.[177] The Meeting adopted various documents, including, *inter alia*, the Methodology for requests of deadline extensions under Articles 3 and 4 of the Convention on Cluster Munitions.[178] In 2019, the Philippines ratified the Convention, and Maldives acceded to it. As at the end of 2019, the Convention had 107 States parties.[179]

(iv) *Anti-personnel Mine-Ban Convention*

The fourth Review Conference of the States Parties to the Convention on the Prohibition of the Use, Stockpiling, Production and Transfer of Anti-personnel Mines and on Their Destruction[180] in Oslo, Norway from 26 to 29 November 2019.[181] The Review Conference adopted the Oslo declaration, pledging promotion and defence of the norms established by the Convention. The Review Conference further adopted the Oslo Action Plan, detailing 50 actions that States parties would take during the period 2020–2024 to support the implementation of the Convention. The Review Conference also adopted a Review of the operation and status of the Convention between 2014 and 2019.[182] The Review Conference was preceded by the Fourth Pledging Conference, two preparatory meetings, a set of informal intersessional meetings held in Geneva earlier that year, as well as meetings carried out by the Convention Commission.[183] The number of States parties remained at 164 in 2019.[184]

---

[172] The protocol text and adherence status are available at https://treaties.unoda.org/t/ccw_p4.

[173] United Nations, *Treaty Series*, vol. 2399, p. 100.

[174] See the Final document (CCW/PV/CONF/2019/5).

[175] The protocol text and adherence status are available at https://treaties.unoda.org/t/ccw_p5.

[176] United Nations, *Treaty Series*, vol. 2688, p. 39.

[177] CCM/MSP/2019/13. Final Report.

[178] See the list of adopted documents in the Final Report CCM/MSP/2019/13, annex II.

[179] The Convention's text and adherence status are available at https://treaties.unoda.org/t/cluster_munitions.

[180] United Nations, *Treaty Series*, vol. 2056, p. 211.

[181] See the Final document (APLC/CONF/2019/5).

[182] See the three documents in the Addendum to the Final document: Texts adopted by the Conference (APLC/CONF/2019/5/Add.1).

[183] *The United Nations Disarmament Yearbook*, vol. 44, 2019, part II, p. 121.

[184] The Convention's text and adherence status are available at https://treaties.unoda.org/t/mine_ban.

(v) *General Assembly*

On 12 December 2019, on the recommendation of the First Committee, the General Assembly adopted the following resolutions concerning conventional arms issues:

- resolution 74/61 entitled "Implementation of the Convention on the Prohibition of the Use, Stockpiling, Production and Transfer of Anti-Personnel Mines and on Their Destruction", by a recorded vote of 169 in favour to none against, with 18 abstentions;
- resolution 74/62 entitled "Implementation of the Convention on Cluster Munitions", by a recorded vote of 144 in favour to 1 against, with 38 abstentions;
- resolution 74/65 entitled "Problems arising from the accumulation of conventional ammunition stockpiles in surplus", without a vote; and
- resolution 74/76 entitled "Convention on Prohibitions or Restrictions on the Use of Certain Conventional Weapons which may be deemed to be Excessively Injurious or to have Indiscriminate Effects", without a vote.

(vi) *Security Council*

In 2019, the Security Council did not adopt a specific resolution on conventional weapons, but it addressed the topic in different resolutions.[185]

(*e*) Regional disarmament activities of the United Nations

(i) *Africa*

Throughout 2019, the United Nations Regional Centre for Peace and Disarmament in Africa (UNREC) maintained its support for African Member States, as well as regional and subregional organizations, in their efforts to promote disarmament, non-proliferation and arms control.[186]

During 2019, the Centre supported the 11 member States of the Economic Community of Central African States (ECCAS) in developing a guide to advance the implementation of the Kinshasa Convention.[187] The Centre convened two additional meetings in 2019 to support the Convention's implementation in the framework of the same project. Separately, with financial support from Japan, the Centre implemented a project in two countries to strengthen the physical security and stockpile management of small arms and light weapons, as well as their ammunition. To support the implementation of Security Council resolution 1540 (2004), the Centre helped organize a capacity-building workshop for Togolese stakeholders involved in the strategic trade in and management of sensitive products.

---

[185] See for example resolution 2462 (2019), para. 27; resolution 2482 (2019), paras. 10–11. See also the Report of the Secretary-General on small arms and light weapons (S/2019/1011).

[186] For more information, see the reports of the Secretary-General on the United Nations Regional Centre for Peace and Disarmament in Africa (A/74/118 (for the period from July 2018 to June 2019) and A/75/120 (for the period from July 2019 to June 2020)) and General Assembly resolution 74/71. See also *The United Nations Disarmament Yearbook*, vol. 44, 2019, part II, p. 144 *et seq.*

[187] Central African Convention for the Control of Small Arms and Light Weapons, their Ammunition and all Parts and Components that can be used for their Manufacture, Repair and Assembly. United Nations *Treaty Series*, vol. 3176. p. 165.

The Centre contributed to a seminar on the International Code of Conduct against Ballistic Missile Proliferation and the threat of missiles, organized by the *Fondation pour la recherche stratégique* on 4 February 2019, in Lomé. Furthermore, from 10 to 15 February 2019, the Centre participated in an intensive course held in Accra on nuclear non-proliferation and security for women in science, technology, engineering and mathematics. The Centre delivered a presentation on the international disarmament machinery as a contribution to that course. The Centre also held two regional workshops on a potential treaty banning the production of fissile material for nuclear weapons or other nuclear explosive devices, one in Equatorial Guinea on 5 and 6 February 2019 and the other in South Africa on 22 and 23 May 2019.

At the request of Youth Awake, a non-governmental organization, the Centre provided capacity-building assistance to 20 young people at a seminar entitled "African youth, the main actor of peace and sustainable development", held from 15 to 19 May 2019 in Kara, Togo. The seminar aimed to foster discussions among participants from Togo's five regions on peace, conflict management, social security for sustainable national cohesion and entrepreneurship.

The Regional Centre assisted the Weapons of Mass Destruction Branch of the Office for Disarmament Affairs and the African Union Commission with organizing a regional meeting for African States parties to the Treaty on the Non-Proliferation of Nuclear Weapons, which was held on 29 and 30 August 2019 in Addis Ababa for 38 States.

On 1 October 2019, the Centre held a discussion with the head of the Arms Trade Treaty secretariat on the current and possible future cooperation between the two entities in support of African Member States in ratifying the Treaty and ensuring that national laws are compliant with its provisions. From 1 to 3 October 2019, the Centre participated in a regional workshop on the implementation of the Arms Trade Treaty in States parties in francophone Africa, organized by the Government of Togo, with funding from the Treaty's voluntary trust fund.

(ii) *Asia and the Pacific*

The United Nations Regional Centre for Peace and Development in Asia and the Pacific (UNRCPD) continued to assist Member States of the region in strengthening their national implementation of the United Nations Programme of Action to Prevent, Combat and Eradicate the Illicit Trade in Small Arms and Light Weapons in All Its Aspects (Programme of Action on Small Arms and Light Weapons), the Arms Trade Treaty and the women, peace and security agenda.[188] The Centre also organized events on various issues related to a potential treaty banning the production of fissile material for nuclear weapons and other nuclear explosive devices, safe and secure ammunition management, Security Council resolution 1540 (2004), and responsible innovation for emerging technologies.

The Centre organized the Regional Outreach Seminar on Trade and Trafficking of Illicit Conventional Ammunition for Southeast Asia, held from 20 to 22 March 2019 in Bangkok

[188] For more information, see the reports of the Secretary-General on the United Nations Regional Centre for Peace and Disarmament in Asia and the Pacific (A/74/112 (for the period from 1 July 2018 to 30 June 2019) and A/75/112 (for the period from 1 July 2019 to 30 June 2020)) and General Assembly resolution 74/69. See also *The United Nations Disarmament Yearbook*, vol. 44, 2019, part II, p. 150 *et seq.*

with funding from Germany. The seminar brought together representatives of Governments from 10 Southeast Asian States. With financial support from the Arms Trade Treaty Voluntary Trust Fund, the Centre and the Government of Kazakhstan co-organized the Arms Trade Treaty Universalization and Implementation Workshop in Nur-Sultan on 3 and 4 July 2019, drawing 32 participants representing Member States in Central Asia and Mongolia.

The Centre also undertook a number of activities related to responsible innovation, including conducting, in cooperation with the Association of Southeast Asian Nations (ASEAN) Foundation and Systems, Applications and Products in Data Processing, a subregional responsible innovation workshop for young innovators attending the ASEAN Data Science Explorers 2019 event, held in Bangkok on 10 October 2019.

From 12 to 15 November, the Centre organized a third subregional workshop for Pacific Island States in Suva, as part of the wider Centre's project on gun violence and illicit small-arms trafficking from a gender perspective, which was funded by the European Union. The eighteenth United Nations-Republic of Korea Joint Conference on Disarmament and Non-proliferation Issues took place in Seoul on 13 and 14 November, drawing 30 participants from Governments.

On 17 and 18 December 2019, in cooperation with the United Nations Regional Centre for Peace and Disarmament in Africa and the Geneva Branch of the Office for Disarmament Affairs, the Centre organized in Bangkok a regional meeting of scientific experts from Asia and Africa to discuss possible ways to advance negotiations of a treaty banning the production of fissile material for nuclear weapons or other nuclear explosive devices and to facilitate the contribution of regional expertise and experience into these negotiations.

(iii) *Latin America and the Caribbean*

The United Nations Regional Centre for Peace, Disarmament and Development in Latin America and the Caribbean (UNLIREC) continued to support Latin American and Caribbean States, at their request, with the implementation of international instruments related to conventional arms and weapons of mass destruction, as well as with adherence to international standards and norms.[189]

In addition to lending its technical and policy support capacities to improve the control of conventional arms, the Regional Centre focused heavily throughout 2019 on advancing dialogue among States on conventional ammunition management at the national and subregional levels. The Centre also provided support to Member States in investigating firearms-related crime scenes, assisting national authorities in their efforts to manage small arms within the private security sector, marking and tracing arms and ammunition, interdicting weapons at entry and exit points, strengthening physical security and stockpile management, and addressing firearms use and possession in school settings.

---

[189] For more information, see the reports of the Secretary-General on the United Nations Regional Centre for Peace, Disarmament and Development in Latin America and the Caribbean (A/74/115 (for the period from July 2018 to June 2019) and A/75/118 (for the period from July 2019 to June 2020)), General Assembly resolution 74/72 See also *The United Nations Disarmament Yearbook*, vol. 44, 2019, part II, p. 148 *et seq.*

To help States combat illicit trafficking in arms and ammunition, as well as their parts and components, the Regional Centre delivered specialized training to 180 officials working at entry and exit points in countries across the region to improve the detection and interdiction of weapons using innovative X-ray identification tools. The Regional Centre also continued to deliver on-site training to officials from the Dominican Republic and Paraguay in support of their efforts to implement the Arms Trade Treaty. Furthermore, the Regional Centre continued assisting States in the region in their implementation of Security Council resolution 1540 (2004).

In addition, the Centre expanded its efforts to help Caribbean States build their forensic ballistic capabilities to combat illicit firearms trafficking in line with the International Tracing Instrument. Throughout 2019, the Centre also continued to engage with beneficiary States to advance the women, peace and security agenda by incorporating gender-responsive programming into armed violence reduction measures.

(iv) *General Assembly*

On 12 December 2019, upon the recommendation of the First Committee, the General Assembly adopted the following resolutions concerning regional disarmament:

- resolution 74/25 entitled "Implementation of the Declaration of the Indian Ocean as a Zone of Peace", by a recorded vote of 134 in favour to 3 against, with 45 abstentions;
- resolution 74/37 entitled "Regional disarmament", without a vote;
- resolution 74/38 entitled "Conventional arms control at the regional and subregional levels", by a recorded vote of 185 in favour to 1 against, with 2 abstentions;
- resolution 74/39 entitled "Confidence-building measures in the regional and subregional context", without a vote; and
- resolution 74/77 entitled "Strengthening of security and cooperation in the Mediterranean region", by a recorded vote of 179 in favour to none against, with 2 abstentions.

(*f*) **Outer space (disarmament aspects)**

The thirty-ninth session of the Inter-Agency Meeting on Outer Space Activities (UN-Space) was held on 28 October 2019 at United Nations Headquarters in New York.[190] The session, organized by the Office for Outer Space Affairs, focused on, *inter alia,* the preparation of the "Space2030" agenda and the coordination of future plans and programmes of common interest for cooperation and exchange of views on current activities in the practical application of space technology and related areas.

(i) *General Assembly*

On 12 December 2019, upon the recommendation of the First Committee, the General Assembly adopted the following resolutions concerning disarmament activities in outer space:

---

[190] See the provisional agenda of the meeting (UN-Space/2019/CRP.1).

- resolution 74/32 entitled "Prevention of an arms race in outer space", by a recorded vote of 183 in favour to 2 against, with no abstentions;
- resolution 74/33 entitled "No first placement of weapons in outer space", by a recorded vote of 128 in favour to 14 against, with 38 abstentions;
- resolution 74/34 entitled "Further practical measures for the prevention of an arms race in outer space", by a recorded vote of 131 in favour to 6 against, with 45 abstentions; and
- resolution 74/67 entitled "Transparency and confidence-building measures in outer space activities", by a recorded vote of 173 in favour to 2 against, with 6 abstentions.

On 13 December 2019, upon the recommendation of the Fourth Committee, the General Assembly adopted resolution 74/82 entitled "International cooperation in the peaceful uses of outer space", without a vote.

(ii) *Security Council*

In 2019, the Security Council did not adopt a specific resolution on disarmament aspects of outer space, nor did it address the topic in other resolutions.

(*g*) Antarctica (arms control aspects)

The Forty-second Antarctic Treaty Consultative Meeting (ATCM) took place in Prague, the Czech Republic from 2 to 11 July 2019.[191] The ATCM adopted the Prague Declaration on the Occasion of the Sixtieth Anniversary of the Antarctic Treaty, confirming that the Antarctic Treaty System was providing for Antarctica's use only for peaceful purposes and free from measures of a military nature.[192] The Treaty was ratified by Slovenia in 2019, bringing the number of States parties to 54.[193]

(*h*) Other disarmament measures and international security

General Assembly

On 12 December 2019, upon the recommendation of the First Committee, the General Assembly adopted the following resolutions:

- resolution 74/24, entitled "Objective information on military matters, including transparency of military expenditures", by a recorded vote of 176 in favour to none against, with 2 abstentions;
- resolution 74/28, entitled "Advancing responsible State behaviour in cyberspace in the context of international security", by a recorded vote of 163 in favour to 10 against, with 6 abstentions;

---

[191] Website of the Secretariat of the Antarctic Treaty: https://www.ats.aq/devAS/Meetings/Past/87.

[192] Appendix 1 to the Final Report. Final Report of the Forty-second Antarctic Treaty Consultative Meeting. Vol. I. 2019. https://documents.ats.aq/ATCM42/fr/ATCM42_fr001_e.pdf.

[193] The treaty's text and adherence status are available at https://treaties.unoda.org/t/antarctic.

- resolution 74/29, entitled "Developments in the field of information and telecommunications in the context of international security", by a recorded vote of 129 in favour to 6 against, with 45 abstentions;
- resolution 74/35, entitled "Role of science and technology in the context of international security and disarmament", without a vote;
- resolution 74/52, entitled "Observance of environmental norms in the drafting and implementation of agreements on disarmament and arms control", without a vote;
- resolution 74/55, entitled "Promotion of multilateralism in the area of disarmament and non-proliferation", by a recorded vote of 127 in favour to 5 against, with 51 abstentions;
- resolution 74/57, entitled "Relationship between disarmament and development", without a vote;
- resolution 74/64, entitled "Youth, disarmament and non-proliferation", without a vote; and
- resolution 74/66, entitled "Strengthening and developing the system of arms control, disarmament and non-proliferation treaties and agreements", by a recorded vote of 179 in favour to none against, with 3 abstentions.

4. Legal aspects of peaceful uses of outer space

(*a*) Legal Subcommittee of the Committee on the Peaceful Uses of Outer Space

The Legal Subcommittee of the Committee on the Peaceful Uses of Outer Space held its fifty-eighth session at the United Nations Office in Vienna from 1 to 12 April 2019.[194]

Under the agenda item "Information on the activities of international intergovernmental and non-governmental organizations relating to space law", the Subcommittee, *inter alia*, agreed that it was important to continue the exchange of information on recent developments in the area of space law between the Subcommittee and international intergovernmental and non-governmental organizations and that such organizations should once again be invited to report to the Subcommittee, at its fifty-ninth session, on their activities relating to space law.[195]

With regard to United Nations treaties on outer space, the Subcommittee reconvened its Working Group on the Status and Application of the Five United Nations Treaties on Outer Space and endorsed the report of the Chair of the Working Group on 11 April 2019.[196] Some delegations expressed the view that wide adherence to the United Nations treaties on outer space contributed to creating a safe, secure and sustainable environment for the development of outer space activities and enhanced the effectiveness of the Legal Subcommittee as the main body for discussing and negotiating international space law.[197] Some delegations expressed the view that the Legal Subcommittee had a mandate to review the content of the five United Nations treaties on outer space in the light of scientific and technical developments, and with a view towards addressing the current challenges presented by the

---

[194] For the Report of the Legal Subcommittee, see A/AC.105/1203.

[195] *Ibid.*, para. 64.

[196] *Ibid.*, paras. 67–68. For the Report of the Chair of the Working Group on the Status and Application of the Five United Nations Treaties on Outer Space, see A/AC.105/1203, Annex I.

[197] *Ibid.*, para. 73.

diversification of space actors and increasing privatization and commercialization of space activities.[198] Some delegations expressed the view that the Registration Convention represented a key facilitator of transparency and confidence-building measures in outer space activities, and that parties to that Convention should provide complete and timely information on the objects they launched, and should maintain their national registers. It was also expressed that training and capacity-building that focused on registration practices was vital for new space actors.[199] Some delegations also expressed that the provisions of the five United Nations treaties on outer space had been clearly and unequivocally formulated.[200] Others expressed the view that, although the status of the five United Nations treaties on outer space as cornerstones of international space law remained unchallenged, it had been clear to the drafters at the time of drafting that future scientific innovations and technological developments would necessitate improvements to the treaties.[201]

Regarding matters related to the definition and delimitation of outer space and the character and utilization of geostationary orbit, the Subcommittee reconvened its Working Group on the Definition and Delimitation of Outer Space and endorsed the report of the Chair of the Working Group.[202]

Regarding the agenda item entitled "National legislation relevant to the peaceful exploration and use of outer space", the Subcommittee agreed that the discussions under the item were important and that they enabled States to gain an understanding of existing national regulatory frameworks, share experiences on national practices and exchange information on national legal frameworks, and encouraged member States to continue to submit to the Secretariat texts of their national space laws and regulations and to provide updates and inputs for the schematic overview of national regulatory frameworks for space activities.[203]

Under the agenda item "Capacity-building in space law", the Subcommittee noted that the Office for Outer Space Affairs had updated the directory of education opportunities in space law,[204] including information on available fellowships and scholarships, and recommended that States members and permanent observers of the Committee inform the Subcommittee, at its fifty-ninth session, of any action taken or planned at the national, regional or international level to build capacity in space law.[205]

As for agenda item "Review and possible revision of the Principles Relevant to the Use of Nuclear Power Sources in Outer Space", some delegations expressed the view that the use of nuclear power sources in outer space should be in conformity with international law.[206] The view was expressed that the space actors responsible for deep space missions with nuclear power sources on board should ensure the traceability and control of

[198] *Ibid.*, para. 75.

[199] *Ibid.*, para. 76.

[200] *Ibid.*, para. 79.

[201] *Ibid.*, para. 81.

[202] *Ibid.*, paras. 85–86. For the Report of the Chair of the Working Group on the Definition and Delimitation of Outer Space, see A/AC.105/1203, Annex II.

[203] *Ibid.*, paras. 121–122.

[204] A/AC.105/C.2/2019/CRP.9.

[205] A/AC.105/1203, paras. 139–140.

[206] *Ibid.*, para. 147.

such missions and control their potentially adverse effects.[207] The view was expressed that international cooperation was the most appropriate tool for disseminating suitable and affordable strategies for minimizing the effects of space debris, in particular debris emanating from platforms with nuclear power sources on board.[208]

Under the agenda item "General exchange of information and views on legal mechanisms relating to space debris mitigation and remediation measures, taking into account the work of the Scientific and Technical Subcommittee", the Subcommittee noted with satisfaction that some States had taken measures to incorporate internationally recognized guidelines and standards related to space debris into the relevant provisions of their national legislation.[209] The Subcommittee agreed that States members of the Committee and international intergovernmental organizations having permanent observer status with the Committee should be invited to further contribute to the compendium of space debris mitigation standards adopted by States and international organizations by providing or updating the information on any legislation or standards adopted with regard to space debris mitigation, using the template provided for that purpose. The Subcommittee also agreed that all other States Members of the United Nations should be invited to contribute to the compendium and encouraged States with such regulations or standards to provide information on them.[210]

Under agenda item "General exchange of information on non-legally binding United Nations instruments on outer space", the Subcommittee noted with appreciation that the Office for Outer Space Affairs had a web page dedicated to non-legally binding United Nations instruments, which included the compendium on mechanisms adopted by States and international organizations in relation to non-legally binding United Nations instruments on outer space. The Subcommittee encouraged States members of the Committee and international intergovernmental organizations having permanent observer status with the Committee to share information on their practices related to non-legally binding United Nations instruments on outer space.[211]

Regarding the agenda item "General exchange of views on the legal aspects of space traffic management", the Subcommittee noted that the space environment was becoming increasingly complex and congested, owing to the growing number of objects in outer space, the diversification of actors in outer space and the increase in space activities, and that the issue of space traffic management could be considered in that context.[212] The Subcommittee took note of a number of measures that were being undertaken at both the national and international levels to improve the safety and sustainability of spaceflight, including the implementation of a national space traffic management policy, international coordination efforts to manage radiofrequency and geostationary orbits through the International Telecommunication Union (ITU), efforts to enhance capabilities and share information related to space situational awareness, the reporting of annual launch plans

---

[207] *Ibid.*, para. 148.

[208] *Ibid.*, para. 149.

[209] *Ibid.*, para. 156.

[210] *Ibid.*, para. 185.

[211] *Ibid.*, para. 189.

[212] *Ibid.*, para. 202.

and the submission of pre-launch notifications regarding space launch vehicles.[213] Several views were expressed, *inter alia*, that a multilateral, comprehensive approach to space traffic management would meet the needs of the growing global space economy.[214] Another view was expressed that States should analyse proposals made to establish, under the auspices of the United Nations, an international platform for the exchange of information on objects and events in outer space, as well as guidelines for long-term sustainability of outer space activities relating to the safety of space operations, as those proposals and guidelines could inform a responsible and systemic approach to space traffic management.[215]

On the agenda item entitled "General exchange of views on the application of international law to small-satellite activities", the Subcommittee agreed that the continuation of its work under the item would provide valuable opportunities for addressing a number of topical issues relating to international and national policy and regulation measures regarding the use of small satellites by various actors.[216] The Subcommittee took note with appreciation of the questionnaire on the application of international law to small-satellite activities,[217] considered by the Working Group on the Status and Application of the Five United Nations Treaties of Outer Space. The Subcommittee noted that the activities involving small satellites, regardless of their size, should be carried out in compliance with existing international regulatory frameworks and certain non-binding instruments in order to guarantee the safety and sustainability of outer space activities.[218]

On the agenda item entitled "General exchange of views on potential legal models for activities in the exploration, exploitation and utilization of space resources", the Subcommittee was informed that the Hague International Space Resources Governance Working Group had developed 19 building blocks for the governance of space resource activities and that the Working Group would continue to explore the need for any future mechanisms for the governance of space resource activities and the form they should take.[219] Some delegations, *inter alia*, expressed the view that there was a growing need to initiate a proper and substantial debate on the issue of the exploration, exploitation and utilization of space resources within the Committee, in particular within the Legal Subcommittee, as the Subcommittee was the primary forum for intergovernmental discussions and negotiations on a future legal framework for space resource exploitation.[220] Some delegations expressed the view that a working group on exploration, exploitation and utilization of space resources should be established as an open-ended intergovernmental group and that the objective of its consultations and negotiations should be to arrive at draft articles for a universal treaty establishing a legally binding international framework for the exploration, exploitation and utilization of space resources.[221]

---

[213] *Ibid.*, para. 203.

[214] *Ibid.*, para. 204.

[215] *Ibid.*, para. 220.

[216] *Ibid.*, para. 224.

[217] A/AC.105/1177, annex I, appendix II.

[218] A/AC.105/1203, para. 231.

[219] *Ibid.*, para. 249.

[220] *Ibid.*, para. 251.

[221] *Ibid.*, para. 267.

Concerning future work, the Subcommittee agreed that five single issues/items for discussion, entitled "General exchange of information and views on legal mechanisms relating to space debris mitigation and remediation measures, taking into account the work of the Scientific and Technical Subcommittee", "General exchange of information on non-legally binding United Nations instruments on outer space", "General exchange of views on the legal aspects of space traffic management", "General exchange of views on the application of international law to small satellite activities" and "General exchange of views on potential legal models for activities in the exploration, exploitation and utilization of space resources", should be included in the agenda of the Subcommittee at its fifty-ninth session.[222]

(*b*) General Assembly

In 2019, the General Assembly adopted five resolutions relating to the legal aspects of the peaceful use of outer space. On 12 December 2019, upon the recommendation of the First Committee, the Assembly adopted resolution 74/32 entitled "Prevention of an arms race in outer space", by a recorded vote of 183 in favour to 2 against, with 0 abstention; resolution 74/33 entitled "No first placement of weapons in outer space", by a recorded vote of 183 in favour to 14 against, with 38 abstentions; resolution 74/34 entitled "Further practical measures for the prevention of an arms race in outer space", by a recorded vote of 131 in favour to 6 against, with 45 abstentions; and resolution 74/67 entitled "Transparency and confidence-building measures in outer space activities", by a recorded vote of 173 in favour to 2 against, with 6 abstentions. On 13 December 2019, the Assembly adopted, upon the recommendation of the Fourth Committee, resolution 74/82 entitled "International cooperation in the peaceful uses of outer space", without a vote.

5. Human rights[223]

(*a*) Sessions of the United Nations human rights bodies and treaty bodies

(i) *Human Rights Council*

The Human Rights Council, established in 2006,[224] meets as a quasi-standing body in three annual regular sessions and additional special sessions as needed. Reporting to the

---

[222] *Ibid.*, para. 271.

[223] This section covers the resolutions adopted, if any, by the Security Council, the General Assembly and the Economic and Social Council. It also includes a selective coverage of the legal activities of the Human Rights Council, in particular activities of Special Rapporteurs and selected resolutions on specific human rights issues. Other legal developments in human rights may be found under the section in the present chapter entitled "Peace and security". The present section does not cover resolutions addressing human rights issues arising in particular States, nor does it cover in detail the legal activities of the treaty bodies (namely, the Human Rights Committee, the Committee on Economic, Social and Cultural Rights, the Committee on the Elimination of Racial Discrimination, the Committee on the Elimination of Discrimination Against Women, the Committee Against Torture, the Committee on the Rights of the Child, the Committee on the Protection of the Rights of All Migrant Workers and Members of their Families and the Committee on the Rights of Persons with Disabilities). Detailed information and documents relating to human rights are available on the website of the Office of the United Nations High Commissioner for Human Rights at https://www.ohchr.org.

[224] General Assembly resolution 60/251 of 15 March 2006. For further details on its establishment, see the United Nations Juridical Yearbook, 2006, chap. III, section 5.

General Assembly, its agenda and programme of work provide the opportunity to discuss all thematic human rights issues and human rights situations that require the attention of the Assembly.

The Council's mandate includes the review on a periodic basis of the fulfilment of the human rights obligations of all Member States, including the members of the Council, over a cycle of four years through the universal periodic review.[225] The Council also assumed the thirty-eight country and thematic special procedures existing under its predecessor, the Commission on Human Rights, while reviewing the mandate and criteria for the establishment of these special procedures.[226] Moreover, based on the previous "1503 procedure", the confidential complaint procedure of the Council allows individuals and organizations to continue to bring complaints revealing a consistent pattern of gross and reliably attested violations of human rights to the attention of the Council.[227]

In 2019, the Human Rights Council held its fortieth, forty-first and forty-second regular sessions.[228] The Council did not hold a special session that year.

(ii) *Human Rights Council Advisory Committee*

The Human Rights Council Advisory Committee was established pursuant to Human Rights Council resolution 5/1 of 18 June 2007.[229] The Advisory Committee is composed of eighteen experts, and functions as a think-tank for the Council, working under its direction and providing expertise in the manner and form requested by the Council, focusing mainly on studies and research-based advice, suggestions for further enhancing its procedural efficiency, as well as further research proposals within the scope of the work set out by the Council. The Advisory Committee held its twenty-second session from 18 to 22 February 2019 and its twenty-third session from 22 to 26 July 2019 in Geneva.[230]

(iii) *Human Rights Committee*

The Human Rights Committee was established under the International Covenant on Civil and Political Rights of 1966[231] to monitor the implementation of the Covenant and

---

[225] The first universal periodic review cycle covered the period 2008–2011. The second universal periodic review cycle covered the period 2012–2016. The third universal periodic review cycle commenced in 2017 and will run through 2021. For a list of States included and calendar of review sessions, see the section Universal Periodic Review at the homepage of the Human Rights Council at http://www.ohchr.org.

[226] Human Rights Council decision 1/102 of 30 June 2006.

[227] More detailed information on the mandate, work and methods of the Human Rights Council is available at the homepage of the Human Rights Council at http://www.ohchr.org/.

[228] For the reports of the Human Rights Council on its fortieth and forty-first sessions, see *Official Records of the General Assembly, Seventy-fourth Session, Supplement No. 53* (A/74/53). For the report of the Human Rights Council on its forty-second session, see *ibid., Seventy-fourth Session, Supplement No. 53A* (A/74/53/Add.1).

[229] The Human Rights Council Advisory Committee replaced the Sub-Commission for the Promotion and Protection of Human Rights as the main subsidiary body of the Human Rights Council.

[230] For the reports of the Advisory Committee on its twenty-second and twenty-third sessions, see A/HRC/AC/22/2 and A/HRC/AC/23/2, respectively.

[231] United Nations, *Treaty Series*, vol. 999, p. 171.

its Optional Protocols[232] in the territory of States parties. The Committee held its 125th session from 4 to 29 March 2019, its 126th session from 1 to 26 July 2019 and its 127th session from 14 October to 8 November 2019 in Geneva.[233] The Committee did not adopt a general comment in 2019. General comment No. 36 on article 6: right to life, adopted at its 124th session from 8 October to 2 November 2018, was distributed on 3 September 2019.[234]

(iv) *Committee on Economic, Social and Cultural Rights*

The Committee on Economic, Social and Cultural Rights was established by the Economic and Social Council[235] to monitor the implementation of the International Covenant on Economic, Social and Cultural Rights of 1966[236] by its States parties. The Committee held its sixty-fifth and sixty-sixth sessions in Geneva from 18 February to 8 March and from 30 September to 18 October 2019, respectively.[237] The Committee did not adopt a general comment in 2019.

(v) *Committee on the Elimination of Racial Discrimination*

The Committee on the Elimination of Racial Discrimination was established under the International Convention on the Elimination of All Forms of Racial Discrimination of 1966[238] to monitor the implementation of this Convention by its States parties. The Committee held its ninety-eighth, ninety-ninth and one-hundredth sessions in Geneva from 23 April to 10 May, from 5 to 29 August, and from 25 November to 13 December 2019, respectively.[239] The Committee did not adopt a general recommendation in 2019.

(vi) *Committee on the Elimination of Discrimination against Women*

The Committee on the Elimination of Discrimination against Women was established under the Convention on the Elimination of All Forms of Discrimination against Women of 1979[240] to monitor the implementation of this Convention by its States parties. The Committee held its seventy-second, seventy-third and seventy-fourth sessions in Geneva from 18 February to 8 March, from 1 to 19 July, and from 21 October to 8 November 2019,

---

[232] Optional Protocol to the International Covenant on Civil and Political Rights, *ibid.*; and Second Optional Protocol to the International Covenant on Civil and Political Rights, *ibid.*, vol. 1642, p. 414.

[233] For the report of the Human Rights Committee on its 125th session, see *Official Records of the General Assembly, Seventy-fourth Session, Supplement No. 40* (A/74/40). For the reports of the Human Rights Committee on its 126th and 127th sessions, see *ibid., Seventy-fifth Session, Supplement No. 40* (A/75/40).

[234] CCPR/C/GC/36.

[235] Economic and Social Council resolution 1985/17 of 28 May 1985.

[236] United Nations, *Treaty Series*, vol. 993, p. 3.

[237] For the reports of the sixty-fifth and sixty-sixth sessions, see *Official Records of the Economic and Social Council, 2020, Supplement No. 2* (E/2020/22).

[238] United Nations, *Treaty Series*, vol. 660, p. 195.

[239] For the report of the ninety-eighth session, see *Official Records of the General Assembly, Seventy-fourth Session, Supplement No. 18* (A/74/18). For the reports of the ninety-ninth and the one-hundredth sessions, see *ibid., Seventy-fifth Session, Supplement No. 18* (A/75/18).

[240] United Nations, *Treaty Series*, vol. 1249, p. 13.

respectively.[241] The Committee revised its joint general recommendation No. 31/general comment No. 18 of the Committee on the Rights of the Child on harmful practices.[242]

(vii) *Committee against Torture*

The Committee against Torture was established under the Convention against Torture and Other Cruel, Inhuman or Degrading Treatment or Punishment of 1984[243] to monitor the implementation of this Convention by its States parties. The Committee held its sixty-sixth, sixty-seventh and sixty-eighth sessions in Geneva from 23 April to 17 May, from 22 July to 9 August, and from 11 November to 6 December 2019, respectively.[244] The Committee did not adopt a general comment in 2019.

The Subcommittee on Prevention of Torture, established in October 2006 under the Optional Protocol to the Convention against Torture and Other Cruel, Inhuman or Degrading Treatment or Punishment,[245] held its thirty-seventh, thirty-eighth and thirty-ninth sessions from 18 to 22 February, from 17 to 21 June, and from 18 to 22 November 2019, respectively.[246]

(viii) *Committee on the Rights of the Child*

The Committee on the Rights of the Child was established under the Convention on the Rights of the Child of 1989[247] to monitor the implementation of this Convention by its States parties. The Committee held its eightieth, eighty-first and eighty-second sessions in Geneva from 14 January to 1 February, from 13 May to 31 May, and from 9 to 27 September 2019, respectively.[248] The Committee adopted general comment No. 24 (2019) on children's rights in the child justice system.[249] The Committee also revised its joint general comment No. 18/general recommendation No. 31 of the Committee on the Elimination of Discrimination against Women, on harmful practices.[250]

---

[241] For the report of the seventy-second session, see *Official Records of the General Assembly, Seventy-fourth Session, Supplement No. 38* (A/74/38). For the reports of the seventy-third and seventy-fourth sessions, see *ibid., Seventy-fifth Session, Supplement No. 38* (A/75/38).

[242] CEDAW/C/GC/31/Rev.1-CRC/C/GC/18/Rev.1.

[243] United Nations, *Treaty Series*, vol. 1465, p. 85.

[244] For the report of the sixty-sixth session, see *Official Records of the General Assembly, Seventy-fourth Session, Supplement No. 44* (A/74/44). For the reports of the sixty-seventh and sixty-eighth sessions, see *ibid., Seventy-fifth Session, Supplement No. 44* (A/75/44).

[245] United Nations, *Treaty Series*, vol. 2375, p. 237.

[246] For details of the thirty-seventh, thirty-eighth and thirty-ninth sessions, see the thirteenth annual report of the Subcommittee (CAT/C/69/3).

[247] United Nations, *Treaty Series*, vol. 1577, p. 3.

[248] For the reports of the eightieth, eighty-first and eighty-second sessions, see *Official Records of the General Assembly, Seventy-fifth Session, Supplement No. 41* (A/75/41).

[249] CRC/C/GC/24.

[250] CEDAW/C/GC/31/Rev.1–CRC/C/GC/18/Rev.1.

(ix) *Committee on the Protection of the Rights of All Migrant Workers and Members of Their Families*

The Committee on the Protection of the Rights of All Migrant Workers and Members of Their Families was established under the International Convention for the Protection of the Rights of All Migrant Workers and Members of Their Families of 1990[251] to monitor the implementation of this Convention by its States parties in their territories. The Committee held its thirtieth and thirty-first sessions in Geneva from 1 to 12 April and from 2 to 11 September 2019, respectively.[252] The Committee did not adopt a general comment in 2019.

(x) *Committee on the Rights of Persons with Disabilities*

The Committee on the Rights of Persons with Disabilities was established under the Convention on the Rights of Persons with Disabilities of 2006[253] and its 2006 Optional Protocol[254] to monitor the implementation of the Convention and the Optional Protocol by States parties. The Committee held its twenty-first and twenty-second sessions in Geneva from 11 March to 5 April and from 26 August to 20 September 2019, respectively.[255] The Committee did not adopt a general comment in 2019.

(xi) *Committee on Enforced Disappearances*

The Committee on Enforced Disappearances was established under the International Convention for the Protection of All Persons from Enforced Disappearance of 2006[256] to monitor the implementation of this Convention by its State parties. The Committee held its sixteenth and seventeenth sessions in Geneva from 8 to 18 April and from 30 September to 11 October 2019, respectively.[257] The Committee did not adopt a general comment in 2019.

(*b*) Racism, racial discrimination, xenophobia and related intolerance

(i) *Human Rights Council*

The Special Rapporteur on contemporary forms of racism, racial discrimination, xenophobia and related intolerance, Ms. Tendayi Achiume, submitted two reports to the Human Rights Council. The first report, submitted pursuant to General Assembly resolution 73/157,

---

[251] United Nations, *Treaty Series*, vol. 2220, p. 3.

[252] For the report of the thirtieth session, see *Official Records of the General Assembly, Seventy-fourth Session, Supplement No. 48* (A/74/48). For the report of the thirty-first session, see *ibid., Seventy-fifth Session, Supplement No. 48* (A/75/48).

[253] United Nations, *Treaty Series*, vol. 2515, p. 3.

[254] *Ibid.*, vol. 2518, p. 283.

[255] For the reports of the twenty-first and twenty-second sessions, see *Official Records of the General Assembly, Seventy-sixth Session, Supplement No. 55* (A/76/55).

[256] General Assembly resolution 61/177 of 20 December 2006, annex.

[257] For the report of the sixteenth session, see *Official Records of the General Assembly, Seventy-fourth Session, Supplement No. 56* (A/74/56). For the report of the seventeenth session, see *ibid., Seventy-fifth Session, Supplement No. 56* (A/75/56).

provided an update on trends in and manifestations of glorification of Nazism, neo-Nazism and related ideologies; and a human rights analysis of efforts by contemporary Nazi, neo-Nazi and other extremist groups to recruit and radicalize young people.[258] The second report addressed the issue of racial equality and extractivism, explaining why racial equality and non-discrimination obligations enshrined in the international human rights framework must be central to reform, regulation and evaluation of the extractivist economy.[259]

Pursuant to Council resolution 38/19, the Office of the United Nations High Commissioner for Human Rights submitted a report to the Human Rights Council summarizing the intersessional high-level panel discussion held on 2 April 2019 on the theme "Incompatibility between democracy and racism: identifying challenges and good practices".[260]

The Working Group of Experts on People of African Descent submitted a report to the Human Rights Council.[261] At its twenty-fourth session, held in Geneva from 25 to 29 March 2019, the Working Group focused on the theme "Data for racial justice".

On 27 September 2019, the Human Rights Council adopted resolution 42/29 entitled "From rhetoric to reality: a global call for concrete action against racism, racial discrimination, xenophobia and related intolerance", without a vote.

(ii) *General Assembly*

The Secretary-General transmitted to the General Assembly two reports of the Special Rapporteur on contemporary forms of racism, racial discrimination, xenophobia and related intolerance, Ms. Tendayi Achiume. The first report, submitted pursuant to resolution 73/157, summarized information received from Member States on actions taken to combat the glorification of Nazism, neo-Nazism and other practices that contribute to fuelling contemporary forms of racism, racial discrimination, xenophobia and related intolerance.[262] The second report, submitted pursuant to General Assembly resolution 73/262, addressed the human rights obligations of Member States in relation to reparations for racial discrimination rooted in slavery and colonialism.[263]

Pursuant to resolution 73/262, the Working Group of Experts on People of African Descent submitted a report to the General Assembly that examined the role of negative racial stereotypes and the stereotyping of people of African descent in perpetuating racially biased decision-making, racial disparities and racial injustice.[264]

The Secretary-General submitted a report entitled "A global call for action for the total elimination of racism, racial discrimination, xenophobia and related intolerance and the comprehensive implementation of and follow-up to the Durban Declaration and Programme of Action".[265] The Secretary-General further submitted a progress report on

---

[258] A/HRC/41/55.

[259] A/HRC/41/54.

[260] A/HRC/42/27.

[261] A/HRC/42/59.

[262] A/74/253.

[263] A/74/321.

[264] A/74/274.

[265] A/74/312.

the Programme of activities for the implementation of the International Decade for People of African Descent,[266] and transmitted a report of the Group of Independent Eminent Experts on the Implementation of the Durban Declaration and Programme of Action.[267]

On 18 December 2019, upon recommendation of the Third Committee, the General Assembly adopted resolution 74/136 entitled "Combating glorification of Nazism, neo-Nazism and other practices that contribute to fuelling contemporary forms of racism, racial discrimination, xenophobia and related intolerance", by a recorded vote of 133 to 2, with 52 abstentions, and resolution 74/137 entitled "A global call for concrete action for the total elimination of racism, racial discrimination, xenophobia and related intolerance and the comprehensive implementation of and follow-up to the Durban Declaration and Programme of Action", by a recorded vote of 135 to 9, with 43 abstentions.

(*c*) Right to development and poverty reduction

(i) *Right to development*

a. Human Rights Council

The Special Rapporteur on the right to development, Mr. Saad Alfarargi, submitted a report to the Human Rights Council pursuant to Council resolution 33/14.[268] The report outlined the activities of the Special Rapporteur since September 2018 and provided guidelines and recommendations on the practical implementation of the right to development.

The United Nations High Commissioner for Human Rights submitted a report to the Human Rights Council summarizing the intersessional meeting for dialogue and cooperation on human rights and the 2030 Agenda for Sustainable Development.[269]

The Working Group on the Right to Development submitted a report on its twentieth session to the Human Rights Council.[270]

The Secretary-General and the United Nations High Commissioner for Human Rights submitted a report on the right to development to both the General Assembly and the Human Rights Council.[271] The report summarized the activities of the Office of the United Nations High Commissioner for Human Rights (OHCHR) on the promotion and realization of the right to development covering the period from June 2018 to May 2019 and analyzed the implementation of the right to development, identifying challenges and making recommendations for their resolution.

On 11 July 2019, the Human Rights Council adopted resolution 41/3 entitled "Enhancement of international cooperation in the field of human rights", by a recorded vote of 28 to 14, with 5 abstentions, and resolution 41/5 entitled "Human rights and international solidarity", by a recorded vote of 32 to 14, with 1 abstention.

---

[266] A/74/308.

[267] A/74/173.

[268] A/HRC/42/38.

[269] A/HRC/40/34.

[270] A/HRC/42/35.

[271] A/HRC/42/29; A/74/167.

On 12 July 2019, the Human Rights Council adopted resolution 41/19 entitled "The contribution of development to the enjoyment of all human rights", by a recorded vote of 33 to 13, with no abstentions.

On 27 September 2019, the Human Rights Council adopted resolution 42/23 entitled "The right to development", by a recorded vote of 27 to 13, with 7 abstentions.

b. General Assembly

The Secretary-General transmitted to the General Assembly the report of the Special Rapporteur on the right to development, Mr. Saad Alfarargi, submitted in accordance with Council resolution 33/14.[272] The report explored the explicit link between the right to development and disaster risk reduction, as well as its practical implications.

On 15 October 2019, the General Assembly adopted resolution 74/4 entitled "Political declaration of the high-level forum on sustainable development convened under the auspices of the General Assembly", without reference to a Main Committee and without a vote.

On 18 December 2019, upon recommendation of the Third Committee, the General Assembly adopted resolution 74/152 entitled "The right to development", by a recorded vote of 138 to 23, with 26 abstentions.

(ii) *Poverty reduction*

a. Human Rights Council

The Special Rapporteur on extreme poverty and human rights, Mr. Philip Alston, submitted a report to the Human Rights Council pursuant to Council resolution 35/19.[273] The report focused on the impact of climate change on human rights, particularly the rights of people living in or near poverty, and on the response of the human rights community, noting its reluctance to engage robustly with climate change.

On 12 July 2019, the Human Rights Council adopted resolution 41/24 entitled "The Social Forum", without a vote.

b. General Assembly

The Secretary-General transmitted to the General Assembly the report of the Special Rapporteur on extreme poverty and human rights, Mr. Philip Alston, submitted in accordance with Council resolution 35/19.[274] The report examined how digital technologies are used within the welfare state. It was recommended in the report that the starting point should be on how welfare budgets could be transformed through technology to ensure a higher standard of living for the vulnerable and disadvantaged.

The Secretary-General submitted three reports to the General Assembly. The first report, entitled "Implementation of the outcome of the World Summit for Social Development and of the twenty-fourth special session of the General Assembly", submitted in accordance

[272] A/74/163.

[273] A/HRC/41/39.

[274] A/74/493.

with General Assembly resolution 73/141, underscored the need to strengthen international cooperation for social development, with particular attention to universal and equitable access to education and health care, and to advance progress in the achievement of the objectives set forth at the World Summit for Social Development and in the 2030 Agenda for Sustainable Development.[275] The second report, entitled "Implementation of the Third United Nations Decade for the Eradication of Poverty (2018–2027)", submitted pursuant to General Assembly resolution 73/246, presented the response of the United Nations system to the theme of the Third United Nations Decade for the Eradication of Poverty (2018–2027), as well as recommendations on how to make the Third Decade effective.[276] The third report, entitled "Eradicating rural poverty to implement the 2030 Agenda for Sustainable Development", submitted pursuant to General Assembly resolution 73/244, examined the state of rural poverty and the gaps and challenges to eradicating it and provided recommendations for overcoming the numerous gaps and challenges.[277]

On 19 December 2019, upon recommendation of the Second Committee, the General Assembly adopted resolution 74/234 entitled "Implementation of the Third United Nations Decade for the Eradication of Poverty", without a vote, and resolution 74/237 entitled "Eradicating rural poverty to implement the 2030 Agenda for Sustainable Development", by a recorded vote of 126 to 49, with 2 abstentions.

(*d*) Right of peoples to self-determination

(i) *Universal realization of the right of peoples to self-determination*

a. Human Rights Council

On 22 March 2019, the Human Rights Council adopted resolution 40/22 entitled "Right of the Palestinian people to self-determination", by a recorded vote of 41 to 3, with 2 abstentions.

b. General Assembly

In accordance with General Assembly resolution 73/160, the Secretary-General submitted a report on the right of peoples to self-determination.[278]

On 3 December 2019, without reference to a Main Committee, the General Assembly adopted resolution 74/10 entitled "Committee on the Exercise of the Inalienable Rights of the Palestinian People", by a recorded vote of 92 to 12, with 61 abstentions.

On 13 December 2019, on the report of the Fourth Committee, the General Assembly adopted resolution 74/95 entitled "Implementation of the Declaration on the Granting of Independence to Colonial Countries and Peoples by the specialized agencies and the international institutions associated with the United Nations", by a recorded vote of 130 to 2, with 52 abstentions, resolution 74/112 entitled "Dissemination of information on decolonization", by a recorded vote of 178 to 3, with 2 abstentions, and resolution 74/113

---

[275] A/74/205.

[276] A/74/210.

[277] A/74/257.

[278] A/74/309.

entitled "Implementation of the Declaration on the Granting of Independence to Colonial Countries and Peoples", by a recorded vote of 134 to 3, with 46 abstentions.

On 18 December 2019, upon recommendation of the Third Committee, the General Assembly adopted resolution 74/139 entitled "The right of the Palestinian people to self-determination", by a recorded vote of 167 to 5, with 11 abstentions, and resolution 74/140 entitled "Universal realization of the right of peoples to self-determination", without a vote.

(ii) *Mercenaries*

a. Human Rights Council

The Working Group on the use of mercenaries as a means of violating human rights and impeding the exercise of the right of peoples to self-determination submitted a report to the Human Rights Council.[279] The report covered the activities of the Working Group from August 2018 to July 2019, and focused on the relationship between private military and security companies and the extractive industry from a human rights perspective.

On 26 September 2019, the Human Rights Council adopted resolution 42/9 entitled "The use of mercenaries as a means of violating human rights and impeding the exercise of the right of peoples to self-determination", by a recorded vote of 29 to 14, with 4 abstentions.

b. General Assembly

In accordance with General Assembly resolution 73/159 and Human Rights Council resolution 33/4, the Secretary-General transmitted the report of the Working Group on the use of mercenaries as a means of violating human rights and impeding the exercise of the right of peoples to self-determination to the General Assembly.[280]

On 18 December 2019, upon recommendation of the Third Committee, the General Assembly adopted resolution 74/138 entitled "Use of mercenaries as a means of violating human rights and impeding the exercise of the right of peoples to self-determination", by a recorded vote of 130 to 52, with 7 abstentions.

(*e*) Economic, social and cultural rights

On 21 March 2019, the Human Rights Council adopted resolution 40/12 entitled "Question of the realization in all countries of economic, social and cultural rights", without a vote.

(i) *Right to food*

a. Human Rights Council

The Special Rapporteur on the right to food, Ms. Hilal Elver, submitted a report to the Human Rights Council on the essential role of fishery workers in contributing to food security and nutrition, and the barriers they face in the enjoyment of their own human rights.[281]

---

[279] A/HRC/42/42.

[280] A/74/244.

[281] A/HRC/40/56.

On 21 March 2019, the Human Rights Council adopted resolution 40/7 entitled "The right to food", without a vote.

b. General Assembly

The Secretary-General transmitted to the General Assembly the interim report of the Special Rapporteur on the right to food, Hilal Elver, submitted pursuant to Assembly resolution 73/171.[282] The report focused on the Sustainable Development Goals as a potentially transformative tool to advance the realization of the right to food, as well as other economic, social and cultural rights.

The Secretary-General submitted a report to the General Assembly, pursuant to Assembly resolution 73/253, entitled "Agriculture development, food security and nutrition".[283] The report highlighted the critical role of a sustainable food systems approach in eradicating poverty, hunger and all forms of malnutrition, promoting sustainable production and consumption, meeting the challenges of urbanization, absorbing the youth labor force and reducing the impact of food systems on biodiversity, natural resources and the climate.

On 18 December 2019, upon recommendation of the Third Committee, the General Assembly adopted resolution 74/149 entitled "The right to food", by a recorded vote of 188 to 2, with no abstentions.

On 19 December 2019, upon recommendation of the Second Committee, the General Assembly adopted resolution 74/242 entitled "Agriculture development, food security and nutrition", without a vote.

(ii) *Right to education*

a. Human Rights Council

The Special Rapporteur on the right to education, Ms. Koumbou Boly Barry, submitted her annual report to the Human Rights Council pursuant to Council resolutions 8/4, 35/2 and 38/9.[284] The report examined the implementation of the right to education and Sustainable Development Goal 4 in the context of the growth of private actors in education.[285]

On 11 July 2019, the Human Rights Council adopted resolution 41/16 entitled "The right to education: follow-up to Human Rights Council resolution 8/4", without a vote.

On 26 September 2019, the Human Rights Council adopted resolution 42/7 entitled "World Programme for Human Rights Education: adoption of the plan of action", without a vote.

b. General Assembly

The Secretary-General transmitted to the General Assembly the report of the Special Rapporteur on the right to education, Ms. Koumbou Boly Barry, submitted in accordance

[282] A/74/164.

[283] A/74/237.

[284] A/HRC/41/37.

[285] A/HRC/41/37.

with Human Rights Council resolutions 8/4 and 26/17.[286] The report focused on the ways in which the right to education contributes to the prevention of atrocity crimes and mass or grave violations of human rights.

On 19 December 2019, the General Assembly, upon recommendation of the Second Committee, adopted resolution 74/223 entitled "Education for sustainable development in the framework of the 2030 Agenda for Sustainable Development", without a vote.

(iii) *Right to an adequate standard of living, including adequate housing*

a. Human Rights Council

The Special Rapporteur on adequate housing as a component of the right to an adequate standard of living, and on the right to non-discrimination in this context, Ms. Leilani Farha, submitted her report to the Human Rights Council pursuant to Council resolution 34/9.[287] The report examined the critical issue of access to justice for the right to housing.

b. General Assembly

The Secretary-General transmitted to the General Assembly the report of the Special Rapporteur on adequate housing as a component of the right to an adequate standard of living, and on the right to non-discrimination in this context.[288] The report examined the right to housing of indigenous peoples and provided guidance for States, indigenous authorities and other actors on how to ensure that their obligations under international human rights law concerning the right to housing are met in conformity with the United Nations Declaration on the Rights of Indigenous Peoples.

(iv) *Access to safe drinking water and sanitation*

a. Human Rights Council

In accordance with Human Rights Council resolution 33/10, the Special Rapporteur on the human right to safe drinking water and sanitation, Mr. Léo Heller, submitted his report to the Human Rights Council.[289] In the report, the Special Rapporteur examined access to water and sanitation beyond the household, with emphasis on the application of the human rights to water and sanitation in public spaces.

On 26 September 2019, the Human Rights Council adopted resolution 42/5 entitled "The human rights to safe drinking water and sanitation", without a vote.

b. General Assembly

The Secretary-General transmitted to the General Assembly the report of the Special Rapporteur on the human right to safe drinking water and sanitation, Léo Heller,

---

[286] A/74/243.

[287] A/HRC/40/61.

[288] A/74/183.

[289] A/HRC/42/47.

submitted pursuant to General Assembly resolution 64/292 and Human Rights Council resolution 33/10.[290] The report focused on the impact of megaprojects on the realization of the human rights to water and sanitation and proposes the megaproject cycle as a framework to clarify how a human rights-based approach can be implemented.

On 18 December 2019, upon recommendation of the Third Committee, the General Assembly adopted resolution 74/141 entitled "The human rights to safe drinking water and sanitation", without a vote.

(v) *Right to health*

a. Human Rights Council

The Special Rapporteur on the right of everyone to the enjoyment of the highest attainable standard of physical and mental health, Mr. Dainius Pūras, submitted a report to the Council pursuant to Council resolution 33/9.[291] In the report, the Special Rapporteur elaborated on the critical role of the social and underlying determinants of health in advancing the realization of the right to mental health, and identified challenges and opportunities associated with a human rights-based approach to action on those determinants.

The Special Rapporteur on the elimination of discrimination against persons affected by leprosy and their family members, Ms. Alice Cruz, submitted a report to the Human Rights Council pursuant to Council resolution 35/9.[292] In the report, the Special Rapporteur focused on the situation of women and children affected by leprosy and their family members.

The Office of the United Nations High Commissioner for Human Rights submitted a report to the Human Rights Council pursuant to Council resolution 38/8.[293] The report contained a summary of discussions held and recommendations made at the consultation on human rights in the response to HIV held in Geneva on 12 and 13 February 2019.

On 11 July 2019, the Human Rights Council adopted resolution 41/10 entitled "Access to medicines and vaccines in the context of the right of everyone to the enjoyment of the highest attainable standard of physical and mental health", without a vote.

On 26 September 2019, the Council adopted resolution 42/16 entitled "The right of everyone to the enjoyment of the highest attainable standard of physical and mental health", without a vote.

b. General Assembly

The Secretary-General transmitted to the General Assembly the report of the Special Rapporteur on the right of everyone to the enjoyment of the highest attainable standard of physical and mental health, Dainius Pūras, submitted in accordance with Human Rights Council resolutions 6/29 and 33/9.[294] In the report, the Special Rapporteur identified features of current health education that limit the capacity of the health-care workforce to

[290] A/74/197.

[291] A/HRC/41/34.

[292] A/HRC/41/47.

[293] A/HRC/41/27.

[294] A/74/174.

function effectively and to play its crucial role in promoting, respecting and fulfilling the right to physical and mental health.

On 10 October 2019, the General Assembly, without reference to a main Committee, adopted resolution 74/2 entitled "Political declaration of the high-level meeting on universal health coverage", without a vote.

On 11 December 2019, the General Assembly, without reference to a main Committee, adopted resolution 74/20 entitled "Global health and foreign policy: an inclusive approach to strengthening health systems", without a vote.

(vi) *Cultural rights*

a. Human Rights Council

The Special Rapporteur in the field of cultural rights, Ms. Karima Bennoune, submitted her report to the Human Rights Council.[295] The report provided an overview of the work of her mandate since its creation in 2009 and suggested strategies for advancing cultural rights over the next decade.

On 21 March 2019, the Human Rights Council adopted resolution 40/6 entitled "Promotion of the enjoyment of the cultural rights of everyone and respect for cultural diversity", without a vote.

b. General Assembly

The Secretary-General transmitted to the General Assembly the report of the Special Rapporteur in the field of cultural rights, Karima Bennoune, submitted in accordance with Human Rights Council resolution 37/12.[296] The report addressed the importance of public spaces for the exercise of cultural rights and identified challenges which must be addressed so that everyone can access and enjoy such spaces.

On 18 December 2019, the General Assembly, on the recommendation of the Third Committee, adopted resolution 74/159 entitled "Human rights and cultural diversity", by a recorded vote of 136 to 55, with no abstentions.

(*f*) Civil and political rights

(i) *Torture*

a. Human Rights Council

The Special Rapporteur on torture and other cruel, inhuman or degrading treatment or punishment, Mr. Nils Melzer, submitted his report to the Human Rights Council pursuant to Council resolution 34/19.[297] The report examined the relationship between corruption and torture or ill-treatment and outlined the predominant patterns of interaction between the two phenomena as well as their systemic root causes.

---

[295] A/HRC/40/53.

[296] A/74/255.

[297] A/HRC/40/59.

The Secretary-General submitted a report to the Human Rights Council on the United Nations Voluntary Fund for Victims of Torture.[298] The report complemented the Secretary-General's report to the General Assembly at its seventy-fourth session and provided information on the activities of the Fund, describing in particular the recommendations for grants adopted by the Board of Trustees of the Fund at its fiftieth session.

b. General Assembly

The Secretary-General transmitted to the General Assembly the interim report of the Special Rapporteur on torture and other cruel, inhuman or degrading treatment or punishment, Nils Melzer, submitted in accordance with General Assembly resolution 72/163.[299] The report considered the relevance of the prohibition of torture and other cruel, inhuman or degrading treatment or punishment to the context of domestic violence.

In accordance with General Assembly resolutions 36/151 and 70/146, the Secretary-General submitted to the General Assembly a report on the United Nations Voluntary Fund for Victims of Torture, which described the outcome of the forty-ninth session of the Board of Trustees of the Fund.[300]

On 28 June 2019, the General Assembly, without reference to a Main Committee, adopted resolution 73/304 entitled "Towards torture-free trade: examining the feasibility, scope and parameters for possible common international standards", by a recorded vote of 81 to 20, with 44 abstentions.

On 18 December 2019, the General Assembly, upon recommendation of the Third Committee, adopted resolution 74/143 entitled "Torture and other cruel, inhuman or degrading treatment or punishment", without a vote.

(ii) *Arbitrary detention, persons deprived of liberty, and extrajudicial, summary and arbitrary execution*

a. Human Rights Council

The Special Rapporteur on extrajudicial, summary or arbitrary executions, Ms. Agnès Callamard, submitted her report to the Human Rights Council, in accordance with Council resolution 35/15.[301] In the report, the Special Rapporteur focused on the investigation of, accountability for and prevention of intentional State killings of human rights defenders, journalists and prominent dissidents, including those who have sought safety abroad.

The Working Group on Arbitrary Detention submitted a report to the Human Rights Council.[302] In the report, the Working Group examined the following thematic issues: deprivation of liberty in the context of conscientious objection to military service; use of registers to avoid arbitrary detention; use of the Working Group's opinions in domestic proceedings; and comprehensive reparations to victims of arbitrary detention.

---

[298] A/HRC/43/25.

[299] A/74/148.

[300] A/74/233.

[301] A/HRC/41/36.

[302] A/HRC/42/39.

On 26 September 2019, the Human Rights Council adopted resolution 42/22 entitled "Arbitrary detention", without a vote.

b. General Assembly

The Secretary-General transmitted to the General Assembly the report of the Special Rapporteur on extrajudicial, summary or arbitrary executions, executions, Agnes Callamard, submitted in accordance with General Assembly resolution 71/198,[303] which focused on the application of death penalty to foreign nationals and the provision of consular assistance by the home State.

(iii) *Enforced disappearances and missing persons*

a. Human Rights Council

The Working Group on Enforced or Involuntary Disappearances submitted its annual report to the Human Rights Council, detailing its activities, communications and cases examined during the period from 3 May 2018 to 22 May 2019.[304]

b. General Assembly

Pursuant to General Assembly resolution 72/183, the Secretary-General submitted to the General Assembly a report entitled "International Convention for the Protection of All Persons from Enforced Disappearance".[305] The report summarized replies received from Governments regarding the implementation of the resolution and contained information on activities carried out in that regard by the Secretary-General, the United Nations High Commissioner for Human Rights and her Office, the Committee on Enforced Disappearances, the Working Group on Enforced or Involuntary Disappearances, and relevant intergovernmental and non-governmental organizations.

The Committee on Enforced Disappearances also submitted the reports of its fifteenth and sixteenth sessions to the General Assembly.[306]

On 18 December, the General Assembly, upon recommendation of the Third Committee, adopted resolution 74/161 entitled "International Convention for the Protection of All Persons from Enforced Disappearance", without a vote.

(iv) *Integration of human rights of women and a gender perspective*[307]

a. Human Rights Council

The Special Rapporteur on violence against women, its causes and consequences, Ms. Dubravka Šimonović, submitted a report to the Human Rights Council.[308] The report

---

[303] A/74/318.

[304] A/HRC/42/40.

[305] A/74/213.

[306] A/74/56.

[307] For more information on the rights of women, see section 6 of this chapter.

[308] A/HRC/41/42.

took stock of the challenges facing the mandate and provided recommendations for establishing a system-wide approach to addressing violence against women, with a view to strengthening the role of the mandate in accelerating the prevention and elimination of such violence.

The Working Group on the issue of discrimination against women in law and in practice submitted a report to the Council analysing the causes of deprivation of liberty of women from a gender perspective.[309]

The Office of the United Nations High Commissioner for Human Rights submitted two reports to the Human Rights Council. The first report presented an analytical study on the integration of a gender-responsive approach into climate action at the local, national, regional and international levels for the full and effective enjoyment of the rights of women.[310] The second report summarized the panel discussion on human rights and climate change that was held on 28 June 2019. The panel discussion in question focused on the effective enjoyment of the rights of women and girls and the promotion and protection of their rights through gender-responsive climate action.[311]

On 21 March 2019, the Human Rights Council adopted resolution 40/5 entitled "Elimination of discrimination against women and girls in sport", without a vote.

On 11 July 2019, the Human Rights Council adopted resolution 41/6 entitled "Elimination of all forms of discrimination against women and girls", without a vote.

On 12 July 2019, the Human Rights Council adopted resolution 41/17 entitled "Accelerating efforts to eliminate all forms of violence against women and girls: preventing and responding to violence against women and girls in the world of work", without a vote.

b. General Assembly

Pursuant to General Assembly resolution 72/149, the Secretary-General submitted a report to the General Assembly.[312] The report outlined the current context with respect to the issue of violence against women and migrant workers and provided information on the measures taken by Member States and activities undertaken within the United Nations system to address this issue and ensure the protection of migrant women's human rights.

The Committee on the Elimination of Discrimination against Women also submitted the reports of its seventieth, seventy-first and seventy-second sessions to the General Assembly.[313]

On 22 May 2019, the General Assembly, without reference to a Main Committee, adopted resolution 73/294 entitled "Twenty-fifth anniversary of the Fourth World Conference on Women", without a vote.

On 18 December 2019, the General Assembly, upon recommendation of the Third Committee, adopted resolution 74/126 entitled "Improvement of the situation of women and girls in rural areas", resolution 74/127 entitled "Violence against women migrant workers", and resolution 74/134 entitled "The girl child", without a vote.

---

[309] A/HRC/41/33.

[310] A/HRC/41/26.

[311] A/HRC/42/26.

[312] A/74/235.

[313] A/74/38.

On 19 December 2019, the General Assembly, upon recommendation of the Second Committee, adopted resolution 74/235 entitled "Women in development", without a vote.

c. Security Council

On 23 April 2019, the Security Council adopted resolution 2467 (2019), which, *inter alia*, reaffirmed its commitment to addressing sexual violence in armed conflict and emphasized the importance of women's participation, the protection of human rights and consistent support for strengthening women's engagement at all levels of decision-making.

On 29 October 2019, the Security Council adopted resolution 2493 (2019) which, *inter alia*, urged Member States to fully implement the women, peace and security agenda, including by ensuring women's full, equal and meaningful participation in all stages of peace processes, and encouraged the creation of safe and enabling environments for civil society, including women peacebuilders and those who protect and promote human rights.

(v) *Trafficking*

a. Human Rights Council

The Special Rapporteur on trafficking in persons, especially women and children, Ms. Maria Grazia Giammarinaro, submitted her annual report to the Human Rights Council.[314] The report emphasized that the long-term social inclusion of victims and survivors of trafficking is a State obligation arising from the duty of due diligence and the right to an effective remedy. It identified key challenges to achieving such inclusion and highlighted promising practices considered innovative and transformative, encouraging their replication, adequate resourcing and wider implementation by States, civil society organizations and the international community.

b. General Assembly

The Secretary-General transmitted to the General Assembly the report of the Special Rapporteur on trafficking in persons, especially women and children, Maria Grazia Giammarinaro, submitted pursuant to Human Rights Council resolution 35/5.[315] In her report, the Special Rapporteur outlined activities undertaken during the reporting period and identified good practices, and proposed guidelines and recommendations for implementing long-term viable remediation responses for workers who are victims of trafficking in persons and severe exploitation in businesses' operations and supply chains.

Pursuant to General Assembly resolution 72/195, the Secretary-General submitted a report to the General Assembly on measures taken by Member States and entities of the United Nations system to implement the resolution.[316] The report also provided information on the status of ratifications and accessions to the Protocol to Prevent, Suppress and Punish Trafficking in Persons, Especially Women and Children, supplementing the United Nations Convention against Transnational Organized Crime, and on efforts by

---

[314] A/HRC/41/46.

[315] A/74/189.

[316] A/74/127.

relevant stakeholders to strengthen implementation of the United Nations Global Plan of Action to Combat Trafficking in Persons.

On 18 December 2019, on the recommendation of the Third Committee, the General Assembly adopted resolution 74/176 entitled "Improving the coordination of efforts against trafficking in persons", without a vote.

(vi) *Freedom of religion or belief, expression and assembly*

a. Human Rights Council

The Special Rapporteur on freedom of religion or belief, Mr. Ahmed Shaheed, submitted a report to the Human Rights Council.[317] In the report, the Special Rapporteur explored the interrelation between freedom of religion or belief and freedom of expression, emphasizing that the two rights are closely linked and mutually reinforcing.

The Special Rapporteur on the promotion and protection of the right to freedom of opinion and expression, Mr. David Kaye, submitted his annual report to the Council.[318] The report examined targeted surveillance in the light of States' obligations under international human rights law and the responsibilities of companies, and proposed a legal and policy framework to enhance regulation, accountability and transparency in the private surveillance industry.

The Special Rapporteur on the rights to freedom of peaceful assembly, Mr. Clément Voule, submitted a report to the Human Rights Council[319] focusing on the opportunities and challenges facing the rights to freedom of peaceful assembly and of association in the digital age.

Pursuant to Human Rights Council resolution 37/38, the United Nations High Commissioner for Human Rights submitted a report to the Human Rights Council entitled "Combating intolerance, negative stereotyping, stigmatization, discrimination, incitement to violence and violence against persons, based on religion or belief".[320] The report provided a comprehensive follow-up to earlier resolutions, presenting conclusions based on information submitted by States regarding measures taken to implement the action plan set out in paragraphs 7 and 8 of the resolution and offering views on potential follow-up measures for further improvement of the plan implementation.

On 21 March 2019, the Human Rights Council adopted resolution 40/10, entitled "Freedom of religion or belief", without a vote.

On 22 March 2019, the Human Rights Council adopted resolution 40/25 entitled "Combating intolerance, negative stereotyping and stigmatization of, and discrimination, incitement to violence and violence against, persons based on religion or belief", without a vote.

On 11 July 2019, the Human Rights Council adopted resolution 41/12 entitled "The rights to freedom of peaceful assembly and of association", without a vote.

---

[317] A/HRC/40/58.

[318] A/HRC/41/35.

[319] A/HRC/41/41.

[320] A/HRC/40/44.

b. General Assembly

The Secretary-General transmitted to the General Assembly the interim report of the Special Rapporteur on freedom of religion or belief, Ahmed Shaheed, submitted in accordance with General Assembly resolution 73/176.[321] The report addressed violence, discrimination and expressions of hostility motivated by antisemitism as impediments to the enjoyment of the right to freedom of religion or belief.

The Secretary-General submitted to the General Assembly a report detailing steps taken by States to combat intolerance, negative stereotyping, stigmatization, discrimination, incitement to violence and violence against persons, based on religion or belief.[322]

The Secretary-General transmitted to the General Assembly the report of the Special Rapporteur on the promotion and protection of the right to freedom of opinion and expression, David Kaye, submitted in accordance with Human Rights Council resolution 34/18.[323] In his report, the Special Rapporteur evaluated the human rights law applicable to the regulation of online "hate speech".

The Secretary-General transmitted to the General Assembly the report of the Special Rapporteur on the rights to freedom of peaceful assembly and of association, Clément Nyaletsossi Voulé, submitted in accordance with Council resolution 41/12.[324] In the report, the Special Rapporteur explored the impacts of violations of the rights to freedom of peaceful assembly and of association on sustainable development, in particular on efforts to reduce economic inequalities and eradicate poverty in all its forms and dimensions as outlined in the 2030 Agenda for Sustainable Development.

The Secretary-General submitted a report to the General Assembly on the safety of journalists and the issue of impunity, pursuant to General Assembly resolution 72/175.[325] The report provided an overview of the situation in relation to the safety of journalists and of the actions taken at the international, regional and national levels.

On 2 April 2019, the General Assembly adopted resolution 73/285 entitled "Combating terrorism and other acts of violence based on religion or belief", without a vote and without reference to a Main Committee.

On 18 December 2019, on the recommendation of the Third Committee, the General Assembly adopted resolution 74/145 entitled "Freedom of religion or belief", without a vote, resolution 74/157 entitled "The safety of journalists and the issue of impunity", without a vote, and resolution 74/164 entitled "Combating intolerance, negative stereotyping, stigmatization, discrimination, incitement to violence and violence against persons, based on religion or belief", without a vote.

---

[321] A/74/358.

[322] A/74/229.

[323] A/74/486.

[324] A/74/349.

[325] A/74/314.

(vii) *Right to life*

a. Human Rights Council

The Office of the United Nations High Commissioner for Human Rights submitted a report to the Human Rights Council pursuant to Council resolutions 26/2 and 36/17.[326] The report summarized the high-level panel discussion on the question of the death penalty, held on 26 February 2019 at the fortieth session of the Council. The panel discussion addressed human rights violations related to the use of the death penalty, in particular with respect to the rights to non-discrimination and equality.

The Secretary-General submitted two reports to the Human Rights Council. The first report (a yearly supplement of the Secretary-General to his quinquennial report on capital punishment), submitted pursuant to Council resolution 36/17, examined the consequences arising at various stages of the imposition and application of the death penalty on the enjoyment of the human rights of persons facing the death penalty and other affected persons.[327] The second report, submitted pursuant to Council resolution 37/26, provided follow-up information from Member States on the implementation of that resolution, with particular attention to activities aimed at raising awareness of the Convention on the Prevention and Punishment of the Crime of Genocide and the realization of educational programmes and projects contributing to the prevention of genocide.[328]

On 27 September 2019, the Human Rights Council adopted resolution 42/24 entitled "The question of the death penalty", by a recorded vote of 26 to 14, with 6 abstentions.

(viii) *Right to privacy*

a. Human Rights Council

The Special Rapporteur on the right to privacy, Mr. Joseph A. Cannataci, submitted a report to the Human Rights Council,[329] which focused on intelligence oversight issues and provided information on the work of the Task Force on Privacy and Personality (privacy and gender) and the Task Force on Health Data.

On 26 September 2019, the Human Rights Council adopted resolution 42/15 entitled "The right to privacy in the digital age", without a vote.

b. General Assembly

The Secretary-General transmitted to the General Assembly the report of the Special Rapporteur on the right to privacy, Joseph A. Cannataci, submitted in accordance with Human Rights Council resolution 28/16.[330] The report summarized the activities of the mandate and presented recommendations concerning the protection and use of health-related data.

---

[326] A/HRC/42/25.

[327] A/HRC/42/28.

[328] A/HRC/41/24.

[329] A/HRC/40/63.

[330] A/74/277.

(ix) *Right to truth*

a. Human Rights Council

The Special Rapporteur on the promotion of truth, justice, reparation and guarantees of non-recurrence, Mr. Fabián Salvioli, submitted a report to the Human Rights Council.[331] In the report, the Special Rapporteur focused on practical experiences of domestic reparation programmes, assessing the conceptual and legal framework, lessons learned and selected challenges, and providing recommendations for their effective design and implementation.

On 26 September 2019, the Human Rights Council adopted resolution 42/17 entitled "Human rights and transitional justice", without a vote.

b. General Assembly

The Secretary-General transmitted to the General Assembly the report of the Special Rapporteur on the promotion of truth, justice, reparation and guarantees of non-recurrence, Fabián Salvioli, submitted in accordance with Human Rights Council resolution 36/7.[332] The report focused on apologies for gross human rights violations and serious violations of international humanitarian law, presenting the Special Rapporteur's assessment of the applicable legal and conceptual framework, surveying existing practices and lessons learned, and providing recommendations for the design and implementation of apologies.

(*g*) Rights of the child

a. Human Rights Council

The Special Representative of the Secretary-General for Children and Armed Conflict, Ms. Virginia Gamba, submitted her annual report to the Human Rights Council.[333] Covering the period from December 2018 to December 2019, the report explored challenges in ending and preventing grave violations and in strengthening the protection of children affected by armed conflicts.

The Secretary-General transmitted to the Human Rights Council the annual report of the Special Representative of the Secretary-General on Violence against Children, Ms. Marta Santos Pais.[334] In the report, the Special Representative provided an overview of major initiatives and developments to sustain and scale up efforts to safeguard children's freedom from violence and advance implementation of the 2030 Agenda for Sustainable Development.

The Special Rapporteur on the sale and sexual exploitation of children, including child prostitution, child pornography and other child sexual abuse material, Ms. Maud De Boer-Buquicchio, submitted a report to the Human Rights Council pursuant to Council resolutions 7/13 and 34/16.[335] The report provided an overview of her activities since her

---

[331] A/HRC/42/45.

[332] A/74/147.

[333] A/HRC/43/38.

[334] A/HRC/40/50.

[335] A/HRC/40/51.

previous report as well as a thematic study on the sale and sexual exploitation of children in the context of sports.

The Office of the United Nations High Commissioner for Human Rights also submitted two reports to the Human Rights Council. The first report, prepared pursuant to Council resolution 37/20, provided an overview of the legal framework and practical measures to empower children with disabilities.[336] The second report, submitted pursuant to Council resolution 35/16, focused on the causes, challenges and response gaps of child, early and forced marriage in humanitarian settings.[337]

On 22 March 2019, the Human Rights Council adopted resolution 40/14 entitled "Rights of the child: empowering children with disabilities for the enjoyment of their human rights, including through inclusive education", without a vote, and resolution 40/15 entitled "Thirtieth anniversary of the Convention on the Rights of the Child", without a vote.

On 11 July 2019, the Human Rights Council adopted resolution 41/8 entitled "Consequences of child, early and forced marriage", without a vote.

b. General Assembly

The Secretary-General submitted three reports to the General Assembly. The first report on the "Status of the Convention on the Rights of the Child" focused on the implementation of the priority themes of the resolutions entitled "Rights of the child" adopted by the General Assembly at its sixty-ninth to seventy-third sessions.[338] The second report, entitled "Follow-up to the outcome of the special session of the General Assembly on children", assessed steps taken in 2018 to achieve a world fit for children and highlighted gaps in achievement as well as strategic shifts necessary to achieve unmet goals.[339] The third report, entitled "The girl child", highlighted the advancements in the legal and normative framework supporting girls living in rural areas.[340]

The Special Representative of the Secretary-General for Children and Armed Conflict submitted her annual report to the General Assembly on activities undertaken in the discharge of her mandate and on progress in advancing the children and armed conflict agenda.[341] Covering the period from August 2018 to July 2019, the report described trends, issues of concern and progress achieved, including the further mainstreaming of child protection across the United Nations system.

In July 2019, Ms. Najat Maalla M'jid succeeded Ms. Santos Pais as Special Representative of the Secretary-General on Violence against Children. She submitted her first report to the General Assembly pursuant to resolution 64/146.[342] The report highlighted action taken at the national and regional levels towards realizing the right of every child to protection from violence, and indicated that the mandate would continue to leverage the 2030 Agenda

---

[336] A/HRC/40/27.

[337] A/HRC/41/19.

[338] A/74/231.

[339] A/74/240.

[340] A/74/246.

[341] A/74/249.

[342] A/74/259.

to accelerate progress towards eliminating all forms of violence against children, including through strengthening partnerships and underscoring the role of children.

The Secretary-General transmitted to the General Assembly the report of the Special Rapporteur on the sale and sexual exploitation of children, including child prostitution, child pornography and any other child sexual abuse material, submitted in accordance with Assembly resolution 73/155.[343] In the report, the Special Rapporteur described the activities undertaken in relation to the discharge of her mandate since her previous report to the assembly.

The Secretary-General transmitted to the General Assembly the report of the Independent Expert leading the global study on children deprived of liberty, Mr. Manfred Nowak, submitted pursuant to General Assembly resolution 72/245.[344] The report summarized the detailed findings of the global study on children deprived of liberty.

On 25 July 2019, the General Assembly, without reference to a Main Committee, adopted resolution 73/327 entitled "International Year for the Elimination of Child Labour, 2021", without a vote.

On 18 December 2019, the General Assembly, on the recommendation of the Third Committee and without a vote, adopted resolution 73/133 entitled "Rights of the child", resolution 74/134 entitled "The girl child", and resolution 74/174 entitled "Countering child sexual exploitation and sexual abuse online".

(*h*) Migrants

a. Human Rights Council

The Special Rapporteur on the human rights of migrants, Mr. Felipe González Morales, submitted a report to the Human Rights Council, in accordance with Human Rights Council resolution 34/21.[345] In the report, the Special Rapporteur presented a thematic study, from a gender perspective, on the impact of migration on migrant women and girls, with a view to deepening understanding of migration as a gendered phenomenon and its implications for human rights.

On 11 July 2019, the Human Rights Council adopted resolution 41/7 entitled "The human rights of migrants", without a vote.

b. General Assembly

The Secretary-General transmitted to the General Assembly the report of the Special Rapporteur on human rights of migrants, Felipe González Morales, submitted pursuant to Human Rights Council resolution 34/21,[346] which contained a study on good practices of gender-responsive migration legislation and policies.

The Secretary-General submitted two reports to the General Assembly pursuant to General Assembly resolution 72/179. The first report on the "Human rights of migrants" covered all aspects of the implementation of that resolution. The report highlighted relevant

---

[343] A/74/162.

[344] A/74/136.

[345] A/HRC/41/38.

[346] A/74/191.

aspects of the international human rights framework regarding international migrants, explored various thematic issues related to the promotion and protection of their rights, summarized information received from governments regarding the implementation of the resolution, and presented conclusions and recommendations on protecting the human rights of migrants.[347] The second report on "Violence against women migrant workers" outlined the context with respect to the problem of violence against women migrant workers and provided information on the measures taken by Member States and activities undertaken within the United Nations system to address this issue and ensure the protection of migrant women's human rights.[348]

On 18 December 2019, the General Assembly, upon recommendation of the Third Committee, adopted resolution 74/127 entitled "Violence against women migrant workers", without a vote, and resolution 74/148 entitled "Protection of migrants", without a vote.

(*i*) Internally displaced persons

a. Human Rights Council

The Special Rapporteur on the human rights of internally displaced persons, Ms. Cecilia Jimenez-Damary, submitted her annual report to the Human Rights Council.[349] In the report, the Special Rapporteur examined the role of national human rights institutions in the protection of the human rights of internally displaced persons, and considered obstacles to their engagement on internal displacement as well as their activities and positive practices at all phases of displacement.

On 11 July 2019, the Human Rights Council adopted resolution 41/15 entitled "Mandate of the Special Rapporteur on the human rights of internally displaced persons", without a vote.

b. General Assembly

The Secretary-General transmitted to the General Assembly the report of the Special Rapporteur on the human rights of internally displaced persons, Cecilia Jimenez-Damary, submitted in accordance with General Assembly resolution 72/182 and Human Rights Council resolution 41/15.[350] In the report, the Special Rapporteur highlighted the situation of internally displaced children suffering and dying because of the lack of rapid and appropriate responses to their specific needs and protection concerns, and the limited capacity and resources available to humanitarian actors to address protection gaps.

The Secretary-General submitted three reports to the General Assembly. The first report, submitted pursuant to General Assembly resolution 72/280, focused on the right of return of refugees and internally displaced persons and their descendants, the prohibition of forced demographic changes, humanitarian access, the importance of preserving the property rights of refugees and internally displaced persons, and the development of a timetable to ensure the prompt voluntary return of all refugees and internally displaced

---

[347] A/74/271.

[348] A/74/235.

[349] A/HRC/41/40.

[350] A/74/261.

persons to their homes.[351] The second report, submitted pursuant to General Assembly resolution 73/136, provided an overview of progress made in improving the international response to natural disasters, and outlined related trends, challenges and thematic issues.[352] The third report updated information contained in the report of the Secretary-General submitted to the Assembly at its seventy-third session and covered the period from 1 July 2018 through 30 June 2019.[353] It included information drawn from the Internal Displacement Monitoring Centre.

On 4 June 2019, the General Assembly, without reference to a Main Committee, adopted resolution 73/298 entitled "Status of internally displaced persons and refugees from Abkhazia, Georgia, and the Tskhinvali region/South Ossetia, Georgia", by a recorded vote of 79 to 15, with 57 abstentions.

On 13 December 2019, the General Assembly, upon recommendation of the Fourth Committee, adopted resolution 74/84 entitled "Persons displaced as a result of the June 1967 and subsequent hostilities", by a recorded vote of 162 to 7, with 11 abstentions.

On 16 December, the General Assembly, without reference to a Main Committee and without a vote, adopted resolution 74/115 entitled "International cooperation on humanitarian assistance in the field of natural disasters, from relief to development".

On 18 December 2019, the General Assembly, upon recommendation of the Third Committee and without a vote, adopted resolution 74/131 entitled "Assistance to refugees, returnees and displaced persons in Africa" and resolution 74/160 entitled "Protection of and assistance to internally displaced persons".

(*j*) Minorities

a. Human Rights Council

The Special Rapporteur on minority issues, Mr. Fernand de Varennes, submitted two reports to the Human Rights Council. The first report, submitted pursuant to Council resolutions 25/5 and 34/6, provided an overview of his activities since his previous report and updated his first thematic report on statelessness as a minority issue, as well as the level of awareness-raising and visibility of minorities and their human rights.[354] The second report drew primarily on the discussions and contributions at the eleventh session of the Forum on Minority Issues held on 29 and 30 November 2018 on the theme "Stateless: a minority issue".[355]

The Office of the United Nations High Commissioner for Human Rights submitted a report to the Human Rights Council entitled "Rights of persons belonging to national or ethnic, religious and linguistic minorities".[356] The report contained information on relevant developments of United Nations human rights bodies and mechanisms, and on the activities undertaken by the Office of the United Nations High Commissioner for Human

351 A/73/880.

352 A/74/319.

353 A/74/322.

354 A/HRC/40/64.

355 A/HRC/40/71.

356 A/HRC/40/30.

Rights at headquarters and in the field that contribute to the promotion of and respect for the provisions of the Declaration on the Rights of Persons Belonging to National or Ethnic, Religious and Linguistic Minorities, and the provisions of relevant international human rights treaties.

b. General Assembly

The Secretary-General transmitted to the General Assembly the report of the Special Rapporteur on minority issues, submitted pursuant to Human Rights Council resolution 34/6.[357] The report provided a summary of the Special Rapporteur's activities since his previous report to the General Assembly, together with a thematic study on the concept of a minority in the United Nations system.

Pursuant to General Assembly resolution 72/184, the Secretary-General submitted a report on the effective promotion of the Declaration on the Rights of Persons Belonging to National or Ethnic, Religious and Linguistic Minorities.[358]

On 18 December 2019, the General Assembly, upon recommendation of the Third Committee, adopted resolution 74/165 entitled "Effective promotion of the Declaration on the Rights of Persons Belonging to National or Ethnic, Religious and Linguistic Minorities", without a vote.

(*k*) Indigenous issues

a. Human Rights Council

The Special Rapporteur on the rights of indigenous peoples, Ms. Victoria Tauli Corpuz, submitted her report to the Human Rights Council.[359] The report summarized activities undertaken since the Special Rapporteur submitted her previous report, analysed issues related to access to justice for indigenous peoples, whether through the ordinary justice system or through their own indigenous justice mechanisms, and explored the interaction and harmonization between ordinary and indigenous justice systems and the opportunities offered by legal pluralism.

Pursuant to resolution 39/13, the United Nations High Commissioner for Human Rights submitted a report containing information on relevant developments relating to human rights bodies and mechanisms, and outlining activities undertaken by the Office of the United Nations High Commissioner for Human Rights at headquarters and in the field to promote and apply the provisions of the United Nations Declaration on the Rights of Indigenous Peoples and related human rights treaties.[360] The High Commissioner also submitted a summary report on the annual half-day panel discussion on the rights of indigenous peoples.[361]

The Expert Mechanism on the Rights of Indigenous Peoples submitted a report to the Human Rights Council providing an overview of its activities during its twelfth session in

---

[357] A/74/160.

[358] A/74/215.

[359] A/HRC/42/37.

[360] A/HRC/42/19.

[361] A/HRC/41/22.

Geneva from 15 to 19 July 2019.[362] The Expert Mechanism also submitted to the Council a study on indigenous peoples' rights in the context of borders, migration and displacement.[363]

On 26 September 2019, the Human Rights Council adopted, without a vote, resolution 42/19 entitled "Human rights and indigenous peoples".

b. General Assembly

The Secretary-General transmitted to the General Assembly the report of the Special Rapporteur on the rights of indigenous peoples, submitted in accordance with Human Rights Council resolution 33/12.[364] In the report, the Special Rapporteur described her activities during the year and examined the right of indigenous peoples to autonomy or self-government as an exercise of their right to self-determination, identifying positive elements in existing arrangements as well as limitations and challenges.

On 18 December 2019, the General Assembly, upon recommendation of the Third Committee, adopted resolution 74/135 entitled "Rights of indigenous peoples", without a vote.

(*l*) Terrorism and human rights

a. Human Rights Council

The Special Rapporteur on the promotion and protection of human rights and fundamental freedoms while countering terrorism, Ms. Fionnuala Ní Aoláin, submitted her report to the Human Rights Council.[365] In her report, the Special Rapporteur examined the impact that measures and practices used to counter terrorism and to prevent and counter extremism have on the protection of human rights for civil society and human rights defenders and addressed the global challenges of protecting civic space arising from the implementation of counter-terrorism law and practice.

The Office of the United Nations High Commissioner for Human Rights submitted a report entitled "Protection of human rights and fundamental freedoms while countering terrorism.[366] The report focused on children as victims and witnesses of terrorist acts, children at perceived risk of recruitment, and those associated or suspected of association with terrorist groups.

On 22 March 2019, the Human Rights Council adopted resolution 40/16 entitled "Mandate of the Special Rapporteur on the promotion and protection of human rights and fundamental freedoms while countering terrorism", without a vote.

On 26 September 2019, the Human Rights Council adopted resolution 42/18 entitled "Terrorism and human rights", without a vote.

---

[362] A/HRC/42/55.

[363] A/HRC/42/56.

[364] A/74/149.

[365] A/HRC/40/52.

[366] A/HRC/40/28.

b. General Assembly

The Secretary-General transmitted to the General Assembly the report of the Special Rapporteur on the promotion and protection of human rights and fundamental freedoms while countering terrorism, Fionnuala Ní Aoláin, submitted in accordance with General Assembly resolution 72/180 and Human Rights Council resolution 40/16.[367] The report addressed the role of "soft law" and new instruments in the creation, enforcement, oversight and regulation of counter-terrorism measures.

The Secretary-General submitted three reports to the General Assembly. The first report, submitted pursuant to resolution 72/284, set out some options for Member States to consider on ways to assess the impact and progress made in the implementation of the United Nations Global Counter-Terrorism Strategy by United Nations entities.[368] The second report, submitted pursuant to General Assembly resolution 50/53, contained information on measures taken to eliminate international terrorism at the national and international levels, on the basis of submissions from Governments and international organizations.[369] The third report, submitted pursuant to General Assembly resolutions 72/180 and 73/174, reviewed developments between 1 July 2017 and 30 June 2019, with reference to recommendations made by international human rights mechanisms.[370]

On 28 June 2019, the General Assembly, without reference to a Main Committee and without a vote, adopted resolution 73/305 entitled "Enhancement of international cooperation to assist victims of terrorism".

On 18 December 2019, the General Assembly, upon the recommendation of the Third Committee and without a vote, adopted resolution 74/147 entitled "Terrorism and human rights", and resolution 74/194 entitled "Measures to eliminate international terrorism".

c. Security Council

On 28 March 2019, the Security Council adopted resolution 2462 (2019) which, *inter alia*, reaffirmed its decision in resolution 1373 (2001) that all States shall prevent and suppress the financing of terrorist acts, called upon States to strengthen efforts to counter and criminalize terrorist financing, and requested follow-up action and reporting through the Council's counter-terrorism architecture.

On 19 July 2019, the Security Council adopted resolution 2482 (2019) which, *inter alia*, called upon Member States to enhance coordination in order to strengthen a global response to linkages between international terrorism and organized crime and emphasized that counter-terrorism measures must comply with States' obligations under international law.

---

[367] A/74/335.

[368] A/73/866.

[369] A/74/151.

[370] A/74/270.

(*m*) Persons with disabilities

a. Human Rights Council

The Special Rapporteur on the rights of persons with disabilities, Ms. Catalina Devandas Aguilar, submitted her annual report to the Human Rights Council.[371] The report provided an overview of the activities undertaken in 2018 and contained a thematic study on disability-specific forms of deprivation of liberty.

The Office of the United Nations High Commissioner for Human Rights submitted a report to the Human Rights Council, which provided an overview of the legal framework and practical measures to empower children with disabilities.[372]

On 22 March 2019, the Human Rights Council adopted resolution 40/14 entitled "Rights of the child: empowering children with disabilities for the enjoyment of their human rights, including through inclusive education", without a vote.

b. General Assembly

The Secretary-General transmitted the report of the Special Rapporteur on the rights of persons with disabilities, Catalina Devandas-Aguilar, submitted in accordance with Human Rights Council resolution 35/6,[373] which examined the situation of older persons with disabilities and provided guidance to States on promoting, protecting and ensuring their human rights and fundamental freedoms, with particular attention to the intersection between ageing and disability.

The Secretary-General submitted a report to the General Assembly pursuant to resolution 72/162, providing a global overview of accessibility for persons with disabilities and presenting ongoing efforts and progress made by Governments, entities of the United Nations system and civil society organizations in advancing accessibility.[374]

On 18 December 2019, the General Assembly, upon recommendation of the Third Committee, adopted resolution 74/144 entitled "Implementation of the Convention on the Rights of Persons with Disabilities and the Optional Protocol thereto: accessibility", without a vote.

On 27 December 2019, the General Assembly, upon recommendation of the Fifth Committee, adopted resolution 74/253 entitled "Enhancing accessibility for persons with disabilities to conferences and meetings of the United Nations system", without a vote.

c. Security Council

On 25 June 2019, the Security Council adopted resolution 2475 (2019) which, *inter alia*, called upon all parties to armed conflict to protect persons with disabilities in situations of risk, including armed conflict, and to ensure their full participation in humanitarian, conflict-prevention, and post-conflict reconstruction processes, in accordance with international law.

---

[371] A/HRC/40/54.

[372] A/HRC/40/27.

[373] A/74/186.

[374] A/74/146.

(*n*) Contemporary forms of slavery

a. Human Rights Council

The Special Rapporteur on contemporary forms of slavery, including its causes and consequences, Ms. Urmila Bhoola, submitted a report to the Human Rights Council.[375] The report assessed current features of slavery and provided indications on how expected changes in the future of work, demographics, migration and the environment may shape slavery in the years to come.

On 26 September 2019, the Human Rights Council adopted resolution 42/10 entitled "Special Rapporteur on contemporary forms of slavery, including its causes and consequences", without a vote.

b. General Assembly

The Secretary-General transmitted to the General Assembly the report of the Special Rapporteur on contemporary forms of slavery, including its causes and consequences, Urmila Bhoola, in accordance with Human Rights Council resolution 33/1,[376] which discussed child slavery and the various forms in which it manifests today.

The Secretary-General submitted to the General Assembly a report on United Nations Voluntary Trust Fund on Contemporary Forms of Slavery,[377] which provided an overview of the work of the Trust Fund, in particular the recommendations for grants to beneficiary organizations that were adopted by the Board of Trustees of the Fund at its twenty-second session, held in Geneva from 26 November to 30 November 2018.

(*o*) Environment and human rights[378]

a. Human Rights Council

The Special Rapporteur on the implications for human rights of the environmentally sound management and disposal of hazardous substances and wastes, Mr. Başkut Tuncak, submitted his report to the Human Rights Council.[379] In his report, the Special Rapporteur presented a final set of principles to help States, businesses and other key actors respect and protect workers from toxic occupational exposures and to provide remedies for violations of their rights.

The Special Rapporteur on the issue of human rights obligations relating to the enjoyment of a safe, clean, healthy and sustainable environment, Mr. David Boyd, submitted a report to the Human Rights Council.[380] In his report, the Special Rapporteur focused on the right to breathe clean air as a component of the right to a healthy environment and

---

[375] A/HRC/42/44.

[376] A/74/179.

[377] A/74/228.

[378] For more information on the environment, see section 8 of this chapter.

[379] A/HRC/42/41.

[380] A/HRC/40/55.

described the negative impact of air pollution on the enjoyment of many human rights, in particular the right to life and right to health.

On 21 March 2019, the Human Rights Council adopted resolution 40/11 entitled "Recognizing the contribution of environmental human rights defenders to the enjoyment of human rights, environmental protection and sustainable development", without a vote.

On 12 July 2019, the Human Rights Council adopted resolution 41/21 entitled "Human rights and climate change", without a vote.

On 26 September 2019, the Human Rights Council adopted resolution 42/21 entitled "Protection of the rights of workers exposed to hazardous substances and wastes", without a vote.

b. General Assembly

The Secretary-General transmitted to the General Assembly the report of the Special Rapporteur on the implications for human rights of the environmentally sound management and disposal of hazardous substances and wastes, Baskut Tuncak, submitted pursuant to Human Rights Council resolution.[381] In the report, the Special Rapporteur outlined the legal basis of the duty to prevent exposure to hazardous substances and wastes and highlighted how exposure prevention is the exception, leading to existential threats to life and health.

The Secretary-General also transmitted to the General Assembly the report of the Special Rapporteur on the issue of human rights obligations relating to the enjoyment of a safe, clean, healthy and sustainable environment, David R. Boyd, submitted in accordance with Human Rights Council resolution 37/8.[382] In the report, the Special Rapporteur discussed the urgent need for action to ensure a safe climate for humanity and illustrated the devastating effects of the current global climate emergency on the enjoyment of human rights, and the crucial role of human rights in catalyzing action to address climate change.

(*p*) Business and human rights

a. Human Rights Council

The open-ended intergovernmental working group on transnational corporations and other business enterprises with respect to human rights presented its report on its fourth session which took place from 15 to 19 October 2018.[383]

The Working Group on the issue of human rights and transnational corporations and other business enterprises submitted two reports to the Human Rights Council. The first report highlighted the differentiated and disproportionate impact of business activities on women and girls.[384] The second report provided an overview of key observations and messages emerging from the seventh Forum on Business and Human Rights, held from 26 to 28 November 2018.[385]

---

[381] A/74/480.

[382] A/74/161.

[383] A/HRC/40/48.

[384] A/HRC/41/43.

[385] A/HRC/41/49.

b. General Assembly

The Secretary-General transmitted to the General Assembly the report of the Working Group on the issue of human rights and transnational corporations and other business enterprises, submitted pursuant to Human Rights Council resolutions 17/4 and 35/7.[386] The report examined what policy coherence on business and human rights means in practice under the Guiding Principles of Business and Human Rights and proposed practical ways to enhance government's capacity, ability and action to achieve this goal, drawing on lessons learned from the development and implementation of national action plans on business and human rights and other relevant policy frameworks.

(*q*) Promotion and protection of human rights

(i) *International promotion and protection*

a. Human Rights Council

The Independent Expert on human rights and international solidarity, Mr. Obiora Okafor, submitted a report to the Human Rights Council.[387] In the report, the Independent Expert engaged with the issue of criminalization or suppression of the rendering of humanitarian assistance to migrants and refugees who enter a State in an irregular manner.

The United Nations High Commissioner for Human Rights submitted two reports to the Human Rights Council. The first report, entitled "Summary of the intersessional meeting for dialogue and cooperation on human rights and the 2030 Agenda for Sustainable Development", provided a summary of the first meeting of the intersessional meetings, held on 16 January 2019.[388] The second report, entitled "Local government and human rights", focused on effective methods to foster cooperation between local government and local stakeholders for the promotion and protection of human rights at their level, including by raising awareness of the Sustainable Development Goals.[389]

The Independent Expert on the promotion of a democratic and equitable international order, Mr. Livingstone Sewanyana, submitted a report to the Human Rights Council.[390] In the report, the Independent Expert examined the intersection of public participation and decision-making in global governance spaces and its impact on a democratic and equitable international order.

On 11 July 2019, the Human Rights Council adopted resolution 41/3 entitled "Enhancement of international cooperation in the field of human rights", by a recorded vote of 28 to 14, with 5 abstentions, and resolution 41/5 entitled "Human rights and international solidarity", by a recorded vote of 32 to 14, with 1 abstention.

On 26 September 2019, the Human Rights Council adopted resolution 42/8 entitled "Promotion of a democratic and equitable international order" by a recorded vote of 25 to 14, with 8 abstentions.

---

[386] A/74/198.

[387] A/HRC/41/44.

[388] A/HRC/40/34.

[389] A/HRC/42/22.

[390] A/HRC/42/48.

On 27 September 2019, the Human Rights Council adopted resolution 42/32 entitled "Enhancement of technical cooperation and capacity-building in the field of human rights", without a vote.

b. General Assembly

The Secretary-General transmitted to the General Assembly the report of the Independent Expert on human rights and international solidarity, Obiora Chinedu Okafor, submitted in accordance with Human Rights Council resolution 35/3.[391] In the report, the Independent Expert examined the challenges that arise in global refugee protection in the absence of human rights-based international solidarity.

The Secretary-General also transmitted to the General Assembly the same report of the Independent Expert on the promotion of a democratic and equitable international order submitted to the Human Rights Council.[392]

On 12 December 2019, the General Assembly, without reference to a Main Committee and without a vote, adopted resolution 74/23 entitled "Promotion of interreligious and intercultural dialogue, understanding and cooperation for peace".

On 13 December 2019, the General Assembly, upon recommendation of the Fourth Committee, adopted resolution 74/82 entitled "International cooperation in the peaceful uses of outer space", without a vote.

On 16 December 2019, the General Assembly, without reference to a Main Committee and without a vote, adopted resolution 74/115 entitled "International cooperation on humanitarian assistance in the field of natural disasters, from relief to development".

On 18 December 2019, the General Assembly, upon recommendation of the Third Committee, adopted resolution 74/150 entitled "Promotion of a democratic and equitable international order", by a recorded vote of 128 to 53, with 8 abstentions, resolution 74/151 entitled "Strengthening United Nations action in the field of human rights through the promotion of international cooperation and the importance of non-selectivity, impartiality and objectivity", without a vote, resolution 74/153 entitled "Enhancement of international cooperation in the field of human rights", without a vote, and resolution 74/178 entitled "International cooperation to address and counter the world drug problem", without a vote.

On 19 December 2019, the General Assembly, upon the Second Committee, adopted resolution 74/206 entitled "Promotion of international cooperation to combat illicit financial flows and strengthen good practices on assets return to foster sustainable development", without a vote.

(ii) *Ombudsman, mediator and other national human rights institutions*

a. Human Rights Council

The Office of the United Nations Commissioner for Human Rights submitted a report to the Human Rights Council entitled "Consultation on the experiences and practices of national human rights institutions in working to support the establishment

[391] A/74/185.

[392] A/74/245.

and maintenance of inclusive societies and the implementation of the 2030 Agenda for Sustainable Development".[393] The report summarized the consultation.

b. General Assembly

The Secretary-General submitted a report to the General Assembly pursuant to General Assembly resolution 72/181.[394] The report provided information on activities undertaken by the Office of the United Nations High Commissioner for Human Rights to establish and strengthen national human rights institutions; on support provided by the United Nations Development Programme and other United Nations agencies, funds and programmes to such institutions; on cooperation between national human rights institutions and the international human rights system; and on support provided by the Office of the High Commissioner to the Global Alliance of National Human Rights Institutions and relevant regional networks.

On 18 December 2019, the General Assembly, upon recommendation of the Third Committee, adopted resolution 74/156 entitled "National human rights institutions", without a vote.

(iii) *Right to promote and protect universally recognized human rights*

a. Human Rights Council

The Special Rapporteur on the situation of human rights defenders, Mr. Michel Forst, submitted a report to the Human Rights Council.[395] In the report, the Special Rapporteur reviewed the situation of women human rights defenders, focusing in particular on the gender-specific risks and obstacles they face.

The Secretary-General submitted a report entitled "Cooperation with the United Nations, its representatives and mechanisms in the field of human rights" which highlighted activities, policy developments and good practices within the United Nations system and beyond to address intimidation and reprisals against those seeking to cooperate or having cooperated with the United Nations, its representatives and mechanisms in the field of human rights.[396]

On 27 September 2019, the Human Rights Council adopted resolution 42/28 entitled "Cooperation with the United Nations, its representatives and mechanisms in the field of human rights", by a recorded vote of 36 to 0, with 11 abstentions.

b. General Assembly

The Secretary-General transmitted to the General Assembly the report of the Special Rapporteur on the situation of human rights defenders, Michel Forst, in accordance with Assembly resolutions 66/164 and 68/181 and Human Rights Council resolutions 16/5 and 25/18.[397] In the report, the Special Rapporteur discussed the persistence of impunity for vi-

---

[393] A/HRC/41/30.

[394] A/74/226.

[395] A/HRC/40/60.

[396] A/HRC/42/30.

[397] A/74/159.

olations committed against human rights defenders and outlined a regulatory framework on the right of access to justice, including the obligation of due diligence in investigations.

On 18 December, the General Assembly, upon recommendation of the Third Committee, adopted resolution 74/146 entitled "Implementing the Declaration on the Right and Responsibility of Individuals, Groups and Organs of Society to Promote and Protect Universally Recognized Human Rights and Fundamental Freedoms through providing a safe and enabling environment for human rights defenders and ensuring their protection", without a vote.

(*r*) Miscellaneous

(i) *Human rights and good governance*

a. Human Rights Council

The Special Rapporteur on the independence of judges and lawyers, Mr. Diego García-Sayán, submitted his annual report to the Human Rights Council, which focused on the exercise of the rights to freedom of expression, association and peaceful assembly by judges and prosecutors, both offline and online.[398]

The Office of the High Commissioner for Human Rights submitted a report to the Human Rights Council pursuant to Council resolution 36/16.[399] The report addressed violence, death and serious injury in situations of deprivation of liberty, drawing on the experience of United Nations and regional human rights mechanisms, as well as submissions from States, civil society and other relevant stakeholders.

On 21 March 2019, the Human Rights Council adopted resolution 40/9 entitled "Human rights, democracy and the rule of law", without a vote.

b. General Assembly

The Secretary-General transmitted to the General Assembly the report of the Special Rapporteur on the independence of judges and lawyers, Diego García-Sayán, submitted pursuant to Human Rights Council resolution 35/11.[400] In the report, the Special Rapporteur examined the role that the Basic Principles on the Independence of the Judiciary have played in guaranteeing judicial independence, and the status of threats and challenges to the independence of judges, lawyers and judicial systems as a whole.

(ii) *Effects of economic reform policies and foreign debt on the full enjoyment of all human rights, particularly economic, social and cultural rights*

a. Human Rights Council

The Office of the High Commissioner for Human Rights submitted a report to the Human Rights Council entitled "Summary of the expert workshop on good practices of

---

[398] A/HRC/41/48.

[399] A/HRC/42/20.

[400] A/74/176.

United Nations-system support to States in preventing and fighting against corruption, with a focus on human rights".[401]

On 21 March 2019, the Human Rights Council adopted resolution 40/4 entitled "The negative impact of the non-repatriation of funds of illicit origin to the countries of origin on the enjoyment of human rights, and the importance of improving international cooperation", by a recorded vote of 31 to 2, with 14 abstentions, and resolution 40/8 entitled "The effects of foreign debt and other related international financial obligations of States on the full enjoyment of all human rights, particularly economic, social and cultural rights", by a recorded vote of 27 to 14, with 6 abstentions.

On 11 July 2019, the Human Rights Council adopted resolution 41/9 entitled "The negative impact of corruption on the enjoyment of human rights", without a vote.

b. General Assembly

The Secretary-General transmitted to the General Assembly the report of the Independent Expert on the effects of foreign debt and other related international financial obligations of States on the full enjoyment of all human rights, particularly economic, social and cultural rights, Juan Pablo Bohoslavsky, submitted pursuant to Human Rights Council resolutions 25/16 and 34/3.[402] The report outlined the negative consequences of austerity measures on economic growth, debt ratios and equality.

(iii) *Unilateral coercive measures*

a. Human Rights Council

The Special Rapporteur on the negative impact of unilateral coercive measures on the enjoyment of human rights, Mr. Idriss Jazairy, submitted his report to the Human Rights Council, in which he considered the impact of unilateral coercive measures on the enjoyment of human rights in eight countries and examined the emergence of international legal norms against the extraterritorial use of unilateral sanctions.[403]

On 21 March 2019, the Human Rights Council adopted resolution 40/3 entitled "The negative impact of unilateral coercive measures on the enjoyment of human rights", by a recorded vote of 27 to 15, with 5 abstentions.

b. General Assembly

The Secretary-General transmitted to the General Assembly the report of the Special Rapporteur on the negative impact of unilateral coercive measures on the enjoyment of human rights, Idriss Jazairy, submitted in accordance with Human Rights Council resolution 27/21 and Assembly resolution 73/167.[404] In the report, the Special Rapporteur addressed legal issues arising from the practice of using unilateral coercive measures.

---

[401] A/HRC/41/20.

[402] A/74/178.

[403] A/HRC/42/46.

[404] A/74/165.

The Secretary-General submitted a report to the General Assembly, pursuant to General Assembly resolution 72/201, on the outcome of the monitoring of the imposition of unilateral coercive measures and an analysis of their impact on affected countries.[405]

On 18 December 2019, the General Assembly, upon recommendation of the Third Committee, adopted resolution 74/154 entitled "Human rights and unilateral coercive measures", by a recorded vote of 135 to 55, with 0 abstentions.

On 19 December 2019, the General Assembly, upon recommendation of the Second Committee, adopted resolution 74/200 entitled "Unilateral economic measures as a means of political and economic coercion against developing countries", by a recorded vote of 122 to 2, with 51 abstentions.

(iv) *Human rights of older persons*

a. Human Rights Council

The Independent Expert on the enjoyment of all human rights by older persons, Ms. Rosa Kornfeld-Matte, submitted her report to the Council.[406] In the report, the Independent Expert described her activities, in particular participation in the third International Conference on the Human Rights of Older Persons, convened in Vienna on 12 and 13 November 2018, and examined the protection of the human rights of older persons in emergency situations.

The Office of the High Commissioner for Human Rights submitted a report to the Human Rights Council entitled "Activities of the Office of the United Nations High Commissioner for Human Rights, the United Nations system and regional organizations to support States' efforts to promote and protect the human rights of older persons".[407] The report contained information on practices and experiences of broader stakeholders, including Member States, national human rights institutions and civil society organizations.

On 26 September 2019, the Human Rights Council adopted resolution 42/12 entitled "The human rights of older persons", without a vote.

b. General Assembly

The Secretary-General submitted a report to the General Assembly entitled "Follow-up to the International Year of Older Persons: Second World Assembly on Ageing", which provided an analysis of ageing-related policies and priorities in the implementation of the 2030 Agenda for Sustainable Development, as reported in the voluntary national reviews presented at the high-level political forum on sustainable development in the period 2016 to 2018.[408]

On 18 December 2019, the General Assembly, upon recommendation of the Third Committee, adopted resolution 74/125 entitled "Follow-up to the Second World Assembly on Ageing", without a vote.

---

[405] A/74/264.

[406] A/HRC/42/43.

[407] A/HRC/41/32.

[408] A/74/170.

(v) *Other issues*

a. Human Rights Council

On 11 July 2019, the Human Rights Council adopted resolution 41/11 entitled "New and emerging digital technologies and human rights", without a vote.

On 12 July 2019, the Human Rights Council adopted resolution 41/20 entitled "Impact of arms transfers on human rights", without a vote.

On 26 September 2019, the Human Rights Council adopted resolution 41/13 entitled "The right to social security", without a vote.

b. General Assembly

On 9 December 2019, the General Assembly adopted resolution 74/16 entitled "Building a peaceful and better world through sport and the Olympic ideal", without reference to a Main Committee and without a vote.

On 18 December 2019, the General Assembly, upon recommendation of the Third Committee, adopted resolution 74/123 entitled "Persons with albinism", without a vote.

6. Women[409]

(*a*) United Nations Entity for Gender Equality and the Empowerment of Women (UN-Women)

UN-Women was established by the General Assembly pursuant to resolution 64/289 of 2 July 2010 as a composite entity to function as a secretariat with the additional role of leading, coordinating and promoting the accountability of the United Nations system in its work on gender equality and the empowerment of women.[410] The Executive Board of UN-Women held four meeting sessions in New York in 2019,[411] during which it adopted nine decisions: decision 2019/1, entitled "Update on the implementation of GA Resolution 72/279 on repositioning of the United Nations development system"; decision 2019/2, entitled "Working methods of the Executive Board"; decision 2019/3, entitled " Financial report and audited financial statements for the year ended 31 December 2017 and Report of the Board Auditors"; decision 2019/4, entitled "Annual Report of the Under-

[409] This section covers the Security Council, the General Assembly, the Economic and Social Council, the Commission on the Status of Women and the United Nations Entity for Gender Equality and the Empowerment of Women (UN-Women). For more detailed information and documents regarding this topic generally, see the website of UN-Women at https://www.unwomen.org/. For information regarding women and human rights, see Chapter III, section A.5(*a*)(vi) and section A.5(*f*) (iv).

[410] It consolidated the mandates and functions of the Office of the Special Adviser on Gender Issues and Advancement of Women, the Division for the Advancement of Women, the United Nations Development Fund for Women and the International Research and Training Institute for the Advancement of Women.

[411] See the reports of the Executive Board of UN-Women: Report on the election of the Bureau, 8 January 2019, and on the first regular session, 12 February 2019 (UNW/2019/1); Report on the annual session of 2019, 18 to 20 June 2019 (UNW/2019/5); Report on the second regular session of 2019, 9 to 10 September 2019 (UNW/2019/9) and the Report of the joint meeting of the Executive Boards of UNDP/UNFPA/UNOPS, UNICEF, UN-Women and WFP, 31 May 2019.

Secretary-General/Executive Director on the Strategic Plan 2018–2021"; decision 2019/5, entitled "Report on the evaluation function of the United Nations Entity for Gender Equality and the Empowerment of Women, 2018"; decision 2019/6, entitled "Report on internal audit and investigation activities for the period from 1 January to 31 December 2018"; decision 2019/7, entitled "Implementation of General Assembly Resolution 72/279 on repositioning of the United Nations development system"; decision 2019/8, entitled "Working methods of the Executive Boards"; and decision 2019/9, entitled "UN-Women policies and procedures to tackle sexual exploitation and abuse and sexual harassment".

(*b*) Commission on the Status of Women

The Commission on the Status of Women was established by the Economic and Social Council in its resolution 11 (II) 21 June 1946 as a functional commission to deal with questions relating to gender equality and the advancement of women. It is the principal global policy-making body in this field and prepares recommendations for and reports to the Economic and Social Council on the promotion of women's rights in political, economic, civil, social and educational fields.

The Commission held its sixty-third session in New York from 11 to 22 March 2019.[412] In accordance with Economic and Social Council resolution 2016/3, the priority theme of the Commission was "Social protection systems, access to public services and sustainable infrastructure for gender equality and the empowerment of women and girls". It also considered as its review theme "Women's empowerment and the link to sustainable development", evaluating progress in the implementation of the agreed conclusions of its sixtieth session.

During its sixty-third session, the Commission adopted decision 63/101 entitled "Information from Non-Self-Governing Territories transmitted under Article 73 (*e*) of the Charter of the United Nations".

(*c*) Economic and Social Council

On 6 June 2019, the Economic and Social Council adopted resolution 2019/2 entitled "Mainstreaming a gender perspective into all policies and programmes in the United Nations system".

On the same day, the Council adopted decision 2019/212 entitled "Report of the Commission on the Status of Women on its sixty-third session and provisional agenda and documentation for the sixty-fourth session"; and decision 2019/213 entitled "Report of the Committee on the Elimination of Discrimination against Women on its seventieth, seventy-first and seventy-second sessions".

On 23 July 2019, it adopted resolution 2019/28 entitled "Situation of and assistance to Palestinian women".

---

[412] For report of the Commission on the Status of Women on its sixty-third session, see *Official Records of the Economic and Social Council, 2019, Supplement No. 7* (E/2019/27-E/CN.6/2019/19).

(*d*) General Assembly

On 18 December 2019, the General Assembly adopted, upon the recommendation of the Third Committee and without a vote, resolution 74/126 entitled "Improvement of the situation of women and girls in rural areas", resolution 74/127 entitled 'Violence against women migrant workers", and resolution 74/128 entitled "Follow-up to the Fourth World Conference on Women and full implementation of the Beijing Declaration and Platform for Action and the outcome of the twenty-third special session of the General Assembly".

On 19 December 2019, the General Assembly adopted, upon the recommendation of the Second Committee and without a vote, resolution 74/235 entitled "Women in development".

(*e*) Security Council

On 23 April 2019, the Security Council adopted resolution 2467 (2019) on Women and peace and security: Sexual violence in conflict.

On 17 September 2019, in its resolution 2489 (2019) on the situation in Afghanistan, the Security Council decided that the Special Representative of the Secretary-General will continue to lead and coordinate the international civilian efforts with a particular focus on supporting gender equality and women's and girls' empowerment, education, and human rights.

On 29 October 2019, the Security Council adopted resolution 2493 (2019) on Women in peace and security.

7. Humanitarian matters

(*a*) Economic and Social Council

On 19 July 2019, the Economic and Social Council adopted resolution 2019/14 entitled "Strengthening of the coordination of emergency humanitarian assistance of the United Nations", without a vote.

(*b*) General Assembly

On 12 December 2019, the General Assembly, upon the recommendation of the First Committee, adopted resolution 74/42 entitled "Humanitarian consequences of nuclear weapons", by a recorded vote of 144 to 13, with 28 abstentions.

On 13 December 2019, the General Assembly, upon the recommendation of the Fourth Committee, adopted resolution 74/83 entitled "Assistance to Palestine refugees" by a recorded vote of 169 to 2, with 9 abstentions.

On 16 December 2019, the General Assembly, without reference to a Main Committee and without a vote, adopted resolution 74/114 entitled "Persistent legacy of the Chernobyl disaster", resolution 74/115 entitled "International cooperation on humanitarian assistance in the field of natural disasters, from relief to development", resolution 74/116 entitled "Safety and security of humanitarian personnel and protection of United Nations personnel", resolution 74/117 entitled "Assistance to the Palestinian people" and resolution 74/118 entitled "Strengthening of the coordination of emergency humanitarian assistance of the United Nations".

On 18 December 2019, the General Assembly, upon the recommendation of the Third Committee and without a vote, adopted resolution 74/131 entitled "Assistance to refugees, returnees and displaced persons in Africa, resolution 74/148 entitled "Protection of migrants", and resolution 74/160 entitled "Protection of and assistance to internally displaced persons".

On 19 December 2019, the General Assembly, upon the recommendation of the Second Committee, adopted resolution 74/218 entitled "Disaster risk reduction", without a vote.

8. Environment

(*a*) United Nations Climate Change Conference in Madrid

The United Nations Climate Change Conference was held in Madrid, Spain, from 2 to 13 December 2019. The twenty-fifth session of the Conference of the Parties to the United Nations Framework Convention on Climate Change, 1992[413] (COP25), the fifteenth session of the Conference of the Parties serving as the meeting of Parties to the Kyoto Protocol, 1997[414] (CMP15), and the second session of the Conference of the Parties serving as the meeting of the Parties to the Paris Agreement, 2015[415] (CMA 2) were held during the Conference.

The Conference of States Parties to the United Nations Framework Convention on Climate Change adopted 18 decisions and one resolution.[416] The Conference of the Parties serving as the meeting of Parties to the Kyoto Protocol adopted seven decisions and one resolution.[417] The second session of the Conference of the Parties serving as the meeting of the Parties to the Paris Agreement adopted nine decisions and one resolution.[418]

(*b*) Economic and Social Council

The High-level Political Forum on Sustainable Development (HLPF), United Nations' central platform for the follow-up and review of the 2030 Agenda for Sustainable Development and the Sustainable Development Goals (SDGs), provides for the full and effective participation of all States Members of the United Nations and States members of specialized agencies. The 2019 session of the HLPF was held from 9 to 18 July 2019, including the three-day ministerial segment from 16 to 18 July 2019. The theme of this year's forum was "Empowering people and ensuring inclusiveness and equality".

In accordance with paragraph 84 of the 2030 Agenda, Member States have decided that the HLPF shall carry out regular voluntary reviews of the 2030 Agenda which will include developed and developing countries as well as the United Nations entities and other stakeholders. The reviews are State-led, involving ministerial and other relevant high-level participants, and provide a platform for partnerships, including through the participation of major groups and other relevant stakeholders. In 2019, 47 countries

---

[413] United Nations, *Treaty Series*, vol. 1771, p. 107.

[414] *Ibid.*, vol. 2303, p. 162.

[415] *Ibid.*, vol. 3156, p. 79.

[416] For the report of the Conference of the Parties, see FCCC/CP/2019/13 and Add. 1 and Add.2.

[417] For the report of the Conference of the Parties, see FCCC/KP/CMP/2019/8 and Add.1.

[418] For the report of the Conference of the Parties, see FCCC/PA/CMA/2019/6 and Add.1.

volunteered to present their national voluntary reviews to the Forum.[419] The 2019 session of the Forum also reviewed six sustainable development goals in depth, including Quality Education (SDG 4); Decent Work and Economic Growth (SDG 8); Reduced Inequalities (SDG 10); Climate Action (SDG 13); Peace, Justice and Strong Institutions (SDG 16); and Partnerships for the Goals (SDG 17).

On 11 July 2019, the Economic and Social Council adopted resolution 2019/8 entitled "Report of the Committee for Development Policy on its twenty-first session", which concerns policy on sustainable development, without a vote. On 23 July 2019, the Economic and Social Council adopted resolution 2019/18 entitled "Education for Justice and the rule of law in the context of sustainable development", without a vote.

(*c*) General Assembly

During the seventy-third session, on 15 January 2019, the Assembly adopted resolution 73/283 entitled "The role of diamonds in fuelling conflict: breaking the link between the illicit transaction of rough diamonds and armed conflict as a contribution to prevention and settlement of conflicts", without reference to a Main Committee and without a vote. On 1 March 2019, the General Assembly adopted resolution 73/284 entitled "United Nations Decade on Ecosystem Restoration (2021–2030)", without reference to a Main Committee and without a vote.

On 9 May 2019, the Assembly adopted resolution 73/292 entitled "The 2020 United Nations Conference to Support the Implementation of Sustainable Development Goal 14: Conserve and sustainably use the oceans, seas and marine resources for sustainable development", without reference to a Main Committee and without a vote. On 28 May 2019, the Assembly adopted resolution 73/297 entitled "Cooperation between the United Nations and the International Fund for Saving the Aral Sea", without reference to a Main Committee and without a vote. On 16 September 2019, the Assembly adopted resolution 73/343 entitled "Tackling illicit trafficking in wildlife", without reference to a Main Committee and without a vote.

During the seventy-fourth session, on 24 and 25 September 2019, Heads of State and Government gathered at the United Nations Headquarters in New York for the High-level Political Forum on Sustainable Development under the auspices of the General Assembly (SDG Summit). The Summit resulted in the adoption of the Political Declaration, entitled "Gearing up for a Decade of Action and Delivery for Sustainable Development",[420] in which leaders called for a decade of action to deliver the Sustainable Development Goals by 2030 and announced actions they are taking to advance the agenda. Subsequently, on 15 October 2019, the General Assembly endorsed the declaration by adopting resolution 74/4 entitled "Political declaration of the high-level political forum on sustainable development convened under the auspices of the General Assembly", without reference to a Main Committee and without a vote.

---

[419] The High-level Political Forum, United Nations central platform for follow-up and review of the 2030 Agenda for Sustainable Development and the Sustainable Development Goals, provides for the full and effective participation of all States Members of the United Nations and States Members of specialized agencies, https://hlpf.un.org/2019.

[420] A/RES/74/4, annex.

On 10 December 2019, the General Assembly, without reference to a Main Committee, adopted: resolution 74/19 entitled "Oceans and the law of the sea", by a recorded vote of 135 in favor, 1 against, with 3 abstentions; resolution 74/18 entitled "Sustainable fisheries, including through the 1995 Agreement for the Implementation of the Provisions of the United Nations Convention on the Law of the Sea", without a vote. On 13 December 2019, the General Assembly, upon the recommendation of the Second Committee and without a vote, adopted resolution 74/81 entitled "Effects of atomic radiation".

On 19 December 2019, upon the recommendation of the Second Committee, the General Assembly adopted the following resolutions without a vote: resolution 74/209 entitled "International Day of Awareness of Food Loss and Waste"; resolution 74/210 entitled "Strengthening cooperation for integrated coastal zone management for achieving sustainable development"; resolution 74/211 entitled "Sustainable tourism and sustainable development in Central America"; resolution 74/212 entitled "International Day of Clean Air for blue skies"; resolution 74/213 entitled "Cooperative measures to assess and increase awareness of environmental effects related to waste originating from chemical munitions dumped at sea"; resolution 74/214 entitled "Sustainable tourism and sustainable development in Central Asia"; resolution 74/217 entitled "Follow-up to the SIDS Accelerated Modalities of Action (SAMOA) Pathway and the Mauritius Strategy for the Further Implementation of the Programme of Action for the Sustainable Development of Small Island Developing States"; resolution 74/218 entitled "Disaster risk reduction"; resolution 74/219 entitled "Protection of global climate for present and future generations of humankind"; resolution 74/220 entitled "Implementation of the United Nations Convention to Combat Desertification in Those Countries Experiencing Serious Drought and/or Desertification, Particularly in Africa"; resolution 74/221 entitled "Implementation of the Convention on Biological Diversity and its contribution to sustainable development"; resolution 74/222 entitled "Report of the United Nations Environment Assembly of the United Nations Environment Programme"; resolution 74/223 entitled "Education for sustainable development in the framework of the 2030 Agenda for Sustainable Development"; resolution 74/225 entitled "Ensuring access to affordable, reliable, sustainable and modern energy for all".

On the same day, the General Assembly also adopted the following resolutions, upon the recommendations of the Second Committee: resolution 74/208 entitled "Oil slick on Lebanese shores", by a recorded vote of 162 in favor, 7 against, with 7 abstentions; resolution 74/215 entitled "Agricultural technology for sustainable development", by a recorded vote of 154 in favor, 2 against, with 26 abstentions; resolution 74/216 entitled "Implementation of Agenda 21, the Programme for the Further Implementation of Agenda 21 and the outcomes of the World Summit on Sustainable Development and of the United Nations Conference on Sustainable Development", by a recorded vote of 131 in favor, 2 against, with 49 abstentions; resolution 74/224 entitled "Harmony with Nature", by a recorded vote of 134 in favor, 2 against, with 45 abstentions; and resolution 74/226 entitled "Combating sand and dust storms", by a recorded vote of 177 in favor, 2 against, with 1 abstention.

9. Law of the Sea

(*a*) Reports of the Secretary-General

Pursuant to paragraph 370 of General Assembly resolution 73/124 of 31 December 2018, the Secretary-General submitted a comprehensive report on oceans and the law of the sea[421] to the General Assembly at its seventy-fourth session, under agenda item 74 entitled "Oceans and the law of the sea".

The first part of the report[422] was prepared to facilitate discussions on the topic of focus of the twentieth meeting of the United Nations Open-ended Informal Consultative Process on Oceans and the Law of the Sea ("Informal Consultative Process"), namely "Ocean Science and the United Nations Decade of Ocean Science for Sustainable Development". The report provided an overview of ocean science and its role (scope of ocean science and its cross-cutting nature for sustainable development); elaborated on gaps in knowledge and ocean science, following a presentation of the current state of knowledge; as well as on means of advancing ocean science and addressing related gaps (implementation of the Convention and its implementing agreement, development of technology and data infrastructures; integration of traditional knowledge, strengthening the science-policy interface and the capacity to carry out research, through the implementation of the United Nations Decade of Ocean Science for Sustainable Development (2021–2030), and by promoting international cooperation and coordination).

The second part of the report[423] provided a comprehensive overview of developments relating to the implementation of the United Nations Convention on the Law of the Sea[424] (the "Convention") and the work of the Organization, its specialized agencies and other institutions in the field of ocean affairs and the law of the sea. The report outlined the developments that had taken place in 2019 with regard to the Convention, including the bodies established thereunder[425] as well as the legal and policy framework;[426] the human dimension;[427] maritime safety and security;[428] climate change;[429] balancing economic growth with environmental protection and social development;[430] and strengthening implementation through integrated and cross-sectoral approaches.[431]

(*b*) Consideration by the General Assembly

(i) *Oceans and law of the sea*

During the seventy-third session, on 9 May 2019, the General Assembly, without reference to a Main Committee, adopted resolution 73/292 entitled "2020 United Nations Conference to Support the Implementation of Sustainable Development Goal 14: Conserve and sustainably use the oceans, seas and marine resources for sustainable development", by which it decided to convene the high-level 2020 United Nations Conference to Support

---

421 A/74/70 and A/74/350.

422 A/74/70.

423 A/74/350.

424 United Nations, *Treaty Series*, vol. 1833, p. 3.

425 A/74/350, chap. III.

426 *Ibid*., chap. II.

427 *Ibid*., chap. IV.

428 *Ibid*., chap. IV.

429 *Ibid*., chap. VI.

430 *Ibid*., chap. VII.

431 *Ibid*., chap. VIII.

the Implementation of Sustainable Development Goal 14: Conserve and sustainably use the oceans, seas and marine resources for sustainable development in Lisbon, from 2 to 6 June 2020, to support the implementation of Sustainable Development Goal 14.[432]

During the seventy-fourth session, the General Assembly considered the agenda item 74 entitled "Oceans and the law of the sea" on 10 December 2019, having before it the following documents: the above-mentioned report of the Secretary-General;[433] the report on the work of the Ad Hoc Working Group of the Whole on the Regular Process for Global Reporting and Assessment of the State of the Marine Environment, including Socioeconomic Aspects ("the Regular Process");[434] the report on the work of the Informal Consultative Process at its twentieth meeting;[435] and the report of the twenty-ninth Meeting of States Parties to the Convention.[436]

On 10 December 2019, the General Assembly, without reference to a Main Committee, adopted resolution 74/19 entitled "Oceans and the law of the sea", by a recorded vote of 135 to 1, with 3 abstentions.

The resolution covers a wide range of ocean issues, such as the implementation of the Convention and related agreements and instruments; capacity-building; the Meeting of States Parties; peaceful settlement of disputes; the Area; effective functioning of the International Seabed Authority (ISA) and the International Tribunal for the Law of the Sea (ITLOS); the continental shelf and the work of the Commission on the Limits of the Continental Shelf (CLCS); maritime safety and security and flag State implementation; marine environment and marine resources; marine biodiversity; marine science; the Regular Process; the Informal Consultative Process; the activities of the Division for Ocean Affairs and the Law of the Sea (DOALOS); and the seventy-fifth session of the General Assembly. The General Assembly decided in the resolution to launch the third cycle of the Regular Process, to cover five years, from 2021 to 2025.

In relation to the Regular Process, the second part of the report of the Secretary-General noted the critical role of the Regular Process as the global mechanism to regularly review the environmental, economic and social aspects of the world's oceans and contribute to the strengthening of the regular scientific assessment of the state of the marine environment in order to enhance the scientific basis for policymaking. The report further noted that the preparation of the second World Ocean Assessment (WOA II), which is expected to be considered by the General Assembly in 2020, would be informed by, inter alia, the two rounds of regional workshops held in 2017 and 2018, respectively, and by a two-day multi-stakeholder dialogue and capacity-building partnership event held in 2019. The conclusions from this event, which provided an opportunity to build awareness and collaboration with respect to capacity-building in support of the Regular Process, have been approved by the twelfth meeting of the Ad Hoc Working Group of the Whole held in 2019.

---

[432] Noting with concern the situation concerning the coronavirus disease 2019 (COVID-19), the General Assembly, in its decision 74/548 of 13 April 2020, decided to postpone the Conference to a later date to be decided by the General Assembly and also decided to set, at a later stage, the new deadlines for its preparatory process.

[433] A/74/70 and A/74/350.

[434] A/74/315.

[435] A/74/119.

[436] SPLOS/29/9.

In its resolution 74/19, the General Assembly endorsed the recommendations adopted by the Ad Hoc Working Group of the Whole at its twelfth meeting and decided to launch the third cycle of the Regular Process from 2021 to 2025. Pursuant to the same resolution, the General Assembly requested the Bureau, with the assistance of the Group of Experts and the secretariat, to develop a draft programme of work for the third cycle, on the basis of the possible outcomes and building blocks of the third cycle prepared by the Bureau and endorsed by the Ad Hoc Working Group of the Whole at its twelfth meeting and taking into account lessons learned from the second cycle, and to report to Member States in advance of the thirteenth meeting of the Ad Hoc Working Group. The Assembly also requested the Secretary-General to prepare the resource requirements for the third cycle of the Regular Process on the basis of the draft programme of work for the third cycle, and to report to Member States in advance of the thirteenth meeting of the Ad Hoc Working Group of the Whole.

(ii) *Intergovernmental Conference on an international legally binding instrument under the United Nations Convention on the Law of the Sea on the conservation and sustainable use of marine biological diversity of areas beyond national jurisdiction*

Pursuant to resolution 73/124, the second and third sessions of the Intergovernmental Conference on an international legally binding instrument under the United Nations Convention on the Law of the Sea on the conservation and sustainable use of marine biological diversity of areas beyond national jurisdiction (the "BBNJ Intergovernmental Conference") took place from 25 March to 5 April 2019 and from 19 to 30 August 2019, respectively, at United Nations Headquarters. The Conference held substantive discussions on the four elements of the package of 2011 set out in paragraph 2 of General Assembly resolution 72/249 and on cross-cutting issues. At the second session, discussions were held on the basis of a "President's aid to negotiations"[437] prepared as requested by the Conference with the aim of facilitating focused discussions and text-based negotiations. At the third session, the negotiations were guided by a draft text of an agreement under the Convention on the conservation and sustainable use of marine biological diversity of areas beyond national jurisdiction.[438] In its resolution 74/19, the General Assembly requested the Secretary-General to convene the fourth session of the Conference from 23 March to 3 April 2020.[439]

(iii) *Sustainable fisheries*

At its meeting on 10 December 2019, the General Assembly also considered agenda item 74 (*b*) entitled "Oceans and the law of the sea: sustainable fisheries, including through the 1995 Agreement for the Implementation of the Provisions of the United Nations Convention on the Law of the Sea of 10 December 1982 relating to the Conservation and Management of Straddling Fish Stocks and Highly Migratory Fish Stocks, and

---

[437] A/CONF.232/2019/1.

[438] A/CONF.232/2019/6, annex.

[439] Noting with concern the situation concerning the coronavirus disease 2019 (COVID-19), the General Assembly, in its decision 74/543 of 11 March 2020, decided to postpone the fourth session of the Conference to the earliest possible available date to be decided by the General Assembly.

related instruments". On the same day, the General Assembly, without reference to a Main Committee, adopted resolution 74/18 entitled, "Sustainable fisheries, including through the 1995 Agreement for the Implementation of the Provisions of the United Nations Convention on the Law of the Sea of 10 December 1982 relating to the Conservation and Management of Straddling Fish Stocks and Highly Migratory Fish Stocks, and related instruments", without a vote.

The resolution is divided into 14 chapters and addresses a number of issues, including: achieving sustainable fisheries; implementation of the 1995 United Nations Fish Stocks Agreement and related fisheries instruments; illegal, unreported and unregulated fishing; monitoring, control and surveillance and compliance and enforcement; fishing overcapacity; large-scale pelagic drift-net fishing; fisheries by-catch and discards; subregional and regional cooperation; responsible fisheries in the marine ecosystem; capacity-building; cooperation within the United Nations system; and activities of DOALOS.

Among other things, the General Assembly noted the agreement at the fourteenth round of informal consultations of States parties to the United Nations Fish Stocks Agreement that the Review Conference on the Agreement should be resumed in 2021, and requested the Secretary-General to resume the Review Conference, convened pursuant to article 36 of the Agreement, in New York for one week in the first part of 2021, with a view to assessing the effectiveness of the Agreement in securing the conservation and management of straddling fish stocks and highly migratory fish stocks, and to render the necessary assistance and provide such services as may be required for the resumption of the Review Conference. The Assembly also took note of the report of the fourteenth round of informal consultations of States parties to the Agreement, focusing on the topic "Performance reviews of regional fisheries management organizations and arrangements" and requested the Secretary-General to convene the fifteenth round of informal consultations of States parties to the Agreement for three days in May 2020: two days to focus on the topic "Implementation of an ecosystem approach to fisheries management" and one day to serve as a preparatory meeting for the resumed Review Conference.

(*c*) Consideration by the Meeting of States Parties to the United Nations Convention on the Law of the Sea

A resumed twenty-eighth Meeting of States Parties[440] was held for the purpose of filling vacancies in the CLCS. The Meeting elected one member of the Commission to fill a seat allocated to the Group of Asia-Pacific States for the remainder of the term of office of the resigning member of the CLCS. No nomination was received from the Group of Eastern European States for the remaining vacancy in the CLCS. The Meeting decided that an election to fill that vacancy would be held at the twenty-ninth Meeting of States Parties if nomination(s) were received from that Group by 10 March 2019. No nominations were received by that deadline.

The twenty-ninth Meeting of States Parties[441] commemorated the twenty-fifth anniversary of the entry into force of the Convention, with opening remarks delivered by the

[440] *See* SPLOS/327.

[441] *See* SPLOS/29/9.

Secretary-General. Delegations underscored the achievements of the Convention as the "constitution for the oceans", recalling that it set out the legal framework within which all activities in the oceans and seas must be carried out. The Meeting took note of the reports presented by ITLOS as well as of the information reported on the ISA and on the CLCS. No nomination was received for the remaining vacancy in the CLCS allocated to the Group of Eastern European States. As was the case at the twenty-seventh, twenty-eighth and resumed twenty-eighth Meetings of States Parties, the Meeting decided that if nomination(s) were received from that Group by an agreed date, a by-election would be held at a resumed twenty-ninth Meeting of States Parties. No nominations were received by the deadline of 16 September 2019.

The Secretary-General's report was also submitted to the twenty-ninth Meeting of States Parties to the Convention, in accordance with article 319 thereof. In their deliberation under agenda item entitled "Report of the Secretary-General under article 319 for the information of States Parties on issues of a general nature, relevant to States Parties, which have arisen with respect to the United Nations Convention on the Law of the Sea", States Parties addressed, *inter alia*, the importance of the oceans and the effective implementation of the Convention, including for the sustainable development of the oceans and seas and their resources, in particular in the context of Goal 14 of the 2030 Agenda for Sustainable Development; the role of the Convention in maintaining international peace and security; and the need for capacity-building and cross-sectoral cooperation and coordination in the sustainable development of the oceans and seas. Delegations expressed support for the ongoing work and progress of the BBNJ Intergovernmental Conference. Delegations highlighted the importance of both ocean science and gender equality for the sustainable development of the ocean and its resources and also addressed: the threats and pressures faced by the marine environment; the adverse effects of climate change on oceans and the related vulnerabilities of developing States; the unsafe movement of people by sea; illegal, unreported, and unregulated fishing; maritime security and safety; situations in specific maritime regions, including the Black Sea, the Sea of Azov and the Strait of Kerch and the South China Sea; and the progress in the work of the institutions established under the Convention.

(*d*) Capacity-Building

The General Assembly has stressed the importance of capacity-building for ensuring that States, especially developing States, are able to fully implement the Convention, benefit from the sustainable development of the oceans and seas and participate fully in global and regional forums.[442] In 2019, DOALOS engaged in capacity-building activities to promote wider appreciation of the Convention and assist in its implementation, including through a training programme on marine scientific research in partnership with the Intergovernmental Oceanographic Commission; through implementation of the Hamilton Shirley Amerasinghe Memorial Fellowship on the Law of the Sea, the United Nations—Nippon Foundation Fellowship and Alumni Programme, and, under the United Nations—Nippon Foundation Sustainable Ocean Programme, two Fellowship Programmes and a training programme in the context of negotiations ongoing in the BBNJ Intergovernmental Conference; and through a technical assistance project to support participating developing

---

[442] UNGA Resolution 74/19, para. 11. See also UNGA Resolution 74/18, para. 228.

States to realize economic benefits from the sustainable use of marine resources, implemented together with the United Nations Conference on Trade and Development.[443]

DOALOS also continued to administer various other trust funds to assist developing States in the implementation of certain provisions of the Convention and to support their participation in various ocean-related forums,[444] while other entities, including intergovernmental organizations, also engaged in capacity-building activities in the ocean sphere.[445] In 2019, particular consideration was given to the need for, and existing opportunities with respect to, capacity-building in the context of ocean science and the United Nations Decade of Ocean Science for Sustainable Development, the topic of focus for the twentieth meeting of the Informal Consultative Process.[446] Together with the transfer of marine technology, capacity-building is one of the issues being considered in the context of the BBNJ Intergovernmental Conference.

10. Crime prevention and criminal justice[447]

(*a*) Commission on Crime Prevention and Criminal Justice

The Commission on Crime Prevention and Criminal Justice (the Commission) was established by the Economic and Social Council in its resolution 1992/1 of 6 February 1992 as a functional commission to deal with a broad scope of policy matters in this field, including combating national and transnational crime, covering organized crime, economic crime and money laundering; promoting the role of criminal law in environmental protection, crime prevention in urban areas, including juvenile crime and violence; and improving the efficiency and fairness of criminal justice administration systems. Aspects of these principal themes are selected for discussion at each of its annual sessions. The Commission also provides substantive and organizational direction for the quinquennial United Nations Congress on Crime Prevention and Criminal Justice.

The Commission held its twenty-eighth session from 20 to 24 May 2019.[448] The main theme for the twenty-eighth session of the Commission was "The responsibility of effective, fair, humane and accountable criminal justice systems in preventing and countering crime motivated by intolerance or discrimination of any kind".

(*b*) Economic and Social Council

On 23 July 2019, the Economic and Social Council, upon the recommendation of the Commission on Crime Prevention and Criminal Justice, adopted the following

[443] UNGA Resolution 74/19, paras. 46–48, 51, 53; A/74/350, paras. 103–108. https://www.un.org/Depts/los/general_assembly/DOALOSList1Sep201831Aug.pdf.

[444] *See* https://www.un.org/Depts/los/general_assembly/TrustFunds.pdf.

[445] *See, e.g.* UNGA Resolution 74/19, paras. 23–24, 26–33, 40–41; A/74/350, paras. 26, 49, 97, 101–102.

[446] A/74/70, particularly paras. 49–56.

[447] For more detailed information and documents regarding this topic generally, see the website of the United Nations Office on Drugs and Crimes at https://www.unodc.org.

[448] See *Official Records of the Economic and Social Council, 2018, Supplement No. 10* and *Supplement No. 10A* (E/2018/30 and Add.1).

resolutions and decisions and recommended their adoptions by the General Assembly: resolution 2019/16 entitled "Integrating sport into youth crime prevention and criminal justice strategies"; resolution 2019/17 entitled "Follow-up to the Thirteenth United Nations Congress on Crime Prevention and Criminal Justice and preparations for the Fourteenth United Nations Congress on Crime Prevention and Criminal Justice"; resolution 2019/18 entitled "Education for Justice and the rule of law in the context of sustainable development"; resolution 2019/19 entitled "Promoting technical assistance and capacity-building to strengthen national measures and international cooperation to combat cybercrime, including information-sharing"; resolution 2019/20 entitled "Countering child sexual exploitation and sexual abuse online"; resolution 2019/21 entitled "Technical assistance provided by the United Nations Office on Drugs and Crime related to counter-terrorism"; resolution 2019/22 entitled "Enhancing transparency in the judicial process"; resolution 2019/23 entitled "Combating transnational organized crime and its links to illicit trafficking in precious metals and illegal mining, including by enhancing the security of supply chains of precious metals"; decision 2019/222 entitled "Report of the Commission on Crime Prevention and Criminal Justice on its reconvened twenty-seventh session"; and decision 2019/223 entitled "Report of the Commission on Crime Prevention and Criminal Justice on its twenty-eighth session and provisional agenda for the twenty-ninth session of the Commission".

(*c*) General Assembly

At the seventy-third session, on 2 April 2019, the General Assembly adopted resolution 73/285, entitled "Combating terrorism and other acts of violence based on religion or belief", without reference to a Main Committee and without a vote. On 20 June 2019, the General Assembly adopted resolution 73/302, entitled "United Nations action on sexual exploitation and abuse", without reference to a Main Committee and without a vote. On 28 June 2019, the General Assembly adopted resolution 73/305, entitled "Enhancement of international cooperation to assist victims of terrorism", without reference to a Main Committee and without a vote.

At the seventy-fourth session, on 18 December 2019, the General Assembly adopted, on the recommendation of the Third Committee and without a vote, the following resolutions: resolution 74/170, entitled "Integrating sport into youth crime prevention and criminal justice strategies"; resolution 74/171, entitled "Follow-up to the Thirteenth United Nations Congress on Crime Prevention and Criminal Justice and preparations for the Fourteenth United Nations Congress on Crime Prevention and Criminal Justice"; resolution 74/172, entitled "Education for Justice and the rule of law in the context of sustainable development"; resolution 74/173, entitled "Promoting technical assistance and capacity-building to strengthen national measures and international cooperation to combat cybercrime, including information-sharing"; resolution 74/174, entitled "Countering child sexual exploitation and sexual abuse online"; resolution 74/175, entitled "Technical assistance provided by the United Nations Office on Drugs and Crime related to counter-terrorism"; resolution 74/176, entitled "Improving the coordination of efforts against trafficking in persons"; resolution 74/177, entitled "Strengthening the United Nations crime prevention and criminal justice programme, in particular its technical cooperation capacity"; and resolution 74/178, entitled "International cooperation to address and counter the world drug problem".

On 27 December 2019, the General Assembly adopted, on the recommendation of the Third Committee, resolution 74/247, entitled "Countering the use of information and communications technologies for criminal purposes", by a recorded vote of 79 in favour, 60 against, with 33 abstentions.

11. International drug control

(*a*) Commission on Narcotic Drugs

The Commission on Narcotic Drugs (CND) was established by the Economic and Social Council in its resolution 9 (I) of 16 February 1946, to assist the Council in supervising the application of the international drug control treaties. In 1991, the General Assembly expanded the mandate of the Commission to enable it to function as the governing body of the United Nations Office on Drugs and Crime. The Economic and Social Council resolution 1999/30 of 28 July 1999 requested the Commission to structure its agenda with two distinct segments: a normative segment for discharging treaty-based and normative functions; and an operational segment for exercising the role of the governing body of the United Nations Office on Drugs and Crime.

The regular and reconvened sixty-second session of the Commission was held in Vienna from 14 to 22 March 2019, and from 12 to 13 December 2019, respectively.[449] The Commission recommended three draft decisions for adoption by the Economic and Social Council. It further brought nine resolutions and 14 decisions to the attention of the Economic and Social Council, the text of which is available in the reports of the Commission.[450]

(*b*) Economic and Social Council

On 23 July 2019, the Economic and Social Council adopted decision 2019/224 entitled "Report of the Commission on Narcotic Drugs on its reconvened sixtieth session"; decision 2019/225 entitled "Report of the Commission on Narcotic Drugs on its sixty-third session and provisional agenda for its sixty-third session"; and decision 2019/226 entitled "Report of the International Narcotics Control Board".

(*c*) General Assembly

On 18 December 2019, the General Assembly adopted, on the recommendation of the Third Committee and without a vote, resolution 74/178 entitled "International cooperation to address and counter the world drug problem".

12. Refugees and displaced persons

[449] For the reports of the sixty-second session of the Commission on Narcotic Drugs, see *Official records of the Economic and Social Council 2019, Supplement No. 8* and *Supplement No. 8A* (E/2019/28 and Add.1).

[450] E/2019/28 and E/2019/28/Add.1.

(*a*) Executive Committee of the Programme of the United Nations High Commissioner for Refugees[451]

The Executive Committee of the Programme of the United Nations High Commissioner for Refugees (UNHCR) was established by the Economic and Social Council in 1958 and functions as a subsidiary organ of the General Assembly, reporting to it through the Third Committee. The Executive Committee meets annually in Geneva to review and approve the programmes and budget of the UNHCR and its intergovernmental and non-governmental partners. The seventieth session of the Executive Committee was held in Geneva from 7 to 11 October 2019.[452]

(*b*) General Assembly

At the seventy-third session, on 4 June 2019, the General Assembly adopted, without reference to a Main Committee, resolution 73/298 entitled "Status of internally displaced persons and refugees from Abkhazia, Georgia, and the Tskhinvali region/South Ossetia, Georgia", by a recorded vote of 79 to 15, with 57 abstentions.

On 19 July 2019, the General Assembly adopted, without reference to a Main Committee, resolution 73/326 entitled "Format and organizational aspects of the international migration review forums", by a recorded vote of 118 to 5, with 3 abstentions.

At the seventy-fourth session, on 13 December 2019, the Assembly adopted, on the recommendation of the Fourth Committee, resolution 74/83 entitled "Assistance to Palestine refugees", by a recorded vote of 169 to 2, with 9 abstentions; resolution 74/84 entitled "Persons displaced as a result of the June 1967 and subsequent hostilities", by a recorded vote of 162 to 7, with 11 abstentions; resolution 74/85 entitled "Operations of the United Nations Relief and Works Agency for Palestine Refugees in the Near East", by a recorded vote of 167 to 6, with 7 abstentions; and resolution 74/86, entitled "Palestine refugees' properties and their revenues", by a recorded vote of 163 to 6, with 12 abstentions.

On 18 December 2019, the General Assembly adopted, on the recommendation of the Third Committee, resolution 74/129 entitled "Enlargement of the Executive Committee of the UNHCR Programme" without a vote; resolution 74/130 entitled "Office of the United Nations High Commissioner for Refugees", by a recorded vote of 179 to 2, with 5 abstentions; resolution 74/131 entitled "Assistance to refugees, returnees and displaced persons in Africa", without a vote; and resolution 74/148 entitled "Protection of migrants", without a vote.

---

[451] For detailed information and documents regarding this topic see the website of the UNHCR at https://www.unhcr.org.

[452] For the report of the United Nations High Commissioner for Refugees on the activities of his Office, see *Official Records of the General Assembly, Seventieth-third Session, Supplement No. 12* (A/74/12 (Part I) and A/74/12 (Part II)). For the report of the sixty-ninth session of the Executive Committee of the High Commissioner's Programme, see *Official Records of the General Assembly, Seventieth Session, Supplement No. 12A* (A/74/12/Add.1).

13. International Court of Justice[453]

(*a*) Organization of the Court

At the end of 2019, the composition of the Court was as follows:

President: Mr. Abdulqawi Ahmed Yusuf (Somalia);

Vice-President: Ms. Xue Hanqin (China);

Judges: Mr. Peter Tomka (Slovakia), Mr. Ronny Abraham (France), Mr. Mohamed Bennouna (Morocco), Mr. Antônio Augusto Cançado Trindade (Brazil), Ms. Joan E. Donoghue (United States of America), Mr. Giorgio Gaja (Italy), Ms. Julia Sebutinde (Uganda), Mr. Dalveer Bhandari (India), Mr. Patrick Lipton Robinson (Jamaica), Mr. James Richard Crawford (Australia), Mr. Kirill Gevorgian (Russian Federation), Mr. Nawaf Salam (Lebanon) and Mr. Iwasawa Yuji (Japan).

The Registrar of the Court was Philippe Gautier (Belgium); the Deputy-Registrar was Jean-Pelé Fomété (Cameroon).

The Chamber of Summary Procedure, comprising five judges, including the President and Vice-President, and two substitutes, which is established annually by the Court in accordance with Article 29 of the Statute of the International Court of Justice to ensure the speedy dispatch of business, was composed as follows:

Members:

President Yusuf;

Vice-President Xue;

Judges Cançado Trindade, Sebutinde and Gevorgian.

Substitute members:

Judges Donoghue and Crawford.

(*b*) Jurisdiction of the Court[454]

Two declarations were made by India and Latvia in 2019 recognizing the compulsory jurisdiction of the Court, as contemplated by Article 36, paragraph 2, of the Statute. Thus, as of 31 December 2019, 74 States had recognized such compulsory jurisdiction.

(*c*) General Assembly

During the seventy-third session, on 22 May 2019, the General Assembly adopted, without reference to a Main Committee, resolution 73/295, entitled "Advisory Opinion of

---

[453] For more information about the Court, see the reports of the International Court of Justice to the General Assembly, *Official Records of the General Assembly, Seventieth-fourth Session, Supplement No. 4* (A/74/4) (for the period 1 August 2018 to 31 July 2019) and *ibid., Seventy-fifth Session, Supplement No. 4* (A/75/4) (for the period 1 August 2019 to 31 July 2020). See also the website of the Court at https://www.icj-cij.org.

[454] For further information regarding the acceptance of the compulsory jurisdiction of the International Court of Justice, see chapter I.4 of *Multilateral Treaties Deposited with the Secretary-General,* available on the website https://treaties.un.org/Pages/ParticipationStatus.aspx.

the International Court of Justice on the legal consequences of the separation of the Chagos Archipelago from Mauritius in 1965", by a recorded vote of 116 to 6, with 56 abstentions.

During the seventy-fourth session, on 30 October 2019, the General Assembly adopted, without reference to a Main Committee, decision 74/505, in which it took note of the report of the International Court of Justice for the period from 1 August 2018 to 31 July 2019.

On 12 December 2019, the Assembly adopted, on the recommendation of the First Committee, resolution 74/59 entitled "Follow-up to the advisory opinion of the International Court of Justice on the legality of the threat or use of nuclear weapons", by a recorded vote of 138 to 33, with 15 abstentions.

14. International Law Commission[455]

(*a*) Membership of the Commission[456]

The membership of the International Law Commission at its seventy-first session consisted of Ali Mohsen Fetais Al-Marri (Qatar), Carlos J. Argüello Gómez (Nicaragua), Bogdan Aurescu (Romania), Yacouba Cissé (Côte d'Ivoire), Concepción Escobar Hernández (Spain), Patrícia Galvão Teles (Portugal), Juan Manuel Gómez Robledo (Mexico), Claudio Grossman Guiloff (Chile), Hussein A. Hassouna (Egypt), Mahmoud D. Hmoud (Jordan), Huikang Huang (China), Charles Chernor Jalloh (Sierra Leone), Ahmed Laraba (Algeria), Marja Lehto (Finland), Shinya Murase (Japan), Sean D. Murphy (United States of America), Hong Thao Nguyen (Viet Nam), Georg Nolte (Germany), Nilüfer Oral (Turkey), Hassan Ouazzani Chahdi (Morocco), Ki Gab Park (Republic of Korea), Chris Maina Peter (United Republic of Tanzania), Ernest Petrič (Slovenia), Aniruddha Rajput (India), August Reinisch (Austria), Juan José Ruda Santolaria (Peru), Gilberto Vergne Saboia (Brazil), Pavel Šturma (Czech Republic), Dire D. Tladi (South Africa), Eduardo Valencia-Ospina (Colombia), Marcelo Vázquez-Bermúdez (Ecuador), Amos S. Wako (Kenya), Michael Wood (United Kingdom of Great Britain and Northern Ireland) and Evgeny Zagaynov (Russian Federation).

(*b*) Seventy-first session of the International Law Commission

The International Law Commission held the first part of its seventy-first session from 29 April to 7 June 2019 and the second part from 8 July to 9 August 2019 at its seat at the United Nations Office at Geneva.[457] The Commission continued its consideration of the following topics: "Crimes against humanity", "Peremptory norms of general international law (*jus cogens*)", "Protection of the environment in relation to armed conflicts", "Succession of

---

[455] Detailed information and documents relating to the work of the International Law Commission may be found on the Commission's website at https://www.un.org/law/ilc/.

[456] Pursuant to article 10 of the Statute of the International Law Commission, the election of the members of the Commission for a five-year term, beginning on 1 January 2017 (until 31 December 2021), took place by secret ballot, at the 40th meeting of the General Assembly at its seventy-first session, held on 3 November 2016.

[457] For the report of the International Law Commission on the work at its seventy-first session, see *Official Records of the General Assembly, Seventy-fourth Session, Supplement No. 10* (A/74/10).

States in respect of State responsibility", "Immunity of State officials from foreign criminal jurisdiction", "General principles of law", and "Sea-level rise in relation to international law".

With respect to the topic "Crimes against humanity", the Commission had before it the fourth report of the Special Rapporteur,[458] as well as comments and observations received from Governments, international organizations and others.[459] The fourth report addressed the comments and observations made by Governments, international organizations and others on the draft articles and commentaries adopted on first reading and made recommendations for each draft article. The Commission adopted, on second reading, the entire set of draft articles on prevention and punishment of crimes against humanity, comprising a draft preamble, 15 draft articles and a draft annex, together with commentaries thereto. The Commission decided, in conformity with article 23 of its statute, to recommend the draft articles on prevention and punishment of crimes against humanity to the General Assembly. In particular, the Commission recommended the elaboration of a convention by the General Assembly or by an international conference of plenipotentiaries on the basis of the draft articles.[460]

With regard to the topic "Peremptory norms of general international law (*jus cogens*)", the Commission had before it the fourth report of the Special Rapporteur,[461] which discussed the question of the existence of regional *jus cogens* and the inclusion of an illustrative list, based on norms previously recognized by the Commission as possessing a peremptory character. Following the plenary debate, the Commission decided to refer the draft conclusion proposed in the fourth report to the Drafting Committee. The Commission subsequently adopted, on first reading, 23 draft conclusions and a draft annex, together with commentaries thereto, on peremptory norms of general international law (*jus cogens*). The Commission decided, in accordance with articles 16 to 21 of its statute, to transmit the draft conclusions, through the Secretary-General, to Governments for comments and observations, with the request that such comments and observations be submitted to the Secretary-General by 1 December 2020.[462]

With respect to the topic "Protection of the environment in relation to armed conflicts", the Commission had before it the second report of the Special Rapporteur,[463] which discussed questions related to the protection of the environment in non-international armed conflicts, and matters related to responsibility and liability for environmental damage. Following the plenary debate, the Commission decided to refer the seven draft principles, as proposed by the Special Rapporteur in her second report, to the Drafting Committee. As a result of its consideration of the topic at the present session, the Commission adopted, on first reading, 28 draft principles, together with commentaries thereto, on protection of the environment in relation to armed conflicts. The Commission decided, in accordance with articles 16 to 21 of its statute, to transmit the draft principles, through the Secretary-General, to Governments, international organizations, including from the United Nations and its Environment Programme, and others, including the International Committee of the Red Cross and the

[458] A/CN.4/725 and Add.1.

[459] A/CN.4/726, Add.1 and Add.2.

[460] *Official Records of the General Assembly, Seventy-fourth Session, Supplement No. 10* (A/74/10), chap. IV.

[461] A/CN.4/727.

[462] *Official Records of the General Assembly, Seventy-fourth Session, Supplement No. 10* (A/74/10), chap. V.

[463] A/CN.4/728.

Environmental Law Institute, for comments and observations, with the request that such comments and observations be submitted to the Secretary-General by 1 December 2020.[464]

With regard to the topic "Succession of States in respect of State responsibility", the Commission had before it the third report of the Special Rapporteur,[465] which addressed introductory issues, including certain general considerations, questions of reparation for injury resulting from internationally wrongful acts committed against the predecessor State as well as its nationals, and technical proposals in relation to the scheme of the draft articles. Following the debate in plenary, the Commission decided to refer draft articles 2, paragraph (*f*), X, Y, 12, 13, 14 and 15, and the titles of Part Two and Part Three, as contained in the third report of the Special Rapporteur, to the Drafting Committee. Upon its consideration of a first report of the Drafting Committee, the Commission provisionally adopted draft articles 1, 2 and 5, with commentaries thereto. Furthermore, the Commission took note of the interim report of the Chair of the Drafting Committee on draft articles 7, 8 and 9 provisionally adopted by the Committee, which was presented to the Commission for information only.[466]

With regard to the topic "Immunity of State officials from foreign criminal jurisdiction", the Commission had before it the sixth[467] and the seventh[468] reports of the Special Rapporteur, which were devoted to addressing procedural aspects of immunity from foreign criminal jurisdiction. In particular, the sixth report, on which the debate was not completed at the seventieth session in 2018, provided an analysis of three components of procedural aspects related to the concept of jurisdiction, namely: (*a*) timing; (*b*) kinds of acts affected; and (*c*) the determination of immunity. The seventh report completed the examination of the procedural aspects of immunity regarding the relationship between jurisdiction and the procedural aspects of immunity; addressed questions concerning the invocation of immunity and the waiver of immunity; examined aspects concerning procedural safeguards related to the State of the forum and the State of the official, considered the procedural rights and safeguards of the official, and proposed nine draft articles. Following the debate in plenary, the Commission decided to refer draft articles 8 to 16 to the Drafting Committee, taking into account the debate and proposals made in plenary. The Commission received and took note of the interim report of the Chair of the Drafting Committee on draft article 8 *ante*, which was presented to the Commission for information only.[469]

With regard to the topic "General principles of law", the Commission had before it the first report of the Special Rapporteur,[470] which addressed the scope of the topic and the main issues to be addressed in the course of the work of the Commission. The report also addressed previous work of the Commission related to general principles of law and provided an overview of the development of general principles of law over time, as well as an initial assessment of certain basic aspects of the topic and future work on the topic. Following the debate in plenary, the Commission decided to refer draft conclusions 1 to 3,

---

[464] *Official Records of the General Assembly, Seventy-fourth Session, Supplement No. 10* (A/74/10), chap. VI.

[465] A/CN.4/731.

[466] *Official Records of the General Assembly, Seventy-fourth Session, Supplement No. 10* (A/74/10), chap. VII.

[467] A/CN.4/722.

[468] A/CN.4/729.

[469] *Official Records of the General Assembly, Seventy-fourth Session, Supplement No. 10* (A/74/10), chap. VIII.

[470] A/CN.4/732.

as contained in the report of the Special Rapporteur, to the Drafting Committee. The Commission subsequently took note of the interim report of the Chair of the Drafting Committee on draft conclusion 1 provisionally adopted by the Committee, which was presented to the Commission for information only.[471]

With respect to the topic "Sea-level rise in relation to international law", the Commission decided to include the topic in its programme of work and established a Study Group, to be co-chaired, on a rotating basis, by Mr. Bogdan Aurescu, Mr. Yacouba Cissé, Ms. Patrícia Galvão Teles, Ms. Nilüfer Oral and Mr. Juan José Ruda Santolaria. The Study Group held one meeting, at which time it agreed on its composition, methods and programme of work, based on the three subtopics identified in the syllabus. The Commission subsequently took note of the joint oral report of the Co-Chairs of the Study Group.[472]

As regards "Other decisions and conclusions of the Commission", the Commission took note of an oral report of the Special Rapporteur on the topic "Provisional application of treaties", Mr. Juan Manuel Gómez Robledo, on the informal consultations convened to consider the draft model clauses on provisional application of treaties, and decided to annex the Special Rapporteur's revised proposal for the draft model clauses to the report, with a view to seeking comments from Governments in advance of the commencement of the second reading of the draft Guide to Provisional Application of Treaties at the seventy-second session of the Commission.[473]

Also, the Commission re-established a Planning Group to consider its programme, procedures and working methods, which in turn decided to re-establish the Working Group on the long-term programme of work, chaired by Mr. Mahmoud D. Hmoud, and the Working Group on methods of work, chaired by Mr. Hussein A. Hassouna.[474]

The Commission decided to include in its long-term programme of work the topics: (*a*) "Reparation to individuals for gross violations of international human rights law and serious violations of international humanitarian law"; and (*b*) "Prevention and repression of piracy and armed robbery at sea".[475]

The Commission received Mr. Abdulqawi Ahmed Yusuf, President of the International Court of Justice and continued its traditional exchanges of information with the Committee of Legal Advisers on Public International Law of the Council of Europe; the Inter-American Juridical Committee; the Asian-African Legal Consultative Organization; and the African Union Commission on International Law. Members of the Commission also held an informal exchange of views with the International Committee of the Red Cross.[476]

Finally, the Commission decided that its seventy-second session would be held in Geneva from 27 April to 5 June and from 6 July to 7 August 2020.[477]

---

[471] *Official Records of the General Assembly, Seventy-fourth Session, Supplement No. 10* (A/74/10), chap. IX.

[472] *Ibid.*, chap. X and XI, sect. B.

[473] *Ibid.*, chap. XI, sect. A, and annex A.

[474] *Ibid.*, chap. XI, sect. D.

[475] *Ibid.*, chap. XI, sect. D, and annexes B and C.

[476] *Ibid.*, chap. XI, sect. F.

[477] *Ibid.*, chap. XI, sect. E.

(*c*) Sixth Committee

The Sixth Committee of the General Assembly considered the agenda item "Report of the International Law Commission on the work of its seventy-first session" at its 23rd to 33rd and 35th meetings, from 28 October to 1 November and on 5, 6 and 20 November 2019.[478] The Chair of the International Law Commission at its seventy-first session introduced the report of the Commission on the work of that session at the 23rd meeting, on 28 October.[479]

At the 35th meeting, on 20 November, the representative of Colombia, on behalf of the Bureau, introduced a draft resolution entitled "Report of the International Law Commission on the work of its seventy-first session".[480] At the same meeting, the representative of Singapore, on behalf of the Bureau, introduced a draft resolution entitled "Crimes against humanity".[481] At the same meeting, the Committee adopted the two draft resolutions without a vote.

(*d*) General Assembly

On 18 December 2019, the General Assembly adopted, on the recommendation of the Sixth Committee and without a vote, resolution 74/186 entitled "Report of the International Law Commission on the work of its seventy-first session". The Assembly expressed its appreciation to the Commission for the work accomplished at its seventy-first session, and recommended that it continue its work on the topics in its current programme, taking into account the comments and observations of Governments. Furthermore, the General Assembly decided that the next session of the Commission be held at the United Nations Office at Geneva from 27 April to 5 June and from 6 July to 7 August 2020.

On the same day, the General Assembly adopted, on the recommendation of the Sixth Committee and without a vote, resolution 74/187 entitled "Crimes against humanity". The Assembly, inter alia, took note of the draft articles on prevention and punishment of crimes against humanity, presented by the Commission, and decided to include in the provisional agenda of its seventy-fifth session an item entitled "Crimes against humanity" and to continue to examine the recommendation of the Commission contained in paragraph 42 of its report on the work of its seventy-first session.

15. United Nations Commission on International Trade Law[482]

(*a*) Fifty-second session of the Commission

The United Nations Commission on International Trade Law (UNCITRAL) held its fifty-second session in Vienna from 8 to 19 July 2019 and adopted its report on 19 July 2019.[483]

---

[478] For the report of the Sixth Committee, see A/74/425. For the summary records, see A/C.6/74/SR.23–33 and 35.

[479] For the ILC report, see *Official Records of the General Assembly, Seventy-fourth Session, Supplement No. 10* (A/74/10).

[480] A/C.6/74/L.20.

[481] A/C.6/74/L.21.

[482] For the membership of the United Nations Commission on International Trade Law, see *Official Records of the General Assembly, Seventy-fourth Session, Supplement No. 17* (A/74/17), para. 4.

[483] *Ibid.*, paras. 1 and 12.

At the session, the Commission adopted the following instruments: (i) the UNCITRAL Model Legislative Provisions on Public-Private Partnerships and the UNCITRAL Legislative Guide on Public-Private Partnerships;[484] (ii) the Practice Guide to the UNCITRAL Model Law on Secured Transactions;[485] and (iii) the UNCITRAL Model Law on Enterprise Group Insolvency and its Guide to Enactment,[486] as well as an additional section of part four of the *UNCITRAL Legislative Guide on Insolvency Law* addressing the obligations of directors of enterprise group companies in the period approaching insolvency.[487]

The Commission took note of the progress made by its Working Groups in their ongoing work on: (*a*) a draft legislative guide on an UNCITRAL limited liability organization (Working Group I (Micro, Small and Medium-sized Enterprises (MSMEs));[488] (*b*) expedited arbitration (Working Group II (Dispute Settlement));[489] (*c*) the possible reform of investor-State dispute settlement (Working Group III (Investor-State Dispute Settlement Reform));[490] (*d*) identity management and trust services (Working Group IV (Electronic Commerce));[491] (*e*) insolvency of micro and small enterprises (Working Group V (Insolvency Law));[492] and (*f*) judicial sale of ships (Working Group VI (Judicial Sale of Ships)).[493]

The Commission approved the publication of the notes by the Secretariat on the main issues of cloud computing contracts, and also authorized the publication of such notes in the form of an online tool in the six official languages of the United Nations.[494]

The Commission welcomed the report on the repository of published information under article 8 of the UNCITRAL Rules on Transparency in Treaty-based Investor-State Arbitration,[495] and expressed its support for continued operation of the repository as a key mechanism for promoting transparency in investor-State arbitration.[496]

The Commission heard a proposal for enlargement of UNCITRAL membership and encouraged its member States to consult with each other and other interested States on the proposal during the intersessional period.[497]

Among other items, the Commission considered its technical cooperation and assistance activities,[498] including through its Regional Centre for Asia and the Pacific,[499] and

---

[484] *Ibid.*, para. 71 and annex I.

[485] *Ibid.*, para. 101.

[486] *Ibid.*, para. 110 and annex II.

[487] *Ibid.*, para. 116.

[488] *Ibid.*, paras. 152–155.

[489] *Ibid.*, paras. 156–158.

[490] *Ibid.*, paras. 159–169.

[491] *Ibid.*, paras. 170–175.

[492] *Ibid.*, paras. 176–183.

[493] *Ibid.*, paras. 184–189.

[494] *Ibid.*, para. 151.

[495] *Ibid.*, *Sixty-eighth Session, Supplement No. 17* (A/68/17), annex I.

[496] *Ibid.*, *Seventy-fourth Session, Supplement No. 17* (A/74/17), para. 292.

[497] *Ibid.*, para. 315.

[498] *Ibid.*, paras. 253–271.

[499] *Ibid.*, paras. 272–278.

proposals for the establishment of other regional centres.[500] It also considered reports of the Secretariat on promotion of ways and means of ensuring a uniform interpretation and application of UNCITRAL legal texts,[501] on the status and promotion of UNCITRAL texts,[502] including through international commercial moot competitions,[503] and on coordination and cooperation with other organizations active in the field of international trade law.[504] The Commission took note of the bibliography of recent writings related to the work of UNCITRAL[505] and considered its role in promoting the rule of law at the national and international levels.[506] It also considered its work programme[507] and its methods of work.[508]

(*b*) Sixth Committee

The Sixth Committee considered the item at its 20th, 21st, 33rd and 34th meetings, on 21 and 22 October and on 6 and 11 November 2019.[509] For its consideration of the item, the Committee had before it the report of the United Nations Commission on International Trade Law on the work of its fifty-second session.[510]

At the 20th meeting, on 21 October, the Chair of the United Nations Commission on International Trade Law at its fifty-second session introduced the report of the Commission on the work of its fifty-second session.

At the 33rd meeting, on 6 November, the representative of Austria, on behalf of several States, introduced a draft resolution entitled "Report of the United Nations Commission on International Trade Law on the work of its fifty-second session".[511] At the same meeting, the representative of Austria, on behalf of the Bureau, introduced the draft resolutions entitled "Model Legislative Provisions on Public-Private Partnerships of the United Nations Commission on International Trade Law"[512] and "Model Law on Enterprise Group Insolvency of the United Nations Commission on International Trade Law".[513] At the 34th meeting, on 11 November, the Committee adopted the three draft resolutions without a vote.

---

[500] *Ibid.*, paras. 279–285.

[501] *Ibid.*, paras. 239–252.

[502] *Ibid.*, paras. 286–289.

[503] *Ibid.*, para. 268.

[504] *Ibid.*, paras. 223–238.

[505] *Ibid.*, paras. 293–294.

[506] *Ibid.*, paras. 295–308.

[507] *Ibid.*, paras. 190–222.

[508] *Ibid.*, paras. 316–318.

[509] For the report of the Sixth Committee, see A/74/423. For the summary records, see A/C.6/74/SR.20, 21, 33 and 34.

[510] *Official Records of the General Assembly, Seventy-fourth Session, Supplement No. 17* (A/74/17).

[511] A/C.6/74/L.7.

[512] A/C.6/74/L.8.

[513] A/C.6/74/L.9.

(*c*) General Assembly

On 18 December 2019, the General Assembly adopted, upon the recommendation of the Sixth Committee and without a vote, resolution 74/182 entitled "Report of the United Nations Commission on International Trade Law on the work of its fifty-second session", resolution 74/183 entitled "Model Legislative Provisions on Public-Private Partnerships of the United Nations Commission on International Trade Law", and resolution 74/184 entitled "Model Law on Enterprise Group Insolvency of the United Nations Commission on International Trade Law".

16. Legal questions dealt with by the Sixth Committee and other related subsidiary bodies of the General Assembly

During the seventy-fourth session of the General Assembly, the Sixth Committee (Legal), in addition to the topics discussed above concerning the International Law Commission and the United Nations Commission on International Trade Law, considered a wide range of topics. The work of the Sixth Committee and of other related subsidiary organs is described below, together with the relevant resolutions and decisions adopted by the General Assembly in 2019.[514] The resolutions and decisions of the General Assembly described in this section were mostly adopted, without a vote, during the seventy-fourth session, on 18 December 2019, on the recommendation of the Sixth Committee, except where otherwise indicated.[515]

(*a*) Responsibility of States for internationally wrongful acts

The draft articles on responsibility of States for internationally wrongful acts were prepared by the International Law Commission and were submitted to the General Assembly at its fifty-sixth session in 2001.[516] The Assembly took note of the draft articles and commended them to the attention of Governments without prejudice to the question of their future adoption or other appropriate action, and decided to include in the provisional agenda of its fifty-ninth session an item entitled "Responsibility of States for internationally wrongful acts".[517] The Assembly had previously considered the item triennially since its fifty-ninth session.

---

[514] For further information and documents regarding the work of the Sixth Committee and the other related subsidiary organs of the General Assembly mentioned in this section, see https://www.un.org/en/ga/sixth/74/74_session.shtml.

[515] The Sixth Committee adopts drafts resolutions, which it recommends for adoption by the General Assembly. These draft resolutions are contained in the reports of the Sixth Committee to the General Assembly on the various agenda items. The Sixth Committee reports also contain information concerning the relevant documentation on the consideration of the items by the Sixth Committee. Resolution 74/258 (Administration of justice at the United Nations) was adopted on 27 December 2019, on the recommendation of the Fifth Committee.

[516] General Assembly resolution 56/83 of 12 December 2001, annex.

[517] *Ibid.*, paras. 1–4.

(i) *Sixth Committee*

During the seventy-fourth session of the General Assembly, the Sixth Committee considered the item at its 13th, 15th, 34th and 35th meetings, on 15 and 16 October and on 11 and 20 November 2019.[518] For its consideration of the item, the Committee had before it the reports of the Secretary-General on this topic.[519]

At its 1st meeting, on 7 October 2019, the Committee decided, pursuant to General Assembly resolution 71/133, to establish a working group on the responsibility of States for internationally wrongful acts open to all States Members of the United Nations or members of specialized agencies or of the International Atomic Energy Agency. The Working Group, which was chaired by Maitê de Sousa Schmitz (Brazil), held three meetings, on 15 and 22 October and 7 November 2019. At its 34th meeting, on 11 November, the Committee heard and took note of the oral report of the Chair of the Working Group.

At the 35th meeting, on 20 November 2019, the representative of Brazil introduced, on behalf of the Bureau, a draft resolution entitled "Responsibility of States for internationally wrongful acts".[520] At the same meeting, the Committee adopted the draft resolution without a vote.

(ii) *General Assembly*

By resolution 74/180 of 18 December 2019, the General Assembly acknowledged the importance and usefulness of the articles on responsibility of States for internationally wrongful acts and the growing number of decisions of international courts, tribunals and other bodies referring to the articles, and commended them once again to the attention of Governments, without prejudice to the question of their future adoption or other appropriate action. The Assembly requested the Secretary-General to invite Governments to submit further written comments on any future action regarding the articles, to update the compilation of decisions of international courts, tribunals and other bodies referring to the articles, and to invite Governments to submit information on their practice in this regard. It further requested the Secretary-General to submit this material well in advance of its seventy-seventh session. Finally, the General Assembly decided to include the item in the provisional agenda of its seventy-seventh session to further examine, within the framework of a working group of the Sixth Committee and with a view to taking a decision, the question of a convention on responsibility of States for internationally wrongful acts or other appropriate action on the basis of the articles.

(*b*) Criminal accountability of United Nations officials and experts on mission

The item entitled "Comprehensive review of the whole question of peacekeeping operations in all their aspects" was included in the agenda of the General Assembly at its nineteenth session, in February 1965, when the General Assembly established the Special

---

[518] For the report of the Sixth Committee, see A/74/421. For the summary records, see A/C.6/74/SR.13, 15, 34 and 35.

[519] A/74/83 and A/74/156.

[520] A/C.6/74/L.16.

Committee on Peacekeeping Operations that was to undertake a comprehensive review of the whole question of peacekeeping operations in all their aspects.[521]

At its sixty-first session, in 2006, the General Assembly decided that the agenda item entitled "Comprehensive review of the whole question of peacekeeping operations in all their aspects", which had been allocated to the Special Political and Decolonization Committee (Fourth Committee), should also be referred to the Sixth Committee for discussion of the report of the Group of Legal Experts on ensuring the accountability of United Nations staff and experts on mission with respect to criminal acts committed in peacekeeping operations,[522] submitted pursuant to General Assembly resolution 59/300.[523] At the same session, the General Assembly decided to establish an *ad hoc* committee, for the purpose of considering the report of the Group of Legal Experts, in particular its legal aspects and to report on its work to the General Assembly under the agenda item entitled "Criminal Accountability of United Nations officials and experts on mission".[524] The Assembly had previously considered this item annually since its sixty-second session.

(i) *Sixth Committee*

During the seventy-fourth session of the General Assembly, the Sixth Committee considered the item at its 7th, 8th and 35th meetings, on 10 October and on 20 November 2019.[525] For its consideration of the item, the Committee had before it the reports of the Secretary-General on this topic.[526]

At the 35th meeting, on 20 November 2019, the representative of Pakistan, on behalf of the Bureau, introduced a draft resolution entitled "Criminal accountability of United Nations officials and experts on mission".[527] At the same meeting, the Committee adopted the draft resolution without a vote.

(ii) *General Assembly*

On 18 December 2019, the General Assembly adopted resolution 74/181, entitled "Criminal accountability of United Nations officials and experts on mission". The General Assembly, *inter alia*, recalled its decision that the consideration of the report of the Group of Legal Experts, in particular its legal aspects, would be continued at the seventy-fifth session in the context of a working group of the Sixth Committee. The Assembly also requested the Secretary-General to report to it at its seventy-fifth session on the implementation of the resolution.

---

[521] General Assembly resolution 2006 (XIX) of 18 February 1965.

[522] A/60/980.

[523] General Assembly decision 61/503A of 13 September 2006.

[524] The Ad Hoc Committee on criminal accountability of United Nations officials and experts on mission was established by General Assembly resolution 61/29 of 4 December 2006. The Ad Hoc Committee held two sessions at United Nations Headquarters in New York, from 9 to 13 April 2007 and from 7 to 9 and on 11 April 2008. For more information, see https://www.un.org/law/criminalaccountability/.

[525] For the report of the Sixth Committee, see A/74/422. For the summary records, A/C.6/74/SR.7, 8 and 35.

[526] A/74/142 and A/74/145.

[527] A/C.6/74/L.14.

(*c*) United Nations Programme of Assistance in the Teaching, Study, Dissemination and Wider Appreciation of International Law

The United Nations Programme of Assistance in the Teaching, Study, Dissemination and Wider Appreciation of International Law was established by the General Assembly at its twentieth session in 1965,[528] to provide direct assistance in the field of international law, as well as through the preparation and dissemination of publications and other information relating to international law. The General Assembly authorized the continuation of the Programme of Assistance annually until its twenty-sixth session, biennially until its sixty-fourth session and annually thereafter.

In the performance of the functions entrusted to him by the General Assembly, the Secretary-General is assisted by the Advisory Committee on the United Nations Programme of Assistance in the Teaching, Study, Dissemination and Wider Appreciation of International Law, the members of which are appointed by the General Assembly.

(i) *Sixth Committee*

The Sixth Committee considered the item at its 22nd and 35th meetings, on 25 October and 20 November 2019.[529] For its consideration of the item, the Committee had before it the report of the Secretary-General.[530]

At the 35th meeting, on 20 November 2019, the representative of Ghana, on behalf of the Bureau, introduced a draft resolution entitled "United Nations Programme of Assistance in the Teaching, Study, Dissemination and Wider Appreciation of International Law".[531] At the same meeting, the Committee adopted the draft resolution, without a vote.

(ii) *General Assembly*

On 18 December 2019, the General Assembly adopted resolution 74/185 entitled "United Nations Programme of Assistance in the Teaching, Study, Dissemination and Wider Appreciation of International Law". In the resolution, the Assembly authorized the Secretary-General to carry out the activities specified in his reports on this item for 2020, to be financed from provisions in the regular budget. The Assembly also requested the Secretary-General to continue to include resources for the activities of the Programme of Assistance in the proposed programme budget for 2021 and authorized the Secretary-General to further expand such activities using voluntary contributions.

(*d*) Diplomatic protection

At its sixty-first session, the General Assembly took note of the draft articles on diplomatic protection adopted by the International Law Commission at its fifty-eighth session, in

---

[528] General Assembly resolution 2099 (XX) of 20 December 1965. For further information on the Programme of Assistance, see https://www.un.org/law/programmeofassistance.

[529] For the report of the Sixth Committee, see A/74/424. For the summary records, see A/C.6/74/SR.22 and 35.

[530] A/74/496.

[531] A/C.6/74/L.15.

2006, and invited Governments to submit comments concerning the recommendation of the Commission that the Assembly elaborate a convention on the basis of the draft articles.[532] The Assembly had considered this item triennially since its sixty-second session.

(i) *Sixth Committee*

The Sixth Committee considered the item at its 13th to 15th, 34th and 35th meetings, on 15 and 16 October and 11 and 20 November 2019.[533] For its consideration of the item, the Committee had before it the report of the Secretary-General.[534]

Pursuant to resolution 71/142 of 13 December 2016, the Committee decided, at its 1st meeting, on 7 October 2019, to establish a Working Group on Diplomatic Protection open to all States Members of the United Nations or members of the Specialized Agencies or of the International Atomic Energy Agency. The Working Group, which was chaired by Thabo Molefe (South Africa), held two meetings, on 16 and 23 October 2019. At its 34th meeting, on 11 November 2019, the Committee heard and took note of the oral report of the Chair of the Working Group.

At the 35th meeting, on 20 November 2019, the representative of South Africa, on behalf of the Bureau, introduced a draft resolution entitled "Diplomatic protection".[535] At the same meeting, the Committee adopted the draft resolution without a vote.

(ii) *General Assembly*

By resolution 74/188 of 18 December 2019, the General Assembly commended once again the articles on diplomatic protection to the attention of Governments and invited them to submit in writing to the Secretary-General any further comments, including comments concerning the recommendation of the Commission to elaborate a convention on the basis of the articles. The Assembly also decided to include the item in the provisional agenda of its seventy-seventh session and invited Governments to focus their statements, in the light of the written comments submitted to the Secretary-General, as well as the views expressed in the debates held at previous sessions, on the question of a convention on diplomatic protection, or any other appropriate action, on the basis of the above-mentioned articles, and also on identifying any difference of opinion on the articles.

(*e*) Consideration of prevention of transboundary harm from hazardous activities and allocation of loss in the case of such harm

The topic "International liability for injurious consequences arising out of acts not prohibited by international law" was included in the programme of work of the Commission in 1978. In 1997, the Commission decided to deal first with prevention aspects of the topic under the subtitle "Prevention of transboundary damage from hazardous activities".

[532] General Assembly resolution 61/35 of 4 December 2006.

[533] For the report of the Sixth Committee, see A/74/426. For the summary records, see A/C.6/74/SR.13–15, 34 and 35.

[534] A/74/143.

[535] A/C.6/74/L.17.

The Commission, in 2001, completed the draft articles on prevention of transboundary harm from hazardous activities and recommended to the General Assembly the elaboration of a convention on the basis of the draft articles.[536]

In 2002, the Commission resumed its work on the second part of the topic under the subtitle "International liability in case of loss from transboundary harm arising out of hazardous activities".[537] In 2006, the Commission completed the liability aspects by adopting draft principles on the allocation of loss in the case of transboundary harm arising out of hazardous activities and recommended to the General Assembly that it endorse the draft principles by a resolution and urge States to take national and international action to implement them.[538] The General Assembly, at its sixty-first session, took note of the principles presented by the Commission and decided to include in the provisional agenda of its sixty-second session an item entitled "Consideration of prevention of transboundary harm from hazardous activities and allocation of loss in the case of such harm".[539] The Assembly had previously considered the item triennially since its sixty-second session.

(i) *Sixth Committee*

The Sixth Committee considered the item at its 21st, 33rd and 34th meetings, on 22 October and on 6 and 11 November 2019.[540] For its consideration of the item, the Committee had before it the reports of the Secretary-General.[541]

At the 33rd meeting, on 6 November 2019, the representative of Czechia, on behalf of the Bureau, introduced a draft resolution entitled "Consideration of prevention of transboundary harm from hazardous activities and allocation of loss in the case of such harm".[542] At the 34th meeting, on 11 November 2019, the Committee adopted the draft resolution without a vote.

(ii) *General Assembly*

By the terms of the resolution 74/189 of 18 December 2019, the General Assembly invited Governments to submit further comments on any future action, in particular on the form of the respective articles and principles, bearing in mind the recommendations made by the Commission in that regard, including in relation to the elaboration of a convention on the basis of the articles, as well as on any practice in relation to the application of the articles and principles. The Assembly also requested the Secretary-General to submit a compilation of decisions of international courts, tribunals and other bodies referring to

---

536 See *Official Records of the General Assembly, Fifty-sixth Session, Supplement No. 10* (A/56/10 and Corr.1).

537 See General Assembly resolution 56/82 of 12 December 2001 and *Official Records of the General Assembly, Fifty-seventh Session, Supplement No.10* (A/57/10 and Corr.1).

538 See *Official Records of the General Assembly, Sixty-first Session, Supplement No.10* (A/61/10).

539 General Assembly resolution 61/36 of 19 December 2006.

540 For the report of the Sixth Committee, see A/74/27. For the summary records, see A/C.6/74/SR.21, 33 and 34.

541 A/74/131, A/74/131/Add.1 and A/74/132.

542 A/C.6/74/L.10.

the articles and the principles. Finally, it decided to include this item in the provisional agenda of its seventy-seventh session.

(*f*) Report of the Special Committee on the Charter of the United Nations and on the Strengthening of the Role of the Organization

(i) *Special Committee on the Charter of the United Nations and on the Strengthening of the Role of the Organization*[543]

The item entitled "Need to consider suggestions regarding the review of the Charter of the United Nations" was included in the agenda of the twenty-fourth session of the General Assembly, in 1969, at the request of Colombia.[544]

At its twenty-ninth session, in 1974, the General Assembly decided to establish an *ad hoc* committee on the Charter of the United Nations to consider any specific proposals that Governments might make with a view to enhancing the ability of the United Nations to achieve its purposes, as well as other suggestions for the more effective functioning of the United Nations that might not require amendments to the Charter.[545]

Meanwhile, another item, entitled "Strengthening of the role of the United Nations with regard to the maintenance and consolidation of international peace and security, the development of cooperation among all nations and the promotion of the rules of international law in relations between States", was included in the agenda of the twenty-seventh session of the General Assembly, at the request of Romania.[546]

At its thirtieth session, the General Assembly decided to reconvene the *ad hoc* committee as the Special Committee on the Charter of the United Nations and on the Strengthening of the Role of the Organization, to examine suggestions and proposals regarding the Charter and the strengthening of the role of the United Nations with regard to the maintenance and consolidation of international peace and security, the development of cooperation among all nations and the promotion of the rules of international law.[547] Since its thirtieth session, the General Assembly has considered the report of the Special Committee annually.

The Special Committee met at United Nations Headquarters from 19 to 27 February 2019 and considered the items "Maintenance of international peace and security", "Peaceful settlement of disputes", "*Repertory of Practice of United Nations Organs* and *Repertoire of the Practice of the Security Council*" and "Working methods of the Special Committee and identification of new subjects".[548]

---

543 For more information, see the website of the Special Committee on the Charter of the United Nations and on the Strengthening of the Role of the Organization, available from https://legal.un.org/committees/charter/.

544 A/7659.

545 General Assembly resolution 3349 (XXIX) of 17 December 1974.

546 A/8792.

547 General Assembly resolution 3499 (XXX) of 15 December 1975.

548 For the report of the Special Committee, see *Official Records of the General Assembly, Seventy-fourth Session, Supplement No. 33* (A/74/33).

(ii) *Sixth Committee*

The Sixth Committee considered the item at its 17th, 18th, 19th and 35th meetings, on 17 and 18 October and on 20 November 2019.[549] For its consideration of the item, the Committee had before it the report of the Special Committee[550] and the reports of the Secretary-General.[551]

At the 35th meeting, on 20 November 2019, the representative of Ethiopia, on behalf of the Bureau, introduced a draft resolution entitled "Report of the Special Committee on the Charter of the United Nations and on the Strengthening of the Role of the Organization",[552] which was adopted at the same meeting without a vote.

(iii) *General Assembly*

On 18 December 2019, the General Assembly adopted resolution 74/190 entitled "Report of the Special Committee on the Charter of the United Nations and on the Strengthening of the Role of the Organization". The Assembly, *inter alia*, requested the Special Committee to continue its consideration of all proposals concerning the question of the maintenance of international peace and security and of the question of the implementation of the provisions of the Charter of the United Nations related to assistance to third States affected by the application of sanctions, to keep on its agenda the question of the peaceful settlement of disputes between States, and to continue to consider, on a priority basis, ways and means of improving the Committee's working methods and enhancing its efficiency.

(*g*) The rule of law at the national and international levels

This item was included in the provisional agenda of the sixty-first session of the General Assembly, in 2006, at the request of Liechtenstein and Mexico.[553] The General Assembly had previously considered the item annually since its sixty-first session.

(i) *Sixth Committee*

The Sixth Committee considered the item at its 8th to 11th and 35th meetings, on 10, 11 and 14 October and on 20 November 2019.[554] For its consideration of the item, the Committee had before it the report of the Secretary-General on strengthening and coordinating United Nations rule of law activities.[555]

At the 35th meeting, on 20 November 2019, the representative of Liechtenstein, on behalf of the Bureau, introduced a draft resolution entitled "The rule of law at the national and international levels".[556] At the same meeting, the Committee adopted the draft resolution without a vote.

---

[549] For the report of the Sixth Committee, see A/74/428. For the summary records, see A/C.6/74/SR.17–19 and 35.

[550] A/74/33.

[551] A/74/152 and A/74/194.

[552] A/C.6/74/L.12.

[553] A/61/142.

[554] For the report of the Sixth Committee, see A/74/429. For the summary records, see A/C.6/74/SR.8–11 and 35.

[555] A/74/139.

[556] A/C.6/74/L.13.

(ii) *General Assembly*

On 18 December 2019, the General Assembly adopted resolution 74/191 entitled "The rule of law at the national and international levels". The General Assembly decided to include this item in the provisional agenda of its seventy-fifth session and invited Member States to focus their comments in the upcoming Sixth Committee debate on the subtopics "Measures to prevent and combat corruption".

(*h*) The scope and application of the principle of universal jurisdiction

This item was included in the provisional agenda of the sixty-fourth session of the General Assembly, in 2009, at the request of the United Republic of Tanzania on behalf of the Group of African States.[557] The General Assembly had previously considered the item annually since its sixty-fourth session.

(i) *Sixth Committee*

The Sixth Committee considered the item at its 14th to 17th, 34th and 35th meetings, from 15 to 17 October and on 11 and 20 November 2019.[558] For its consideration of the item, the Committee had before it the reports of the Secretary-General submitted to the General Assembly at its sixty-fifth to seventy-fourth sessions.[559]

At its 1st meeting, on 7 October, the Committee established a working group open to all Member States and relevant observers to the General Assembly pursuant to General Assembly resolution 73/208 to continue to undertake a thorough discussion of the scope and application of the principle of universal jurisdiction. The Working Group held two meetings, on 18 and 24 October. At its 34th meeting, on 11 November, the Committee heard and took note of the oral report of the Chair of the Working Group.

At the 35th meeting, on 20 November, the representative of the Gambia, on behalf of the Bureau, introduced a draft resolution entitled "The scope and application of the principle of universal jurisdiction".[560] At the same meeting, the Committee adopted the draft resolution without a vote.

(ii) *General Assembly*

In resolution 74/192 of 18 December 2019, the General Assembly, *inter alia*, invited Member States and relevant observers, as appropriate, to submit, by 24 April 2020, information and observations on the scope and application of universal jurisdiction, including, where appropriate, information on the relevant applicable international treaties, their national legal rules and judicial practice. The Assembly further requested the Secretary-General to prepare and submit to it, at its seventy-fifth session, a report based on such

---

[557] A/63/237/Rev.1.

[558] For the report of the Sixth Committee, see A/74/430. For the summary records, see A/C.6/74/SR.14–17, 34 and 35.

[559] A/65/181, A/66/93, A/66/93/Add.1, A/67/116, A/68/113, A/69/174, A/70/125, A/71/111, A/72/112, A/73/123, A/73/123/Add.1 and A/74/144.

[560] A/C.6/74/L.6.

information and observations. Moreover, the Assembly decided that the Sixth Committee should, at the seventy-fifth session, establish a working group open to all Member States and relevant observers to the General Assembly to continue its consideration of the item.

(*i*) The law of transboundary aquifers

At its sixty-third session, in 2008, the General Assembly, under the item entitled "Report of the International Law Commission on the work of its sixtieth session", considered chapter IV of the report of the Commission, which contained the draft articles on the law of transboundary aquifers, together with commentaries, and a recommendation that the Assembly take note of the draft articles on the law of transboundary aquifers in a resolution and annex those articles to the resolution. The General Assembly, subsequently, welcomed the conclusion of the work of the Commission on the law of transboundary aquifers and its adoption of the draft articles and a detailed commentary on the subject; took note of the draft articles, the text of which was annexed to its resolution; commended them to the attention of Governments without prejudice to the question of their future adoption or other appropriate action; encouraged the States concerned to make appropriate bilateral or regional arrangements for the proper management of their transboundary aquifers, taking into account the provisions of the draft articles; and decided to include the item in the provisional agenda of its sixty-sixth session with a view to examining, in particular, the question of the form that might be given to the draft articles.[561] The Assembly further considered this item at its sixty-sixth, sixty-eighth and seventy-first sessions.

(i) *Sixth Committee*

The Sixth Committee considered the item at its 21st, 34th and 35th meetings, on 22 October and 11 and 20 November 2019.[562]

At the 34th meeting, on 11 November, the representative of Israel, on behalf of the Bureau, introduced a draft resolution entitled "The law of transboundary aquifers".[563] At the 35th meeting, on 20 November, the Committee adopted the draft resolution without a vote.

(ii) *General Assembly*

On 18 December 2019, the General Assembly adopted resolution 74/193 entitled "The law of transboundary aquifers". The Assembly, *inter alia*, once again commended the draft articles annexed to its resolution 68/118 to the attention of Governments as guidance for bilateral or regional agreements and arrangements for the proper management of transboundary aquifers, and encouraged the International Hydrological Programme of the United Nations Educational, Scientific and Cultural Organization to continue its contribution by providing further scientific and technical assistance upon the consent of

---

[561] General Assembly resolution 63/124 of 11 December 2008.

[562] For the report of the Sixth Committee, see A/74/431. For the summary records, see A/C.6/74/SR.21, 34 and 35.

[563] A/C.6/74/L.11.

the recipient State and within its mandate. The Assembly further decided to include the item in the provisional agenda of its seventy-seventh session.

(*j*) Measures to eliminate international terrorism

This item was included in the agenda of the twenty-seventh session of the General Assembly in 1972, further to an initiative of the Secretary-General.[564] At that session, the General Assembly decided to establish the *ad hoc* committee on International Terrorism, consisting of 35 members.[565]

At its fifty-first session, the General Assembly established an *ad hoc* committee to elaborate an international convention for the suppression of terrorist bombings and, subsequently, an international convention for the suppression of acts of nuclear terrorism, to supplement related existing international instruments, and thereafter to address means of further developing a comprehensive legal framework of conventions dealing with international terrorism.[566] Through the work of the Committee, the General Assembly has thus far adopted three counter-terrorism instruments.

(i) *Sixth Committee*

The Sixth Committee considered the item at its 3rd to 7th, 34th and 35th meetings, from 8 to 10 October and on 11 and 20 November 2019.[567] For its consideration of the item, the Committee had before it the report of the Secretary-General on measures to eliminate international terrorism.[568]

At its 1st meeting, on 7 October 2019, the Committee established a Working Group with a view to finalizing the process on the draft comprehensive convention on international terrorism, as well as discussions on the item included in its agenda by General Assembly resolution 54/110 concerning the question of convening a high-level conference under the auspices of the United Nations. The Working Group was open to all States Members of the United Nations or members of the specialized agencies or of the International Atomic Energy Agency. The Working Group held three meetings, as well as informal consultations, on 21 and 24 October and on 7 November. At its 34th meeting, on 11 November, the Committee heard and took note of the oral report by the Chair of the Working Group on the work of the Working Group and on the results of the informal consultations held during the current session.[569]

---

[564] A/8791, Add.1 and Add.1/Corr.1.

[565] General Assembly resolution 3034 (XXVII) of 18 December 1972.

[566] General Assembly resolution 51/210 of 17 December 2016.

[567] For the report of the Sixth Committee, see A/74/432. For the summary records, see A/C.6/74/SR.3–7, 34 and 35.

[568] A/74/151.

[569] See A/C.6/74/SR.34.

At the 35th meeting, on 20 November, the representative of Canada, on behalf of the Bureau, introduced a draft resolution entitled "Measures to eliminate international terrorism".[570] At the same meeting, the Committee adopted the draft resolution without a vote.

(ii) *General Assembly*

On 18 December 2019, the General Assembly adopted resolution 74/194 entitled "Measures to eliminate international terrorism". The Assembly, *inter alia*, decided to recommend that the Sixth Committee, at the seventy-fifth session of the General Assembly, establish a working group with a view to finalizing the process on the draft comprehensive convention on international terrorism as well as discussions on the item included in its agenda by General Assembly resolution 54/110, while encouraging all Member States to redouble their efforts during the intersessional period towards resolving any outstanding issues.

(*k*) Revitalization of the work of the General Assembly

This item, which was included in the agenda of the forty-sixth session of the General Assembly in 1991, had originally been proposed for inclusion in the draft agenda of that session by the President of the General Assembly at its forty-fifth session.[571] The General Assembly had previously considered the question at its forty-sixth to forty-eighth, fifty-second to fifty-third, and annually since fifty-fifth sessions.[572]

(i) *Sixth Committee*

The Sixth Committee considered the item at its 34th and 35th meetings, on 11 and 20 November 2019.[573]

At the 35th meeting, on 20 November, the Chair introduced a draft decision containing the provisional programme of work of the Committee for the seventy-fifth session of the General Assembly, as proposed by the Bureau.[574] At the same meeting, the Committee adopted the draft decision.

(ii) *General Assembly*

In its decision 74/521, the General Assembly noted that the Sixth Committee has decided to adopt the provisional programme of work for the seventy-fifth session of the General Assembly, as proposed by the Bureau.

---

570 A/C.6/74/L.18.

571 See General Assembly decision 45/461 of 16 September 1991.

572 At its fifty-fourth session, the General Assembly decided to defer consideration of the item (General Assembly decision 54/491).

573 For the report of the Sixth Committee, see A/74/445. For the summary records, see A/C.6/74/SR.34 and 35.

574 A/C.6/74/L.22.

(*l*) Administration of justice at the United Nations

The General Assembly had previously considered the item at its fifty-fifth to fifty-seventh sessions, at its fifty-ninth session and at its sixty-first to sixty-ninth sessions, in the framework of both the Fifth and Sixth Committee, with the aim of introducing a new system for handling internal disputes and disciplinary matters in the United Nations.

At its sixty-second session, the General Assembly decided to establish: (*a*) a two-tier formal system of administration of justice, comprising a first instance United Nations Dispute Tribunal and an appellate instance United Nations Appeals Tribunal; (*b*) the Office of Administration of Justice, comprising the Office of the Executive Director and the Office of Staff Legal Assistance and the Registries for the United Nations Dispute Tribunal and the United Nations Appeals Tribunal; (*c*) a single integrated and decentralized Office of the Ombudsman for the United Nations Secretariat, funds and programmes with branches in several duty stations and a new mediation division; (*d*) the Internal Justice Council; and (*e*) the Management Evaluation Unit in the Office of the Under-Secretary-General for Management.[575]

At its sixty-third session, the General Assembly adopted the statutes of the United Nations Dispute Tribunal and the United Nations Appeals Tribunal; it also decided that those Tribunals would be operational as of 1 July 2009; and further decided that all persons who had access to the Office of the Ombudsman under the previous system would also have access to the new informal system.[576]

Outstanding legal matters have been considered by the Sixth Committee in the ensuing years. These matters included, *inter alia*, the rules of procedure of the two tribunals, the scope *ratione personae* of the administration of justice system and the scope and functioning of the Office of Staff Legal Assistance (OSLA).

(i) *Sixth Committee*

The Sixth Committee considered the item at its 17th and 34th meetings, on 17 October and 11 November 2019.[577] For its consideration of the item, the Committee had before it the report of the Secretary-General on the activities of the Office of the United Nations Ombudsman and Mediation Services,[578] the report of the Secretary-General on the administration of justice at the United Nations,[579] and the report of the Internal Justice Council on the administration of justice at the United Nations.[580]

At the 34th meeting, on 11 November 2019, the Committee received a report on the results of the informal consultations and authorized its Chair to send a letter to the President of the General Assembly with a request that it be brought to the attention of the Chair of the Fifth Committee and circulated as a document of the General Assembly. The letter was circulated as an annex to the document A/C.5/74/10.

---

575 General Assembly resolution 62/228.

576 General Assembly resolution 63/253.

577 For the summary records of the Sixth Committee, see A/C.6/74/SR.17 and A/C.6/74/SR.34.

578 A/74/171.

579 A/74/172.

580 A/74/169.

(ii) *General Assembly*

On 27 December 2019, the General Assembly adopted, on the recommendation of the Fifth Committee and without a vote, resolution 74/258 entitled "Administration of justice at the United Nations". The Assembly, *inter alia*, invited the Sixth Committee to consider the legal aspects of the report of the Secretary-General on the administration of justice, without prejudice to the role of the Fifth Committee as the Main Committee of the General Assembly responsible for administrative and budgetary matters.

(*m*) Report of the Committee on Relations with the Host Country

(i) *Committee on Relations with the Host Country*

The Committee on Relations with the Host Country was established by the General Assembly at its twenty-sixth session, in 1971.[581] In 2019, the Committee was composed of the following 19 Member States: Bulgaria, Canada, China, Costa Rica, Côte d'Ivoire, Cuba, Cyprus, France, Honduras, Hungary, Iraq, Libya, Malaysia, Mali, Russian Federation, Senegal, Spain, United Kingdom of Great Britain and Northern Ireland and the United States of America.

In 2019, the Committee held five meetings: the 292nd to 296th meetings. At its 296th meeting, on 29 October 2019, the Committee approved a number of recommendations and conclusions, which were contained in chapter IV of its report.[582]

(ii) *Sixth Committee*

The Sixth Committee considered the item at its 33rd and 35th meetings, on 6 and 20 November 2019.[583] For its consideration of the item, the Committee had before it the report of the Committee on Relations with the Host Country.[584]

At the 35th meeting, on 20 November, the representative of Cyprus, also on behalf of Bulgaria, Canada, Costa Rica and Côte d'Ivoire, introduced a draft resolution entitled "Report of the Committee on Relations with the Host Country".[585] At the same meeting, the Committee adopted the draft resolution without a vote.

(iii) *General Assembly*

On 18 December 2019, the General Assembly adopted resolution 74/195 entitled "Report of the Committee on Relations with the Host Country". The Assembly, *inter alia*, endorsed the recommendations and conclusions contained in the report of the Committee

---

[581] General Assembly resolution 2819 (XXVI) of 15 December 1971.

[582] *Official Records of the General Assembly, Seventy-fourth session, Supplement No. 26* (A/74/26), chap. IV.

[583] For the report of the Sixth Committee, see A/74/434. For the summary records, see A/C.6/74/SR.33 and 35.

[584] *Official Records of the General Assembly, Seventy-fourth session, Supplement No. 26* (A/74/26).

[585] A/C.6/74/L.19.

on Relations with the Host Country and decided to include the item in the provisional agenda of its seventy-fifth session.

(*n*) Observer Status in the General Assembly

(i) *Sixth Committee*

The Committee considered requests for observer status in the General Assembly for the Cooperation Council of Turkic-speaking States, for the Eurasian Economic Union, for the Community of Democracies, for the Ramsar Convention on Wetlands Secretariat, for the Global Environment Facility, for the Group of Seven Plus, for the International Organization of Employers, for the International Trade Union Confederation, and for the Boao Forum for Asia at its 19th, 20th, 24th and 35th meetings, on 18, 21 and 29 October and on 20 November 2019.[586]

(ii) *General Assembly*

In its resolution 74/196 of 18 December 2019, the General Assembly granted observer status to the Group of Seven Plus.

By its decisions 74/523 to 74/530 of 18 December 2019, the General Assembly decided to defer a decision on the request for observer status for the Cooperation Council of Turkic-speaking States, for the Eurasian Economic Union, for the Community of Democracies, for the Ramsar Convention on Wetlands Secretariat, for the Global Environment Facility, for the International Organization of Employers, for the International Trade Union Confederation, and for the Boao Forum for Asia, respectively, to its seventy-fifth session.

17. International Residual Mechanism for Criminal Tribunals[587]

(*a*) Organization of the International Residual Mechanism for Criminal Tribunals[588]

By resolution 1966 (2010) of 22 December 2010, the Security Council, acting under Chapter VII of the Charter of the United Nations, decided to establish the International Residual Mechanism for Criminal Tribunals (IRMCT) with two branches, the branch for the International Criminal Tribunal for Rwanda (ICTR) which commenced functioning on 1 July 2012 and the branch for the International Tribunal for the Former Yugoslavia (ICTY) which commenced functioning on 1 July 2013, to carry out a number of essential

[586] For the reports of the Sixth Committee, see A/74/435 to A/74/443, respectively. For the summary records, see A/C.6/74/SR. 19, 20, 24 and 35.

[587] Further information regarding the judgments of the International Residual Mechanism for Criminal Tribunal is contained in chapter VII of this publication.

[588] For more information, see, for the period 1 July 2018 to 30 June 2019, the seventh annual report of International Residual Mechanism for Criminal Tribunals dated 1 August 2019 (A/74/267–S/2019/622). See also, for the period 1 July 2019 to 30 June 2020, the eighth annual report of International Residual Mechanism for Criminal Tribunals, dated 30 July 2020 (A/75/276–S/2020/763).

functions of the Tribunals after their closure. By the same resolution, the Security Council also decided to adopt the Statute of IRMCT, contained in the annex.

On 15 January 2019, at its 66th plenary meeting, the General Assembly, by General Assembly resolution 73/145, elected Mustapha El Baaj (Morocco) as a judge of the International Residual Mechanism for Criminal Tribunals for a term of office until 30 June 2020.

On 19 January 2019, the Mechanism saw a change in leadership, with Judge Carmel Agius (Malta) assuming the presidency and taking over from Judge Theodor Meron (United States).[589]

On 28 January 2019, the Secretary-General appointed Mahandrisoa Edmond Randrianirina (Madagascar) for a term of office expiring on 30 June 2020, and Claudia Hoefer (Germany) on 19 February 2019 for a term of office expiring on 30 June 2020.

On 19 July 2019, Judge Ben Emmerson (United Kingdom) resigned.

At the end of 2019, the President of the Mechanism was Judge Carmel Agius (Malta), the Prosecutor was Serge Brammertz (Belgium), and the Registrar was Olufemi Elias (Nigeria).

At the end of 2019, the IRMCT was composed of the following 24 judges: Carmel Agius (President, Malta), Theodor Meron (United States of America), Jean-Claude Antonetti (France), Joseph E. Chiondo Masanche (United Republic of Tanzania), William Hussein Sekule (United Republic of Tanzania), Lee G. Muthoga (Kenya), Alphons M.M. Orie (Netherlands), Burton Hall (Bahamas), Florence Rita Arrey (Cameroon), Vagn Prüsse Joensen (Denmark), Liu Daqun (China), Prisca Matimba Nyambe (Zambia), Aminatta Lois Runeni N'gum (Zimbabwe/Gambia), Seon Ki Park (Republic of Korea), José Ricardo de Prada Solaesa (Spain), Gberdao Gustave Kam (Burkina Faso), Graciela Susana Gatti Santana (Uruguay), Ivo Nelson de Caires Batista Rosa (Portugal), Seymour Panton (Jamaica), Elizabeth Ibanda-Nahamya (Uganda), Yusuf Aksar (Turkey), Mustapha El Baaj (Morocco), Mahandrisoa Edmond Randrianirina (Madagascar) and Claudia Hoefer (Germany).[590]

(*b*) General Assembly

On 23 October 2019, the General Assembly adopted, without reference to a Main Committee, decision 74/504, taking note of the seventh annual report of the International Residual Mechanism for Criminal Tribunals.

On 27 December 2019, the General Assembly adopted, on the recommendation of the Fifth Committee and without a vote, resolution 74/259 entitled "Financing of the International Residual Mechanism for Criminal Tribunals".

(*c*) Security Council

In 2019, the Security Council held two meetings related to the work of the International Residual Mechanism for Criminal Tribunals. The two meetings took the form of debates and no decisions were adopted by the Council under this item in 2019.[591]

---

[589] A/74/267–S/2019/622.

[590] A/75/276–S/2020/763.

[591] Repertoire of the Practice of the Security Council, 2019, p. 110.

B. General review of the legal activities of intergovernmental organizations related to the United Nations

1. Food and Agriculture Organization of the United Nations[592]

(a) Membership

As of 31 December 2019, the membership of the Food and Agriculture Organization of the United Nations (FAO) remained unchanged at 194 members, two associate members and one member organization.

(b) Constitutional and general legal matters

(i) *Governing bodies*

In 2019, the 41st session of the FAO Conference was convened. By resolution 4/2019,[593] the Conference appointed Mr. Qu Dongyu as the new Director-General of the FAO, setting out the terms and conditions of appointment in light of the recommendations of the General Committee to the Conference. In anticipation of the election of the new Director-General, guidance was circulated by the Secretary-General of the Conference of the FAO providing that, in order to protect the secrecy of the ballot, the Elections Officer could require any member of delegations or the secretariat participating in the supervision of any vote by secret ballot to dispose of any kind of electronic device prior to entering the room where the count is to take place, and that this requirement may be enforced by any means deemed relevant by the Elections Officer. Subsequently, immediately prior to the elections for the office of Director-General, the General Committee of the Conference of the FAO noted that, further to consultation with the Independent Chairperson of the Council of the FAO, the Director-General had decided that (i) electronic recording devices—defined as any device which could be used to record images, including but not limited to cameras, mobile phones or smartwatches—should not be allowed within the polling area; (ii) electors should leave any such devices in a basket at the entrance to the polling area before entering; and (iii) electors should show the tellers that they do not have electronic devices. Such arrangements were summarized in a document[594] submitted by the Secretariat for consideration by the Committee on Constitutional and Legal Matters of the FAO (see section (ii) below).

(ii) *Committee on Constitutional and Legal Matters*

In 2019, the 108th and 109th sessions of the Committee on Constitutional and Legal Matters (CCLM) were held. During these sessions, the CCLM considered and reviewed a number of substantive constitutional matters and draft resolutions. These included the

---

[592] For official documents and more information about the Food and Agriculture Organization of the United Nations, see http://www.fao.org.

[593] Report of the 41st session of the Conference of FAO, Rome, 22–29 June 2019, paras. 26–29.

[594] See FAO, *Voting procedures under Rule XII, paragraph 10 of the General Rules of the Organization*, CCLM 109/2.

proposed Amendments to the Convention Placing the International Poplar Commission within the framework of FAO (see point (iii) below).[595] Moreover, the CCLM considered voting procedures under Rule XII, paragraph 10 of the General Rules of the Organization, including the procedures and practices adopted prior to the 41st session of the Conference in order to ensure the complete secrecy of the ballot during the election of the Director-General (see section (i) above). In this regard, the CCLM considered that a broader analysis of the FAO's voting procedures should be carried out in light of the rules and best practices of other United Nations Common System agencies. Accordingly, the CCLM requested the Secretariat to prepare a comparative analysis addressing voting procedures, including preventive measures and mechanisms to enforce the Organization's rules and procedures related to voting and possible non-compliance with such rules.[596] At the time of writing, work continues on this matter, which is the subject of consultations with regional groups by the Independent Chairperson of the Council and will also be considered by the CCLM.

The relevant Reports of the CCLM were approved by the Council at its 161st[597] and 163rd[598] sessions.

(iii) *Statutory bodies*

Statutory bodies may be established under article VI and article XIV of the Constitution of the FAO.[599]

In 2019, the 161st session of the Council endorsed the Draft Conference resolution entitled "Amendments to the Convention Placing the International Poplar Commission within the framework of FAO" (the Convention), following endorsement by the CCLM[600] of the proposed amendments to the Convention adopted by the International Poplar Commission (IPC) in February 2019. The main amendments to the Convention concerned (i) expanding the scope of the Convention to cover not only poplars but also other tree species that have similar growth patterns and uses in the tropics and subtropics, and consequently changing the name of the Convention to "Convention on the International Commission on Poplars and Other Fast-Growing Trees Sustaining People and the Environment"; (ii) allowing member nations and associate members of the FAO that are not members of the IPC to attend sessions of the Commission as observers, and non-member States of the FAO that are Members of the United Nations, any of its Specialized Agencies or the International Atomic Energy Agency to be represented, upon request, as observers at sessions of the Commission, subject to the provisions relating to the granting of observer status to Nations adopted by the Conference of the FAO; (iii) expanding the functions of the Commission; (iv) providing for the possibility of the receipt of voluntary contributions by the IPC; and (v) replacing the

---

[595] Report of the 108th session of the Committee on Constitutional and Legal Matters, Rome, 11–12 March 2019, paras. 7–9.

[596] Report of the 109th session of the Committee on Constitutional and Legal Matters, Rome, 21–22 October 2019, paras. 6–8.

[597] Report of the 161st session of the Council, Rome, 8–12 April 2019, para. 20.

[598] Report of the 163rd session of the Council, Rome, 2–6 December 2019, para. 12.

[599] See FAO, *Basic Texts of the Food and Agriculture Organization of the United Nations: 2017 edition*, vol. I, p. 3, available at https://www.fao.org/4/mp046e/mp046e.pdf.

[600] Report of the 161st session of the Council, Rome, 8–12 April 2019, para. 20, letter *d*) and annex G.

words "chairman" or "chairmen" as included in the text of the Convention with "chairperson" or "chairpersons" for the sake of linguistic gender-neutrality. The amendments were finally adopted by the Conference by resolution 17/2019.[601]

Finally, during 2019, a number of processes began which are likely to have constitutional and legal implications and which will be addressed by the FAO Governing Bodies in 2020.

(*c*) Treaties, Commissions and other Statutory Bodies established under the auspices of the FAO

As of 31 December 2019, the FAO Director-General exercised Depositary functions in respect of the following treaties:[602]

(*a*) Seventeen multilateral treaties adopted under article XIV of the FAO Constitution.

(*b*) Nineteen multilateral treaties concluded outside the framework of the FAO.

(i) *Entry into force of treaties and amendments thereto*

In 2019, no new treaties were adopted or entered into force. As noted in paragraph (*b*) (iii) above, amendments to the Convention Placing the International Poplar Commission within the framework of the FAO were approved and entered into force in 2019.

(ii) *Depositary actions*

During 2019, a total of 13 depositary actions concerning treaties deposited with the Director General of FAO were recorded. With regard to treaties established under article XIV of the FAO Constitution,[603] depositary actions related to the 2001 International Treaty on Plant Genetic Resources for Food and Agriculture (ITPGRFA), the 2009 Agreement on Port State Measures to Prevent, Deter and Eliminate Illegal, Unreported and Unregulated Fishing (PSMA). As concerns treaties outside the framework of the FAO[604] in respect of which the Director-General exercises depositary functions, depositary actions related to the 1966 International Convention for the Conservation of Atlantic Tunas (ICCAT), the 1991 Regional Convention on Fisheries Cooperation Among African

---

[601] Report of the 41st session of the Conference, Rome 22–29 June 2019, para. 80 and appendix K.

[602] This does not include the FAO Constitution, bilateral agreements adopted under article 15 of the International Treaty on Plant Genetic Resources for Food and Agriculture and treaties that are no longer in force.

[603] Under the provisions of article XIV of the FAO Constitution, the Conference may "approve and submit to Member Nations conventions or agreements concerning questions relating to food and agriculture (…)" and the Council may "approve and submit to Member Nations agreements concerning questions relating to food and agriculture which are of particular interest to Member Nations of geographical areas specified in such agreements (…)". Information on depositary actions regarding multilateral treaties established under article XIV of the FAO Constitution is available at http://www.fao.org/treaties/results/en/?search=adv&subj_coll=ArticleXIV.

[604] Information on depositary actions regarding multilateral treaties concluded outside the FAO framework in respect of which the FAO Director-General exercises depositary functions and their status is available at http://www.fao.org/treaties/results/en/?search=adv&subj_coll=No_ArticleXIV.

States Bordering the Atlantic Ocean (COMHAFAT), and the 2006 Southern Indian Ocean Fisheries Agreement (SIOFA).

(*d*) Cash-based transfers schemes

In 2019, the FAO standardized its internal rules and procedures applicable to the design, management and implementation of cash-based transfers schemes. Cash-based transfers involve the provision of money to individuals or households within the context of regular and emergency projects. The FAO uses both unconditional and conditional cash-based transfers, in combination with other assistance modalities such as in-kind agricultural inputs and technical training. The above rules and procedures aim to reinforce control and manage corporate risks related to cash-based transfers, by establishing risk management processes applicable to vendors (*i.e.* financial service providers) responsible for disbursement to beneficiaries, and by setting specific rules for beneficiary identification, selection and data management within the context of cash-based transfers.

(*e*) New Policies on the prevention of Sexual Harassment and Whisteblower protection

In the course of 2019, the FAO continued to implement the corporate Action Plan for the Prevention of Sexual Exploitation and Abuse (PSEA) and Sexual Harassment (PSH) developed in 2018,[605] and to update its policies in alignment with ongoing United Nations initiatives to eradicate sexual harassment, sexual exploitation and abuse, to create a safe workplace, and to ensure a zero-tolerance environment with respect to such behaviour. In February 2019, the FAO issued a new Policy on the Prevention of Sexual Harassment,[606] following the United Nations System Model Policy on Sexual Harassment endorsed by the United Nations System Chief Executives Board for Coordination (CEB) and adapted to the specific institutional and legal framework of the Organization. The FAO was one the first United Nations agencies to adopt the United Nations Reference Model incorporating the uniform definition of sexual harassment. In particular, the new Policy on PSH enhances three key areas: reporting, investigation and decision making, outreach and support.

---

[605] The Action Plan for the Prevention of Sexual Exploitation and Abuse and Sexual Harassment was presented at the 159th session of the Council in the context of the FAO Corporate Policy, Processes and Measures on the PSH and PSAE. The Action Plan reflects the key priority areas of work identified by the Task Force on Addressing Sexual Harassment within the Organizations of the United Nations System established by the United Nations System Chief Executives Board for Coordination (CEB) in 2017, and sets out detailed and time bound deliverables with designation of responsibilities for internal management purposes.

[606] Administrative Circular No. 2019/01—*FAO Policy on Sexual Harassment*, issued on 13 February 2019, which replaces Administrative Circular No. 2015/03—*Policy on the Prevention of Harassment, Sexual Harassment and Abuse of Authority*, issued on 15 January 2015. The issuance of the new Policy had been announced in 2018, in the context of the FAO's revamped strategy against PHS and PSEA, as established by Administrative Circular No. 2018/02—*Zero tolerance on sexual harassment and sexual exploitation or abuse*, issued on 21 February 2018.

As part of the implementation of the above-mentioned Action Plan, in August 2019 the FAO issued a new Whistleblower Protection Policy,[607] which incorporates best practices criteria as recommended by a recent review of the United Nations System Joint Inspection Unit.[608]

(*f*) Legislative assistance (LEGN)

The FAO provides technical legal assistance in the drafting of legal instruments, the formulation of model laws, legislative reviews, setting-up of implementation infrastructure and oversight mechanisms, strengthening of institutional capacities and frameworks, and the development of practical legal tools for food and agriculture and natural resources, including land, forestry and fisheries. In 2019, the Development Law Branch (LEGN) of the FAO Legal Office provided such legal assistance to FAO member nations under 124 national, regional and global projects.

During 2019, LEGN advanced its collaboration with a number of other United Nations System entities, including: the United Nations Environment Programme (UNEP), the United Nations Framework Convention on Climate Change (UNFCCC), the United Nations Office on Drugs and Crime (UNODC), the World Health Organization (WHO), the International Union for Conservation of Nature (IUCN) and the International Maritime Organization's International Maritime Law Institute (IMO-IMLI). Furthermore, the FAO expanded its strategic collaboration with various international and regional institutions, among which are: the World Organisation for Animal Health (OIE), the Convention on International Trade in Endangered Species of Wild Fauna and Flora (CITES), the African Union Commission (AUC), the Pacific Islands Forum Fisheries Agency (FFA), the International Bar Association (IBA), the Wildlife Conservation Society (WCS), the Centre de coopération internationale en recherche agronomique pour le développement (CIRAD), the Center for International Forestry Research (CIFOR) and the Community of Latin American and Caribbean States (CELAC). In addition, LEGN consolidated its collaboration with some of its targeted strategic partners. For example, it cooperated closely with the Pan-African Parliament (PAP) and the Parlatino, as well as numerous national parliaments in both regions to strengthen the capacities of parliamentarians to actively contribute to legislating for zero hunger by 2030.

LEGN took further steps to reach new audiences, including leading universities and research centres, to advance knowledge and raise awareness on key emerging areas, foremost among which was food fraud.

LEGN provided direct legislative support to national authorities in many technical areas, including food security and nutrition (FSN), the right to adequate food (RTF), antimicrobial resistance (AMR), the Agreement on Port States Measures (PSMA), Illegal, Unreported and Unregulated (IUU) fishing, Sustainable Wildlife Management (SWM), Small-scale Fisheries (SSF), contract farming, food safety, food loss and waste (FLW), school food and nutrition (SFN), and responsible investments in agriculture and land

---

[607] Administrative Circular No. 2019/06—*FAO Whistleblower Protection Policy*, issued on 14 August 2019. The new Policy replaces Administrative Circular No. 2011/05—*Whistleblower Protection Policy* dated 9 February 2011.

[608] JIU/REP/2018/4, Review of Whistle-Blower Policies and Practices in United Nations System Organization.

tenure. LEGN assisted FAO member nations with the elaboration of framework and sectoral laws—some of which are currently in the consultation phase such as the Model Law on FSN in Africa—while others were adopted during the year, including national laws on family farming in Paraguay,[609] as well as on FLW in Peru and in El Salvador.[610] LEGN also supported FAO member nations by undertaking national assessments, including legal and institutional assessments on FSN and the RTF in numerous countries to guide evidence-based decision-making to achieve SDG2.

LEGN undertook several capacity-strengthening training and other events on different multidisciplinary issues for a variety of stakeholders. Among those were LEGN-led webinars and regional workshops on AMR in Africa, Asia and Latin America,[611] multisectoral training on FSN and RTF in Africa and Latin America,[612] as well as on combatting IUU fishing in Asia-Pacific, Africa and the Caribbean.[613]

In addition, 2019 witnessed LEGN strengthening a number of thematic diagnostic tools, such as one on climate change and agriculture building on earlier collaborations with other partners, and on SWM to assess statutory and customary laws and enforcement and implementation across sectors.[614]

(*g*) Legislative studies, Legal Papers Online and other technical papers (LEGN)

In 2019, LEGN published extensively on numerous crucial areas for achieving the SDGs under the FAO's mandate. As reflected in the Bibliography, some of the areas covered include due diligence, tenure and agricultural investment, climate change, fisheries, plant and animal health, SWM, AMR, as well as overarching issues such as the RTF and FSN. In addition, LEGN developed technical publications for targeted audiences, such as thematic legal briefs for parliamentarians on seven critical areas within their mandate for achieving zero hunger by 2030.

In 2019, work continued on the collection, translation and dissemination of information on food, agriculture and natural resources management legislation and policies through the free online database, FAOLEX.[615] With over 173,000 records in its collection, FAOLEX registered over 3,000 daily users in 2019 and introduced 8,640 new

---

[609] More information can be found at http://www.fao.org/legal-services/stories/detail/en/c/1273897/.

[610] More information can be found at http://www.fao.org/legal-services/stories/detail/en/c/1274471/.

[611] As part of the tripartite (FAO, WHO and the OIE) AMR collaboration and the formulation and implementation of four donor-funded global projects across four continents and involving more than 25 countries.

[612] Including the implementation of a joint FAO/PAP technical cooperation project to strengthen the capacities of parliamentarians on RTF and FSN across Africa, foremost among which the members of the Pan-African Parliamentary Alliance for Food and Nutrition Security, as well as under the long-standing collaboration with Parliamentary Fronts against Hunger in Latin America and the Caribbean as part of the Hunger Free Latin America and the Caribbean Initiative.

[613] As part of the work involving 28 countries across the three regions.

[614] The assessment is being undertaken in eight countries in Africa, the Caribbean and the Pacific regions.

[615] Available at https://www.fao.org/faolex/en/.

legislative texts and 936 new policies into the database. FAOLEX also added and broadened its in-house collaborations to create and expand subset databases like Agroecology Lex, Aqualex, AMR-Lex, Codex Alimentarius, Family Farming Lex, Pastoralist Knowledge Hub, PortLex, Right to Food Around the Globe, SoilLex, Timber-Lex and WildlifeLex.

(*h*) Employment-related matters

During 2019, and as per previous years, the FAO continued to address claims by staff and non-staff personnel before national authorities concerning employment-related matters. Many of these matters related to the payment of benefits, including social security benefits, on the basis of national legislation, as well as to requests for disclosure of information and data related to FAO personnel.

The FAO maintained the established position of the United Nations System. In these cases, FAO recalled its immunity from every form of legal process, the international character of the employment relationship between the Organization and its personnel, the application of the Organization's rules—as distinct from national laws and procedures—to the employment contracts, and the provision for alternative dispute settlement mechanisms under the Organization's legal framework.

2. International Fund for Agricultural Development[616]

(*a*) Governing Council

(i) *Application for non-original membership*

The Republic of Poland became a member of the International Fund for Agricultural Development (IFAD) in 2019. The application for membership presented by the republic of Poland and the President's task of notifying the Secretary General of the United Nations on this decision was recommended by the Executive Board and then approved by the Governing Council at its forty-second session according to the resolution 205/XLII as contained in page 2 of document GC 42/L.2. The membership of Poland would become effective upon the deposit of its instrument of accession within the United Nations Treaty Section.

(ii) *Amendments to the Policies and Criteria for IFAD Financing*

In accordance with the recommendation of the Executive Board, the Governing Council adopted resolution 207/XLII, as contained in section III of document GC 42/L.7 on 14 February 2019, approving the proposed revisions. The proposed revisions include both the update of Financing Terms and the Non-Concessional Borrowing Policy (NCBP).

With regard to the update of financing terms, an amendment is required for the following proposed changes: (i) introduction of differentiated maturity and grace periods for ordinary term financing; (ii) introduction of currency-specific loan pricing determined by the Executive Board for highly concessional terms and blend terms financing; and

[616] For official documents and more information about the International Fund for Agricultural Development, see http://www.ifad.org/.

(iii) change in the frequency of review and revision of the IFAD service charge and the reference interest rate of rate setting from a semi-annual basis to a quarterly basis. For the NCBP, an amendment is needed to allow for the application of disincentive measures that would result in a deviation from the standard financing terms for which a country would normally be eligible. The amendments to the Policies and Criteria for IFAD Financing became effective on the date of their adoption by the Governing Council.

(iii) *Proposed Amendments to the basic legal texts of IFAD to facilitate the Fund's engagement with the private sector*

The Governing Council adopted the resolutions approving the recommendation of the Executive Board, as contained in annex I of document GC 42/L.8 and Corr.1, to engage with the private sector with flexibility by allowing IFAD to lend to private sector organizations and enterprises, including investment funds. In proposing this new framework, IFAD is endeavouring to diversify its lending portfolio by broadening the scope of lending to include private sector counterparties and invest in equity funds and other financing methods targeting rural SMEs and smallholder cooperatives. The amendments to the Agreement Establishing IFAD would take effect from the date of the approval by the Executive Board of the revised IFAD Private-Sector Strategy.[617]

(vi) *IFAD's Transition Framework*

In accordance with the recommendation of the Executive Board at its 125th session in December 2018, the Governing Council considered and took note of the IFAD Transition Framework document, as contained in document GC 42/L.9. This Framework would continue to evolve along with IFAD's and borrowing countries' capacities and contexts to ensure a smooth, predictable, sustainable and equitable transition for borrowers by providing expanded and tailored lending and non-lending support.

(*b*) Executive Board

(i) *Proposals for Streamlining the Approval of IFAD-funded Projects and Programmes*

The Executive Board, at its 126th session, reviewed the proposals for streamlining the approval of projects and programmes and approved the following: (*a*) raising the funding threshold of the lapse-of-time procedure (LOT) from US$25 million to US$40 million (inclusive); (*b*) reducing the time required for approval of LOT proposals to 21 calendar days rule 24 of the Rules of Procedure of the Executive Board; and (*c*) delegating certain authority to the President to approve additional financing as per document EB 2019/126/R.48/Rev.2.

---

[617] The Proposed Amendments to the Basic Legal Texts of IFAD to Facilitate the Fund's Engagement with the Private Sector, which were adopted by the Governing Council in February 2019, entered into force on date of 10 September 2019.

(ii) *Concessional partner loan agreement proposals*

To mobilize additional resources during the period of the Eleventh Replenishment of IFAD's Resources (IFAD11) and possibly beyond, the Executive Board approved the proposals for concessional partner loans from Finland, India and France, as contained in documents EB 2019/126/R.28, EB 2019/126/R.29 and EB 2019/126/R.49 respectively.

(iii) *IFAD's Appeals Process: Assessment and Recommendations*

The Executive Board, at its 126th session, unanimously approved the Fund's withdrawal from the jurisdiction of the Administrative Tribunal of the International Labour Organization and its submission to the jurisdiction of the United Nations Appeals Tribunal. The detailed decision as contained in document EB 2019/126/C.R.P.1/Rev.2 and the related document (EB 2019/126/R.35), together with the IFAD Staff Association position paper would be publicly disclosed, and IFAD would undertake a communications effort to further engage with staff and ensure that the benefits of this change were clear.

(iv) *Partnership Agreements and Memoranda of Understanding*

Partnership Agreements and Memoranda of Understanding entered into by IFAD in 2019 include, but not limited to, the following:

a. Memorandum of Understanding with the Korea Rural Economic Institute

At its 126th session in May 2019, the Executive Board authorized the President to negotiate and finalize a memorandum of understanding with the Korea Rural Economic Institute to seek opportunities for collaboration in thematic areas related to agricultural and rural development including: rural poverty eradication; rural transformation; climate change; food and nutrition security; small and medium-sized rural enterprises and cooperatives; rural women and youth employment; and any other areas as may be agreed upon between the parties from time to time. The memorandum of understanding was signed on 13 May 2019 (EB 2019/127/INF.6).

b. Memorandum of understanding between the Asian Infrastructure Investment Bank and IFAD

The Executive Board authorized the President to negotiate and finalize a memorandum of understanding with the Asian Infrastructure Investment Bank (AIIB) aimed at establishing a common framework whereby both institutions can explore possible opportunities for cooperation on matters of common interest. The memorandum of understanding between IFAD and AIIB was signed on 12 July 2019. (EB 2019/127/INF.7).

(v) *IFAD Private Sector Engagement Strategy 2019–2024*

With the strong support expressed by members, the Executive Board, at its 127th session, approved the IFAD Private Sector Engagement Strategy 2019–2024 as contained in document EB 2019/127/R.3. Any new financial instrument proposed thereunder would be subject to the prior review of the Audit Committee and approval of the Executive Board. The progress in implementing the strategy would be reported regularly to the Board by Management.[618] IFAD would be the first United Nations agency to directly offer financial instruments to the private sector.

(vii) *Revision of IFAD's Project Procurement Guidelines*

The Executive Board approved the revised Project Procurement Guidelines for application to financing agreements in accordance with their terms and conditions. Upon approval, these Guidelines will replace the Project Procurement Guidelines adopted by the Executive Board at its hundredth session in September 2010.

(viii) *Anti-Money Laundering and Countering the Financing of Terrorism Policy*

The Executive Board approved the IFAD Anti-Money Laundering and Countering the Financing of Terrorism Policy, which would be revised to incorporate the amendments set forth in its addendum. Management will provide an update of the procedures for the implementation of this policy developed by the internal working group to the Audit Committee and to the Board, and ensure that external auditor would have a look into the procedures. The General Conditions for Agricultural Development Financing related to this policy and templates, especially for future projects with private sectors would be reviewed and developed further.[619]

(ix) *Sovereign borrowing framework loan from Canada*

The Executive Board approved the proposal that IFAD Management enter into a non-legally binding loan arrangement with the Department of Foreign Affairs, Trade and Development of Canada for a loan up to CAD$ 150 million. The arrangement is financially sustainable and adheres to the parameters set out in the SBF, as detailed in document EB 2019/128/R.42 and in its corrigendum.

(x) *Debt Sustainability Framework Reform*

Increasing commitments directly to lower-income countries on a replenishment-by-replenishment basis in a transparent and predictable manner is a way to preserve IFAD's financial sustainability and provides flexibility for members to pledge additional resources. The Executive Board approved the Debt Sustainability Framework Reform as contained in document EB 2019/128/R.44, and the transmittal of the draft resolution provided in annex IV of the DSF Reform document to the Governing Council including the recommendation that the Governing Council adopt the draft resolution at its forty-third session.

---

[618] The progress in implementing the strategy includes updates on the Agribusiness Capital Fund (ABC Fund), greater evidence of the appetite for IFAD financing, information on operational modalities and updates on capacity-building.

[619] EB 2019/128/R.41.

3. International Labour Organization[620]

(*a*) Legal Activities and Decisions

(i) *Adoption of a Declaration, a Convention with an accompanying Recommendation and resolutions during its 108th (Centenary) session (Geneva, June 2019)*[621]

At its 108th session, the International Labour Conference adopted a Declaration and one international labour Convention with an accompanying Recommendation. It also adopted ten resolutions, of which three are highlighted below.

a. The ILO Centenary Declaration for the Future of Work and the related resolution

At its 108th session, the International Labour Conference adopted the ILO Centenary Declaration for the Future of Work to mark the 100th anniversary of the ILO.[622]

This Declaration is the sixth declaration adopted by the Conference. Under the ILO's established practice, a declaration is a Conference resolution. It is a solemn instrument of a non-binding nature where principles of lasting importance are enunciated at the highest level. The Preamble of the Centenary Declaration refers to three previous Declarations of the same significance: the Declaration concerning the aims and purposes of the ILO (Declaration of Philadelphia), 1944;[623] the Declaration on Fundamental Principles and Rights at Work, 1998;[624] and the Declaration on Social Justice for a Fair Globalization, 2008.[625]

The Centenary Declaration looks at the major challenges and opportunities for the future of work, ranging from technology to climate change, from demographic shifts to the need for new skills. It provides guidance for dealing with these pressing issues and a platform for cooperation with other organizations in the international system. It is also a reaffirmation of the ILO's constitutional mandate and the critical role of social dialogue and international labour standards in the fulfilment of this mandate.

Together with the Declaration, the Conference adopted the resolution on the ILO Centenary Declaration for the Future of Work.[626] In this resolution, the Conference invited the ILO Governing Body to ensure the follow-up on, and regular review and implementation

---

[620] For official documents and more information about the International Labour Organization, see http://ilo.org.

[621] The texts adopted at the 108th session (2019) of the International Labour Conference are available in English, French and Spanish at https://www.ilo.org/ilc/ILCSessions/108/reports/texts-adopted/lang--en/index.htm.

[622] See https://www.ilo.org/sites/default/files/wcmsp5/groups/public/@ed_norm/@relconf/documents/meetingdocument/wcms_711674.pdf.

[623] See https://normlex.ilo.org/dyn/nrmlx_en/f?p=1000:62:0::NO:62:P62_LIST_ENTRIE_ID:2453907:NO.

[624] See https://www.ilo.org/ilo-declaration-fundamental-principles-and-rights-work/about-declaration/text-declaration-and-its-follow.

[625] See https://www.ilo.org/sites/default/files/wcmsp5/groups/public/@dgreports/@cabinet/documents/genericdocument/wcms_371208.pdf.

[626] See https://www.ilo.org/sites/default/files/wcmsp5/groups/public/@ed_norm/@relconf/documents/meetingdocument/wcms_711659.pdf.

of the Centenary Declaration. In addition, the Conference specifically requested the Governing Body to: (i) consider, as soon as possible, proposals for including safe and healthy working conditions in the ILO's framework of fundamental principles and rights at work; (ii) request the Director-General to submit to the Governing Body proposals aimed at promoting greater coherence within the multilateral system. In this resolution, the Conference also called for the completion, at the earliest opportunity, of the process of ratification of the Instrument of Amendment to the ILO Constitution, 1986, in order to definitively democratize the functioning and composition of the ILO governing bodies.

In a resolution adopted on 16 September 2019, the United Nations General Assembly welcomed the adoption of the ILO Centenary Declaration for the Future of Work and encouraged its implementation.[627]

b. Convention and Recommendation concerning the elimination of violence and harassment in the world of work and the related resolution

At its 108th session (2019), the International Labour Conference adopted the first-ever standards on the elimination of violence and harassment in the world of work, namely the Violence and Harassment Convention (No. 190) and Recommendation (No. 206), 2019. The texts of the Convention and Recommendation were achieved through tripartite consensus and were adopted with wide support. Their adoption reaffirms the ILO's crucial standard-setting role and provides a historic opportunity to shape a future of work based on dignity and respect.

The Convention calls for the right of everyone to a world of work free from violence and harassment to be respected, promoted and realized. It provides the first common definition of the term "violence and harassment", which is understood to refer to a "range of unacceptable behaviours and practices, or threats thereof, whether a single occurrence or repeated, that aim at, result in, or are likely to result in physical, psychological, sexual or economic harm, and includes gender-based violence and harassment". The Convention also defines "gender-based violence and harassment" as "violence and harassment directed at persons because of their sex or gender, or affecting persons of a particular sex or gender disproportionately, and includes sexual harassment." The Convention foresees that definitions in national laws and regulations may provide for a single concept or separate concepts.

The Convention and the Recommendation provide for a common framework grounded on the adoption of an inclusive, integrated and gender-responsive approach for the prevention and elimination of violence and harassment in the world of work, which envisages action that ranges from protection and prevention, enforcement and remedies, to guidance, training and awareness-raising. They take into account the different and complementary roles that governments, employers and workers, as well as their respective organizations, play in preventing and addressing violence and harassment, and they recognize that this requires members to respect, promote and realize the fundamental principles and rights at work. The Convention also provides that members shall require employers to take appropriate steps to prevent violence and harassment in the world of work, specifying that such steps should be commensurate with employers' degree of control.

---

[627] A/RES/73/342.

Calling for the adoption of a gender-responsive approach, the Convention acknowledges that gender-based violence and harassment disproportionately affects women and girls and provides for specific measures in this regard, while recognizing the need to tackle underlying causes and risk factors. The instruments also recognize the effects of domestic violence, and require measures, so far as is reasonably practicable, to mitigate its impact in the world of work.

The Convention applies to all sectors, whether private or public, both in the formal and informal economy, and whether in urban or rural areas. It acknowledges that there are groups disproportionately affected by violence and harassment, and highlights the importance of ensuring the right to equality and non-discrimination for such groups. It also requires the identification of specific sectors, occupations and work arrangements in which there is more exposure to violence and harassment in consultation with employers' and workers' representatives, and the adoption of appropriate protection measures.

These instruments provide the guiding compass for a comprehensive approach to eliminate violence and harassment, so that the issue can be addressed in its diverse and evolving forms, and in the different contexts in which it originates and escalates. Having received the deposit of ratification instruments from Fiji and Uruguay, Convention No. 190 will enter into force on 25 June 2021.

The resolution concerning the elimination of violence and harassment in the world of work invited governments to ratify the Violence and Harassment Convention, 2019, and to implement, in consultation with employer and worker organizations, the Violence and Harassment Convention and Recommendation, 2019. It also invited the Governing Body to request the ILO Director-General to develop a comprehensive strategy for the wide ratification of the Convention and effective implementation of the instruments. Such strategy was approved by the ILO Governing Body at its 337th session (24 October–7 November 2019).

c. Resolution concerning the status of the judges of the Administrative Tribunal of the International Labour Organization

On 17 June 2019, the International Labour Conference adopted a resolution granting the judges of the ILO Administrative Tribunal the status of "officials other than office officials" and thereby extended to them the privileges and immunities under article VI, Section 19 of the 1947 Convention on the Privileges and Immunities of the Specialized Agencies. The resolution accordingly amended paragraph 1 of article III of the Statute of the ILO Administrative Tribunal.

The resolution aligned the status of the judges of the Administrative Tribunal of the International Labour Organization with that of the judges of the United Nations Dispute and Appeals Tribunals who are considered officials other than Secretariat officials.

d. Other resolutions adopted by the International Labour Conference

The following resolutions were also adopted by the International Labour Conference:

- Resolution concerning the arrears of contributions of Sierra Leone
- Resolution concerning the arrears of contributions of Somalia
- Resolution concerning the adoption of the Programme and Budget for 2020–21 and the allocation of the budget of income among member States

- Resolution concerning the scale of assessments of contributions to the budget for 2020–21
- Resolution concerning the composition of the Administrative Tribunal of the International Labour Organization
- Resolution concerning the appointments to the ILO Staff Pension Committee (United Nations Joint Staff Pension Board)
- Resolution concerning the financial report and audited consolidated financial statements for the year ended 31 December 2018

(*b*) The Standards Review Mechanism Tripartite Working Group

The Standards Review Mechanism Tripartite Working Group (SRM TWG)[628] held its fifth meeting in September 2019. During this meeting, the SRM TWG reviewed seven international labour Conventions and Recommendations concerning employment policy, and examined the follow-up to be taken to a further instrument falling within that subject area that had previously been determined to be outdated, and made corresponding recommendations.[629] In addition, the SRM TWG discussed how to give effect to the 2017 and 2018 Governing Body decisions calling for the Office to prepare proposals for possible standard-setting items on the topics of biological hazards, ergonomics and manual handling, chemical hazards and guarding of machinery.[630]

In November 2019, the ILO Governing Body took a number of decisions based on the recommendations of the SRM TWG.[631] In relation to the review of the seven instruments on employment policy, the Governing Body classified five instruments as up to date and two instruments (Unemployment Convention, 1919 (No. 2) and Fee-Charging Employment Agencies Convention (Revised), 1949 (No. 96)) as outdated. The Governing Body decided to place on the agenda of the 110th session (2021) of the Conference an item concerning the withdrawal of the Fee Charging Employment Agencies Convention, 1933 (No. 34), which had already been decided to be outdated; and to place on the agenda of the 119th session (2030) of the Conference an item concerning the abrogation or withdrawal,

---

[628] The Standards Review Mechanism is an in-built mechanism of the ILO standards policy, established by the Governing Body in 2011. It is part of a series of actions taken by the ILO to ensure that it has a clear, robust and up-to-date body of international labour standards serving as a global reference. The SRM operates through a working group composed of representatives of the ILO tripartite constituents. The mandate of the SRM Tripartite Working Group (SRM TWG) is to undertake a review of international labour standards and to make recommendations to the Governing Body on the status of the standards examined, the identification of gaps in coverage, including those requiring new standards and practical and time-bound action as appropriate.

[629] The Standards Initiative: Report of the fifth meeting of the Standards Review Mechanism Tripartite Working Group, GB.337/LILS/1 (Annex I, Recommendations of the SRM TWG).

[630] The Standards Initiative: Report of the fifth meeting of the Standards Review Mechanism Tripartite Working Group, GB.337/LILS/1 (Annex I, Recommendations of the SRM TWG, para. 9).

[631] ILO Governing Body 337th session, Geneva, October-November 2019, GB.337/LILS/PV, para. 35 and The Standards Initiative: Report of the fifth meeting of the Standards Review Mechanism Tripartite Working Group, GB.337/LILS/1.

as relevant, of Convention No. 96.[632] It noted the SRM TWG's intention to evaluate the follow-up involving tailored plans of action concerning Convention No. 2 in 2026. In addition, the Governing Body requested the Office to initiate the preparation of proposals for possible standard-setting items on the topics of biological hazards, ergonomics and manual handling, chemical hazards and guarding of machinery, for consideration for inclusion in future agendas of the Conference; and be guided by the recommendations of the SRM TWG in preparing those standard-setting proposals for inclusion in the agenda of the Conference at the earliest dates possible and as a matter of institutional priority. The Governing Body also adopted the SRM TWG's recommendations on additional non-normative follow-up, including promotional campaigns and the development of tools in relation to public employment services, and job creation and decent work in SMEs and the establishment of an enabling environment for sustainable SMEs.

(c) Guidance documents submitted to the Governing Body of the International Labour Office

(i) *Conclusions of the Meeting of Experts on Cross-border Social Dialogue*

At its 337th session (October 2019), the Governing Body approved the conclusions of the Meeting of Experts on Cross-border Social Dialogue held in February 2019.[633] The overall aim of the conclusions is to enhance the contribution of cross-border social dialogue to the promotion of decent work in an increasingly interconnected world of work. They contain a set of recommendations both for the constituents and for the ILO, aimed at providing guidance on the future work of the Organization in this area. The deliberations at the Meeting of Experts were based on an Office report,[634] which provided a review of existing standards, the practices developed at various levels and the instances that pave the way for cross-border social dialogue.

The conclusions concern a variety of forms of cross-border social dialogue, including: cross-border social dialogue in regional economic communities, bilateral and multilateral trade agreements and interregional arrangements; cross-border social dialogue related to international instruments relevant to the promotion of fundamental principles and rights at work and human rights due diligence; cross-border social dialogue through transnational company agreements; and multi-stakeholder dialogue related to corporate social responsibility/responsible business conduct policies and initiatives adopted by enterprises.

---

[632] ILO Governing Body 337th session, Geneva, October-November 2019, GB.337/INS/PV, para. 51 and Proposals for the withdrawal of the Fee-Charging Employment Agencies Convention, 1933 (No. 34), and the abrogation of the Fee-Charging Employment Agencies Convention (Revised), 1949 (No. 96), GB.337/INS/2(Add.1).

[633] ILO Governing Body 337th session, Geneva, October-November 2019, GB.337/INS/PV, para. 51 and Proposals for the withdrawal of the Fee-Charging Employment Agencies Convention, 1933 (No. 34), and the abrogation of the Fee-Charging Employment Agencies Convention (Revised), 1949 (No. 96), GB.337/INS/2(Add.1).

[634] ILO, 2019. *Cross-border social dialogue*, Report for discussion at the Tripartite Meeting of Experts on Cross-border social dialogue, Geneva 12–14 February 2019.

(ii) *The Meeting of Experts on Defining Recruitment Fees and Related Costs*

At its 335th session (March 2019), the Governing Body approved the publication and dissemination of the definition of recruitment fees and related costs, adopted by the Meeting of Experts on Defining Recruitment Fees and Related Costs held in November 2018, which should be read together with the General principles and operational guidelines for fair recruitment of 2016 recognizing the principle that workers shall not be charged directly or indirectly, in whole or in part, any fees or related costs for their recruitment.[635] The agreed definition of recruitment fees covers all types of recruitment, in all sectors and for all workers, regardless of whether they were recruited nationally or internationally. Experts determined, among other things, that related costs were expenses integral to the recruitment and placement process within and across borders, taking into account that the widest set of related recruitment costs were incurred for international recruitment.

(iii) *The Joint ILO–UNESCO Committee of Experts on the Application of the Recommendations concerning Teaching Personnel*

At its 335th session (March 2019), the Governing Body took note of the report of the 13th session of the Joint ILO–UNESCO Committee of Experts on the Application of the Recommendations concerning Teaching Personnel (CEART) held in October 2018.[636] At that session, the CEART examined and made recommendations regarding a number of issues affecting teaching personnel, including teachers and the future of work; privatization and education; technical and vocational education and training conditions at the upper secondary and tertiary levels; the assessment and evaluation of higher education personnel; and financing for education. The CEART also examined a number of allegations from teacher unions regarding the application of the Recommendations concerning Teaching Personnel. The CEART furthermore adopted a declaration entitled "Education is not a commodity: Teachers, the right to education and the future of work".

(iv) *The Subcommittee on Wages of Seafarers of the Joint Maritime Commission*

At its 335th session (March 2019), the Governing Body took note of the report of the Subcommittee on Wages of Seafarers of the Joint Maritime Commission which met in Geneva in November 2018. The purpose of the meeting was to update the minimum monthly basic pay or wage figure for able seafarers referred to in the Maritime Labour Convention, 2006, as amended, (Guideline B2.2.4), which revised a similar provision in the Seafarers' Wages, Hours of Work and the Manning of Ships Recommendation, 1996 (No. 187), and to make the appropriate recommendation to the Governing Body. The Subcommittee adopted a resolution concerning the ILO minimum monthly basic pay or wage for able seafarers in which, among other things, it agreed to update the current ILO

---

[635] ILO Governing Body, 335th session (March 2019), GB.335/PV, para. 563. Report of the Director-General. Second Supplementary Report: Report of the Meeting of Experts on Defining Recruitment Fees and Related Costs (Geneva, 14–16 November 2018), GB.335/INS/14/2.

[636] ILO Governing Body, 335th session (March 2019), GB.335/PV, para. 725. The Joint ILO–UNESCO Committee of Experts on the Application of the Recommendations concerning Teaching Personnel, 13th session, Final report, CEART/13/2018/10.

minimum basic wage for an able seafarer and agreed on the figure to be used as the basis for recalculation purposes.[637]

(*d*) Legal advisory services and training

With respect to international labour standards, in 2019, the ILO provided technical assistance in reporting and other international labour standards related obligations, including capacity building and assistance with implementation and reform of national legislation. Assistance included training on the content of selected international labour standards; research to generate information on the status of implementation of international labour standards, including legislative gap analyses; advice on elements that will enable tripartite constituents to take the relevant decisions aiming at full implementation; legal advice on the revision or drafting of legislation and regulations in the light of international labour standards, best comparative labour practices and the comments of the ILO's supervisory bodies; and strengthening the data collection and reporting capacity of tripartite constituents. The ILO, in collaboration with its International Training Centre in Turin, delivered training courses to legal professionals at various levels (interregional, regional, sub regional and national), collected judicial decisions in which domestic and international courts have relied on international labour standards and the work of ILO supervisory bodies, and developed an online self-guided training package on the judicial use of international labour law sources. The ILO also engaged with the constituents through conferences and tripartite meetings. With respect to the Violence and Harassment Convention (No. 190) and Recommendation (No. 206), 2019, the ILO provided technical assistance in the elaboration of pre-ratification analysis in 10 countries and in the undertaking of several reforms of national legislation.

(*e*) Committee on Freedom of Association

At its last meetings (March and June 2019), the Committee on Freedom of Association had before it more than 42 cases concerning 25 countries from all parts of the world, for which it presented interim or final conclusions, or for which the examination was adjourned pending the arrival of information from governments. Many of these cases have been before the Committee on more than one occasion. Moreover, 24 new cases have been submitted to it since the last meeting of the Committee of Experts. The Committee on Freedom of Association has drawn the attention of the Committee of Experts to the legislative aspects of Cases Nos 3246 and 3247 (Chile), 3296 (Mozambique), 2318 (Cambodia), 3128 (Zimbabwe), 3284 (El Salvador), 3317 (Panama), 3021 (Turkey) and 3076 (Republic of Maldives).

---

[637] ILO Governing Body, 335th session (March 2019), GB.335/PV, para. 725. The Subcommittee on Wages of Seafarers of the Joint Maritime Commission. Final report. Updating of the minimum monthly basic pay or wage figure for able seafarers, SWJMC/2018/6, appendix III.

(*f*) Representations submitted under article 24 of the ILO Constitution and complaints made under article 26 of the ILO Constitution

In 2019, the Governing Body considered the developments in two representations submitted under article 24 of the ILO Constitution by industrial associations of employers or workers, alleging that a member State that has ratified a Convention has failed to secure within its jurisdiction the effective observance of that Convention.

The Governing Body also considered the developments in three complaints (Bangladesh, Chile and the Bolivarian Republic of Venezuela) made under article 26 of the Constitution alleging that a member State that has ratified a Convention is not securing its effective observance.

4. International Monetary Fund[638]

(*a*) Membership

(i) *Accession to membership*

No new countries became members of the International Monetary Fund (IMF) in 2019. As of 31 December 2019, the membership of the IMF consisted of 189 member countries.

(ii) *Status and obligations under article VIII or article XIV of the IMF's Articles of Agreement*

Under article VIII, Sections 2, 3, and 4 of the IMF's Articles of Agreement, members of the IMF may not, without the IMF's approval (i) impose restrictions on the making of payments and transfers for current international transactions; or (ii) engage in any discriminatory currency arrangements or multiple currency practices. Notwithstanding these provisions, pursuant to article XIV, Section 2 of the IMF's Articles of Agreement, when a member joins the IMF, it may notify the IMF that it intends to avail itself of the transitional arrangements under article XIV of the IMF's Articles of Agreement that allow the member to maintain and adapt to changing circumstances the restrictions on payments and transfers for current international transactions that were in effect on the date on which it became a member. Article XIV of the IMF's Articles of Agreement does not, however, permit a member, after it joins the IMF, to introduce new restrictions on the making of payments and transfers for current international transactions without the IMF's approval.

The total number of countries that have accepted the obligations of article VIII, Sections 2, 3, and 4, as of December 31, 2019, was 172. Seventeen countries continued to avail themselves of the transitional arrangements under article XIV.

(iii) *Overdue financial obligations to the IMF*

As of December 31, 2019, members with protracted arrears (*i.e.*, financial obligations that are overdue by six months or more) involving the general resources of the IMF were

---

[638] For official documents and more information about the International Monetary Fund, see https://www.imf.org/.

Somalia and Sudan. In addition, Somalia and Sudan have protracted overdue Trust Fund and/or Structural Adjustment Facility obligations not involving the general resources of the IMF. Article XXVI, Section 2(*a*) of the IMF's Articles of Agreement provides that if "a member fails to fulfill any of its obligations under this Agreement, the [IMF] may declare the member ineligible to use the general resources of the [IMF]." Such declarations of ineligibility were in place at end-December 2019 with respect to Somalia and Sudan, whose arrears are subject to sanctions under article XXVI.

(*b*) Key policy decisions of the IMF

In 2019, the IMF took steps to move ahead with a number of major policy reforms that would allow it to meet the evolving needs of its members and to adjust to changes in the global economy, as follows:

(i) *The 2018–19 review of facilities for low-income countries (LICs)*

On May 24, 2019, the Executive Board of the IMF concluded the 2018–19 Review of Facilities for Low-Income Countries—Reform Proposals ("Facilities Review") and the companion Review of the Financing of the Fund's Concessional Assistance and Debt Relief to Low-Income Countries ("Financing Review").[639]

The reform package enhanced support for LICs by: (i) providing higher levels of access to concessional financing, favoring the needs of the poorest and most vulnerable LICs; (ii) responding to the specific challenges faced by countries in fragile or post-conflict situations and by countries vulnerable to natural disasters, including through higher access limits under the Rapid Credit Facility (RCF); and (iii) improving the flexibility of Poverty Reduction and Growth Trust (PRGT) instruments through reforms to the Standby Credit Facility (SCF) and the Extended Credit Facility (ECF) to allow better tailoring of program design to countries' diverse circumstances. The reform package is consistent with maintaining the self-sustainability of the PRGT financing framework. The policy also increased access limits under the Rapid Financing Instrument (RFI), the emergency lending instrument available to all IMF member countries. The RFI access limits increase expands the scope for providing financial support to countries in fragile situations and/or vulnerable to natural disasters that are not eligible for concessional financing while preserving broad harmonization of access limits across the RFI and the RCF.

This Facilities Review was part of a wider policy work agenda relating to the Fund's support for LICs. The companion paper on the Review of the Financing of the Fund's Concessional Assistance and Debt Relief to LICs analyzed the impact of the reforms on the PRGT financing framework. The parallel Review of the PRGT Interest Rate Structure aligned the interest rates on loans extended under the SCF and the ECF, resulting in a continued zero-interest rate charge for the period July 2019–June 2021.[640]

---

[639] Press release available at https://www.imf.org/en/News/Articles/2019/06/06/pr19202-imf-executive-board-approvesreform-package-to-enhance-support-to-low-income countries.

[640] Press release available at https://www.imf.org/en/News/Articles/2019/06/26/pr19239-exec-board-modifies-prgt-intr-rate-mechapprove-zero-rate-all-lic-lend-facilities-june-2021.

The Facilities Review follows the May 2019 Board paper on Building Resilience in Developing Countries Vulnerable to Large Natural Disasters which set out a three-pillar approach to resilience-building as a useful framework for analyzing policy options in a systematic fashion and for identifying key priorities. In the meeting on May 1, 2019, Directors noted that the Fund has a valuable role to play in supporting country efforts to build resilience to natural disasters, as part of its surveillance and capacity building activities. A coherent resilience strategy should fit within a medium-term macroeconomic policy framework that is consistent with maintaining debt sustainability, including under adverse shocks—an area of core Fund expertise. Staff could also contribute through analysis of the economic impact of disasters and of trade-offs between public investment and debt accumulation. Directors agreed that the Fund's lending toolkit was sufficiently flexible to provide support for disaster-vulnerable countries that face a BoP need, but most saw scope to increase access limits as well as to use the toolkit in non-traditional ways to support resilience-building. Directors encouraged giving special attention to countries prone to natural disasters in the upcoming FSAP Review and Comprehensive Surveillance Review.[641]

(ii) *The 2018 review of program design and conditionality*

On May 3, 2019, the Executive Board of the IMF discussed staff papers reviewing the design, conditionality, and performance of IMF-supported programs ongoing during the period September 2011 to end-2017.[642]

Executive Directors welcomed the first comprehensive stocktaking of the Fund's lending operations since the 2008 global financial crisis. They noted the finding that three-quarters of Fund-supported programs had achieved success or some success, despite the extremely challenging post-crisis environment. Directors agreed that there is room for improvement, drawing lessons for future program design from success and failure and case studies. They broadly agreed with the findings and, with some caveats, supported the key recommendations, some of which would require further discussions in the upcoming reviews of relevant Fund policies.

Directors welcomed the finding that Fund-supported programs were generally well-tailored to country needs and perceived as being consistent with the principle of uniformity of treatment. However, they saw scope for better tailoring and streamlining program objectives and structural conditions, particularly for fragile and small States, in light of their economic circumstances and capacity constraints. Many Directors also encouraged staff to ensure the application of the 2017 Staff Guidance Note on the Fund's Engagement with Small Developing States, and to integrate critical resilience-building measures into the programs.

(iii) *Strategy for IMF Engagement on Social Spending*

On May 2, 2019, the Executive Board of the International Monetary Fund (IMF) discussed a policy paper outlining a strategy to guide IMF engagement on social spending

---

[641] Press release available at https://www.imf.org/en/News/Articles/2019/06/25/pr19241-exec-board-discusses-building-resiliencedeveloping-countries-vulnerable-natural-disasters.

[642] Press release available at https://www.imf.org/en/News/Articles/2019/05/20/pr19174-imf-executiveboard-discusses-2018-review-of-program-design-and-conditionality.

issues to enhance its effectiveness.[643] Executive Directors welcomed the proposed strategy to guide Fund engagement on social spending issues. They noted that the Fund has made considerable progress in its treatment of social spending over recent years and that the proposed framework is expected to strengthen the Fund's engagement on social spending issues by making it more systematic and effective in surveillance and Fund-supported programs. Directors welcomed that the strategy reflected consultations with a broad set of stakeholders, including civil society, academics, and international development institutions.

Directors appreciated that the proposed strategy will be guided by an assessment of the macro-criticality of specific social spending issues. They agreed that social spending can become macro-critical through three key channels: fiscal sustainability, spending adequacy, and spending efficiency. In this context, Directors underlined the need for a sufficiently granular framework to assess macro-criticality. Directors emphasized that staff should continue to provide policy advice on sustainable financing of social spending with an increased focus on the quality of such spending for improving social outcomes. Directors also highlighted the importance of underpinning both surveillance and program policy advice on social spending with in-depth analytical work as appropriate and supported by capacity development where necessary. Directors noted the importance of technical assistance to help ensure adequate data availability and quality, and to help create fiscal space—both through domestic revenue mobilization and improved spending efficiency—to finance increases in social spending where needed. A number of Directors noted that the distributive effects of taxation and other revenue sources should be considered together with the effects of social spending.

(iv) *International corporate tax*

On February 21, 2019, the Executive Board of the IMF discussed a paper setting out the current state of international income tax arrangements.[644] Executive Directors welcomed the opportunity to take stock of recent developments in international aspects of corporate taxation, and offered preliminary observations on alternative proposals currently being debated. They acknowledged the importance of these issues to all Fund members in their efforts to raise revenues in an efficient and equitable manner, and the potential for significant cross-border spillovers.

Directors welcomed the significant progress made in addressing corporate tax avoidance and enhancing multilateral cooperation, notably by the G-20/OECD project on Base Erosion and Profit Shifting, and the Inclusive Framework that has broadened the scope of cooperation to many non-OECD countries. At the same time, they noted that there remain shortcomings in current international tax arrangements, and that many countries face pressures to introduce unilateral action. Directors agreed that much remains to be done to find sustainable global solutions, building on the progress achieved so far to ensure fairness, inclusiveness, and broad consensus, although their views differed on the extent of needed reforms and the roles of relevant bodies.

---

[643] Press release available at https://www.imf.org/en/News/Articles/2019/06/13/pr19217-imf-executive-board-supports-newstrategy-for-engagement-on-social-spending.

[644] Press release available at https://www.imf.org/en/Publications/Policy-Papers/Issues/2019/03/08/Corporate-Taxation-in-the-GlobalEconomy-46650.

As an important element of the current debate, Directors welcomed the discussion on tax challenges associated with digitalization. They recognized that this is a difficult issue, technically and politically, and that views on whether special treatment is needed, and if so in what form, continue to differ widely. For the long term, a number of Directors considered that it would not be desirable or feasible to design ring-fenced solutions. Directors looked forward to the final report from the OECD to the G-20 in 2020, which could serve as a basis for a cooperative approach going forward.

(v) *Selection process for IMF Managing Director*

On September 5, 2019, the Board of Governors of the IMF approved the proposal by the Executive Board to remove the age limit for the position of IMF Managing Director.[645] Approval of the proposal required a simple majority of the votes cast, with a minimum participation requirement of a majority of Governors holding two-thirds of the total voting power. Voting ran from August 21 to September 4.

Since 1951, the IMF's By-Laws had prohibited the appointment of a candidate aged 65 or over as Managing Director, and had also prohibited the Managing Director from serving past his/her 70th birthday. The amendment to the By-Laws adopted by the Board of Governors brought the Managing Director's terms of appointment into line with those of members of the IMF Executive Board, which the Managing Director chairs, and those of the President of the World Bank Group, who are not subject to an age limit.

The IMF Executive Board engaged in the selection of a successor to outgoing Managing Director Christine Lagarde, who stepped down on September 12, 2019.[646]

On September 25, 2019, the IMF Executive Board selected Kristalina Georgieva to serve as IMF Managing Director and Chair of the Executive Board for a five-year term starting on October 1, 2019.[647]

5. International Maritime Organization[648]

(*a*) Membership

As of 31 December 2019, the membership of the International Maritime Organization (IMO) stood at 174. In August 2019, the Federated States of Micronesia and the Islamic Republic of Afghanistan expressed interest in joining the Organization.

---

[645] Press release available at https://www.imf.org/en/News/Articles/2019/09/05/pr19325-imf-executive-board-governors-remove-agelimit-for-the-position-of-managing-director.

[646] Press release available at https://www.imf.org/en/News/Articles/2019/07/16/pr19281-statement-imf-executive-board-managingdirector-lagarde-resigns-selection-process-starts.

[647] Press release available at https://www.imf.org/en/News/Articles/2019/09/25/pr19351-imf-executive-board-selects-kristalinageorgieva-as-managing-director.

[648] For official documents and more information about the International Maritime Organization, see http://www.imo.org.

(*b*) Review of the legal activities

(i) *Significant legal activities, developments and decisions*

a. Regulatory scoping exercise on Maritime Autonomous Surface Ships

The Maritime Safety Committee (MSC) and the Legal Committee (LEG) took the first steps in how safe, secure and environmentally sound Maritime Autonomous Surface Ships (MASS) operations may be addressed in IMO instruments. To this end, the Committees approved a framework for a regulatory scoping exercise (RSE) with a target completion year of 2020, including preliminary definitions of MASS and degrees of autonomy, as well as a methodology for conducting the exercise and a plan of work. The exercise envisaged a two-step approach: an initial review of the instruments under the purview of MSC with an agreed methodology and an analysis of the most appropriate way of addressing MASS operations. The results of the second step would be submitted in 2020 for final consideration. A review of analyses entered in GISIS during the RSE in the Facilitation Committee (FAL), LEG and MSC regarding different conventions under their purview, identified potential common gaps and/or themes that may require clarification.

LEG would carry out a gap analysis of liability and compensation treaties developed under the auspices of IMO. Particular consideration is given to the impact of MASS on seafarers. A web platform based on similar framework and methodology as undertaken by the MSC would be used to facilitate the work. The aim was to complete the review and analysis for consideration by LEG at its next session in 2020.

MSC invited volunteering member States to submit the results of the first step to the Intersessional Working Group, which took place in September 2019, and agreed on the result of the first step of the RSE, and commenced the second step.

On the deadline of the first stage of the second step (*i.e.* initial stage), *i.e.* 15 November 2019, all volunteering member States had completed the initial analysis of the most appropriate way(s) of addressing MASS operations and imported the results in the MASS module.

b. Safety in polar waters

MSC approved the guidance for navigation and communication equipment intended for use on ships operating in polar waters. The guidance includes recommendations on temperature and mechanical shock testing, and on how to address ice accretion and battery performance in cold temperatures. This is expected to be an important tool in support of the implementation of the mandatory Polar Code.

The Assembly adopted a resolution urging member States to implement, on a voluntary basis, interim safety measures of the Polar Code on ships not certified under the SOLAS Convention.

c. Piracy and maritime security

In 2019, the Organization received reports of 190 incidents of piracy and armed robbery against ships which occurred worldwide, as compared to 223 incidents reported in 2018, a decrease of 15 per cent. Based on the data received it also emerges that the areas most affected by acts of piracy and armed robbery against ships in 2019 were West Africa (67 incidents), Straits of Malacca and Singapore (45 incidents) and the South China

Sea (31 incidents), followed by South America (Pacific) (14 incidents) and South America (Caribbean) (12 incidents). The number of incidents that took place in the Gulf of Guinea (West Africa) decreased in 2019 by 14 compared to 2018, when 81 incidents were reported. However, the number of incidents involving kidnap and missing crew increased from 11 in 2018 to 20 in 2019, with a total of 151 crew members reported as kidnapped/missing. This is the highest number so far on record.

The number of incidents of piracy and armed robbery against ships in the Straits of Malacca and Singapore increased to 45, from 8 incidents reported in 2018. About 70 per cent of the 2019 incidents targeted a steaming ship, compared to approximately 34 per cent of incidents worldwide in 2018. The number of incidents of piracy and armed robbery against ships reported in the South China Sea has gradually decreased, with 31 incidents reported to the Organization in 2019. A decreasing trend is identifiable since 2013, when 142 incidents were reported. These include incidents that have occurred in the waters off the Philippines and Indonesia, and in the area of the Sulu–Celebes Sea (waters between the Philippines and Malaysia). Further details, including regional trends and developments throughout 2019 are provided in the Secretariat's Reports on acts of piracy and armed robbery against ships, Annual Report—2019, which would be released in April 2020.

In June 2019, MSC established the G7++ Friends of the Gulf of Guinea, a forum to coordinate international efforts and encourage interested parties to participate towards eradication of piracy in the Gulf of Guinea, the first meeting was held on 2 July 2019. This group is open to all interested member States, NGOs and IGOs.

(ii) *Seafarer abandonment cases*

The Legal Committee discussed the growing number of cases of abandonment and recognised the need for collective action to address the issue. Proposals for guidelines on cooperation between flag and port States to resolve seafarer abandonment cases will be discussed at its next session.

In 2017 and 2018, the cases reported increased drastically. In 2017, there were 55 cases reported, 14 of which were resolved that year and 8 of which were resolved in 2018. In 2018, the total number of reported cases was 44 and of those, 15 cases had been resolved as of 31 December 2018. Of the cases reported in 2018, eight involved flag States which had not ratified the MLC, 2006.

a. Addressing fraudulent ship registration

Fraudulent registration and related unlawful practices include the registration of vessels without the knowledge or approval of the relevant national maritime administration. Fraudulent registration of ships prevents lawful registries from exercising effective jurisdiction and control over vessels at sea, deprives lawful registries from obtaining legitimate revenue while unjustly enriching fraudulent actors and exacts unjustified reputational harms on States when vessels engage in illicit activities under the cloak of a fraudulent registration. Furthermore, fraudulently registered ships may not be in compliance with safety and environmental protection standards, endangering the vessels' crew and posing an increased threat of damage to the marine environment.

To address this problem, the IMO Assembly, at its thirty-first session, in December 2019, approved resolution A.1142(31) on Measures to prevent the fraudulent registration and fraudulent registries of ships urging governments to provide information on their registries of ships and communicate it to the Organization. The resolution includes a procedure for communicating this information to IMO, including information on the name of national governmental body(ies) and authorized or delegated entities in charge of ship registration. Its aim is to allow the IMO Secretariat to verify the information, through the appropriate channels, and to populate the new comprehensive database of registries in the publicly available Contact Points Module in the Global Integrated Shipping Information System (GISIS). The IMO Secretariat has improved the display of information on ships which have been confirmed as not legally registered. In such a case, a "false flag" is shown for the particular ship in the module on Ship and company particulars in GISIS.

Furthermore, LEG agreed that IMO should work with the United Nations Security Council to establish an easily searchable database, by IMO number and vessel name, of vessels currently the subject of, or designated pursuant to, United Nations Security Council resolutions. The Committee further agreed on recommended best practices to assist in combating fraudulent registration of ships and will consider, at its future sessions, effective enforcement measures to discourage the practice and to prevent ships with fraudulent registration from operating.

b. Reduction of greenhouse gas emissions from ships

The Marine Environment Protection Committee (MEPC) approved the Programme of follow-up actions of the initial strategy on the reduction of greenhouse gas (GHG) emissions from ships, setting out a vision to reduce GHG emissions from international shipping up to 2023[649].

Feeding into the process towards adoption of a revised Strategy in 2023 will be the data collection system on fuel oil consumption of ships over 5,000 gross tons, which began on 1 January 2019. IMO undertook the fourth IMO GHG study, which will provide an update of emissions estimates for international shipping for the period 2012 to 2018.

Moreover, the MEPC adopted the 2018 Guidelines on the method of calculation of the attained Energy Efficiency Design Index (EEDI) for new ships, incorporating updates to the 2014 Guidelines.

The MEPC also approved several measures to support the objectives set out in the initial IMO strategy on reduction of GHG emissions from ships, in line with the Paris Agreement temperature goals under UNFCCC and the United Nations 2030 Agenda for Sustainable Development. The measures aim in particular to strengthen existing requirements for new ships to be more energy efficient and to encourage cooperation with ports to reduce emissions from shipping. The Committee also approved a procedure for the impact assessment of new measures proposed and agreed to establish a multi-donor trust fund for GHG.

---

[649] The initial strategy refers to a range of candidate short-, mid- and long-term measures. Short term measures could be finalized and agreed between 2018 and 2023; mid-term measures, between 2023 and 2030; and long-term measures, beyond 2030.

c. Implementation of sulphur 2020 limit

A new 0.50 per cent limit on sulphur in ships' fuel oil will be in force from 1 January 2020, under the MARPOL treaty. The MEPC adopted a comprehensive set of guidance and guidelines to support the consistent implementation of the new limit which will be applicable globally—while in designated emission control areas (ECAs) the limit will be even lower, at 0.10 per cent.

The MEPC adopted a MARPOL amendment to prohibit the carriage of non-compliant fuel oil for combustion purposes for propulsion or operation on board a ship—unless the ship has an exhaust gas cleaning system ("scrubber") fitted.

Sulphur oxides (SOx) are known to be harmful to human health, causing respiratory symptoms and lung disease. In the atmosphere, SOx can lead to acid rain, which can harm crops, forests and aquatic species, and contributes to the acidification of the oceans. Consistent implementation of the 0.50 per cent sulphur limit for all ships will ensure a level playing field and is expected to improve the environment and human health.

d. Marine plastic pollution

The MEPC also adopted an Action Plan with a completion date of 2025 to enhance existing regulations and introduce new measures to reduce marine plastic litter from all ships, including fishing vessels. The plan supports IMO's commitment to UN 2030 Sustainable Development Goal 14 (SDG 14) on conservation and sustainable use of the oceans.

Both macroplastics (such as plastic bags, water bottles and fishing gear) and microplastics (small plastic particles generally five millimetres or less in size) in the marine environment result in harmful effects on marine life, biodiversity and human health. Studies demonstrate that, despite the existing regulatory framework to prevent marine plastic litter from ships, discharges into the sea continue to occur. A Correspondence Group was established to finalize a draft strategy to address marine plastic litter from ships, based on discussions held in 2019 and report to MEPC in 2020.

e. Ballast Water Management Convention implementation

The International Convention for the Control and Management of Ships' Ballast Water, 2004 (BWM Convention) entered into force in September 2017 and has to date been ratified by 81 States, representing 80.76 per cent of world merchant shipping tonnage. Amendments to the treaty, relating to implementation timelines, entered into force on 13 October 2019. MEPC 74 approved five ballast water management systems that make use of Active Substances.

The BWM Convention aims to stop the spread of potentially invasive aquatic species in ships' ballast water and requires ships to manage their ballast water to remove, render harmless or avoid the uptake or discharge of aquatic organisms and pathogens within ballast water and sediments. In October 2019, the Code for the approval of the ballast water management systems will become mandatory. The MEPC approved amendments to the BWM Convention concerning commissioning testing of ballast water management systems and the form of the International Ballast Water in 2020.

f. Conventions and agreements not yet into force

Hong Kong International Convention for the Safe and Environmentally Sound Recycling of Ships, 2009

As of 1 October 2019, there were 13 contracting States to the Convention, representing approximately 29.42 per cent of the gross tonnage of the world's merchant shipping. The combined annual ship recycling volume of the contracting States during the preceding 10 years is 1,729,478 GT, *i.e.* 0.44 per cent of the merchant shipping tonnage of the same States.

2010 Convention on Liability and Compensation for Damage in Connection with the Carriage of Hazardous and Noxious Substances by Sea

The 2010 Convention on the liability and compensation for the damage in connection with the carriage of hazardous and noxious substances by sea (2010 HNS Convention), has as of 1 October 2019, five contracting States (Canada, Norway, Turkey, Denmark and South Africa), four of which have more than 2 million 3 units of gross tonnage. The treaty provides a global regime for liability and compensation in the event of an incident involving the international or domestic carriage by sea of Hazardous and Noxious Substances, such as chemicals, LPG and LNG. All States are encouraged to ratify the 2010 HNS Protocol to enable its entry into force as soon as possible.

Cape Town Agreement of 2012 on the Implementation of the Provisions of the 1993 Protocol relating to the Torremolinos International Convention for the Safety of Fishing Vessels, 1977

As of 1 October 2019, there were 11 contracting States to the Agreement, with an aggregate number of fishing vessels of 24 meters in length and over operating on the high seas equivalent to 1413. This Agreement effectively updates and revises the Torremolinos Protocol of 1993 relating to the Torremolinos International Convention for the Safety of Fishing Vessels, 1977, which is not intended to enter into force.

In October 2019, IMO and the Government of Spain organized Ministerial Conference on Fishing Vessel Safety and Illegal, Unreported and Unregulated (IUU) Fishing, in Torremolinos, Málaga, Spain that aimed at promoting the ratification of the Cape Town Agreement. During the conference, nearly 50 States signed the Torremolinos Declaration, publicly indicating their determination to ratify the Agreement by the target date of 11 October 2022 (tenth anniversary of the adoption of the Agreement).

6. United Nations Educational, Scientific and Cultural Organization[650]

(*a*) International regulations

The texts of all UNESCO standard-setting instruments adopted by the General Conference or by International Conference of States, as well as the list of States parties to the conventions, can be found on UNESCO's website.[651]

---

[650] For official documents and more information about the United Nations Educational, Scientific and Cultural Organization, see https://www.unesco.org/.

[651] See http://www.unesco.org/legal_instruments.

(i) *Entry into force of instruments previously adopted*

The Revised Convention on the Recognition of Studies, Certificates, Diplomas, Degrees and Other Academic Qualifications in Higher Education in African States, adopted in Addis Ababa (Ethiopia) on 12 December 2014, entered into force on 15 December 2019 in accordance with its article V.2.

(ii) *Instruments adopted by the General Conference of UNESCO at its 40th session (12—27 November 2019)*

The General Conference adopted at its 40th session, on 25 November 2019, the Global Convention on the Recognition of Qualifications in Higher Education (40 C/Resolution 85).

The General Conference also adopted at its 40th session, on 25 November 2019, the Recommendation on Open Educational Resources (OER) (40 C/Resolution 57).

(iii) *Instruments adopted by the International Conference of States*

The Regional Convention on the Recognition of Studies, Diplomas and Degrees in Higher Education in Latin America and the Caribbean was adopted in Buenos Aires (Argentina) on 13 July 2019 by an International Conference of UNESCO member States of the Latin America and the Caribbean Region.

(iv) *Proposals concerning the preparation of new instruments*

The General Conference, at its 40th session, invited the Director-General to submit to it at its 41st session in 2021 a draft text of a recommendation on the ethics of artificial intelligence (40 C/Resolution 37). The General Conference also invited the Director-General to submit to it at the earliest possible session (preferably the 41st session) a draft text of a recommendation on open science (40 C/Resolution 24).

The UNESCO Office of International Standards and Legal Affairs organized the first UNESCO Conventions Ceremony on the margins of the 40th session of the General Conference. On that occasion, in the presence of the Director-General, three States signed different conventions and eight States deposited 10 instruments of ratification. The deposit of some of these instruments during the Ceremony enabled the entry into force of the 2014 Revised Convention on the Recognition of Studies, Certificates, Diplomas, Degrees and Other Academic Qualifications in Higher Education in African States on 15 December 2019. In view of the success of this new event for the ratification and implementation of international standards adopted by UNESCO, the organization of other signature and ratification ceremonies along the lines of this Ceremony are foreseen in the future.

(*b*) Human rights

Examination of cases and questions concerning the exercise of human rights coming within UNESCO's fields of competence.

The Committee on Conventions and Recommendations met in private sessions at UNESCO Headquarters from 3 to 5 April 2019 and from 9 to 11 October 2019 in order to examine communications which had been transmitted to it in accordance with decision 104 EX/3.3 of the Executive Board.

At its April 2019 session, the Committee examined six communications of which three were examined with a view to determining their admissibility or otherwise, two were examined as to their substance and one was examined for the first time. One communication was struck from the list because it was considered as having been settled. The examination of the other five communications were deferred. The Committee presented its report to the Executive Board at its 206th session.

At its October 2019 session, the Committee examined five communications of which three were examined with a view to determining their admissibility or otherwise, one was examined as to the substance and one was examined for the first time. The examination of these five communications were deferred. The Committee presented its report to the Executive Board at its 207th session.

7. United Nations Industrial Development Organization[652]

(*a*) Constitutional matters

On 7 March 2019, the Federated States of Micronesia deposited with the Secretary-General of the United Nations an instrument of accession to the Constitution of UNIDO. The Constitution entered into force for the Federated States of Micronesia on 7 March 2019 in accordance with its article 25(2) *c*.

On 1 April 2019, Antigua and Barbuda deposited with the Secretary-General of the United Nations an instrument of ratification to the Constitution of UNIDO. The Constitution entered into force for Antigua and Barbuda on 1 April 2019 in accordance with its article 25(2) *c*.

(*b*) Agreements and other arrangements concluded in 2019

Information on agreements and other arrangements concluded in 2019 is available in Appendix G to the 2019 Annual Report of the United Nations Industrial Development Organization (UNIDO).

8. Universal Postal Union[653]

(*a*) Membership

As of 31 December 2019, the membership of the Universal Postal Union (UPU) remained unchanged at 192 members.

---

[652] For official documents and more information about the United Nations Industrial Development Organization, see http://www.unido.org.

[653] For official documents and more information about the Universal Postal Union, see http://www.upu.int.

(*b*) Agreements concluded by the Universal Postal Union

On 29 March and 4 April 2019, the UPU and the Ministry of Internal Affairs and Communications of Japan signed a memorandum of cooperation concerning the implementation of Recommendation C 14/2016.[654] The memorandum was concluded with the aim of fostering the development of a global policy at the UPU level on risk reduction and management and emergency assistance activities.

On 2 April 2019, the UPU and the FutureLab Consulting Inc. signed a letter of intent in relation to blockchain technology and applications in postal services. The letter was concluded with the aim of enhancing communication and information sharing, improving access to basic services, and strengthening operations efficiency in logistics, financial services and e-commerce delivery.

On 25 June and 29 July 2019, the UPU concluded a memorandum of understanding with the Burgundy School of Business. The memorandum was concluded with the purpose of establishing a framework within which the two parties may cooperate to further their shared goals and objectives.

On 28 June 2019, the UPU and the Ministry of Transport, Communication and Primary Sector of Aruba signed a letter of intent in relation to the potential launch of a feasibility study aimed at establishing a hub for e-commerce activities in the Caribbean region.

On 30 June and 29 July 2019, the UPU concluded a memorandum of understanding with the Global Alliance of Data-Driven Marketing Associations. This memorandum aims to establish a framework within which the two parties may cooperate to further their shared goals and objectives.

9. World Health Organization[655]

(*a*) Institutional and administrative matters

(i) *Constitutional developments*

No new amendments to the Constitution were proposed or adopted, and neither of the two current amendments entered into force. The current amendments are the amendment to article 7 and the amendment to article 74 of the Constitution. The amendment to article 7 of the Constitution was adopted by the Eighteenth World Health Assembly by resolution WHA18.48 of 20 May 1965. The amendment to article 74 of the Constitution was adopted by the thirty-first World Health Assembly by resolution WHA31.18 of 18 May 1978. Respectively, they have been accepted by 98 and 112 member States. Amendments shall come into force for all members when adopted by a two-thirds vote of the Health Assembly and accepted by two-thirds of the members in accordance with their respective constitutional processes.

---

[654] Resolution C 14/2016 entitled "Promotion of disaster risk management measures in the field of development cooperation" was adopted by the 26th UPU Congress in Istanbul in 2016.

[655] For official documents and more information about the World Health Organization, see https://www.who.int.

(ii) *WHO Governance*

The WHO Executive Board at its 144th session in January 2019 adopted a series of amendments to its Rules of Procedure regarding: the deadline for submitting proposals; reference to non-State actors in official relations with WHO invited to attend Board sessions in an observer capacity; and replacement of gender-specific language with both feminine and masculine forms in the English version of its Rules of Procedure (decisions EB144(3) and EB144(4)). At its 145th session, the Executive Board also confirmed a series of amendments to the Staff Rules concerning the effective date of amendments to the Staff Rules, definitions, payments and deductions, annual leave and retirement.

The seventy-second World Health Assembly in May 2019 established the salaries of staff in ungraded positions and of the Director-General (resolution WHA72.13). At the same session, the Health Assembly also adopted amendments to its Rules of Procedure regarding: replacement of gender-specific language with both feminine and masculine forms in the English version of its Rules of Procedure (decision WHA72(21)); as well as the requirements for including items on its provisional agenda, the deadline for submitting proposals and reference to non-State actors in official relations invited to attend sessions of the Health Assembly in an observer capacity (decision WHA72(22)).

Through decision EUR/RC69(1), the sixty-ninth session of the WHO Regional Committee for Europe adopted amendments to its Rules of Procedure to include reference to non-State actors in official relations with WHO and adopted the long-term schedules of membership to the Executive Board and the Standing Committee of the Regional Committee.

The Governing Council of the WHO International Agency for Research in Cancer (a WHO institution established by the World Health Assembly) at its sixty-first session in May 2019 decided to admit Hungary as a Participating State in the Agency, pursuant to article XII of the Statute of the Agency (resolution GC/61/R1). The Governing Council also took note of the decision of Turkey to withdraw from the Agency with effect from 3 June 2019 (resolution GC/61/R17).

(iii) *Agreements with WHO member States*

In July 2019, the WHO Regional Office for Europe concluded an agreement with the Ministry of Health of the Russian Federation concerning a financial contribution provided by the Russian Federation in the area of noncommunicable diseases, including the establishment and operational support of a WHO geographically dispersed office on noncommunicable diseases.

In September 2019, the WHO Regional Office for Europe concluded a host agreement with the Federal Public Service Public Health, Food Chain Safety and Environment of Belgium concerning the WHO Office to the European Union.

(*b*) Other Normative Developments and Activities

(i) *International Health Regulations (2005) ("IHR (2005)")*

In 2019, the WHO Director-General convened an IHR Emergency Committee for the outbreak of Ebola virus disease occurring in the Democratic Republic of the Congo on four occasions. Following the 17 July 2019 meeting, the Director-General determined that the Ebola outbreak constituted a public health emergency of international concern and issued temporary recommendations.

The Emergency Committee regarding ongoing events and context involving transmission and international spread of poliovirus was convened four times. Following each meeting, the Director-General maintained the public health emergency of international concern and issued corresponding temporary recommendations.

(ii) *WHO Global Code of Practice on the International Recruitment of Health Personnel*

The WHO Global Code of Practice on the International Recruitment of Health Personnel is a comprehensive, multilateral framework that was adopted by the World Health Assembly and is aimed at advancing cooperation and information sharing on health worker migration. It establishes ethical principles and practices for the international recruitment of health personnel and the strengthening of health systems. Although non-binding in nature, it includes a robust monitoring framework. The second review of the relevance and effectiveness of the Code was conducted over the period May 2019 to January 2020 and findings will be submitted to the seventy-third World Health Assembly in 2020. To facilitate the review process, the Director-General constituted a WHO Expert Advisory Group consisting of 12 member State representatives and eight individual experts. The Expert Advisory Group's findings reaffirm the centrality of the Code to the universal health coverage and health security agenda.

(iii) *Supporting National Law Reform Efforts on WHO Mandated Topics*

During 2019, Headquarters, Regional, and Country Offices of WHO continued to provide technical cooperation to a number of member States in connection with the development, assessment, or review of various areas of health legislation and WHO-mandated topics.

(iv) *Multilateral treaties under WHO auspices*

Belgium, Cabo Verde, Croatia, Czech Republic, Fiji, Kuwait, Luxembourg, Nigeria and Sweden acceded to the Protocol to Eliminate Illicit Trade in Tobacco Products in 2019. By the end of 2019, there were 58 parties to the Protocol.

(v) *Other normative developments*

In May 2019, the seventy-second World Health Assembly adopted the eleventh revision of the WHO International Statistical Classification of Diseases and Related Health Problems (ICD-11), which will come into effect on 1 January 2022 (resolution WHA72.15). ICD-11 is a key WHO instrument that provides the diagnostic classification standard for all clinical and research purposes. Transitional arrangements will apply for at least five years starting from 1 January 2022 and as long as necessary to enable member States to compile and report statistics using previous revisions of the ICD.

At the same session, the Health Assembly also amended Footnote 1 of the Standard Material Transfer Agreement 2 (SMTA2) contained in Annex 2 to the Pandemic Influenza Preparedness Framework in order to address the issue of indirect use of PIP biological materials by companies (decision WHA72(12)). The PIP Framework is a key WHO normative instrument, adopted by consensus by the sixty-fourth World Health Assembly and whose objective is the sharing of influenza viruses and equitable access to vaccines and other benefits, on an equal footing.

Through correspondence dated 24 January 2019, the WHO Director-General notified the United Nations Secretary-General of the recommendations made by the WHO Expert Committee on Drug Dependence on the international scheduling of cannabis and cannabis-related substances under the 1961 Single Convention on Narcotic Drugs and the 1971 Convention on Psychotropic Substances. If adopted by the United Nations Commission on Narcotic Drugs, the recommendations would entail a change to the current international control regime of cannabis and cannabis-related substances. In March 2019, the Commission on Narcotic Drugs decided to postpone the voting on the WHO recommendations.

10. International Atomic Energy Agency[656]

(*a*) Membership

In 2019, Saint Lucia became a member State of the International Atomic Energy Agency (IAEA). By the end of the year, there were 171 member States.

(*b*) Multilateral treaties under IAEA auspices

(i) *Convention on the Physical Protection of Nuclear Material*[657]

In 2019, Benin and Chad became parties to the Convention. By the end of the year, there were 159 parties.

(ii) *Amendment to the Convention on the Physical Protection of Nuclear Material*[658]

In 2019, Benin, Chad, Comoros, and Saint Kitts and Nevis became parties to the Amendment. By the end of the year, there were 122 parties.

(iii) *Convention on Early Notification of a Nuclear Accident*[659]

In 2019, Benin and Ecuador became parties to the Convention. By the end of the year, there were 124 parties.

---

656 For official documents and more information about the International Atomic Energy Agency, see http://www.iaea.org.

657 United Nations, *Treaty Series*, vol. 1456, p. 101.

658 *Ibid.*, vol. 3132, no. A-24631.

659 *Ibid.*, vol. 1439, p. 275.

(iv) *Convention on Assistance in the Case of a Nuclear Accident or Radiological Emergency*[660]

In 2019, Benin and Ecuador became parties to the Convention. By the end of the year, there were 119 parties.

(v) *Convention on Nuclear Safety*[661]

In 2019, Benin, Bolivia, and Morocco became parties to the Convention. By the end of the year, there were 88 parties.

(vi) *Joint Convention on the Safety of Spent Fuel Management and on the Safety of Radioactive Waste Management*[662]

In 2019, Benin and Bolivia became parties to the Convention. By the end of the year, there were 82 parties.

(vii) *Vienna Convention on Civil Liability for Nuclear Damage*[663]

In 2019, Benin and Rwanda became parties to the Convention. By the end of the year, there were 42 parties.

(viii) *Optional Protocol Concerning the Compulsory Settlement of Disputes*[664]

In 2019, the status of the Protocol remained unchanged with two parties.

(ix) *Protocol to Amend the Vienna Convention on Civil Liability for Nuclear Damage*[665]

In 2019, Benin became a party to the Protocol. By the end of the year, there were 14 parties.

(x) *Joint Protocol Relating to the Application of the Vienna Convention and the Paris Convention*[666]

In 2019, Benin and Montenegro became parties to the Protocol. By the end of the year, there were 30 parties.

---

[660] *Ibid.*, vol. 1457, p. 133.

[661] *Ibid.*, vol. 1963, p. 293.

[662] *Ibid.*, vol. 2153, p. 303.

[663] *Ibid.*, vol. 1063, p. 265.

[664] *Ibid.*, vol. 2086, p. 94.

[665] *Ibid.*, vol. 2241, p. 270.

[666] *Ibid.*, vol. 1672, p. 293.

(xi) *Convention on Supplementary Compensation for Nuclear Damage*[667]

In 2019, Benin became a party to the Convention. By the end of the year, there were 11 parties.

(xii) *Regional Co-operative Agreement for Research, Development and Training Related to Nuclear Science and Technology, 2017*[668]

In 2019, the status of the Agreement remained unchanged with 17 parties.

(xiii) *African Regional Co-operative Agreement for Research, Development and Training Related to Nuclear Science and Technology (AFRA)—(Fifth Extension)*[669]

In 2019, the status of the Fifth Extension of the Agreement remained unchanged with 41 parties.

(xiv) *First Agreement to Extend the Co-operation Agreement for the Promotion of Nuclear Science and Technology in Latin America and the Caribbean (ARCAL)*[670]

In 2019, the status of the Agreement remained unchanged with 21 parties.

(xv) *Co-operative Agreement for Arab States in Asia for Research, Development and Training Related to Nuclear Science and Technology (ARASIA)—(Second Extension)*[671]

In 2019, the status of the Second Extension of the Agreement remained unchanged with 9 parties.

(xvi) *Agreement on the Establishment of the ITER International Fusion Energy Organization for the Joint Implementation of the ITER Project*[672]

In 2019, the status of the Agreement remained unchanged with 7 parties.

---

[667] *Ibid.*, vol. 3038, p. 41.

[668] *Ibid.*, vol. 3282, no. I-55546.

[669] *Ibid.*, vol. 1566, p. 359 and document INFCIRC/377 and INFCIRC/377/Add.20 (fifth extension).

[670] United Nations, *Treaty Series*, vol. 3072, p. 261 and documents INFCIRC/582 and INFCIRC/582/Add.4 (extension of the agreement).

[671] United Nations, *Treaty Series*, vol. 2203, p. 355 and documents INFCIRC/613 and INFCIRC/613/Add.3 (second extension).

[672] United Nations, *Treaty Series*, vol. 2491, p. 207 and document INFCIRC/702.

(xvii) *Agreement on the Privileges and Immunities of the ITER International Fusion Energy Organization for the Joint Implementation of the ITER Project*[673]

In 2019, the status of the Agreement remained unchanged with 6 parties.

(*c*) Safeguards Agreements

During 2019, a Safeguards Agreement pursuant to the Treaty on the Non-Proliferation of Nuclear Weapons (NPT)[674] between the IAEA and Benin, and a Protocol Additional thereto, entered into force.[675] In addition, a Safeguards Agreement pursuant to the NPT between the IAEA and the State of Palestine[676] was signed, but had not entered into force as of 31 December 2019. A Safeguards Agreement pursuant to the NPT between the IAEA and Sao Tome and Principe, and a Protocol Additional thereto, were approved by the IAEA Board of Governors.

In 2019, a Protocol Additional to the Safeguards Agreement pursuant to the NPT between the IAEA and Ethiopia entered into force.[677] Moreover, a Protocol Additional to the Safeguards Agreement pursuant to the Treaty for the Prohibition of Nuclear Weapons in Latin America and the NPT between the IAEA and Bolivia (Plurinational State of) was approved by the IAEA Board of Governors and signed, but had not entered into force as of 31 December 2019.

(*d*) Revised supplementary agreements concerning the provision of technical assistance by the IAEA (RSA)

In 2019, Eritrea, Guyana, Saint Lucia, Saint Vincent and the Grenadines, and Trinidad and Tobago signed an RSA with the IAEA. By the end of the year, there were 141 States parties to an RSA.

(*e*) IAEA legislative assistance activities

In 2019, the Agency continued to provide legislative assistance to its member States. Country specific bilateral legislative assistance was provided to 17 member States through written comments and advice on drafting national nuclear legislation. The Agency also reviewed the legal framework of countries embarking on a nuclear power programme as part of various Integrated Nuclear Infrastructure Review missions. Short-term scientific visits to Agency Headquarters were organized for a number of individuals, allowing them to gain further practical experience in nuclear law.

The Agency organized the ninth session of the Nuclear Law Institute in Vienna, Austria, from 30 September to 11 October 2019, a comprehensive two-week course intended to enable participants to acquire a solid understanding of all aspects of nuclear law, as well as to develop the necessary skills to draft, amend or review their national nuclear

---

[673] United Nations, *Treaty Series*, vol. 2491, p. 317 and document INFCIRC/703.

[674] *Ibid.*, vol. 729, p. 161.

[675] Reproduced in IAEA Document: INFCIRC/930.

[676] See IAEA Annual Report 2019, Table A6. Conclusion of safeguards agreements, additional protocols and small questions protocols (as of 31 December 2019).

[677] Reproduced in IAEA Document: INFCIRC/261/Add.1.

legislation. Sixty-five participants from 56 IAEA member States from Africa, Asia and the Pacific, Europe and Latin America and the Caribbean attended the training.

Two Regional Workshops on Nuclear Law were conducted for the Asia and the Pacific Region in Jakarta, Indonesia, in August, and in Vienna, Austria, in December, which were attended by over 60 participants from 27 member States of the region. National workshops on nuclear law were also organized in seven member States. In addition, a meeting for legal advisers of regulatory bodies was organized for the first time in July, which allowed to identify ways to expand training opportunities and reference material for the benefit of the exercise of the legal support function in regulatory bodies.

(*f*) Conventions

(i) *Convention on Nuclear Safety (CNS)*

An Officers' Turnover Meeting was held in Vienna in March, where the officers of the Seventh Review Meeting to the Convention on Nuclear Safety shared experience and feedback on the preparations and conduct of the previous review meetings with the officers elected for the Eighth CNS Review Meeting. At the Meeting, incoming and outgoing officers also discussed the peer review process in detail, including key documents, thereby ensuring the transfer of knowledge on obligations under the CNS, its processes and the role of the officers concerned.

At an additional Officers' Meeting, held in Vienna in September, officers for the Eighth CNS Review Meeting approved templates to further enhance the peer review process to be used at that meeting, discussed the organization of topical sessions on safety culture and aging management, and also considered the possibility of using an electronic tool for handling questions during these sessions.

(ii) *Joint Convention on the Safety of Spent Fuel Management and on the Safety of Radioactive Waste Management (Joint Convention)*

In preparation for the Fourth Extraordinary Meeting of the Joint Convention, a working group was established by the contracting parties to the Joint Convention. The working group was open to all contracting parties and mandated to initiate a discussion on proposals as well as further develop and elaborate upon them in order to facilitate consensus-building at the Fourth Extraordinary Meeting. Proposals for amendments to the Joint Convention itself were excluded from the scope of the working group.

The Agency facilitated two meetings of that working group in July and in November, respectively. At these meetings, participants discussed, inter alia, actions to improve the peer review process including measures in response to the increased number of contracting parties as well as possible amendments to the Joint Convention guidance documents. Between meetings, a number of draft working papers were made available to contracting parties.

(iii) *Promotional activities related to the CNS and to the Joint Convention*

The Agency continued to promote adherence to the CNS and the Joint Convention. As part of these efforts, in addition to the regular outreach, tailored promotional activities were carried out in 2019. In particular, the Agency held a Regional Workshop to promote adherence to the Joint Convention in October 2019 in Centurion, South Africa, and facilitated a Joint Workshop to promote adherence to the CNS and the Joint Convention held in August 2019 in Vienna.

(iv) *The Convention on the Physical Protection of Nuclear Material (CPPNM) and its Amendment*

The fifth annual Technical Meeting of Representatives of States Parties to the CPPNM and the CPPNM Amendment was held at IAEA Headquarters in Vienna on 11 November 2019. Representatives from 64 parties to the CPPNM and its Amendment and to the CPPNM only participated. As in previous years, the meeting considered matters within the scope of the CPPNM and the Amendment in order for the States parties to better understand their enhanced commitments and responsibilities under the Amendment and to share experiences and lessons learned in the implementation of those commitments and responsibilities.

In 2019, the IAEA also convened two meetings of legal and technical experts_ in preparation for the 2021 Conference of the Parties to the Amendment to the Convention on the Physical Protection of Nuclear Material (2021 Conference), from 22 to 25 July and from 12 to 15 November, respectively. The aim was to facilitate the review, at the 2021 Conference, of the implementation of the CPPNM as amended and its adequacy as concerns the preamble, the whole of the operative part and the annexes in the light of the then prevailing situation, as foreseen in article 16.1 thereof. Over 100 experts from 70 parties to the CPPNM and its Amendment, as well as parties to the CPPNM only, participated in the two meetings.

The Agency continued in 2019 to promote universal adherence to the Amendment to the CPPNM through technical meetings, regional workshops and other activities. Two regional events were convened to promote universalization, one for English-speaking African countries in July and one for Latin American countries in October, and an international seminar on the CPPNM and its Amendment was held in Vienna in May.

(*g*) Civil liability for nuclear damage

The International Expert Group on Nuclear Liability (INLEX) continues to serve as the Agency's main forum for questions related to nuclear liability. The 19th Meeting of INLEX took place in Vienna, Austria, in May 2019. The Group concluded its discussions on transportable nuclear power plants and also discussed, inter alia, liability issues concerning cyberattacks, jurisdiction under the Joint Protocol Relating to the Application of the Vienna Convention and the Paris Convention, and the different amounts of compensation available under the various nuclear liability conventions.

In addition, a Workshop on Civil Liability for Nuclear Damage for European Countries was held in Bucharest in April. Participants were given an overview of the international nuclear liability regime and of its implementation in national laws.

11. International Organization of Migration[678]

(a) Membership

The Republic of Uzbekistan became the 173rd member of the Organization on 15 March 2019, the date of its submission to the IOM Director General of the confirmation of ratification of the IOM Constitution. On 27 November 2018, at its 109th session, the Council of the International Organization for Migration adopted resolution No. 1367[679] admitting the Republic of Uzbekistan as a member of the Organization, as of the date of such submission by the Republic of Uzbekistan to the Director General.

(b) International Migration Review Forums

In resolution 73/326 of the General Assembly of the United Nations on Format and organizational aspects of the International Migration Review Forum (IMRF),[680] the IOM Director General was requested, as Coordinator of the United Nations Network on Migration, to assist, upon requests by member States, in the preparation and organization of regional reviews in the implementation of the Global Compact for Safe, Orderly and Regular Migration (Global Compact), and to facilitate the policy debate at the IMRF, focusing on challenges in the implementation of the Global Compact, including links with the 2030 Agenda, the capacity-building mechanism and contemporary and emerging issues related to migration. This policy debate will also consider possible guidance for the United Nations system towards improving system-wide effectiveness and coherence and supporting Member States in implementing the GCM, upon request of Member States, based on their national policies and priorities. As part of the processes, IOM's International Dialogues on Migration, among others, are invited to contribute.

12. Organization for the Prohibition of Chemical Weapons[681]

(a) Membership

In 2019, the number of member States of the Organization for the Prohibition of Chemical Weapons (OPCW) remained unchanged, namely 193.

(b) Legal status, privileges and immunities and international agreements

In 2019, the OPCW continued to negotiate privileges and immunities agreements with member States in accordance with paragraph 50 of article VIII of the Convention in

---

678 For official documents and more information about the International Organization of Migration, see https://www.iom.int/.

679 Full text of Resolution No. 1367: https://governingbodies.iom.int/system/files/en/council/109/C-109-RES-1367-%20Admission%20New%20Member%20Uzbekistan.pdf.

680 GA resolution 73/326.

681 For official documents and more information about the Organization for the Prohibition of Chemical Weapons, see http://www.opcw.org.

order to ensure their effective entry into force. The total number of such agreements concluded by the Organisation stood at 55 at the end of the reporting period.

During 2019, the OPCW concluded a number of international agreements, including technical agreements, voluntary contribution agreements, agreements concerning the provision of Junior Professional Officers for appointment with the OPCW, and exchanges of letters and memoranda of understanding, which entail substantial undertakings at the policy level or are intended to facilitate the day-to-day work of the Technical Secretariat in support of the objectives of the Convention.

(*c*) Legislative assistance activities[682]

Throughout 2019, the Technical Secretariat of the OPCW continued to provide assistance, upon request, in support of the States parties' efforts to develop and adopt national legislative and other measures to implement their obligations under the Convention, in particular under article VII of the Convention. The Technical Secretariat also assisted States parties wishing to update their legal framework. The OPCW continued to provide tailor-made assistance on national implementation of the Convention to requesting States parties, pursuant to: (*a*) subparagraph 38(*e*) of article VIII of the Convention; (*b*) the decision on national implementation measures of article VII obligations adopted by the Conference of the States Parties ("the Conference") at its fourteenth session[683]; and (*c*) paragraph 9.103(*c*) of the Report of the Third Special Session of the Conference of the States Parties to Review the Operation of the Chemical Weapons Convention.[684]

In its implementation support efforts, the Technical Secretariat of the OPCW acted in accordance with the decision of the Conference regarding the implementation of article VII obligations, as adopted by the Conference at its eighth session,[685] as well as other decisions of the Conference concerning the implementation of article VII obligations.[686] These decisions focused on, among other things, the obligations of States parties to designate or establish a National Authority to serve as the national focal point for effective liaison with the OPCW and other States parties, as required by paragraph 4 of article VII of the Convention, as well as the steps necessary to enact national implementing legislation, including penal legislation and administrative measures, to implement the Convention, as required by paragraph 1 of article VII of the Convention.

With a total of 191 States parties (99 per cent) having designated or established a National Authority as at 31 July 2019, only two States parties are yet to fulfil the requirement under article VII (4) of the CWC, which mandates such establishment or designation. There has been steady progress in the status of implementation of article VII of the Convention. With regard to the adoption of the necessary legislative and/or administrative measures, 160 States parties (83 per cent) have adopted national implementing legislation.

---

[682] OPCW, document EC-92/DG.9, C-24/DG.10, dated 26 August 2019.

[683] OPCW, document C-14/DEC.12, dated 4 December 2009.

[684] OPCW, document RC-3/3*, dated 19 April 2013.

[685] OPCW, document C-8/DEC.16, dated 24 October 2003.

[686] OPCW, document C-10/DEC.16 dated 11 November 2005; C-11/DEC.4 dated 6 December 2006; C-12/DEC.9 dated 9 November 2007; C-13/DEC.7 dated 5 December 2008; and C-14/DEC.12 dated 4 December 2009.

Of these, as at 31 July 2019, 119 States parties (62 per cent) have legislation covering all the initial measures. Additionally, the number of States parties that have enacted penal legislation containing the requisite prohibitions and penalties that will enable them to prosecute perpetrators of Convention-related offences at the domestic level has increased. 147 States parties (76 per cent) have enacted laws containing the prohibitions on chemical weapons under paragraph 1 of article I of the Convention, and 146 States parties (76 per cent) have applicable penal sanctions in the event of their violation. 131 States parties (68 per cent) have incorporated the prohibitions in the Annex on Implementation and Verification (the "Verification Annex") pertaining to scheduled chemicals into their domestic legal framework, and 130 States parties (67 per cent) have applicable penal sanctions in the event of their violation. For States parties that possess industrial facilities declarable under the Convention, 109 States parties (56 per cent) have adopted additional implementing measures pertaining to declarable industrial facilities.

As required under article VII (5) of the CWC, 165 States parties (85 per cent) have submitted information to the Secretariat on the legislative and administrative measures they have taken to implement various aspects of the Convention as at 31 July 2019, out of which 148 States parties (77 per cent) have provided copies of the relevant texts of the adopted measures.

The Technical Secretariat continued to maintain formal and informal working contact with States parties with which it had built a relationship through technical assistance programmes, visits, and consultations, particularly in order to identify additional needs for assistance, to follow up on assistance already provided, and to coordinate future assistance activities. During 2019, the Secretariat provided, upon request, comments on the texts of three draft laws. The Secretariat also reviewed the texts of legislation that were provided as article VII submissions to determine whether they meet the requirements of the Convention and met with a number of States parties to discuss the status of their implementation of article VII.

The Technical Secretariat organised three sessions of the Internship Programme for Legal Drafters and National Authority Representatives, in the reporting period 2018–2019, which were attended by eight States parties. During the sessions, the Secretariat emphasised the elements of comprehensive implementing legislation that address current and emerging issues, including terrorism. The participating States parties developed road maps detailing the steps and activities for the adoption of draft legislation that will also serve as the basis for monitoring and follow-up by the Secretariat.

In the same reporting period, the Secretariat implemented the fourth and fifth sessions of the Influential Visitors Programme with Chile and Togo, respectively. The programme is targeted at States parties that are in the final stages of adoption of implementing legislation. Under the programme, National Authority representatives, along with key high-level officials from States parties who may facilitate the process of the adoption of legislation, are invited to the OPCW Headquarters for a series of meetings to sensitise them to Convention-related issues.

The Secretariat organised two subregional stakeholders' fora on implementation of the Convention and subregional cooperation, which were held in Tirana, Albania, for States parties in the Western Balkans and in Nairobi, Kenya, for States parties in East Africa. The participating States parties exchanged views on challenges and best practices in national implementation of the Convention and ways to strengthen subregional cooperation.

In the same reporting period, a second workshop on the role of implementing legislation on the Convention in addressing threats arising from non-State actors was organised for States parties in Asia and was held in Kuala Lumpur, Malaysia from 9 to 11 April 2019. The workshop was aimed at raising the awareness of relevant stakeholders from States parties on how implementing legislation on the Convention can serve as an effective tool in addressing threats involving toxic chemicals, including chemical terrorism, arising from non-State actors. The workshop was attended by over 50 participants from 12 States parties in Asia, as well as representatives from a number of international and regional organisations.

The Secretariat also provided support to national awareness-raising and legislative assistance workshops upon the request of States parties. On 26 and 27 March 2019, the Secretariat provided technical support to a national legal workshop on the implementation of the Convention held in Bandar Seri Begawan, Brunei Darussalam. The event was organised by the Ministry of Defence of Brunei Darussalam and was attended by over 40 representatives from 12 government ministries and agencies. The workshop was aimed at supporting Brunei Darussalam in finalising the draft text of its implementing legislation on the Convention. From 20 to 22 June 2019, the Secretariat also provided technical support to a national awareness-raising and legislative assistance workshop held in Issyk-Kul, Kyrgyzstan. The event was co-organised by the Ministry of Economy of Kyrgyzstan and the Organisation for Security and Co-operation in Europe and was attended by 25 representatives from 11 government ministries and agencies. The workshop was aimed at assisting Kyrgyzstan in finalising the draft text of regulations that would fill in the gaps in its legislative framework on the Convention.

The Secretariat, in cooperation with the National Authority of Qatar, organised a round-table discussion on the role of parliamentarians in enhancing national implementation of the Convention. The event took place on 7 April 2019 in Doha, Qatar, in the margins of the 140th Assembly of the Inter-Parliamentary Union (IPU). Parliamentarians from Bangladesh, Chile, Mongolia, Qatar, and Spain participated in the event and shared their views on how parliaments can play a more active role in enhancing national implementation of the Convention. The Secretariat will continue to collaborate and engage with the IPU on issues related to the legal implementation of the Convention.

The Secretariat participated in a number of events organised by other entities in order to raise awareness of the Convention. Furthermore, the Secretariat met with States parties in the margins of the Annual Meeting of National Authorities, as well as the regional meetings of representatives of National Authorities, in order to discuss the status of their implementation of article VII and to offer technical assistance.

The Secretariat continued to support bilateral cooperation between National Authorities on various issues, including through the Mentorship/Partnership Programme, in which National Authorities that have proven to be effective in the implementation of their obligations under the Convention provide guidance to National Authorities that require additional support for enhancing their effective functioning. The programme is part of the efforts of the Secretariat to enhance the technical support and assistance provided to States parties in support of their national implementation efforts by facilitating an exchange of visits between National Authorities. During the reporting period, representatives of the National Authority of Togo visited Morocco and vice versa; representatives of the National Authority of the Gambia visited the United Kingdom of Great Britain and Northern Ireland; and representatives of the National Authority of Afghanistan visited India. The mentor countries shared their technical expertise, experiences, and good practices in the process of developing, adopting, and implementing their respective legislation on the Convention with their partner countries, as well as on other relevant thematic issues.

(*d*) Other normative developments and activities of the Policy-Making Organs

(i) *Expanding chemical laboratory capabilities*

The Organisation continued to conclude grant arrangements with States parties in the framework of the Note S/1512/2017 entitled "Upgrading the OPCW Chemical Laboratory to a Centre for Chemistry and Technology" in order to support the acquisition, construction, and operation of a new Centre for Chemistry and Technology. The objective of the Centre is to upgrade and ultimately replace the existing OPCW Laboratory and Equipment Store in order to ensure that the Organisation keeps pace with evolving chemical threats and science and technology demands. It also aims at enhancing the capacity of the Secretariat to provide training and capacity building activities to State parties.[687]

(ii) *Adoption of decisions under article XV of the Chemical Weapons Convention to change the Annex on Chemicals*

During its twenty-fourth session held from 25 to 29 November 2019, the Conference of the States Parties adopted by consensus two proposals for technical changes to Schedule 1 of the Annex on Chemicals to the Chemical Weapons Convention, which were submitted, respectively, by Canada, the Netherlands, and the United States of America, jointly, and by the Russian Federation.[688] The Joint Proposal by Canada, the Netherlands, and the United States of America, adopted on 27 November 2019, added two families of toxic chemicals to Schedule 1(A) of the Annex on Chemicals to the Chemical Weapons Convention.[689] The Proposal by the Russian Federation, adopted on 27 November 2019, added toxic chemicals to Schedule 1(A) of the Annex on Chemicals to the Chemical Weapons Convention.[690] This marked the first time that changes have been introduced to the Annex on Chemicals since the adoption of the Convention.

The Director-General, as required under subparagraph 5(*f*) of article XV of the Convention, notified all States parties and the Secretary-General of the United Nations, in his capacity as the Depositary of the Convention, of the decisions adopted by the Conference.[691] Consistent with subparagraph 5(*g*) of article XV of the Convention, the changes to Schedule 1 of the Annex on Chemicals will enter into force for all States parties on 7 June 2020, 180 days from the date of notification by the Director-General of their approval.[692]

---

[687] OPCW, document para. 9.59(*o*), RC-4/3/Rev.1, dated 30 November 2018.

[688] OPCW, document C-24/5, dated 29 November 2019.

[689] OPCW, document C-24/DEC.4, dated 27 November 2019.

[690] OPCW, document C-24/DEC.5, dated 27 November 2019.

[691] OPCW, documents L/ODG/221840/19, dated 10 December 2019 and NV/ODG/221841/19, dated 10 December 2019.

[692] OPCW, document NV/ODG/221841/19, dated 10 December 2019.

(iii) *Transition to biennial programme and budget*

During its twenty-fourth session, the Conference of the States Parties approved the OPCW's transition from an annual to a biennial programme and budget cycle, with a view to the first biennial programme and budget covering the period 2022–2023 being prepared in 2021 for the consideration and adoption by the Conference at its twenty-sixth session.[693]

13. World Trade Organization[694]

(*a*) Membership

In 2019, the World Trade Organization (WTO) membership counted 164 members. No new members joined the Organization during the year.

(i) *WTO accessions*

Applications for WTO membership are examined in individual Accession Working Parties, which are established by the Ministerial Conference/General Council. The legal framework of WTO accessions is set out in article XII of the Marrakesh Agreement Establishing the World Trade Organization. As a result of bilateral and multilateral negotiations with WTO members, acceding States/separate customs territories undertake trade liberalizing commitments on market access; specific commitments on WTO rules; and agree to comply with the WTO Agreement.

(ii) *On-going accessions in 2019*

In 2019, the following States/separate customs territories were in the process of acceding to the WTO (in alphabetical order):

1. Algeria
2. Andorra
3. Azerbaijan
4. Bahamas
5. Belarus
6. Bhutan
7. Bosnia and Herzegovina
8. Comoros, Union of the
9. Equatorial Guinea
10. Ethiopia
11. Holy Sea
12. Islamic Republic of Iran
13. Iraq
14. Lebanese Republic
15. Libya
16. Sao Tomé and Principe
17. Serbia
18. Somalia
19. South Sudan
20. Sudan
21. Syrian Arab Republic
22. Timor-Leste
23. Uzbekistan

---

693 OPCW, document C-24/DEC.11, dated 28 November 2019.

694 For official documents and more information about the World Trade Organization, see http://www.wto.org.

On 31 October 2019 Curaçao applied to join the WTO (WT/ACC/CUW/1).

(*b*) Dispute Settlement

The General Council convenes as the Dispute Settlement Body (DSB) to deal with disputes arising under the Marrakesh Agreement Establishing the World Trade Organization; the multilateral trade agreements covering trade in goods, trade in services, and trade-related aspects of intellectual property rights; and, under a specific decision, the plurilateral trade agreement on government procurement. The DSB has the sole authority to establish dispute settlement panels, adopt panel and Appellate Body reports, maintain surveillance over the implementation of recommendations and rulings contained in such reports, and authorize suspension of concessions in the event of non-compliance with those recommendations and rulings.[695]

(i) *Requests for consultations received and panels established*

During 2019, the DSB received 19 requests for consultations (the first formal step in dispute settlement proceedings) pursuant to article 4 of the Understanding on Rules and Procedures Governing the Settlement of Disputes (DSU). The DSB established 11 new panels relating to 13 individual complaints. The DSB established panels in the following disputes:

- European Union—Anti-Dumping Measures on Certain Cold-Rolled Flat Steel Products from Russia (DS521) complaint by the Russian Federation
- United States—Tariff Measures on Certain Goods from China (DS543) complaint by China
- Turkey—Additional Duties on Certain Products from the United States (DS561) complaint by the United States
- United States—Safeguard Measure on Imports of Crystalline Silicon Photovoltaic Products (DS562) complaint by China
- Turkey—Additional Duties on Imports of Air Conditioning Machines from Thailand (DS573) complaint by Thailand
- Qatar—Certain Measures Concerning Goods from the United Arab Emirates (DS576) complaint by the United Arab Emirates
- United States—Anti-Dumping and Countervailing Duties on Ripe Olives from Spain (WT/DS577) complaint by the European Union
- Morocco—Definitive Anti-Dumping Measures on School Exercise Books from Tunisia (DS578) complaint by Tunisia
- India—Measures Concerning Sugar and Sugarcane (DS579) complaint by Brazil, (DS580) complaint by Australia, (DS581) complaint by Guatemala
- Turkey—Certain measures Concerning the Production, Importation and Marketing of Pharmaceutical Products (DS583) complaint by the European Union
- India—Additional Duties on Certain Products from the United States (DS585) complaint by the United States

---

[695] Further information on WTO dispute settlement in 2019 can be found in the WTO Annual Report 2020.

(ii) *Appellate Body and Panel reports adopted by the DSB*

In 2019, the DSB adopted the following seven panel reports in eight separate disputes and four Appellate Body reports in five disputes:

- Brazil—Certain Measures Concerning Taxation and Charges (DS472, DS497) complaints by the European Union and Japan (Panel and Appellate Body reports)
- Ukraine—Anti-Dumping Measures on Ammonium Nitrate (DS493) complaint by the Russian Federation (Panel and Appellate Body reports)
- Korea—Import Bans, and Testing and Certification Requirements for Radionuclides (DS495) complaint by Japan (Panel and Appellate Body reports)
- Korea—Anti-Dumping Duties on Pneumatic Valves from Japan (DS504) complaint by Japan (Panel and Appellate Body reports)
- China—Domestic Support for Agricultural Producers (DS511) complaint by the United States (Panel report)
- Russia—Measures Concerning Traffic in Transit (DS512) complaint by Ukraine (Panel report)
- China—Tariff Rate Quotas for Certain Agricultural Products (DS517) complaint by the United States (Panel report)

In addition, as of 31 December 2019, there were a number of appeals still pending before the Appellate Body. From 10 December 2019, however, following the expiry of the terms of office of two of the three remaining Appellate Body members, the Appellate Body was reduced to one member and could no longer compose Divisions (of three Appellate Body members) to hear new appeals. The Appellate Body also advised on 10 December 2019 that it was suspending consideration of nine pending appeals.

(*c*) Amendment of the Trade Policy Review Mechanism Contained in Annex 3 to the Marrakesh Agreement Establishing the World Trade Organization

The amendments resulting from the General Council Decision circulated in document T/L/1014 and transmitted to members in document WT/Let/1276, to paragraph C(ii) of the Trade Policy Review Mechanism contained in Annex 3 to the WTO Agreement, took effect for all WTO members, in accordance with the provisions of article X:8 of the WTO Agreement, on 1 January 2019, pursuant to paragraph 2 of the Decision (WT/LET/1423).

(*d*) Acceptances of Protocols

(i) *Agreement on Trade-Related Aspects of Intellectual Property Rights (TRIPS)*

The amended TRIPS Agreement incorporating a decision on patents and public health will enter into force when two thirds of WTO members have accepted the change. During 2019, Burundi (WT/LET/1455) and Cuba (WT/LET/1437) accepted the amended agreement. Members that are yet to accept the amendment currently have until 31 December 2021 to do so (WT/L/1081).

(ii) *Government Procurement Agreement (GPA) and the Protocol Amending the Government Procurement Agreement*

The amended GPA, which streamlines and modernizes the 1994 WTO Agreement on Government Procurement, entered into force on 6 April 2014. During 2019, Australia deposited instruments of acceptance of the agreement and the amended agreement, which then entered into on 5 May 2019 (WT/LET/1429).

In addition, parties to the GPA approved the United Kingdom's accession to the Agreement, in its own right, once it leaves the European Union (GPA/CD/2 and Add.1).

(iii) *Agreement on Trade Facilitation*

The Agreement on Trade Facilitation entered into force on 22 February 2017 when the WTO obtained acceptance of the Agreement from two thirds of its 164 members. This Protocol of Amendment, which was officially opened for acceptance on 27 November 2014, inserts the Agreement on Trade Facilitation into the WTO Agreement. During 2019, Ecuador (WT/LET/1424), Angola (WT/LET/1431), Morocco (WT/LET/1435), Egypt (WT/LET/1439), Tajikistan (WT/LET/1444), Maldives (WT/LET/1447), Guinea (WT/LET/1451), and Burundi (WT/LET/1454) accepted the Protocol.

(iv) *Civil Aircraft Agreement*

On 24 June 2019, North Macedonia accepted the Protocol Amending the Annex to the Agreement on Trade in Civil Aircraft (document TCA/9). The Protocol entered into force for North Macedonia on 24 July 2019 (WT/LET1442).[696]

14. International Criminal Court[697]

(*a*) Situations under Preliminary Examination[698]

Before the Office of the Prosecutor (OTP or Office) opens an investigation, it conducts a preliminary examination into a situation in order to determine whether it meets the legal criteria established by the Rome Statute (Statute),[699] and whether there is a reasonable basis to proceed with an investigation. Pre-Trial Chamber (PTC) III has interpreted "reasonable

---

[696] See also the Basic Instruments and Selected Documents of the World Trade Organization (WTO BISD 2019) for further information on other WTO legal instruments, decisions and reports issued by WTO bodies in 2019.

[697] For official documents and more information on the International Criminal Court, see http://www.icc-cpi.int.

[698] The Office of the Prosecutor, Report on Preliminary Examination Activities 2019, 5 December 2019, available at: https://www.icc-cpi.int/sites/default/files/itemsDocuments/191205-rep-otp-PE.pdf.

[699] Rome Statute of the International Criminal Court, Rome, 1998, United Nations, *Treaty Series*, vol. 2187, p. 3.

basis" as a "sensible or reasonable justification for a belief that a crime falling within the jurisdiction of the Court has been or is being committed."[700]

During the preliminary examination reporting period,[701] the OTP (i) continued preliminary examinations of the situations in Colombia, Guinea, Iraq/United Kingdom, Nigeria, Palestine, the Philippines, Ukraine and Venezuela;[702] and (ii) completed and closed the preliminary examination of the situation in Bangladesh/Myanmar.[703] Although completed, the preliminary examination related to the situation in Afghanistan was still subject to further litigation before the Appeals Chamber (AC) after the initial rejection by PTC II of the Office's request to proceed with an investigation.[704] Concerning the situation of the Registered Vessels of Comoros, Greece and Cambodia, although the preliminary examination has been closed since 2014, the issue of the reconsideration of the Prosecutor's decision not to investigate remained subject to litigation, with the Prosecutor confirming her decision not to investigate in December 2019.[705] The OTP published a report on its preliminary examination activities on 5 December 2019.[706]

The OTP continued to analyse information received alleging the commission of crimes potentially falling within the Court's jurisdiction. Between 1 January 2019 and 31 December 2019, the Office received 814 communications pursuant to article 15 of the Statute. Of these, 617 were manifestly outside the Court's jurisdiction; 48 warranted further analysis; 120 were linked to a situation already under preliminary examination; and 29 were linked to an ongoing investigation or prosecution.

(i) *The Situation in Colombia*

Colombia deposited its instrument of ratification to the Statute on 5 August 2002. The ICC therefore has jurisdiction over Rome Statute crimes committed on the territory of Colombia or by its nationals from 1 November 2002 onwards. However, the Court may exercise jurisdiction over war crimes committed since 1 November 2009 only, in accordance

---

[700] *Situation in the Republic of Burundi*, Public Redacted Version of "Decision Pursuant to Article 15 of the Rome Statute on the Authorization of an Investigation into the Situation in the Republic of Burundi", ICC-01/17-X-9-US-Exp, 25 October 2017 (ICC-01/17-9-Red), 9 November 2017, para. 30.

[701] The Office of the Prosecutor, "Report on Preliminary Examination Activities 2019", 5 December 2019, para. 17. Available at: https://www.icc-cpi.int/itemsDocuments/191205-rep-otp-PE.pdf.

[702] *Ibid.*, para. 21.

[703] *Ibid.*, para. 18.

[704] In December 2019, a hearing was held to receive oral arguments in the appeals of the victims and the Prosecutor against PTC II's decision not to authorize an investigation: *Situation in the Islamic Republic of Afghanistan*, Transcript of hearing, 4 December 2019, ICC-02/17-T-001-ENG; Transcript of hearing, 5 December 2019, ICC-02/17-T-002-ENG; Transcript of hearing, 6 December 2019, ICC-02/17-T-003-ENG.

[705] *Situation on Registered Vessels of the Union of the Comoros, the Hellenic Republic and the Kingdom of Cambodia*, Notice of Prosecutor's Final Decision under rule 108(3), as revised and refiled in accordance with the PTC's request of 15 November 2018 and the AC's judgment of 2 September 2019, ICC-01/13-99, 2 December 2019.

[706] The Office of the Prosecutor, "Report on Preliminary Examination Activities 2019", 5 December 2019. Available at: https://www.icc-cpi.int/itemsDocuments/191205-rep-otp-PE.pdf.

with Colombia's declaration under article 124 of the Statute excluding war crimes from the jurisdiction of the Court for a seven-year period.[707]

Opened in June 2004, the preliminary examination of the situation in Colombia remains ongoing.[708] In the course of the reporting period, the OTP continued to receive communications pursuant to article 15 of the Statute in relation to this situation.[709]

During the reporting period, the OTP continued its factual and legal assessment of information relating to the status, progress and genuineness of national proceedings carried out by the Colombian authorities under the ordinary justice, the Justice and Peace Law and the Special Jurisdiction for Peace (SJP) systems.[710]

Further, the OTP held consultations with national authorities; gathered additional information on the areas of focus of the preliminary examination; and held multiple meetings with State authorities, international organisations, international NGOs and Colombian civil society in The Hague and New York.[711] The OTP reiterated on several occasions its support for the peace process and the implementation of sound transitional justice measures in Colombia.[712]

The Prosecutor held various meetings with Colombian authorities, including with President H.E. Iván Duque, the Minister of Foreign Affairs, the High Presidential Counsellor for Stabilization and the former Attorney General.[713] In the course of these meetings, the Prosecutor exchanged views with the Colombian authorities on several aspects relevant to the preliminary examination, including on matters relating to the status of national proceedings relevant to the Office's analysis as well as on legislative developments that could have an impact on proceedings addressing Rome Statute crimes. The Prosecutor expressed her continued support for the authorities' efforts to ensure justice to the victims in accordance with the peace agreement, as well as the principles, values and requirements of the Rome Statute.

In the context of its ongoing admissibility assessment, the information assessed during the reporting period indicates that the Colombian authorities have taken meaningful steps to address conduct amounting to ICC crimes, as outlined in the 2012 Interim Report.[714] In this context, the OTP had identified the following potential cases that would form the focus of its preliminary examination: (i) proceedings relating to the promotion and expansion of paramilitary groups; (ii) proceedings relating to forced displacement; (iii) proceedings relating to sexual crimes; and, (iv) false positive cases. In addition, the OTP decided to:

---

707 *Ibid.*, para. 86.

708 *Ibid.*, para. 133.

709 *Ibid.*, para. 86.

710 *Ibid.*, para. 93.

711 *Ibid.*, para. 129.

712 *Ibid.*, para. 130.

713 *Ibid.*, para. 131.

714 ICC-OTP, Situation in Colombia, Interim Report, November 2012, paras. 197–224. Available at: https://www.icc-cpi.int/NR/rdonlyres/3D3055BD-16E2-4C83-BA85-35BCFD2A7922/285102/OTPCOLOMBIAPublicInterimReportNovember2012.pdf.

(v) follow-up on the Legal Framework for Peace and other relevant legislative developments, as well as jurisdictional aspects relating to the emergence of "new illegal armed groups".[715]

The Colombian authorities appear to have made progress towards the fulfilment of their duty to investigate and prosecute conduct amounting to war crimes and crimes against humanity under the Rome Statute, and thereby also address the forms of conduct underlying the potential cases identified by the Office.[716] During 2020, the OTP will continue assessing the genuineness of the proceedings carried out under the ordinary justice system, the Justice and Peace Law tribunals and the SJP, as well as contextual and legislative developments that may impact the effective conduct of their operations.[717] In this context, the Office will closely follow individual proceedings that should arise from relevant "macro" cases under the SJP, as well as the identification of cases selected for further steps, including investigations and prosecutions.[718]

Given the scale, complexity and long-term nature of the domestic proceedings being undertaken by the three national jurisdictions dealing with such conduct, the Office will also seek to conceptualize during 2020 the preparation of relevant benchmarks which could enable the Office to complete its preliminary examination, subject to the continued satisfaction of certain conditions, such as: the absence of manifest gaps in the scope of national proceedings or of factors vitiating their genuineness, and the imposition of effective penal sanctions that serve appropriate sentencing objectives of retribution, rehabilitation, restoration and deterrence.[719] This would also be subject to the possibility for the OTP to revisit its assessment in due course based on a change in circumstances. The Office will engage during 2020 in a series of consultations with the authorities and all other relevant stakeholders in this regard.[720]

(ii) *The Situation in Guinea*

Guinea deposited its instrument of ratification to the Statute on 14 July 2003. The ICC therefore has jurisdiction over Rome Statute crimes committed on the territory of Guinea or by Guinean nationals from 1 October 2003 with no end date. The preliminary examination of the situation in Guinea was opened on 14 October 2009[721] and remains ongoing. The OTP continued to receive communications pursuant to article 15 in relation to the situation in Guinea.[722]

During the reporting period, the OTP continued to assess the Guinean authorities' efforts to conduct genuine national proceedings relating to the 28 September 2009 events

[715] The Office of the Prosecutor, "Report on Preliminary Examination Activities 2019", 5 December 2019, para. 91. Available at: https://www.icc-cpi.int/itemsDocuments/191205-rep-otp-PE.pdf.

[716] *Ibid.*, para. 132.

[717] *Ibid.*

[718] *Ibid.*

[719] *Ibid.*, para. 133.

[720] *Ibid.*

[721] ICC Prosecutor confirms situation in Guinea under examination, 14 October 2009. Available at: https://www.icc-cpi.int//Pages/item.aspx?name=otp-stat-guinea-09-10-14.

[722] The Office of the Prosecutor, "Report on Preliminary Examination Activities 2019", 5 December 2019, para. 134. Available at: https://www.icc-cpi.int/itemsDocuments/191205-rep-otp-PE.pdf.

in the Conakry stadium, regarding which the OTP found a reasonable basis to believe that crimes against humanity were committed.

Since national proceedings have been ongoing, the Office's assessment has focused on whether the national authorities are willing and able to conduct genuine investigations and prosecutions, including the question of whether there has been unjustified delay which in the circumstances is inconsistent with an intent to bring the persons concerned to justice.[723]

The national investigation was completed in December 2017. On 25 June 2019, the Supreme Court rejected the appeal in cassation lodged by a number of parties to the proceedings challenging parts of the panel of judges' closing orders decision referring the case to trial.[724] With no more legal remedies available to challenge the completion of the national investigation in December 2017, the Supreme Court's decision concluded the investigation phase of the 28 September 2009 events case.[725]

During the reporting period, the OTP closely examined the work of the steering committee tasked with the logistical organisation of the trial and the implementation of its decisions.[726] The Office also assessed the impact of possible procedural and political factors that could potentially obstruct the holding of a trial or unjustifiably delay its organisation. In this respect, the Office has continued to encourage relevant stakeholders to support the organisation of the trial.

In particular, the Office has remained in regular contact with the Guinean authorities, national and international civil society organisations and other international partners supporting the national authorities in their efforts to organise a fair and impartial trial.[727] The Office has also continued liaising with international partners focusing on sexual and gender-based crimes, such as the United Nations Team of Experts on the Rule of Law and Sexual Violence in Conflict and its judicial expert deployed to support national proceedings.

In April and October 2019, the Office conducted its seventeenth and eighteenth missions to Conakry.[728] During both missions, the Office held meetings with the former and the new Minister of Justice (*ad interim*), the General Prosecutor of the Conakry Appeals Court, members of the steering committee, civil society, victims' counsel and the diplomatic community in Conakry, including the Office of the United Nations High Commissioner for Human Rights, the United Nations Development Programme and the European Union.[729] The Office also continued to meet on multiple occasions with national civil society organisations and victims' representatives, which included a meeting between the Prosecutor and Guinean civil society representatives on the margins of the ASP in December 2018.[730]

Despite the limited progress in the work of the steering committee, the Minister of Justice announced on 29 October 2019, during the OTP's visit to Conakry, that the trial

[723] *Ibid.*, para. 140.

[724] *Ibid.*, para. 141.

[725] *Ibid.*, para. 142.

[726] *Ibid.*, para. 147.

[727] *Ibid.*

[728] *Ibid.*, para. 148.

[729] *Ibid.*

[730] *Ibid.*

will take place at the latest in June 2020.[731] On 11 November 2019, the Prosecutor issued a public statement highlighting the Office's main findings during its visit to Conakry in October 2019 and commending the announcement of a concrete date for the commencement of the trial, but expressing her concern about the lack of progress made by the steering committee in the organisation of the trial.[732] The statement also included an intended preventive aspect following reports of numerous episodes of violence in Guinea in October and November 2019, occurring mainly in the context of state repression of demonstrations against a possible amendment of the Guinean Constitution.

The Office will closely examine the implementation of all the basic conditions for the organisation of the trial in June 2020.[733] To this end, the Office will pursue its regular exchanges with the Guinean authorities to discuss all aspects of the organisation of the trial, and encourage, as appropriate, relevant national and international stakeholders towards the organisation of a trial. Based on the information gathered over the next reporting period, the Office will continue to conduct its admissibility assessment for the purpose of determining whether the ongoing national proceedings are vitiated by an unwillingness or inability to genuinely carry out the proceedings within a reasonable delay.

(iii) *The Situation in Iraq/United Kingdom*

Iraq is not a State party to the Statute and has not lodged a declaration under article 12(3) accepting the jurisdiction of the Court.[734] In accordance with article 12(2)(*b*) of the Statute, acts on the territory of a non-State party will fall within the jurisdiction of the Court only when the person accused of the crime is a national of a State that has accepted jurisdiction. The United Kingdom ("UK") deposited its instrument of ratification to the Statute on 4 October 2001. The ICC therefore has jurisdiction over Rome Statute crimes committed on UK territory or by UK nationals from 1 July 2002 onwards.

On 13 May 2014, the Prosecutor announced that the preliminary examination of the situation in Iraq, previously concluded in 2006, was re-opened,[735] following the submission of further information on alleged crimes in a communication dated 20 January 2014, submitted by the European Center for Constitutional and Human Rights and Public Interest Lawyers (ECCHR), alleging the responsibility of UK officials for war crimes involving systematic detainee abuse in Iraq from 2003 until 2008.[736] During the reporting period, the OTP continued to receive communications pursuant to article 15 of the Statute.[737]

---

731 *Ibid*., para. 146.

732 Statement of ICC Prosecutor, Fatou Bensouda, at the conclusion of her Office's mission to Conakry, Guinea, 11 November 2019. Available at: https://www.icc-cpi.int/Pages/item.aspx?name=191111-otp-statement-guinea.

733 The Office of the Prosecutor, "Report on Preliminary Examination Activities 2019", 5 December 2019, para. 152. Available at: https://www.icc-cpi.int/itemsDocuments/191205-rep-otp-PE.pdf.

734 *Ibid*., para. 156.

735 Prosecutor of the International Criminal Court, Fatou Bensouda, re-opens the preliminary examination of the situation in Iraq, 13 May 2014. Available at: https://www.icc-cpi.int//Pages/item.aspx?name=otp-statement-iraq-13-05-2014.

736 *Ibid*., para. 154.

737 The Office of the Prosecutor, "Report on Preliminary Examination Activities 2019", 5 December 2019, para. 153. Available at: https://www.icc-cpi.int/itemsDocuments/191205-rep-otp-PE.pdf.

During 2019, the Office focused on bringing its determination on the scope and genuineness of domestic proceedings to a conclusion.[738] In so doing, the Office has maintained contact with relevant actors, including the UK authorities, who have continued to cooperate with the Office, and with article 15 senders.[739] In this context, in July 2019, the Office received a new submission from the ECCHR, one of the two main senders of article 15 communications. The Office has also interacted with the UK authorities on issues related to the preliminary examination.

In addition, the Office sought to finalize its gravity assessment, taking into consideration: (i) the gravity of the alleged crimes, including their scale, nature, manner of commission, and impact; and (ii) the persons or groups of persons most responsible for the alleged crimes committed. This assessment will also be revisited in the light of any additional findings made as a result of its inquiries outlined above.[740]

The Office has also followed a proposal made in May 2019 by the former Defence Secretary, calling for "a statutory presumption against prosecution of current or former personnel for alleged offences committed outside the UK in the course of duty more than 10 years previously, and which have been the subject of a previous investigation."[741] The initial proposal, which the Office understands was to govern both Northern Ireland and more recent conflicts such as in Afghanistan and Iraq, would stipulate that prosecutions in such circumstances should not be considered to be in the public interest, except in exceptional circumstances.[742]

The Office understands that the above proposal remains subject to public consultation and no white paper setting out the specific text of draft legislation has as yet been introduced.[743] Nonetheless, were such domestic legislation to be adopted, the Office would need to consider its potential impact on the ability of the UK authorities to investigate and/or prosecute crimes allegedly committed by members of the British armed forces in Iraq, against the standards of inactivity and genuineness set out in article 17 of the Statute.

During the reporting period, the Office made significant progress towards finalising its assessment of the situation in Iraq/UK. At the same time, the Office has had to assess the impact of certain relevant developments during the year.[744] During 2020, the Office will seek to ascertain whether the allegations of a lack of genuineness can be substantiated in order to enable it to come to a final determination with respect to the preliminary examination as early as practically possible.[745]

(iv) *The Situation in Nigeria*

Nigeria deposited its instrument of ratification to the Statute on 27 September 2001. The ICC therefore has jurisdiction over Rome Statute crimes committed on the territory of Nigeria or by its nationals from 1 July 2002 onwards.

---

[738] *Ibid.*, para. 164.

[739] *Ibid.*, para. 172.

[740] *Ibid.*, para. 171.

[741] *Ibid.*, para. 173.

[742] *Ibid.*

[743] *Ibid.*, para. 174.

[744] *Ibid.*, para. 175.

[745] *Ibid.*

The preliminary examination of the situation in Nigeria opened on 18 November 2010 and remains ongoing.[746] During the reporting period, the Office continued to receive communications pursuant to article 15 in relation to this situation.

During the reporting period, the Office has sought to finalize its factual and legal assessment of information received on alleged crimes and gathered additional information on relevant national proceedings conducted by the Nigerian authorities.[747]

The Office has been able to arrive at subject-matter determinations on the majority of allegations concerning crimes against humanity and war crimes allegedly committed by Boko Haram members and members of the Nigerian Security Forces (NSF) from 2009 until early 2019.[748] During the reporting period, the Office has updated its subject-matter assessment to include alleged crimes occurring after March 2015. Based on its updated subject-matter assessment, two new potential cases were identified by the Office, one with respect to Boko Haram and one with respect to the NSF.[749]

The Office has also examined article 15 communications with respect to allegations of crimes not related to the armed conflict between the NSF and Boko Haram.[750] In this context, the Office has noted with deep concern allegations of ongoing evidence tampering and of the alleged destruction of evidence.

The Office has focused on a number of apparent challenges facing the Nigerian authorities in their efforts to combat criminality and their impact on the Office's assessment under articles 17(2) and 17(3), including the absence of legislative provisions addressing certain categories of conduct; the persistence of the armed conflict; inadequate investigation files; an over-reliance on confession-based evidence; a lack of forensic evidence; limited cooperation between investigators and prosecutors at pre-investigation stages; logistical difficulties, inadequate security for counsels, and the challenges of converting military intelligence to admissible evidence.[751]

From 24 to 27 June 2019, the Office conducted a technical mission to Abuja to discuss the status of its preliminary examination activities with the country's authorities and with other relevant partners and stakeholders.[752] In October 2019, the Prosecutor conducted a two-day mission to Abuja, Nigeria.[753] It was her fourth mission to this country. During her visit, the Prosecutor met with the Vice-President of Nigeria, H.E. Mr. Yemi Osinbajo, to discuss the Nigerian Government's support for and cooperation with the preliminary examination of the situation in Nigeria. During her visit, the Nigerian Government assured

---

[746] The Office of the Prosecutor, "Report on Preliminary Examination Activities 2019", 5 December 2019, para. 176. Available at: https://www.icc-cpi.int/itemsDocuments/191205-rep-otp-PE.pdf.

[747] *Ibid.*, para. 194.

[748] *Ibid.*, para. 181.

[749] *Ibid.*, para. 189.

[750] *Ibid.*, para. 188.

[751] *Ibid.*, para. 193.

[752] International Criminal Court, Annual report of the International Criminal Court to the United Nations on its activities in 2018/19, A/74/324 23 August 2019, para. 52. Available at: https://www.icc-cpi.int/Pages/item.aspx?name=190823-icc-report-unga.

[753] The Office of the Prosecutor, "Report on Preliminary Examination Activities 2019", 5 December 2019, para. 195. Available at: https://www.icc-cpi.int/itemsDocuments/191205-rep-otp-PE.pdf.

the Prosecutor of Nigeria's commitment to the ICC and its cooperation with the Office's preliminary examination.

In October 2019, the Office held a fourth technical meeting with Nigerian authorities at the Ministry of Justice in Abuja to gather additional information on national proceedings conducted with respect to the ten potential cases identified and to review its findings to date.[754]

The Office also continued to engage with international partners supporting the Nigerian judiciary's activity in relation to crimes that could fall under the jurisdiction of the ICC.[755] This included the presentation of its preliminary findings to Nigerian prosecuting authorities in a workshop organized by a partner NGO in June 2019 and aimed at reinforcing Nigeria's capacity to address complex and serious crimes.

Throughout the reporting period, the Office maintained close contact with relevant partners and stakeholders in the situation in Nigeria, including international and Nigerian NGOs, communication senders, and diplomatic actors.[756] In particular, the Office also continued liaising with international partners focusing on SGBC, such as the Office of the United Nations Special Representative on Sexual Violence in Conflict.[757]

In 2020, the Office will continue to urge the Nigerian authorities to tangibly demonstrate that they are indeed fulfilling their primary responsibility to investigate and prosecute ICC crimes, in the absence of which the Office will need to come to its own determination with respect to the admissibility of the potential cases it has identified and on whether the requirements of article 15 have been met.[758]

(v) *The Situation in Palestine*

On 1 January 2015, the Government of the State of Palestine lodged a declaration under article 12(3) of the Statute accepting the jurisdiction of the ICC over alleged crimes committed "in the occupied Palestinian territory, including East Jerusalem, since June 13, 2014."[759] On 2 January 2015, the State of Palestine acceded to the Statute by depositing its instrument of accession with the United Nations Secretary-General. The Statute entered into force for the State of Palestine on 1 April 2015.

The situation in Palestine has been under preliminary examination since 16 January 2015.[760] During the reporting period, the OTP continued to receive communications pursuant to article 15 in relation to this situation.[761]

---

[754] *Ibid.*, para. 196.

[755] *Ibid.*, para. 197.

[756] *Ibid.*, para. 198.

[757] *Ibid.*

[758] *Ibid.*, para. 199.

[759] Declaration Accepting the Jurisdiction of the International Criminal Court, 31 December 2014. Available at: https://www.icc-cpi.int/iccdocs/PIDS/press/Palestine_A_12-3.pdf.

[760] The Prosecutor of the International Criminal Court, Fatou Bensouda, opens a preliminary examination of the situation in Palestine, 16 January 2015. Available at: https://www.icc-cpi.int/Pages/item.aspx?name=pr1083.

[761] The Office of the Prosecutor, "Report on Preliminary Examination Activities 2019", 5 December 2019, para. 200. Available at: https://www.icc-cpi.int/itemsDocuments/191205-rep-otp-PE.pdf.

On 22 May 2018, the OTP received a referral from the State of Palestine under articles 13(*a*) and 14 of the Statute regarding the situation in Palestine since 13 June 2014.[762] On 24 May 2018, the Presidency of the Court assigned the Situation in Palestine to PTC I.[763]

On 20 December 2019, the Prosecutor announced that the preliminary examination into the Situation in Palestine had concluded and that there was a reasonable basis to proceed with an investigation into the situation in Palestine, pursuant to article 53(1) of the Statute.[764] While concluding that the Court has jurisdiction and the scope of the Court's territorial jurisdiction extends to the West Bank, including East Jerusalem, and Gaza, the Prosecutor recognized the controversy that surrounds this issue as well as the importance of resolving it prior to commencing an investigation. Accordingly, she requested from PTC I a jurisdictional ruling, pursuant to article 19(3) of the Statute, on the scope of the territorial jurisdiction of the International Criminal Court (ICC or the Court) under article 12(2)(a) of the Rome Statute in Palestine.[765]

In working towards bringing the preliminary examination to a conclusion and a decision under article 53(1), the Office has sought to finalize its subject-matter analysis of alleged conduct in Gaza and in the West Bank as well as attendant admissibility assessments concerning complementarity and gravity, while continuing to receive and carefully review additional information provided by relevant actors.[766]

In addition to the above, the Office also received and gathered information regarding other crimes allegedly committed by both sides in relation to the violence that has occurred in the context of the protests held along the Israel-Gaza border since 30 March 2018 and throughout 2019.[767]

Throughout the reporting period, the Office continued to engage and consult with relevant stakeholders, including officials of Palestine and Israel, intergovernmental and non-governmental organizations, and members of civil society.[768]

The Office also continued to monitor relevant developments in the region closely, and to assess new allegations and information available concerning the alleged commission of Rome Statute crimes and any related national proceedings.[769] The Office also followed with

---

[762] Statement by ICC Prosecutor, Mrs Fatou Bensouda, on the referral submitted by Palestine, 22 May 2018. Available at: https://www.icc-cpi.int/Pages/item.aspx?name=180522-otp-stat.

[763] *Situation in the State of Palestine*, Decision assigning the situation in the State of Palestine to PTC I, ICC-01/18-1, 24 May 2018.

[764] Statement of ICC Prosecutor, Fatou Bensouda, on the conclusion of the preliminary examination of the Situation in Palestine, and seeking a ruling on the scope of the Court's territorial jurisdiction, 20 December 2019. Available at: https://www.icc-cpi.int/Pages/item.aspx?name=20191220-otp-statement-palestine.

[765] The request was refiled on 22 January 2020, following the decision of PTC I on 21 January 2020. See *Situation in the State of Palestine*, Prosecution request pursuant to article 19(3) for a ruling on the Court's territorial jurisdiction in Palestine, ICC-01/18-12, 22 January 2020. See also *Situation in the State of Palestine*, Decision on the Prosecutor's Application for an extension of the page limit, ICC-01/18-11, 21 January 2020.

[766] The Office of the Prosecutor, "Report on Preliminary Examination Activities 2019", 5 December 2019, paras. 221 and 225. Available at: https://www.icc-cpi.int/itemsDocuments/191205-rep-otp-PE.pdf.

[767] *Ibid.*, para. 226.

[768] *Ibid.*, para. 228.

[769] *Ibid.*, para. 229.

concern proposals advanced during the recent electoral campaign in Israel, to be tabled to the Knesset, for Israel to annex the Jordan Valley in the West Bank.

(vi) *The Situation in the Philippines*

The Philippines deposited its instrument of ratification to the Statute on 30 August 2011.[770] On 17 March 2018, the Government of the Philippines deposited a written notification of withdrawal from the Statute with the United Nations Secretary-General.[771] Pursuant to article 127 of the Statute, the withdrawal took effect one year after this date, on 17 March 2019. The ICC retains jurisdiction over the Rome Statute crimes committed on the territory of the Philippines or by its nationals during the period when it was a State party to the Statute, namely between 1 November 2011 and 16 March 2019.[772]

The OTP initiated a preliminary examination of the situation in the Philippines on 8 February 2018.[773] During the reporting period, the Office continued to receive communications pursuant to article 15 in relation to this situation.[774]

The Office sought to finalize its subject-matter analysis of such alleged conduct as well as attendant admissibility assessments concerning complementarity and gravity.[775] It gathered, received, and analyzed information from a wide range of sources. The Office reviewed hundreds of media and academic articles, reports, databases, legal submissions, primary documents, press releases and public statements by intergovernmental, governmental and non-governmental organizations, and other relevant sources, including such that was received through article 15 communications submitted directly to the Office.[776] Consistent with standard practice, the Office has subjected such information to rigorous source evaluation, including an independent and thorough assessment of the reliability of sources and credibility of information received.[777] In connection with this process, the Office has continued to take steps to verify the seriousness of information received and corroborate a number of relevant factual issues.

In the context of its assessment of subject-matter jurisdiction, the Office further examined particular features of the "war on drugs" campaign and implementation,

---

[770] ICC-OTP, Republic of the Philippines. Available at: https://www.icc-cpi.int/philippines.

[771] The United Nations, C.N.138.2018.TREATIES-VXIII.10, 17 March 2018. Available at: https://treaties.un.org/doc/Publication/CN/2018/CN.138.2018-Eng.pdf.

[772] Regarding the ICC's exercise of jurisdiction over crimes committed on territories of States parties that have later deposited a withdrawal notice, *see* further: *Situation in the Republic of Burundi*, Public Redacted Version of "Decision Pursuant to Article 15 of the Rome Statute on the Authorization of an Investigation into the Situation in the Republic of Burundi", ICC-01/17-X-9-US-Exp, 25 October 2017, ICC-01/17-9-Red, 9 November 2017, para. 24.

[773] Statement of the Prosecutor of the International Criminal Court, Mrs Fatou Bensouda, on opening Preliminary Examinations into the situations in the Philippines and in Venezuela, 8 February 2018. Available at: https://www.icc-cpi.int/Pages/item.aspx?name=180208-otp-stat.

[774] The Office of the Prosecutor, "Report on Preliminary Examination Activities 2019", 5 December 2019, para. 231. Available at: https://www.icc-cpi.int/itemsDocuments/191205-rep-otp-PE.pdf.

[775] *Ibid.*, para. 249.

[776] *Ibid.*

[777] *Ibid.*

independently documented and analyzed relevant individual alleged incidents, and conducted an analysis of relevant patterns and trends. With respect to the legal assessment, the Office has analyzed the information available to determine whether the alleged conduct of State actors and/or other individuals (such as vigilantes) amounts to the crimes against humanity of murder, torture, other inhumane acts or rape.[778] Such analysis was conducted with a view to identifying potential cases likely to arise from any potential investigation into the situation and the persons or groups of persons who may bear the greatest responsibility for the identified alleged crimes.

In addition, the Office has gathered information relevant to the determinations on admissibility.[779] For example, the Office collected and assessed open-source information on any relevant national proceedings being conducted by Philippine authorities. The Office also monitored proceedings that appear to remain ongoing and took steps to obtain further information pertinent to the complementarity assessment.

Throughout the reporting period, the Office continued to engage and consult with relevant stakeholders in order to address a range of matters relevant to the preliminary examination and to seek further information to inform its assessment of the situation.[780] For example, the Office held a number of meetings and was in contact with such stakeholders, including various civil society organizations.

The Office also followed with concern reports of threats and other measures apparently taken against human rights defenders, including those who have criticized the war on drugs campaign.[781] The Office will continue to closely monitor such reports, as well as other relevant developments in the Philippines.

During 2020, the Office will aim to finalize the preliminary examination in order to enable the Prosecutor to reach a decision on whether to seek authorization to open an investigation into the situation in the Philippines.[782]

(vii) *The Situation in Ukraine*

Ukraine is not a Party to the Statute. However, on 17 April 2014, the Government of Ukraine lodged a declaration under article 12(3) of the Statute accepting the jurisdiction of the Court over alleged crimes committed on its territory from 21 November 2013 to 22 February 2014.[783] On 25 April 2014, the Prosecutor opened a preliminary examination of the situation in Ukraine relating to the so-called "Maidan events."[784]

On 8 September 2015, the Government of Ukraine lodged a second declaration under article 12(3) of the Statute accepting the jurisdiction of the ICC in relation to alleged

---

[778] *Ibid.*, para. 250.

[779] *Ibid.*, para. 251.

[780] *Ibid.*, para. 252.

[781] *Ibid.*, para. 253.

[782] *Ibid.*, para. 254.

[783] Available at: https://www.icc-cpi.int/itemsDocuments/997/declarationRecognitionJuristiction09-04-2014.pdf. See also: https://www.icc-cpi.int/ukraine.

[784] The Prosecutor of the International Criminal Court, Fatou Bensouda, opens a preliminary examination in Ukraine, 25 April 2014. Available at: https://www.icc-cpi.int/Pages/item.aspx?name=pr999&ln=en.

crimes committed on its territory from 20 February 2014 onwards, with no end date.[785] On 29 September, based on Ukraine's second declaration under article 12(3), the Prosecutor announced the extension of the preliminary examination to include alleged crimes occurring after 20 February 2014 in Crimea and eastern Ukraine.[786]

The situation in Ukraine has been under preliminary examination since 25 April 2014. During the reporting period, the Office continued to receive communications under article 15 of the Statute in relation to crimes alleged to have been committed since 21 November 2013.[787]

In early 2019, the Office completed its preliminary analysis of subject-matter jurisdiction and assessed that there was a reasonable basis to believe that a number of crimes under the Statute had been committed both in the context of the situations in Crimea and in eastern Ukraine.[788] The Office examined a large volume of information regarding a number of allegations of crimes that occurred in the context of the situation that led up to the occupation, and during the occupation of the territory of Crimea and the events that occurred in eastern Ukraine. In conducting this analysis, the Office examined several forms of alleged conduct and considered the various legal qualifications under the Statute.

In 2019, the Office has also reviewed additional information related to the period specified in Ukraine's first declaration under article 12(3) of the Statute and is conducting a thorough legal assessment of the information to determine whether it would alter the previous assessment of the alleged crimes that occurred in the context of the Maidan events.[789]

During the reporting period, the OTP moved the focus of its preliminary examination of the situation in Ukraine to the assessment of admissibility.[790] The Office continued to receive information from a variety of sources to conduct a preliminary "mapping" of the different investigative and prosecutorial authorities conducting investigations and proceedings relevant to the potential cases that would likely be the focus of any investigation and to identify the existence of multiple and overlapping jurisdictions with regard to conduct of relevance to the ICC's jurisdiction.

In relation to Crimea, the Office has identified multiple existing criminal proceedings being conducted by the authorities, including conduct and persons that would likely be the focus of any investigation of crimes allegedly committed in Crimea.[791] In relation to these relevant proceedings identified, the Office is currently seeking further information for purposes of assessing whether the specific conduct that is the focus of these national proceedings is the same as that identified in the potential cases identified by the Office.

---

[785] Available at: https://www.icc-cpi.int/iccdocs/other/Ukraine_Art_12-3_declaration_08092015.pdf#search=ukraine.

[786] ICC Prosecutor extends preliminary examination of the situation in Ukraine following second article 12(3) declaration, 29 September 2015. Available at: https://www.icc-cpi.int/Pages/item.aspx?name=pr1156.

[787] The Office of the Prosecutor, "Report on Preliminary Examination Activities 2019", 5 December 2019, para. 255. Available at: https://www.icc-cpi.int/itemsDocuments/191205-rep-otp-PE.pdf.

[788] *Ibid.*, para. 267.

[789] *Ibid.*, para. 287.

[790] *Ibid.*, para. 281.

[791] *Ibid.*, para. 283.

In relation to eastern Ukraine, the Office has also identified a number of existing proceedings carried out by Ukrainian authorities and the Office is currently seeking further information for purposes of assessing whether the specific conduct that is the focus of these national proceedings is the same as that identified in the potential cases identified by the Office.[792]

For purposes of the admissibility assessment, the Office is also considering whether, based on the information available, the crimes allegedly committed in eastern Ukraine and in Crimea respectively are sufficiently grave within the meaning and requirements of the Statute to justify the opening of an investigation, in particular considering their scale, nature, manner of commission, and their impact on victims and affected communities.[793]

During the reporting period, the Office held a number of meetings with stakeholders both at the seat of the Court and during a mission to Ukraine in June 2019, to discuss existing proceedings and a range of issues of other relevance to the preliminary examination.[794] During its June mission to Ukraine, the Office communicated to the Ukrainian authorities and civil society stakeholders its preliminary findings in relation to alleged crimes in eastern Ukraine and Crimea, and discussed with them the (phase 3) assessment of admissibility, and additional information of relevance to the Office's analysis in that regard.[795]

The Office will seek to finalize its assessment of the admissibility of potential cases that would likely be the focus of any investigation, both in relation to Crimea and eastern Ukraine, in order to enable the Prosecutor to come to a determination under article 15(3) of the Statute.[796] In this regard, the Office is gathering additional information on relevant national proceedings and engaging with the Ukrainian authorities, civil society and other relevant stakeholders. Given the open-ended nature of Ukraine's acceptance of ICC jurisdiction, the Office will also continue to consider allegations of new crimes committed in Ukraine.[797]

(viii) *The Situation in Venezuela*

Venezuela deposited its instrument of ratification to the Statute on 7 June 2000. The ICC therefore has jurisdiction over Rome Statute crimes committed on the territory of Venezuela or by its nationals from 1 July 2002 onwards.

The OTP initiated a preliminary examination into the situation in Venezuela on 8 February 2018.[798]

On 27 September 2018, the Office received a referral from a group of States parties to the Statute regarding the alleged perpetration of crimes against humanity committed in

---

[792] *Ibid.*, para. 284.

[793] *Ibid.*, para. 285.

[794] *Ibid.*, para. 286.

[795] *Ibid.*

[796] *Ibid.*, para. 288.

[797] *Ibid.*

[798] Statement of the Prosecutor of the International Criminal Court, Mrs Fatou Bensouda, on opening Preliminary Examinations into the situations in the Philippines and in Venezuela, 8 February 2018. Available at: https://www.icc-cpi.int/Pages/item.aspx?name=180208-otp-stat.

Venezuela since 12 February 2014.[799] On 28 September 2018, the Presidency of the Court assigned the situation to PTC I.[800]

During the reporting period, the Office examined several forms of alleged conduct and their possible legal qualifications under the Statute.[801] In particular, the Office analyzed and evaluated the information available to determine whether it provides a reasonable basis to believe that the alleged crimes against actual or perceived opponents of the Government in the context of the anti-government protests and related political unrest from at least April 2017 amount to crimes against humanity under article 7 of the Statute.[802]

The Office has almost concluded its subject-matter assessment.[803] In particular, the Office has analyzed multiple article 15 communications, together with publicly available material, including reports from Venezuelan and international civil society organizations and think-tanks, the United Nations Office of the High Commissioner for Human Rights, the United Nations Working Group on Arbitrary Detention, the Inter-American Commission on Human Rights and the Organization of American States.[804] The Office has also continued engaging with multiple stakeholders and information providers in efforts to address relevant information gaps.

The Office expects to finalize its assessment of subject-matter jurisdiction in early 2020.[805] Should the assessment result in a positive finding, the Office will proceed to an assessment of admissibility. The Office will also continue to record allegations of crimes to the extent that they may fall within the jurisdiction of the Court.[806]

(*b*) Completed preliminary examinations

(i) *The Situation in Bangladesh/Myanmar*

Bangladesh deposited its instrument of ratification to the Statute on 23 March 2010.[807] The ICC therefore has jurisdiction over crimes committed on or after 1 June 2010 on the territory of Bangladesh, pursuant to article 12(2)(*a*) of the Statute, or by its nationals, pursuant to article 12(2)(*b*) of the Statute.[808]

---

[799] Referral of the situation in Venezuela under Article 14 of the Rome Statute submitted by the Republic of Argentina, Canada, the Republic of Colombia, the Republic of Chile, the Republic of Paraguay and the Republic of Peru. Available at: https://www.icc-cpi.int/itemsDocuments/180925-otp-referral-venezuela_ENG.pdf.

[800] *Situation in the Bolivarian Republic of Venezuela,* Decision assigning the situation in the Bolivarian Republic of Venezuela to PTC I, ICC-02/18-1, 28 September 2018.

[801] The Office of the Prosecutor, "Report on Preliminary Examination Activities 2019", 5 December 2019, para. 75. Available at: https://www.icc-cpi.int/itemsDocuments/191205-rep-otp-PE.pdf.

[802] *Ibid.*

[803] *Ibid.*, para. 81.

[804] *Ibid.*

[805] *Ibid.*, para. 83.

[806] *Ibid.*

[807] Assembly of State Parties, Bangladesh. Available at: https://asp.icc-cpi.int/en_menus/asp/states%20parties/asian%20states/Pages/bangladesh.aspx.

[808] *Situation in the People's Republic of Bangladesh/Republic of the Union of Myanmar,* Decision Pursuant to Article 15 of the Rome Statute on the Authorisation of an Investigation into the Situation in the People's

On 9 April 2018, the OTP filed a Request seeking a ruling from the PTC on the exercise of jurisdiction pursuant to article 12(2)(*a*) of the Statute.[809] On 6 September 2018, PTC I issued a decision confirming that the Court may exercise jurisdiction over the alleged deportation of the Rohingya people from Myanmar to Bangladesh, as well as potentially other crimes under article 7 of the Statute.[810]

During the reporting period, the Office completed its comprehensive assessment of statutory criteria for a determination of whether there is a reasonable basis to proceed with an investigation into the situation in Bangladesh/Myanmar pursuant to article 53(1) of the Statute.[811]

The Office further engaged with relevant stakeholders, including victims' groups and civil society, both at the seat of the Court and during missions to Bangladesh.[812] In Cox's Bazar, the delegation visited refugee camps and met with government authorities, humanitarian agencies and NGOs, as well as a number of victims' representatives. The delegation also exchanged views with representatives of various agencies, including the UN, members of the diplomatic community and academics.[813]

On 26 June 2019, the Presidency assigned the situation to PTC III.[814] On 4 July 2019, following the Office's preliminary examination process, the Prosecutor requested authorization from PTC III to investigate the situation in Bangladesh/Myanmar in the period since 9 October 2016.[815] On the same day, the Prosecutor notified victims and victims' representatives seeking to make representations to PTC III on the Prosecutor's request that the deadline for so doing was 28 October 2019. PTC III received views on the Prosecutor's request by or on behalf of hundreds of thousands of alleged victims.[816]

On 14 November 2019, PTC III authorized the commencement of an investigation into this situation.[817] The Chamber authorized an investigation in relation to any crime, including any future crime, within the jurisdiction of the Court committed at least in part on the territory of Bangladesh or on the territory of any other State party or State making a declaration under article 12(3) of the Statute, if the alleged crime is sufficiently linked to the

---

Republic of Bangladesh/Republic of the Union of Myanmar, ICC-01/19-27, 14 November 2019, para. 113.

809 The Office of the Prosecutor, Prosecution's Request for a Ruling on Jurisdiction under Article 19(3) of the Statute, ICC-RoC46(3)-01/18-1, 9 April 2018.

810 Decision on the "Prosecution's Request for a Ruling on Jurisdiction under Article 19(3) of the Statute", ICC-RoC46(3)-01/18-37, 6 September 2018.

811 The Office of the Prosecutor, "Report on Preliminary Examination Activities 2019", 5 December 2019, para. 292. Available at: https://www.icc-cpi.int/itemsDocuments/191205-rep-otp-PE.pdf.

812 *Ibid.*, para. 293.

813 *Ibid.*

814 *Situation in the People's Republic of Bangladesh/Republic of the Union of Myanmar*, Decision on the constitution of PTC III and on the assignment of the situation in the People's Republic of Bangladesh/Republic of the Union of Myanmar, ICC-01/19-1, 25 June 2019.

815 *Situation in the People's Republic of Bangladesh/Republic of the Union of Myanmar*, Request for authorisation of an investigation pursuant to article 15, ICC-01/19-7, 4 July 2019.

816 The Office of the Prosecutor, "Report on Preliminary Examination Activities 2019", 5 December 2019, paras. 294–295. Available at: https://www.icc-cpi.int/itemsDocuments/191205-rep-otp-PE.pdf.

817 *Situation in the People's Republic of Bangladesh/Republic of the Union of Myanmar*, Decision Pursuant to Article 15 of the Rome Statute on the Authorisation of an Investigation into the Situation in the People's Republic of Bangladesh/Republic of the Union of Myanmar, ICC-01/19-27, 14 November 2019.

situation as described in the decision, irrespective of the nationality of the perpetrators.[818] As for the time period, the Chamber authorized the investigation of crimes allegedly committed on or after 1 June 2010, the date of entry into force of the Statute for Bangladesh, and, in relation to crimes allegedly committed at least in part on the territory of other States parties, after the date of entry into force of the Statute for those States parties.[819]

Subsequent to PTC III's decision, and in accordance with article 18 of the Statute, the Office notified all States parties and those States which would normally exercise jurisdiction over the alleged crimes concerned of its initiation of an investigation into this situation.[820] In accordance with PTC III's authorization decision, the Office has commenced its investigation into the situation in Bangladesh/Myanmar.[821] The Office will pursue its mandate independently, impartially and objectively, and will examine allegations against all groups or parties within the situation in order to assess whether persons belonging to those groups or parties bear criminal responsibility under the Statute.[822]

(ii) *The Situation in the Islamic Republic of Afghanistan*

Afghanistan deposited its instrument of ratification to the Statute on 10 February 2003. The ICC therefore has jurisdiction over Rome Statute crimes committed on the territory of Afghanistan or by its nationals since 1 May 2003, with no end-date.[823]

The preliminary examination of the situation in the Islamic Republic of Afghanistan was announced in 2007.[824] On 20 November 2017, the OTP requested authorization from PTC III to initiate an investigation into alleged war crimes and crimes against humanity committed in Afghanistan, as well as similar crimes sufficiently linked to the situation and committed on the territory of other State parties to the Rome Statute.[825]

The situation was reassigned to PTC II on 16 March 2018,[826] and on 12 April 2019, PTC II had unanimously rejected the request of the Prosecutor to proceed with an investigation on alleged crimes against humanity and war crimes committed on the territory of the Islamic Republic of Afghanistan.[827] The Prosecutor requested leave to appeal

---

[818] The Office of the Prosecutor, "Report on Preliminary Examination Activities 2019", 5 December 2019, para. 297. Available at: https://www.icc-cpi.int/itemsDocuments/191205-rep-otp-PE.pdf.

[819] *Ibid.*

[820] The Office of the Prosecutor, "Report on Preliminary Examination Activities 2019", 5 December 2019, para. 300. Available at: https://www.icc-cpi.int/itemsDocuments/191205-rep-otp-PE.pdf.

[821] *Ibid.*, para. 301.

[822] *Ibid.*

[823] *Ibid.*

[824] The Office of the Prosecutor, "Report on Preliminary Examination Activities 2017", 4 December 2017, para. 230. Available at: https://www.icc-cpi.int/itemsDocuments/2017-PE-rep/2017-otp-rep-PE_ENG.pdf.

[825] *Situation in the Islamic Republic of Afghanistan,* Public redacted version of "Request for authorisation of an investigation pursuant to article 15", 20 November 2017, ICC-02/17-7-Conf-Exp, ICC-02/17-7-Red, 20 November 2017.

[826] *Situation in the Islamic Republic of Afghanistan,* Decision assigning judges to divisions and recomposing Chambers, ICC-02/17-30, 16 March 2018, p. 6.

[827] *Situation in the Islamic Republic of Afghanistan,* Decision Pursuant to Article 15 of the Rome Statute on the Authorisation of an Investigation into the Situation in the Islamic Republic of Afghanistan,

the decision on 7 June 2019.[828] On 17 September 2019, PTC II granted in part the request of the Prosecutor for Leave to Appeal the "Decision Pursuant to Article 15 of the Rome Statute on the Authorisation of an Investigation into the Situation in the Islamic Republic of Afghanistan."[829] From 4 to 6 December 2019, the AC held a hearing.[830] During the duration of the reporting period, the decision of the AC to authorize the Prosecutor to commence an investigation into alleged crimes under the jurisdiction of the Court in relation to the situation in the Islamic Republic of Afghanistan was still pending.

(iii) *The Situation of Registered Vessels of the Union of the Comoros, the Hellenic Republic and the Kingdom of Cambodia*

The Prosecutor's decision not to investigate the situation referred by the Government of the Comoros, the Comoros' successful request for review of that decision, and the filing of the Prosecutor's reconsideration of her decision (again declining to investigate) has previously been reported. On 15 November 2018, PTC I again directed the Prosecutor to reconsider her decision not to investigate.[831] In the decision, the Chamber requested the Prosecutor to reconsider, by 15 May 2019, her decision not to investigate, and to do so in accordance with the decision of 16 July 2015 issued by PTC I on the first request of the Comoros to review the Prosecutor's decision not to investigate.

Having been granted leave to appeal this decision by the PTC, on 11 February 2019, the Prosecutor filed her appeal brief.[832] On 1 May 2019, the AC held a hearing with the Prosecutor, the Comoros and the victims. On 3 May 2019, the Chamber issued an order scheduling the delivery of the judgment for 2 September 2019 and suspending the time limit set by the PTC for the Prosecutor to reconsider her decision until then.[833] On 2 September 2019, the AC delivered its judgment and rejected the appeal of the Prosecutor against the decision of PTC I on the application for judicial review by the Comoros.[834] The AC nevertheless maintained,

ICC-02/17-33, 12 April 2019.

[828] *Situation in the Islamic Republic of Afghanistan,* Request for Leave to Appeal the "Decision Pursuant to Article 15 of the Rome Statute on the Authorisation of an Investigation into the Situation in the Islamic Republic of Afghanistan", ICC-02/17-34, 7 June 2019.

[829] *Situation in the Islamic Republic of Afghanistan,* Decision on the Prosecutor and Victims' Requests for Leave to Appeal the 'Decision Pursuant to Article 15 of the Rome Statute on the Authorisation of an Investigation into the Situation in the Islamic Republic of Afghanistan', ICC-02/17-62, 17 September 2019.

[830] *Situation in the Islamic Republic of Afghanistan,* Transcript of hearing, 4 December 2019, ICC-02/17-T-001-ENG; Transcript of hearing, 5 December 2019, ICC-02/17-T-002-ENG; Transcript of hearing, 6 December 2019, ICC-02/17-T-003-ENG.

[831] *Situation on Registered Vessels of the Union of the Comoros, the Hellenic Republic and the Kingdom of Cambodia,* Decision on the "Application for Judicial Review by the Government of the Union of the Comoros", ICC-01/13-68, 15 November 2018.

[832] *Situation on Registered Vessels of the Union of the Comoros, the Hellenic Republic and the Kingdom of Cambodia,* Prosecution Appeal Brief, ICC-01/13-85, 11 February 2019.

[833] *Situation on Registered Vessels of the Union of the Comoros, the Hellenic Republic and the Kingdom of Cambodia,* Scheduling Order for delivery of judgment on the appeal of the Prosecutor against the decision of PTC I of 15 November 2018 entitled 'Decision on the "Application for Judicial Review by the Government of the Union of the Comoros"', ICC-01/13-97, 3 May 2019.

[834] *Situation on Registered Vessels of the Union of the Comoros, the Hellenic Republic and the Kingdom of Cambodia,* Judgment on the appeal of the Prosecutor against PTC I's 'Decision on the "Application for Judicial Review by the Government of the Union of the Comoros"', ICC-01/13-98, 2 September 2019.

Judge Chile Eboe-Osuji and Judge Luz del Carmen Ibáñez Carranza dissenting, that the 'ultimate decision' as to whether or not to initiate an investigation is that of the Prosecutor.

On 2 December 2019, the Prosecutor notified her decision that there is no reasonable basis to proceed with an investigation.[835]

(*c*) Situations under investigation

(i) *The Situation in Burundi*

Burundi deposited its instrument of ratification to the Rome Statute on 21 September 2004. On 27 October 2016, Burundi submitted a notification of withdrawal from the Statute, which became effective on 27 October 2017.[836] The ICC may therefore exercise its jurisdiction over crimes listed in the Rome Statute committed on the territory of Burundi or by its nationals from 1 December 2004 to 26 October 2017.

On 25 October 2017, PTC III issued its decision authorizing the Prosecutor to open an investigation *proprio motu* regarding crimes allegedly committed in Burundi or by Burundian nationals outside Burundi since 26 April 2015.[837] The Prosecutor is authorized to extend her investigation to crimes committed before 26 April 2015 or continued after 26 October 2017, if certain legal requirements are met.

a. Judicial proceedings

In its decision authorizing an investigation, the PTC observed that the Court retains jurisdiction over any crime within its jurisdiction up to and including 26 October 2017,[838] regardless of Burundi's withdrawal.

The PTC found a reasonable basis to believe that a widespread and systematic attack against the Burundian civilian population has been carried out by State agents and groups, together with members of the "Imbonerakure", pursuant to a State policy to suppress dissenting views.[839]

b. Investigations

The Office of the Prosecutor conducted missions in connection to investigations into the crimes alleged to have been committed as part of the situation in Burundi, also to build and maintain relevant cooperation networks.[840]

---

[835] *Situation on Registered Vessels of the Union of the Comoros, the Hellenic Republic and the Kingdom of Cambodia*, Notice of Prosecutor's Final Decision under rule 108(3), as revised and refiled in accordance with the PTC's request of 15 November 2018 and the AC's judgment of 2 September 2019, ICC-01/13-99, 2 December 2019.

[836] The United Nations, C.N.805.2016.TREATIES-XVIII.10, 28 October 2016. Available at: https://treaties.un.org/doc/Publication/CN/2016/CN.805.2016-Eng.pdf.

[837] *Situation in the Republic of Burundi*, Public Redacted Version of "Decision Pursuant to Article 15 of the Rome Statute on the Authorization of an Investigation into the Situation in the Republic of Burundi", ICC-01/17-X-9-US-Exp, 25 October 2017, ICC-01/17-9-Red, 9 November 2017.

[838] *Ibid.*, para. 24.

[839] *Ibid.*, para. 48.

[840] International Criminal Court, "Report on the Activities of the International Criminal Court", ICC-ASP/18/9, 21 October 2019, para. 11. Available at: https://asp.icc-cpi.int/iccdocs/asp_docs/ASP18/ICC-ASP-18-9-ENG.pdf.

(ii) *The Situation in the Central African Republic*

The Central African Republic ("CAR") ratified the Rome Statute on 3 October 2001 and referred the situation in its territory since 1 July 2002 to the ICC. The Court therefore may exercise its jurisdiction over crimes listed in the Rome Statute committed on the territory of CAR or by its nationals from 1 July 2002 onwards.[841]

The ICC's investigation in CAR I focused on alleged war crimes and crimes against humanity committed in the context of a conflict in CAR since 1 July 2002, with the peak of violence in 2002 and 2003.[842]

Judicial proceedings

The Prosecutor v. *Jean-Pierre Bemba Gombo*

On 8 June 2018, by majority, the AC granted Mr. Bemba's appeal against conviction,[843] and reversed the convictions for the crimes against humanity of murder and rape, and the war crimes of murder, rape, and pillaging, entered by Trial Chamber ("TC") III. In particular, the AC identified defects in the form of the charges and errors in some of the findings required for responsibility under article 28(*a*) of the Statute (concerning his alleged failure to take all necessary and reasonable measures in response to crimes committed by his subordinates). Two judges of the AC, dissenting, would have dismissed Mr. Bemba's appeal in its entirety, and affirmed his convictions.

On 8 March 2019, Mr. Bemba filed a claim for compensation and damages before PTC II.[844] Mr. Bemba requested compensation in the amount of no less than €68.6 million following his acquittal by the AC. In the alternative, he requested no less than €42.4 million for damages to his property caused through the seizure/freezing of his assets or, failing that, his claim for financial loss to be submitted to binding arbitration under UNCITRAL Rules. On 9 May 2019, PTC II held a hearing during which the parties presented orally their observations on Mr. Bemba's claim. The decision denying Mr. Bemba's claim is pending.[845]

The Prosecutor v. *Jean-Pierre Bemba Gombo, Aimé Kilolo Musamba, Jean-Jacques Mangenda Kabongo, Fidèle Babala Wandu, and Narcisse Arido*

On 8 March 2018, the AC issued its judgment on the appeals of the five convicted persons in the Court's first case relating to offences against the administration of justice pursuant to article 70 of the Statute.[846] It confirmed convictions for giving false testimony

---

[841] *Ibid.*

[842] *Ibid.*

[843] *Prosecutor* v. *Jean-Pierre Bemba Gombo,* Judgment on the appeal of Mr. Jean-Pierre Bemba Gombo against TC III's "Judgment pursuant to Article 74 of the Statute", ICC-01/05-01/08-3636-Red, 8 June 2018.

[844] *Prosecutor* v. *Jean-Pierre Bemba Gombo,* Second Public Redacted Version of "Mr. Bemba's claim for compensation and damages", ICC-01/05-01/08-3673-Red2, 19 March 2019.

[845] *"International Criminal Court, "Report on the Activities of the International Criminal Court"*, ICC-ASP/18/9, 21 October 2019, para. 16. Available at: https://asp.icc-cpi.int/iccdocs/asp_docs/ASP18/ICC-ASP-18-9-ENG.pdf.

[846] *Prosecutor* v. *Jean-Pierre Bemba Gombo et al.,* Judgment on the appeals of the Prosecutor, Mr. Jean-Pierre Bemba Gombo, Mr. Fidèle Babala Wandu and Mr. Narcisse Arido against the decision of TC VII entitled "Decision on Sentence pursuant to Article 76 of the Statute", ICC-01/05-01/13-2276-Red, 8 March 2018.

and corruptly influencing witnesses under articles 70(1)(*a*) and (70)(1)(*c*) of the Statute and, on a technical basis, reversed the convictions of Mr. Bemba, Mr. Kilolo and Mr. Mangenda for presenting evidence that the party knew was false or forged under article 70(1)(*b*).

The same day, the AC ruled on the appeals by three of the convicted persons and by the Prosecutor against the sentences imposed by TC VII. Mr. Babala's and Mr. Arido's sentences of six months' and 11 months' imprisonment, respectively, were confirmed.[847] Based on the Prosecutor's appeal, the AC reversed Mr. Bemba's, Mr. Kilolo's, and Mr. Mangenda's sentences and remanded the matter back to TC VII, noting that their convictions had been partially reversed.

Following the AC's acquittal of Mr. Bemba in the Main Case, on 12 June 2018, TC VII ordered Mr. Bemba's provisional release with specific conditions for the remainder of the re-sentencing proceedings.[848]

TC VII issued its decision on re-sentencing on 17 September 2018[849] in the following terms:

- Mr. Bemba was sentenced to one year imprisonment and a fine of €300,000.
- Mr. Kilolo was sentenced to 11 months of imprisonment and a fine of €30,000.
- Mr. Mangenda was sentenced to 11 months of imprisonment.

The TC ordered the deduction from the convicted persons' sentence, of the time they had spent in detention pursuant to an order of the Court and, accordingly, considered the sentences of imprisonment as served.

The fines were ordered to be paid to the Court within three months of the TC's decision and thereafter transferred to the Trust Fund for Victims.

The sentences of Mr. Kilolo and Mr. Mangenda are final. On 18 October 2018, Mr. Bemba filed his notice of appeal against the re-sentencing decision,[850] followed by his document in support of appeal on 17 December 2018.[851] On 27 November 2019, the AC rejected all three grounds of appeal of Mr. Bemba and confirmed the re-sentencing decision.[852]

---

[847] *Prosecutor* v. *Jean-Pierre Bemba Gombo et al.*, Public Redacted Judgment on the appeals of Mr. Jean-Pierre Bemba Gombo, Mr. Aimé Kilolo Musamba, Mr. Jean-Jacques Mangenda Kabongo, Mr. Fidèle Babala Wandu and Mr. Narcisse Arido against the decision of TC VII entitled "Judgment pursuant to Article 74 of the Statute", ICC-01/05-01/13-2275-Red, 8 March 2018.

[848] *Prosecutor* v. *Jean-Pierre Bemba Gombo et al.*, Decision on Mr. Bemba's Application for Release, ICC-01/05-01/13-2291, 12 June 2018.

[849] *Prosecutor* v. *Jean-Pierre Bemba Gombo et al.*, Decision Re-sentencing Mr. Jean-Pierre Bemba Gombo, Mr. Aimé Kilolo Musamba and Mr. Jean-Jacques Mangenda Kabongo, ICC-01/05-01/13-2312, 17 September 2018.

[850] *Prosecutor* v. *Jean-Pierre Bemba Gombo et al.*, Notice of appeal, ICC-01/05-01/13-2313, 18 October 2018.

[851] *Prosecutor* v. *Jean-Pierre Bemba Gombo et al.*, Article 82(1)(*a*) Appeal of Mr. Jean-Pierre Bemba Gombo against the decision of TC VII entitled "Decision Re-sentencing Mr. Jean-Pierre Bemba Gombo, Mr. Aimé Kilolo Musamba and Mr. Jean-Jacques Mangenda Kabongo, ICC-01/05-01/13-2315, 17 December 2018.

[852] *Prosecutor* v. *Jean-Pierre Bemba Gombo et al.*, Judgment on the appeal of Mr. Jean-Pierre Bemba Gombo against the decision of TC VII of 17 September 2018 entitled 'Decision Re-sentencing Mr. Jean-Pierre Bemba Gombo, Mr. Aimé Kilolo Musamba and Mr. Jean-Jacques Mangenda Kabongo', ICC-01/05-01/13-2351, 27 November 2019.

(iii) *The Situation in the Central African Republic II*

The ICC's investigation in CAR II has focused on alleged war crimes and crimes against humanity committed in the context of a conflict in CAR since 1 August 2012. The 2012 conflict reportedly involved alleged crimes by both Muslim Séléka and Christian anti-Balaka groups; the violence allegedly led to thousands of deaths and left hundreds of thousands displaced.

a. Judicial proceedings

The Prosecutor v. *Alfred Yekatom and Patrice-Edouard Ngaïssona*

On 17 November 2018, Mr. Yekatom was surrendered to the ICC by the Central African authorities and transferred to the ICC detention center. On 12 December 2018, Mr. Ngaïssona was arrested in France by the French authorities, and was transferred to the ICC on 23 January 2019, following the completion of necessary national proceedings.[853] They were surrendered on charges of crimes against humanity and war crimes allegedly committed at various sites in the Central African Republic.

On 20 February 2019, the Chamber decided to join the cases against the two suspects.[854] The confirmation of charges hearing was held from 19 September 2019 to 11 October 2019.[855] On 11 December 2019, PTC II issued a unanimous decision partially confirming the charges of war crimes and crimes against humanity brought by the Prosecutor against Alfred Yekatom and Patrice-Edouard Ngaïssona and committed them to trial before a TC.[856]

b. Investigations

The investigations initiated by the OTP on 24 September 2014 in CAR II continued[857]. The Office conducted numerous missions to CAR and the wider region, in connection to its active investigations into both sides of the conflict in CAR.

The Office has maintained and further strengthened cooperation with CAR authorities, as well as other countries in the region, in particular neighboring countries. Furthering and sustaining cooperation of international and regional organizations, NGOs and other relevant entities remained a priority.[858]

---

[853] International Criminal Court, "Report on the Activities of the International Criminal Court", ICC-ASP/18/9, 21 October 2019, para. 22. Available at: https://asp.icc-cpi.int/iccdocs/asp_docs/ASP18/ICC-ASP-18-9-ENG.pdf.

[854] ICC PTC II joins Yekatom and Ngaïssona cases, 20 February 2019. Available at: https://www.icc-cpi.int/Pages/item.aspx?name=PR1439.

[855] ICC concludes confirmation of charges hearing in Yekatom and Ngaïssona case. Available at: https://www.icc-cpi.int/Pages/item.aspx?name=pr1487.

[856] Yekatom and Ngaïssona case: ICC PTC II confirms part of the charges of war crimes and crimes against humanity and commits suspects to trial, 11 December 2019, Available at: https://www.icc-cpi.int/Pages/item.aspx?name=PR1506. *See further Prosecutor* v. *Alfred Yekatom and Patrice-Edouard Ngaïssona*, Decision on the confirmation of charges against Alfred Yekatom and Patrice-Edouard Ngaïssona, ICC-01/14-01/18-403-Red, 11 December 2019 (public redacted version on 20 December 2019).

[857] International Criminal Court, "Report on the Activities of the International Criminal Court", ICC-ASP/18/9, 21 October 2019, paras. 24–26. Available at: https://asp.icc-cpi.int/iccdocs/asp_docs/ASP18/ICC-ASP-18-9-ENG.pdf.

[858] *Ibid.*, para. 25.

The OTP continued to monitor and encourage national proceedings. In line with its Strategic Goals, the Office shared expertise and best practices with domestic judicial actors, including the CAR Special Criminal Court.[859]

(iv) *The Situation in Côte d'Ivoire*

On 18 April 2003, Côte d'Ivoire ratified the Statute and lodged a declaration pursuant to article 12(3) accepting the jurisdiction of the Court for crimes committed as of 19 September 2002.[860] On 3 October 2011, PTC III authorized the opening of a *proprio motu* investigation in the situation in Côte d'Ivoire.[861]

The investigation has focused on alleged crimes against humanity committed during the 2010/2011 post-electoral violence in the country. According to reports, the upsurge erupted after Presidential election results between opponents Mr. Laurent Gbagbo and Mr. Alassane Ouattara were disputed.

a. Judicial proceedings

The Prosecutor v. *Laurent Gbagbo and Charles Blé Goudé*

On 15 January 2019, TC I, by majority, acquitted Laurent Gbagbo and Charles Blé Goudé of all charges.[862] The Prosecutor appealed their unconditional release, and on 1 February 2019, upon hearing the appeal, the AC imposed conditions on the release of Mr. Gbagbo and Mr. Blé Goudé so as to ensure their future appearance before the Court as may be required.[863] On 16 July 2019, the TC issued a decision in which it gave its reasons for acquitting the accused.[864]

On 16 September 2019, the Prosecutor filed a notice of appeal before the AC, seeking reversal of the majority's decision acquitting Laurent Gbagbo and Charles Blé Goudé.[865] Appeal proceedings continue into the next reporting period, in 2020.

The Prosecutor v. *Simone Gbagbo*

---

[859] *Ibid.*, para. 26.

[860] Déclaration de Réconnaissance de la Compétence de la Cour Pénale Internationale, 18 Avril 2003. Available at: https://www.icc-cpi.int/NR/rdonlyres/FF9939C2-8E97-4463-934C-BC8F351BA013/279779/ICDE1.pdf.

[861] *Situation in the Republic of Côte d'Ivoire,* Corrigendum to "Decision Pursuant to Article 15 of the Rome Statute on the Authorisation of an Investigation into the Situation in the Republic of Côte d'Ivoire", ICC-02/11-14-Corr, 15 November 2011.

[862] ICC TC I acquits Laurent Gbagbo and Charles Blé Goudé from all charges, 15 January 2019, Available at: https://www.icc-cpi.int/Pages/item.aspx?name=pr1427.

[863] ICC Appeals Chamber to impose conditions on Laurent Gbagbo and Charles Blé Goudé upon their release following their acquittal, 1 February 2019. Available at: https://www.icc-cpi.int/Pages/item.aspx?name=pr1436.

[864] *Prosecutor* v. *Laurent Gbagbo and Charles Blé Goudé,* Reasons for oral decision of 15 January 2019 on the Requête de la Défense de Laurent Gbagbo afin qu'un jugement d'acquittement portant sur toutes les charges soit prononcé en faveur de Laurent Gbagbo et que sa mise en liberté immédiate soit ordonnée, ICC-02/11-01/15-1263, 16 July 2019.

[865] *Prosecutor* v. *Laurent Gbagbo and Charles Blé Goudé,* Corrected version of "Prosecution Notice of Appeal", 16 September 2019, ICC-02/11-01/15-1270, ICC-02/11-01/15-1270-Corr, 17 September 2019.

Execution of the arrest warrant issued for Simone Gbagbo (on 29 February 2012)[866] was still pending during the reporting period.[867]

b. Investigations

The OTP continued investigations of alleged crimes committed by all parties to the conflict during the post-election period.[868]

(v) *The Situation in Darfur, Sudan*

Sudan is not a State party to the Rome Statute. However, since the United Nations Security Council referred the situation to the Court in Resolution 1593, on 31 March 2005,[869] the ICC may exercise its jurisdiction over crimes committed in Darfur, Sudan, or by its nationals from 1 July 2002 onwards.

The ICC investigation, which opened in June 2005,[870] has produced several cases with suspects ranging from Sudanese Government officials, Militia/Janjaweed leaders, and leaders of the Resistance Front, and has involved charges that include genocide, war crimes and crimes against humanity.[871]

a. Judicial proceedings

The Prosecutor v. *Omar Hassan Ahmad Al-Bashir*

On 11 December 2017, PTC II found that the Hashemite Kingdom of Jordan had failed to comply with its obligations under the Statute by failing to arrest and surrender Omar Al-Bashir to the Court while he was on Jordanian territory, and referred the matter to the ASP and United Nations Security Council.[872]

On 6 May 2019, the AC confirmed the PTC's finding that Jordan had failed to comply with its obligation to cooperate with the Court but reversed the decision to refer Jordan to the ASP and United Nations Security Council.[873] The AC confirmed that the official

---

[866] *Prosecutor* v. *Simone Gbagbo*, Warrant of Arrest for Simone Gbagbo, ICC-02/11-01/12-1, 29 February 2012.

[867] ICC-OTP, Simone Gbagbo Case. Available at: https://www.icc-cpi.int/cdi/simone-gbagbo#7.

[868] International Criminal Court, "Report on the Activities of the International Criminal Court", ICC-ASP/18/9, 21 October 2019, para. 37, Available at: https://asp.icc-cpi.int/iccdocs/asp_docs/ASP18/ICC-ASP-18-9-ENG.pdf.

[869] The United Nations, S/RES/1593 (2005), 31 March 2005, Available at: https://www.icc-cpi.int/nr/rdonlyres/85febd1a-29f8-4ec4-9566-48edf55cc587/283244/n0529273.pdf.

[870] The Prosecutor of the ICC opens investigation in Darfur, 6 June 2005. Available at: https://www.icc-cpi.int/Pages/item.aspx?name=the+prosecutor+of+the+icc+opens+investigation+in+darfur.

[871] Available at: https://www.icc-cpi.int/darfur.

[872] *Prosecutor* v. *Omar Al-Bashir,* Decision under article 87(7) of the Rome Statute on the non-compliance by Jordan with the request by the Court for the arrest and surrender of Omar Al-Bashir, ICC-02/05-01/09-309, 11 December 2017.

[873] *Prosecutor* v. *Omar Al-Bashir,* Judgment in the Jordan Referral re Al-Bashir Appeal, ICC-02/05-01/09-397-Corr, 6 May 2019.

position of a suspect does not preclude a State party's duty to cooperate with the Court, as provided in the Statute.

The cases against Messrs Harun, Hussein, Kushayb and Banda

The execution of arrest warrants issued for Messrs Ahmad Muhammad Harun (arrest warrant issued on 27 April 2007),[874] Abdel Raheem Muhammad Hussein (arrest warrant issued on 1 March 2012),[875] Ali Muhammad Ali Abd-Al-Rahman (also known as Ali Kushayb, arrest warrant issued on 27 April 2007)[876] and Abdallah Banda Abakaer Nourain (arrest warrant issued on 11 September 2014),[877] were still pending during the reporting period.[878]

b. Investigations

The OTP continued to collect documentary and other evidence, conduct witness interviews and monitor trends that could constitute as crimes under the Rome Statute.[879]

As highlighted in the Prosecutor's December 2018 and June 2019 briefings[880] to the United Nations Security Council pursuant to United Nations Security Council Resolution 1593 (2005), given the changes on the ground in Sudan, she called for cooperation from the new government of Sudan as well as renewed collective efforts to secure the execution from the new government of Sudan of the outstanding arrest warrants. The OTP continued to make progress with its investigations, notwithstanding resource and cooperation challenges, and lack of access to the territory of Sudan.

(vi) *The Situation in the Democratic Republic of the Congo*

In April 2002, the Democratic Republic of Congo ("DRC") ratified the Rome Statute and in April 2004, referred the situation in its territory since 1 July 2002 to the ICC.[881]

---

[874] *Prosecutor* v. *Ahmad Muhammad Harun and Ali Muhammad Ali Abd-Al-Rahman ("Ali Kushayb")*, Warrant of Arrest for Ahmad Harun, ICC-02/05-01/07-2, 28 April 2007.

[875] *Prosecutor* v. *Abdel Raheem Muhammad Hussein*, Warrant of Arrest for Abdel Raheem Muhammad Hussein, ICC-02/05-01/12-2, 01 March 2012.

[876] *Prosecutor* v. *Ahmad Muhammad Harun and Ali Muhammad Ali Abd-Al-Rahman ("Ali Kushayb")*, Warrant of Arrest for Ali Kushayb, ICC-02/05-01/07-3-Corr, 27 April 2007.

[877] *Prosecutor* v. *Abdallah Banda Abakaer Nourain*, Warrant of arrest for Abdallah Banda Abakaer Nourain, ICC-02/05-03/09-606, 11 September 2014.

[878] ICC-OTP, Harun and Kushayb Case. Available at: https://www.icc-cpi.int/darfur/harunkushayb; ICC-OTP, Hussein Case. Available at: https://www.icc-cpi.int/darfur/hussein; ICC-OTP, Banda Case. Available at: https://www.icc-cpi.int/darfur/banda.

[879] International Criminal Court, "Report on the Activities of the International Criminal Court", ICC-ASP/18/9, 21 October 2019, para. 49, Available at: https://asp.icc-cpi.int/iccdocs/asp_docs/ASP18/ICC-ASP-18-9-ENG.pdf.

[880] Statement to the United Nations Security Council on the Situation in Darfur, pursuant to UNSCR 1593 (2005), 14 December 2018. Available at: https://www.icc-cpi.int/Pages/item.aspx?name=181214-stat-otp-UNSC-1593; Statement to the United Nations Security Council on the Situation in Darfur, pursuant to UNSCR 1593 (2005), 18 December 2019. Available at: https://www.icc-cpi.int/Pages/item.aspx?name=2019-12-19-otp-stat-UNSC-sudan.

[881] ICC-OTP, Democratic Republic of the Congo. Available at: https://www.icc-cpi.int/drc.

The Court may therefore exercise its jurisdiction over crimes listed in the Rome Statute committed on the territory of the DRC or by its nationals from 1 July 2002 onwards.[882]

The investigation to date has been focused on alleged war crimes and crimes against humanity committed mainly in eastern DRC, in the Ituri region and the North and South Kivu Provinces.[883]

a. Judicial proceedings

The Prosecutor v. *Bosco Ntaganda*

TC VI delivered its judgment on 8 July 2019, finding Mr. Ntaganda guilty of five counts of crimes against humanity and thirteen counts of war crimes, committed in Ituri, DRC, in 2002 and 2003.[884] The Chamber found Mr. Ntaganda liable as a direct perpetrator for parts of the charges of three of the crimes (murder as a crime against humanity and as a war crime, and persecution as a crime against humanity), and as an indirect co-perpetrator for the other parts of these crimes and for the remaining crimes.

On 9 September 2019, both Mr. Ntaganda and the Prosecutor filed notices of appeal against TC VI's judgment.[885]

On 7 November 2019, TC VI unanimously sentenced Bosco Ntaganda to a total of 30 years of imprisonment.[886] On 9 December 2019, Mr. Ntaganda filed a notice of appeal against his sentence.[887]

Appeal proceedings in all three matters continue into the next reporting period, in 2020.

The Prosecutor v. *Sylvestre Mudacumura*

Execution of the arrest warrant issued for Sylvestre Mudacumura (issued on 13 July 2012) was still pending during the reporting period.[888]

b. Investigations

During the reporting period, the Office continued to engage with the authorities, including to secure cooperation in the context of the ongoing proceedings before the Court, to encourage the arrest/surrender of Mr. Mudacumura subject to a warrant for arrest as well as to encourage national investigations.[889]

---

[882] *Ibid.*

[883] *Ibid.*

[884] *Prosecutor* v. *Bosco Ntaganda,* Judgment, ICC-01/04-02/06-2359, 8 July 2019.

[885] International Criminal Court, "Report on the Activities of the International Criminal Court", ICC-ASP/18/9, 21 October 2019, para. 54, Available at: https://asp.icc-cpi.int/iccdocs/asp_docs/ASP18/ICC-ASP-18-9-ENG.pdf.

[886] *Prosecutor* v. *Bosco Ntaganda*, Sentencing judgment, ICC-01/04-02/06-2442, 7 November 2019.

[887] *Prosecutor* v. *Bosco Ntaganda*, Notice of Appeal against Sentencing Judgment (ICC-01/04-02/06-2442), ICC-01/04-02/06-2448, 9 December 2019.

[888] ICC-OTP, Mudacumura Case. Available at: https://www.icc-cpi.int/drc/mudacumura.

[889] International Criminal Court, "Report on the Activities of the International Criminal Court", ICC-ASP/18/9, 21 October 2019, para. 57, Available at: https://asp.icc-cpi.int/iccdocs/asp_docs/ASP18/ICC-ASP-18-9-ENG.pdf.

(vii) *The Situation in Georgia*

Georgia ratified the Rome Statute on 5 September 2003.[890] The ICC therefore may exercise its jurisdiction over crimes listed in the Rome Statute committed on the territory of Georgia or by its nationals from 1 December 2003 onwards. On 27 January 2016, PTC I granted the Prosecutor's request to open an investigation *proprio motu* in the situation in Georgia, in relation to crimes against humanity and war crimes in the context of an international armed conflict between 1 July and 10 October 2008.[891]

Investigations

The OTP continued to investigate alleged crimes in the situation in Georgia and continues to call upon all parties, including the Russian Federation and South Ossetia, to cooperate with its investigations, and welcomed the efforts of those who have done so.[892]

From 6 to 10 May 2019, the Registry, the Office of the Prosecutor and the Trust Fund for Victims carried out a joint outreach mission to Georgia.[893] The delegation met with civil society representatives, victims and members of affected communities, local authorities and the diplomatic community, legal professionals and academics, and media representatives. A key objective of the mission was to explain the investigation in Georgia and the broader work of the Court to those audiences.

(viii) *The Situation in the Republic of Kenya*

Kenya ratified the Rome Statute on 15 March 2005.[894] The Court therefore may exercise its jurisdiction over crimes listed in the Rome Statute committed on the territory of Kenya or by its nationals from 1 June 2005 onwards.[895] On 31 March 2010, PTC II granted the Prosecutor's request to open an investigation *proprio motu* in the situation in Kenya, in relation to crimes against humanity committed between 1 June 2005 and 26 November 2009.[896]

ICC investigations have focused on alleged crimes against humanity committed in the context of post-election violence in Kenya in 2007/2008, in six of the eight Kenyan Provinces: Nairobi, North Rift Valley, Central Rift Valley, South Rift Valley, Nyanza Province and Western Province.[897]

---

[890] ICC-OTP, Georgia. Available at: https://www.icc-cpi.int/georgia.

[891] *Situation in Georgia*, Decision on the Prosecutor's Request for Authorization of an Investigation, ICC-01/15-12, 27 January 2016.

[892] International Criminal Court, "Report on the Activities of the International Criminal Court", ICC-ASP/18/9, 21 October 2019, para. 66, Available at: https://asp.icc-cpi.int/iccdocs/asp_docs/ASP18/ICC-ASP-18-9-ENG.pdf.

[893] *Ibid.*, para. 67.

[894] ICC-OTP, Kenya. Available at: https://www.icc-cpi.int/kenya.

[895] *Ibid.*

[896] *Situation in the Republic of Kenya*, Corrigendum of the Decision Pursuant to Article 15 of the Rome Statute on the Authorization of an Investigation into the Situation in the Republic of Kenya, ICC-01/09-19-Corr, 31 March 2010.

[897] ICC-OTP, Kenya. Available at: https://www.icc-cpi.int/kenya.

On 26 November 2019, the Prosecutor published the outcome of an internal Kenya situation review exercise following the receipt of a report in February 2018 by a panel of independent external experts.[898]

a. Judicial proceedings

The cases against Messrs Barasa, Gicheru and Bett

The execution of arrest warrants issued for Walter Osapiri Barasa (on 2 August 2013),[899] and Paul Gicheru and Philip Kipkoech Bett (on 10 March 2015)[900] were still pending during the reporting period.[901]

b. Investigations

The OTP continued to receive information on the alleged commission of crimes under the jurisdiction of the Court.[902] It also continued stressing the importance of the surrender and transfer to the Court of individuals subject to ICC warrants in the Kenya situation for alleged instances of article 70 offences against the administration of justice.[903]

(ix) *The Situation in Libya*

Libya is not a party to the Rome Statute.[904] However, on 26 February 2011, in Resolution 1970 (2011), the United Nations Security Council unanimously referred the situation in Libya since 15 February 2011 to the ICC.[905] The ICC may therefore exercise its jurisdiction over crimes listed in the Rome Statute committed on the territory of Libya or by its nationals from 15 February 2011 onwards.[906]

The United Nations Security Council referred the situation to the ICC, "condemning the violence and use of force against civilians, deploring the gross and systematic violations of human rights, including the repression of peaceful demonstrators, expressing deep

---

[898] Statement of the Prosecutor, Fatou Bensouda, on external expert review and lessons drawn from the Kenya situation, 26 November 2019. Available at: https://www.icc-cpi.int/Pages/item.aspx?name=191126-otp-statement-kenya.

[899] *Prosecutor* v. *Walter Osapiri Barasa,* Warrant of arrest for Walter Osapiri Barasa, ICC-01/09-01/13-1-Red2, 26 September 2013.

[900] *Prosecutor* v. *Paul Gicheru and Philip Kipkoech Bett,* Order unsealing the warrant of arrest and other documents, ICC-01/09-01/15-11, 10 September 2015. See also: *Prosecutor* v. *Paul Gicheru and Philip Kipkoech Bett,* Decision on the "Prosecution's Application under Article 58(1) of the Rome Statute", ICC-01/09-01/15-1-Red, 10 September 2015.

[901] ICC-OTP, Barasa Case. Available at: https://www.icc-cpi.int/kenya/barasa; ICC-OTP, Gicheru and Bett Case. Available at https://www.icc-cpi.int/kenya/gicheru-bett.

[902] International Criminal Court, "Report on the Activities of the International Criminal Court", ICC-ASP/18/9, 21 October 2019, para. 71, Available at: https://asp.icc-cpi.int/iccdocs/asp_docs/ASP18/ICC-ASP-18-9-ENG.pdf.

[903] *Ibid.*

[904] ICC-OTP, Libya. Available at: https://www.icc-cpi.int/libya.

[905] The United Nations, S/RES/1970 (2011), 26 February 2011. Available at: http://unscr.com/en/resolutions/doc/1970.

[906] ICC-OTP, Libya. Available at: https://www.icc-cpi.int/libya.

concern at the deaths of civilians, and rejecting unequivocally the incitement to hostility and violence against the civilian population made from the highest level of the Libyan government,"[907] then under Muammar Mohammed Abu Minyar Gaddafi.

a. Judicial proceedings

The Prosecutor v. *Saif Al-Islam Gaddafi*

On 5 June 2018, Saif Al-Islam Gaddafi challenged the admissibility of the case pursuant to articles 17(1)(*c*), 19 and 20(3) of the Statute.[908] On 5 April 2019, PTC I rejected his admissibility challenge and found that his case was admissible before the ICC.[909] On 10 April 2019, Saif Al-Islam Gaddafi filed an appeal against PTC I's decision rejecting his challenge to the admissibility of the case.[910] On 11 June 2019, the Prosecutor filed a response.[911]

The Prosecutor v. *Al-Tuhamy Mohamed Khaled*

The warrant of arrest against Al-Tuhamy Mohamed Khaled, issued on 18 April 2013 and made public on 24 April 2017,[912] remains unexecuted. The OTP, in cooperation with the ICC Registry, continues its efforts to secure his arrest and surrender to the Court.[913]

The Prosecutor v. *Mahmoud Mustafa Busayf Al-Werfalli*

On 4 July 2018, PTC I issued a second warrant of arrest against Mr. Al-Werfalli[914] for alleged murder as a war crime in the context of an eighth incident of 24 January 2018, when he allegedly killed 10 persons outside the Bi'at al-Radwan Mosque in Benghazi, Libya. The Prosecutor made public calls for his immediate arrest and surrender to the Court, including at the United Nations Security Council, which referred the situation in Libya to the ICC Prosecutor through Resolution 1970 (2011).[915]

---

[907] *Ibid.*, para. 1.

[908] *Prosecutor* v. *Saif Al-Islam Gaddafi,* Admissibility Challenge by Dr. Saif Al-Islam Gadafi pursuant to Articles 17(1)(*c*), 19 and 20(3) of the Rome Statute, ICC-01/11-01/11-640, 5 June 2018.

[909] *Prosecutor* v. *Saif Al-Islam Gaddafi,* Decision on the 'Admissibility Challenge by Dr. Saif Al-Islam Gadafi pursuant to Articles 17(1)(*c*), 19 and 20(3) of the Rome Statute', ICC-01/11-01/11-662, 5 April 2019.

[910] *Prosecutor* v. *Saif Al-Islam Gaddafi,* Defence Appeal against PTC I's "Decision on the 'Admissibility Challenge by Dr. Saif Al-Islam Gadafi pursuant to Articles 17(1)(*c*), 19 and 20(3) of the Rome Statute'" and Application for extension of time to file the Appeal Brief, ICC-01/11-01/11-663, 10 April 2019.

[911] *Situation in Libya,* Prosecution Response to Mr. Saif Al-Islam Gaddafi's Appeal against the "Decision on the 'Admissibility Challenge by Dr. Saif Al-Islam Gadafi pursuant to Articles 17(1)(*c*), 19 and 20(3) of the Rome Statute'" (ICC-01/11-01/11-669), ICC-01/11-01/11-671, 11 June 2019.

[912] *Prosecutor* v. *Al-Tuhamy Mohamed Khaled,* Decision on Reclassification of the Warrant of Arrest, ICC-01/11-01/13-18, 24 April 2017; *Prosecutor* v. *Al-Tuhamy Mohamed Khaled,* Warrant of Arrest for Al-Tuhamy Mohamed Khaled with under seal and ex parte Annex, ICC-01/11-01/13-1, 18 April 2013.

[913] Office of the Prosecutor, Seventeenth Report of the Prosecutor of the International Criminal Court to the United Nations Security Council pursuant to UNSCR 1970 (2011), 8 May 2019, para. 8. Available at: https://www.icc-cpi.int/Pages/item.aspx?name=190508-rep-otp-UNSC-libya.

[914] *Prosecutor* v. *Mahmoud Mustafa Busayf Al-Werfalli,* Second Warrant of Arrest, ICC-01/11-01/17-13, 4 July 2018.

[915] The United Nations, S/RES/1970 (2011), 26 February 2011. Available at: http://unscr.com/en/resolutions/doc/1970.

b. Investigations

The OTP conducted numerous missions to collect documentary and other evidence as well as to conduct witness interviews.[916] As highlighted in the Prosecutor's reports of 2 November 2018 and 8 May 2019 to the Security Council[917], the OTP continued to advance investigations relating to both existing and potential new cases and called for State support to secure execution of the outstanding arrest warrants. In its investigative activities, the OTP received close cooperation from relevant States, as well as the United Nations Support Mission in Libya and other international organizations. With a view to closing the impunity gap, as per its Strategic Plan, the OTP has also continued to pursue its strategy of cooperation with a number of States and organisations to support national investigations and prosecutions that relate to human smuggling and trafficking through Libya.[918]

(x) *The Situation in Mali*

Mali ratified the Rome Statute on 16 August 2000 and referred the situation in its territory since January 2012 to the ICC.[919] The Court therefore may exercise its jurisdiction over crimes listed in the Rome Statute committed in the territory of Mali or by its nationals from 1 July 2002 onwards.[920]

The investigations in Mali have focused on alleged war crimes committed mainly in three northern regions of Gao, Kidal and Timbuktu, with incidents also occurring in the south in Bamako and Sévaré.[921]

a. Judicial proceedings

The Prosecutor v. *Al Hassan Ag Abdoul Aziz Ag Mohamed Ag Mahmoud ("Mr. Al Hassan")*

On 4 July 2019, Mr. Al Hassan submitted a challenge to the admissibility of the case, arguing that the charges are insufficiently grave to satisfy the gravity threshold.[922] On

[916] International Criminal Court, "Report on the Activities of the International Criminal Court", ICC-ASP/18/9, 21 October 2019, para. 73, Available at: https://asp.icc-cpi.int/iccdocs/asp_docs/ASP18/ICC-ASP-18-9-ENG.pdf.

[917] Office of the Prosecutor, Sixteenth Report of the Prosecutor of the International Criminal Court to the United Nations Security Council pursuant to UNSCR 1970 (2011), 2 November 2018. Available at: https://www.icc-cpi.int/Pages/item.aspx?name=181102-rep-otp-UNSC-libya; Office of the Prosecutor, Seventeenth Report of the Prosecutor of the International Criminal Court to the United Nations Security Council pursuant to UNSCR 1970 (2011), 8 May 2019. Available at: https://www.icc-cpi.int/Pages/item.aspx?name=190508-rep-otp-UNSC-libya.

[918] International Criminal Court, "Report on the Activities of the International Criminal Court", ICC-ASP/18/9, 21 October 2019, para. 73, Available at: https://asp.icc-cpi.int/iccdocs/asp_docs/ASP18/ICC-ASP-18-9-ENG.pdf.

[919] République du Mali, Renvoi de la Situation au Mali, 13 Juillet 2012. Available at: https://www.icc-cpi.int/NR/rdonlyres/A245A47F-BFD1-45B6-891C-3BCB5B173F57/0/ReferralLetterMali130712.pdf.

[920] ICC-OTP, Mali. Available at: https://www.icc-cpi.int/mali.

[921] *Ibid.*

[922] *Prosecutor* v. *Al Hassan*, Public redacted version of "Submissions for the confirmation of charges", ICC-01/12-01/18-394-Red, 9 July 2019.

27 September 2019, PTC I rejected the admissibility challenge;[923] Mr. Al Hassan's appeal against this decision is pending before the AC.[924]

The confirmation of charges hearing took place between 8 July 2019 and 17 July 2019.[925] On 30 September 2019, PTC I issued a unanimous decision, confirming the charges of war crimes and crimes against humanity against Mr. Al Hassan and committed him to trial before a TC.[926]

On 21 November 2019, the Presidency constituted TC X, which will be in charge of the case against Mr. Al Hassan.[927]

b. Investigations

The OTP conducted several missions for the purpose of collecting evidence, screening and interviewing witnesses, and securing the continued cooperation of its partners, including States in the Sahel region.[928] It continued to receive cooperation from the national authorities and other parties, including United Nations entities—in particular the United Nations Multidimensional Integrated Stabilization Mission in Mali and the United Nations Educational, Scientific and Cultural Organization.[929]

(xi) *The Situation in Uganda*

In June 2002, Uganda acceded to the Statute and in January 2004 it referred the situation in its territory since 1 July 2002 to the Court.[930] The ICC therefore may exercise its jurisdiction over crimes listed in the Rome Statute committed on the territory of Uganda or by its nationals from 1 July 2002 onwards.[931]

The focus of the investigations to date has been on alleged war crimes and crimes against humanity committed in the context of a conflict between the Lord's Resistance Army and the national authorities in Northern Uganda since 1 July 2002.[932]

---

[923] *Prosecutor* v. *Al Hassan*, Decision on the Admissibility Challenge raised by the Defence for Insufficient Gravity of the Case, ICC-01/12-01/18-459-tENG, 27 September 2019.

[924] *Prosecutor* v. *Al Hassan*, Notice of Appeal of the PTC's "Décision relative à l'exception d'irrecevabilité pour insuffisance de gravité de l'affaire soulevée par la défense" (ICC-01/12-01/18-459), ICC-01/12-01/18-462, 4 October 2019.

[925] *Prosecutor* v. *Al Hassan*, Rectificatif à la Décision relative à la confirmation des charges portées contre Al Hassan Ag Abdoul Aziz Ag Mohamed Ag Mahmoud, ICC-01/12-01/18-461-Corr-Red, 13 November 2019, para. 26.

[926] *Ibid.*

[927] Al Hassan case: ICC Presidency constitutes TC X, 21 November 2019. Available at: https://www.icc-cpi.int/Pages/item.aspx?name=pr1498.

[928] International Criminal Court, "Report on the Activities of the International Criminal Court", ICC-ASP/18/9, 21 October 2019, para. 78, Available at: https://asp.icc-cpi.int/iccdocs/asp_docs/ASP18/ICC-ASP-18-9-ENG.pdf.

[929] International Criminal Court, Annual report of the International Criminal Court to the United Nations on its activities in 2018/19, A/74/324 23 August 2019, para. 30. Available at: https://www.icc-cpi.int/Pages/item.aspx?name=190823-icc-report-unga.

[930] President of Uganda refers situation concerning the Lord's Resistance Army (LRA) to the ICC, 29 January 2004. Available at: https://www.icc-cpi.int/news/icc-president-uganda-refers-situation-concerning-lords-resistance-army-lra-icc.

[931] ICC-OTP, Uganda. Available at: https://www.icc-cpi.int/uganda.

[932] *Ibid.*

a. Judicial proceedings

The Prosecutor v. *Dominic Ongwen*

Mr. Ongwen's trial on 70 counts of crimes against humanity and war crimes resumed on 18 September 2018 with the opening statements of the Defence, followed by Defence presentation of evidence.[933] On 14 March 2019, Mr. Ongwen applied for leave to appeal the decision of TC IX on his motions alleging defects in the decision on the confirmation of charges.[934] Leave to appeal was granted on 1 April 2019.[935] On 17 July 2019, the AC issued its judgment rejecting the appeal, finding that TC IX did not err in its interpretation of rule 134 of the Rules and did not improperly exercise its discretion when dismissing *in limine* Mr. Ongwen's motions alleging defects in the decision on the confirmation of charges.[936]

The Prosecutor v. *Joseph Kony and Vincent Otti*

The request for the arrest and surrender of Messrs Kony[937] and Otti[938] remains outstanding.[939]

b. Investigations

The OTP conducted several missions including for trial support purposes, and continued to encourage national proceedings in relation to both parties to the conflict.[940]

(*d*) Outstanding Requests for Arrest and Surrender

Requests for arrest and surrender publicly issued by the Court are outstanding against 14 individuals:

---

[933] International Criminal Court, Annual report of the International Criminal Court to the United Nations on its activities in 2018/19, A/74/324 23 August 2019, para. 90. Available at: https://www.icc-cpi.int/Pages/item.aspx?name=190823-icc-report-unga.

[934] *Prosecutor* v. *Dominic Ongwen*, Defence Request for Leave to Appeal 'Decision on Defence Motions Alleging Defects in the Confirmation Decision (ICC-02/04-01/15-1476), notified 7 March 2019, ICC-02/04-01/15-1480, 14 March 2019.

[935] *Prosecutor* v. *Dominic Ongwen*, Decision on Defence Request for Leave to Appeal a Decision on Motions Alleging Defects in the Confirmation Decision, ICC-02/04-01/15-1493, 1 April 2019.

[936] Ongwen case: ICC Appeals Chamber confirms the Trial Chamber's decision on motions requesting dismiss of the charges, 17 July 2019. Available at: https://www.icc-cpi.int/Pages/item.aspx?name=pr1472. *See further Prosecutor* v. *Dominic Ongwen*, Judgment on the appeal of Mr. Dominic Ongwen against Trial Chamber IX's 'Decision on Defence Motions Alleging Defects in the Confirmation Decision', ICC-02/04-01/15-1562, 17 July 2019.

[937] *Prosecutor* v. *Joseph Kony et al.*, Request for arrest and surrender of Joseph Kony issued on 8 July 2005 as amended on 27 September 2005 (2), ICC-02/04-01/05-29, 26 September 2005; *Prosecutor* v. *Joseph Kony et al.*, Warrant of Arrest for Joseph Kony issued on 8th July 2005 as amended on 27th September 2005, ICC-02/04-01/05-53.

[938] *Prosecutor* v. *Joseph Kony et al.*, Warrant of Arrest for Vincent OTTI, ICC-02/04-01/05-54, 08 July 2005.

[939] ICC-OTP, Kony *et al.* Case. Available at: https://www.icc-cpi.int/uganda/kony.

[940] International Criminal Court, "Report on the Activities of the International Criminal Court", ICC-ASP/18/9, 21 October 2019, para. 93, Available at: https://asp.icc-cpi.int/iccdocs/asp_docs/ASP18/ICC-ASP-18-9-ENG.pdf.

– Darfur: Ahmad Harun,[941] since 2007; Omar Al Bashir,[942] since 2009; Abdel Raheem

[941] *Prosecutor* v. *Ahmad Muhammad Harun and Ali Muhammad Ali Abd-Al-Rahman ("Ali Kushayb")*, Warrant of Arrest for Ahmad Harun, ICC-02/05-01/07-2, 28 April 2007. *See* also: *Prosecutor* v. *Ahmad Muhammad Harun and Ali Muhammad Ali Abd-Al-Rahman ("Ali Kushayb")*, Request to the Republic of the Sudan for the Arrest and Surrender of Ahmad Harun, ICC-02/05-01/07-13-tEN, 4 June 2007; *Prosecutor* v. *Ahmad Muhammad Harun and Ali Muhammad Ali Abd-Al-Rahman ("Ali Kushayb")*, Demande d'Arrestation et de Remise d'Ahmad Harun Adressée à la République Arabe d'Egypte, à l'Etat d'Erythrée, à la République Fédérale Démocratique d'Ethiopie et à la Jamahiriya Arabe Libyenne, ICC-02/05-01/07-15-Corr, 4 June 2007.

[942] *Prosecutor* v. *Omar Al-Bashir*, Warrant of Arrest for Omar Hassan Ahmad Al Bashir, ICC-02/05-01/09-10, 4 March 2009; *Prosecutor* v. *Omar Al-Bashir*, Second Warrant of Arrest for Omar Hassan Ahmad Al Bashir, ICC-02/05-01/09-95, 12 July 2010. *See* also: *Prosecutor* v. *Omar Al-Bashir*, Request to the Republic of the Sudan for the Arrest and Surrender of Omar Al Bashir, ICC-02/05-01/09-5, 5 March 2009; *Prosecutor* v. *Omar Al-Bashir*, Request to All States Parties to the Rome Statute for the Arrest and Surrender of Omar Al Bashir, ICC-02/05-01/09-7, 6 March 2009; *Prosecutor* v. *Omar Al-Bashir*, Request to all United Nations Security Council Members that Are Not States Parties to the Rome Statute for the Arrest and Surrender of Omar Al Bashir, ICC-02/05-01/09-8, 6 March 2009; *Prosecutor* v. *Omar Al-Bashir*, Request to the State of Qatar for the Arrest and Surrender of Omar Al Bashir, ICC-02/05-01/09-9, 6 March 2009; *Situation in Darfur, Sudan*, Supplementary Request to the Republic of the Sudan for the Arrest and Surrender of Omar Hassan Ahmad Al Bashir, ICC-02/05-01/09-101, 21 July 2010; *Prosecutor* v. *Omar Al-Bashir*, Supplementary Request for the Arrest and Surrender of Omar Hassan Ahmad Al Bashir to States that Were United Nations Security Council Members on 4 March 2009 and Are Not States Parties to the Rome Statute, ICC-02/05-01/09-100, 21 July 2010; *Prosecutor* v. *Omar Al-Bashir*, Supplementary Request to All United Nations Security Council Members that Are Not States Parties to the Rome Statute for the Arrest and Surrender of Omar Hassan Ahmad Al Bashir, ICC-02/05-01/09-97, 21 July 2010; *Prosecutor* v. *Omar Al-Bashir*, Supplementary Request to All States Parties to the Rome Statute for the Arrest and Surrender of Omar Hassan Ahmad Al Bashir, ICC-02/05-01/09-96, 21 July 2010; *Prosecutor* v. *Omar Al-Bashir*, Request for Arrest and Surrender for Omar Hassan Ahmad Al-Bashir, ICC-02/05-01/09-165, 10 October 2013; *Prosecutor* v. *Omar Al-Bashir*, Request for Arrest and Surrender for Omar Hassan Ahmad Al Bashir, ICC-02/05-01/09-170, 20 November 2013; *Prosecutor* v. *Omar Al-Bashir*, Request for arrest and surrender for Omar Hassan Ahmad Al Bashir to the United Arab Emirates, ICC-02/05-01/09-225, 24 February 2015; *Prosecutor* v. *Omar Al-Bashir*, Request for arrest and Surrender for Omar Hassan Ahmad Al Bashir to the Kingdom of Bahrain, ICC-02/05-01/09-226, 25 February 2015; *Prosecutor* v. *Omar Al-Bashir*, Request for arrest and Surrender for Omar Hassan Ahmad Al Bashir to the Republic of Indonesia, ICC-02/05-01/09-236, 16 April 2015; *Prosecutor* v. *Omar Al-Bashir*, Request for the Arrest and Surrender for Omar Hassan Ahmad Al Bashir to the Republic of India, ICC-02/05-01/09-252, 26 October 2015; *Prosecutor* v. *Omar Al-Bashir*, Demande d'arrestation et de remise d'Omar Hassan Ahmad Al Bashir adressée à la République de Guinée *équatoriale*, ICC-02/05-01/09-272, 24 November 2016; *Prosecutor* v. *Omar Al-Bashir*, Request to the Republic of Kazakhstan for Cooperation in the Arrest and Surrender of Omar Hassan Ahmad Al-Bashir, ICC-02/05-01/09-304, 31 August 2017; *Prosecutor* v. *Omar Al-Bashir*, Request to the Republic of Belarus for Cooperation in the Arrest and Surrender of Omar Hassan Ahmad Al-Bashir, ICC-02/05-01/09-395, 4 December 2018.

Muhammad Hussein,[943] since 2012; and Abdallah Banda,[944] since 2014;

- DRC: Sylvestre Mudacumura,[945] since 2012;
- Uganda: Joseph Kony[946] and Vincent Otti,[947] since 2005;
- Kenya: Walter Osapiri Barasa,[948] since 2013; Paul Gicheru and Philip Kipkoech Bett,[949] since 2015;

---

[943] *Prosecutor* v. *Abdel Raheem Muhammad Hussein,* Warrant of Arrest for Abdel Raheem Muhammad Hussein, ICC-02/05-01/12-2, 01 March 2012. See also: *Prosecutor* v. *Abdel Raheem Muhammad Hussein,* Request to the Republic of the Sudan for the arrest and surrender of Abdel Raheem Muhammad Hussein, ICC-02/05-01/12-4, 13 March 2012; *Prosecutor* v. *Abdel Raheem Muhammad Hussein,* Request to all States Parties to the Rome Statute for the arrest and surrender of Abdel Raheem Muhammad Hussein, ICC-02/05-01/12-5, 13 March 2012; *Prosecutor* v. *Abdel Raheem Muhammad Hussein,* Request to United Nations Security Council Members not States Parties to the Rome Statute for the arrest and surrender of Abdel Raheem Muhammad Hussein, ICC-02/05-01/12-6, 13 March 2012; *Prosecutor* v. *Abdel Raheem Muhammad Hussein,* Request for the Arrest and Surrender of Abdel Raheem Muhammad Hussein to the United Arab Emirates, ICC-02/05-01/12-36, 22 December 2016.

[944] *Prosecutor* v. *Abdallah Banda Abakaer Nourain,* Warrant of arrest for Abdallah Banda Abakaer Nourain, ICC-02/05-03/09-606, 11 September 2014. See also: *Prosecutor* v. *Abdallah Banda Abakaer Nourain, Sudan,* Request to States Parties for the arrest and surrender of Abdallah Banda Abakaer Nourain, ICC-02/05-03/09-627, 16 January 2015; *Prosecutor* v. *Abdallah Banda Abakaer Nourain,* Request to the Republic of the Sudan for the arrest and surrender of Abdallah Banda Abakaer Nourain, ICC-02/05-03/09-626, 16 January 2015.

[945] *Prosecutor* v. *Sylvestre Mudacumura,* Décision relative à la requête déposée par le Procureur en vertu de l'article 58, ICC-01/04-01/12-1-Red-tFRA, 13 July 2012. See also *Prosecutor* v. *Sylvestre Mudacumura,* Demande d'arrestation et de remise de Sylvestre Mudacumura adressée à la République démocratique du Congo, ICC-01/04-01/12-2, 28 August 2012.

[946] *Prosecutor* v. *Joseph Kony et al.*, Warrant of Arrest for Joseph Kony issued on 8th July 2005 as amended on 27th September 2005, ICC-02/04-01/05-53, 28 September 2005. See also: *Prosecutor* v. *Joseph Kony et al.*, Public redacted version—Decision to Issue Requests for Arrest and Surrender to the Central African Republic, ICC-02/04-01/05-224-Red, 11 June 2015; *Prosecutor* v. *Joseph Kony et al.*, Request to the Democratic Republic of the Congo for Arrest and Surrender of Joseph Kony, ICC-02/04-01/05-30, 27 September 2005.

[947] *Prosecutor* v. *Joseph Kony et al.*, Warrant of Arrest for Vincent Otti, ICC-02/04-01/05-54, 08 July 2005. See also: *Prosecutor* v. *Joseph Kony et al.*, Public redacted version—Decision to Issue Requests for Arrest and Surrender to the Central African Republic, ICC-02/04-01/05-224-Red, 11 June 2015.

[948] *Prosecutor* v. *Walter Osapiri Barasa,* Warrant of arrest for Walter Osapiri Barasa, ICC-01/09-01/13-1-Red2, 26 September 2013.

[949] *Prosecutor* v. *Paul Gicheru and Philip Kipkoech Bett,* Order unsealing the warrant of arrest and other documents, ICC-01/09-01/15-11, 10 September 2015. See also: *Prosecutor* v. *Paul Gicheru and Philip Kipkoech Bett,* Decision on the "Prosecution's Application under Article 58(1) of the Rome Statute", ICC-01/09-01/15-1-Red, 10 September 2015.

- Libya: Saif Al-Islam Gaddafi since 2011;[950] Al-Tuhamy Mohamed Khaled since 2013;[951] Mahmoud Mustafa Busyf Al-Werfalli since 2017;[952] and
- Côte d'Ivoire: Simone Gbagbo, since 2012.[953]

(*e*) Victims' participation in the proceedings: recent developments

One of the fundamental mandates of the ICC is the participation of victims in the judicial proceedings as well as their possibility to receive reparations in case of a conviction of an accused.

The Victims Participation and Reparations Section ("VPRS") in the Registry acts as the first liaison body between victims and the ICC. A small team of lawyers, specialized field staff and data processing specialists acts as the entry point for victims' applications, legal analysis and liaison with the ICC's Chambers.

In 2019, the VPRS received close to 3000 victim representations[954] and applications for participation in the proceedings and/or for reparations.[955] The largest number of documents received in 2019 are related to: (i) the confirmation of charges proceedings in the case of *The Prosecutor* v. *Al Hassan Ag Abdoul Aziz Ag Mohamed Ag Mahmoud* ("*Al Hassan* case") (just over 800); (ii) the confirmation of charges proceedings in the case of *The Prosecutor* v. *Alfred Yekatom and Patrice-Edouard Ngaïssona* ("*Yekatom and*

[950] *Prosecutor* v. *Saif Al-Islam Gaddafi,* Warrant of Arrest for Saif Al-Islam Gaddafi, ICC-01/11-01/11-3, 27 June 2011. See also *Prosecutor* v. *Saif Al-Islam Gaddafi,* Request to the Libyan Arab Jamahiriya for the arrest and surrender of Muammar Mohammed Abu Minyar Gaddafi, Saif Al-Islam Gaddafi and Abdullah Al-Senussi, ICC-01/11-01/11-5, 4 July 2011; *Prosecutor* v. *Saif Al-Islam Gaddafi,* Request to States neighboring the Libyan Arab Jamahiriya for the arrest and surrender of Muammar Mohammed Abu Minyar Gaddafi, Saif Al-Islam Gaddafi and Abdullah Al-Senussi, ICC-01/11-01/11-6, 4 July 2011; *Prosecutor* v. *Saif Al-Islam Gaddafi,* Request to the United Nations Security Council Members that are not States Parties to the Rome Statute for the arrest and surrender of Muammar Mohammed Abu Minyar Gaddafi, Saif Al-Islam Gaddafi and Abdullah Al-Senussi, ICC-01/11-01/11-8, 4 July 2011; *Prosecutor* v. *Saif Al-Islam Gaddafi,* Request to all States Parties to the Rome Statute for the arrest and surrender of Muammar Mohammed Abu Minyar Gaddafi, Saif Al-Islam Gaddafi And Abdullah Al-Senussi, ICC-01/11-01/11-7, 7 July 2011.

[951] *Prosecutor* v. *Al-Tuhamy Mohamed Khaled,* Decision on Reclassification of the Warrant of Arrest, ICC-01/11-01/13-18, 24 April 2017; *Prosecutor* v. *Al-Tuhamy Mohamed Khaled,* Warrant of Arrest for Al-Tuhamy Mohamed Khaled with under seal and ex parte Annex, ICC-01/11-01/13-1, 18 April 2013.

[952] *Prosecutor* v. *Mahmoud Mustafa Busayf Al-Werfalli,* Warrant of Arrest, ICC-01/11-01/17-2, 15 August 2017; *Prosecutor* v. *Mahmoud Mustafa Busayf Al-Werfalli,* Second Warrant of Arrest, ICC-01/11-01/17-13, 4 July 2018. See also: *Situation in Libya,* Request to Libya for cooperation in the arrest and surrender of Mahmoud Mustafa Busayf Al-Werfalli, ICC-01/11-01/17-3, 21 August 2017.

[953] *Prosecutor* v. *Simone Gbagbo*, Warrant of Arrest for Simone Gbagbo, ICC-02/11-01/12-1, 29 February 2012. See also: *Prosecutor* v. *Simone Gbagbo*, Demande d'arrestation et de remise de Simone Gbagbo, ICC-02/11-01/12-6, 22 March 2012.

[954] When the Prosecutor intends to commence an investigation on her own volition, she needs to seek a Pre-Trial Chamber's authorization (article 15(3) of the Rome Statute). As part of this process, victims may make so-called 'representations' to the Pre-Trial Chamber on the matter. This process is facilitated by the VPRS.

[955] This figure includes also the supplementary information provided by the victims to complement their application forms for participation and/or reparations.

Ngaïssona case") (1256); (iii) the reparations phase in the case of *The Prosecutor against* v. *Ahmad Al Faqi Al Mahdi* ("*Al Mahdi* case") in the situation in the Republic of Mali; (iv) the reparation phase in the case of *The Prosecutor against Thomas Lubanga* (328); and (v) the article 15(3) process [*i.e.* the request of the ICC Prosecutor to the Chamber to open an investigation] in the situation in the People's Republic of Bangladesh/Republic of the Union of Myanmar ("Bangladesh/Myanmar situation") (343).

In 2019, the VPRS submitted more than seven hundred formal/substantive communications with various interlocutors (Chambers, parties and participants, experts, victims groups, civil society organizations, governmental international and national organizations, etc.) and submitted 80 court filings, including reports on legal representation of victims, victim representations, systems for victims' participation to be adopted in judicial proceedings, and victim applications for participation and/or reparations. In doing so, the VPRS assisted victims and their representatives, the Chambers and the Trust Fund for Victims ("TFV") with analytical reports containing legal analysis of applications and the result of consultations with relevant stakeholders, also on cultural, political and other contextual aspects.

The VPRS also conducted victim-related activities in the field through designated Registry staff in various duty stations in a number of situations before the ICC. Notably, the VPRS carried out a number of missions in relation to the Bangladesh/Myanmar situation, with a view to reaching out to as many Rohingya victims as possible and to collect their views about the Court opening an investigation pertaining to their situation (which has in the meantime been authorised). The VPRS also strengthened its online dissemination of relevant information and continued the training of relevant stakeholders as to how to engage with often vulnerable victims in relation to ICC proceedings. The VPRS also conducted several reparations-related missions to the Democratic Republic of the Congo in order to carry out, *inter alia*, a victim mapping exercise for reparations in the case of *The Prosecutor* v. *Bosco Ntaganda*.

In relation to activities relating to potential new investigations by the Prosecutor, the VPRS continued the preliminary mapping of communities of potentially affected persons in relevant situations. It also engaged in further developing networks of reliable local partners and contact points for potential future victim participation and/or reparations proceedings before the ICC.

Other relevant activities included the liaison with a range of internal and external actors aimed at building support networks for the VPRS mandate in different legal proceedings before the ICC; identifying pools of reliable intermediaries in the field; and supporting victims' legal representatives. The VPRS's general field activities in reaching out to affected victims' communities focused on providing accurate information on victim participation and reparations before the ICC; conducting consultations with victims and key civil society actors; as well as preparing and, as appropriate, delivering key messages in the field in response to judicial developments.

The VPRS has continued, throughout 2019, to develop objectives as well as key performance indicators of its activities and output following the ICC's strategic goals as an institution. The VPRS also continued developing the VPRS "Mobile Application module": this is an application form for victims on ICC-issued mobile IT devices which ICC staff will be using in the field in their interactions with victims. In practice, this will allow ICC staff to take relevant statements and information from victims in the field through a tablet device, adding significantly to the security of information and the efficiency of workflows. In addition, victims of ICC crimes are able to submit relevant information and, importantly, application forms online through the ICC's website. This does not make the direct human interaction less important, but it adds to the efficient and secure data flow and general accessibility of the ICC for victims, and allows the Registry to better focus its resources in order to reach out to *all* affected communities as effectively as possible.

(*f*) In-house legal representation of victims in the proceedings: the Role of the Office of Public Counsel for Victims (the "OPCV")

The Office of Public Counsel for Victims (the "OPCV") is an independent office within the Court which falls within the Registry only for administrative purposes.[956] This independence is a prerequisite for carrying out the mandate of assisting legal representatives of victims, and assisting and representing victims. It allows the Office to work without being subjected to pressure of any kind and preserves the privileged relationship between victims and their counsel. As a consequence, in the performance of their mandate, Counsel from the Office and members of their teams are bound by the Code of Professional Conduct for Counsel before the ICC.

In 2019, the Office has provided assistance to external counsel in virtually all situations and cases before the Court. Said support has included the provision of legal advice and research, as well as the appearance at hearings on their behalf.

Under regulation 81(4)(*e*) of the Regulations of the Court, the mandate to provide support and assistance to victims includes direct legal representation in court proceedings.[957] In this regard, Chambers have adopted a practice whereby Counsel of the Office are appointed as legal representative for unrepresented applicants or victims in specific proceedings (such as admissibility) and/or for victims participating in the proceedings. Counsel have been appointed to represent victims participating at different stages, including at the pre-trial, trial and reparations phases. When appointed as legal representatives, the mandate of Counsel of the Office does not differ from the one of external counsel appointed as legal representatives. Therefore, in fulfilling their mandate, members of the Office enjoy the same rights and prerogatives as external counsel and they are bound by the same obligations.

In 2019, Counsel from the OPCV were appointed as common legal representatives in the *Yekatom & Ngaïssona* case (2 teams) at pre-trial; in the *Ongwen* case at trial; in the *Ntaganda* case (2 teams) in appeal and reparations; in the *Gbabgo & Blé Goudé* case in appeal, in the *Lubanga* and *Katanga* reparations proceedings, and remained appointed in the proceedings following the acquittal of Mr. Bemba. Furthermore, Counsel remained appointed to represent victims in the *Kony et al.* case, as well as victims and applicants in the DRC and Uganda situations. Finally, Counsel represented the interests of victims having communicated with the Court in admissibility proceedings under article 19 of the Rome Statute and in the proceedings deriving from article 53 of the Rome Statute (Situation

---

[956] Regulation 81 of the Regulations of the Court as amended on 2 November 2011, entered into force on 29 June 2012. For an overview of the interpretation by Chamber of the role and mandate of the Office, please refer to the OPCV, Representing Victims before the International Criminal Court, A Manual for Legal Representatives—5th Revised Edition, January 2020, pp. 227–239.

[957] Counsel from the Office may "[represent] *a victim or victims throughout the proceedings, on the instruction or with the leave of the Chamber, when this is in the interests of justice*".

in the Islamic Republic of Afghanistan, Situation in the State of Palestine, Situation on Registered Vessels of the Union of the Comoros, the Hellenic Republic of Greece and the Kingdom of Cambodia). More than 7,000 victims were represented by Counsel from the OPCV. Victims represented reside in 22 countries.

The involvement of the Office in multiple situations and cases, and in different capacities, has allowed its members to gain specific and extensive experience on victims' issues, including the handling of a high number of victims given the fact that they are assigned simultaneously to several proceedings.

In performing their tasks, members of the Office take into account concerns relating to the security and safety of victims, and endeavor to respect the will of victims, as well as the language spoken by them and the specificities related to gender and children issues.

In fulfilling its role of representing the general interests of victims and raising the awareness on victims' rights and prerogatives under the Rome Statute and the Rules of Procedure and Evidence (the "RPE"), members of the Office were involved in outreach activities for the judiciary, the legal profession and civil society in countries where investigations and/or cases are ongoing, as well as in other countries.

(*g*) Developments concerning the relationship between the ICC and the UN

In 2019, the ASP issued the following resolutions which address, among others, the Court's relationship with the United Nations:

- ICC-ASP/18/Res.1—Resolution of the Assembly of States Parties on the proposed programme budget for 2020, the Working Capital Fund for 2020, the scale of assessment for the apportionment of expenses of the International Criminal Court, financing appropriations for 2020 and the Contingency Fund;[958]
- ICC-ASP/18/Res.3—Resolution on cooperation;[959]
- ICC-ASP/18/Res.6—Strengthening the International Criminal Court and the Assembly of States Parties.[960]

[958] Available at https://asp.icc-cpi.int/iccdocs/asp_docs/ASP18/ICC-ASP-18-Res1-ENG.pdf.

[959] Available at https://asp.icc-cpi.int/iccdocs/asp_docs/ASP18/ICC-ASP-18-Res3-ENG.pdf.

[960] Available at https://asp.icc-cpi.int/iccdocs/asp_docs/ASP18/ICC-ASP-18-Res6-ENG.pdf.

Chapter IV

TREATIES CONCERNING INTERNATIONAL LAW CONCLUDED UNDER THE AUSPICES OF THE UNITED NATIONS AND RELATED INTERGOVERNMENTAL ORGANIZATIONS

A. Treaties concerning international law concluded under the auspices of the United Nations

In 2019, the Convention on the Facilitation of Border Crossing Procedures for Passengers, Luggage and Load-luggage Carried in International Traffic by Rail, Geneva, 22 February 2019, was concluded under the auspices of the United Nations.[1]

B. Treaties concerning international law concluded under the auspices of intergovernmental organizations related to the United Nations

1. International Labour Organization

On 21 June 2019, the International Labour Conference adopted the Convention (No. 190) Concerning the Elimination of Violence and Harassment in the World of Work.[2]

2. United Nations Educational, Scientific and Cultural Organization

In 2019, the following instruments were concluded under the auspices of the United Nations Educational, Scientific and Cultural Organization (UNESCO):

- Regional Convention on the Recognition of Studies, Diplomas and Degrees in Higher Education in Latin America and the Caribbean, Buenos Aires, 13 July 2019.[3]
- Global Convention on the Recognition of Qualifications concerning Higher Education, Paris, 25 November 2019.[4]

[1] Not reproduced herein. For the text of the Agreement, see *Multilateral Treaties Deposited with the Secretary-General*, chapter XI.C.7.

[2] United Nations, *Treaty Series*, vol. 3444, No. I-56938.

[3] United Nations, *Treaty Series*, No. I-57559.

[4] United Nations, *Treaty Series*, No. I-57727.

3. United Nations World Tourism Organization

At its twenty-third session, held in St. Petersburg, Russian Federation, on 12 September 2019, the General Assembly of the World Tourism Organization adopted the following instruments:

- Framework Convention on Tourism Ethics.[5]
- Optional Protocol to the Framework Convention on Tourism Ethics.[6]

4. Universal Postal Union

On 26 September 2019, at its Extraordinary Congress held in Geneva, the Universal Postal Union adopted the Second Additional Protocol to the Universal Postal Convention.[7]

[5] World Tourism Organization, General Assembly, resolution A/RES/722(XXIII), Adoption of the Framework Convention on Tourism Ethics and its Optional Protocol (twenty-third session, Saint Petersburg, Russian Federation, 9–13 September 2019); the Convention and Optional Protocol were adopted under this resolution and opened for signature thereafter.

[6] *Ibid.*

[7] Universal Postal Union, *Decisions of the 2019 Extraordinary Congress* (Geneva), Second Additional Protocol to the Universal Postal Convention, available at https://www.upu.int/en/universal-postal-union/about-upu/acts [Last access: 26/12/2025]

Chapter V

DECISIONS OF THE ADMINISTRATIVE TRIBUNALS OF THE UNITED NATIONS AND RELATED INTERGOVERNMENTAL ORGANIZATIONS[1]

A. Decisions of the United Nations Dispute Tribunal

In 2019, the United Nations Dispute Tribunal ("UNDT" or "Tribunal") in New York, Geneva and Nairobi issued a total of 159 judgments and 570 orders.[2] Summaries of six selected judgments are reproduced below.[3]

1. *Judgment No. UNDT/2019/004 (14 January 2019): Younis* v. *Secretary-General of the United Nations*[4]

Receivability (UNDT)—*Ratione materiae*—Administrative decision—Learning and development opportunities—Terms and conditions of employment

The staff member was on a temporary appointment at the D-1 level from mid-November 2016 until about 2 May 2017. During this temporary assignment, the staff member received a special post allowance at the D-1 level. In March 2017, the Office of Human Resources Management ("OHRM") announced that it was receiving nominations for the United Nations Leaders Programme (the "Programme") designed for staff members at the Director level. In particular, the announcement stated that "staff members serving on D1 post on temporary assignment for at least 3 months or more" were eligible to apply. On 2 August 2017, the staff member received an e-mail from OHRM confirming his nomination for the Programme; however, on 21 August 2017, OHRM informed that the staff member was no longer eligible to attend the Programme as, according to the standard operating

---

[1] For general information on the administration of justice at the United Nations, see chapter III, part A, section 16 (*k*) of this publication. In view of the large number of judgments rendered by the administrative tribunals of the United Nations and related intergovernmental organizations, only those judgments which address significant issues of United Nations administrative law or are otherwise of general interest have been summarized in the present edition of the Yearbook.

[2] See A/75/162, para. 5 and table 7. For the texts of the judgments and orders of the UNDT, see https://www.un.org/en/internaljustice/undt/judgments-orders.shtml. A digest of the case law of the United Nations Dispute Tribunal and United Nations Appeals Tribunal for 2009–2019 is available at https://www.un.org/en/internaljustice/assets/pdf/E-OAJ%20Jurisprudential%20Digest%20WEB%202009-2019.pdf.

[3] The summaries provided are for illustrative purposes only and are not authoritative, representative or exhaustive. Some UNDT judgments summarized may have been overturned on appeal by UNAT. For the full list of judgments by the UNDT and the latest developments, consult the website of the Office of the Administration of Justice at https://www.un.org/en/internaljustice.

[4] Judge Ebrahim-Carstens (New York).

procedures, the end of the temporary D-1 level assignment "should be beyond the selected course date". The staff member contested the decision finding him ineligible to attend the Programme. He alleged that he had been discriminated against as two other staff members in similar circumstances were allowed to attend. As relief, he sought an apology, an official investigation to determine accountability, a reinstatement of his nomination to the Programme, and financial remedy for stress.

First, UNDT found that the staff member's application was receivable on the grounds that learning and development opportunities are for the benefit of the staff members, which under the Staff Regulations and Rules form the terms and conditions of their employment, and, as such, the decision relating to learning and development opportunities was an administrative decision subject to judicial review. On the merits, UNDT concluded that a strong expectation of the training benefit was created for the staff member in this case and that, at the very least, OHRM had a discretion to reconsider the staff member's situation in light of the particular circumstances being, inter alia, that another ineligible staff member had been accorded the benefit to participate, that the staff member had already been nominated, approved and endorsed, and in light of the last-minute and late notification of refusal. UNDT granted the staff member's application and directed the parties to attempt to resolve the issue of appropriate relief.

2. *Judgment No. UNDT/2019/016 (31 January 2019): Nikolarakis* v. *Secretary-General of the United Nations*[5]

Revision of judgment—Receivability (UNDT)—Discovery of decisive fact—Unknown fact—Definition of party—Applicant and respondent—Counsel—Legal representative

In August 2017, UNDT rendered Judgment No. UNDT/2017/068 (the "Judgment"), ordering rescission of the contested "decision to exclude [the staff member] from the recruitment exercise" for an S-3 level position, or alternatively, payment of USD 20,000 as compensation in lieu of rescission, together with USD 5,000 for loss of opportunity for career advancement and for loss of job security. One of the main factors in UNDT's assessment of compensation was its assumption that the staff member had been deprived of an opportunity to compete for an S-3 level appointment for a significant period of time. In October 2017, the Administrative Law Section ("ALS"), the Secretary-General's Counsel, filed an application for revision of the Judgment, contending that certain decisive facts were unknown to UNDT and ALS at the time the Judgment was rendered. Specifically, ALS requested UNDT to take note of the new job opening at the Department of Safety and Security that was issued in April 2017 for thirteen S-3 level vacancies, for which the staff member was invited to an interview (and following which he was appointed to an S-3 level position in March 2018). UNDT noted that ALS had not been informed of developments regarding the staff member's application for the said S-3 level position and considered whether a "party", within the meaning of UNDT Statute and Rules of Procedure, was to be understood as solely an applicant and/or a respondent or also to include their counsel.

UNDT found that article 12(1) of its Rules of Procedure, which states that "a party may present his or her case to the [UNDT] in person, or may designate counsel from [the Office

[5] Judge Ebrahim-Carstens (New York).

of Staff Legal Assistance] or counsel authorized to practice law in a national jurisdiction", makes a clear distinction between a "party" and his or her "counsel". Consequently, UNDT concluded that one of the fundamental conditions for granting a revision of judgment was not present in this case since the party applying for revision, meaning the Secretary-General or the Administration at large, had known about the ongoing recruitment exercise for the S-3 level position (even though it was unknown to ALS at the time the Judgment was rendered) and, on a strictly technical basis, based on this fact alone, the application for revision of the Judgment was not receivable. To do justice to the parties, particularly as the staff member had been appointed to the S-3 level position, UNDT granted the parties the possibility to settle the matter informally, failing which UNDT would make a final determination on the matter on the papers before it.

3. *Judgment No. UNDT/2019/032 (26 February 2019): Ladu* v. *Secretary-General of the United Nations*[6]

SUMMARY DISMISSAL—STANDARD OF PROOF—DUE PROCESS—PROPORTIONALITY OF THE SANCTION FOR SECURITY OFFICERS—ROLE OF COUNSEL AS AN OFFICER OF THE TRIBUNAL

In February 2019, UNDT rendered Judgment No. UNDT/2019/032 (the "Judgment"), dismissing the Applicant's challenge to the "Respondent's decision to summarily dismiss [the staff member] for misconduct". The Applicant also sought reinstatement, "two years' net base salary with all allowances for loss of employment" and "one year's salary as compensation for violation of his due process rights" and full payment of the "remaining months of his contract". UNDT reviewed three issues in the case—whether a case of misconduct was established against the Applicant by clear and convincing evidence, whether the Applicant's due process rights were respected during the investigations and disciplinary proceedings and whether the disciplinary sanction was disproportionate. UNDT referred to the standard of proof as outlined in Judgment UNAT-2011/164, para. 2: "Clear and convincing proof requires more than a preponderance of the evidence but less than proof beyond a reasonable doubt—it means that the truth of the facts asserted is highly probable."

UNDT noted that the facts forming the basis for the disciplinary measure were not disputed by the Applicant. The Applicant only disputed the disciplinary process and the proportionality of the sanction of summary dismissal. UNDT identified no due process breaches. UNDT rejected the assertion that the Applicant's alleged poor English skills played a role during the disciplinary process as the Applicant gave testimony in English during the hearing. The role of Security Officer came with the need for increased trust in the protection of staff and property of the United Nations. An enhanced level of trust, if broken, tended to support proportionality of a more severe sanction. UNDT held that the role of legal representation must be approached with a sense of responsibility and candor. Counsel had the role of an officer of the Tribunal and must act with integrity and refrain from making ridiculous submissions.

---

[6] Judge Nkemdilim Izuako (Nairobi).

4. *Judgment No. UNDT/2019/085 (16 May 2019): Avramoski* v. *Secretary-General of the United Nations*[7]

Refusal to correct the date of entry on duty (EOD) as an administrative decision—Decision affecting the terms and conditions of a staff member—Decision triggering the deadline for a management evaluation request—Data entry in ERP system as an expression of an administrative decision—Temporal jurisdiction of UNDT

The Applicant, a Budget and Finance Assistant with the United Nations Multidimensional Integrated Stabilization Mission in the Central African Republic (MINUSCA), challenged the Administration's refusal to amend her entry-on-duty (EOD) date in Umoja from 2 September 2008 to 28 February 2000. She argued that she had served continuously with the Organization since 2000 and that the recorded EOD incorrectly reflected a break in service. The Administration maintained that, following her separation from UNMIS on 1 September 2008, she had been reappointed to the United Nations Logistics Base (UNLB) effective 2 September 2008 in accordance with the rules then applicable to movements between special and established missions, which required a new appointment and a reset EOD. In 2018, the Applicant requested correction of the EOD entry, but the Field Personnel Division confirmed that the date had been properly reset and declined to make a retroactive change. After management evaluation, the Applicant applied to the UNDT seeking correction of the EOD and related adjustments, while the Respondent raised objections as to receivability and defended the lawfulness of the 2008 reappointment.

UNDT held that the Respondent's refusal to retroactively change a reappointment to a transfer, which would create an appointment which continues instead of a new appointment, thereby changing the EOD, constituted an administrative decision. The deadline for challenging such a decision in a management evaluation request was 60 days starting from the notification of such decision. An entry in Umoja could, under certain conditions, serve as evidence that the decision was taken not to make a retroactive change. An entry of the EOD on the Personnel Action form may not be as sufficient as notification because it may not be as obvious to find. UNDT confirmed that an administrative decision must have direct legal consequences affecting a staff member's terms or conditions of appointment and must not only be a prefatory act for subsequent decisions. The EOD date was relevant for several legal effects, for example eligibility for continuous appointment, accrual of entitlements, and determination of retirement age. Umoja evidenced that the Applicant was reappointed, which implied a break in service. Given the time that had passed since the decision on reappointment was taken, it was not within the temporal jurisdiction of UNDT and had no unlawful impact on the Applicant's terms or conditions of appointment.

5. *Judgment No. UNDT/2019/124 (5 July 2019): Gueben* v. *Secretary-General of the United Nations*[8]

Remand from UNAT to Administration—Exercise of discretion for granting a permanent appointment—Conformity of decision with UNAT Judgment remand to Administration—Administrative practice—Non-discrimination—Termination indemnity

The Applicant, a former P-4 language professional with the United Nations Assistance to the Khmer Rouge Trials (UNAKRT), challenged the decision not to grant him a

[7] Judge Agnieszka Klonowiecka-Milart (Nairobi).

[8] Judge Teresa Bravo (Geneva).

permanent appointment following a second reconsideration of his suitability ordered after earlier litigation. The Applicant had originally been denied conversion to a permanent appointment in the Secretariat-wide exercise conducted under ST/SGB/2009/10. After successive judicial proceedings, including UNAT Judgment 2016-UNAT-692, the matter was remanded for an individualized reassessment of his qualifications, competencies and transferable skills. By letter of 17 March 2017, the Acting ASG/OHRM informed the Applicant that he was not considered suitable for conversion, noting in particular that he had not passed the Language Competitive Examination (LCE) and did not meet the Secretariat requirements for language professional posts, including proficiency in additional official languages. The Administration also considered the operational context of UNAKRT as a downsizing entity and the likelihood of the Applicant's services being required beyond that entity. After management evaluation upheld the decision, the Applicant filed an application with UNDT, alleging non-compliance with UNAT's instructions, discriminatory treatment *vis-à-vis* non-language professional staff, and unlawful reliance on requirements not expressly set out in the Staff Rules. He sought conversion to a permanent appointment or, alternatively, compensation, including a termination indemnity and moral damages.

Considering that UNAKRT was a downsizing entity, UNDT found it reasonable for the Administration to evaluate the Applicant's transferable skills in the context of the requirements for language professional staff within the Secretariat. UNAT Judgment 2016-UNAT-692 expected the Administration to strictly adhere to its directives, where UNAT explicitly instructed the ASG/OHRM to consider, on an individual and separate basis, each staff member's respective qualifications, competencies, conduct and transferrable skills when determining each of their application for conversion to a permanent appointment and not to give predominance or such overwhelming weight to the consideration of the finite mandate of an Organization so as to fetter or limit the exercise of discretion in deciding whether to grant a permanent appointment to any individual staff member. UNDT was of the view that there was no evidence of a discriminatory treatment of the Applicant *vis-à-vis* non-language staff. The Applicant's situation was not equivalent to the situation of non-language professional staff because the latter possess skills that were common to the broader Secretariat and were not subject to the same requirements as language professional staff.

6. *Judgment No. UNDT/2019/129/Corr.1 (23 July 2019): Applicant* v. *Secretary-General of the United Nations*[9]

COMPLAINT OF HARASSMENT—DUTY OF CONFIDENTIALITY—DEADLINE FOR INVESTIGATION PROCESS—INVESTIGATION PRIVILEGE—DISCLOSURE OF INVESTIGATION REPORT—MORAL DAMAGES—COMPENSATION

The Applicant, a staff member of the Office of Internal Oversight (OIOS) in Vienna, challenged the decision not to pursue disciplinary action against his supervisor following a complaint of prohibited conduct under ST/SGB/2008/5. After initially being informed that his complaint did not warrant investigation, the matter proceeded to a fact-finding investigation by a panel, which concluded that while there was a factual basis for certain allegations, they were insufficient to justify disciplinary proceedings, though managerial action was recommended. The Acting ASG/OHRM decided not to initiate disciplinary measures

[9] Judge Teresa Bravo (Geneva).

and the USG/OIOS informed the Applicant accordingly. The Applicant alleged procedural flaws in the investigation, including breach of confidentiality, lack of transparency, bias in the composition of the investigation panel, and unreasonable delay, and sought rescission of the decision, disclosure of the report, and compensation for moral harm.

UNDT recalled that the *onus* lay on an applicant to demonstrate a breach of confidentiality imputable to the Administration and found insufficient evidence that the contents of the complaint had been improperly disclosed. It reaffirmed established jurisprudence that the Organization was not obliged to disclose the full investigation report following a process under ST/SGB/2008/5, absent extraordinary circumstances. The Tribunal further reiterated that the investigation of disciplinary charges was a prerogative of the Organization and that it could not compel the Administration to initiate disciplinary action, as the Administration was better placed to assess whether misconduct is established. However, the Tribunal found that, although the investigation itself had been properly conducted, it was excessively protracted and failed to meet the timeframes envisaged in the applicable framework, leaving the Applicant in prolonged uncertainty. Applying the principles governing moral damages—requiring a breach of a fundamental right, harm caused by the Administration's act or omission, and supporting evidence—the Tribunal concluded that the undue delay caused the Applicant stress and anxiety and awarded USD 5,000 in moral damages. All other claims were dismissed.

B. Decisions of the United Nations Appeals Tribunal

In 2019, the United Nations Appeals Tribunal ("UNAT" or "Appeals Tribunal") issued a total of 82 judgments and 23 orders.[10] The summaries of eight of those decisions are reproduced below.[11]

1. *UNAT Order No. 353 (2019) (6 September 2019): Nouinou* v. *Secretary-General of the United Nations*[12]

Abuse of process—Abusive conduct—Serious accusations against Judges—Code of Conduct for Legal Representatives and Litigants in Person

Following the dismissal of the staff member's appeal against a UNDT judgment, the staff member filed two motions which UNAT denied. The staff member subsequently filed further motions which UNAT rejected on the ground that they were clearly without merit and frivolous and constituted an abuse of process. UNAT warned the staff member that if she kept abusing the process, it would have to award costs against her pursuant to article 9(2) of the Appeals Tribunal Statute. The staff member then proceeded to file an application for revision of judgment as well as two further motions. UNAT granted the motion for confidentiality but denied the second motion finding that the staff member's

[10] See A/75/162, table 9. For the texts of the judgments and orders of the UNAT, see https://www.un.org/en/internaljustice/unat/judgments-orders.shtml. A digest of the case law of the United Nations Dispute Tribunal and United Nations Appeals Tribunal for 2009–2019 is available at https://www.un.org/en/internaljustice/assets/pdf/E-OAJ%20Jurisprudential%20Digest%20WEB%202009-2019.pdf.

[11] The summaries provided are for illustrative purposes only and are not authoritative, representative or exhaustive.

[12] Judge Martha Halfeld, Duty Judge.

derogatory, baseless and abusive statements and accusations against UNAT Judges violated the Code of Conduct for Legal Representatives and Litigants in Person which required a party to "maintain the highest standards of integrity and ... at all times act honestly, candidly, fairly, courteously, in good faith" and "assist the Tribunals in maintaining the dignity and decorum of proceedings". UNAT found that the staff member's abusive conduct warranted an award of costs pursuant to article 9(2) of the Appeals Tribunal Statute and ordered that she pay, within 15 calendar days of the issuance of the Order, USD 600 in costs failing which she would be refused access to prosecute any further cases before UNAT.

2. *Judgment No. 2019-UNAT-912 (29 March 2019): Clemente* v. *United Nations Joint Staff Pension Board*[13]

UNJSPF—Surviving spouse—Widow's benefit—Previous marriage—Validity of marriage—Null and void marriage—Marital status—Interpretation of marriage—Domestic law—Private international law—Common law marriage

A staff member employed at United Nations Office at Geneva ("UNOG") married her late husband in the Philippines in March 1995 and remained married to him for 20 years, until his death. Her late husband participated in the United Nations Joint Staff Pension Fund (the "Fund" or "UNJSPF") from October 1999 to November 2015 as a staff member of World Intellectual Property Organization ("WIPO"), and he listed her as his spouse throughout his participation in the Fund. Both WIPO and the United Nations reported their marital status to the Fund, and the Swiss authorities granted them residence status as spouses. However, his previous marriage was not annulled until August 1996, approximately one year after his marriage to the staff member. Divorce is not recognized under Philippine law. A marriage may be dissolved only by the death of a spouse or by annulment. The Fund informed the staff member that, based on its review of Philippine law, her marriage to her late husband was considered void on the ground of bigamy, as it had been contracted prior to the annulment of his first marriage. Accordingly, the Fund rejected the staff member's request for a widow's benefit under article 34 of its Regulations. The staff member appealed the decision, arguing that her marital relationship with her late husband constituted a common-law marriage and that, under Philippine law, a void or voidable marriage was deemed valid until declared otherwise in judicial proceedings. She further stated that her marriage had not been the subject of any judicial proceedings for a declaration of nullity.

UNAT considered article 34 of the UNJSPF Regulations which provided that a widow's benefit would be payable to the surviving spouse of a participant who was entitled to a retirement benefit at the date of his death, if she was married to the deceased at the date of his separation from service and remained married to him until his death. In accordance with general principles of private international law, the validity of a marriage must be assessed and determined in accordance with the law of the place where the marriage was celebrated, being the law of the Philippines. The Supreme Court of the Philippines had ruled on various occasions that although a second marriage might be presumed to be legally void if it was celebrated while a first marriage was still subsisting, it would be presumptively valid until declared a nullity by a court. Illegal juridical acts were often deemed to exist in municipal legal systems until they were set aside by a court in appropriate proceedings because they had

[13] Judge John Raymond Murphy, Presiding, Judge Martha Halfeld and Judge Richard Lussick.

legal consequences that could not be overlooked. A marriage may be hypothetically a nullity, but remained effective and was, in reality, valid until a judicial declaration to the contrary.

UNAT found that there was no evidence that the staff member's marriage had been the subject of any legal proceedings for a declaration of nullity in the Philippines. The marriage was accordingly recognized by the competent authorities of the Philippines. Her presumptively valid marriage was extant at the date her late husband separated from service and she remained so married to him until his death. Accordingly, UNAT set aside the decision of the Standing Committee of the UNJSPB and ordered that the staff member be paid a widow's benefit under article 34.

3. *Judgment No. 2019-UNAT-914 (29 March 2019): Oglesby* v. *United Nations Joint Staff Pension Fund*[14]

DISCRIMINATION—SEX DISCRIMINATION—SEXUAL ORIENTATION—SAME-SEX MARRIAGE—EQUAL TREATMENT—MARITAL STATUS—MARRIAGE AFTER SEPARATION FROM SERVICE—UNJSPF—SURVIVOR'S BENEFITS—WIDOWER'S BENEFIT—PROSPECTIVE SURVIVOR—COMPETENCE OF TRIBUNAL—POWER TO GRANT RELIEF

A former staff member married his same-sex partner of 36 years in New York in April 2018, 20 years after his separation from service in December 1998. At the time of his separation from service, same-sex marriage was not legally recognized in any jurisdiction and he was therefore unable to marry his partner. The day after the marriage, he visited the New York office of the United Nations Joint Staff Pension Fund ("UNJSPF" or "the Fund") to inquire whether his husband could be recognized as his surviving spouse. He was advised that, as he had not been married at the time of his separation from service in 1998, his husband did not meet a fundamental eligibility requirement for a widower's benefit under articles 34 and 35 of the UNJSPF Regulations and would therefore not be recognized as his surviving spouse.

The Fund further advised that in 2016 the United Nations Joint Staff Pension Board ("UNJSPB" or "the Pension Board") had extended the interpretation of marriage to include unions and registered partnerships legally entered into in the jurisdiction where the status was established and conferring rights comparable to those of marriage, including pension rights. However, the application of those guidelines was not retroactive. Moreover, under the expanded recognition framework, *de facto* unions and registered partnerships in New York were not accepted as equivalent to marriage, as they did not confer the same rights and obligations, including pension rights. The Fund informed him of the option to purchase an annuity—a periodic lifetime benefit payable to a spouse married after separation from service—in favour of his husband under article 35*ter* of the Regulations, which would become effective 18 months after the date of marriage.

The former staff member requested the Fund to interpret the relevant provisions in a constructive and humane manner, noting that he had served the Organization for approximately 25 years, was 79 years old and was being treated for a serious heart condition. He argued that the annuity was not a viable alternative, as it would lapse if he did not survive until its effective date. The Standing Committee of the UNJSPB upheld the decision not to recognize his husband as a prospective survivor. The former staff member appealed that decision, contending that articles 34 and 35 discriminated against persons in same-sex

[14] Judge John Raymond Murphy, Presiding, Judge Sabine Knierimand and Judge Martha Halfeld.

relationships and were inconsistent with Article 8 of the Charter of the United Nations and article 7 of the Universal Declaration of Human Rights, which prohibit discrimination on impermissible grounds, including sexual orientation and marital status.

UNAT found that, at the time of his separation from service, the former staff member was not married to his husband; their relationship did not enjoy a status comparable to marriage under United States law; the Regulations did not provide for retrospective recognition of the 2018 marriage; and the Regulations specifically addressed his situation by providing for an annuity under article 35*ter*. UNAT therefore concluded that, under the express terms of articles 34 and 35, the spouse was not entitled to a survivor's benefit.

Nonetheless, UNAT observed that "there was ... merit in [the appellant's] line of argument" that the differentiation between spouses in heterosexual marriages and persons in same-sex relationships was unfair and discriminatory. UNAT held, however, that it lacked the remedial authority to grant the relief sought. It emphasized that it did not have the competence to apply the Charter of the United Nations or the Universal Declaration of Human Rights directly, nor the power to invalidate internal or subsidiary legislative provisions on that basis. UNAT further noted that it was not a constitutional court and that its jurisdiction, under article 2 (9) of its Statute, was limited to determining whether there had been non-observance of the UNJSPF Regulations. It concluded that the UNJSPF had acted in accordance with its Regulations and that any continuing discrimination on the grounds of sexual orientation inconsistent with the Charter would be a matter for the Secretary-General or the General Assembly. Accordingly, UNAT concluded that the appeal "regrettably" had to fail.

4. *Judgment No. 2019-UNAT-918 (29 March 2019): Nadasan* v. *Secretary-General of the United Nations*[15]

Standard of review—Disciplinary sanction—Misconduct—Sexual harassment—Separation from service—Standard of proof—Proportionality of sanction—Procedural errors—Investigation—Witnesses

A former staff member challenged the Administration's decision to separate him from service with compensation in lieu of notice and payment of a termination indemnity. The decision was based on a finding that he had engaged in sexual harassment. UNDT dismissed his application in its entirety, concluding that the material facts underlying the disciplinary measure had been sufficiently established by documentary evidence and that the disciplinary sanction imposed was proportionate. In reaching that conclusion, UNDT found, inter alia, that the former staff member had repeatedly contacted the complainant by telephone, email and through Facebook, notwithstanding her repeated and clear requests that he cease contact. UNDT determined that the evidence demonstrated that his conduct was continuous, of a sexual nature and unwelcome. UNDT further found that the former staff member's due process rights had been respected.

UNAT held that UNDT had not erred in finding that the documentary evidence was sufficient to establish that the former staff member had engaged in sexual harassment amounting to serious misconduct, and that the sanction of separation from service with compensation in lieu of notice and payment of a termination indemnity was proportionate and lawful. UNAT further found that the principal requirements of due process had been met and dismissed the appeal.

---

[15] Judge Sabine Knierim, Presiding, Judge Martha Halfeld and Judge John Raymond Murphy.

5. *Judgment No. 2019-UNAT-939 (28 June 2019): Delaunay* v. *Registrar of the International Court of Justice*[16]

DUTY TO PROTECT STAFF—HARASSMENT—COMPENSATION—MORAL DAMAGES—LEGAL FEES

From 2009, the staff member served as a medical doctor at the International Court of Justice ("ICJ") under a 25 per cent part-time arrangement. Concurrently, she was engaged as a medical doctor on a contractual basis with the European Patent Office ("EPO"). In 2010, she informed the Security Service of the Registry of a "medical emergency situation" involving the Head of the ICJ Library. In March 2013, she informed the Registrar of a second incident, again involving the Head of the Library. The Head of the Library, in turn, complained that the staff member had interfered in the management of her service, failed to provide medical assistance to a staff member visibly in distress and breached medical ethics. She further alleged that the medical doctor had been the subject of similar complaints at EPO and before the French Medical Board. She followed up on several occasions, copying other recipients, including the ICJ President and the Staff Committee, on her correspondence.

In September 2013, the Registry informed the staff member of the allegations against her and of the Registrar's decision to initiate an investigation. She responded, indicating that she wished to "formally complain" of harassment and requesting that appropriate measures be taken and that "a disciplinary or investigative process" be undertaken. She subsequently submitted a formal complaint alleging defamation and slander by the Head of the Library. On the same day, the Registrar appointed a panel to investigate the allegations made by the two staff members against each other.

In January 2014, the panel submitted its report to the Registrar, concluding that the Head of the Library had verbally assaulted the medical doctor in March 2013; that nearly all of the allegations made against the medical doctor were unsupported by evidence and had been shown to be deliberate falsehoods; and that the Head of the Library had harassed the medical doctor. In April 2014, the Registrar informed the staff member that he had concluded that the Head of the Library had engaged in misconduct through acts of harassment and defamation against her and that disciplinary action would be taken in the form of termination of the Head of the Library's employment. The Registry also informed the staff member that most of the allegations made against her had not been substantiated.

In November 2017, the staff member submitted a document to the Registrar alleging that senior officials had prior knowledge that the Head of the Library posed a risk to her subordinates and that the ICJ had breached its duty to protect staff from harassment. In January 2019, the Conciliation Committee issued its report recommending payment of USD 1,000 "for the moral damage [she had] suffered as a result of the Administration having exceed[ed] her consent in the handling of her personal information". The staff member appealed.

UNAT held that the ICJ had breached its duty to protect the staff member from harassment by another staff member. It found that, once senior management had become aware of the incidents, it should reasonably have foreseen the risk of further incidents and failed to take appropriate measures to protect staff. UNAT awarded USD 12,500 in compensation for the harm suffered, in particular damage to the staff member's reputation during the investigations, and awarded EUR 3,630 in legal fees.

---

[16] Judge John Murphy, Presiding, Judge Dimitrios Raikos and Judge Martha Halfeld.

6. *Judgment No. 2019-UNAT-941 (28 June 2019): Dieng* v. *Secretary-General of the United Nations*[17]

MANAGEMENT EVALUATION—EXTENSION OF TIME—GOOD FAITH—ESTOPPEL—RECEIVABILITY (UNDT)—*RATIONE TEMPORIS*

The staff member filed a request for management evaluation contesting his reassignment to a different office. The Management Evaluation Unit ("MEU") confirmed receipt of the request and advised, in writing, that, pursuant to staff rule 11.2 (*d*) of the Staff Rules, the management evaluation was to be completed within 45 calendar days of receipt of the request, that is, no later than 23 July 2018. The MEU further advised that, in the event of any delay in completing the management evaluation, and pursuant to staff rule 11.4 (*a*), the 90-calendar-day time limit for filing an application with UNDT would begin to run from 23 July 2018, or from the date on which the management evaluation was completed, if earlier, unless that deadline had been extended by the Secretary-General in order to facilitate informal resolution.

Subsequently, MEU informed the staff member, again in writing, that the contested decision had been upheld and that, since its response had been issued prior to the expiry of the 90-day deadline for filing an application with UNDT, receipt of the management evaluation set a new deadline for submission of the application. The staff member thereafter filed an application with UNDT contesting the decision. UNDT dismissed the application as time-barred.

UNAT recalled its established jurisprudence to the effect that, where no response to a request for management evaluation is received, a staff member has 90 days from the date on which the response is due to file an application with UNDT. If a response is received after the expiry of that 90-day time limit, such receipt does not restart the time limit for filing an application with UNDT.

Since MEU's response had been received after the expiry of the 90-day period, it did not reset the time limit for filing an application. Accordingly, UNDT did not initially err in law in concluding that the staff member's application was not receivable *ratione temporis*, as it had been filed outside the applicable regulatory time limit.

However, applying the principles of good faith and the regularity of administrative proceedings to the specific facts of the case, UNAT found that UNDT had erred in dismissing the application as time-barred. UNAT held that MEU was competent only to make recommendations regarding the suspension or extension of relevant deadlines in the management evaluation process, whereas the authority to extend such deadlines was reserved to the Secretary-General, who had not exercised that authority in the present case. Although not required to do so, MEU had advised the staff member that the 90-calendar-day period for filing an application with the UNDT began to run from 23 July 2018. Relying on that representation, the staff member filed his application outside the original regulatory time limit.

UNAT concluded that, in the circumstances, and in application of the principles of good faith and the regularity of administrative proceedings, UNDT had erred in dismissing the application as time-barred. Moreover, the Secretary-General was estopped, in the circumstances of the case, from raising the defence that the application for judicial review was time-barred. UNAT therefore remanded the case to UNDT for consideration on the merits.

---

[17] Judge Dimitrios Raikos, Presiding, Judge Richard Lussick and Judge Deborah Thomas-Felix.

7. *Judgment No. 2019-UNAT-949 (25 October 2019): Sheffer* v. *Secretary-General of the International Maritime Organization*[18]

REQUIREMENT OF NEUTRAL FIRST INSTANCE PROCESS UNDER THE UNAT STATUTE—REMAND—ADVISORY NATURE OF THE STAFF APPEALS BOARD'S DECISION—DISTINCTION BETWEEN RECOMMENDATION AND DECISION

In 2017, a staff member of the International Maritime Organization ("IMO") submitted a request for the upward reclassification of his post. The request was denied. The staff member challenged the non-classification decision before the IMO Staff Appeals Board ("SAB"), arguing that his post should be upgraded. SAB concluded that the impugned decision had been taken in accordance with established IMO procedures and recommended that it be maintained. The Secretary-General of IMO accepted SAB's recommendation and decided to maintain Mr. Sheffer's post at the G-7 level.

UNAT held that SAB had merely provided advice to the Secretary-General of IMO and had not itself taken a final decision. The Secretary-General of IMO, as the final decision-maker, could not be regarded as a neutral component of the process, since he was both the representative of the employer and the original decision-maker whose determination was being challenged.

UNAT therefore remanded the case to SAB, requiring it to reconsider and decide the matter in compliance with the requirement that a neutral first-instance process include a written decision issued by a neutral body.

8. *Judgment No. 2019-UNAT-975 (25 October 2019): Reilly* v. *Secretary-General of the United Nations*[19]

JURISDICTION AND COMPETENCE OF THE APPEALS TRIBUNAL—APPEAL AGAINST CASE MANAGEMENT OR INTERLOCUTORY ORDER—RECEIVABILITY—END OF A JUDGE'S TERM—REASSIGNMENT OF CASES—LEGAL INTERPRETATION OF GENERAL ASSEMBLY RESOLUTIONS—JUDICIAL INDEPENDENCE—FAIR TRIAL

A newly assigned judge of UNDT issued case management or interlocutory Order No. 54 (GVA/2019) and Order No. 55 (GVA/2019), notifying the parties of the reassignment of cases previously pending before an *ad litem* judge whose term had ended. The judge proposed a course of action in the reassigned cases and sought the views of the parties on that course of action, allowing them to raise any objections.

On appeal, appellants submitted that removal of a "sitting judge" exceeded jurisdiction of UNDT and constituted a reviewable and correctable error.

UNAT referred to General Assembly resolution 73/276, which had extended "the positions of the two *ad litem* judges in Geneva and Nairobi and the current incumbent judges [...] pending the nomination of candidates by the Internal Justice Council and the appointment of the aforementioned four half-time judges by the General Assembly, which should take place no later than 31 December 2019". UNAT observed that the term of the *ad litem* judge in Geneva had been extended only "pending" or "while waiting" for appointment of the four half-time judges, which was to occur no later than 31 December 2019. UNAT

---

[18] Judge John Murphy, Presiding, Judge Dimitrios Raikos and Judge Deborah Thomas-Felix.

[19] Judge Kanwaldeep Sandhu, Presiding, Judge Sabine Knierim and Judge John Raymond Murphy.

considered that this interpretation was not unreasonable and accorded with intent of the legislative branch and with context and object of the legislative provisions.

UNAT further noted that article 4(1) of the UNDT Statute provides that UNDT "shall be composed of three full-time judges and six half-time judges" and that General Assembly decision 73/408C set out the full composition of UNDT. There was no mention of *ad litem* judges or their mandate in resolution 73/276 or in the UNDT Statute.

Based on the interpretation of resolution 73/276 and decision 73/408C read together, UNAT concluded that there had been no "removal" or "replacement" of the *ad litem* judge and that the term expired upon appointment of the half-time judges to UNDT.

UNAT also observed that, unlike the Statute of the International Court of Justice, the UNDT Statute contained no provision allowing judges to remain seized of matters beyond the expiry of their terms. Unlike the practice of the International Criminal Tribunal for the Former Yugoslavia, neither General Assembly nor the UNDT Statute conferred authority to extend the mandate of *ad litem* judges or to permit them to remain seized of matters beyond the expiry of their terms.

C. Decisions of the Administrative Tribunal of the International Labour Organization[20]

In 2019, the Administrative Tribunal of the International Labour Organization adopted a total of 150 judgments at its 127th and 128th sessions.[21]

D. Decisions of the World Bank Administrative Tribunal[22]

In 2019, the Administrative Tribunal of the World Bank adopted a total of 25 judgments and four orders at its spring and fall sessions: 14 judgments and one order were rendered on

[20] The Administrative Tribunal of the International Labour Organization is competent to hear complaints alleging non-observance, in substance or in form, of the terms of appointment of officials and of the staff regulations of international organizations that have recognized the competence of the Tribunal. For a list of those organizations, see http://www.ilo.org/tribunal/membership/lang--en/index.htm. The Tribunal is also competent to hear disputes with regard to the execution of certain contracts concluded by the International Labour Organization and disputes relating to the application of the regulations of the former Staff Pension Fund of the International Labour Organization. For more information about the Administrative Tribunal of the International Labour Organization and the full texts of its judgments, see http://www.ilo.org/tribunal/lang--en/index.htm.

[21] See https://www.ilo.org/dyn/triblex/triblexmain.showlist.

[22] The World Bank Administrative Tribunal is competent to hear and pass judgment upon any applications alleging non-observance of the contract of employment or terms of appointment, including all pertinent regulations and rules in force at the time of the alleged non-observance, of members of the staff of the International Bank for Reconstruction and Development, the International Development Association and the International Finance Corporation, the Multilateral Investment Guarantee Agency and the International Centre for the Settlement of Investment Disputes (collectively "the Bank Group"). The Tribunal is open to any current or former member of the staff of the Bank Group, any person who is entitled to a claim upon a right of a member of the staff as a personal representative or by reasons of the staff member's death and any person designed or otherwise entitled to receive payment under

26 April 2019 at the conclusion of the Tribunal's spring session, and eleven judgments and three orders were rendered on 25 October 2019 at the conclusion of the Tribunal's fall session.[23]

E. Decisions of the Administrative Tribunal of the International Monetary Fund[24]

The Administrative Tribunal of the International Monetary Fund issued two Judgments and one Order in 2019, which are summarized below.

1. *Judgment No. 2019-1 (5 April 2019): Mr. "LL", Applicant* v. *International Monetary Fund, Respondent*

Staff retirement plan—Offset of workers' compensation annuity against disability person—Separation for medical reasons—Separation benefits Fund payments—Remedies ordered by tribunal include interests on retroactive payments

Applicant filed an application challenging a series of decisions taken by the Fund following a work-related injury that resulted in a career-ending disability.

Applicant was separated from employment for medical reasons pursuant to General Administrative Order ("GAO") No. 16. At the time of his separation, the Administration Committee of the Staff Retirement Plan ("SRP" or "Plan") determined that Applicant, an SRP participant, did not qualify for a disability pension in terms of section 4.3 of the Plan. Separating from the Fund without access to a disability pension, Applicant was granted Separation Benefits Fund ("SBF") payments, pursuant to GAO No. 16. Applicant opted to take part of his SBF benefits as paid leave, bridging him to an early retirement pension under SRP section 4.2 (which he began to receive in due course), and the remainder as a lump-sum payment.

Applicant also filed a request for workers' compensation benefits, which was rejected as untimely. After the Fund later waived its timeliness defense, the Workers' Compensation Claim Administrator determined that Applicant was eligible for benefits associated with "temporary" but not "permanent" total disability; that is, Applicant was not entitled to a workers' compensation annuity. Applicant challenged that determination before the Fund's Grievance Committee, which, following a hearing, recommended that the workers' compensation decision be reconsidered. The Grievance Committee found that the Claim Administrator had failed to apply governing standards and to take account of up-to-date medical records. Upon reconsideration, the Claim Administrator awarded Applicant a workers' compensation annuity of 66–2/3 percent of his final pensionable remuneration, in accordance with GAO No. 20, section 5.01.1.

---

any provision of the Staff Retirement Plan. For more information on the World Bank Administrative Tribunal and full texts of its decisions, see https://tribunal.worldbank.org (accessed on 16 January 2025).

[23] See https://tribunal.worldbank.org/judgments-orders-all (accessed on 16 January 2025).

[24] The Administrative Tribunal of the International Monetary Fund became operational on 1 January 1994. The Tribunal is competent to pass judgment upon any application: (*a*) by a member of the staff challenging the legality of an administrative act adversely affecting him; or (*b*) by an enrollee in, or beneficiary under, any retirement or other benefit plan maintained by the Fund as employer challenging the legality of an administrative act concerning or arising under any such plan which adversely affects the applicant. The complete jurisprudence of the IMF Administrative Tribunal may be accessed electronically at http://www.imf.org/tribunal.

Following a further recommendation of the Grievance Committee, Fund Management made Applicant's workers' compensation annuity retroactive to the date that his early retirement pension had commenced. Additionally, it required Applicant to repay (pro-rated over a four-year period) the lumpsum SBF (*i.e.*, medical separation) benefit he had earlier been granted, on the ground that he was now receiving a workers' compensation annuity. Fund Management then referred questions relating to the "coordination" of Applicant's workers' compensation annuity and SRP pension benefits to the SRP Administration Committee, which took the following decisions: (i) to replace Applicant's early retirement pension with a disability pension, retroactive to his early retirement date; and (ii) to pay Applicant a "coordinated" disability pension and workers' compensation annuity, which was (*a*) capped at the amount payable to him as a workers' compensation annuity, (*b*) financed in part by the SRP, and (*c*) reduced by the amount of the commutation payment Applicant had taken on his early retirement pension.

The case before the Tribunal arose from fifteen grievances filed by Applicant with the Fund's Grievance Committee, the decisions of Fund Management accepting the Grievance Committee's recommendations, and from the subsequent rulings by the SRP Administration Committee relating to Applicant's pension entitlements in light of the later award of a workers' compensation annuity.

Following consideration of the arguments of the parties, including through oral proceedings, the Administrative Tribunal rendered a judgment in which it sustained that the SRP Administration Committee erred when it replaced his early retirement pension with a disability pension and "coordinated" that pension with his workers' compensation annuity in the manner described above. In the view of the Tribunal, the SRP Administration Committee misinterpreted and misapplied SRP section 10.5, which grants the Committee discretionary authority to offset workers' compensation payments against "such part of [a] disability pension provided hereunder, in such equitable manner as the Administration Committee shall decide."

The Tribunal found no basis in the Fund's law to pay Applicant a single "coordinated" annuity rather than a separate SRP pension and workers' compensation annuity. Furthermore, capping that annuity at the amount Applicant would have received as a workers' compensation annuity meant that the Committee had failed to give any weight to Applicant's years of service and contributions under the Plan. The Tribunal concluded that "... it will not ordinarily be equitable for the Committee to permit the [workers' compensation] annuity to be offset against that portion of the disability pension that the SRP participant had, in effect, accrued as a result of contributions made by both the participant and the Fund during the participant's employment." Rather, concluded the Tribunal, the plain meaning of SRP section 10.5 was that Applicant would retain both an SRP pension and a separate workers' compensation annuity.

The Tribunal additionally addressed the financing arrangement that the Committee had applied to the single annuity. The Tribunal concluded that the blending of Applicant's SRP pension and workers' compensation annuity, such that assets of the SRP were used to finance Applicant's workers' compensation benefits, was plainly contrary to the Plan. SRP sections 9.1 and 13.2 make clear that the assets of the Plan may be used only to pay the Plan's liabilities, and the Plan's liabilities may be paid only from the assets of the Plan. Accordingly, the Committee's decisions wrongfully deprived Applicant of his SRP pension, fully financed by the Plan, and a separate workers' compensation annuity, fully financed by the IMF.

In concluding that the Committee misinterpreted and misapplied SRP section 10.5, the Tribunal expressly rejected the Committee's reliance on a 1992 decision of the Fund's Executive Board. The Tribunal held that the Committee's discretion under SRP section 10.5 was a narrow one, confined by the terms of the Plan. In relying on a Board decision that did not represent an amendment to the Plan, and was contrary to it, the Committee had exceeded the margin of its discretionary authority.

In addition to sustaining Applicant's challenge to the decisions of the SRP Administration Committee, the Tribunal also concluded that the Fund abused its discretion when it decided to require Applicant, on the basis of his later having been granted a workers' compensation annuity, to repay the amount of the lumpsum SBF payment he had received pursuant to GAO No. 16 upon his separation for medical reasons. Neither the Fund's internal law nor Applicant's separation arrangements letter provided a basis for that decision.

Although the Tribunal concluded that Applicant had prevailed on his principal claims, it did not sustain the following complaints: that the Fund wrongfully (i) breached a "duty of care" to take preventative measures to ensure Applicant's health and safety; (ii) failed to provide compensation for alleged injury to his spouse; (iii) failed to provide compensation for lost personal effects; (iv) failed to provide him with "special sick leave" for workers' compensation related absence; (v) failed to compensate him for alleged tax consequences of the Fund's determination of his disability-related benefits; and (vi) failed to provide compensation for alleged procedural irregularities, delays, and failures to address confusion in the Fund's laws on disability.

Pursuant to the remedial authority granted by its Statute, the Tribunal rescinded the contested decisions of the SRP Administration Committee, along with the decision of Fund Management requiring Applicant to repay the lumpsum separation payment he had been granted under GAO No. 16. The Tribunal also ordered measures to "correct the effects" (Statute, article XIV, section 1) of those rescinded decisions. Going forward, Applicant will be paid: (i) an early retirement pension (SRP section 4.2), retroactive to the date of his eligibility for such pension, paid solely by the SRP Retirement Fund; and (ii) a separate workers' compensation annuity (GAO No. 20) retroactive to the date of his separation from the Fund, paid solely by the IMF.

In restoring retroactively Applicant's rightful entitlements under the Fund's internal law, the Tribunal ordered that the Fund pay Applicant interest on those past due payments. Additionally, the Tribunal ordered the Fund to reimburse Applicant the total amount of his legal fees and costs incurred in pursuing his case before the Tribunal.

2. *Order No. 2019-1 (10 October 2019):*
Ms. "PP", Applicant v. *International Monetary Fund, Respondent*
(Applicant's Request for Provisional Relief and Respondent's Motion to Dismiss in Part)

Disciplinary reprimand—Order to terminate household employee—Suspension of contested decision—Irreparable harm—Motion to Dismiss in Part—Jurisdiction of the Tribunal

Applicant filed an Application challenging the decision of the Director of the Human Resources Department ("HRD") that Applicant "failed to afford … fair and reasonable treatment" to a G-5 household employee and "engaged in conduct that reflected adversely on the Fund," in violation of Fund rules. The HRD Director decided, as a "disciplinary" measure, that Applicant would receive a formal written reprimand, which is to remain in her personnel file for three years.

In addition to the "disciplinary" decision, the HRD Director took another decision, characterized by the Fund as an "administrative" decision. That decision (*a*) directed Applicant to end the employment of a different G-5 employee, who remained employed in Applicant's household, and (*b*) stated that the Fund would not be able to support applications made by Applicant for G-5 visas in the future. The "administrative" decision stated that the HRD Director was "obliged to make the [decision] in the interests of the Fund," due to the "position communicated to [the Fund] by the [U.S.] State Department." The Application challenges both the "disciplinary" decision and the "administrative" decision.

In Order No. 2019-1, the Tribunal decided two matters preliminary to its consideration of the merits of the Application, namely, Applicant's request for provisional relief and the Fund's motion to dismiss part of the Application.

In her Application, Applicant requested provisional relief in the form of an order: "(1) prohibiting the Fund from requiring [the current G-5 employee]'s dismissal from [Applicant]'s home during the pendency of this case; and (2) requiring the Fund to secure all necessary visa actions by the State Department (*e.g.* an I94 renewal) to permit [the G-5 employee]'s continued employment by [Applicant] during the pendency of this case."

The Fund, for its part, filed a Motion to Dismiss in Part, seeking to dismiss that portion of the Application challenging the "administrative" decision. The Fund contended that the decision to terminate Applicant's eligibility to hire G-5 employees was a decision of the U.S. State Department rather than of the Fund, and, accordingly, that the Tribunal lacked jurisdiction to decide that claim.

As to Applicant's Request for Provisional Relief, the Tribunal emphasized that provisional relief is an extraordinary measure that it will order only in limited circumstances. Provisional relief is an exception to the ordinary rule (stated in article VI, section 4, of the Tribunal's Statute) that the filing of an application shall not have the effect of suspending the implementation of the decision contested.

The Tribunal considered the following questions: Does Applicant seek suspension of a decision contested in the Tribunal? Has Applicant shown "irreparable harm" to her in the absence of the provisional relief she seeks? May Applicant assert a request for provisional relief based on alleged "irreparable harm" to the current G-5 employee?

The Tribunal observed that part of Applicant's request for provisional relief did not seek suspension of a decision contested in the Tribunal, and the Tribunal denied it on that basis. As to the part of the request that did seek suspension of a decision contested in the Tribunal, *i.e.*, that Applicant terminate the employment of her current G-5 employee, the Tribunal concluded that Applicant had not met the test of showing that she would suffer "irreparable harm" in the absence of the relief she sought. The Tribunal observed that Applicant had been on notice for more than a year that her current G-5 employee must leave her household and had had ample opportunity to make alternate employment arrangements with non-G-5 visa holders. With respect to Applicant's attempt to assert alleged "irreparable harm" on behalf of her current G-5 employee, the Tribunal concluded that Applicant had not met the requirements for securing provisional relief as envisaged by the Commentary on the Statute, which concerns itself with the employment relationship between the Fund and its own staff members. Accordingly, the Tribunal denied Applicant's Request for Provisional Relief.

As to the Fund's Motion to Dismiss in Part, the Tribunal decided that although its Statute and Rules of Procedure do not expressly provide for a motion to dismiss part of an application (in contrast to summary dismissal of an application *in toto*) before a full exchange of pleadings on the merits of the case, neither do they exclude that possibility. The Tribunal concluded that in the unusual context of the expedited exchange of preliminary pleadings on Applicant's request for preliminary relief, in which the Fund's arguments opposing provisional relief and seeking to dismiss part of the Application were closely related, the Motion to Dismiss in Part was admissible. On the merits of the Fund's Motion, however, the Tribunal decided that it would better serve the interests of justice to decide all of the issues of the case, including Applicant's challenge to the decision affecting her eligibility to hire G-5 employees, following a full briefing on the merits of the Application. Accordingly, the Tribunal dismissed the Motion to Dismiss in Part. In taking that decision, the Tribunal stated that the Fund had the right to raise in its pleadings on the merits its argument that the Tribunal lacked jurisdiction over Applicant's challenge to the "administrative" decision.

3. *Judgment No. 2019-2 (17 December 2019): Mr. "OO", Applicant* v. *International Monetary Fund, Respondent*

NON-CONVERSION OF FIXED TERM APPOINTMENT—STANDARD OF REVIEW—"PERFORMANCE" DISTINGUISHED FROM "CAREER POTENTIAL"—B-LEVEL DIVERSITY HIRING INITIATIVE—FAIR TREATMENT—REMEDY FOR INTANGIBLE INJURY

Applicant challenged the non-conversion of his fixed-term appointment to an open-ended appointment. The governing Fund law during the relevant period required that three criteria be satisfied for conversion, namely, that the appointee meets "performance" requirements, the appointee demonstrates "career potential" with the Fund, and there is a "staffing need" on the part of the Fund. The Fund grounded the non-conversion of Applicant's appointment on the latter two criteria. Applicant challenged the Fund's reliance on those criteria, given the context of his recruitment through the Fund's B-Level Diversity Hiring Initiative ("Initiative"). The Initiative provided central funding for a limited number of three-year, fixed-term appointments at the B-Level for staff members recruited from underrepresented regions of the world. The central funding covered the cost to a department of employing, for three years, an Initiative recruit in a job that was not part of the department's complement of full-time equivalent ("FTE") positions.

The Tribunal began by addressing Applicant's contention that the Initiative, and/or the terms of his recruitment through the Initiative, meant that the Fund could not ground the non-conversion decision on either of its stated reasons. After reviewing the arguments of the parties and the record of the case, the Tribunal concluded that the Fund's discretionary authority to decide whether to convert Applicant's fixed-term appointment to an open-ended appointment was not constrained by his recruitment through the Initiative, either as a matter of Fund law or as a matter of expectation created. Accordingly, the Fund could rely on the usual criteria for conversion of fixed-term appointments.

The Tribunal next considered whether the non-conversion decision represented an abuse of the Fund's discretion. The Tribunal noted that Applicant's case was the first to come before it in which the Fund had not based the contested non-conversion decision on failure to meet "performance" requirements. The Tribunal accordingly had to decide how to apply the abuse of discretion standard in deciding a challenge to a non-conversion decision taken on the ground that the fixed-term appointee, although meeting "performance" standards, had failed to demonstrate "career potential." The Tribunal contrasted the assessment of "performance," which will necessarily be a backward-looking exercise, with the assessment of "career potential," which requires managers to project the fixed-term appointee's future trajectory. "To the extent that the assessment of 'career potential' will rely in part on the evaluation of the individual's 'performance' to date," said the Tribunal, "that aspect of the assessment is reviewable under the standards applicable to other performance-based decisions." Insofar as the projection of "career potential" calls upon managers to make a judgment about the staff member's likely future contribution to the Fund, "it will be informed by managerial expertise, including knowledge of the institution. As such, it will be entitled to a considerable degree of deference by the Tribunal."

Applying that standard of review, the Tribunal considered whether Applicant had established that the Fund had failed to provide him with (*a*) assignments that afforded a fair opportunity to demonstrate "career potential" and (*b*) adequate notice of alleged shortcomings that would figure in the assessment of his "career potential" and opportunity to remedy them. In assessing whether a fixed-term appointee has been given adequate notice of "performance" shortcomings that will reflect adversely in an assessment of "career potential," said the Tribunal, "what is important is that the fixed-term appointee is given notice (*a*) of observed shortcomings and (*b*) that these may figure in the decision whether the appointment will be converted to open-ended status." The Tribunal found that this had been done in Applicant's case. The Tribunal also decided that, in taking the measure of Applicant's "career potential," it was not unreasonable for managers to have considered Applicant's possibilities for future promotion. Furthermore, although Applicant's "performance" was deemed to fall within the "Effective" range, it was within managers' discretionary authority to make a considered determination that his "career potential" fell short of that required for conversion of his fixed-term appointment. In the view of the Tribunal, Applicant's fixed-term performance monitoring identified a pattern of shortcomings relating to competencies in managerial leadership and initiative that reasonably could have led managers to conclude that Applicant lacked potential for a career with the Fund. Accordingly, the Tribunal concluded that the Fund did not abuse its discretion in taking the non-conversion decision on the ground that Applicant did not demonstrate "career potential" with the Fund.

Having sustained the non-conversion decision on the ground of lack of "career potential," the Tribunal did not find it necessary to decide whether the decision might also be sustained on the basis of lack of "staffing need." (The Fund had described the two criteria as independently sufficient bases for the non-conversion decision.)

The Tribunal additionally decided that Applicant had not established that the non-conversion decision was improperly motivated by bias or discrimination.

The Tribunal next considered whether the Fund had treated Applicant fairly in relation to his appointment under the Initiative, given the purposes of the Initiative. The Fund had explained that the Initiative was to "provide top candidates *entrée* to the Fund from which they could learn the institutional culture, build networks, and make themselves more competitive for B-Level vacancies as they arose." Recruitment through the Initiative differed from the usual fixed-term appointment process in that it provided funding for Applicant's B-Level position for a three-year term without any provision for continuation of the position at the conclusion of the term. Accordingly, said the Tribunal, supervisors' usual responsibilities, including to provide "suitable assignments, clear expectations, appropriate guidance, and timely feedback" (Fund's Guidelines for Conversion of Fixed-Term Appointments), were heightened by the uneasy fit between the Initiative and the usual fixed-term appointment process, as well as by the obligation under the Initiative to "facilitate ... integration" of Initiative recruits into the Fund. Having reviewed the record of the case, the Tribunal concluded that the challenges faced as an Initiative recruit were amplified in Applicant's case by managerial lapses in integrating him into the work of his department. In particular, following the departure of the senior official who had championed Applicant's recruitment, the official's successor did not initially demonstrate support for incorporating Applicant in the work of the relevant part of the department. In the view of the Tribunal, the purposes of the Initiative and fairness to Applicant required that the new manager be advised of Applicant's program and undertake proactive measures to support its success. As managers had failed to meet this obligation, the Tribunal concluded that the Fund failed to treat Applicant fairly in relation to his appointment under the Initiative, given the purposes of the Initiative. Pursuant to the remedial authority granted by its Statute, the Tribunal awarded Applicant compensation to correct the effects of the intangible injury consequent to that failure of fair treatment. The Tribunal set the amount of compensation at the sum equivalent to nine months of Applicant's salary at the time of the lapse of his fixed-term appointment. The Tribunal additionally ordered the Fund to reimburse Applicant fifty percent of the total amount of his legal fees and costs.

Chapter VI

SELECTED LEGAL OPINIONS OF THE SECRETARIATS OF THE UNITED NATIONS AND RELATED INTERGOVERNMENTAL ORGANIZATIONS*

A. Legal opinions of the Secretariat of the United Nations

(Issued or prepared by the Office of Legal Affairs)

1. Privileges and immunities

(*a*) Letter from the Chef de Cabinet, Executive Office of the Secretary-General, to the Permanent Representative of [Member State] regarding the actions of the Secretariat taken in connection with the servicing of the Credentials Committee of the Second High-Level United Nations Conference on South-South Cooperation (BAPA+40 Conference)

Representation of Member States before intergovernmental organs and conferences of the United Nations—Functions of Secretariat in servicing credentials committee—Credentials committee Member State-led process—Circulation by Secretariat of communications received relating to representation of Member States solely for information and without prejudice to action by credentials committee

22 March 2019

Excellency,

I write with reference to your letter dated 19 March 2019 addressed to the Secretary-General.

I wish to take this opportunity to set forth the position of the Secretariat concerning the actions it has taken in connection with the servicing of the Credentials Committee of the Second High-Level United Nations Conference on South-South Cooperation, also referred to as the BAPA+40 Conference.

The Secretariat acts in all cases to ensure that its actions respect and do not undermine a Member States-led process for determining the representatives of States before the intergovernmental organs of the United Nations and its conferences. In exercising its functions, the Secretariat shares and circulates communications it receives, as it is for the Chair of the Credentials Committee and its members to decide on the appropriate course of action.

With respect to the Conference, the Credentials Committee had been tasked to examine credentials of representatives and report to the Conference without delay. Accordingly, the Secretariat circulated to States that were to be appointed to the Credentials Committee,

* This chapter contains legal opinions and other similar legal memoranda and documents.

all communications it had received relating to the representation of [Member State] before the Conference. The circulation of the various communications was solely to inform the members of the Committee of the communications that had been received relevant to the work of the Committee. It was without prejudice to any action that the Committee may take. In circulating such communications, the Secretariat acted consistent with the standard practice of the Committee.

I also wish to take this opportunity to confirm that, as requested, your letter dated 19 March 2019 will be issued as an official document of the United Nations General Assembly, under agenda item 3 (*b*).

...

[*Signed*]

(*b*) Memorandum from Under-Secretary-General for Legal Affairs and United Nations Legal Counsel to the Chief *ad interim*, Petitions and Urgent Actions Section, Office of the United Nations High Commissioner for Human Rights, regarding the competence of the Committee on the Elimination of Racial Discrimination to consider a matter brought to the attention of the Committee pursuant to article 11 of the International Convention on the Elimination of All Forms of Racial Discrimination

Law of treaties—Recognition of States—Establishment of treaty relations between parties to multilateral treaty—Effects of statement of non-recognition by party to multilateral treaty and statement excluding establishment of treaty relations—Participation in multilateral treaty does not itself imply recognition of all other parties—Statement excluding treaty relations prevents establishment of such relations—Procedure and jurisdiction of human rights treaty bodies—Inter-State communications under the Convention on the Elimination of All Forms of Racial Discrimination—Question of substantive human rights as between parties between which treaty relations not established—Rights *erga omnes partes*—Peremptory rules of general international law (*jus cogens*)—Objective obligations under human rights treaties—Practice of States parties to the Convention on the Elimination of All Forms of Racial Discrimination suggests that parties consider Convention to establish objective obligations

23 July 2019

1. I refer to your memorandum, dated [date], by which you have transmitted to us the following question posed by the Committee on the Elimination of Racial Discrimination ("the Committee"):

> "As a matter of public international law, or of treaty law and practice of the United Nations, does the objection of the [State A], dated [date] ([document symbol]), to the accession by the [State B] to the International Convention on the Elimination of All Forms of Racial Discrimination, dated [date], of itself legally preclude the Committee from examining a communication filed by either State against the other under articles 11 to 13 of the Convention?"

2. You have mentioned in your memorandum that the Committee has also sought the views of the Office of Legal Affairs on the role which the following elements might play in the consideration of the above-mentioned question:

- The *jus cogens* or *erga omnes* character of the prohibition of racial discrimination as enshrined in the Convention;
- The requirement that treaty reservations should be compatible with the object and purpose of the treaty, and the applicability of this requirement to objections; and
- The protest of the [State A] against the objection by other States parties to the establishment of treaty relations between them and the [State A].

Background

3. The International Convention on the Elimination of All Forms of Racial Discrimination* (the "Convention") was concluded on 7 March 1966 and entered into force on 4 January 1969. Pursuant to its article 17, the Convention "is open for signature by any State Member of the United Nations or member of any of its specialized agencies, by any State Party to the Statute of the International Court of Justice, and by any other State which has been invited by the General Assembly of the United Nations to become a Party to this Convention" and "is subject to ratification." Pursuant to its Article 18, the Convention is "open to accession by any State referred to in article 17, paragraph 1, of the Convention" and "[a]ccession shall be effected by the deposit of an instrument of accession with the Secretary-General of the United Nations."

4. [State A] deposited its instrument of ratification on [date], which contained a reservation stating that "[t]he [State A] does not consider itself bound by the provisions of Article 22 of the said Convention". In accordance with its Article 19, paragraph 2, the Convention entered into force for [State A] on [date] ([document symbol]). The [State B] deposited its instrument of accession on [date] without any reservation; and the Convention entered into force for it on [date] ([document symbol]). In connection with Article 17 of the Convention, it is recalled that the [State B] has, since [year], been a member of a specialized agency of the United Nations, namely, [name of the specialized agency].

5. In a communication that was submitted to the depositary on [date] ([document symbol]), [State A] stated as follows:

> "'[State B]' does not satisfy the criteria for statehood under international law and lacks the legal capacity to join the aforesaid convention both under general international law and the terms of bilateral [State A]-[State B] agreements.
>
> "The Government of [State A] does not recognize '[State B]' as a State, and wishes to place on record, for the sake of clarity, its position that it does not consider '[State B]' a party to the Convention and regards the [State B] request for accession as being without legal validity and without effect upon [State A]'s treaty relations under the Convention."

6. In a communication that was submitted to the depositary on [date] ([document symbol]), the [State B] stated as follows:

* International Convention on the Elimination of All Forms of Racial Discrimination (New York, 1966), United Nations, *Treaty Series*, vol. 660, p. 1.

"The Government of the [State B] regrets the position of [State A], the occupying Power, and wishes to recall United Nations General Assembly resolution [resolution symbol and date] according [State B] 'non-member observer State status in the United Nations'. In this regard, [State B] is a State recognized by the United Nations General Assembly on behalf of the international community.

"As a State Party to the International Convention on the Elimination of all forms of Racial Discrimination, which entered into force on [date], the [State B] will exercise its rights and honor its obligations with respect to all States Parties. The [State B] trusts that its rights and obligations will be equally respected by its fellow States Parties."

7. Paragraphs 1 and 2 of article 11 of the International Convention on the Elimination of All Forms of Racial Discrimination provide as follows:

"1. If a State Party considers that another State Party is not giving effect to the provisions of this Convention, it may bring the matter to the attention of the Committee. The Committee shall then transmit the communication to the State Party concerned. Within three months, the receiving State shall submit to the Committee written explanations or statements clarifying the matter and the remedy, if any, that may have been taken by that State.

"2. If the matter is not adjusted to the satisfaction of both parties, either by bilateral negotiations or by any other procedure open to them, within six months after the receipt by the receiving State of the initial communication, either State shall have the right to refer the matter again to the Committee by notifying the Committee and also the other State."

8. We understand that the [State B] sent a communication concerning [State A] to the Committee on [date]. The communication, among other things, states that:

"[t]he [State B] exercises this right under Arts. 11–13 CERD, inherent in its status of being a member of CERD, given the urgency of the situation in the Occupied [State B] Territory ('OPT') and the blatant, and indeed ever increasing, violations by [State A] as the occupying power, of CERD which have taken place, and continue to take place in the OPT ever since [State A] occupied [territory A], [territory B], as well as [territory C], in [year]".

9. By a note verbale, dated [date], addressed to the secretariat of the Committee (the secretariat), [State A] stated that:

"[i]n light of [State A]'s official objection to the purported [State B] accession and the absence of treaty relations between [State A] and the [State B] entity under the Convention, it follows that Article 11 cannot and should not be activated with respect to [State A] in this situation, and that the Committee lacks the jurisdiction to initiate the mechanisms and procedures of this provision, including the initial transmission of the reported [State B] communication, … [and] requests that the Committee decline to proceed with any [State B] request pursuant to Article 11 of the Convention with respect to [State A]."

10. The secretariat transmitted the communication of the [State B] to [State A] on [date]. On the same day, the secretariat further informed both States Parties of the decision that had been adopted by the Committee at its [number] session, on [date], according to which, "[w]ithout considering the substance of [the [State B]'s] communication", the Committee had decided:

"1. To request the Secretary-General of the United Nations to transmit the communication submitted by the [State B] to the State Party concerned, the [State A]; 2. To invite the [State A] to submit to the Committee; within three months, "written explanations or statements clarifying the matter and the remedy, if any, that may been taken by that State", as provided for by Article 11, para 1, of the said Convention".

This was followed by a number of communications to the Committee from [State A] and from the [State B], dated [date], [date], [date], [date] and [date], each of which was transmitted by the Secretariat to the other State party.

11. In a Note Verbale dated [date], the secretariat, referring to paragraph 2 of article 11 of the Convention, informed both States Parties that the deadline for referring the matter again to the Committee was [date], adding that "[t]his reminder does not imply that any decision has been adopted on the admissibility of the matter under consideration". Acting consistently with article 11, paragraph 2, of the Convention, the [State B] subsequently referred the matter again to the Committee on [date].

12. At its [number] session, held in Geneva from [date] to [date], the Committee decided to give the opportunity to [State A] to inform the Committee whether it wished to supply any relevant information on the issues of the jurisdiction of the Committee or the admissibility of the communication from the [State B], including the question of the exhaustion of all available domestic remedies, and to give to the [State B] the opportunity to respond to the submission by [State A]. This decision was communicated to [State A] and to the [State B] by notes verbales, dated [date], from the secretariat. The Committee also decided to examine any preliminary question at its [number] session, which was to take place from [date] to [date].

13. Subsequently, a number of communications were sent to the two States, including a communication to [State A], dated [date], from the Committee's Working Group on communications that stated as follows: "No action undertaken by the Committee under article 11 of the Convention prejudges the issue of jurisdiction of the Committee. The Committee will not address the merits of the case, envisaged by article 12 of the Convention, nor any preliminary issue other than the issue of jurisdiction raised by the [State A], before having established whether it has jurisdiction to deal with the inter-state communication of reference." Moreover, the Committee sent a communication, dated [date], to both States which stated that "[t]he object of the upcoming proceedings [during the 98th session] is precisely to determine whether there is in respect of the Convention a treaty relation between the [State A] and the [State B], which would allow for the application of the articles 12 and 13 of the Convention." The Committee subsequently informed the two States that the relevant proceedings would be pursued during the Committee's [number] session to be held in [month and year].

14. We understand that the Committee has asked the question quoted in paragraph 1 above in the light of the above events.

Treaty relations between [State A] and the [State B]

15. As mentioned above, following the [State B]'s accession to the Convention on [date], [State A] submitted a communication dated [date], stating as follows:

> "The Government of [State A] does not recognize '[State B]' as a State, and wishes to place on record, for the sake of clarity, its position that it does not consider '[State B]' a party to the Convention and it regards the [State B] request for accession as being without legal validity and without effect upon [State A]'s treaty relations under the Convention."

16. This statement raises two questions: first, the legal validity or otherwise of the [State B]'s accession to the Convention and, secondly, the effects of [State A]'s statement

that it regards that accession as being "without effect upon [State A]'s treaty relations under the Convention".

17. As for the first of these questions, it is recalled that, on [date], the General Assembly adopted resolution [resolution symbol], in which it decided to "accord to [State B] non-member observer State status in the United Nations". In consequence of this resolution, the Secretary-General, acting in his capacity as depositary, has, since that date, regarded the [State B] as a "State" for the purpose of participation in those multilateral treaties for which he acts as depositary. He has accordingly accepted in deposit instruments by which the [State B] has expressed its consent to be bound by those treaties that are open to participation by "all States".

18. Moreover, as has already been mentioned, the [State B] has been a Member State of [name of specialized agency] since [year]. It is therefore a "State … member of any of [the United Nations] specialized agencies" within the meaning of articles 17 and 18 of the Convention. The Secretary-General accordingly accepted in deposit the [State B]'s instrument of accession to the Convention on [date].

19. In light of the above, and meeting a necessary and sufficient criterion laid down in the Convention for participation in it and having completed the steps laid down in the Convention for establishing its consent to be bound by it, this Office considers that the [State B] therefore is and must be considered to be a State party to the Convention.

20. The further question therefore arises of whether or not, because of [State A]'s statement, there exist treaty relations under the Convention between [State A] and the [State B].

21. In its statement, [State A] declares that it "does not recognize '[State B]' as a State" and "regards the [State B] request for accession as being … without effect upon [State A]'s treaty relations under the Convention".

22. Statements of this kind are quite common in the practice of States with respect to multilateral treaties that are deposited with the Secretary-General. The International Law Commission considered their legal nature in the context of its study of "the law and practice relating to reservations".

23. In his third report on that topic, the Special Rapporteur, Mr. Alain Pellet, proposed the following draft guideline, entitled "reservations relating to 'non-recognition'":

> "A unilateral statement by which a State purports to exclude the application of a treaty between itself and one or more other States which it does not recognize constitutes a reservation, regardless of the date on which it is made" (*Yearbook of the International Law Commission*, 1998, vol. II, pt. 1, at p. 253, para. 177).

24. The Commission considered this proposed draft guideline at its fiftieth session in 1998. A number of the Commission's members raised questions regarding the qualification of such statements as reservations, arguing that the legal regime of reservations under the 1969 Vienna Convention on the Law of Treaties* could not apply to them. Thus, it was pointed out *inter alia* that, unlike reservations, these statements are made by States at any time, not only when signing or establishing their consent to be bound by a treaty; that they are made even with respect to treaties that contain provisions excluding, or permitting only specific types of, reservations; and that they do not concern the legal effect of

* Vienna Convention on the Law of Treaties (Vienna, 1969), United Nations, *Treaty Series*, vol. 1155, p. 331.

the treaty itself or its provisions, but rather the capacity of the non-recognized entity to be bound by the treaty. At the same time, the Commission noted that these statements cannot be qualified as interpretative declarations, as they do not purport to interpret the treaty in respect of which they are made.

25. In light of these arguments, the Special Rapporteur proposed the following, revised draft guideline in his fourth report:

> "A unilateral statement by which a State indicates that its participation in a treaty does not imply recognition of an entity which it does not recognize as a State does not constitute either a reservation or an interpretative declaration, even if it purports to exclude the application of the treaty between the declaring State and the non-recognized entity" (*Yearbook of the International Law Commission 1999*, vol. II (part 1), at p. 137, para. 53).

26. Ultimately, the Commission adopted the following guideline, entitled "Statements of non-recognition", and included it in its Guide to Practice:

> "A unilateral statement by which a State indicates that its participation in a treaty does not imply recognition of an entity which it does not recognize is outside the scope of the present Guide to Practice, even if it purports to exclude the application of the treaty between the declaring State and the non-recognized entity" (*Yearbook of the International Law Commission 2011*, vol. II (part 2), at p. 27, Guideline 1.5.1).

27. In its accompanying commentary, the Commission differentiated between two forms that statements of non-recognition can take: one by which a party indicates that its participation in a treaty does not imply recognition of a non-recognized entity and another by which a party further indicates that its statement excludes the application of the treaty between itself and the non-recognized entity (*Yearbook of the International Law Commission,* 2011, vol. II, pt. 3, at p. 69, para. 2). The statement by [State A] is of this second type.

28. The Commission considered that the first type of statement does not have any legal effects (*loc. cit.*, para. 4). Indeed, it is now well established that participation in a multilateral treaty does not in itself imply recognition of every one of the parties to it (*loc. cit.*).

29. The second type of statement has a different nature and objective and specifically aims at preventing the application of the treaty between the State making the statement and the non-recognized entity. The Commission affirmed that such a statement "clearly purports to have (and does have) a legal effect on the application of the treaty, which is entirely excluded, but only in the relations between the declaring State and the non-recognized entity" (*loc. cit.*, para. 5).

30. The International Law Commission did not further elaborate. It considered such statements, like statements of the first kind, to be neither reservations nor interpretative declarations and so to fall outside the scope of its study. (*loc. cit.*, p. 70, para. 13). Nevertheless, States being free, by virtue of their sovereignty, to choose whether and with which other States to enter into treaty relations, it is difficult to see why statements of the second kind would not have the legal effect that the Commission attributed to them.

31. This being so, [State A]'s present statement is to be regarded as having had the effect of preventing the establishment of treaty relations under the Convention between it and the [State B].

32. That said, it may be noted that the International Court of Justice is currently seized of similar questions in the case concerning the *[case name]*. In that case, the [State B]

seeks to found the jurisdiction of the Court on article I of the Optional Protocol to the Vienna Convention on Diplomatic Relations concerning the Compulsory Settlement of Disputes. The [State C] has informed the Court of the communications that it has submitted to the Secretary-General in his capacity as depositary of the Convention and its Optional Protocol in which it declared that it did not consider itself to be in a treaty relationship with the applicant. By an Order dated [date], the Court decided that the written pleadings in the case should first address the question of jurisdiction of the Court and that of the admissibility of the application. The [State B] was to file its Memorial by [date]. The [State C] is due to file its Counter-Memorial by [date].

Treaty relations and the right to trigger the processes in articles 11 to 13

33. There therefore being no bilateral treaty relations under the Convention between [State A] and the [State B], [State A] does not owe any obligations under the Convention to the [State B] and the [State B] is not vested by the Convention with any correlative rights to require of [State A] the performance of the obligations that the Convention imposes on it (and *vice versa*).

34. The question consequently arises whether the absence of any such right on the part of the [State B] precludes the Committee from examining its communication under article 11 of the Convention.

35. As with any treaty, the Convention consists of a series of legal relations between the States that are party to it, consisting of obligations and correlative rights to require the performance of those obligations.

36. In the case of the Convention, as with other multilateral treaties for the protection of human rights, these relationships of rights and obligations are of two different kinds, at least in the case of the substantive rights and obligations deriving from the provisions in its Part I.

37. First, there are rights to require the performance of obligations that are vested in the State or States that would be injured in the event that those obligations are breached. In any given situation, there may be one such State or perhaps more than one; but not every State party will be vested with such a right. As an "injured" State, that State party may claim from a State party responsible for a breach the various forms of reparation known to international law, consistently with what is provided in Chapter II of Part Two of the International Law Commission's Draft Articles on Responsibility of States for Internationally Wrongful Acts (*Yearbook of the International Law Commission 2001*, vol. II (part 2), at pp. 26–30).

38. Secondly, there are rights to require the performance of obligations that are vested in every State party to the Convention, regardless of whether or not it would be injured in the event that those obligations are breached. In the event of a breach, every State party may claim from a responsible State only certain forms of reparation—cessation of the breach and guarantees that it will not be repeated. It may also claim from it the performance of the obligations of reparation that it owes to the injured State or States. Looked at from the point of view of obligations rather than rights, each State party owes this form of obligation in any given situation to every other State party to the Convention: that is, the obligations are owed *erga omnes partes*. This category of obligations is

reflected in article 48, paragraph 1 (*a*), of the Draft Articles on Responsibility of States for Internationally Wrongful Acts (*loc. cit.*)

39. Obligations and rights of the first type clearly do not exist as between [State A] and the [State B]. If [State A] conducts itself in a manner that is not consistent with any of the substantive provisions of the Convention, the [State B] therefore cannot assert that it is an injured State and, as such, claim from [State A] full reparation for any harm that may thereby be caused to it.

40. The same applies also in the case of obligations and rights of the second type. It may be true that, if it engages in an activity that is not consistent with any of the substantive provisions of the Convention, [State A] will thereby breach obligations that it owes under the Convention towards every other State party and so violate the correlative rights to the performance of that obligation that the Convention vests in each of them. However, it will not thereby breach any obligation under the Convention towards the [State B].

41. The fact that every other State party would be able to invoke its rights under the Convention to require [State A] to put an end to its breach and to provide guarantees against its repetition does not necessarily entail that the Convention vests the [State B] with those same rights. Rights of this second kind are just as much rights that are created by the Convention as are rights of the first kind; and just as the absence of treaty relations under the Convention between [State A] and the [State B] entails that the [State B] is not vested with rights of the first kind under the Convention *vis-à-vis* [State A], it equally entails that right of the second kind are not vested in it, either.

42. It should be emphasized that this—the fact that, if [State A] engaged in an activity that is not consistent with the any of the substantive provisions of the Convention, it would not thereby breach any obligations owed under the Convention towards the [State B]—does not entail that [State A] would not thereby violate any of the obligations that it may owe to the [State B] under other sources of international law. To the extent that the substantive provisions of the Convention are reflective of general customary international law, [State A] could, by engaging in an activity that is not consistent with them, violate rights that are vested in the [State B] under that body of law. However, it would not thereby violate any right of the [State B] under the Convention, since no such right is vested in it. This is so whatever the nature of the right that is vested in the [State B] under customary international law may be—whether it is of the first or of the second kind—and whatever the nature of the correlative obligation may be—whether it is of the first kind or of the second—that is, an obligation *erga omnes*.

43. The same holds true if and to the extent that any of the substantive provisions of the Convention may be reflective of a peremptory rule of general international law (*jus cogens*). As far as the law of treaties is concerned, the fact that a rule is a peremptory norm of international law renders void any treaty or international agreement that is in conflict with it (article 53 of the Vienna Convention on the Law of Treaties). However, the nature of [State A]'s statement is one that precludes the creation of treaty relations under the Convention between it and the [State B]. It is not its actual or intended effect to create a new treaty obligation, let alone one that is in conflict with any of the substantive provisions of the Convention.

44. The same analysis would also apply in the event that any of [State A]'s activities should constitute a serious breach of an obligation under a peremptory norm of general international law (*jus cogens*). Any such breach could cause to arise, as a matter of general

international law, the specific legal consequences that are set out in Chapter III of Part Two of the International Law Commission's Draft Articles on the Responsibility of States for Internationally Wrongful Acts (*loc. cit.* above); but there would still be no violation of any right of the [State B] under the Convention, since no such right is vested in it.

45. The possible status of any of the substantive provisions of the Convention as a norm of *jus cogens* therefore has no bearing on the answer to the question at hand.

46. In view of this analysis, it would appear that the absence of treaty relations under the Convention between [State A] and the [State B] has the consequence that it is not possible for the [State B] to trigger the procedures that are set out in article 11 of the Convention—that is, it cannot submit a communication alleging that [State A] is not giving effect to the provisions of the Convention that would have the effect of empowering the Committee to examine that communication. The right to trigger those procedures would only exist if the [State B] is vested with rights under the Convention to require [State A] that it give effect to the Convention's provisions; and that, in the absence of treaty relations between them, it does not.

47. It would only be otherwise if the substantive obligations that the Convention imposes upon the States Parties to it are of such a nature that the right to require their performance does not, at least in certain respects, depend upon the existence of bilateral treaty relations under the Convention between the two States concerned or, alternatively, if those obligations are of such a nature that it is not possible for a State party to take action the effect of which would be that the right to require their performance would not vest in any other State party.

48. There are certain indications in the case law of certain human rights bodies that this may indeed be the case. Thus, the European Commission of Human Rights as long ago as 1961 took the position that "the obligations undertaken by the High Contracting Parties in the [European Convention on Human Rights] are essentially of an objective character, being designed rather to protect the fundamental rights of individual human beings from infringement by any of the High Contracting Parties than to create subjective and reciprocal rights for the High Contracting Parties themselves" (*Austria* v. *Italy*, no. 788/60, Decision of the Commission as to admissibility of 11 January 1961, A/60/922, p. 18; reaffirmed in *France, Norway, Denmark, Sweden, Netherlands* v. *Turkey*, nos. 9940–9944/82, Decision of the Commission as to admissibility of 6 December 1983, paras. 38–43, in *Alparslan Temeltasch* v. *Switzerland*, no. 9116/80, Report of the Commission of 5 March 1983, para. 63, and in *Cyprus* v. *Turkey*, no. 25781/94, Report of the Commission of 4 June 1999, para. 71).

49. In similar vein, the European Court of Human Rights has stated that the Convention "comprises more than mere reciprocal engagements between contracting States", since it "creates, over and above a network of mutual, bilateral undertakings, objective obligations which, in the words of the Preamble, benefit from a 'collective enforcement'" (*Ireland* v. *United Kingdom*, no. 5310/71, Judgment of 18 January 1978, para. 239).

50. The Inter-American Court of Human Rights, in its Advisory Opinion of 24 September 1982 on *The effect of reservations on the entry into force of the American Convention on Human Rights*, referred to the *Austria* v. *Italy* precedent of the European Commission noted above and held that "modern human rights treaties in general, and the American Convention in particular, are not multilateral treaties of the traditional type

concluded to accomplish the reciprocal exchange of rights for the mutual benefit of the contracting States" (Advisory Opinion No. OC-2/82 of 24 September 1982, at para. 29). It went on to affirm that, "[i]n concluding these human rights treaties, the States can be deemed to submit themselves to a legal order within which they, for the common good, assume various obligations, not in relation to other States, but towards all individuals within their jurisdiction" (para. 29). Human rights treaties such as the American Convention are thus best seen, the Court stated, as a "framework enabling States to make binding unilateral commitments not to violate the human rights of individuals within their jurisdiction" (para. 33).

51. In 1999, the Inter-American Court forcefully reaffirmed this analysis and stated that "[t]he American Convention and the other human rights treaties are inspired by a set of higher common values (centered around the protection of the human person), are endowed with specific supervisory mechanisms, are applied as a collective guarantee, embody essentially objective obligations, and have a special character that sets them apart from other treaties, [...which instead...] govern mutual interests between and among the States Parties" (*Case of Ivcher-Bronstein* v. *Peru*, Judgment on Competence of 24 September 1999, para. 42).

52. As indicated by this body of case law, the "objective" or "non-reciprocal" nature of the substantive obligations under the European Convention on Human Rights and, likewise, under the American Convention on Human Rights stems, at least in part, from the fundamental notion that those obligations are subject to a system of collective guarantee and collective enforcement. Any State party may enforce the obligations of any other State party under those conventions and, in doing so, does not thereby invoke a right to the performance of a correlative obligation that is owed to it by that latter State party. Thus, in the case of the European Convention, any State party may trigger the operation of the machinery of collective enforcement that that Convention creates, without thereby invoking a right that is correlative to the obligation that is alleged to have been breached. This also holds true in the case of the American Convention in the event that the two States concerned have both deposited a declaration under article 45 or article 62 of the Convention, and have therefore recognized the competence of the Commission established by the Convention to receive and examine communications alleging that another State party has violated a human right set out in the Convention or if they have accepted the jurisdiction of the Court established by the Convention on all matters relating to the Convention's interpretation or application.

53. Following from this fundamental principle, it has been held that no State party to the European Convention can do anything that would prevent another State party from triggering in respect of it the machinery for the collective enforcement of the Convention that the Convention creates. Thus, the European Commission of Human Rights has affirmed that "to accept that a Government may void 'collective enforcement' of the Convention under Art. 24, by asserting that they do not recognise the Government of the applicant State, would defeat the purpose of the Convention" (*Cyprus* v. *Turkey*, no. 8007/77, Report of the Commission of 4 October 1983, para. 48, quoting and reaffirming paras. 43 of its Interim report on the State of the Proceedings of 12 July 1980). The fact that Turkey did not recognize the applicant as the Government of Cyprus and so did not consider it capable of lodging an application in its name therefore did not prevent the Commission from considering the complaints that Cyprus had made against it, nor did it absolve Turkey from its obligation to cooperate with the Commission in the proceedings. Significantly, the Commission also affirmed that the ability to trigger the system of

collective enforcement that the Convention creates "does not of itself envisage any direct rights or obligations between the High Contracting Parties concerned" (*loc. cit.*, quoting and reaffirming para. 40 of its Interim Report).

54. The European Court of Human Rights took a similar position in its 1995 judgment on preliminary objections in the case of *Loizidou* v. *Turkey* (no. 15318/89, Judgment on Preliminary Objections of 23 March 1995, para. 41). Thus, the Court affirmed that "recognition of an applicant Government by a respondent Government is not a precondition for either the institution of proceedings under Article 24 of the Convention or the referral of cases to the Court under Article 48". The Court added that, "[i]f it were otherwise, the system of collective enforcement which is a central element in the Convention system could be effectively neutralised by the interplay of recognition between individual Governments and States" (*ibid.*). The fact that the Government of Turkey did not accept the capacity of the applicant Government to represent the State and people of Cyprus was therefore irrelevant and the Court was not prevented for that reason from considering the case that Cyprus had referred to it.

55. In similar vein, in the 1999 *Case of Ivcher-Bronstein* v. *Peru* mentioned above, the Inter-American Court of Human Rights confirmed the "objective" nature of the obligations under the Convention and affirmed that the "international settlement of human rights cases (entrusted to tribunals like the Inter-American and European Courts of Human Rights) cannot be compared to the peaceful settlement of international disputes involving purely interstate litigation (entrusted to a tribunal like the International Court of Justice)" (*Case of Ivcher-Bronstein* v. *Peru*, Judgment on Competence of 24 September 1999, para. 48). The Court thus cited with approval the words of the European Court in the case of *Soering* v. *the United Kingdom*, that "regard must be had to [the European Convention's] special character as a treaty for the collective enforcement of human rights" and that "its provisions must [therefore] be interpreted so as to make its safeguards practical and effective" (*loc. cit.*, para. 44). No analogy could therefore be made between declarations that States may make under Article 36, paragraph, 2, of the Statute of the International Court of Justice and those that States Parties may make under the American Convention recognizing the jurisdiction of the Inter-American Court (*loc. cit.*, para. 47); and, while States may be able to withdraw the former, States Parties to the American Convention cannot withdraw the latter. Peru purported withdrawal of its declaration recognizing the Court's jurisdiction was consequently inadmissible (*loc. cit.*, para. 56); and the Court was accordingly able to proceed to consider the merits of the case that the that the Inter-American Commission on Human Rights had filed with it concerning alleged violations by Peru of Mr. Ivcher-Bronstein's rights.

56. In the case of regional human rights treaties, there is therefore a body of case law that would seem to support the proposition that one State party cannot, by any unilateral action such as a statement of non-recognition, bar any other State party from taking steps to enforce those treaties by triggering the operation of the collective machinery that those treaties create.

57. If this is indeed the case, the question arises whether the same principle applies also to multilateral conventions for the protection of human rights in general and to the Convention in particular.

58. Echoing the European and Inter-American case law, the Human Rights Committee has taken the position in its General Comment No. 24 (52) that human rights

treaties "are not a web of inter-State exchanges of mutual obligations" and that "[t]he principle of inter-State reciprocity has no place" in respect of them (CCPR/C/21/Rev.1/Add.6, reproduced in A/50/40, Vol. I, Annex V, at para.17; see also para. 7; and *cf.* the recommendation 3 of the working group on reservations of the Inter-Committee Meeting of human rights treaty bodies, HRI/MC/2007/5, at para. 16 [19]). The Committee accordingly considered that the provisions of the Vienna Convention on the Law of Treaties regarding objections to reservations are "inappropriate to address the problem of reservations to human rights treaties"; and it considered it "open to question", because of the "special characteristics" of human rights treaties such as the International Covenant on Civil and Political Rights, "what effect objections have between States *inter se*" (*loc. cit.*), specifically, whether they can have the effect of preventing the application of those treaties between the objecting State and the reserving State.

59. The Committee on Human Rights has thus come close to adopting, if it has not actually adopted, the analysis of the nature of the substantive obligations created by human rights treaties that has been espoused in the jurisprudence under the European and American conventions—an analysis that is antithetical to the notion that one State party can prevent another State party from invoking its failure to comply with its obligations under the Convention and requiring it to conform its conduct with those obligations (*cf. the Joint Separate Opinion of Judges Higgins, Elaraby,* Kooijmans, Owada and Simma in *Armed Activities on the Territory of the Congo (New Application: 2002) (Democratic Republic of the Congo* v. *Rwanda), Jurisdiction and Admissibility, Judgment, ICJ Reports 2006*, p. 4 at p. 69, para. 16).

60. In a separate, but related, line of reasoning, the Committee on Human Rights considered it to be part of the object and purpose of the Covenant "to provide an efficacious supervisory machinery for the obligations undertaken" by States parties (*loc. cit.* above, para. 7). Reservations designed to remove the "supportive guarantee" that this machinery represents would be contrary to that object and purpose and so be impermissible (*cf.* the Joint Separate Opinion of Judges Higgins, Elaraby, Kooijmans, Owada and Simma *loc. cit.* above, at p. 70, para. 21). From this, the Committee drew the conclusion that a State may not formulate a reservation the effect of which would be to exclude the obligation to present periodic reports to the Committee (*loc. cit.*, para. 11). One could also draw from it the further conclusion that, where a human rights treaty creates machinery for considering inter-State complaints regarding its implementation that (unlike that in the Covenant) is automatically applicable to States parties, reservations that would exclude the competence of that machinery, either in whole or in part, would also be impermissible. Certainly, the Committee was of the view that a reservation that would exclude its competence to interpret the Covenant would be so (*loc. cit.*).

61. This analysis would support an argument that, regardless of the juridical nature of the rights and obligations that are created by a human rights treaty, one State party to such a treaty cannot take action the effect of which would be that another State party could not trigger in respect of it any enforcement machinery that the treaty creates. Indeed, article 20, paragraph 2, of the Convention specifically stipulates that "a reservation the effect of which would inhibit the operation of any of the bodies established by the Convention [shall not] be allowed". A reservation that would inhibit the Committee established under the Convention from examining any communication that might be made by a specific State party would seem to fall within the scope of this stipulation, just as much as one that would

inhibit it from examining a communication by any State party. If such a reservation is impermissible, a statement of the kind at issue here would arguably be impermissible, also.

62. There is no evidence, however, that such an analysis is supported by States Parties to the Covenant. Indeed, several seem to have taken a different view of the matter. Thus, the United States, the United Kingdom and France each submitted observations on the Committee's General Comment No. 24 (52), maintaining that, notwithstanding anything that the Committee might have said to the contrary, the rules set out in articles 20 and 21 of the Vienna Convention on the Law of Treaties do in fact apply in respect of reservations to the Covenant that are not incompatible with its object and purpose (see respectively: A/50/40, vol. I, Annex VI A, section 5; A/50/40 Vol. I, Annex VI B, at paras. 5, 13 and 15; and A/51/40, Vol. I, Annex VI, at para. 10). They accordingly considered that a State party is able to object to a permissible reservation and to do so in a manner that, as contemplated in article 21, paragraph 3, of the Vienna Convention, prevents the entry into force of the Covenant as between itself and the reserving State—a position that is corroborated by the practice of States parties to the Covenant in responding to reservations (*Multilateral Treaties Deposited with the Secretary General*, Chapter IV, no. 4). The United Kingdom specifically affirmed that the practice of States parties demonstrates that they do in fact regard its substantive provisions as creating "a network of mutual bilateral undertakings" between the States parties to it (A/50/40, vol. I, Annex VI B., at para. 5).

63. As for the Convention itself, the Committee on the Elimination of Racial Discrimination seems at one point to have taken an approach similar to that of the Human Rights Committee. Thus, in 1997, the Committee decided to propose the topic of reservations to treaties for consideration by the Sub-Commission of the Commission on Human Rights on Prevention of Discrimination and Protection of Minorities. In explaining its proposal, the note that the secretariat prepared for the Committee (see CERD/C/SR.1189, para. 52) stated that the "concept of reciprocity" cannot be applied to treaties for the promotion of human rights (E/CN.4/1997/Sub.2/1997/31, at p. 3). Six years later, in a Preliminary Opinion on reservations to treaties on human rights that was prepared for the Committee by three of its members, it was similarly stated that "human rights treaties are not a web of inter-State exchange[s] of mutual obligations" and that the implementation of the Convention is therefore, as in the case of other human treaties, "not a matter of reciprocity". At the same time, however, the Preliminary Opinion makes clear that its authors considered the Convention as, at least in part, a matter of "State to State relationships and commitments" and that becoming party to the Convention is a matter of establishing "relationships between different States parties" (CERD/C/62/Misc.20/rev.3, at p. 2).

64. This latter analysis is borne out by the Committee's consideration in [year] of [State D]'s sixth periodic report under article 9, paragraphl (*b*), of the Convention ([document symbol]). Indeed, the Committee there seems to have taken the view that the Convention consists solely of commitments that are owed State to State in the normal manner and that it is possible for one State party to prevent those relationships from arising *vis-à-vis* another specific State party.

65. Thus, [State D]'s sixth periodic report stated that [State A]'s occupation of the [territory D] prevented the application of the Convention in those territories and then made a number of allegations regarding [State A]'s activities there ([paragraph number]). The [State D] representative repeated this in introducing his country's report before the

Committee ([document symbol and paragraph number]). A member of the Committee raised a point of order, stating that this represented a communication by a State party to the effect that another State party is not giving effect to the provisions of the Convention, within the meaning of article 11, paragraph 1, and that the Committee had consequently to follow the procedures set out in that article ([paragraph number]). In response, the representative of [State D] recalled that, on its accession to the Convention, his country had made a statement that its doing so did not signify that [State D] was thereby entering into a relationship with [State A] regarding any matter regulated by the Convention. He also stated that his country was not invoking article 11 in this particular case ([paragraph number]). Pursuant to the Committee's rules of procedure, the Chairman ruled that the relevant portion of [State D]'s report did not constitute a communication under article 11, paragraph 1, of the Convention ([paragraph number]). Explaining his ruling, he stated, among other things, that States Parties to the Convention had not raised any objection to the reservation made by [State D] at the time of its accession, yet article 11, paragraph 2, clearly implied that a relationship under the Convention must exist between two States Parties concerned ([document symbol and paragraph number]). An appeal having been made against the Chairman's ruling, it was put to a vote. His ruling was then upheld by 11 votes to 2, with 1 abstention ([document symbol and paragraph number]).

66. The fact that, in the present case, the Committee, consistently with article 11, paragraph 1, of the Convention, transmitted the communication of the [State B] to [State A] does not entail that it has now rejected this analysis. Its decision at its [number] session to give [State A] the opportunity to inform the Committee whether it wished to supply any relevant information on the issues of the Committee's jurisdiction or the admissibility of the [State B]'s communication clearly indicates that it has yet to consider the issue.

67. The practice of States Parties to the Convention in formulating and reacting to reservations to it and in making and reacting to statements of non-recognition would seem to indicate that they consider that the legal relationships established by the Convention are ones of the normal kind—namely, that they consist of obligations with correlative rights to require their performance—and that it is consequently possible for a State party to prevent those relationships from arising between it and another State party at the same time that those relationships exist between it and other States Parties. There is nothing in that practice to suggest that States Parties consider that the Convention creates a layer of "objective" obligations and rights, over and on top of the obligations and rights of a "reciprocal" nature. Indeed, the fact that several States Parties evidently consider that, by objecting to reservations, it is possible to prevent the entry into force of the Convention between themselves and reserving States concerned suggests that they do not (see the objection by Austria to the reservation of Saudi Arabia, of Cyprus to the declaration by Turkey, of Denmark to the reservation of Yemen, of Finland to the reservation of Yemen, of France to the reservation of Saudi Arabia, of Germany to the reservations of Saudi Arabia and Thailand, of Mexico to the reservation of Yemen, of the Netherlands to the reservation of Yemen, of Norway to the reservation of Saudi Arabia, of Romania to the reservation of Thailand, of Spain to the reservation of Saudi Arabia, of Sweden to the reservation of Yemen and to the declaration of Turkey and of the United Kingdom to the declaration of Turkey and to the reservations of Thailand and Grenada: *Multilateral Treaties Deposited with Secretary-General*, Chapter IV, no. 2).

68. There is also nothing in the practice of the States Parties to the Convention that would suggest that they consider that a State party cannot take action that would result in articles 11 to 13 of the Convention not applying as between that State and other States Parties. Indeed, it would appear from the Committee's consideration of [State D]'s sixth periodic report, discussed above, that the Committee considered this to be entirely possible.

Conclusion

69. The following conclusions can be drawn in the light of the preceding analysis:

(1) A State party to the Convention is able, through a unilateral statement that is suitably framed, to prevent the creation of obligations and rights under the Convention between itself and another specific State party.

(2) [State A]'s communication of [date] is framed in such a manner as to have that effect as between itself and the [State B].

(3) There is nothing, either in the juridical nature of the legal relationships that are established between States Parties to the Convention or about the provisions of article 11, 12 and 13 of the Convention that would bar one State party from taking action, by means of a unilateral statement suitably framed, the effect of which would be that a right does not vest in another specific State party to submit a valid and effective communication against it under article 11, paragraph 1, and so trigger the operation of the procedures set out in those articles.

(4) [State A]'s communication of [date] is suitably framed to have that effect *vis-à-vis* the [State B].

(5) [State A]'s communication of [date] therefore, of itself, precludes the Committee from examining a communication filed by the [State B] against it under articles 11 to 13 of the Convention (and *vice versa*).

B. Legal opinions of the secretariats of intergovernmental organizations related to the United Nations

1. International Labour Organization

(Submitted by the Office of the Legal Adviser of the International Labour Office)

Legal opinion rendered during the 106th session of the International Labour Conference (June 2019) regarding questions concerning the legal aspects of the possible recognition of occupational safety and health as a fifth category of fundamental principles and rights at work in the ILO Centenary Declaration for the Future of Work

Fundamental principles and rights at work—No legal impediment to International Labour Conference recognizing additional fundamental principle and right at work through same process as ILO Centenary Declaration—Procedural options include amending declaration or adoption of additional declaration—Relevant instruments could be identified at time of adoption or

LATER STAGE—AMENDMENT OF CENTENARY DECLARATION WOULD NOT ENSURE ACCEPTANCE OF PRINCIPLE BY STATES PARTY TO TREATIES REFERRING TO DECLARATION

In response to questions concerning the possible recognition of a fifth category of fundamental principles and rights at work, the Legal Adviser indicated that while it would, of course, belong to the Conference or the Governing Body to determine to which Convention or Conventions a fifth fundamental principle and right at work would apply, there had been several important developments over the past 20 years pointing at an emerging consensus about the fundamental character and importance of the Occupational Safety and Health Convention, 1981 (No. 155),* and the Promotional Framework for Occupational Safety and Health Convention, 2006 (No. 187),** among all occupational safety and health (OSH) standards. Both instruments underlined the importance of applying a systems approach to OSH management and of progressively establishing the goal of a preventative safety and health culture. The relevant instruments could be identified either at the time of negotiating the adoption of a new declaration, or at a later stage, as the Declaration should not necessarily include an express reference to the Convention or Conventions concerned. Second, as regards the role of the Standards Review Mechanism (SRM) in the consideration of the relevant instruments, it was correct to say that the SRM's mandate was principally to identify standards in need of revision and therefore the SRM process was of little relevance to the current deliberations on the potential selection of fundamental OSH Conventions. Third, in response to whether it was possible to amend the 1998 Declaration through the ILO Centenary Declaration, the Legal Adviser expressed the view that, legally speaking, there was nothing to prevent the Conference as the supreme deliberative and executive organ of the Organization from adopting a declaration that would supplement or otherwise modify, in whole or in part, an earlier declaration. The Conference had therefore the authority 20 years after having recognized the prominence of four categories of fundamental principles and rights at work to "elevate" another principle, namely the workers' right to a safe and healthy working environment, to the same level of prominence. The legal consequence of the recognition of a new fundamental principle would be that the 1998 Declaration, as well as all other formal instruments referring to four categories of fundamental principles and rights at work, should be henceforth considered implicitly amended—by virtue of the principle that a later law repealed an earlier law or *lex posterior derogat priori*—but only to the extent that the ILO Centenary Declaration would specifically modify the scope and content of their provisions. Fourth, with respect to whether it would be necessary, following the identification of OSH as a fifth fundamental principle and right at work, to refer to two separate authoritative declarations, he considered that that would not appear to be necessary since the 1998 Declaration would have to be read and understood in the light of subsequent developments, such as the adoption of a Centenary Declaration and any additional elements that the latter would possibly bring in the field of OSH and fundamental principles and rights at work. Strictly speaking, no formal revision of the 1998 Declaration seemed to be required although such a possibility lay within the discretionary powers of the Conference. Among the declarations that had been

* Convention (No. 155) concerning Occupational Safety and Health and the Working Environment (Geneva, 1983), United Nations, *Treaty Series*, vol. 1331, p 279.

** Convention (No. 187) concerning the Promotional Framework for Occupational Safety and Health (Geneva, 2006), *ibid.*, vol. 2564, p. 291.

formally amended in the past, the 1964 Declaration concerning the Policy of "Apartheid" of the Republic of South Africa and the MNE Declaration were just two examples. Fifth, in relation to what would happen if the Conference or the Governing Body could not agree on the relevant Convention or Conventions despite the ILO Centenary Declaration elevating OSH to the status of a fundamental principle and right at work, the Legal Adviser indicated that such eventuality had not yet been considered but he believed that an institutional solution should in principle always be possible.[1]

The Legal Adviser, responding to further observations, reiterated that there was no legal impediment to the Conference recognizing a new fundamental principle and right at work through the ILO Centenary Declaration. That would involve the same sovereign organ, the same procedure and the same constitutional logic that also underpinned the 1998 Declaration, namely that the protection of workers' safety and health had a clear and solid constitutional basis—both the preamble of the Constitution and the Declaration of Philadelphia contained express references to protection of disease and injury and adequate protection for the life and health of workers—so that Members had an obligation arising from the very fact of their membership to respect the principles concerning the fundamental right which was the subject of the Convention or Conventions recognized as fundamental in the area of OSH. The Conference could decide to either formally revise the 1998 Declaration or to do so through the adoption of a new declaration. The explanations given aimed at clarifying what was legally feasible, without expressing preference for any specific option. Finally, with respect to the question raised about the implications of the possible adoption of a new declaration supplementing the 1998 Declaration on the numerous multilateral agreements that made express reference to the 1998 Declaration, he noted that a formal revision of the 1998 Declaration would give more visibility to the recognition of OSH as a new fundamental principle and would facilitate the "reading" of the Declaration especially in the context of trade agreements, such as the 2018 trade agreement between the United States, Mexico and Canada, that made explicit reference to the 1998 Declaration. It should be borne in mind, however, that a formal amendment of the 1998 Declaration could not ensure by itself the acceptance of the new fundamental principle by States parties to those trade agreements.[2]

---

[1] Provisional Record No. 6-B (Rev.), International Labour Conference 108th Session, Geneva, June 2019, para. 1002.

[2] Provisional Record No. 6-B (Rev.), International Labour Conference 108th Session, Geneva, June 2019, para. 1011.

2. United Nations Industrial Development Organization

(Submitted by the Legal Adviser of the United Nations Industrial Development Organization)

(*a*) Internal e-mail message to the UNIDO Chief of Financial Department and to the Human Resource Officer concerning subsidization of after-service self-insurance (ASHI)

Acquired rights of staff members—Social security—After-service health insurance (ASHI)—Legality of lowering rate of subsidization—Rate of ASHI subsidization treated as acquired right—Past changes only applied to future staff members

Dear colleagues,

LEG has prepared the attached talking points on the rate of subsidization of ASHI in preparation for possible discussions in the context of the informal working group on PBC-related issues.

Talking points
Rate of subsidization of ASHI

1. The Office of Legal Affairs (LEG) was asked to provide an opinion concerning the legality of lowering the rate of subsidization of after-service health insurance (ASHI) from 75 per cent to 50 per cent. This question was also examined in 1999.

2. The rates of subsidization of health insurance, including ASHI, were established by the Director General pursuant to his authority under staff regulation 8.2.* The rate of subsidization of ASHI is inextricably linked to the rate of subsidization of in-service health insurance. Staff members are subsidized at the rate of 50 per cent in the expectation that, if eligible for ASHI, the subsidy will increase to 75 per cent upon retirement. At the United Nations, the health insurance subsidy is effectively higher at 67 per cent for both current staff members and retirees.

3. To avoid legal liabilities, UNIDO is very cautious about making changes to the system of ASHI. For example, when the conditions of eligibility were tightened (*i.e.* the minimum period of service was increased from 5 to 10 years), the change was only applied prospectively to new staff members.

4. Several reports have examined the subject of ASHI in recent years, including reports by the ICSC, the Secretary-General, and the External Auditor of UNIDO. None of the reports recommended lowering the subsidy for ASHI:

- The ICSC pointed out that the subsidy is higher in the comparator (US) and other civil services and recommended keeping the subsidy at its current level. The General Assembly accepted that recommendation in 2014.

* Available at https://www.unido.org/overview/legal-resources/basic-legal-documents/staff-regulations-and-rules.

- The Secretary-General stated in his most recent report on the management of ASHI that there is no argument for reducing the subsidy and that a reduction would amount to an inappropriate transfer of an organizational obligation to the staff.
- The External Auditor stated in his report for 2017 that UNIDO has the responsibility towards its employees to be able to cover ASHI in future and recommended that UNIDO consider the partial funding of its ASHI liabilities.

5. The Legal Adviser concluded that:

- In practice, UNIDO treats the rate of subsidization of ASHI as an acquired right of current staff members, *i.e.*, a right that must be respected even if the rules are changed.
- As things stand, there are no grounds for the Director General to reduce the subsidy. If the subsidy were lowered, there would be a high risk of prolonged and disruptive litigation and that UNIDO would be found to be in breach of its obligations.
- If necessary, the subsidy could be lowered prospectively for new staff recruited after a certain date. Given the ongoing discussions in the common system, it is advisable for UNIDO to act in concert with other agencies.

1 February 2019

(*b*) Internal e-mail message to the UNIDO Chief of Cabinet concerning the proposed award of a decoration of honor to the UNIDO Director General by the Minister of the [State]

Gifts and honours—Director General is approving authority for acceptance of gifts, honours and remuneration by UNIDO staff members—Director General may not accept decoration or honour from Government if doing so would compromise or be seen as compromising independence and loyalty to UNIDO

I refer to your urgent email of [date] forwarding an email of the same date from [Name] on the above-mentioned subject. You sought my advice on the proposed award of a decoration of honour to the Director General on [date] by the Minister of [Ministry] of the [State].

In view of the clarifications that [Name] provided in her email of [date], namely, that the proposed award ("[title]") is not a gift and that it recognizes the contribution of public servants to the enhanced development of the country, and the fact that under UNIDO/DGB/(M).115 of 1 March 2010 (Code of Ethical Conduct), the Director General is the approving authority for acceptance of gifts, honours and remuneration by UNIDO staff members, I limit myself to the following comments.

The decision on whether to accept the decoration/honour lies with the Director General, as the highest approving authority under the DG bulletin. As a legal matter, the Director General may not accept a decoration/honour from a Government if by doing so his independence and loyalty to the Organization would be compromised (or be seen as being compromised). Under the given circumstances, I do not see a basis for questioning the Director General's status or impartiality were he to accept the proposed decoration of honor.

10 June 2019

(*c*) Internal e-mail message to the Director of the UNIDO Department of External Relations concerning the privileges and immunities of UNIDO Goodwill Ambassadors

Status of goodwill ambassadors—Goodwill ambassadors may be considered experts on mission—Status may be clarified in terms of reference—Relevant obligations under headquarters agreement apply

I refer to your email of [date] asking for urgent feedback on whether the Director General's letter of designation of a UNIDO goodwill ambassador may state that he or she has the status of an expert on mission for UNIDO.

The proposal is, in principle, acceptable from a legal perspective. LEG is ready to review the draft letter of designation in due course. I suggest that you also add a new section to the terms of reference for goodwill ambassadors as follows:

Legal Status

Without prejudice to any other privileges and immunities accorded to them, Goodwill Ambassadors shall enjoy during the period of their missions, including the time spent on journeys in connection with their missions, the status of expert on mission for UNIDO under the Convention on the Privileges and Immunities of the United Nations[*] or Annex XVII to the Convention on the Privileges and Immunities of the Specialized Agencies,[**] as applicable.

In [State], the provisions of the Convention on the Privileges and Immunities of the United Nations are supplemented by the provisions of the Headquarters Agreement of UNIDO.[***] In terms of article XIII, section 44, of the Headquarters Agreement, UNIDO must communicate to the Government of [State] a list of experts on mission for UNIDO. UNIDO should therefore notify the Government of the names of goodwill ambassadors in the same way as it does for other experts and consultants.

[...]

21 June 2019

[*] Convention on the Privileges and Immunities of the United Nations (New York, 1946), United Nations, *Treaty Series*, vol. 1, p. 15.

[**] Annex XVII—United Nations Industrial Development Organization (UNIDO)—to the Convention on the Privileges and Immunities of the Specialized Agencies (Vienna, 1987), *ibid.*, vol. 1482, p. 244. See also Convention on the Privileges and Immunities of the Specialized Agencies (New York, 1947), *ibid.*, vol. 33, p. 261.

[***] Agreement regarding the Headquarters of the United Nations Industrial Development Organization (New York, 1967), *ibid.*, vol. 600, p. 94.

(*d*) Internal e-mail message to the Director of the UNIDO Department of External Relations concerning several legal questions on the resumed forty-seventh session of the Industrial Development Board

Rules of procedure of the Industrial Development Board—Resumed sessions—Session adjourned but not closed may be resumed—Rule 8.2 regulating notification of new session does not apply—Additional agenda not required in resumed session—Additional documents in-session documentation—Delegations need not reregister for resumed session—Officers and bureau continue in office for resumed session—Rule 84 on circulation of proposals applies—Required majorities for voting in Board and General Conference

Reference is made to your email of [date] asking for urgent advice on a number of questions in connection with the resumption of IDB.47 and the procedure for adoption of the programme and budgets for the next biennium. I confirm my availability for a meeting to discuss the matter prior to [date] and respond to your questions below.

1. Having asked for objections from the plenary, the President of the Board adjourned the forty-seventh session in line with rule 9 of the Rules of Procedure of the Board. Are we therefore correct in asserting, that the forty-seventh session is ongoing and that the resumption of the session will not constitute a new session (either regular [Rule 3] or special [Rule 4])?

LEG: The forty-seventh session is not ongoing as such. If the Board decided to adjourn the forty-seventh session temporarily under rule 9 of its rules of procedure, then its meetings will be a continuation of the same session once they resume. There is no question of there being a new session if the forty-seventh session was not closed but was merely adjourned.

2. Following from 1 above:

a) The timing of the notification for the resumption is not governed by Rule 8.2, as it is neither a regular nor a special session. While we will of course endeavour to get the notification out as soon as possible once a date is known (further to the consultations by [initials]), do we have to abide by the "not later than fourteen days before the opening date of the session" in Rule 8.2 (b)?

LEG: I agree that rule 8.2 does not regulate the timing of the Director General's notification of the opening date and place of a resumed session of the Board. Under rule 9, the Board could adjourn for a short or a long period. As a practical matter, the period of notification depends on the period of the adjournment. A reasonable position for the Secretariat to take would be that the notification will go out immediately after the date of the resumption has been set.

b) There is no need for an additional agenda, as the already adopted agenda for the forty-seventh session continues to be "active" and the two items (5 (c) on the scale of assessments and 6 on the programme and budgets) are still to be closed;

LEG: I agree. (The approach was different with respect to the resumed seventeenth session of the General Conference in view of the precedent set by the first session of the Conference.)

c) Any additional documentation that will be required by the consultations for the resumed session will fall under the category of "in-session documentation" (Rule 16), rather than "pre-session documentation" (Rule 15);

LEG: Rule 15 relates to the distribution of documentation required for consideration of items on the provisional agenda. Therefore, it does not appear to govern the present situation. If extensive additional documents are required once the session has resumed, rule 16 on in-session documentation will apply.

d) The registrations of the delegations to the forty-seventh session of the Board (Rule 21.3) continue to be "active". However, for practical reasons, in the notification sent out for the resumed session (2 (a) above), we will request Permanent Missions register any changes in their delegation from those already registered;

LEG: I agree that delegations do not need to re-register but may be asked to inform the Director General of changes in their composition.

e) The bureau of the Board (Rules 23–27) continues to be the one elected at the forty-seventh session.

LEG: This is also my view.

Any proposal coming out of the consultations and approved by the resumed session of the Board in line with the above, would constitute an "other proposal" and would therefore need to be submitted to the GC at least one day prior to its consideration in the GC, unless the President of the GC would decide otherwise, with the consent of the Conference (Rule 84 of the Rules of Procedure of the GC).

LEG: If decisions of the Board adopting the programme and budgets are usually treated by the Conference as proposals within the meaning of rule 84 of its rules of procedure, then the requirements on circulation in rule 84 would apply in this case as well.

4. Following from the above, therefore, the resumed session of the Board could, technically, also take place the day before the GC;

LEG: I agree that the Board could resume its forty-seventh session the day before the opening of the General Conference and close the session on the same day.

5. In the case of a vote on the programme and budgets, the majorities required would be:

a) At the IDB: two-thirds majority of the members of the Board present and voting (Article 14.3 of the Constitution and Rule 51.2 (a));

LEG: This is correct.

b) At the GC: two-thirds majority of the Members present and voting, in case the vote is on the proposal considered by the Board (Article 14.4 (a) of the Constitution and Rule 92.2 (c) of the Rules of Procedure of the GC), or two-thirds majority of all Members, in case the proposal approved by the Board is further amended (Article 14.4 (b) and 14.6 of the Constitution and Rules 87 and 92.1 (c));

LEG: This is correct.

c) Following from (b) above, if the Board approves a proposal with a two-thirds majority of Members of the Board present and voting, and at the GC an amendment is proposed, the amendment:

i. Would require a meeting of the PBC and subsequently the IDB, meeting concurrently with the Conference, to allow for their consideration of the amendments to what was adopted by the Board (Rule 87 of the Rules of Procedure of the GC).

LEG: This is correct.

ii. Should the proposed amendment then be passed by the Board (with a majority of two-thirds of the Board Members present and voting), would it become a proposal of the Board and therefore require a majority at the GC of two-thirds of Members present and voting (92.2), or two-thirds of all Members (87)?

LEG: The relevant rule is rule 87.2 of the rules of procedure of the Conference: proposed amendments to the programme and budgets adopted by the Board shall be subject to the procedure set out in rule 87.1, which requires the Conference to approve the amendments by a two-thirds majority of all Members.

12 July 2019

(*e*) Internal e-mail message to the Director of the UNIDO Department of External Relations concerning UNIDO's share of the contribution to the United Nations Resident Coordinator (UNRC) system for the period 2020–2021

United Nations resident coordinator system—Cost-sharing by Sustainable Development Group member entities—UNIDO contribution determined on basis of Agency to Agency Contribution Agreement

Kindly refer to the request of the chair of an informal meeting of the IDB.47 held on [date] for a legal opinion on the amount of UNIDO's share of the contribution to the United Nations Resident Coordinator (UNRC) system for the period 2020–2021. In particular, the issue presented for legal advice was whether the amount of the contribution to be doubled pursuant to General Assembly resolution 72/279 is USD 1,552,998, which represents the amount that UNIDO paid as its contribution for the period 2018–2019.

Please find attached the requested legal opinion.

[…]

I. Introduction

1. The Secretariat has been requested to provide a legal opinion on the amount of UNIDO's share of the contribution to the United Nations Resident Coordinator (UNRC) system for the period 2020–2021. In particular, the issue presented is whether the amount of the contribution to be doubled pursuant to General Assembly resolution 72/279[1] is USD 1,552,998, which represents the amount of *UNIDO's past contribution* for the period 2018–2019.[2]

2. The legal opinion concludes that doubling UNIDO's past contribution (USD 1,552,998) is not in accordance with resolution 72/279. Doubling UNIDO's contribution under the current UNDG cost-sharing arrangement should be determined by the cost-sharing formula that applies to all contributing UNDG member entities.

---

[1] See General Assembly resolution 72/279 of 31 May 2018.

[2] The United Nations Secretariat has informed UNIDO that, according to its records, UNIDO's share amounts to USD 1,318,560 per annum, or USD 2,637,121 per annum following General Assembly resolution 72/279. Cf. Letter dated [date] from [Name], UN Assistant Secretary-General for Development Coordination, to […], UNIDO Director General.

II. Background

3. In its resolution 72/279 on the repositioning of the UN development system, the General Assembly decided, inter alia, to establish a hybrid funding model to support a reformed Resident Coordinator system. As concerns the UN Development Group (renamed, UN Sustainable Development Group) agency cost-sharing pillar of the hybrid funding model, the General Assembly decided "to provide sufficient funding in line with the report of the Secretary-General, on an annual basis starting from 1 January 2019, through: … (*b*) Doubling the current *United Nations Development Group cost-sharing arrangement* among United Nations development system entities".[3] The General Assembly also called upon "all Member States in the relevant governing bodies of all United Nations development system entities to ensure that all entities double their agreed contributions under the *current United Nations Development Group cost-sharing arrangement*".[4]

A. The UN Agency to UN Agency Contribution Agreement

4. As a legal matter, the share of UNIDO's contribution to the UNRC system is established pursuant to a UN Agency to UN Agency Contribution Agreement signed in January 2014, which has been amended on two occasions[5] (unless the context otherwise requires, references to "Agreement" shall hereafter refer to the Agreement as amended and presently in force).

5. The Agreement is composed of 11 parts, which are lettered A to K, and three Annexes, which are numbered 1 to 3. According to part A ("Summary"), the "Contribution Amount" is expressed as follows:

> "USD 763,181 for the period 1/1/2018–31/12/2018, and USD 789,817 for the period 1/1/2019–31/12/2019.
>
> Each Agency's Contribution towards the Activities for calendar year 2016 and thereafter shall be determined through a consultative process among the Agencies convened by UN DOCO before December 1st, 2014 and every year or second year thereafter depending on the contributing agency's budget approval cycle."

6. Part B of the Agreement ("Contribution") reflects the foregoing provision and makes clear that the Contribution shall be made "in accordance with the UNDG cost-sharing formula (Annex 2)".

7. Part A of the Agreement also identifies Annexes 1, 2 and 3, as follows:

> "1) 'UNDG Review of Funding Modalities in Support of the RC System. Summary Note' (22 May 2013).
>
> 2) UNDG cost-sharing formula.
>
> 3) RC system standard structure model and budget for UNDG cost-sharing."

8. Part H of the Agreement ("Amendments") provides as follows:

> "The present Agreement, including its Annexes, may be modified or amended only by written agreement between the two Agencies. Notwithstanding the foregoing, any proposed modification or amendment to the method of assessment of a Contributing

---

[3] See General Assembly resolution 72/279 of 31 May 2018, paragraph 10.

[4] See General Assembly resolution 72/279 of 31 May 2018, paragraph 12.

[5] UNIDO signed the first amendment (Amendment 1) in March 2016 and the second amendment (Amendment 2) in May 2018.

Agency's annual contribution as specified in Section B above, or to the UNDG cost-sharing formula set in Annex 2, shall be subject to consultation and agreement amongst UNDG member organizations prior to the modification or amendment of relevant provisions in the present Agreement."

B. Amendments 1 and 2 to the Agreement

a) Amendment 1

9. Annex 2 was amended in 2016 pursuant to "Amendment 1" to the Agreement. According to Amendment 1, "Annex 2 shall be replaced by the new Annex 2 hereby attached with the revised UNDG cost-sharing formula".

10. The new Annex 2 includes three tables, which are numbered 1 to 3. Table 1 provides formula-relevant data in respect of the participating UNDG entities, such as staff count, expenditures, and number of UNDAFs. Tables 2 and 3 break down the elements in the cost-sharing formula and specify the total to be contributed by each entity. According to table 2, UNIDO's share in respect of 2016 amounted to USD 1,274,092; according to table 3, UNIDO's share in respect of 2017 amounted to USD 1,318,560.

11. The amounts in Annex 2, however, were not reflected as the "Contribution Amount" in the Agreement as amended by Amendment 1. The Agreement as amended by Amendment 1 specifies a "Contribution Amount" of "USD 763,181 for the period 1/1/2016–31/12/2016, and USD 789,817 for the period 1/1/2017–31/12/2017".

12. The explanation for the discrepancy lies in the understanding that the parties reached at the time of the conclusion of Amendment 1. UNIDO explained that UNIDO's share according to the cost-sharing formula included costs that were attributable to non-Member States of UNIDO. Based on the scale of assessments corresponding to 2016–2017, UNIDO Member States accounted for only 59.9 per cent of the UN scale. UNIDO thus offered to pay in respect of 2016 USD 1,274,092 x 0.599 = USD 763,181. It was also agreed to pay in respect of 2017 an amount proportionately similar, USD 1,318,560 x 0.599 = USD 789,817. With this understanding as to the amounts to pay in respect of 2016 and 2017, Amendment 1 was signed in March 2016.

b) Amendment 2

13. The Agreement was subsequently amended in 2018 for a second time ("Amendment 2"). The sole amendment concerned the Contribution Amount, which was defined as "USD 763,181 for the period 1/1/2018–31/12/2018, and USD 789,817 for the period 1/1/2019–31/12/2019". As in the case of Amendment 1, all other terms and conditions of the Agreement, except as so amended, remained unchanged and continued in full force and effect. Thus, Amendment 2 did not modify either the cost-sharing formula or the formula-relevant data as contained in Annex 2 of the Agreement.

III. Legal Opinion

14. In its resolution 72/279, the General Assembly decided to double the current UNDG cost-sharing arrangement among UN development system entities. It called upon all Member States in the relevant governing bodies of all UN development system entities to ensure that all entities double their agreed contributions under the current

UNDG cost-sharing arrangement. Therefore, the key issue is to determine what the General Assembly refers to as *the current UNDG cost-sharing arrangement.*

15. In the case of UNIDO, the principal legal instrument that defines its obligations to contribute to the UNDG cost-sharing arrangement is the Agreement. The Agreement stipulates in Annex 2 the terms of the current UNDG cost-sharing formula. Under said formula, three elements determine the Organization's share of the UNDG cost-sharing arrangement: 1) annual base fee, which is contributed by all UNDG members; 2) amount based on the Organization's staff size and expenditures, where the contribution is calculated in proportion to the Organization's share of the total UNDG staff count and UNDG expenditures; and 3) amount based on the Organization's participation in UN Development Assistance Frameworks (UNDAFs) and Integrated Strategic Frameworks (ISFs), which is referred to as system-load. Annex 2 further stipulates that the UNRC system funding requirements will be subject to adjustments for a variety of factors, such as inflation based on ICSC salary scales, changes in the country classifications of non-crisis countries, CEB financial and personnel statistics, and statistics on agency participation in UNDAFs and ISFs.

16. Under the Agreement, the "agreed contributions under the current UNDG cost-sharing arrangement" can only be understood by reference to Annex 2 to the Agreement. Any other figure, while agreed in respect of a specific period (2018–2019, for example), would not constitute an amount agreed under the current UNDG cost-sharing arrangement. The cost-sharing arrangement is determined by a cost-sharing formula, which is outlined in Annex 2. Under the formula, the number of Member States is not a factor. It follows that the Contribution Amount which UNIDO recently paid under the Agreement represents an amount that, although agreed to by the parties, is not under the current UNDG cost-sharing arrangement. As the Assistant Secretary-General for Development Coordination has written,

> "The cost-sharing formula devised is a function of how much 'use' entities avail of the coordination system, calculated using proxy indicators such as staff numbers and UNDAF budgets. ... As such, the number of Member States that belong to individual UNSDG entities is not directly relevant to the calculation."[6]

17. Furthermore, none of the amendments to the Agreement revised the cost-sharing formula to take account of the composition of a contributing agency's membership. The reduced amounts which UNIDO paid pursuant to the amendments did not amend the current UNDG cost-sharing arrangement. As indicated above, pursuant to part H of the Agreement any modification or amendment to the UNDG cost-sharing arrangement shall be subject to consultation and agreement amongst UNDG member organizations.

IV. Conclusion

18. As a legal matter, the amount of UNIDO's share of the contribution to the UNRC system for the period 2020–2021 should be determined by the cost-sharing formula that applies to all contributing UNDG member entities. Therefore, the amount of USD 1,552,998, which represents the reduced amount that UNIDO paid as its contribution for the period 2018–2019, is not the amount to be doubled pursuant to General Assembly resolution 72/279.

---

[6] Letter dated [date] from [Name], UN Assistant Secretary-General for Development Coordination, to [...], UNIDO Director General.

(*f*) External e-mail message to the Legal Adviser of [a United Nations Organization] concerning amendment of the UNIDO Constitution: New obligations/fundamental change

Amendments to UNIDO Constitution—Amendments regulated by article 23 of UNIDO Constitution—Amendments not qualified by nature

Kindly refer to your email of [date] asking us if the Constitution of UNIDO has a provision that prescribes different procedures for its amendment if such amendment implies "new obligations" for Member States or involves a "fundamental change" of the Constitution and whether there has been any interpretive decision or guidance by our supreme policymaking organ.

I wish to inform you that amending the Constitution of UNIDO is regulated by Article 23 of the Constitution as follows:

> 1. At any time after the second regular session of the Conference any Member may propose amendments to this Constitution. Texts of proposed amendments shall be promptly communicated by the Director General to all Members and shall not be considered by the Conference until ninety days after the dispatch of such communication.
>
> 2. Except as specified in paragraph 3, an amendment shall come into force and be binding on all Members when:
>
> (*a*) It is recommended by the Board to the Conference;
>
> (*b*) It is approved by the Conference by a two-thirds, majority of all Members;
>
> (*c*) Two-thirds of the Members have deposited instruments of ratification, acceptance or approval of the amendment with the Depositary.
>
> 3. An amendment relating to Article 6, 9, 10, 13, 14 or 23 or to Annex 11 shall come into force and be binding on all Members when:
>
> (*a*) It is recommended by the Board to the Conference by a two-thirds majority of all members of the Board;
>
> and
>
> (*b*) It is approved by the Conference by a two-thirds majority of all Members;
>
> (*c*) Three-fourths of the Members have deposited instruments of ratification, acceptance or approval of the amendment with the Depositary.

As can be seen, Article 23 qualifies neither the nature of an amendment nor does it prescribe different procedures for an amendment if such amendment implies "new obligations" for Member States or involves a "fundamental change" of the Constitution.

UNIDO's Constitution has not been amended so far and the General Conference has not provided any guidance beyond that provided in Article 23.

21 August 2019

(*g*) Inter-office memorandum to the UNIDO Director General concerning a Judgment of the [State A] Supreme Court of [date] in a dispute between an UNIDO consultant and the [Regional health insurance fund]

STATUS OF AFFILIATE PERSONNEL—SOCIAL SECURITY—ISA-HOLDERS AND CONSULTANTS NOT UNIDO OFFICIALS—ISA-HOLDERS AND CONSULTANTS NOT EXCLUDED FROM HOST COUNTRY SOCIAL SECURITY SYSTEM UNDER UNIDO HEADQUARTERS AGREEMENT

1. The purpose of this memorandum is to report briefly on a recent judgment concerning UNIDO delivered by the Supreme Court of [State A] (*Name*).

2. The case concerned a dispute over whether a consultant of UNIDO, [Name], was entitled to receive the [State A] child-care allowance from [Month A] to [Month B] [year], while she was still a national of [State B]. In [year], the responsible *[Regional health insurance fund]* claimed back the amount of the child-care allowance it had paid to [Name] for that period (some [currency and amount]). The *[Regional health insurance fund]* wrongly argued that [Name] had been an official of UNIDO at the time and, accordingly, that she had not been eligible to receive the allowance by virtue of Section 39(*b*) of the Headquarters Agreement.

3. Section 39(*b*) of the Headquarters Agreement disqualifies officials of UNIDO (*i.e.* staff members)[1] from receiving the [State A] child-care allowance unless they are [State] nationals or stateless persons resident in [State A]. The Headquarters Agreement contains no such exclusion in respect of experts on mission for UNIDO (*i.e.* consultants or ISA-holders).

4. UNIDO provided written confirmation that [Name] was an ISA-holder and that she did not have the status of an official of UNIDO. [Name]'s initial appeals were nonetheless unsuccessful. In a judgment dated [date], the Labour and Social Court of [city] (...) found that [Name] was indeed an official of UNIDO and that she was therefore liable to refund the amount in question. On [date], the Regional Court of [city] (...) upheld the judgment of the first court.

5. In its judgment dated [date], the Supreme Court concluded that the lower courts had erred and that [Name]'s appeal should succeed: as an ISA-holder, she did not qualify to be an official of UNIDO and was not excluded from receiving the [State A] child-care allowance under the Headquarters Agreement.

6. The judgment of the Supreme Court is significant for the following reasons:

- The Supreme Court is the highest instance in civil and criminal matters in [State A]. Its judgment affirms that, under the Headquarters Agreement of UNIDO, which is law in [State A], only staff members appointed by the Director General are officials of UNIDO.
- The Supreme Court rejected the lower courts' broad interpretation of the term "official" as including ISA-holders, an interpretation that would have had far-reaching implications for the privileges and immunities of all of UNIDO's consultants if it had been allowed to stand.
- In reaching its conclusion, the Supreme Court cited UNIDO's note verbale of [date] confirming that the Director General had not appointed [Name] as an official and that she had the status of an expert on mission. The court's reliance on this communication

---

[1] In terms of Section 1(*h*) of the Headquarters Agreement, the expression "official of UNIDO" means "the Director-General and all members of the staff of the UNIDO, except those who are locally recruited and assigned to hourly rates".

(one of several sent in the course of the case) demonstrates the value of official intervention in private legal matters that affect the interests of UNIDO.

7. Finally, [Name] is to be commended for pursuing the matter all the way to the Supreme Court despite the personal financial risk involved. Since the Supreme Court ordered the *[Regional health insurance fund]* to reimburse [Name] the legal costs of her appeals, there is no need for the Organization to consider an *ex gratia* payment.

13 September 2019

(*h*) External e-mail to the Legal Adviser of [a United Nations Organization] concerning the legal framework of the Staff Council of UNIDO

STAFF RELATIONS—STAFF REPRESENTATIVE BODIES—UNIDO STAFF UNION ORGAN OF UNIDO AND NOT INDEPENDENT LEGAL PERSON—FUNCTIONS OF STAFF REPRESENTATIVES OFFICIAL FUNCTIONS—FINANCIAL AND ADMINISTRATIVE FRAMEWORK OF STAFF UNION

This is with reference to your email of [date] concerning the legal framework of the Staff Council of UNIDO. The attached answers to your questions are based on input kindly provided by our Staff Council.

The accompanying statutes and administrative circular are not confidential. The staff regulations and rules and the Headquarters Agreement of UNIDO are published at [Website].

[...]

Questionnaire on the Staff Council of UNIDO

(1) The independent personality and status of the Staff Council vis-à-vis the organization.

The Staff Union and its executive organ, the Staff Council, were constituted in accordance with staff regulation 5.2 and staff rule 105.01. The Staff Union does not have independent legal personality and is part of the Organization.

(2) The independent status of the members of the Staff Council as distinct from their status as staff members of the organization.

Members of staff elected to the Staff Council are known as staff representatives. The functions of staff representatives are official functions. Staff representatives have the same rights, duties, obligations and privileges as other staff members under the staff regulations and rules. In addition, they enjoy protection against any discriminatory treatment or prejudicial action based on their status or activities as staff representatives. See Administrative Circular UNIDO/DA/PS/AC.80 dated 28 March 1991 on facilities to be provided to staff representatives.

(3) Financial and accounting matters; for example: (1) whether the Staff Council has a separate accounting system; (2) whether the Staff Council purchases goods and services by its own means or through the normal procurement process of the organization; (3) how the Staff Council claims VAT exemption: on its own or through the organization; (4) what is the legal basis for the practice relating to points (1), (2) and (3)?

The budget, funds and accounts of the Staff Union are administered in accordance with the financial rules of the Staff Union and the financial rules of the Staff Council. See chapter XII and Annex C to the Statutes of the Staff Union. The Staff Council procures goods and services in accordance with the provisions of the Statutes and the procurement rules of UNIDO. The Staff Council claims reimbursement of VAT payments on a quarterly basis through the Department of Finance of UNIDO. The right to reimbursement derives from article VII of the Headquarters Agreement of UNIDO.

(4) Auditing: is the Staff Council subject to internal and external auditing (e.g., the Staff Council's financial and other reports, etc)?

In accordance with article 33 of the Statutes, the accounts of the Staff Union are audited by independent auditors appointed by the Staff Council.

(5) Whether your organization establishes separate and independent positions for the Staff Council, outside the normal organizational structure or the organization itself.

For administrative purposes, the Staff Council is "hosted" under the Directorate of Corporate Management and Operations. The President of the Staff Council is currently released from her assigned duties on a 100 per cent basis. The post of Staff Council Assistant is an established Secretariat post.

(6) Whether the members of the Staff Council are subject to performance appraisal as regards their work related to the Staff Council.

Staff representatives are elected by and accountable to the members of the Staff Union. Their performance as staff representatives is not subject to appraisal under the permanence management system of the Organization.

(7) Whether the Staff Council in your organization has a governing instrument such as a charter, and, if so, whether this charter and related documents form part of the organization's documentation, or whether they are exclusively the documentation of the Staff Council.

The Statutes of the Staff Union are adopted by the members of the Union and approved by the Director General of UNIDO. See staff rule 105.01(*b*).

(8) Any other issue you may deem of relevance.

N/A.

25 September 2019

(*i*) Internal e-mail to the Director of the UNIDO Department of External Relations concerning the interpretation of Rule 101 of the Rules of Procedure of the General Conference on balloting

Rules of Procedure of UNIDO General Conference—Elections to Industrial Development Board and Programme and Budget Committee—Secret ballot must be held unless, in absence of objection, General Conference decides to proceed without ballot—In absence of agreement within regional group, member States should present nominations individually

I refer to your email of [date] asking me to confirm your understanding of Rule 101 (Balloting) of the Rules of Procedure of the UNIDO General Conference. I also refer to our telephone conversation of this afternoon in the course of which I sought some clarifications and shared my views on the meaning of Rules 100 (Elections), 101 (Balloting) and 102 (Elections to the Industrial Development—IDB) and the Programme and Budget Committee—PBC).

Your reading of the Rule 101 is that "if any Member State wanted to make their opposition to one of the nominees known during the General Conference, this opposition would not result in the need to have the actual balloting exercise, as it would not change the number of places to be filled or the number of nominations at hand."

I wish to inform you that in accordance with Rule 100, para. 1, "[a]ll elections shall be held by secret ballot unless, in the absence of any objection, the Conference decides to proceed without taking a ballot on an agreed candidate or list of candidates." In other words, as long as there is an objection to a candidate or a list of candidates or a proposal (*e.g.* from the President) to dispense with the balloting exercise, there must be a secret ballot even when the number of candidates equals or is less than the number of places to be filled.

You also mentioned that even though you have received confirmations from the regional chairs of lists B and D that the respective members of each list have agreed on certain candidates, there are still certain countries in each list who object to a certain candidate. I advised you to confirm with the respective chairs that if there is no agreed list, their correspondence should be withdrawn and the interested members of the relevant list should be asked immediately to present in writing their nominations for the IDB and PBC as soon as possible. You may also suggest to a known objecting Member State that they may wish to absent themselves from the room when the Conference starts the consideration of a certain candidate. I recall that upon my suggestion to the Chair of list D prior at GC.[number], several objecting States to the nomination of [State] left the room at the time of a decision on [State] as they did not wish to press for a vote and politicize GC.[number] session.

29 October 2019

(*j*) Internal e-mail to the Director of the UNIDO Department of External Relations concerning the change of [State]'s candidate for the post of External Auditor

External auditor function—Nominations by member States—In absence of rule otherwise, member State may substitute nominee

I refer to your email of [date] informing me that effective [date], [Name A], the candidate of [State] for the post of the External Auditor of UNIDO, is no longer Chairman nor a member of the Audit Board of the [State]. [State] is now considering nominating [Name B], Chairman of the Audit Board of the [State], as its candidate for the post of External Auditor. As I informed [Name C] over the phone on the same date, [State] may send a note verbale to UNIDO about their new nomination provided that they have not passed any deadline. [Name C] informed me later that the deadline for submission of nominations is a secretariat deadline for the purpose of effectively managing the nominations. I promised to reply in writing.

PMO in its information note of [date] informed Permanent Missions as follows:

> "In decision GC.6/Dec.18, the General Conference requested the Director General, in future, to invite proposals from Member States for the appointment of an External Auditor and to submit such proposals to the Programme and Budget Committee for consideration. … "

In compliance with that decision, a note verbale dated [date] was sent to Member States, asking them to inform the Director General by [date] of their interest in providing the services of an External Auditor. The proposals thus received were to be submitted to the Programme and Budget Committee at its thirty-fifth session, to be held from [date]. [State] submitted its nomination on [date]. Included as part of the information which [State] provided about its nominee was the end date of [Name A]'s tenure, which was stated to be in [date].

I note that all nominations for the post of the External Auditor have been examined by the PBC and the IDB in conformity with decision GC.6/Dec.18 and the Secretariat's note of [date]. Both the PBC and the IDB have taken note of the information provided by the Secretariat and did not recommend any particular candidate to the General Conference. The end date of [Name A]'s tenure ([Month and year]), which was brought to the attention of the PBC and the IDB, did not, apparently, raise any issue.

The Financial Regulations and Rules and the Rules of Procedures of the General Conference have not fixed any statutory deadline for submission of nominations for the position of External Auditor. The General Conference's decision GC.6/Dec.18 requested the Secretariat to invite proposals from Member States for the appointment of an External Auditor and to submit such proposals to the Programme and Budget Committee for consideration. The Secretariat has clearly complied with this decision. I do not interpret the General Conference's decision as barring [State] from submitting a new candidate. Nor, in my opinion, is it possible to bar the General Conference from considering [State]'s new candidate. Although a member state may challenge [State]'s new candidate on the grounds that the nomination was not considered by the PBC/IDB, it is for the General Conference to decide what to do with the late nomination.

In short, the Secretariat may wish to inform [State] that, if it wishes to proceed with the nomination, it may submit a new note verbale with the change of nominee (and other relevant information) for the General Conference's consideration.

30 October 2019

(*k*) Internal e-mail to the UNIDO Administrative Assistant concerning the proposed Director General's membership of the Joint Committee [Name of the Committee] of the [United Nations Specialized Agency A] and [United Nations Specialized Agency B]

Inter-agency coordination—Participation of Director-General in committees of other specialized agencies—Director-General works exclusively for benefit of UNIDO—Membership by Director-General in governing structures of other international organizations risks compromising independence and impartiality of Director-General as chief administrative officer

I refer to your email of late [date] concerning the above-mentioned subject. Attached to your email was an email dated [date] from [Name], Senior Policy Officer at the [UN Specialized Agency A], which invites the Director General to become a member of the Joint Committee on the [Name of the Committee]. The [Committee]'s mandate is to "consider all matters affecting the remuneration and other benefits of the Executive Directors of the [UN Specialized Agency A] ([UN Specialized Agency B]) and of their Alternates, and to make such recommendations for any action by the Board[s] of Governors on the said matters as the Joint Committee shall deem advisable." The [Committee] is chaired by the Governor who is the joint Chairman of the Annual Meetings of the [UN Specialized

Agency A] and [UN Specialized Agency B]. The [Committee] also has two members, who are former Governors or Alternate Governors of the [UN Specialized Agency A] and/ or [UN Specialized Agency B]. UNIDO's Director General, [...], is a former Alternate Governor of the [UN Specialized Agency A]. The [Committee] will meet twice, once in [city] on the margins of the 2020 Spring Meetings in [Month A], and once more in [Month B] in a still undetermined location. Each [Committee] meeting lasts one to two days and the total commitment over a six-month period is 5–6 days, including time spent studying the background documentation.

The [UNIDO office] has already obtained the views of [UNIDO Department] and the [UNIDO office] on the matter and now wishes to seek further advice from LEG.

As a legal matter, I recall that the Director General should work exclusively for the benefit of UNIDO and be responsible and accountable solely to policy-making organs of UNIDO. See Article 11(3)-(4) of the UNIDO Constitution.

Regardless of the terms of reference of the [Committee], it cannot be excluded that the [Committee] will formulate proposals and policies that create the appearance of conflict of interests for the Director General (Staff regulations 1.1 and 1.3 refers).

In view of the provisions of the staff regulations, I think it would not be appropriate or advisable for the Director General to accept the [UN Specialized Agency A]'s invitation. UNIDO's practice is for its officials not to advise the membership of national and international committees. Appointment to the governing structures of another intergovernmental organization such as the [UN Specialized Agency A] may risk compromising, or appearing to compromise, the independence and impartiality required of the Director General as the chief administrative officer of UNIDO. Even if the membership of [Committee] is in a personal capacity, it would be all but impossible to distinguish personal from official capacities in practice. At any rate, no distinction is made between personal and official capacities under staff regulations 1.1 and 1.3.

In conclusion, whether or not to accept the invitation is mainly a policy decision for the Director General. Should the Director General decide to decline the invitation, he may thank the [UN Specialized Agency A] for its invitation and add that, while the rules of UNIDO prevent him from sitting on the [Committee] at this stage, he would be interested to consider membership of the [Committee] once his term of office expires in early [month and year].

15 November 2019

(*l*) Internal e-mail to the UNIDO Staff Council President concerning the amendment to the Statutes of the Staff Union

STAFF RELATIONS—STAFF REPRESENTATIVE BODIES—PRUDENTIAL REASONS FOR OFFICE OF LEGAL AFFAIRS NOT TO GIVE LEGAL OPINION TO STAFF REPRESENTATIVE BODY—AMENDMENT OF STATUTES OF STAFF REPRESENTATIVE BODY

Reference is made to your email of [date], which asks whether an amendment to the Statutes of the Staff Union to change the duration of the tenure of the Staff Council President to 2 years requires clearance by the Director General and, if so, what would be the procedure to follow.

Given that the issues you raise directly concern an internal matter of the Staff Union, I consider it appropriate for prudential reasons not to express a legal opinion. As I am sure you will understand, the Office of Legal Affairs plays a key role in advising the DG and management, in general, and, therefore, it must not be seen as actually or potentially being involved in how the Staff Union organizes itself. Nonetheless, and despite not having all relevant facts, I would like to note the following.

The Statutes of the Staff Union explicitly provide for an amendment procedure (cf. Art. 34[1]). The amendment procedure is, however, silent on the matter of the Director General's approval of amendments to the Statutes.

I also note that the Director General's agreement to Staff Council election procedures is explicitly referenced in staff regulation 5.2 and staff rule 105.01(*c*).[2] The issue of the Staff Council President's tenure would seem to be related, at least indirectly, to such election procedures.

Finally, the Statutes of the Staff Union have been amended before; therefore, you may wish to follow the Staff Council's past practice on the matter. My understanding is that the President of the Staff Council has, in the past, written to the Director General in accordance with staff rule 105.01(*b*)[3] to notify him of proposed amendments to the Statutes and of the reasons therefor. In his memorandum, the President of the Staff Council informed the Director General that the revised Statutes would be submitted to the Director General for his agreement after having been adopted by staff members following a referendum (IOM from [Name] to DG, dated [date], ref. [...], refers).

21 November 2019

[1] "1. The Statutes may be amended by a majority vote in a referendum of the active members of the Union. A decision to hold such a referendum shall be made by a two-thirds majority of the Council or at the written request of at least 20 per cent of the active members of the Union.

2. Amendments to these Statutes shall enter into force on the third working day following the referendum in which they have been approved, unless otherwise specified in the amendment."

[2] Staff Regulation 5.2: "A staff representative body ... shall be organized in such a way as to afford equitable representation to all staff, by means of elections that shall take place at least biennially under electoral regulations drawn up by the staff representative body and agreed to by the Director-General."

Staff Rule 105.01(*c*): "...The election of the Staff Council shall be organized by the polling officers, who are selected by the staff, under electoral regulations drawn up by the Council and agreed to by the Director-General, in such a way as to ensure the complete secrecy and fairness of the vote."

[3] "Staff members may form a Staff Union. The functions of the Staff Union shall be as described in its statute, which shall be adopted by the members of the Union and agreed to by the Director-General."

Part Three

JUDICIAL DECISIONS ON QUESTIONS RELATING TO THE UNITED NATIONS AND RELATED INTERGOVERNMENTAL ORGANIZATIONS

Chapter VII

DECISIONS AND ADVISORY OPINIONS OF INTERNATIONAL TRIBUNALS

A. International Court of Justice[1]

The International Court of Justice is the principal judicial organ of the United Nations. It was established in June 1945 by the Charter of the United Nations and began work in April 1946.

1. Judgments

(*a*) *Application of the International Convention for the Suppression of the Financing of Terrorism and of the International Convention on the Elimination of All Forms of Racial Discrimination (Ukraine* v. *Russian Federation)*, Preliminary Objections, Judgment, 8 November 2019.

(*b*) *Jadhav (India* v. *Pakistan)*, Judgment, 17 July 2019.

(*c*) *Certain Iranian Assets (Islamic Republic of Iran* v. *United States of America)*, Preliminary Objections, Judgment, 13 February 2019.

2. Advisory Opinions

Legal Consequences of the Separation of the Chagos Archipelago from Mauritius in 1956, Advisory Opinion, 25 February 2019.

3. Selected Orders[2]

Application of the International Convention on the Elimination of All Forms of Racial Discrimination (Qatar v. *United Arab Emirates)*, Provisional Measures, Order of 14 June 2019.

---

[1] The texts of the judgments, advisory opinions and orders are published in the *ICJ Reports*. Summaries of judgments, advisory opinions and orders of the Court are provided in English and French on its website http://www.icj-cij.org. In addition, the summaries can be found in all six official languages of the United Nations on the website of the Codification Division of the United Nations Office of Legal Affairs, http://www.un.org/law/ICJsummaries/. For more information about the Court's activities, see Report of the International Court of Justice, *Official Records of the General Assembly, Seventy-fourth Session, Supplement No. 4* (A/74/4) and *Seventy-fifth Session, Supplement No. 4* (A/75/4), for the periods of 1 August 2018 to 31 July 2019 and 1 August 2019 to 31 July 2020, respectively.

[2] Only orders of the International Court of Justice concerning provisional measures, intervention or the discontinuance of proceedings are included in this section.

4. Pending cases as at 31 December 2019

(*a*) *Application of the Convention on the Prevention and Punishment of the Crime of Genocide (The Gambia* v. *Myanmar)* (2019–).

(*b*) *Guatemala's Territorial, Insular and Maritime Claim (Guatemala/Belize)* (2019–).

(*c*) *Relocation of the United States Embassy to Jerusalem (Palestine* v. *United States of America)* (2018–).

(*d*) *Alleged Violations of the 1955 Treaty of Amity, Economic Relations, and Consular Rights (Islamic Republic of Iran* v. *United States of America)* (2018–).

(*e*) *Appeal Relating to the Jurisdiction of the ICAO Council under Article II, Section 2, of the 1944 International Air Services Transit Agreement (Bahrain, Egypt and United Arab Emirates* v. *Qatar)* (2018–).

(*f*) *Appeal Relating to the Jurisdiction of the ICAO Council under Article 84 of the Convention on International Civil Aviation (Bahrain, Egypt, Saudi Arabia and United Arab Emirates* v. *Qatar)* (2018–).

(*g*) *Application of the International Convention on the Elimination of All Forms of Racial Discrimination (Qatar* v. *United Arab Emirates)* (2018–).

(*h*) *Arbitral Award of 3 October 1899 (Guyana* v. *Venezuela)* (2018–).

(*i*) *Application of the International Convention for the Suppression of the Financing of Terrorism and of the International Convention on the Elimination of All Forms of Racial Discrimination (Ukraine* v. *Russian Federation)* (2017–).

(*j*) *Certain Iranian Assets (Islamic Republic of Iran* v. *United States of America)* (2016–).

(*k*) *Immunities and Criminal Proceedings (Equatorial Guinea* v. *France)* (2016–).

(*l*) *Dispute over the Status and Use of the Waters of the Silala (Chile* v. *Bolivia)* (2016–).

(*m*) *Maritime Delimitation in the Indian Ocean (Somalia* v. *Kenya)* (2014–).

(*n*) *Alleged Violations of Sovereign Rights and Maritime Spaces in the Caribbean Sea (Nicaragua* v. *Colombia)* (2013–).

(*o*) *Question of the Delimitation of the Continental Shelf between Nicaragua and Colombia beyond 200 nautical miles from the Nicaraguan Coast (Nicaragua* v. *Colombia)* (2013–).

(*p*) *Armed Activities on the Territory of the Congo (Democratic Republic of the Congo* v. *Uganda)* (1999–).

(*q*) *Gabčíkovo-Nagymaros Project (Hungary/Slovakia)* (1993–).

B. International Tribunal for the Law of the Sea[3]

The International Tribunal for the Law of the Sea is an independent permanent tribunal established by the United Nations Convention on the Law of the Sea, 1982.[4]

---

[3] For more information about the Tribunal's activities, including relating to orders and judgments rendered in 2019, see the Annual report of the International Tribunal for the Law of the Sea for 2019 (SPLOS/30/2) and the Tribunal's website at http://www.itlos.org.

[4] United Nations, *Treaty Series*, vol. 1833, p. 3.

The Agreement on Cooperation and Relationship between the United Nations and the International Tribunal for the Law of the Sea,[5] signed by the Secretary-General of the United Nations and the President of the Tribunal on 18 December 1997, establishes a mechanism for cooperation between the two institutions.

1. Judgments

Case No. 25—The M/V "Norstar" Case (Panama v. *Italy)*, Judgment, 10 April 2019.

2. Advisory Opinions

No advisory opinions were delivered by the International Tribunal for the Law of the Sea in 2019.

3. Selected Orders[6]

(*a*) *Case No. 27—The M/T "San Padre Pio" (No. 2) Case (Switzerland* v. *Nigeria)*, Provisional Measures, Order of 6 July 2019.

(*b*) *Case No. 28—Case Concerning the Detention of Three Ukrainian Naval Vessels (Ukraine* v. *Russian Federation)*, Provisional Measures, Order of 15 May 2019.

4. Pending cases as at 31 December 2019

(*a*) *Case No. 29—The M/T "San Padre Pio" (No. 2) Case (Switzerland/Nigeria)* (2019–).

(*b*) *Case No. 28—Dispute concerning delimitation of the maritime boundary between Mauritius and Maldives in the Indian Ocean (Mauritius/Maldives)* (2019–).

C. International Criminal Court[7]

The International Criminal Court is an independent permanent court established by the Rome Statute of the International Criminal Court, 1998.[8] The Relationship Agreement between the United Nations and the International Criminal Court, signed by the Secretary-General of the United Nations and the President of the Court on 4 October 2004, outlines the relationship between the two institutions.[9]

---

[5] *Ibid.*, vol. 2000, p. 468.

[6] Only orders of the International Tribunal for the Law of the Sea concerning provisional measures, prompt release, intervention or the discontinuance of proceedings are included in this section.

[7] For more information about the Court's activities, see Report of the International Criminal Court, for the period 1 August 2018 to 31 July 2019 (A/74/324) and the period 1 August 2019 to 31 July 2020 (A/74/324), as well as the Court's website at http://www.icc-cpi.int.

[8] United Nations, *Treaty Series*, vol. 2187, p. 3.

[9] *Ibid.*, vol. 2283, p. 195.

In 2019, the following situations were under investigation by the Office of the Prosecutor: Uganda,[10] Democratic Republic of the Congo,[11] Central African Republic,[12] Darfur (the Sudan),[13] Kenya,[14] Libya,[15] Côte d'Ivoire,[16] Mali,[17] Central African Republic II,[18] Georgia,[19],Burundi[20] and Bangladesh/Myanmar.[21]

On 12 April 2019, Pre-Trial Chamber II rejected the request of the Prosecutor to open an investigation *proprio motu* into the situation in Afghanistan.[22] On 17 September 2019, Pre-Trial Chamber II granted in part the request of the Prosecutor and Victims to appeal the rejection of the request.[23] At the end of 2019, the appeal was pending.

Additionally, in 2019 the Office of the Prosecutor continued its preliminary examinations in Colombia, Guinea, Iraq/United Kingdom of Great Britain and Northern Ireland, Nigeria, the Philippines, the State of Palestine, Ukraine and the Bolivarian Republic of Venezuela.

On 15 November 2018, following a request for review presented by the Government of the Union of the Comoros, Pre-Trial Chamber I requested the Prosecutor to reconsider her decision, dated 6 November 2014, to close the preliminary examination regarding the situation on Registered Vessels of Comoros, Greece and Cambodia, in accordance with the Chamber's 16 July 2015 Decision.[24] On 11 February 2019, the Prosecutor appealed the

---

[10] The situation was referred to the Court by Uganda in January 2004.

[11] The situation was referred to the Court by the Democratic Republic of the Congo in April 2004.

[12] The situation was referred to the Court by the Central African Republic in December 2004. The referral pertains to crimes within the jurisdiction of the Court committed anywhere on the territory of the Central African Republic since 1 July 2002.

[13] On 31 March 2005, the Security Council referred the situation in Darfur, the Sudan, to the Prosecutor of the Court by Security Council resolution 1593 (2005), adopted on 31 March 2005.

[14] On 31 March 2010, Pre-Trial Chamber II granted the Prosecutor's request to open an investigation *proprio motu* into the situation in Kenya.

[15] On 26 February 2011, the Security Council referred the situation in Libya to the Prosecutor of the Court by Security Council resolution 1970 (2011), adopted on 26 February 2011.

[16] On 3 October 2011, Pre-Trial Chamber III granted the Prosecutor's request to open an investigation *proprio motu* into the situation in Côte d'Ivoire.

[17] The situation was referred to the Court by Mali in July 2012.

[18] The situation was referred to the Court by the Central African Republic in May 2014. The referral pertains to crimes allegedly committed on the Central African Republic territory since 1 August 2012.

[19] On 27 January 2016, Pre-Trial Chamber I granted the Prosecutor's request for authorisation to open an investigation *proprio motu* into the situation in Georgia.

[20] On 25 October 2017, Pre-Trial Chamber III granted the Prosecutor's request to open an investigation *proprio motu* into the situation in Burundi.

[21] On 14 November 2019, Pre-Trial Chamber III granted the Prosecutor's request to open an investigation *proprio motu* into the situation in Bangladesh/Myanmar.

[22] *Situation in the Islamic Republic of Afghanistan*, Pre-Trial Chamber II, Decision Pursuant to Article 15 of the Rome Statute on the Authorisation of an Investigation into the Situation in the Islamic Republic of Afghanistan, ICC-02/17-33, 12 April 2019.

[23] *Situation in the Islamic Republic of Afghanistan*, Pre-Trial Chamber II, Decision on the Prosecutor and Victims' Requests for Leave to Appeal the 'Decision Pursuant to Article 15 of the Rome Statute on the Authorisation of an Investigation into the Situation in the Islamic Republic of Afghanistan', ICC-02/17-62, 17 September 2019.

[24] *Situation on Registered Vessels of the Union of the Comoros, the Hellenic Republic and the Kingdom of Cambodia*, Pre-Trial Chamber I, Decision on the "Application for Judicial Review by the

decision.[25] On 2 September 2019, the Appeals Chamber delivered its judgment and rejected the appeal of the Prosecutor.[26] On 2 December 2019, the Prosecutor notified her decision that there was no reasonable basis to proceed with an investigation.[27]

Situations and cases before the Court as at 31 December 2019

(*a*) Situation in Uganda

(i) *Judgment delivered by the Appeals Chamber*

The Prosecutor v. *Dominic Ongwen*, Case No. ICC-02/04-01/151562, Judgment on the appeal of Mr Dominic Ongwen against Trial Chamber IX's "Decision on Defence Motions Alleging Defects in the Confirmation Decision", Appeals Chamber, 17 July 2019.

(ii) *Pending cases and proceedings*

(*a*) *The Prosecutor* v. *Joseph Kony and Vincent Otti*, Case No. ICC-02/04-01/05.

(*b*) *The Prosecutor* v. *Dominic Ongwen*, Case No. ICC-02/04-01/15.

(*b*) Situation in the Democratic Republic of the Congo

(i) *Judgments delivered by the Trial Chambers*

(*a*) *The Prosecutor* v. *Bosco Ntaganda*, Case No. ICC-01/04-02/06-2442, Trial Chamber VI, Sentencing Judgment, 7 November 2019.

(*b*) *The Prosecutor* v. *Bosco Ntaganda*, Case No. ICC-01/04-02/06-2359, Trial Chamber VI, Judgment, 8 July 2019.

(ii) *Judgments delivered by the Appeals Chamber*

The Prosecutor v. *Thomas Lubanga Dyilo*, Case No. ICC-01/04-01/06-3466, Appeals Chamber, Judgment on the appeals against Trial Chamber II's "Decision Setting the Size of the Reparations Award for which Thomas Lubanga Dyilo is Liable", 18 July 2019

Government of the Union of the Comoros", 15 November 2018, No. ICC-01/13-68.

[25] *Situation on Registered Vessels of the Union of the Comoros, the Hellenic Republic and the Kingdom of Cambodia*, Prosecution Appeal Brief, ICC-01/13-85, 11 February 2019.

[26] *Situation on Registered Vessels of the Union of the Comoros, the Hellenic Republic and the Kingdom of Cambodia*, Appeals Chamber, Judgment on the appeal of the Prosecutor against PTC I's 'Decision on the "Application for Judicial Review by the Government of the Union of the Comoros"', ICC-01/13-98, 2 September 2019.

[27] *Situation on Registered Vessels of the Union of the Comoros, the Hellenic Republic and the Kingdom of Cambodia*, Notice of Prosecutor's Final Decision under rule 108(3), as revised and refiled in accordance with the PTC's request of 15 November 2018 and the AC's judgment of 2 September 2019, ICC-01/13-99, 2 December 2019.

(iii) *Pending cases and proceedings*

(*a*) *The Prosecutor* v. *Thomas Lubanga Dyilo*, Case No. ICC-01/04-01/06.

(*b*) *The Prosecutor* v. *Bosco Ntaganda*, Case No. ICC-01/04-02/06.

(*c*) *The Prosecutor* v. *Germain Katanga*, Case No. ICC-01/04-01/07.

(*d*) *The Prosecutor* v. *Sylvestre Mudacumura*, Case No. ICC-01/04-01/12.

(*c*) Situation in Darfur, the Sudan

(i) *Judgment delivered by the Appeals Chamber*

The Prosecutor v. *Omar Hassan Ahmad Al Bashir*, Case No. ICC-02/05-01/09-397, Judgment in the Jordan Referral re Al-Bashir Appeal, Appeals Chamber, 06 May 2019.

(ii) *Pending cases and proceedings*

(*a*) *The Prosecutor* v. *Ahmad Muhammad Harun ("Ahmad Harun") and Ali Muhammad Ali Abd-Al-Rahman ("Ali Kushayb")*, Case No. ICC-02/05-01/07.

(*b*) *The Prosecutor* v. *Omar Hassan Ahmad Al Bashir*, Case No. ICC-02/05-01/09.

(*c*) *The Prosecutor* v. *Abdallah Banda Abakaer Nourain*, Case No. ICC-02/05-03/09.

(*d*) *The Prosecutor* v. *Abdel Raheem Muhammad Hussein*, Case No. ICC-02/05-01/12.

(*d*) Situation in Kenya

Pending cases and proceedings

(*a*) *The Prosecutor* v. *Walter Osapiri Barasa*, Case No. ICC-01/09-01/13.

(*b*) *The Prosecutor* v. *Paul Gicheru and Philip Kipkoech Bett*, Case No. ICC-01/09-01/15.

(*e*) Situation in Libya

Pending cases and proceedings

(*a*) *The Prosecutor* v. *Saif Al-Islam Gaddafi*, Case No. ICC-01/11-01/11.

(*b*) *The Prosecutor* v. *Al-Tuhamy Mohamed Khaled*, Case No. ICC-01/11-01/13.

(*c*) *The Prosecutor* v. *Mahmoud Mustafa Busayf Al-Werfalli*, Case No. ICC-01/11-01/17.

(*f*) Situation in Côte d'Ivoire

(i) *Judgment delivered by the Trial Chambers*

The Prosecutor v. *Laurent Gbagbo and Charles Blé Goudé*, Case No. ICC-02/11-01/15-1263, Reasons for oral decision of 15 January 2019 on the Requête de la Défense de Laurent Gbagbo afin qu'un jugement d'acquittement portant sur toutes les charges soit prononcé en faveur de Laurent Gbagbo et que sa mise en liberté immédiate soit ordonnée, 16 July 2019.

(ii) *Judgment delivered by the Appeals Chamber*

The Prosecutor v. *Laurent Gbagbo and Charles Blé Goudé*, Case No. ICC-02/11-01/15-1251-Red, Public Redacted Judgment on the Prosecutor's appeal against the oral decision of Trial Chamber I pursuant to article 81(3)(*c*)(*i*) of the Statute, Appeals Chamber, 1 February 2019.

(iii) *Pending cases and proceedings*[28]

(*a*) *The Prosecutor* v. *Laurent Gbagbo and Charles Blé Goudé*, Case No. ICC-02/11-01/15.

(*b*) *The Prosecutor* v. *Simone Gbagbo*, Case No. ICC-02/11-01/12.

(*g*) Situation in Mali

Pending cases and proceedings

(*a*) *The Prosecutor* v. *Ahmad Al Faqi Al Mahdi*, Case No. ICC-01/12-01/15.

(*b*) *The Prosecutor* v. *Al Hassan Ag Abdoul Aziz Ag Mohamed Ag Mahmoud*, Case No. ICC-01/12-01/18.

(*h*) Situation in the Central African Republic II

Pending cases and proceedings

The Prosecutor v. *Alfred Yekatom and Patrice-Edouard Ngaïssona*, Case No. ICC-01/14-01/18.

(*i*) Situation on Registered Vessels of the Union of the Comoros, the Hellenic Republic and the Kingdom of Cambodia

Judgment delivered by the Appeals Chamber

Situation on Registered Vessels of the Union of the Comoros, the Hellenic Republic and the Kingdom of Cambodia, Case No. ICC-01/13-98, Appeals Chamber, Judgment on the appeal of the Prosecutor against Pre-Trial Chamber I's "Decision on the 'Application for Judicial Review by the Government of the Union of the Comoros'", 2 September 2019.

---

[28] On 11 March 2015, Trial Chamber I joined the Gbagbo case (ICC-02/11-01/11) and the Blé Goudé case (ICC-02/11-02/11).

D. International Residual Mechanism for Criminal Tribunals[29]

The International Residual Mechanism for Criminal Tribunals was established in 2010 by Security Council resolution 1966 (2010), adopted on 22 December 2010.[30] The Mechanism was created to carry out certain residual functions of the International Criminal Tribunal for the former Yugoslavia[31] and the International Criminal Tribunal for Rwanda,[32] including trial and appellate proceedings, the supervision and enforcement of sentences, and tracking the remaining fugitives.

1. Judgments delivered by the Appeals Chamber

(*a*) *Prosecutor* v. *Augustin Ngirabatware*, Case No. MICT-12-29-R, Review Judgment, 27 September 2019.

(*b*) *Prosecutor* v. *Radovan Karadžić*, Case No. MICT-13-55-A, Judgment, 20 March 2019.

2. Pending cases and proceedings as at 31 December 2019

(*a*) *Prosecutor* v. *André Ntagerura*, Case No. MICT-19-119 (2019–).

(*b*) *Prosecutor* v. *Anselme Nazbonimpa et al.*, Case No. MICT-18-116 (2018–).

(*c*) *Prosecutor* v. *Petar Jojić and Vjerica Radeta*, Case No. MICT-17-111-R90 (2017–).

(*d*) *Prosecutor* v. *Ratko Mladić*, Case No. MICT-13-56 (2017–).

(*e*) *Prosecutor* v. *Jovica Stanišić and Franko Simatović*, Case No. MICT-15-96 (2015–).

(*f*) *Prosecutor* v. *Félicien Kabuga*, Case No. MICT-13-38 (2013–).

---

[29] The texts of the orders, decisions and judgments are available on the Mechanism's website at http://www.irmct.org/. For more information about the Mechanism's activities, see the Seventh and Eighth annual reports of the International Residual Mechanism for Criminal Tribunals, for the period 1 July 2018 to 30 June 2019 (A/74/267–S/2019/622) and 1 July 2019 to 30 June 2020 (A/75/276–S/2020/763), respectively.

[30] The Statute of the Mechanism is contained in the annex to the resolution.

[31] The International Tribunal for the Prosecution of Persons Responsible for Serious Violations of International Humanitarian Law in the Territory of the Former Yugoslavia since 1991 (International Criminal Tribunal for the former Yugoslavia) was a subsidiary body of the United Nations Security Council, established by Security Council Resolution 827 (1993), adopted on 25 May 1993). The Statute of the Tribunal is annexed to the report of the Secretary-General pursuant to Security Council resolution 808 (1993) of 22 February 1993 (S/25704 and Add.1). The Tribunal closed on 31 December 2017. The texts of the indictments, decisions and judgments are published in the *Judicial Reports/Recueils judiciaires* of the International Criminal Tribunal for the former Yugoslavia. The texts are also available in English and French on the legacy website of the International Criminal Tribunal for the former Yugoslavia at https://www.icty.org.

[32] The International Criminal Tribunal for Rwanda was a subsidiary body of the United Nations Security Council, established by Security Council resolution 955 (1994), adopted on 8 November 1994. The Statute of the Tribunal is in the annex to the resolution. The Tribunal closed on 31 December 2015. The texts of the orders, decisions and judgments are published in the *Recueil des ordonnances, decisions et arrêts/Reports of Orders, Decisions and Judgements* of the International Criminal Tribunal for Rwanda. The texts are also available in English and French on the legacy website of the International Criminal Tribunal for Rwanda at https://unictr.irmct.org/en.

(*g*) *Prosecutor* v. *Augustin Bizimana*, Case No. MICT-13-39 (2012–).

(*h*) *Prosecutor* v. *Protais Mpiranya*, Case No. MICT-12-02 (2012–).

E. Extraordinary Chambers in the Courts of Cambodia[33]

The Agreement between the United Nations and the Royal Government of Cambodia concerning the prosecution under Cambodian law of crimes committed during the period of Democratic Kampuchea, signed in Phnom Penh on 6 June 2003,[34] entered into force on 29 April 2005 and established the Extraordinary Chambers in the Courts of Cambodia to prosecute crimes committed during the period of Democratic Kampuchea.

No judgments were delivered by the Extraordinary Chambers in the Courts of Cambodia in 2019.

Pending cases and proceedings as at 31 December 2019

(*a*) *Khieu Samphân*, Case No. 002/02 (2010–).

(*b*) *Meas Muth*, Case No. 003 (2009–).

(*c*) *Yim Tith*, Case No. 004 (2009–).

(*d*) *Ao An*, Case No. 004/02 (2009–).

F. Special Tribunal for Lebanon[35]

The Special Tribunal for Lebanon was established in 2007 pursuant to the Agreement between the United Nations and the Lebanese Republic on the establishment of a Special Tribunal for Lebanon, dated 22 January and 6 February 2007,[36] and to the Security Council resolution 1757 (2007) adopted on 30 May 2007 to prosecute persons responsible for the attack of 14 February 2005 resulting in the death of former Lebanese Prime Minister Rafiq Hariri and in the death or injury of other persons.

1. Judgments

No judgments were delivered by the Special Tribunal for Lebanon in 2019.

---

[33] The texts of the judgments, decisions and orders of the Extraordinary Chambers in the Courts of Cambodia are available on its website at http://www.eccc.gov.kh. For more information on the Court's activities, see the Report of the Secretary-General on the Request for a subvention to the Extraordinary Chambers in the Courts of Cambodia of 20 September 2019 (A/74/359).

[34] United Nations, *Treaty Series*, vol. 2329, p. 117.

[35] The texts of the indictments, decisions and orders of the Special Tribunal for Lebanon are available on the International Criminal Court Legal Tools database at https://www.legal-tools.org. For more information on the Tribunal's activities, see the Tenth and Eleventh Annual Reports of the Special Tribunal for Lebanon, for the periods 1 March 2018 to 28 February 2019 and 1 March 2019 to 28 February 2020, respectively, available at an archived version of the Tribunal's website at https://swap.stanford.edu/was/20231214151815/https://www.stl-tsl.org/en/documents/annual-reports.

[36] United Nations, *Treaty Series*, vol. 2461, p. 257.

2. Pending cases and proceedings as at 31 December 2019

(*a*) *Salim Jamil Ayyash*, Case No. STL-18-10 (2018–).

(*b*) *Salim Jamil Ayyash, Hassan Habib Merhi, Hussein Hassan Oneissi and Assad Hassan Sabra*, Case No. STL-11-01 (2011–).

G. Residual Special Court for Sierra Leone[37]

The Special Court for Sierra Leone[38] was an independent court established by the Agreement between the United Nations and the Government of Sierra Leone on the Establishment of a Special Court for Sierra Leone, 2002.[39] The Special Court was mandated to try those who bore the greatest responsibility for serious violations of international humanitarian law and Sierra Leonean law committed in the territory of Sierra Leone since 30 November 1996.

As the Special Court completed its mandate and finished its judicial activities in 2013, the Residual Special Court for Sierra Leone superseded the Special Court. The Residual Special Court was established pursuant to an Agreement between the United Nations and the Government of Sierra Leone on the Establishment of a Residual Special Court for Sierra Leone,[40] signed in 2010 and entered into force in 2012.

The purpose of the Residual Special Court is to carry out the continuing obligations of the Special Court after its closure in 2013, such as witness protection, supervision of prison sentences, and management of the Special Court's archives. Johnny Paul Koroma is the only indicted person by the Special Court who is not in custody. Should he be arrested, the Residual Special Court will have jurisdiction to try him.

No judgments were delivered by the Residual Special Court for Sierra Leone in 2019.

[37] The texts of the decisions delivered by the Residual Special Court for Sierra Leone are available at the Residual Special Court's website at http://www.rscsl.org. For more information on the Residual Special Court's activities, see the Fifth Annual Report of the President of the Residual Special Court for Sierra Leone, available from https://rscsl.org/annual-report/sixth-annual-report-2019/.

[38] The texts of the judgments and decisions delivered by the Special Court for Sierra Leone are available at the Residual Special Court's website at http://www.rscsl.org. For more information on the Court's activities, see the Eleventh and Final Report of the President of the Special Court for Sierra Leone, available from https://rscsl.org/annual-report/eleventh-annual-report/.

[39] For the text of the Agreement and the Statute of the Special Court dated 26 January 2002, see United Nations, *Treaty Series*, vol. 2178, p. 137.

[40] Ibid., vol 2871, p. 333.

Chapter VIII

DECISIONS OF NATIONAL TRIBUNALS

[No decision or advisory opinion from national tribunals on questions relating to the United Nations and related intergovernmental organizations to be reported for 2019.]

Part Four

BIBLIOGRAPHY

A. International organizations in general

1. General

Bordin, F.L., *The Analogy between States and International Organizations* (United Kingdom: Cambridge University Press, 2019). 296 p.

Daugirdas, K., Reputation as a Disciplinarian of International Organizations, *American Journal of International Law*, vol. 113 (2019): p. 221–271.

Dingwerth, K., *et al.* (eds), *International Organizations Under Pressure: Legitimating Global Governance in Challenging Times* (Oxford: Oxford University Press, 2019). 336 p.

Klabbers, J., Interminable Disagreement: Reflections on the Autonomy of International Organisations, *Nordic Journal of International Law*, vol. 88 (2019): p. 111–133.

Klabbers, J., Notes on the Ideology of International Organizations Law: The International Organization for Migration, State-Making, and the Market for Migration, *Leiden Journal of International Law*, vol. 32 (2019): p. 383–400.

Marcoux, J., *International Investment Law and Globalization: Foreign Investment, Responsibilities and Intergovernmental Organizations* (London: Routledge, 2019). 274 p.

Quayle, P., and Gao, X. (eds), *International Organizations and the Promotion of Effective Dispute Resolution* (Leiden, The Netherlands: Brill, Nijhoff, 2019). 254 p.

von Borzyskowski, I., and Vabulas, F., Hello, Goodbye: When do States Withdraw from International Organizations? *The Review of International Organizations*, vol. 14 (2019): p. 335–366.

2. Particular Questions

Arditi, L., The Role of Practice in International Organizations: The Case of Government Recognition by the International Monetary Fund, *International Organizations Law Review* (2019): p. 1–55.

Heathcote, G., *Feminist Dialogues on International Law: Successes, Tensions, Futures*, First ed. (Oxford, UK: Oxford University Press, 2019). 229 p.

Kamto, M., and Tyagi, Y., *The Access of Individuals to International Justice/L'accès de l'individu à la justice internationale* (Leiden; Boston: Brill, Nijhoff, 2019). 576 p.

3. Responsibility of International Organizations

Chinkin, C.M., United Nations Accountability for Violations of International Human Rights Law (Volume 395), in Hague Academy of International Law (ed), *Collected Courses of the Hague Academy of International Law* (Leiden; Boston: Brill, 2019). p. 199–320.

Okada, Y., Effective Control Test at the Interface between the Law of International Responsibility and the Law of International Organizations: Managing Concerns Over the Attribution of UN Peacekeepers' Conduct to Troop-Contributing Nations, *Leiden Journal of International Law*, vol. 32 (2019): p. 275–297.

Spagnolo, A., The Boundaries of the Duty of Care of International Organizations Towards their Civilian Personnel Deployed Abroad: Insights from the Recent ILOAT Case-Law, *Diritti umani e diritto internazionale*, vol. 3 (2019): p. 561–578.

Voulgaris, N., *Allocating International Responsibility between Member States and International Organisations* (Oxford: Hart Publishing Limited, 2019). 264 p.

B. United Nations

1. General

Ivanenko, V., La Fédération de Russie et l'Organisation des Nations Unies: les fondements juridico-institutionnels et les modalités de la coopération mutuelle au plan économique et social, in Fines, F., *et al.* (eds), *La puissance russe, entre émergence et renaissance* (Paris: Éditions A. Pedone, 2019). p. 99–112.

Laval, P., Les Nations Unies et l'idée de gouvernance, *Revue générale de droit international public*, vol. 123 (2019): p. 849–863.

Lieblich, E., At Least Something: The UN Special Committee on the Problem of Hungary, 1957–1958, *European Journal of International Law*, vol. 30 (2019): p. 843–876.

Nindler, R., The United Nations' Capability to Manage Existential Risks with a Focus on Artificial Intelligence, *International Community Law Review*, vol. 21 (2019): p. 5–34.

White, N.D., The Legacy of the League of Nations: Continuity or Change? *Revista Española de Derecho Internacional*, vol. 71 (2019): p. 277–284.

2. Security Council

Aitken, H., Policing the Police: Security Council Monitoring of States' Sanctions Implementation Obligations, *New York University Journal of International Law and Politics*, vol. 51 (2019): p. 705–771.

Ali, N., Through a Glass Darkly: The ICC, the UNSC and the Quest for Justice in International Law, *International Criminal Law Review*, vol. 19 (2019): p. 669–697.

Corell, H., UN Security Council Reform—The Council Must Lead by Example, *Max Planck Yearbook of United Nations Law*, vol. 22 (2019): p. 1–33.

Cusato, E., Overcoming the "Logic of Exception": A Critique of the UN Security Council's Response to Environmental Damage from the 1990–91 Gulf War, *Asian Journal of International Law*, vol. 9 (2019): p. 75–97.

Dörfler, T., *Security Council Sanctions Governance: The Power and Limits of Rules* (Abingdon, Oxon; New York, NY: Routledge, 2019). 240 p.

Fry, J.D., and Chong, A., UN Security Council Resolution of International Water Disputes, *Georgetown Journal of International Law*, vol. 50 (2019): p. 363–423.

Galand, A.S., *UN Security Council Referrals to the International Criminal Court: Legal Nature, Effects and Limits* (Leiden: Brill Nijhoff, 2019). 268 p.

Graf-Brugère, A., *La « menace contre la paix » dans la pratique du conseil de sécurité des Nations Unies: Réflexions sur un concept de droit international* (Zürich: Schulthess Juristische Medien, 2019). 316 p.

Isanga, J.M., Resurgent Cold War and U.N. Security Council Reform Opportunities, *Denver Journal of International Law and Policy*, vol. 47 (2019): p. 73–117.

Istrefi, K., *European Judicial Responses to Security Council Resolutions: A Consequentialist Assessment* (Leiden; Boston: Brill Nijhoff, 2019). 203 p.

Iyi, J., Re-Thinking the Authority of the UN Security Council to Refer Nationals of Non-Party States to the ICC, *Netherlands International Law Review*, vol. 66 (2019): p. 391–417.

Kaye, D., Legitimacy, Collective Authority and Internet Governance: A Reflection on David Caron's Study of the UN Security Council, *Ecology Law Quarterly*, vol. 46 (2019): p. 135–147.

Lippold, M., The Interpretation of UN Security Council Resolutions between Regional and General International Law: What Role for General Principles? in Fitzmaurice, M., *et al.* (eds), *General Principles and the Coherence of International Law* (Leiden; Boston: Brill Nijhoff, 2019). p. 149–176.

Mégret, F., Peering Behind the 'Institutional Veil' to Assess State Behaviour in the Security Council: Does/Should ICC Membership Make a Difference? *International Criminal Law Review*, vol. 19 (2019): p. 938–978.

Mpunga Biayi, P., Le Conseil de Sécurité des Nations Unies et les droits de l'homme, *Revue québécoise de droit international*, vol. 32 (2019): p. 173–201.

Paige, T.P., *Petulant and Contrary: Approaches by the Permanent Five Members of the UN Security Council to the Concept of 'Threat to the Peace' Under Article 39 of the UN Charter* (Leiden; Boston: Brill Nijhoff, 2019). 330 p.

Proulx, V., International Civil Individual Responsibility and the Security Council: Building the Foundations of a General Regime, *Michigan Journal of International Law*, vol. 40 (2019): p. 215–287.

Shirazyan, S., Building A Universal Counter-Proliferation Regime: The Institutional Limits of United Nations Security Council Resolution 1540, *Journal of National Security Law & Policy*, vol. 10 (2019): p. 1–44.

Tzanakopoulos, A., La Russie et le Conseil de Sécurité des Nations Unies: les trois époques de la pratique, *Revue générale de droit international public*, vol. 123 (2019): p. 91–100.

Van der Linden, H., Climate Change Mitigation and the U.N. Security Council: A Just War Analysis, in Kling, J. (ed), *Pacifism, Politics, and Feminism: Intersections and Innovations* (Leiden; Boston: Brill Rodopi, 2019). p. 117–136.

White, P.B., Cunningham, D.E., and Beardsley, K.C., The United Nations Security Council and Conflict Prevention in Self-Determination Disputes, in Wilkenfeld, J. (ed), *Research Handbook on Mediating International Crises* (Cheltenham, UK; Northampton, MA, USA: Edward Elgar Publishing, 2019). p. 167–182.

Williams, P.R., and Pearlman, S., Use of Force in Humanitarian Crises: Addressing the Limitations of U.N. Security Council Authorization, *Case Western Reserve Journal of International Law*, vol. 51 (2019): p. 211–221.

3. International Court of Justice

Allen, S., Legal Consequences of the Separation of the Chagos Archipelago from Mauritius in 1965 (I.C.J.), *International Legal Materials*, vol. 58 (2019): p. 445–602.

Black-Branch, J., International Obligations Concerning Disarmament and the Cessation of the Nuclear Arms Race: Justiciability Over Justice in the Marshall Islands Cases at the International Court of Justice, *Journal of Conflict and Security Law*, vol. 24 (2019): p. 449–472.

Dimetto, M., The use (and Abuse) of Investment Case Law before the ICJ: The Legitimate Expectations Doctrine, *Rivista di diritto internazionale*, vol. 102 (2019): p. 786–806.

Islam, M.R., The Case of Palestine Against the USA at the ICJ: A Non-Starter or Precedent-Setter? *Georgia Journal of International and Comparative Law*, vol. 48 (2019): p. 27.

Nucup, N.B., Infallible or Final?: Revisiting the Legitimacy of the International Court of Justice as the "Invisible" International Supreme Court, *The Law & Practice of International Courts and Tribunals*, vol. 18 (2019): p. 145–162.

Polonskaya, K., International Court of Justice: The Role of Consent in the Context of Judicial Propriety Deconstructed in Light of Chagos Archipelago, *The Law & Practice of International Courts and Tribunals*, vol. 18 (2019): p. 189–218.

Puma, G., Preliminary Questions in the ICJ Advisory Opinion on the Legal Consequences of the Separation of the Chagos Archipelago from Mauritius in 1965, *Zeitschrift für ausländisches öffentliches Recht und Völkerrecht = Heidelberg journal of international law*, vol. 79 (2019): p. 841–880.

Salas Kantor, B., and Zavala Achurra, M.E., The Principle of Res Judicata before the International Court of Justice: In the Midst of Comradeship and Divorce between International Tribunals, *Journal of International Dispute Settlement*, vol. 10 (2019): p. 288–306.

Wojcikiewicz Almeida, P., International Procedural Regulation in the Common Interest: The Role of Third-Party Intervention and Amicus Curiae before the ICJ, *Law and Practice of International Courts and Tribunals*, vol. 18 (2019): p. 163–188.

C. Intergovernmental organizations related to the United Nations

1. General Agreement on Tariffs and Trade

Fang, M.M., Shades of Green: Mapping the Parameters of the GATT Article III:8(*a*) Government Procurement Derogation in the Renewable Energy Transition, *Journal of World Investment & Trade*, vol. 20 (2019): p. 553–576.

2. International Centre for Settlement of Investment Disputes

Butler, N., Non-Disputing Party Participation in ICSID Disputes: *Faux Amici*? *Netherlands International Law Review*, vol. 66 (2019): p. 143–178.

3. International Civil Aviation Organization

American Bar Association, An Interview with ICAO Council President Olumuyiwa Benard Aliu, *The Air and Space Lawyer*, vol. 32 (2019): p. 9–11.

4. International Labour Organization

Kilpatrick, C., Taking the Measure of Changing Labour Mobilization at the International Labour Organisation in the Wake of the EU Sovereign Debt Crisis, *International and Comparative Law Quarterly*, vol. 68 (2019): p. 665–697.

Plouffe-Malette, K., De l'OIT à l'OMC. L'interdiction d'importation des produits intégrant le travail forcé et les pires formes de travail des enfants: un appel à la morale ? *Revue québécoise de droit international*, vol. 32 (2019): p. 239–248.

Vijeyarasa, R., A Move in the Right Direction? the Model Law Against Trafficking in Persons and the ILO Operational Indicators, *International Migration*, vol. 57 (2019): p. 177–191.

5. International Maritime Organization

Chircop, A., The IMO Initial Strategy for the Reduction of GHGS from International Shipping: A Commentary, *International Journal of Marine and Coastal Law*, vol. 34 (2019): p. 482–512.

6. International Monetary Fund

Arditi, L., The Role of Practice in International Organizations: The Case of Government Recognition by the International Monetary Fund, *International Organizations Law Review* (2019): p. 1–55.

7. Organization for the Prohibition of Chemical Weapons

Orakhelashvili, A., The Attribution Decision Adopted by the OPCW's Conference of States Parties and its Legality, *International Organizations Law Review* (2019): p. 1–18.

Rajah, T.M., Dawson, G., and Aylett, L., The Chemical Weapons Convention and the Contribution of the Organisation for the Prohibition of Chemical Weapons to Sustainable Development, *Journal of Conflict and Security Law*, vol. 24 (2019): p. 617–629.

8. United Nations Educational, Scientific and Cultural Organization

Mahoney, K.T., "Why did Constantinople Get the Works? That's Nobody's Business but the Turks." A New Approach to Cultural Property Claims and Geographic Renaming Under the 1970 UNESCO Convention, *Brooklyn Journal of International Law*, vol. 44 (2019): p. 762–794.

9. World Bank Group

Brunori, M., Protecting Access to Land for Indigenous and Non-Indigenous Communities: A New Page for the World Bank? *Leiden Journal of International Law*, vol. 32 (2019): p. 501–516.

Cabrera Ormaza, M.V., and Ebert, F.C., The World Bank, Human Rights, and Organizational Legitimacy Strategies: The Case of the 2016 Environmental and Social Framework, *Leiden Journal of International Law*, vol. 32 (2019): p. 483–500.

Dann, P., and Riegner, M., The World Bank's Environmental and Social Safeguards and the Evolution of Global Order, *Leiden Journal of International Law*, vol. 32 (2019): p. 537–559.

Houghton, R., Looking at the World Bank's Safeguard Reform through the Lens of Deliberative Democracy, *Leiden Journal of International Law*, vol. 32 (2019): p. 465–482.

Jokubauskaite, G., The World Bank Environmental and Social Framework in a Wider Realm of Public International Law, *Leiden Journal of International Law*, vol. 32 (2019): p. 457–463.

Lewis, C., and Söderbergh, C., The World Bank's New Environmental and Social Framework: Some Progress but Many Gaps regarding the Rights of Indigenous Peoples, *International Journal of Human Rights*, vol. 23 (2019): p. 63–86.

Liang, W., The World Bank and the Creation of the International Center for Settlement of Investment Disputes: Legality and Legitimacy, in Quayle, P., and Gao, X. (eds), *International Organizations and the Promotion of Effective Dispute Resolution* (Leiden, The Netherlands: Brill, Nijhoff, 2019). p. 103–120.

Van Den Meerssche, D., International Law as Insulation—The Case of the World Bank in the Decolonization Era, *Journal of the History of International Law*, vol. 21 (2019): p. 459–484.

Van Den Meerssche, D., Performing the Rule of Law in International Organizations: Ibrahim Shihata and the World Bank's Turn to Governance Reform, *Leiden Journal of International Law*, vol. 32 (2019): p. 47–69.

10. World Health Organization

Burci, G.L., The World Health Organization at 70: Challenges and Adaptation Introductory Notes, *International Organizations Law Review*, vol. 16 (2019): p. 229–241.

Fuchs, C., Process is Due: The World Health Organization Prequalification of Medicines, *Emory Law Journal*, vol. 68 (2019): p. 643–684.

Kamradt-Scott, A., The International Health Regulations (2005): Strengthening their Effective Implementation and Utilisation, *International Organizations Law Review*, vol. 16 (2019): p. 242–271.

Klabbers, J., The Normative Gap in International Organizations Law: The Case of the World Health Organization, *International Organizations Law Review*, vol. 16 (2019): p. 272–298.

11. World Trade Organization

Babu, R.R., WTO and the Protection of Public Morals, *Asian Journal of WTO and International Health Law and Policy*, vol. 13 (2018): p. 333–354.

Dufour, G., La compétence de l'OMC en matière de change: Le cas des dévaluations monétaires compétitives au regard de l' article XV du GATT, *Revue de droit international et de droit comparé*, vol. 96 (2019): p. 237–257.

Hahn, M., Challenges for the Rule of Law in the WTO, *ZEuS Zeitschrift für Europarechtliche Studien*, vol. 22 (2019): p. 349–368.

Suttle, O., Rules and Values in International Adjudication: The Case of the WTO Appellate Body, *International and Comparative Law Quarterly*, vol. 68 (2019): p. 399–441.

Valles, C., Pogoretskyy, V., and Yanguas, T., Challenging Unwritten Measures in the World Trade Organization: The Need for Clear Legal Standards, *Journal of International Economic Law*, vol. 22 (2019): p. 459–482.

D. Other legal issues

1. Aggression

de Souza Dias, T., The Activation of the Crime of Aggression before the International Criminal Court: Some Overlooked Implications Arising for States Parties and Non-States Parties to the Rome Statute, *Journal of Conflict and Security Law*, vol. 24 (2019): p. 567–591.

Hartig, A., Post Kampala: The Early Implementers of the Crime of Aggression, *Journal of International Criminal Justice*, vol. 17 (2019): p. 485–493.

Kreβ, C., Du déclenchement de la compétence de la Cour Pénale Internationale à l'égard du crime d'agression, *African Journal of International and Comparative Law*, vol. 27 (2019): p. 546–563.

Lubell, N., and Wood, M., The ILA's 2018 Report on Aggression and the Use of Force, *Journal on the Use of Force and International Law*, vol. 6 (2019): p. 4–11.

Orozco Torres, L.E., *El crimen de agresión en derecho internacional contemporáneo* (Valencia: Tirant lo Blanch, 2019). 394 p.

Sarkin, J., and Almeida, J., Understanding the Activation of the Crime of Aggression at the International Criminal Court: Progress and Pitfalls, *Wisconsin International Law Journal*, vol. 36 (2019): p. 518–551.

Trahan, J., Revisiting the Role of the Security Council Concerning the International Criminal Court's Crime of Aggression, *Journal of International Criminal Justice*, vol. 17 (2019): p. 471–483.

Warren, C.C., Prosecuting the Crime of Aggression as a Complement: A Framework to Promote the International Criminal Court's Legitimacy in Head-of-State Prosecutions, *The George Washington International Law Review*, vol. 51 (2019): p. 231–288.

Weisbord, N., *The Crime of Aggression: The Quest for Justice in an Age of Drones, Cyberattacks, Insurgents, and Autocrats* (Princeton, NJ: Princeton University Press, 2019). 272 p.

2. Collective Security

Friman, J., Deblurring the Concept of a Breach of the Peace as a Component of Contemporary International Collective Security, *Journal on the Use of Force and International Law*, vol. 6 (2019): p. 12–51.

Villegas Delgado, C.A., Naciones Unidas y su estrategia global contra el terrorismo: una aproximación desde la perspectiva del Estado de Derecho y la legalidad internacional, in Orozco Torres, L.E., Téllez Carvajal, E., and Delgado, C.V. (eds), *Sociedad global, ciber (in)seguridad y terrorismo(s): retos y alternativas* (Valencia: Tirant lo Blanch, 2019): p. 175–200.

3. Commercial Arbitration

Binder, P., and United Nations Commission on International Trade Law, *International Commercial Arbitration and Mediation in UNCITRAL Model Law Jurisdictions*, Fourth ed. (Alphen aan den Rijn, The Netherlands: Kluwer Law International, 2019). 1092 p.

Devendra, I.C., State Responsibility for Corruption in International Investment Arbitration, *Journal of International Dispute Settlement*, vol. 10 (2019): p. 248–287.

4. Diplomatic Protection

Polanco Lazo, R., *The Return of the Home State to Investor-State Disputes: Bringing Back Diplomatic Protection?* (Cambridge: Cambridge University Press, 2019). 342 p.

5. Disarmament

Barber, R., Uniting for Peace Not Aggression: Responding to Chemical Weapons in Syria without Breaking the Law, *Journal of Conflict and Security Law*, vol. 24 (2019): p. 71–110.

Black-Branch, J., International Obligations Concerning Disarmament and the Cessation of the Nuclear Arms Race: Justiciability Over Justice in the Marshall Islands Cases at the International Court of Justice, *Journal of Conflict and Security Law*, vol. 24 (2019): p. 449–472.

Black Branch, J., and Fleck, D. (eds), *Nuclear Non-Proliferation in International Law—Volume IV—Human Perspectives on the Development and Use of Nuclear Energy* (The Hague: T.M.C. Asser Press, 2019). p. 257–293.

Casey-Maslen, S., The Status of Nuclear Deterrence Under International Law in Light of the Treaty on the Prohibition of Nuclear Weapons, *Yearbook of International Humanitarian Law (2018)*, vol. 21 (2019): p. 23–57.

Casey-Maslen, S., *Treaty on the Prohibition of Nuclear Weapons: A Commentary* (Oxford, United Kingdom: Oxford University Press, 2019). 304 p.

Colangelo, A.J., and Hayes, P., An International Tribunal for the use of Nuclear Weapons, *Journal for Peace and Nuclear Disarmament*, vol. 2 (2019): p. 219–252.

Datan, M., and Scheffran, J., The Treaty is Out of the Bottle: The Power and Logic of Nuclear Disarmament, *Journal for Peace and Nuclear Disarmament*, vol. 2 (2019): p. 114–132.

Lodgaard, S., Arms Control and World Order, *Journal for Peace and Nuclear Disarmament*, vol. 2 (2019): p. 1–18.

Nave, E., The Importance of the Arms Trade Treaty for the Implementation of the Sustainable Development Goals, *Journal of Conflict and Security Law*, vol. 24 (2019): p. 297–324.

Schneebaum, S.M., What Does International Law Have to Say about Nuclear Weapons? And What Does This Have to Say About International Law? *SAIS Review of International Affairs*, vol. 39 (2019): p. 149–158.

6. Environmental Questions

Bendel, J., The Provisional Measures Orders in International Environmental Disputes: A Case for International Courts and Tribunals, *Nordic Journal of International Law*, vol. 88 (2019): p. 489–524.

Caraballo Maqueira, L., La COP 21 y el Acuerdo de París, análisis crítico, in Sandoval Cervantes, D., Melgarito Rocha, B.E., and Caraballo Maqueira, L. (eds), *Derecho, lucha de clases y reconfiguración del capital en nuestra América Vol.1* (Ciudad de Buenos Aires, Argentina: CLACSO—Consejo Latinoamericano de Ciencias Sociales, 2019). p. 255–262.

Desai, B.H., and Sidhu, B.K., Climate Change as a Common Concern of Humankind: Some Reflections on the International Law-Making Process, in Jaria-Manzano, J., and Borràs. S. (eds), *Research Handbook on Global Climate Constitutionalism* (Northampton: Edward Elgar Publishing, 2019). p. 153–175.

Diz Pereira Pinto, D., The Ecosystem Approach as a Frame for SDG 14 Implementation, *Ocean Yearbook*, vol. 33 (2019): p. 187–206.

Duyck, S., Delivering on the Paris Promises? Review of the Paris Agreement's Implementing Guidelines from a Human Rights Perspective, *Climate Law*, vol. 9 (2019): p. 202–223.

Fernández Fernández, E., and Malwé, C., The Emergence of the 'Planetary Boundaries' Concept in International Environmental Law: A Proposal for a Framework Convention, *Review of European, Comparative & International Environmental Law*, vol. 28 (2019): p. 48–56.

Ferrey, S., Counter-Intuitive Climate Forcing: Post Paris Agreement Corporate Incentives, *Climate Law*, vol. 43 (2019): p. 629.

Ferris, E., Climate Change, Migration, Law and Global Governance, *North Carolina Journal of International Law*, vol. 44 (2019): p. 425–459.

Freestone, D. (ed), *Conserving Biodiversity in Areas Beyond National Jurisdiction* (Leiden; Boston: Brill Nijhoff, 2019). 341 p.

George, E., Shareholder Activism and Stakeholder Engagement Strategies: Promoting Environmental Justice, Human Rights, and Sustainable Development Goals, *Wisconsin International Law Journal*, vol. 36 (2019): p. 298–365.

Gervasi, M., On the United States' Decision to Withdraw from and Cease Implementation of the Paris Agreement on Climate Change, *Chinese Journal of International Law*, vol. 18 (2019): p. 777–809.

Gonzalez, C.G., Climate Justice and Climate Displacement: Evaluating the Emerging Legal and Policy Responses, *Wisconsin International Law Journal*, vol. 36 (2019): p. 366–396.

Goodman, C., and Matley, H., Law Beyond Boundaries: Innovative Mechanisms for the Integrated Management of Biodiversity Beyond National Jurisdiction, *ICES Journal of Marine Science*, vol. 75 (2018): p. 402–404.

Guruswamy, L., Sustainable Development: Energy, Justice, and Women, *Wisconsin International Law Journal*, vol. 36 (2019): p. 397–423.

Khubchandani, M., The United States and the Paris Agreement on Climate Change, *Max Planck Yearbook of United Nations Law Online*, vol. 22 (2019): p. 70–82.

Laina, E., Promoting the Progressive Development of International Environmental Law, *Environmental Policy and Law*, vol. 48 (2019): p. 362–372.

Lawrence, P., and Reder, M., Equity and the Paris Agreement: Legal and Philosophical Perspectives, *Journal of Environmental Law*, vol. 31 (2019): p. 511–531.

Lim, M., *Charting Environmental Law Futures in the Anthropocene* (Singapore: Springer, 2019). 242 p.

Mayer, B., Climate Assessment as an Emerging Obligation Under Customary International Law, *International and Comparative Law Quarterly*, vol. 68 (2019): p. 271–308.

Mickelson, K., Common Heritage of Mankind as a Limit to Exploitation of the Global Commons, *European Journal of International Law*, vol. 30 (2019): p. 635–663.

Moreira, C., and Francine, N., A Brief Overview of Sustainable Development: How a Debated Concept with a Much-Contested Legal Nature Could Perform a Valuable Role in the Decision-Making, *Brazilian Journal of International Law*, vol. 61 (2019): p. 16–37.

Murphy, A., The United Nations Security Council and Climate Change: Mapping a Pragmatic Pathway to Intervention, *Carbon & Climate Law Review*, vol. 13 (2019): p. 50–62.

Narváez Moncayo, A.E., Los principios del Derecho Internacional Ambiental, *Derecho y Cambio Social*, iss. 56 (2019): p. 370–387.

Nordquist, M.H., Moore, J.N., and Long, R.J. (eds), *The Marine Environment and United Nations Sustainable Development Goal 14: Life Below Water* (Leiden, The Netherlands: Brill Nijhoff, 2019). 421 p.

Peel, J., and Lin, J., Transnational Climate Litigation: The Contribution of the Global South, *American Journal of International Law*, vol. 113 (2019): p. 679–726.

Pickering, J., *et al.*, Global Climate Governance between Hard and Soft Law: Can the Paris Agreement's 'Crème Brûlée' Approach Enhance Ecological Reflexivity? *Journal of Environmental Law*, vol. 31 (2019): p. 1–28.

Popovski, V., *The Implementation of the Paris Agreement on Climate Change* (Abingdon, Oxon; New York, NY: Routledge, 2019). 316 p.

Prete, G., and Cournil, C., Staging International Environmental Justice: The International Monsanto Tribunal, *Political and Legal Anthropology Review*, vol. 42 (2019): p. 191–209.

Rajamani, L., Integrating Human Rights in the Paris Climate Architecture: Contest, Context, and Consequences, *Climate Law*, vol. 9 (2019): p. 180–201.

Rios Rodriguez, J., L'érosion côtière en droit international universel et régional, *Revue juridique de l'environnement*, vol. 44 (2019): p. 79–88.

¿Sarmiento E., J.P., Protocolo de Montreal y el Convenio de Viena? ¿Un caso exitoso en Derecho Internacional de protección global del medio ambiente? *Revista de Derecho*, vol. 52 (2019): p. 6–12.

Sohnle, J., Lavallée, S., and Trudeau, H., Le droit international de l'environnement (01/2017–07/2019) ou ruser à la maniere d'Ulysse, *Revue juridique de l'environnement*, vol. 44 (2019): p. 769–786.

Stephens, T., The Role and Relevance of Nationally Determined Contributions Under the Paris Agreement to Ocean and Coastal Management in the Anthropocene, *Ocean Yearbook*, vol. 33 (2019): p. 250–267.

Streck, C., Unger, M.v., and Kramer, N., From Paris to Katowice: Cop-24 Tackles the Paris Rulebook, *Journal for European Environmental & Planning Law*, vol. 16 (2019): p. 165–190.

Thieffy, P., Le rôle du secteur privé dans le Pacte mondial pour l'environnement, *Journal du droit international*, vol. 146 (2019): p. 739–754.

Van der Linden, H., Climate Change Mitigation and the U.N. Security Council: A Just War Analysis, in Kling, J. (ed), *Pacifism, Politics, and Feminism: Intersections and Innovations* (Leiden; Boston: Brill Rodopi, 2019). p. 117–136.

Viñuales, J.E., The Protocol on Water and Health as a Strategy for Global Water Governance Integration, *International and Comparative Law Quarterly*, vol. 68 (2019): p. 175–192.

Voigt, C., How a 'Global Pact for the Environment' Could Add Value to International Environmental Law, *Review of European, Comparative & International Environmental Law*, vol. 28 (2019): p. 13–24.

Zoma, L., Perception et effectivité du droit de l'environnement: entre influence des niveaux de développement et nécessité de réduire les disparités, *Revue juridique de l'environnement*, vol. 44 (2019): p. 321–338.

7. Financing

Basak, R., and van der Werf, E., Accountability Mechanisms in International Climate Change Financing, *International Environmental Agreements: Politics, Law and Economics*, vol. 19 (2019): p. 297–313.

Chen, J., Financing the Sustainable Development Goals: The Role of African Sovereign Wealth Funds, *New York University Journal of International Law & Politics*, vol. 51 (2019): p. 1259–1292.

8. Friendly Relations and Cooperation among States

Criddle, E.J., and Fox-Decent, E., Mandatory Multilateralism, *American Journal of International Law*, vol. 113 (2019): p. 272–325.

9. Human Rights

Abashidze, A., and Koneva, A., The Process of Strengthening the Human Rights Treaty Body System: The Road Towards Effectiveness or Inefficiency? *Netherlands International Law Review*, vol. 66 (2019): p. 357–389.

Adami, R., *Women and the Universal Declaration of Human Rights* (New York; London; Routledge, 2020). 174 p.

Álvarez Rodríguez, I., Caminante, se hace camino al andar. Comunidad LTGBI, derechos humanos y Naciones Unidas, *Estudios de Deusto*, vol. 67 (2019): p. 127–163.

Anderson, A., *et al.*, Imminence in Refugee and Human Rights Law: A Misplaced Notion for International Protection, *International and Comparative Law Quarterly*, vol. 68 (2019): p. 111–140.

Barnes, M.M., The United Nations Guiding Principles on Business and Human Rights, the State Duty to Protect Human Rights and the State-Business Nexus, *Revista de Direito Internacional*, vol. 15 (2018): p. 42–64.

Becker, M.A., and Nouwen, S.M.H., International Commissions of Inquiry: What Difference do They Make? Taking an Empirical Approach, *European Journal of International Law*, vol. 30 (2019): p. 819–841.

Bellier, I., and Hays, J., *Échelles de gouvernance et droits des peuples autochtones* (Paris: L'Harmattan, 2019). 302 p.

Bertotti, S., Separate or Inseparable?: How Discourse Interpreting Law and Politics as Separable Categories Shaped the Formation of the UN Human Rights Council's Universal Periodic Review, *International Journal of Human Rights*, vol. 23 (2019): p. 1140–1165.

Burger, J., After the Declaration: Next Steps for the Protection of Indigenous Peoples' Rights, *The International Journal of Human Rights*, vol. 23 (2019): p. 22–33.

Cabrera Ormaza, M.V., and Ebert, F.C., The World Bank, Human Rights, and Organizational Legitimacy Strategies: The Case of the 2016 Environmental and Social Framework, *Leiden Journal of International Law*, vol. 32 (2019): p. 483–500.

Callamard, A., Towards International Human Rights Law Applied to Armed Groups, *Netherlands Quarterly of Human Rights*, vol. 37 (2019): p. 85–100.

Camacho, O.L., Intersexuales en estado de excepción: violencias contra las corporeidades diversas, *American University International Law Review*, vol. 34 (2019): p. 535–566.

Chan, A.W., The Need for a Shared Responsibility Regime between State and Non-State Actors to Prevent Human Rights Violations Caused by Cyber-Surveillance Spyware, *Brooklyn Journal of International Law*, vol. 44 (2019): p. 795–830.

Collinge, D., The Missing Link: Bringing United Nations' Protection of Civilians Mandates Under the Framework of International Human Rights Law, *Journal of International Peacekeeping*, vol. 23 (2019): p. 82–104.

Cristancho Díaz, J.R., Capacidad jurídica de las personas con discapacidad: ¿Derecho fundamental absoluto? *Revista Chilena de Derecho y Ciencia Política*, vol. 10 (2019): p. 31–56.

de Beco, G., The Indivisibility of Human Rights and the Convention on the Rights of Persons with Disabilities, *International and Comparative Law Quarterly*, vol. 68 (2019): p. 141–160.

de Frouville, O., and Tavernier, J., *La Déclaration universelle des droits de l'Homme, 70 ans après: les fondements des droits de l'Homme au défi des nouvelles technologies: actes du colloque des 13 et 14 décembre 2018* (Paris: Editions A. Pedone, 2019). 288 p.

de la Rasilla, I., The World Court of Human Rights: Rise, Fall and Revival? *Human Rights Law Review*, vol. 19 (2019): p. 585–603.

Fassbender, B., and Traisbach, K. (eds), *The Limits of Human Rights* (Oxford, UK: Oxford University Press, 2019). 416 p.

Fernández Liesa, C.R., Los actores no estatales y el derecho internacional de los derechos humanos, *Revista Derechos y Libertades*, iss. 41 (2019): p. 117–147.

Ferstman, C., *et al.* (eds), *Contemporary Human Rights Challenges: The Universal Declaration of Human Rights and its Continuing Relevance* (London; New York: Routledge, Taylor & Francis Group, 2019). 238 p.

Genser, J., *The UN Working Group on Arbitrary Detention: Commentary and Guide to Practice* (Cambridge: Cambridge University Press, 2019). 630 p.

Gilbert, J., and Lennox, C., Towards New Development Paradigms: The United Nations Declaration on the Rights of Indigenous Peoples as a Tool to Support Self-Determined Development, *International Journal of Human Rights*, vol. 23 (2019): p. 104–124.

Gómez Isa, F., La declaración de las Naciones Unidas sobre los Derechos de los Pueblos Indígenas: un hito en el proceso de reconocimiento de los derechos indígenas, *Revista Española de Derecho Internacional*, vol. 71 (2019): p. 119–138.

Gomez, C.E., The International Criminal Court's Decision on the Rohingya Crisis: The Need for a Critical Redefinition of Trans-Border Jurisdiction to Address Human Rights, *California Western International Law Journal*, vol. 50 (2019): p. 177–205.

Guild, E., Basaran, T., and Allinson, K., From Zero to Hero? An Analysis of the Human Rights Protections within the Global Compact for Safe, Orderly and Regular Migration (GCM), *International Migration*, vol. 57 (2019): p. 43–59.

Igbinedion, S.A., Finding Value for the Right to Development in International Law, *African Human Rights Law Journal*, vol. 19 (2019): p. 395–417.

Joseph, S., and Jenkin, E., The United Nations Human Rights Council: Is the United States Right to Leave this Club? *American University International Law Review* vol. 35 (2019): p. 75–132.

Kadelbach, S., Rensmann, T., and Rieter, E. (eds), *Judging International Human Rights: Courts of General Jurisdiction as Human Rights Courts* (Cham, Switzerland: Springer International Publishing, 2019). 684 p.

Kanter, A.S., Do Human Rights Treaties Matter: The Case for the United Nations Convention on the Rights of People with Disabilities, *Vanderbilt Journal of Transnational Law*, vol. 52 (2019): p. 577–609.

Khoury-Bisharat, H., The Unintended Consequences of the Goldstone Commission of Inquiry on Human Rights Organizations in Israel, *European Journal of International Law*, vol. 30 (2019): p. 877–901.

Kim, H.J., Are UN Investigations into Human Rights Violations a Viable Solution? An Assessment of UN Commissions of Inquiry, *Journal of Human Rights Practice*, vol. 11 (2019): p. 96–115.

McCall-Smith, K., Treaty Bodies: Choreographing the Customary Prohibition Against Torture, *International Community Law Review*, vol. 21 (2019): p. 344–368.

McGregor, L., Murray, D., and Ng, V., International Human Rights Law as a Framework for Algorithmic Accountability, *International and Comparative Law Quarterly*, vol. 68 (2019): p. 309–343.

Megret, F., Beyond UN Accountability for Human Rights Violations: Host State Inertia and the Neglected Potential of Sovereign Protection, *International Organizations Law Review*, vol. 16 (2019): p. 68–104.

Méndez Silva, R., Terrorismo y Derechos Humanos: Revisión de las resoluciones de la Asamblea General y del Consejo de Seguridad de las Naciones Unidas, *Anuario hispano-luso-americano de derecho internacional*, vol. 24 (2019): p. 19–52.

Nowak, M., Birk, M., and Monina, G., *The United Nations Convention Against Torture and its Optional Protocol: A Commentary* (Oxford: Oxford University Press, 2019). 1360 p.

Pietrafesa, A., Violencia de género, Internet y el derecho a la libertad de expresión: un nuevo desafío para el derecho internacional de los derechos humanos, *American University International Law Review*, vol. 34 (2019): p. 567–586.

Pocar, F., *International Human Rights Institutions and Enforcement* (Cheltenham, UK: Edward Elgar Publishing Limited, 2019). 1,856 p.

Rajamani, L., Integrating Human Rights in the Paris Climate Architecture: Contest, Context, and Consequences, *Climate Law*, vol. 9 (2019): p. 180–201.

Ramcharan, B.G., *Modernizing the UN Human Rights System* (Boston: Brill, 2019). 242 p.

Ramcharan, R., and Ramcharan, B.G. (eds), *Asia and the Drafting of the Universal Declaration of Human Rights* (Singapore: Palgrave Macmillan, 2019). 255 p.

Riccardi, A., The Universal Declaration of Human Rights in Twenty Years of ICC Practice: An International Law Perspective, *International Criminal Law Review*, vol. 19 (2019): p. 1057–1080.

Scheinin, M., *Human Rights Norms in "Other" International Courts* (Cambridge: Cambridge University Press, 2019). 413 p.

Shikhelman, V., Implementing Decisions of International Human Rights Institutions—Evidence from the United Nations Human Rights Committee, *European Journal of International Law*, vol. 30 (2019): p. 753–777.

Skivenes, M., and Søvig, K.H. (eds), *Child Rights and International Discrimination Law: Implementing Article 2 of the United Nations Convention on the Rights of the Child* (New York, NY: Routledge, 2019). 214 p.

Tan, D., Filling the Lacuna: De Facto Regimes and Effective Power in International Human Rights Law, *New York University Journal of International Law and Politics*, vol. 51 (2019): p. 435–491.

Tobin, J., *The UN Convention on the Rights of the Child: A Commentary* (Oxford, UK: Oxford University Press, 2019). 1872 p.

Voss, M.J., The Use (Or Misuse) of Amendments to Contest Human Rights Norms at the UN Human Rights Council, *Human Rights Review*, vol. 20 (2019): p. 397–422.

Wagner, B., Kettemann, M.C., and Vieth, K. (eds), *Research Handbook on Human Rights and Digital Technology: Global Politics, Law and International Relations* (Cheltenham, UK; Northampton, MA: Edward Elgar Publishing, 2019): p. 113–128.

Wheatley, S., *The Idea of International Human Rights Law* (Oxford, United Kingdom; New York, NY: Oxford University Press, 2019). 215 p.

10. International Administrative Law

Collins, R., The League of Nations and the Emergence of International Administration: Finding the Origins of International Institutional Law, *Revista Española de Derecho Internacional*, vol. 71 (2019): p. 285–294.

da Silva Bravo, T., The United Nations' Internal Justice System and Fair Trial Rights of International Staff Members in Disciplinary Proceedings, in Pinto de Albuquerque, P. (ed), *Judicial Power in a Globalized World: Liber Amicorum Vincent De Gaetano* (Cham: Springer, 2019). p. 559–577.

Spagnolo, A., The Boundaries of the Duty of Care of International Organizations Towards their Civilian Personnel Deployed Abroad: Insights from the Recent ILOAT Case-Law, *Diritti umani e diritto internazionale*, vol. 3 (2019): p. 561–578.

11. International Commercial Law

Ahmed, M., Reflections on the UNCITRAL Convention on the Enforcement of Mediation Settlement Agreements and Model Law, *Lloyd's Maritime and Commercial Law Quarterly*, iss. 2 (2019): p. 259–269.

Block-Lieb, S., Soft and Hard Strategies: The Role of Business in the Crafting of International Commercial Law, *Michigan Journal of International Law*, vol. 40 (2019): p. 433–478.

Brunner, C., and Gottlieb, B., *Commentary on the UN Sales Law (CISG)* (Alphen aan den Rijn, The Netherlands: Wolters Kluwer, 2019). 752 p.

Devaux, C., *La fabrique du droit du commerce international réguler les risques de capture* (Bruxelles: Bruylant, 2019). 456 p.

Gabriel, H.D., The Use of Soft Law in the Creation of Legal Norms in International Commercial Law: How Successful Has It Been? *Michigan Journal of International Law*, vol. 40 (2019): p. 413–432.

Joutsen, M., The United Nations: Organised Crime on the Agenda of the United Nations, in Gilmour, S., and Allum, F. (eds), *Handbook of Organised Crime and Politics.* (Cheltenham, UK: Edward Elgar Publishing, 2019). p. 468–481.

Mankowski, P., *Commercial Law Article-by-Article Commentary.* (München, Germany: Germany Nomos Oxford Hart, 2019). 1531 p.

Murphy, S.D., Anniversary Commemoration and Work of the International Law Commission's Seventieth Session, *American Journal of International Law*, vol. 113 (2019): p. 90–108.

12. International Criminal Law

Adem, S.H., *Palestine and the International Criminal Court* (Berlin, Germany: T.M.C. Asser Press, 2019). 228 p.

Ali, N., Through a Glass Darkly: The ICC, the UNSC and the Quest for Justice in International Law, *International Criminal Law Review*, vol. 19 (2019): p. 669–697.

Ballin, E.H., The Value of International Criminal Justice: How Much International Criminal Justice Can the World Afford? *International Criminal Law Review*, vol. 19 (2019): p. 201–213.

Bradfield, P., Preserving Vulnerable Evidence at the International Criminal Court—The Article 56 Milestone in *Ongwen, International Criminal Law Review*, vol. 19 (2019): p. 373–411.

Bocchese, M., After Ratification: Predicting State Compliance with ICC Treaty Obligations, *International Criminal Law Review*, vol. 19 (2019): p. 635–668.

Brown, C., Sexual Exploitation and Abuse in Conflict: An International Crime? *American University International Law Review*, vol. 34 (2019): p. 503–533.

Caeiro, P., and Costa, J., Joint Criminal Enterprise on the Decline: A Step Further in the 'Self-Becoming' of International Criminal Law? *International Criminal Law Review*, vol. 19 (2019): p. 214–233.

Cedrangolo, U., The Accountability for International Crimes Perpetrated by Children, *International Criminal Law Review*, vol. 19 (2019): p. 698–723.

Chigara, B.A., Towards a *Nemo Judex in Parte Sua* Critique of the International Criminal Court? *International Criminal Law Review*, vol. 19 (2019): p. 412–444.

Djukić, D., *The Right to Appeal in International Criminal Law* (Leiden; Boston: Brill, Nijhoff, 2019). 294 p.

Eggett, C., The Role of Principles and General Principles in the 'Constitutional Processes' of International Law, *Netherlands International Law Review*, vol. 66 (2019): p. 197–217.

Eltringham, N., *Genocide Never Sleeps: Living Law at the International Criminal Tribunal for Rwanda* (Cambridge, United Kingdom; New York, NY: Cambridge University Press, 2019). 226 p.

Emmanuel Adouki, D.E., *Les vingt ans du Traité de Rome: portant Statut de la Cour pénale internationale* (Paris: Bayonne Institut universitaire Varenne, 2019). 282 p.

Estrada Tanck, D., El principio de igualdad ante la ley en el derecho internacional = The principle of equality before the law in International Law. *Cuadernos de derecho transnacional*, vol. 11 (2019): p. 322–339.

Fernández Arribas, G., Corte Penal Internacional y crimen de agresión: el levantamiento de inmunidades mediante la remisión de asuntos por el Consejo de Seguridad, *Revista Española de Derecho Internacional*, vol. 71 (2019): p. 195–222.

Fernández Arribas, G., The Narrow Protection of Cultural Properties and Historical Monuments in the Rome Statute: Filling the Gap, *International Community Law Review*, vol. 29 (2019): p. 129–146.

Fisher, K.J., International Criminal 'Lawfare' and its Potential Effects on Post-Conflict Positive Peace, *International Criminal Law Review*, vol. 19 (2019): p. 724–745.

Grey, R., *Prosecuting Sexual and Gender-Based Crimes at the International Criminal Court: Practice, Progress and Potential* (Cambridge, United Kingdom; New York, NY: Cambridge University Press, 2019). 367 p.

Grey, R., *et al.*, Gender-Based Persecution as a Crime Against Humanity: The Road Ahead, *Journal of International Criminal Justice*, vol. 17 (2019): p. 957–979.

Hathaway, O.A., *et al.*, What is a War Crime? *The Yale Journal of International Law*, vol. 44 (2019): p. 53–113.

Heinze, A., The 20th Anniversary of the Rome Statute, *Criminal Law Forum*, vol. 30 (2019): p. 109–135.

Hola, B., Mulgrew, R., and van Wijk, J., Introduction: National Prosecutions of International Crimes: Sentencing Practices and (Negotiated) Punishments, *International Criminal Law Review*, vol. 19 (2019): p. 1–14.

Jackson, M., Virtuous Accomplices in International Criminal Law, *International and Comparative Law Quarterly*, vol. 68 (2019): p. 817–835.

Jones, A., A Quiet Transformation? Efficiency Building in the "Fall" of International Criminal Justice, *International Criminal Law Review*, vol. 19 (2019): p. 445–474.

Katz, C., Le refus de la protection des groupes politiques par la Convention sur la prévention et la répression du génocide: une exclusion contestable, une finalité entamée, *Revue trimestrielle des droits de l'homme*, vol. 30 (2019): p. 349–364.

Keitner, C.I., The ICC and Non-Party States: Consistency and Consensus Revisited, *Georgia Journal of International and Comparative Law*, vol. 47 (2019): p. 629–634.

Kenny, C., and McDermott, Y., The Expanding Protection of Members of a Party's Own Armed Forces Under International Criminal Law, *International and Comparative Law Quarterly*, vol. 68 (2019): p. 943–976.

Lafontaine, F., and Larocque, F., *Doing Peace the Rights Way: Essays in International Law and Relations in Honour of Louise Arbour* (Cambridge; Antwerp; Chicago: Intersentia, 2019). 508 p.

Levy, A., Rohingya in Myanmar: The United Nations' Failure to Enforce Violations of Crimes Against Humanity and Genocide (Note), *The George Washington International Law Review*, vol. 51 (2019): p. 321–343.

Liss, R., Crimes Against the Sovereign Order: Rethinking International Criminal Justice, *American Journal of International Law*, vol. 113 (2019): p. 727–771.

MacCall-Smith, K., Smith, R.K.M., and Yahyaoui Krivenko, E., Reservations to the Convention on the Prevention and Punishment of the Crime of Genocide, in Hodson, L., and Lavers, T., *Feminist Judgements in International Law* (Oxford; London; New York; New Delhi; Sydney: Hart, 2019). p. 55–81.

Magliveras, K.D., The Withdrawal of African States from the ICC: Good, Bad or Irrelevant? *Netherlands International Law Review*, vol. 66 (2019): p. 419–439.

Mälksoo, L., Civilizational Diversity as Challenge to the (False) Universality of International Law, *Asian Journal of International Law*, vol. 9 (2019): p. 155–164.

McDonald, N., The Role of Due Diligence in International Law, *International and Comparative Law Quarterly*, vol. 68 (2019): p. 1041–1054.

Megiddo, T., Beyond Fragmentation: On International Law's Integrationist Forces, *The Yale Journal of International Law*, vol. 44 (2019): p. 115–147.

Nimigan, S., The Malabo Protocol, the ICC, and the Idea of 'Regional Complementarity', *Journal of International Criminal Justice*, vol. 17 (2019): p. 1005–1029.

Nuridzhanian, G., Ne Bis in Idem in Article 20(3) of the Rome Statute and Non-State Courts, *The Law & Practice of International Courts and Tribunals*, vol. 18 (2019): p. 219–239.

Omorogbe, E.Y., The Crisis of International Criminal Law in Africa: A Regional Regime in Response? *Netherlands International Law Review*, vol. 66 (2019): p. 287–311.

O'Rourke, M., Prolonged Impunity as a Continuing Situation of Torture or Ill-Treatment? Applying a Dignity Lens to so-called 'Historical' Cases, *Netherlands International Law Review*, vol. 66 (2019): p. 101–141.

Owiso, O., The International Criminal Court and Reparations: Judicial Innovation or Judicialisation of a Political Process? *International Criminal Law Review*, vol. 19 (2019): p. 505–531.

Riccardi, A., The Universal Declaration of Human Rights in Twenty Years of ICC Practice: An International Law Perspective, *International Criminal Law Review*, vol. 19 (2019): p. 1057–1080.

Soler, C., *The Global Prosecution of Core Crimes Under International Law* (The Hague: T.M.C. Asser Press, 2019). 590 p.

de Souza Dias, T., The Nature of the Rome Statute and the Place of International Law before the International Criminal Court, *Journal of International Criminal Justice*, vol. 17 (2019): p. 507–535.

Sterio, M., and Scharf, M.P. (eds), *The Legacy of Ad Hoc Tribunals in International Criminal Law: Assessing the ICTY's and the ICTR's most Significant Legal Accomplishments.* (Cambridge, United Kingdom; New York, NY, USA: Cambridge University Press, 2019). 376 p.

Sweeney, C., Accountability for Syria: Is the International Criminal Court Now a Realistic Option? *Journal of International Criminal Justice*, vol. 17 (2019): p. 1083–1115.

Tolbert, D., Looking Forward and Looking Back: How can the International Criminal Court (ICC) Navigate in a Complicated and Largely Hostile World? *Georgia Journal of International and Comparative Law*, vol. 47 (2019): p. 659–667.

Tomkiewicz, V., Les réparations collectives devant la Cour pénale international, *Journal du droit international*, vol. 146 (2019): p. 49–77.

Tsilonis, V., *The Jurisdiction of the International Criminal Court* (Cham: Springer, 2019). 283 p.

de Vries, B., Could International Fact-Finding Missions Possibly Render a Case Inadmissible for the ICC? Remarks on the Ongoing Attempts to Include International Criminal Law in Fact-Finding, *Journal of Conflict and Security Law*, vol. 24 (2019): p. 593–616.

13. International Economic Law

Boisson de Chazournes, L., International Economic Law and the Quest for Universality, *Leiden Journal of International Law*, vol. 32 (2019): p. 401–414.

Esis, I., El rol de las instituciones arbitrales en el desarrollo del arbitraje internacional, *Revista de Direito Internacional*, vol. 16 (2019): p. 37–52.

Ruiz Fabri, H., Understanding International Economic Law in Unsettling Times: A Feminist Approach, *The Journal of World Investment & Trade*, vol. 20 (2019): p. 3–14.

14. International Terrorism

Bakhteeva, E., *et al.*, Elements of Crime and Evidence of International Terrorism, *Dilemas Contemporáneos: Educación, Política y Valore*, vol. VI (2019): p. 1–13.

Cocchini, A., ¿Hacia una responsabilidad objetiva del Estado que «no puede» combatir el terrorismo internacional? *Anuario Español de Derecho Internacional*, vol. 35 (2019): p. 297–331.

López-Muñoz, J., Conexiones entre el crimen organizado y el terrorismo, in López-Muñoz, J. (ed), *Criminalidad organizada y terrorismo: Formas criminales paradigmáticas* (Madrid: Dykinson, 2019). p. 295–312.

Méndez Silva, R., Terrorismo y Derechos Humanos: Revisión de las resoluciones de la Asamblea General y del Consejo de Seguridad de las Naciones Unidas, *Anuario hispano-luso-americano de derecho internacional*, vol. 24 (2019): p. 19–52.

Villegas Delgado, C.A., Naciones Unidas y su estrategia global contra el terrorismo: una aproximación desde la perspectiva del Estado de Derecho y la legalidad internacional, in Orozco Torres, L.E., Téllez Carvajal, E., and Delgado, C.V. (eds), *Sociedad global, ciber (in)seguridad y terrorismo(s): retos y alternativas* (Valencia: Tirant lo Blanch, 2019): p. 175–200.

15. International Trade Law

Adelus, E., Global Law-Making in Insolvency Law: The Role for the United Nations Commission for International Trade Law, *Uniform Law Review*, vol. 24 (2019): p. 175–213.

Brunner, C., and Gottlieb, B., *Commentary on the UN Sales Law (CISG)* (Alphen aan den Rijn, The Netherlands: Wolters Kluwer, 2019). 752 p.

Butler, N., Non-Disputing Party Participation in ICSID Disputes: *Faux Amici? Netherlands International Law Review*, vol. 66 (2019): p. 143–178.

Butler, P., 40 Years Convention on the International Sale of Goods (CISG): Even More Important Today than 40 Years Ago to Encourage Trade? *Zeitschrift für vergleichende Rechtswissenschaft: einschließlich der ethnologischen Rechts—und der Gesellschaftsforschung*, vol. 118 (2019): p. 231–256.

Coppelli Ortiz, G., Entre el libre comercio y el proteccionismo. Impacto de los obstáculos sobre la equidad en el comercio en el marco de la Agenda 2030, *Anuario Español de Derecho Internacional*, vol. 35 (2019): p. 333–371.

Duke, A., What does the CISG have to Say about Smart Contracts: A Legal Analysis (Comment), *Chicago Journal of International Law*, vol. 20 (2019): p. 141–177.

Mariniello, T., Judicial Control Over Prosecutorial Discretion at the International Criminal Court, *International Criminal Law Review*, vol. 19 (2019): p. 979–1013.

Montineri, C., The United Nations Commission on International Trade Law (UNCITRAL) and the Significance of the Singapore Convention on Mediation, *Cardozo Journal of Conflict Resolution*, vol. 20 (2019): p. 1023–1036.

Nerlich, V., Audiences of the International Criminal Court, *International Criminal Law Review*, vol. 19 (2019): p. 1046–1056.

Sterio, M., and Scharf, M.P. (eds), *The Legacy of Ad Hoc Tribunals in International Criminal Law: Assessing the ICTY's and the ICTR's most Significant Legal Accomplishments* (Cambridge, United Kingdom; New York, NY, USA: Cambridge University Press, 2019). 376 p.

Trachtman, J.P., Functionalism, Fragmentation, and the Future of International (Trade) Law, *The Journal of World Investment & Trade*, vol. 20 (2019): p. 15–31.

16. International Tribunals

Amoulgam, A.K., Examens préliminaires à la Cour pénale internationale: fondements juridiques, pratique du Bureau de la Procureure et développements judiciaires, *Revue québécoise de droit international*, vol. 32 (2019): p. 173–202.

Bekou, O., Dealing with Non-Cooperation at the ICC: Towards a More Holistic Approach, *International Criminal Law Review*, vol. 19 (2019): p. 911–937.

Carcano, A., On the Governance of International Judicial Institutions: The Development of Performance Indicators for the International Criminal Court, *Max Planck Yearbook of United Nations Law Online*, vol. 22 (2019): p. 83–113.

Cottin, A., and Kyriakou, P.A., Revisiting the Dispute Requirement in International Interpretation Proceedings: Deeds, Not Words, *Journal of International Dispute Settlement*, vol. 10 (2019): p. 307–327.

Crow, K., The Opacity of Proportionality in International Courts: Could Categories Clarify? *The George Washington International Law Review*, vol. 51 (2019): p. 289–320.

Galand, A.S., The Nature of the Rome Statute of the International Criminal Court (and its Amended Jurisdictional Scheme), *Journal of International Criminal Justice*, vol. 17 (2019): p. 933–956.

Ginsburg, T., International Courts and Democratic Backsliding, *Berkeley Journal of International Law*, vol. 37 (2019): p. 265–288.

Ikamto, M., and Tyagi, Y. (eds), *The Access of Individuals to International Justice/L'accès de l'individu à la justice internationale* (Leiden; Boston: Brill, Nijhoff, 2019). 576 p.

Nadège Samba-Vouka, M., La saisine de la Cour pénale internationale par le Conseil de Sécurité de l›Organisation des Nations unies, in Emmanuel, D. (ed), *Les vingt ans du Traité de Rome: portant Statut de la Cour pénale internationale* (Bayonne: Institut Universitaire Varenne, 2019). p. 197–224.

Oxman, B.H., Nonparticipation and Perceptions of Legitimacy, *Berkeley Journal of International Law*, vol. 37 (2019): p. 235–248.

Pinto de Albuquerque, P., and Wojtyczek, K. (eds), *Judicial Power in a Globalized World: Liber Amicorum Vincent De Gaetano* (Cham: Springer, 2019). 671 p.

Salas Kantor, B., and Zavala Achurra, M.E., The Principle of Res Judicata before the International Court of Justice: In the Midst of Comradeship and Divorce between International Tribunals, *Journal of International Dispute Settlement*, vol. 10 (2019): p. 288–306.

Suttle, O., Rules and Values in International Adjudication: The Case of the WTO Appellate Body, *International and Comparative Law Quarterly*, vol. 68 (2019): p. 399–441.

Wuschka, S., Procedural Aspects of the Obligation of Non-Recognition before International Investment Tribunals, in Fach Gomez, K., Gourgourinis, A., and Titi, C. (eds), *European Yearbook of International Economic Law*, Special Issue (Cham: Springer, 2019). p. 129–151.

17. International Waterways

de Cossío Klüver, M.A., Un recurso natural invisible: los acuíferos transfronterizos, *Agenda Internacional*, vol. 26 (2019): p. 137–157.

McCaffrey, S.C., *The Law of International Watercourses* (Oxford: Oxford University Press, 2019). 642 p.

Perry, H.J.M., Kirby Lecture in International Law 2018: The Duality of Water: Conflict or Co-operation, *The Australian Year Book of International Law*, vol. 36 (2019): p. 1–27.

Viñuales, J.E., The Protocol on Water and Health as a Strategy for Global Water Governance Integration, *International and Comparative Law Quarterly*, vol. 68 (2019): p. 175–192.

Weber, C.M., Protection and Use of Transboundary Groundwater Resources Under Public International Law—An Analysis of the UN International Law Commission's Draft Articles on the Law of Transboundary Aquifers, *Max Planck Yearbook of United Nations Law*, vol. 22 (2019): p. 114–141.

18. Intervention and humanitarian intervention

Adams, S., The Responsibility to Protect and the Fate of the Rohingya, *Global Responsibility to Protect*, vol. 11 (2019): p. 435–450.

Aldoghmi, H.S., R2P and Refugee Protection: Framing the Responsibility to Protect Prima Facie Refugees Fleeing Mass Atrocity Crimes, *Global Responsibility to Protect*, vol. 11 (2019): p. 104–134.

Gómez Isa, F., The UNDRIP: An Increasingly Robust Legal Parameter, *International Journal of Human Rights*, vol. 23 (2019): p. 7–21.

Henderson, S., The Evolution of the Principle of Non-Intervention? R2P and Overt Assistance to Opposition Groups, *Global Responsibility to Protect*, vol. 11 (2019): p. 365–393.

López-Casamayor Justicia, A., Armas letales autónomas a la luz del derecho internacional humanitario: legitimidad y responsabilidad, *Cuadernos de estrategia*, iss. 201 (2019): p. 177–213.

Nguyen, Q.T.T., Rethinking the Legality of Intervention by Invitation: Toward Neutrality, *Journal of Conflict and Security Law*, vol. 24 (2019): p. 201–238.

O'Donnell, T., Vulnerability and the International Law Commission's Draft Articles on the Protection of Persons in the Event of Disasters, *International and Comparative Law Quarterly*, vol. 68 (2019): p. 573–610.

Pınar Gözen, E., UN General Assembly Dialogues on the Responsibility to Protect and the Use of Force for Humanitarian Purposes, *Global Responsibility to Protect*, vol. 11 (2019): p. 313–332.

Rankin, M., The 'Responsibility to Prosecute' Core International Crimes? The Case of German Universal Jurisdiction and the Syrian Government, *Global Responsibility to Protect*, vol. 11 (2019): p. 394–410.

Sassòli, M., *International Humanitarian Law: Rules, Solutions to Problems Arising in Warfare and Controversies* (Cheltenham: Edward Elgar Publishing, 2019). 720 p.

Simm, G., Disaster Militarism? Military Humanitarian Assistance and Disaster Relief, *Max Planck Yearbook of United Nations Law*, vol. 22 (2019): p. 347–375.

Thakur, R., Global Justice and National Interests: How R2P Reconciles the Two Agendas on Atrocity Crimes, *Global Responsibility to Protect*, vol. 11 (2019): p. 411–434.

Todeschini, V., The Impact of International Humanitarian Law on the Principle of Systemic Integration, *Journal of Conflict and Security Law*, vol. 23 (2018): p. 359–382.

Visser, L., May the Force be with You: The Legal Classification of Intervention by Invitation, *Netherlands International Law Review*, vol. 66 (2019): p. 21–45.

19. Jurisdiction

Gomez, C.E., The International Criminal Court's Decision on the Rohingya Crisis: The Need for a Critical Redefinition of Trans-Border Jurisdiction to Address Human Rights, *California Western International Law Journal*, vol. 50 (2019): p. 177–205.

Jervis, C.E.M., Jurisdictional Immunities Revisited: An Analysis of the Procedure Substance Distinction in International Law, *European Journal of International Law*, vol. 30 (2019): p. 105–128.

Langer, M., and Eason, M., The Quiet Expansion of Universal Jurisdiction, *European Journal of International Law*, vol. 30 (2019): p. 779–817.

Staiano, F., Universal Jurisdiction over Transnational Maritime Crimes Beyond Piracy, *Rivista di diritto internazionale*, vol. 102 (2019): p. 663–693.

20. Law of Armed Conflict

Almila, E., Protecting Children from Sexual Violence in Armed Conflict Under International Humanitarian Law Discrepancies between Conventions and Practice of International Criminal Courts and Tribunals, *Journal of International Humanitarian Legal Studies*, vol. 10 (2019): p. 217–239.

Fach Gómez, K., Gourgourinis, A., and Titi, C. (eds), *International Investment Law and the Law of Armed Conflict* (Cham: Springer International Publishing, 2019). 536 p.

Gordon, N., and Perugini, N., 'Hospital Shields' and the Limits of International Law, *European Journal of International Law*, vol. 30 (2019): p. 439–463.

Lewis, D.A., The Notion of "Protracted Armed Conflict" in the Rome Statute and the Termination of Armed Conflicts Under International Law: An Analysis of Select Issues, *International Review of the Red Cross*, vol. 101 (2020): p. 1091–1115.

Mammadov, U., and Huseynov, T., Protecting Environmental Human Rights in Armed Conflict Situations, *Environmental Policy and Law*, vol. 49 (2019): p. 101–110.

Sassòli, M., *International Humanitarian Law: Rules, Solutions to Problems Arising in Warfare and Controversies* (Cheltenham: Edward Elgar Publishing, 2019). 720 p.

Smith, T., Critical Perspectives on Environmental Protection in Non-International Armed Conflict: Developing the Principles of Distinction, Proportionality and Necessity, *Leiden Journal of International Law*, vol. 32 (2019): p. 759–779.

21. Law of the Sea

Bastid Burdeau, G., The Respect of Other States' Rights (Freedom of Navigation and Other Rights and Freedoms Set Out in the LOSC) as a Limitation to the Military Uses of the EEZ by Third States, *The International Journal of Marine and Coastal Law*, vol. 34 (2019): p. 117–127.

Beckman, R., Davenport, T., and Phan, H.D. (eds), *The Timor-Leste/Australia Conciliation: A Victory for UNCLOS and Peaceful Settlement of Disputes* (Singapore: World Scientific, 2019). 338 p.

Beckman, R.C., *et al.* (eds), *High Seas Governance: Gaps and Challenges* (Brill/Nijhoff: Brill/Nijhoff, 2019). 318 p.

Black, J.A., A New Custom Thickens: Increased Coastal State Jurisdiction within Sovereign Waters, *Boston University International Law Journal*, vol. 37 (2019): p. 355–393.

Boyle, A., Litigating Climate Change Under Part XII of the LOSC, *The International Journal of Marine and Coastal Law*, vol. 34 (2019): p. 458–481.

Caddell, R., and Molenaar, E.J. (eds), *Strengthening International Fisheries Law in an Era of Changing Oceans* (Oxford, UK; Portland, Oregon: Hart Publishing, 2019). 512 p.

Chircop, A., Koivurova, T., and Singh, K., Is There a Relationship between UNDRIP and UNCLOS? *Ocean Yearbook*, vol. 33 (2019): p. 90–130.

Delfour-Samama, O., La pêche profonde en mer, un défi pour une pêche durable, *Revue juridique de l'environnement*, vol. 44 (2019): p. 275–289.

Fife, R.E., Obligations of 'Due Regard' in the Exclusive Economic Zone: Their Context, Purpose and State Practice, *The International Journal of Marine and Coastal Law*, vol. 34 (2019): p. 43–55.

Forteau, M., The Legal Nature and Content of 'Due Regard' Obligations in Recent International Case Law, *The International Journal of Marine and Coastal Law*, vol. 34 (2019): p. 25–42.

Freestone, D., Sustainable Development, Ocean Governance and Marine Protected Areas, *Asia-Pacific Journal of Ocean Law and Policy*, vol. 4 (2019): p. 127–141.

Freestone, D., and Schofield, C.H., Securing Ocean Spaces for the Future?: The Initiative of the Pacific SIDS to Develop Regional Practice Concerning Baselines and Maritime Zone Limits, *Ocean Yearbook*, vol. 33 (2019): p. 58–89.

Gjerde, K.M., Clark, N.A., and Harden-Davies, H.R., Building a Platform for the Future: The Relationship of the Expected New Agreement for Marine Biodiversity in Areas Beyond National Jurisdiction and the UN Convention on the Law of the Sea, *Ocean Yearbook*, vol. 33 (2019): p. 1–44.

Goodman, C., and Matley, H., Law Beyond Boundaries: Innovative Mechanisms for the Integrated Management of Biodiversity Beyond National Jurisdiction, *ICES Journal of Marine Science*, vol. 75 (2018): p. 402–404.

Gupta, S., Historic Fishing Rights in Foreign Exclusive Maritime Zones: Preserved or Proscribed by UNCLOS? *The Korean Journal of International and Comparative Law*, vol. 7 (2019): p. 226–248.

Hamamoto, S., The Genesis of the 'Due Regard' Obligations in the United Nations Convention on the Law of the Sea, *The International Journal of Marine and Coastal Law*, vol. 34 (2019): p. 7–24.

Hasan, M.M., and Jian, H., Spratly Island Dispute in the South China Sea: Potential Solutions, *Journal of East Asia and International Law*, vol. 12 (2019): p. 145–168.

de Herdt, S., Meaningful Responses to Unilateralism in Undelimited Maritime Areas, *The Journal of Territorial and Maritime Studies*, vol. 6 (2019): p. 5–26.

Hoogeland, M., *et al.*, Case Note: The South China Sea Dispute and the Role of UNCLOS in the Settlement of the Dispute, *Revue québécoise de droit international* (2019): p. 93–116.

Ishii, Y., The 'Due Regard' Obligation and the Peaceful and Economic Uses of the EEZ Other than Fisheries, *The International Journal of Marine and Coastal Law*, vol. 34 (2019): p. 73–88.

Ivanova, E., The Cross-Fertilization of UNCLOS, Custom and Principles Relating to Procedure in the Jurisprudence of UNCLOS Courts and Tribunals, *Max Planck Yearbook of United Nations Law Online*, vol. 22 (2019): p. 142–170.

Jacobsson, M., Institutional Arrangements for the Ocean: From Zero to Indefinite? *Ecology Law Quarterly*, vol. 46 (2019): p. 149–162.

Klein, N., The Timor Sea Conciliation and Lessons for Northeast Asia in Resolving Maritime Boundary Disputes, *The Journal of Territorial and Maritime Studies*, vol. 6 (2019): p. 30–50.

Lando, M., *Maritime Delimitation as a Judicial Process* (Cambridge: Cambridge University Press, 2019). 432 p.

Lathrop, C.G., Roach, J.A., and Rothwell, D.R. (eds), *Baselines Under the International Law of the Sea. Reports of the International Law Association Committee on Baselines Under the International Law of the Sea* (Leiden: Koninklijke Brill NV, 2019). 190 p.

Long, R.J., Restoring Marine Environmental Damage: Can the Costa Rica v Nicaragua Compensation Case Influence the BBNJ Negotiations? *Review of European Community and International Environmental Law*, vol. 28 (2019): p. 244–257.

de Lucia, V., and Iavicoli, V., From Outer Space to Ocean Depths: The 'Spacecraft Cemetery' and the Protection of the Marine Environment in Areas Beyond National Jurisdiction, *California Western International Law Journal*, vol. 49 (2019): p. 345–389.

Ma, D., Obligation to Exchange Views Under Article 283 of the United Nations Convention on the Law of the Sea: An Empirical Approach for Improvement, *Journal of East Asia and International Law*, vol. 12 (2019): p. 305–320.

McCreath, M., and Scanlon, Z., The Dispute Concerning the Delimitation of the Maritime Boundary between Ghana and Côte d'Ivoire: Implications for the Law of the Sea, *Ocean Development & International Law*, vol. 50 (2019): p. 1–22.

McLaughlin, R., Article 110 of the Law of the Sea Convention 1982 and Jurisdiction Over Vessels without Nationality, *The George Washington International Law Review*, vol. 51 (2019): p. 373–406.

Michelot, A., Le « système Océan », un enjeu de solidarité écologique, *Revue juridique de l'environnement*, vol. 44 (2019): p. 231–242.

Nordquist, M.H., Moore, J.N., and Long, R.J. (eds), *The Marine Environment and United Nations Sustainable Development Goal 14: Life Below Water* (Leiden, The Netherlands: Brill Nijhoff, 2019). 421 p.

Ong, D.M., Prospects for Cooperation Over Shared Natural Resources in the Continental Shelf Beyond 200 Nautical Miles and Implications of Article 82 of the UNCLOS for Land-Locked, Developing States in Semi-Enclosed Seas, in Zou, K. (ed), *Maritime Cooperation in Semi-Enclosed Seas: Asian and European Experiences* (Leiden; Boston: Brill Nijhoff, 2019). p. 106–128.

Olorundami, F.A., Should the Diaoyu/Senkaku Islands be Classified as Islands Or Rocks?: An Examination in Light of the South China Sea Arbitration Award / Fayokemi Ayodeji Olorundami, *The International Journal of Marine and Coastal Law*, vol. 34 (2019): p. 325–349.

Onele, J., Revisiting Unilateral Exploitation of Mineral Resources in Disputed Water Under United Nations Convention on the Law of the Sea: Any New Matter Arising? *Journal of International Dispute Settlement*, vol. 10 (2019): p. 160–173.

Oral, N., International Law as an Adaptation Measure to Sea-Level Rise and its Impacts on Islands and Offshore Features, *The International Journal of Marine and Coastal Law*, vol. 34 (2019): p. 415–439.

Oral, N., Navigating the Oceans: Old and New Challenges for the Law of the Sea for Straits used for International Navigation, *Berkeley Journal of International Law*, vol. 37 (2019): p. 317–344.

Oude Elferink, A.G., Exploring the Future of the Institutional Landscape of the Oceans Beyond National Jurisdiction, *Review of European Community and International Environmental Law*, vol. 28 (2019): p. 236–243.

Papanicolopulu. I. (ed), *Gender and the Law of the Sea* (Leiden; Boston: Brill Nijhoff, 2019). 366 p.

Payne, C.R., New Law for the High Seas, *Ecology Law Quarterly*, vol. 46 (2019): p. 191–214.

Phan, H.D., International Courts and State Compliance: An Investigation of the Law of the Sea Cases, *Ocean Development & International Law*, vol. 50 (2019): p. 70–90.

Prezas, I., Foreign Military Activities in the Exclusive Economic Zone: Remarks on the Applicability and Scope of the Reciprocal 'Due Regard' Duties of Coastal and Third States, *The International Journal of Marine and Coastal Law*, vol. 34 (2019): p. 97–116.

Quince, C., *The Exclusive Economic Zone* (Wilmington, Delaware: Vernon Press, 2019). 292 p.

Ranganathan, S., Ocean Floor Grab: International Law and the Making of an Extractive Imaginary, *European Journal of International Law*, vol. 30 (2019): p. 573–600.

Redgwell, C., Treaty Evolution, Adaptation and Change: Is the LOSC 'Enough' to Address Climate Change Impacts on the Marine Environment? *The International Journal of Marine and Coastal Law*, vol. 34 (2019): p. 440–457.

Ricard, P., The Limitations on Military Activities by Third States in the EEZ Resulting from Environmental Law, *The International Journal of Marine and Coastal Law*, vol. 34 (2019): p. 144–165.

Saunders, I., Artificial Islands and Territory in International Law, *Vanderbilt Journal of Transnational Law*, vol. 52 (2019): p. 643–684.

Scanlon, Z., Safeguarding the Legitimacy of Illegal, Unreported and Unregulated Fishing Vessel Listings, *International and Comparative Law Quarterly*, vol. 68 (2019): p. 369–398.

Schatz, V.J., and Koval, D., Russia's Annexation of Crimea and the Passage of Ships through Kerch Strait: A Law of the Sea Perspective, *Ocean Development & International Law*, vol. 50 (2019): p. 275–297.

Schmalenbach, K., and Pleiel, J., An Ocean of Plastic: What Can a Future "Treaty on Biodiversity in Areas Beyond National Jurisdiction" Contribute to Solving a Global Problem, *Archiv des Völkerrechts*, vol. 57 (2019): p. 1–25.

Schofield, C., and Freestone, D., Islands Awash Amidst Rising Seas: Sea Level Rise and Insular Status Under the Law of the Sea, *The International Journal of Marine and Coastal Law*, vol. 34 (2019): p. 391–414.

Scovazzi, T., 'Due Regard' Obligations, with Particular Emphasis on Fisheries in the Exclusive Economic Zone, *The International Journal of Marine and Coastal Law*, vol. 34 (2019): p. 56–72.

Seta, M., The Contribution of the International Organization for Standardization to Ocean Governance, *RECIEL Review of European, Comparative & International Environmental Law*, vol. 28 (2019): p. 304–313.

Smith, J., International Law and Western Sahara's Maritime Area, *Ocean Development & International Law*, vol. 50 (2019): p. 117–140.

Song, Y., The July 2016 Arbitral Award, Interpretation of Article 121(3) of the UNCLOS, and Selecting Examples of Inconsistent State Practices, *Ocean Development & International Law*, vol. 49 (2018): p. 247–261.

Stephens, T., The Role and Relevance of Nationally Determined Contributions Under the Paris Agreement to Ocean and Coastal Management in the Anthropocene, *Ocean Yearbook*, vol. 33 (2019): p. 250–267.

Strauss, M.J., The Future of Baselines as the Sea Level Rises: Guidance from Climate Change Law, *The Journal of Territorial and Maritime Studies*, vol. 6 (2019): p. 27–43.

Tanaka, Y., *The South China Sea Arbitration: Toward an International Legal Order in the Oceans* (Oxford; New York: Hart, 2019). 312 p.

Thomé, N., L'impact de l'érosion et de la submersion sur les délimitations maritimes, *Revue juridique de l'environnement*, vol. 44 (2019): p. 57.

Treves, T., 'Due Regard' Obligations Under the 1982 UN Convention on the Law of the Sea: The Laying of Cables and Activities in the Area, *The International Journal of Marine and Coastal Law*, vol. 34 (2019): p. 167–194.

Valdez, A.I., Beyond the Arbitral Ruling: A Transboundary Environmental Impact Assessment in the South China Sea, *Asian Journal of International Law*, vol. 9 (2019): p. 251–274.

van Logchem, Y., The Rights and Obligations of States in Disputed Maritime Areas: What Lessons can be Learned from the Maritime Boundary Dispute between Ghana and Cote d'Ivoire? *Vanderbilt Journal of Transnational Law*, vol. 52 (2019): p. 121–177.

Vázquez Gómez, E., La protección de la diversidad biológica marina más allá de la jurisdicción nacional. Hacia un nuevo acuerdo de aplicación de la Convención de Naciones Unidas sobre el Derecho del mar, *Revista Electrónica de Estudios Internacionales*, iss. 37 (2019): p. 1–29.

del Vecchio, A., and Virzo, R. (eds), *Interpretations of the United Nations Convention on the Law of the Sea by International Courts and Tribunals* (Cham, Switzerland: Springer International Publishing, 2019). 444 p.

Verlag, D.K., *China and the Law of the Sea: China's Artificial Islands in the South China Sea* (Hamburg: Verlag Dr. Kovač, 2019). 197 p.

Vrancken, P.H.G., State Jurisdiction to Investigate and Try Fisheries Crime at Sea, *Marine Policy: The International Journal for Economics Planning and Politics of Ocean Exploitation*, vol. 105 (2019): p. 129–139.

Wong, Y., Reasonable Restrictions on Freedom of High Seas by "Marine Protected Areas on the High Seas": An Empirical Research, *Journal of East Asia and International Law*, vol. 12 (2019): p. 245–268.

Xu, Q., Reflections on the Presence of Third States in International Maritime Boundary Delimitation, *Chinese Journal of International Law*, vol. 18 (2019): p. 91–128.

Zou, K.(ed), *Maritime Cooperation in Semi-Enclosed Seas: Asian and European Experiences* (Leiden; Boston: Brill/ Nijhoff, 2019). 254 p.

22. Law of Treaties

Chesterman, S., *et al.* (eds), *The Oxford Handbook of United Nations Treaties* (New York: Oxford University Press, 2019). 736 p.

Djeffal, C., How Post-Positivism Sheds Light on Treaty Interpretation: Celebrating the VCLT Rule of Interpretation, in Siliquini-Cinelli, L. (ed), *Legal Positivism in a Global and Transnational Age* (Cham: Springer, 2019). p. 277–294.

Eqbal, M.T., International Organizations and Reservations to Treaties: A Critical Review of the International Law Commission's Work, *Indian Journal of International Law*, vol. 58 (2018): p. 399–424.

Gervasi, M., The ILC Guide to Practice on Reservations to Treaties Put to the Test in the *Hossam Ezzat* Case before the African Commission on Human and People's Rights, *Rivista Di Diritto Internazionale*, vol. 102 (2019): p. 109–136.

Gragl, P., and Fitzmaurice, M., The Legal Character of Article 18 of the Vienna Convention on the Law of Treaties, *International and Comparative Law Quarterly*, vol. 68 (2019): p. 699–717.

Harris, C., Claims with an Ulterior Purpose: Characterising Disputes Concerning the "Interpretation or Application" of a Treaty, *The Law & Practice of International Courts and Tribunals*, vol. 18 (2019): p. 279–299.

Hayashi, M., Non-Proliferation Treaty and Nuclear Disarmament: Article VI of the NPT in Light of the ILC Draft Conclusions on Subsequent Agreements and Practice, *International Community Law Review*, vol. 22 (2020): p. 84–106.

Klingler, J., Parkhomenko, Y., and Salonidis, C. (eds), *Between the Lines of the Vienna Convention?: Canons and Other Principles of Interpretation in Public International Law* (Alphen aan den Rijn: Wolters Kluwer, 2019). 472 p.

Novak, F., La conducta ulterior de las partes como regla principal de interpretación de los tratados, *Revista Española de Derecho Internacional*, vol. 71 (2019): p. 101–124.

Panjwani, P., The Role of Travaux in Interpreting BIT Provisions: Are Tribunals Over-Prepared to Resort to Preparatory Works? *Journal of World Investment & Trade*, vol. 20 (2019): p. 473–512.

Suresh Bhat, S., A Study of the Issue of 'Relevant Rules' of International Law for the Purposes of Interpretation of Treaties Under Article 31(3)(*c*) of the Vienna Convention on the Law of Treaties, *International Community Law Review*, vol. 29 (2019): p. 190–219.

Wang, Y.A., The Dynamism of Treaties, *Maryland Law Review*, vol. 78 (2019): p. 828–881.

Woolaver, H., From Joining to Leaving: Domestic Law's Role in the International Legal Validity of Treaty Withdrawal, *European Journal of International Law*, vol. 30 (2019): p. 73–104.

23. Natural Resources

Feichtner, I., Mining for Humanity in the Deep Sea and Outer Space: The Role of Small States and International Law in the Extraterritorial Expansion of Extraction, *Leiden Journal of International Law*, vol. 32 (2019): p. 255–274.

Handl, G., and Svendsen, K. (eds), *Managing the Risk of Offshore Oil and Gas Accidents: The International Legal Dimension* (Cheltenham, UK; Northampton, MA: Edward Elgar Publishing, 2019). 488 p.

Lanfranchi, M., Gestion durable des ressources minérales marines et droit international, *Journal du droit international*, vol. 146 (2019): p. 717–738.

24. Non-governmental Organizations

Dani, C., Humanitarian Aid and the Responsibility to Protect: NGOs between Neutrality and Instrumentalization, *Die Friedens-Warte*, vol. 92 (2019): p. 25–39.

Evangelidis, E., and O'Donnell, T., NGOs and the International Law Commission Draft Articles on the Protection of Persons in the Event of Disasters: A Relationship of Mutual or Grudging Respect? *Yearbook of International Disaster Law*, vol. 1 (2019): p. 116–147.

25. Outer Space Law

Castillo Argañaraz, L.F., Las actividades espaciales y la responsabilidad internacional, *Perspectivas Revista de Ciencias Sociales*, iss. 8 (2019): p. 301–313.

Feichtner, I., Mining for Humanity in the Deep Sea and Outer Space: The Role of Small States and International Law in the Extraterritorial Expansion of Extraction, *Leiden Journal of International Law*, vol. 32 (2019): p. 255–274.

Froehlich, A., and Seffinga, V. (eds), *The United Nations and Space Security: Conflicting Mandates between UNCOPUOS and the CD* (Cham, Switzerland: Springer, 2019). 129 p.

Imhof, P., L'utilisation militaire de l'espace extra-atmosphérique est-elle licite selon le droit international public? *Quebec Journal of International Law*, vol. 32 (2019): p. 203–241.

Kyriakopoulos, G.D., and Manoli, M. (eds), *The Space Treaties at Crossroads: Considerations De Lege Ferenda* (Cham, Switzerland: Springer, 2019). 197 p.

de Lucia, V., and Iavicoli, V., From Outer Space to Ocean Depths: The 'Spacecraft Cemetery' and the Protection of the Marine Environment in Areas Beyond National Jurisdiction, *California Western International Law Journal*, vol. 49 (2019): p. 345–389.

Tapio, J., and Soucek, A., 'National Implementation of Non-Legally Binding Instruments: Managing Uncertainty in Space Law?', *Air and Space Law*, vol. 44 (2019): p. 565–582.

26. Peaceful Settlement of Disputes

Hill-Cawthorne, L., International Litigation and the Disaggregation of Disputes: Ukraine/Russia as a Case Study, *International and Comparative Law Quarterly*, vol. 68 (2019): p. 779–815.

Hioureas, C.G., The Singapore Convention on International Settlement Agreements Resulting from Mediation: A New Way Forward? *Berkeley Journal of International Law*, vol. 37 (2019): p. 215–224.

Jiménez Sánchez, C., El arreglo pacífico de controversias en el Sáhara Occidental, ¿intractable conflicto es aún posible una solución? = Peace settlement of disputes in Western Sahara, intractable conflict or it is possible to reach a solution? *Anuario español de derecho internacional*, vol. 35 (2019): p. 451–486.

Liang, W., The World Bank and the Creation of the International Center for Settlement of Investment Disputes: Legality and Legitimacy, in Quayle, P., and Gao, X. (eds), *International Organizations and the Promotion of Effective Dispute Resolution* (Leiden, The Netherlands: Brill, Nihjoff, 2019): p. 103–120.

McLachlan, C., The Assault on International Adjudication and the Limits of Withdrawal, *International and Comparative Law Quarterly*, vol. 68 (2019): p. 499–537.

Murphy, S.D., Seventh Annual Charles N. Brower Lecture: A Century of Dispute Settlement through International Law (1919–2019): The Role of Multilateralism: Remarks, *Proceedings of the ASIL Annual Meeting*, vol. 113 (2019): p. 299–311.

Robles, A.C.J., *The South China Sea Arbitration: Understanding the Awards and Debating with China* (Brighton: Sussex Academic Press, 2019). 335 p.

Tomuschat, C., Enforcement of International Law: From the Authority of Hard Law to the Impact of Flexible Methods, *Zeitschrift für ausländisches öffentliches Recht und Völkerrecht (ZaöRV)*, vol. 79 (2019): p. 579–631.

Verbist, H., United Nations Convention on International Settlement Agreements Resulting from Mediation, *b-Arbitra*, vol. 2019 (2019): p. 53–86.

27. Peacekeeping and related activities

Braga Matijascic, V., and de Macedo Braga, C., United Nations Peace Operations: Evolution, Challenges, and New Dynamics, *NUPRI Working Paper*, vol. WP 02 (2019): p. 1–15.

Cavalcante, F., *Peacebuilding in the United Nations: Coming into Life* (Cham, Switzerland: Palgrave Macmillan, 2019). 323 p.

Charara, L., The Legal Architecture of United Nations Peacekeeping: A Case Study of UNIFIL, *Michigan Journal of International Law*, vol. 40 (2019): p. 385–409.

de Coning, C., and Peter, M. (eds), *United Nations Peace Operations in a Changing Global Order* (Cham: Springer International Publishing, 2019). 333 p.

Davies, S.E., and True, J., *The Oxford Handbook of Women, Peace and Security* (New York: Oxford University Press, 2019). 898 p.

Gilder, A., The Effect of 'Stabilization' in the Mandates and Practice of UN Peace Operations, *Netherlands International Law Review*, vol. 66 (2019): p. 47–73.

Laurence, M., An 'Impartial' Force? Normative Ambiguity and Practice Change in UN Peace Operations, *International Peacekeeping*, vol. 26 (2019): p. 256–280.

Mudgway, C., *Sexual Exploitation and Abuse by UN Peacekeepers: Towards a Hybrid Solution* (London: Routledge, Taylor & Francis Group, 2019). 170 p.

Okada, Y., Effective Control Test at the Interface between the Law of International Responsibility and the Law of International Organizations: Managing Concerns Over the Attribution of UN Peacekeepers' Conduct to Troop-Contributing Nations, *Leiden Journal of International Law*, vol. 32 (2019): p. 275–297.

Okada, Y., What's Wrong with Behrami and Saramati?: Revisiting the Dichotomy between UN Peacekeeping and UN-Authorized Operations in Terms of Attribution, *Journal of Conflict & Security Law*, vol. 24 (2019): p. 343–371.

Oswald, B., Durham, H., and Bates, A. (eds), *Documents on the Law of UN Peace Operations* (Oxford, United Kingdom: Oxford University Press, 2019). 704 p.

Ryngaert, C., and Spijkers, O., The End of the Road: State Liability for Acts of UN Peacekeeping Contingents After the Dutch Supreme Court's Judgment in Mothers of Srebrenica (2019), *Netherlands International Law Review*, vol. 66 (2019): p. 537–553.

Strydom, H., Mali and the Sahel: Making Peace in another Rough Neighbourhood, *Netherlands International Law Review*, vol. 66 (2019): p. 75–99.

van Leeuwen, J., Addressing the Gap: Accountability Mechanisms for Peacekeepers Accused of Sexual Exploitation and Abuse, *Victoria University of Wellington law review*, vol. 50 (2019): p. 135–156.

White, N.D., Peacekeeping Doctrine: An Autonomous Legal Order? *Nordic Journal of International Law*, vol. 88 (2019): p. 86–110.

28. Piracy

Eruaga, O.A., and Mejia, M., Piracy and Armed Robbery Against Ships: Revisiting International Law Definitions and Requirements in the Context of the Gulf of Guinea, *Ocean Yearbook*, vol. 33 (2019): p. 421–455.

Horsley, E.F., State-Sponsored Ransomware through the Lens of Maritime Policy, *Georgia Journal of International and Comparative Law*, vol. 47 (2019): p. 669–681.

Odeke, A., You are Free to Commit Piracy and Armed Robbery Against Ships but Please do Not do it in this Place: Geographical Scope of Piracy and Armed Robbery Against Ships Under UNCLOS and Related International Instruments, *Journal of Maritime Law and Commerce*, vol. 50 (2019): p. 407–449.

29. Political and Security Questions

Amann, D.M., Legal Consequences of the Separation of the Chagos Archipelago from Mauritius in 1965, *American Journal of International Law*, vol. 113 (2019): p. 784–791.

Barber, R., Accountability for Crimes Against the Rohingya: Possibilities for the General Assembly Where the Security Council Fails, *Journal of International Criminal Justice*, vol. 17 (2019): p. 557–584.

Caflisch, L., La valeur des cartes dans la preuve des frontières internationales, *Revue generale de droit international public*, vol. 123 (2019): p. 619–651.

Damrosch, L.F., The Legitimacy of Economic Sanctions as Countermeasures for Wrongful Acts, *Ecology Law Quarterly*, vol. 46 (2019): p. 95–110.

Davies, S.E., and True, J., *The Oxford Handbook of Women, Peace, and Security* (New York: Oxford University Press, 2019). 898 p.

Goulet, J., La cour pénale internationale face au défi des contestations africaines sur sa légitimité, *Revue Québécoise de Droit International*, vol. 32 (2019): p. 107–126.

Kantorowicz-Reznichenko, E., The Enforcement of International Law, in Hosli, M.O., Selleslaghs, J. (eds), *The Changing Global Order: Challenges and Prospects* (Cham: Springer, 2019): p. 361–384.

Kraska, J., Maritime Interdiction of North Korean Ships Under UN Sanctions, *Berkeley Journal of International Law*, vol. 37 (2019): p. 369–392.

Lages de Oliveira, R., Migración internacional y derecho: una reflexión en clave de Derechos Humanos, *Anales de la Universidad de Chile*, iss. 16 (2019): p. 27–45.

Menkes, M.J., The Legality of US Investment Sanctions Against Iran before the ICJ: A Watershed Moment for the Essential Security and Necessity Exceptions, *The Canadian Yearbook of International Law*, vol. 56 (2019): p. 328–364.

Nahlawi, Y., Overcoming Russian and Chinese Vetoes on Syria through Uniting for Peace, *Journal of Conflict and Security Law*, vol. 24 (2019): p. 111–143.

Pozo Serrano, P., La retirada de Estados Unidos del Plan de Acción Integral Conjunto y la reimposición de sanciones a Irán: aspectos jurídicos y políticos, *Anuario Español de Derecho Internacional*, vol. 35 (2019): p. 219–259.

Riordan, S., *The Geopolitics of Cyberspace: A Diplomatic Perspective* (Leiden; Boston: Brill, 2019). 84 p.

Rodriguez, M., Disinformation Operations Aimed at (Democratic) Elections in the Context of Public International Law: The Conduct of the Internet Research Agency during the 2016 US Presidential Election, *International Journal of Legal Information*, vol. 47 (2019): p. 149–197.

Rose, C., Kubiciel, M., and Landwehr, O. (eds), *The United Nations Convention Against Corruption: A Commentary* (Oxford, United Kingdom: Oxford University Press, 2019). 800 p.

Shahabuddin, M., Post-Colonial Boundaries, International Law, and the Making of the Rohingya Crisis in Myanmar, *Asian Journal of International Law*, vol. 9 (2019): p. 334–358.

Sierzputowski, B., The Data Embassy Under Public International Law, *International and Comparative Law Quarterly*, vol. 68 (2019): p. 225–242.

Téllez-Núñez, A., Una mirada a la vivencia del derecho internacional desde la perspectiva de las sanciones económicas unilaterales, *Revista Derecho del Estado*, vol. 42 (2019): p. 311–338.

30. Progressive Development and Codification of International Law

Arcari, M., Les instruments non conventionnels de la Commission du Droit International des Nations Unies: succès ou échec de la codification? *Revista da Faculdade de Direito*, vol. 75 (2019): p. 375–394.

Azaria, D., The International Law Commission's Return to the Law of Sources of International Law, *FIU Law Review*, vol. 13 (2019): p. 989–1006.

Baylis, E., The International Law Commission's Soft Law Influence, *FIU Law Review*, vol. 13 (2019): p. 1007–1025.

Bernstorff, J.v., and Dann, P. (eds), *The Battle for International Law: South-North Perspectives on the Decolonization Era* (Oxford: Oxford University Press, 2019). 496 p.

D'Aspremont, J., The Four Lives of Customary International Law, *International Community Law Review*, vol. 21 (2019): p. 229–256.

Delerue, F., Reinterpretation or Contestation of International Law in Cyberspace? *Israel Law Review*, vol. 52 (2019): p. 295–326.

Díaz Galán, E.C., La Indefinición jurídica del asilo diplomático al hilo de la práctica internacional: «una figura olvidada», *Anuario Español de Derecho Internacional*, vol. 35 (2019): p. 405–450.

Eggett, C., The Role of Principles and General Principles in the 'Constitutional Processes' of International Law, *Netherlands International Law Review*, vol. 66 (2019): p. 197–217.

Galvão Teles, P., The ILC's Past Practice on Progressive Development and Codification of International Law—An Empirical Analysis Focusing on the Law of the Sea, Law of Treaties and State Responsibility, *FIU Law Review*, vol. 13 (2019): p. 1027–1042.

Gosalbo Bono, R., Consideraciones en torno a la distinción entre el fondo y la forma en el Derecho internacional (público y privado), *Revista Española de Derecho Internacional*, vol. 71 (2019): p. 23–62.

Gradoni, L., UN-Procedural Customary Law, *Journal of International Dispute Settlement*, vol. 10 (2019): p. 175–199.

Imran Kanu, M., 70 Years of the International Law Commission, its Future Role in the Changing Landscape of International Law and the Small-Developing States Nexus, *FIU Law Review*, vol. 13 (2019): p. 1043–1064.

Joyner, D.H., Why I Stopped Believing in Customary International Law, *Asian Journal of International Law*, vol. 9 (2019): p. 31–45.

Kugala, J., The Legitimacy of Rules of Customary International Law and the Right to Justification. *Zeitschrift für ausländisches öffentliches Recht und Völkerrecht = Heidelberg Journal of International Law*, vol. 79 (2019): p. 785–813.

Lippold, M., Reflections on Custom Critique and on Functional Equivalents in the Work of Jean d'Aspremont, *International Community Law Review*, vol. 21 (2019): p. 257–282.

Lusa Bordin, F., A Glass Half Full? The Character, Function and Value of the Two-Element Approach to Identifying Customary International Law, *International Community Law Review*, vol. 21 (2019): p. 283–306.

Mayer, B., Climate Assessment as an Emerging Obligation Under Customary International Law, *International and Comparative Law Quarterly*, vol. 68 (2019): p. 271–308.

Mora-Carvajal, D.A., Aproximación positivista a la unidad y la coherencia de un derecho internacional fragmentado, *Revista de la Facultad de Derecho y Ciencias Políticas*, vol. 49 (2019): p. 81–101.

Moreno, A., La obligación de negociar en el derecho internacional: un análisis a la luz de la clasificación de las obligaciones de comportamiento y de resultado, *Agenda Internacional*, vol. 26 (2019): p. 293–311.

Morton, J.S., Reflections on the International Law Commission and its Role in World Affairs, *FIU Law Review*, vol. 13 (2019): p. 1065–1073.

Oral, N., The International Law Commission and the Progressive Development and Codification of Principles of International Environmental Law, *FIU Law Review*, vol. 13 (2019): p. 1075–1100.

Pacholska, M., New Kids on the Block: International Organizations as Customary Rules Creators, *International Community Law Review*, vol. 21 (2019): p. 325–343.

Pronto, A.N., Codification and Progressive Development of International Law: A Legislative History of Article 13(1)(*a*) of the Charter of the United Nations, *FIU Law Review*, vol. 13 (2019): p. 1101–1123.

Rimmer, S.H., and Ogg, K. (eds), *Research Handbook on Feminist Engagement with International Law* (Northampton, Massachusetts: Edward Elgar Publishing, 2019). 592 p.

Roeben, V., Institutions of International Law: How International Law Secures Orderliness in International Affairs, *Max Planck Yearbook of United Nations Law Online*, vol. 22 (2019): p. 187–217.

Šturma, P., The International Law Commission between Codification, Progressive Development, or a Search for a New Role, *FIU Law Review*, vol. 13 (2019): p. 1125–1135.

Tladi, D., Codification, Progressive Development, New Law, Doctrine, and the Work of the International Law Commission on Peremptory Norms of General International Law (Jus Cogens): Personal Reflections of the Special Rapporteur, *FIU Law Review*, vol. 13 (2019): p. 1137–1150.

von Bernstorff, J., and Dann, P. (eds), *The Battle for International Law: South-North Perspectives on the Decolonization Era* (Oxford: Oxford University Press, 2019). 496 p.

Wiessner, S., and González, C.L., The ILC at its 70th Anniversary: Its Role in International Law and its Impact on U.S. Jurisprudence, *FIU Law Review*, vol. 13 (2019): p. 1151–1174.

Wood, M., Customary International Law and the General Principles of Law Recognized by Civilized Nations, *International Community Law Review*, vol. 21 (2019): p. 307–324.

31. Recognition of States

Cambridge University Press, Recognition in the Context of the Israeli-Palestinian Conflict Proceedings of an International Workshop Held at the Hebrew University of Jerusalem, 5 November 2018, *Israel Law Review*, vol. 52 (2019): p. 367–412.

Grzybowski, J., The Paradox of State Identification: De Facto States, Recognition, and the (Re-) Production of the International, *Theory International Theory*, vol. 11 (2019): p. 241–263.

Yusuf, H.O., and Chowdhury, T., The U.N. Committee of 24's Dogmatic Philosophy of Recognition: Toward a *Sui Generis* Approach to Decolonization, *Indiana Journal of Global Legal Studies*, vol. 26 (2019): p. 437–460.

32. Refugees and internally displaced persons

Aldoghmi, H.S., R2P and Refugee Protection: Framing the Responsibility to Protect Prima Facie Refugees Fleeing Mass Atrocity Crimes, *Global Responsibility to Protect*, vol. 11 (2019): p. 104–134.

Anderson, A., *et al.*, Imminence in Refugee and Human Rights Law: A Misplaced Notion for International Protection, *International and Comparative Law Quarterly*, vol. 68 (2019): p. 111–140.

Foster, M., and Lambert, H., *International Refugee Law and the Protection of Stateless Persons* (Oxford: Oxford University Press, 2019). 254 p.

Goodwin-Gill, G.S., The Office of the United Nations High Commissioner for Refugees and the Sources of International Refugee Law, *International and Comparative Law Quarterly*, vol. 69 (2020): p. 1–41.

Juste Ruiz, J., El Derecho internacional de las migraciones: entre la crisis y la renovación, *Anuario Español de Derecho Internacional*, vol. 35 (2019): p. 535–551.

Pozo Serrano, P., El Pacto Mundial sobre los refugiados: límites y contribución a la evolución del derecho internacional de los refugiados, *Revista Electrónica de Estudios Internacionales*, iss. 38 (2019): p. 1–29.

Reichel, E., Navigating between Refugee Protection and State Sovereignty: Legitimating the United Nations High Commissioner for Refugees, in Weise, T., *et al.* (eds), *International Organizations Under Pressure: Legitimating Global Governance in Challenging Times* (Oxford: Oxford University Press, 2019). p. 195–231.

Reyes, E., Environmental Refugees? Rethinking What's in a Name, *North Carolina Journal of International Law*, vol. 44 (2019): p. 461–486.

Singh Juss, S., *Research Handbook on International Refugee Law* (Cheltenham, UK; Northampton, MA: Edward Elgar Publishing, 2019). 480 p.

Türk, V., The Promise and Potential of the Global Compact on Refugees, *International Journal of Refugee Law*, vol. 30 (2019): p. 575–583.

33. Right of Asylum

Juste Ruiz, J., El Derecho internacional de las migraciones: entre la crisis y la renovación, *Anuario Español de Derecho Internacional*, vol. 35 (2019): p. 535–551.

Querton, C., Gender and the Boundaries of International Refugee Law: Beyond the Category of 'Gender-Related Asylum Claims', *Netherlands Quarterly of Human Rights*, vol. 37 (2019): p. 379–397.

34. Rule of Law

Brock, L., Between Sovereign Judgment and the International Rule of Law: The Protection of People from Mass Atrocities, in Albert, M., and Lang, A.F.J. (eds), *The Politics of International Political Theory: Reflections on the Works of Chris Brown.* (Cham: Palgrave Macmillan, 2019): p. 87–115.

Grondin, O., *et al.*, Les amnisties des crimes internationaux: recherche sur l'état du droit, *Revue québécoise de droit international*, vol. 32 (2019): p. 1–24.

Hahn, M., Challenges for the Rule of Law in the WTO, *ZEuS Zeitschrift für Europarechtliche Studien*, vol. 22 (2019): p. 349–368.

Janse, R., Why did the Rule of Law Revive? *Hague Journal on the Rule of Law*, vol. 11 (2019): p. 341–348.

Jean, M.. La politique internationale de l'état de droit. Observations critiques, *Revue Québécoise de Droit International*, vol. 32 (2019): p. 147–171.

Koskenniemi, M., Imagining the Rule of Law: Rereading the Grotian 'Tradition', *European Journal of International Law*, vol. 30 (2019): p. 17–52.

Kriebaum, U., Rule of Law Notions in Human Rights Law, *ZEuS Zeitschrift für Europarechtliche Studien*, vol. 22 (2019): p. 369–382.

Lachenmann, F., Sustainable Development Goal 16 at a Cross-Roads, *Max Planck Yearbook of United Nations Law*, vol. 22 (2019): p. 171–186.

Loiselle, M., The Penholder System and the Rule of Law in the Security Council Decision-Making: Setback or Improvement? *Leiden Journal of International Law*, vol. 33 (2019): p. 139–156.

Reinisch, A., The UN Concept of the Rule of Law, *ZEuS Zeitschrift für Europarechtliche Studien*, vol. 22 (2019): p. 337–348.

Živković, V., Fair and Equitable Treatment between the International and National Rule of Law, *Journal of World Investment & Trade*, vol. 20 (2019): p. 513–552.

35. Self-defence

Müllerson, R., Self-Defence Against Armed Attacks by Non-State Actors, *Chinese Journal of International Law*, vol. 18 (2019): p. 751–775.

Servín Rodríguez, C.A., La legítima defensa en Derecho Internacional Penal: análisis de sus elementos con particular referencia a los crímenes de guerra, *Nuevo Foro Penal*, vol. 15 (2019): p. 1–46. (in two different journals)

Servín Rodríguez, C.A., La legítima defensa en Derecho Internacional Penal: análisis de sus elementos con particular referencia a los crímenes de guerra, *Revista Digital Mundo Asia Pacífico*, vol. 5 (2019): p. 230–275.

Tzimas, T., Self-Defense by Non-State Actors in States of Fragmented Authority, *Journal of Conflict and Security Law*, vol. 24 (2019): p. 175–199.

de Wet, E., The Invocation of the Right to Self-Defence in Response to Armed Attacks Conducted by Armed Groups: Implications for Attribution, *Leiden Journal of International Law*, vol. 32 (2019): p. 91–110.

36. Self-determination

Black-Branch, J., The 'Inalienable Right' to Nuclear Energy Under the Nuclear Non-Proliferation Treaty: Indigenous Rights of Consultation, Self-Determination and Environmental Protection of Aboriginal Lands, in Black Branch, J., and Fleck, D. (eds), *Nuclear Non-Proliferation in International Law—Volume IV—Human Perspectives on the Development and use of Nuclear Energy* (The Hague: T.M.C. Asser Press, 2019). p. 257–293.

Bossacoma Busquets, P., *Morality and Legality of Secession: A Theory of National Self-Determination* (Cham: Palgrave Macmillan, 2019). 393 p.

Chiatoh, V.M., Self-Determination and Territorial Integrity: Southern Cameroons and the Republic of Cameroun, *African Journal of International and Comparative Law*, vol. 27 (2019): p. 629–653.

Mosses, M., Revisiting the Matthew and Hunter Islands Dispute in Light of the Recent Chagos Advisory Opinion and Some Other Relevant Cases: An Evaluation of Vanuatu's Claims Relating to the Right to Self-Determination, Territorial Integrity, Unlawful Occupation and State Responsibility Under International Law, *Netherlands International Law Review*, vol. 66 (2019): p. 475–506.

Weismann, P., Peoples' Right to Self-Determination: The Case of the Chagos Archipelago, *International Community Law Review*, vol. 21 (2019): p. 463–479.

White, P.B., Cunningham, D.E., and Beardsley, K.C., The United Nations Security Council and Conflict Prevention in Self-Determination Disputes, in Wilkenfeld, J. (ed), *Research Handbook on Mediating International Crises* (Cheltenham, UK; Northampton, MA, USA: Edward Elgar Publishing, 2019). p. 167–182.

37. State Immunity

Beer, Y., Save the Injured—Don't Kill IHL: Rejecting Absolute Immunity for 'Shielding Hospitals', *European Journal of International Law*, vol. 30 (2019): p. 465–480.

Cartes Rodríguez, J.B., Reflexiones en torno a la inmunidad de jurisdicción penal de los Jefes de Estado ante la comisión de crímenes internacionales en el marco del Estatuto de Roma, *Anuario Español de Derecho Internacional*, vol. 35 (2019): p. 487–531.

Jervis, C.E.M., Jurisdictional Immunities Revisited: An Analysis of the Procedure Substance Distinction in International Law, *European Journal of International Law*, vol. 30 (2019): p. 105–128.

Kates, P., Immunity of State Owned Enterprises: Striking a New Balance, *New York University Journal of International Law and Politics*, vol. 51 (2019): p. 1223–1258.

Nouwen, S.M.H., Return to Sender: Let the International Court of Justice Justify or Qualify International Criminal Court Exceptionalism regarding Personal Immunities, *The Cambridge Law Journal*, vol. 78 (2019): p. 596–611.

Ruys, T., The Role of State Immunity and Act of State in the NM Cherry Blossom Case and the Western Sahara Dispute, *International and Comparative Law Quarterly*, vol. 68 (2019): p. 67–90.

Ruys, T., Angelet, N., and Ferro, L. (eds), *The Cambridge Handbook of Immunities and International Law* (Cambridge, United Kingdom: Cambridge University Press, 2019). 790 p.

Tladi, D., The International Law Commission's Recent Work on Exceptions to Immunity: Charting the Course for a Brave New World in International Law? *Leiden Journal of International Law*, vol. 32 (2019): p. 169–187.

Wood, M., Lessons from the ILC's Work on 'Immunity of State Officials': Melland Schill Lecture, 21 November 2017, *Max Planck Yearbook of United Nations Law*, vol. 22 (2019): p. 34–69.

38. State Responsibility

Cassella, S., Responsabilité(s) de l'État pour le risque global lié aux changements climatiques, *Revue générale de droit international public*, vol. 123 (2019): p. 363–389.

Chan, A.W., The Need for a Shared Responsibility Regime between State and Non-State Actors to Prevent Human Rights Violations Caused by Cyber-Surveillance Spyware, *Brooklyn Journal of International Law*, vol. 44 (2019): p. 795–830.

Devendra, I.C., State Responsibility for Corruption in International Investment Arbitration, *Journal of International Dispute Settlement*, vol. 10 (2019): p. 248–287.

Mackenzie-Gray Scott, R., State Responsibility for Complicity in the Internationally Wrongful Acts of Non-State Armed Groups, *Journal of Conflict and Security Law*, vol. 24 (2019): p. 373–407.

Riaño Tovar, C.E., La sucesión de Estados y la responsabilidad internacional: ¿un evento tan antiguo como vigente en el Derecho Internacional?, in Abello-Galvis, R., and Arévalo-Ramírez, W. (eds), *Derecho Internacional Público, Derecho Internacional de la Inversión Extranjera: Reflexiones y Diálogos* (Bogotá D.C.: Editorial Universidad del Rosario). p. 23–56.

Ryngaert, C., and Spijkers, O., The End of the Road: State Liability for Acts of UN Peacekeeping Contingents After the Dutch Supreme Court's Judgment in Mothers of Srebrenica (2019), *Netherlands International Law Review*, vol. 66 (2019): p. 537–553.

Sander, B., Democracy Under the Influence: Paradigms of State Responsibility for Cyber Influence Operations on Elections, *Chinese Journal of International Law*, vol. 18 (2019): p. 1–56.

Soler, C., The State Obligation to Cooperate Under International Law, in Soler, C. (ed), *The Global Prosecution of Core Crimes Under International Law* (The Hague: T.M.C. Asser Press, 2019). p. 165–208.

Webb, P., and Garciandia, R., State Responsibility for Modern Slavery: Uncovering and Bridging the Gap, *International and Comparative Law Quarterly*, vol. 68 (2019): p. 539–571.

39. State Sovereignty

Besson, S., International Courts and the Jurisprudence of Statehood, *Transnational Legal Theory: A Quarterly Journal*, vol. 10 (2019): p. 30–64.

Brock, L., Between Sovereign Judgment and the International Rule of Law: The Protection of People from Mass Atrocities, in Albert, M., and Lang, A.F.J. (eds), *The Politics of International Political Theory: Reflections on the Works of Chris Brown* (Cham: Palgrave Macmillan, 2019). p. 87–115.

Laval, P., La conception de la souveraineté dans les opinions séparées des juges russes au sein des Cours internationales, *Revue générale de droit international public*, vol. 123 (2019): p. 7–23.

Megret, F., Beyond UN Accountability for Human Rights Violations: Host State Inertia and the Neglected Potential of Sovereign Protection, *International Organizations Law Review*, vol. 16 (2019): p. 68–104.

Reichel, E., Navigating between Refugee Protection and State Sovereignty: Legitimating the United Nations High Commissioner for Refugees, in Weise, T., *et al.* (eds), *International Organizations Under Pressure: Legitimating Global Governance in Challenging Times* (Oxford: Oxford University Press, 2019). p. 195–231.

Smith, L.V., Sovereignty Under the League of Nations Mandates: The Jurists' Debates, *Journal of the History of International Law / Revue d'histoire du droit international*, vol. 21 (2019): p. 563–587.

Talmon, S., The United States Under President Trump: Gravedigger of International Law, *Chinese Journal of International Law*, vol. 18 (2019): p. 645–668.

40. State Succession

Müller, A.T., The Effectiveness-Legitimacy Conundrum in the International Law of State Formation, in Bersier Ladavac, N., Bezemek, C., and Schauer, F. (eds), T*he Normative Force of the Factual: Legal Philosophy between is and Ought* (Cham, Switzerland: Springer, 2019). p. 79–95.

Riaño Tovar, C.E., La sucesión de Estados y la responsabilidad internacional: ¿un evento tan antiguo como vigente en el Derecho Internacional?, in Abello-Galvis, R., and Arévalo-Ramírez, W. (eds), *Derecho Internacional Público, Derecho Internacional De La Inversión Extranjera: Reflexiones y Diálogos* (Bogotá D.C.: Editorial Universidad Del Rosario). p. 23–56.

41. Transitional Justice

Baker, C., and Obradovic-Wochnik, J., Mapping the Nexus of Transitional Justice and Peacebuilding, in Lemay-Hébert, N. (ed), *Handbook on Intervention and Statebuilding* (Cheltenham, UK; Northampton, MA, USA: Edward Elgar Publishing, 2019). p. 184–197.

Cepeda Rodríguez, E., and Pérez Niño, W.F., Derechos sociales y justicia transicional: experiencias internacionales y el caso colombiano, *Revista Mexicana de Ciencias Políticas y Sociales*, vol. 64 (2019): p. 77–107.

García Martín, L., Challenging the Transitional Justice Paradigm: Addressing ESRs Violations in Transitional Justice Processes, *Anuario Español de Derecho Internacional*, vol. 35 (2019): p. 655–677.

Gidley, R., *Illiberal Transitional Justice and the Extraordinary Chambers in the Courts of Cambodia* (New York, NY: Springer Berlin Heidelberg, 2019). 250 p.

Grover, L., Transitional Justice, International Law and the United Nations, *Nordic Journal of International Law*, vol. 88 (2019): p. 359–397.

Wambua, M., Transitional Justice and Peacebuilding: The ICC and TJRC Processes in Kenya, *African Conflict and Peacebuilding Review*, vol. 9 (2019): p. 54–71.

42. Use of Force

Beaucillon, C., Limiting Third States' Military Activities in the EEZ: 'Due Regard Obligations' and the Law on the Use of Force Applied to Nuclear Weapons, *The International Journal of Marine and Coastal Law*, vol. 35 (2019): p. 128–143.

Brown, D., Measuring First Use of Force: Methods, Results, and Implications, *Journal on the Use of Force and International Law*, vol. 6 (2019): p. 83–112.

Lubell, N., and Wood, M., The ILA's 2018 Report on Aggression and the Use of Force, *Journal on the Use of Force and International Law*, vol. 6 (2019): p. 4–11.

Pınar Gözen, E., UN General Assembly Dialogues on the Responsibility to Protect and the Use of Force for Humanitarian Purposes, *Global Responsibility to Protect*, vol. 11 (2019): p. 313–332.

Rodríguez Rodríguez, J., El uso de la fuerza contra actores no estatales. Una crítica a la teoría "unwilling or unable" desde el Derecho Internacional vigente, *Revista de las Facultades de Derecho y Ciencias Económicas y Empresariales*, iss. 107 (2019): p. 1–31.

van der Steenhoven, N., Conduct and Subsequent Practice by States in the Application of the Requirement to Report Under UN Charter Article 51, *Journal on the Use of Force and International Law*, vol. 5 (2019): p. 242–272.

Williams, P.R., and Pearlman, S., Use of Force in Humanitarian Crises: Addressing the Limitations of U.N. Security Council Authorization, *Case Western Reserve Journal of International Law*, vol. 51 (2019): p. 211–221.

The United Nations System

PRINCIPAL ORGANS

GENERAL ASSEMBLY

Subsidiary Organs
- Disarmament Commission
- Human Rights Council
- International Law Commission
- Joint Inspection Unit (JIU)
- Main committees
- Standing committees and ad hoc bodies

Funds and Programmes[1]
UNDP United Nations Development Programme
- **UNCDF** United Nations Capital Development Fund
- **UNV** United Nations Volunteers

UNEP[8] United Nations Environment Programme
UNFPA United Nations Population Fund
UN-HABITAT[8] United Nations Human Settlements Programme
UNICEF United Nations Children's Fund
WFP World Food Programme (UN/FAO)

Research and Training
UNIDIR United Nations Institute for Disarmament Research
UNITAR United Nations Institute for Training and Research
UNSSC United Nations System Staff College
UNU United Nations University

Other Entities
ITC International Trade Centre (UN/WTO)
UNCTAD[1,8] United Nations Conference on Trade and Development
UNHCR[1] Office of the United Nations High Commissioner for Refugees
UNOPS[1] United Nations Office for Project Services
UNRWA[1] United Nations Relief and Works Agency for Palestine Refugees in the Near East
UN-WOMEN[1] United Nations Entity for Gender Equality and the Empowerment of Women

Related Organizations
CTBTO Preparatory Commission for the Comprehensive Nuclear-Test-Ban Treaty Organization
IAEA[1,3] International Atomic Energy Agency
ICC International Criminal Court
IOM[1] International Organization for Migration
ISA International Seabed Authority
ITLOS International Tribunal for the Law of the Sea
OPCW[3] Organization for the Prohibition of Chemical Weapons
WTO[1,4] World Trade Organization

Peacebuilding Commission

HLPF
High-level Political Forum on Sustainable Development

SECURITY COUNCIL

Subsidiary Organs
- Counter-Terrorism Committee
- International Residual Mechanism for Criminal Tribunals
- Military Staff Committee
- Peacekeeping operations and political missions
- Sanctions committees (ad hoc)
- Standing committees and ad hoc bodies

ECONOMIC AND SOCIAL COUNCIL

Functional Commissions
- Crime Prevention and Criminal Justice
- Narcotic Drugs
- Population and Development
- Science and Technology for Development
- Social Development
- Statistics
- Status of Women
- United Nations Forum on Forests

Regional Commissions[8]
ECA Economic Commission for Africa
ECE Economic Commission for Europe
ECLAC Economic Commission for Latin America and the Caribbean
ESCAP Economic and Social Commission for Asia and the Pacific
ESCWA Economic and Social Commission for Western Asia

Other Bodies[10]
- Committee for Development Policy
- Committee of Experts on Public Administration
- Committee on Non-Governmental Organizations
- Permanent Forum on Indigenous Issues

UNAIDS Joint United Nations Programme on HIV/AIDS
UNGEGN United Nations Group of Experts on Geographical Names
UNGGIM Committee of Experts on Global Geospatial Information Management

Research and Training
UNICRI United Nations Interregional Crime and Justice Research Institute
UNRISD United Nations Research Institute for Social Development

Specialized Agencies[1,5]
FAO Food and Agriculture Organization of the United Nations
ICAO International Civil Aviation Organization
IFAD International Fund for Agricultural Development
ILO International Labour Organization
IMF International Monetary Fund
IMO International Maritime Organization
ITU International Telecommunication Union
UNESCO United Nations Educational, Scientific and Cultural Organization
UNIDO United Nations Industrial Development Organization
UNWTO World Tourism Organization
UPU Universal Postal Union
WHO World Health Organization
WIPO World Intellectual Property Organization
WMO World Meteorological Organization
WORLD BANK GROUP[7]
- **IBRD** International Bank for Reconstruction and Development
- **IDA** International Development Association
- **IFC** International Finance Corporation

SECRETARIAT

Departments and Offices[9]
EOSG Executive Office of the Secretary-General
DCO Development Coordination Office
DESA Department of Economic and Social Affairs
DGACM Department for General Assembly and Conference Management
DGC Department of Global Communications
DMSPC Department of Management Strategy, Policy and Compliance
DOS Department of Operational Support
DPO Department of Peace Operations
DPPA Department of Political and Peacebuilding Affairs
DSS Department of Safety and Security
OCHA Office for the Coordination of Humanitarian Affairs
OCT Office of Counter-Terrorism
ODA Office for Disarmament Affairs
OHCHR Office of the United Nations High Commissioner for Human Rights
OIOS Office of Internal Oversight Services
OLA Office of Legal Affairs
OOSA Office for Outer Space Affairs
OSAA Office of the Special Adviser on Africa
SRSG/CAAC Office of the Special Representative of the Secretary-General for Children and Armed Conflict
SRSG/SVC Office of the Special Representative of the Secretary-General on Sexual Violence in Conflict
SRSG/VAC Office of the Special Representative of the Secretary-General on Violence Against Children
UNDRR United Nations Office for Disaster Risk Reduction
UNODC[1] United Nations Office on Drugs and Crime
UNOG United Nations Office at Geneva
UN-OHRLLS Office of the High Representative for the Least Developed Countries, Landlocked Developing Countries and Small Island Developing States
UNON United Nations Office at Nairobi
UNOP[2] United Nations Office for Partnerships
UNOV United Nations Office at Vienna
UN YOUTH United Nations Youth Office

INTERNATIONAL COURT OF JUSTICE

TRUSTEESHIP COUNCIL[6]

Notes:

1 Member of the United Nations System Chief Executives Board for Coordination (CEB).
2 The United Nations Office for Partnerships is the focal point vis-a-vis the United Nations Foundation, Inc.
3 IAEA and OPCW report to the Security Council and the General Assembly (GA).
4 WTO has no reporting obligation to the GA, but contributes on an ad hoc basis to GA and Economic and Social Council (ECOSOC) work on, inter alia, finance and development issues.
5 Specialized agencies are autonomous organizations whose work is coordinated through ECOSOC (intergovernmental level) and CEB (inter-secretariat level).
6 The Trusteeship Council suspended operations on 1 November 1994, as Palau, the last United Nations Trust Territory, became independent on 1 October 1994.
7 International Centre for Settlement of Investment Disputes (ICSID) and Multilateral Investment Guarantee Agency (MIGA) are not specialized agencies in accordance with Articles 57 and 63 of the Charter, but are part of the World Bank Group.
8 The secretariats of these organs are part of the United Nations Secretariat.
9 The Secretariat also includes the following offices: the Ethics Office, United Nations Ombudsman and Mediation Services, and the Office of Administration of Justice.
10 For a complete list of ECOSOC Subsidiary Bodies see un.org/ecosoc.

This Chart is a reflection of the functional organization of the United Nations System and for informational purposes only. It does not include all offices or entities of the United Nations System.

Published by the United Nations Department of Global Communications 23-00013 – July 2023

Printed and bound by CPI Group (UK) Ltd, Croydon, CR0 4YY
06/10/2026
14976391-0002